CONSERVATION
OF NATURAL RESOURCES

■ CONSERVATION ■
OF NATURAL RESOURCES

Gary A. Klee

Department of Geography and Environmental Studies
San Jose State University

Prentice Hall, Englewood Cliffs, New Jersey 07632

Library of Congress Cataloging-in-Publication Data

KLEE, GARY A.
   Conservation of natural resources/Gary A. Klee.
     p.   cm.
   Includes bibliographical references.
   ISBN 0-13-168469-8
    1. Conservation of natural resources.   2. Natural resources—
Management.   3. Conservation of natural resources—United States.
4. Natural resources—United States—Management.   I. Title.
S938.K54   1991   89-23164
333.7'2'0973—dc20   CIP

Editorial/production supervision
  and interior design: KATHLEEN M. LAFFERTY
Photo research: BARBARA SCOTT
Cover design: BRUCE KENSELAAR
Cover photographs: GARY A. KLEE
Manufacturing buyer: PAULA MASSENARO

©1991 by Prentice-Hall, Inc.
A Division of Simon & Schuster
Englewood Cliffs, New Jersey 07632

Printed in the United States of America

10 9 8 7 6 5 4 3 2 1

ISBN 0-13-168469-8

Prentice-Hall International (UK) Limited, *London*
Prentice-Hall of Australia Pty. Limited, *Sydney*
Prentice-Hall Canada Inc., *Toronto*
Prentice-Hall Hispanoamericana, S.A., *Mexico*
Prentice-Hall of India Private Limited, *New Delhi*
Prentice-Hall of Japan, Inc., *Tokyo*
Simon & Schuster Asia Pte. Ltd., *Singapore*
Editora Prentice-Hall do Brasil, Ltda., *Rio de Janeiro*

*For my loving wife, Helen, the computer wiz,
and my ''perfect'' daughter, Laura, the little
UCLA Bruin. Without their continual support,
this book would never have seen the light.*

CONTENTS

3   SOIL RESOURCE MANAGEMENT   49

4   WATER RESOURCES   77

5   WATER RESOURCE MANAGEMENT   103

6   RANGELAND RESOURCES AND THEIR MANAGEMENT   143

7   FOREST RESOURCE MANAGEMENT   169

8   WILDLIFE RESOURCES   199

13   NONFUEL MINERAL RESOURCES   330

14   CONSERVATION AND RENEWABLES: THE SOFT ENERGY PATH   359

PREFACE

Conservation of Natural Resources is about Americans and their efforts to conserve their natural resource heritage. It is a look at the many successes and failures of their politics, laws, organizations, and other social institutions that have affected the utilization, conservation, or protection of their country's natural resources. Consequently, it is a book that goes beyond the narrow confines of the traditional academic disciplines of geography, biology, and history to provide the *interdisciplinary* perspective that is required for devising solutions to today's many natural resource management problems.

For almost 20 years, I have had the good fortune to teach courses in natural resource management at the University of Wisconsin–Superior, San Diego State University, and The Pennsylvania State University, and, since 1977, at San Jose State University. At the first three universities, courses in resource management were part of the curricula of the geography department. Within these geography departments, the course that I primarily taught was called the *Conservation of Natural Resources*. At San Jose State University, the *Resources for the Future* course is taught within the Environmental Studies Program, which is now part of the Department of Geography and Environmental Studies. Regardless of the exact title of the course, it was always designed to be an advanced class, going beyond the introductory geography or introductory environmental studies course.

What makes this book unique to the field of geography and environmental studies? First, it focuses on *resource management tools, techniques, and policy strategies for the preprofessional*, rather than on a liberal arts introduction to environmental studies for the lower-level student who is pursuing general elective credit. Second, it emphasizes the *applied geographic and environmental planning perspective*, rather than the more traditional biological perspective. Third, it has a *minimum amount of discussion about the past abuses of a resource*. Students are tired of hearing about what we have done wrong, and a brief reminder is usually sufficient. Fourth, it has a *maximum amount of discussion about how to protect a resource*. Students are practical—they simply want to know what can be done to improve a forest, to protect prime agricultural land, or to preserve an open space. In sum, I have attempted to pull together the most current, innovative, interesting, and useful tools, techniques, and policy strategies for students training to be natural resource managers. While the text stresses methodology rather than theory, it also attempts to reappraise traditional strategies of resource management and, I hope, to suggest some new ideas worthy of serious consideration.

This book should be particularly useful to professors who teach courses in natural resource management in the upper levels of environmental studies programs. These instructors will appreciate the availability of a preprofessional text that provides the details concerning resource management tools, techniques, and policy strategies for the student training for professional service. Professors of geography will, I hope, appreciate my geographical perspective and use of numerous spatial illustrations (e.g., maps and aerial photographs). Environmental scientists will appreciate the scientific explanations of environmental degradation, as well as the descriptions of efforts to monitor changes within the environment. Professors of natural science and biology will appreciate the underlying basis of the discussion: ecosystems, biomes, and human/plant/animal interactions. Professors of urban planning may also find the book of use, since almost every resource chapter includes a discussion of natural resource management problems and strategies within the urban context. For example, the chapter on wildlife has a section on wildlife within the city, and the chapter on forestry has a section on urban forestry.

BOOK AND CHAPTER ORGANIZATION

The book is organized into 14 chapters. Chapter 1, on the history of natural resource management in America, introduces you to the key conservationists, institutions, policies, and resource management problems of the various major periods in American history. With this background, the reader can then turn to separate chapters that cover specific resource categories, such as soil, water, and wildlife.

Each of the resource chapters is organized into five major topics or sections: (1) management tools and techniques, (2) conservation policy strategies, (3) innovative ideas and success stories, (4) prospects for the future, and (5) personal action. In the first section of each chapter, I have tried to get to the nitty-gritty or how-to aspect of the subject, which is generally skimmed over in most introductory textbooks on environmental studies. After briefly reviewing the negative environmental impacts associated with a particular resource, the second section of each chapter looks in depth at the policy strategies related to that resource. For example, any discussion of nonfuel minerals must discuss such things as the federal laws and international treaties, leasing controls, pollution and safety controls, as well as land reclamation requirements related to that resource. The third section discusses the more innovative and unusual means that have been used to restore, to enhance, or to preserve a natural resource. These sections serve two purposes: (1) they illustrate that environmental degradation *can* be corrected if there is a will to do it, and (2) they provide working models for future resource managers and environmental quality planners. In the fourth section of each chapter, the current status of a particular resource in the United States is identified. I then project (when possible) the status of that resource 10 to 30 years from now, depending upon which management strategy is used in the meantime. Emphasis is placed on identifying the pros and cons that must be weighed in any resource management decision. The final section of each major resource chapter is geared to answer what *you personally can do right now* to help restore, maintain, or preserve a particular resource. These sections conclude with a discussion of career opportunities available in the management of the particular resource being discussed.

ACKNOWLEDGMENTS

Where does one begin when acknowledging the help of others? Certainly, I must thank the professors of geography at the University of Oregon where I earned my Ph.D. They introduced me to George Perkins Marsh, Aldo Leopold, and Carl Sauer. Although the above authors and others helped ''brainwash'' me into a particular way of thinking, it was not until I stumbled onto an edition of Raymond Dasmann's *Environmental Conservation* that all the pieces of my professional life began to come together. I can still recall thinking, ''Ah yes, it's natural resource management that I am really interested in! Finally, I have found my academic niche.'' To these professors and writers, and to a host of other individuals, not to mention my ever-critical graduate students, I remain forever indebted.

I would also like to thank the many reviewers who critically studied and commented upon early drafts of this book. Special thanks must go to the geographers/reviewers who provided encouragement and suggestions: John Allen, University of Connecticut; Jacquelyn Beyer, University of Colorado; Kent Barnes, Salem State University; Don Hagan, Northwest Missouri State University; Warren Johnson, San Diego State University; Philip Pryde, San Diego State University; Marilyn Silberfein, Temple University; Imre Sutton, California State University, Fullerton; Robert Walker, Florida State University; and Jeffrey Zinn, Congressional Research Service, Library of Congress.

Finally, I must thank the editors and staff of Prentice Hall. I especially want to express my appreciation to Dan Jorannstad, senior editor for geography at Prentice Hall, and to Kathleen Lafferty, my production editor. Without their friendly support and great attention to detail, this book would not have made the mark.

A NOTE TO THE STUDENT

What follows are a few suggestions to help in your use of this book.

Keep some definitions in mind. By **resources** or **natural resources,** I am referring to all forms of naturally occuring matter or energy that is considered useful or essential by human societies. It is important to remember that natural resources are defined by a *cultural appraisal,* in that their exploitation depends on a society's perception of the natural resource as a commodity, on the society's ability to discover its whereabouts, and on the society's ability to exploit it. During World War II, for example, traditional Micronesian islanders did not perceive the bauxite on their islands as a natural resource. By contrast, the more technologically advanced Japanese culture, which had colonized those islands, mined the bauxite for the aluminum production necessary for military machinery. To the Micronesians, bauxite was not a natural resource; to the Japanese, it was, indeed, a natural resource to be exploited. It is easy, therefore, to see how natural resources are the link between a people (or a cultural group) and their physical environment.

This book will concentrate on America's soil, water, grassland, forest, wildlife, wilderness and open-space, marine and freshwater fisheries, and nonfuel and fuel mineral resources. For the sake of brevity, a separate chapter on air resources was not included, but components of the subject have been integrated into the other chapters (e.g., the effects of acid rain on forests are discussed in the chapter on forest resource management).

The term *resources* can be subdivided into two categories—renewable and nonrenewable. **Renewable resources,** also known as *income* resources, are those commodities that can continuously replenish themselves in the course of natural events *within the limits of human time.* Solar energy, for example, is incoming, or inexhaustible. If managed properly, so are soil, water (abiotic), freshwater (biotic), marine life, wildlife, grassland, and forest. This division is not quite as simple as it sounds, however. Renewable resources need time for recycling or renewing; for example, trees need time to grow and animals need time to reproduce. Certain fast-growing forests can be considered renewable, whereas others, such as the Old Growth stands in the Pacific Northwest that are 500 to 1000 years old, must be classified nonrenewable. Although generally classified as a renewable resource, many forms of wildlife face critical survival thresholds that threaten their very existence. In addition, some resources are renewable in one respect (e.g., soil resources and soil fertility), whereas they are nonrenewable in other respects (e.g., soil resources and soil erosion). **Nonrenewable resources,** on the other hand, are more clearly definable. These are the *capital* or "money in the bank" resources that do not naturally replenish themselves within the limits of human time. Examples of these are fossil fuels, minerals, and such construction materials as sand and gravel.

Because of ever-growing populations and increased technology, societies worldwide have made attempts to conserve their renewable and nonrenewable resources through various forms of resource management. By **conservation,** I refer to the rational use of the environment to provide for the highest sustainable quality of life for the greatest number of people *and other organisms.* Definitions by other authors have rightfully used such words or phrases as "wise resource use," "maintenance of diversity of life," "protection and improvement of resources," and "greatest good for the greatest number." My definition of conservation, however, is broader than most authors since I include the newer concepts of "restoration," "resilience," "regeneration," and "recycling." Regardless of which set of words or phrases you use, such expressions all encompass the notion of *sustaining* resources so that some level of *permanence* or well-being can be brought to human society and the planet's natural ecosystems.

To conserve resources requires some form of resource management, whether it be inadvertent or intentional. By *inadvertent resource management,* I refer to the unintentional or spinoff actions of a society that affect the availability and exploitation of local resources. In Oceania, for example, this would entail discussing and analyzing magico-religious taboos, traditional land and lagoon tenure systems, social stratification, and various forms of population control, such as celibacy, abortion, and infanticide. Although not usually inspired by conservation, these aspects of Oceanic cultures can be viewed as a form of resource management. This book, however, will concentrate on the *intentional resource management* practices of American society. In other words, it will look at the *conscious efforts* that Americans have made to conserve and to protect their abundant (but declining) natural resource heritage.

Use the news media. Environmental issues are a growing concern to Americans and other citizens of the planet, and these issues are increasingly being covered by various forms of local, national, and international news. Clip articles from your newspaper, magazine, and journal subscriptions to supplement what you are reading in the text. Share these items of information with your instructor. It is no secret that instructors get some of their best teaching materials and ideas from their students!

Identify local resource problems and players. Regardless of the chapter resource category (e.g., soil, water, wildlife), identify if and where similar problems (e.g., soil erosion, water contamination, loss of wildlife habitat) exist in your city or county. Once you have identified a topic of special interest to you, get permission to go to the site with a camera and topographic map, shoot some color slides that illustrate resource management problems and/or solutions, interview some key agency representatives and local concerned citizens, do some additional reading about the local situation, then request to give a slide presentation in your class. If nothing else, turn one or two of your normal Sunday outings into a "resource investigation." In other words, that day at the beach can also include a brief investigation of coastal erosion, loss of wetland habitat, or plastic debris that affects marine life; the hike in the forest can include a look at forest succession, timber harvesting techniques, or whether dead or down woody material is available for wildlife, and so on. Everything you do, every single day, has something to do with a natural resource, whether it is drinking a cup of coffee, writing a letter, or driving to school. *Once you start seeing elements of the planet as natural resources, you will never see the world the same again.* Now is the time to start seeing the world as a natural resource manager or environmental planner.

Always be asking yourself "What am I willing to do personally to improve America's (and thus the world's) natural resource predicament?" This book makes many suggestions as to how individuals can personally get involved in bringing about positive change in terms of our natural resource heritage. Ninety-nine percent of you are not going to pick up on all these suggestions and become some kind of "environmental messiah." *I certainly am no environ-mental saint myself.* For example, I commute a long distance to work so that I can live by the coast (although I drive a small, "recycled" 25-year-old car with good gas mileage, and I make the commute only three days a week); I recently bought a house with lots of energy-inefficient windows (although I plan to replace the existing glass with double-pane windows eventually); and I have a large lawn that I knowingly overwater to keep "greener than green" (although next year I will be replacing one-third of that lawn with drought-tolerant, thus water-conserving, landscaping). On the environmental plus side, however, I compost all kitchen scraps, I recycle (newspapers, aluminum cans, glass), and I rarely if ever use pesticides. Sometimes, however, I get so mad at the damage done by gophers that I resort to the unmentionable! The point that I wish to stress is that you are not likely to reach ecological sainthood, but you can strive to be moving in that direction. For every ecological sin, counter that negative action with a positive one of approximate equal value in terms of environmental impact.

Constantly be thinking "Do I want to make a career in natural resource management?" Are you concerned about the current state of the environment? Do certain things upset you, such as visiting cities that are choked with dirty air or drinking water that you suspect to be contaminated or seeing forests, grasslands, or parks that have been degraded? Do you also have a hatred of needless waste (gas-guzzling automobiles, excessive packaging), or landscape uglification (litter, hills upon hills of clearcut forests), or vandalism (graffti-covered buildings or fences; trees that have been cut up, hacked to death, or poisoned). If you have ever thought that someone should be out there *protecting* that pristine wilderness or *preserving* those prime agricultural lands or *conserving* our forest heritage, then you should give some serious thought to being just that individual. As a natural resource manager, you would be practicing *land stewardship,* caring for the earth and all its creatures. As in rearing one's own child, *it gives meaning to life.* When reading the following chapters, constantly be asking yourself: What can I do that would really give meaning to my life?

Gary A. Klee

CONSERVATION
OF NATURAL RESOURCES

HISTORY OF AMERICAN NATURAL RESOURCE MANAGEMENT

There are two ways of living: a man may be casual and simply exist, or constructively and deliberately try to do something with his life. The constructive idea implies constructiveness not only about one's own life, but about that of society, and the future possibilities of mankind.

Julian Huxley,
Essays of a Biologist, 1923

The 1970s was a decade of heightened environmental awareness. One element was a new sense of limits: a sense that natural resource exploitation and environmental contamination had to be controlled. The international celebration of Earth Day in 1970 served to herald a new era of environmental awareness, and, consequently, a number of universities developed courses, programs, and departments to match the mounting public concern for the environment.

It was a period when colleges and universities began to see that traditional academic disciplines were not addressing the critical environmental questions that bombarded the industrialist, businessperson, lawmaker, and homeowner. It became obvious that new courses, new programs, and new departments had to be created that focused strictly on the basic question, *What is the proper role of humans on Earth?* and its spinoff question, *How can humans best live in harmony with their environment?* In fact, many students who read this textbook are taking courses that were developed during the late 1970s environmental movement. This "environmentalism"—which is still considered a fad by some—has now become *institutionalized* in business, government, public schools, universities, and our overall way of life.

The true strength of environmentalism, however, lies in the roots of conservation in the American mind. Although the decade of the 1970s witnessed an explosion of environmental awareness, conservation and love of the earth are deeply rooted in the hearts of Americans. The contemporary environmental movement, which began in the 1970s, is only the most recent wave in a long tradition of conservation—a tradition that includes such well-known individuals as Emerson, Thoreau, Bartram, Jefferson, Marsh, Roosevelt, Pinchot, Muir, and hundreds of others.

These individuals all had one thing in common: a respect and love of the earth, a hatred of needless waste, and a desire to conserve and preserve our natural heritage. This chapter explores their story in greater detail.

ANTECEDENTS TO THE CONSERVATION MOVEMENT

The American Indian: ''First Ecologist'' or ''Miscast Ecologist''?

The American conservation movement has traditionally idolized Native Americans for what is perceived to be their ability to live in harmony with the land. A statement from historian Douglas Strong (1971, pp. 7–8) is but one of innumerable examples that could be cited:

> The continent's original inhabitants, the Indians, had used the land far differently [than the European invaders]. They held it in reverence, believing that they and all other living plants and animals were part of nature. . . . To abuse it [the land], or to exploit it for selfish personal gain, or in any way disturb the basic harmony between themselves and their environment, would have violated their most fundamental beliefs. So they ''walked lightly on the land,'' and their tenure left few scars.

Vecsey and Venables (1980) and Hughes (1983) have similarly discussed the ecological traditional lifestyles of the Indian peoples. One merely has to visit the offices of today's American environmental organizations, such as the Sierra Club or the National Wildlife Federation, to find photographs of Indians in landscapes (Figure 1-1) or posters of American Indian chiefs and their famous quotes regarding the sacredness of Mother Earth. Because of this long-standing tradition of respect for Native Americans and their land practices, it is worthwhile to take a closer look at those whom many still call our ''First Ecologists'' or ''First Conservationists.''

Depending on the authority one consults, the region north of the Rio Grande supported between one to ten million Native Americans just prior to the coming of the Europeans. Geographer Ned Greenwood (1980) has mapped the various aboriginal cultural regions of North America (Figure 1-2), thus reminding us that ''American Indians'' were no more one cultural group than the continent of Europe is one country. For example, he notes that Adena and Hopewell cultures of the ''Northeastern Woodland Indians'' cultural region supplemented their hunting and gathering practices with a form of horticulture that emphasized ''rainfall cultivation.'' ''Slope terracing'' was also practiced to increase arable land. By contrast, the Hohokam peoples of the ''Southwestern Village Indians'' built extensive canal and water diversion systems to irrigate their crops. According to Greenwood (1980, p. 198), at the peak of their devel-

FIGURE 1-1 The first ecologist? A Crow Indian blending into the landscape of his homeland, the Black Canyon. (Photo by Edward Curtis, 1905. Courtesy of the National Anthropological Archives, Smithsonian Institution, Photo No. 75-8112.)

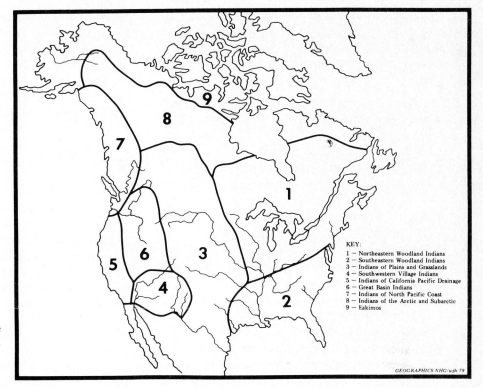

KEY:
1 — Northeastern Woodland Indians
2 — Southeastern Woodland Indians
3 — Indians of Plains and Grasslands
4 — Southwestern Village Indians
5 — Indians of California Pacific Drainage
6 — Great Basin Indians
7 — Indians of North Pacific Coast
8 — Indians of the Arctic and Subarctic
9 — Eskimos

GEOGRAPHICS·NHG/wjh·79

FIGURE 1-2 Aboriginal cultural regions of North America, A.D. 1600–1700. (From Ned Greenwood, "North America." In Gary A. Klee, ed., *World Systems of Traditional Resource Management* [London: Edward Arnold, 1980], p. 196.)

opment "the Hohokam had constructed over 200 miles (320 kilometers) of main canals which averaged 7 feet (2.25 meters) in depth and 30 feet (9.23 meters) in width, and watered over 200,000 acres (81,000 hectares)." Nonhorticultural groups also existed, such as the Hokancoahuiltecan-speaking tribes within the California coastal drainage. Here the tribes practiced hunting and gathering, with the acorn being the primary staple. Although their specific practices were different, the Indian cultures of the Great Basin, the North Pacific Coast, the Boreal forest zone, and the Arctic were also nonhorticultural.

From the above, it should be clear that it is not always easy to generalize about the Indian impact on the land. However, most historians, geographers, and anthropologists would agree that the flora and fauna of pre-Columbian North America suffered little pressure from these early peoples. However, they would also probably agree that the American Indian did not always live in "blissful harmony" with nature. For example, these early hunting bands used fire to drive animals into traps, to clear land for crops, and to create new grazing areas for livestock, thus dramatically altering the natural landscape. These early societies may also have caused the extinction of certain animals, such as the *Mastodon Americanus*, the *Bison antiquus*, and the Camelops. According to many, it was not so much "Indian land ethic" that protected the land, but rather their relatively small population. For example, Greenwood (1980, p. 200) notes that

> . . . at the time of European discovery only about 1 million people inhabited 4.8 billion acres (7.5 million square miles or 2.9 billion hectares). . . . Today [1980] this same land area supports some 250 million individuals who cultivate between 500 and 550 million acres (200–220 million hectares) each year.

The controversy over North American Indians and their actual impact on the environment will no doubt continue. For a detailed and interesting discussion, consult conservationist Max Nicholson's *The Environmental Revolution: A Guide for the New Masters of the World* (1970).

There is no question, however, that traditional cultures, including the American Indians, had numerous conservation techniques (Klee 1980, Greenwood 1980), and that there is renewed interest by scientists and academicians in identifying, analyzing, and possibly applying some of these traditional conservation techniques or concepts to modern systems of resource management. An illustration of this is the effort being made by the International Union for the Conservation of Nature and Natural Resources (IUCN) Commission on Traditional Ecological Knowledge. In the August 1985 issue (p. 1) of their occasional newsletter, entitled *Tradition, Conservation, & Development,* the Commission outlined their mission as follows:

- To promote the synthesis and use of traditional ecological knowledge and resource management practices of rural communities as an effective basis for modern and sustainable resource management systems, and for nature and natural resource conservation;

- To develop and promote effective ways of harnessing, recording, analyzing and applying traditional ecological knowledge for the conservation of nature and natural resources;

- To develop simple methods based on traditional ecological knowledge, for use by rural communities and others, for the assessment and monitoring of the conservation of nature and natural resources;

- To collaborate with groups with related interests, both within and without the Commission, and to liaise with appropriate external agencies, to foster the achievement of conservation objectives through the application of traditional ecological knowledge.

American universities have also developed research and internship programs to record, analyze, and possibly apply traditional conservation techniques to modern resource management practices. For example, Steve Gleissman directs The Agroecology Program at the University of California at Santa Cruz, which sets up internship opportunities for students to observe traditional agricultural techniques in Mexico. These conservation techniques (e.g., diversified cropping) are then tried on university experimental plots that are more analogous to modern systems of agriculture. Further research needs to be done on North American Indian traditional conservation techniques (e.g., floodwater farming, rainfall culture, sand mulching, field placement, and plow patterns) to see if there are any concepts or lessons in conservation that might be applicable to our modern systems of resource management.

Native Americans may be America's first conservationists; they are also at the forefront of today's antinuclear movement. One reason is that substantial amounts of U.S. uranium reserves, essential to nuclear processing, are located on land populated by Indians and Chicanos on the Colorado Plateau (New Mexico, Colorado, Arizona, and Utah). On their lands, winds blow across 100-million-ton piles of tailings, which are the byproduct of uranium mining. These winds carry radioactive radon gas into their agricultural crops, homes, and water supplies. Health concerns about this situation have resulted in widespread community organizing and in educational efforts by native people on the reservations and in the pueblos. It is for this reason that many Native American activists are leading the way in calling for the greater use of renewable energy sources.

Not all environmentalists, however, view the Native American as an "ecological saint." Recently, some authors, such as Steinhart (1984) and Williams (1986), have attacked the long venerated American Indian, thus giving the American environmental movement a sudden anti-Indian sentiment. They maintain that the Indian is really a "miscast ecologist," citing their general abuse of natural resources on their reservation lands and the specific killing of certain animals (e.g., the bald eagle) that are protected by national laws. Rather than strip American Indians of any further treaty rights, other scholars, such as Schwarz (1987), have called for environmentalists to seek mutually agreeable trade-offs (e.g., the opening up of certain national forest lands to Native Americans in exchange for the surrender of some of their treaty rights). Schwarz uses the opening up of Alaskan wilderness lands to the Inuit cultural group as a model.

Whether "first ecologist" or "miscast ecologist," Native Americans were certainly the first inhabitants of the North American continent that practiced conservation techniques that are worthy of our study, and these techniques have a possible application in modern systems of natural resource management. For that reason alone, Native Americans must be included in any study of American environmental history.

The Colonialists and a New Land Policy

By 1607, the first colonialists had begun to settle the Atlantic shores of North America (Table 1-1). To these early immigrants, this was a continent of dark woods and dense thickets, wild animals and savages—all in all, a hideous and desolate wilderness to be conquered.

According to Stewart Udall (1963)—former secretary of the Department of the Interior under presidents Kennedy and Johnson, and a respected conservationist—the colonists brought three things with them that changed the policy toward land within the region. First, they brought a new technology based

TABLE 1-1
Chronology of historical events, key conservationists, important books (1607–1849)

YEAR	HISTORICAL EVENTS	KEY CONSERVATIONISTS	IMPORTANT BOOKS
1607	Jamestown settled by the London Company		
1620	Pilgrims land at Plymouth		
1756–1763	French and Indian War		
1776	American Declaration of Independence and Revolution		
1769	Daniel Boone begins exploring the American wilderness	Daniel Boone (1734–1820)	
1789–1797	George Washington (first U.S. president)	George Washington (1732–1799) Patrick Henry (1736–1799) William Bartram (1739–1823)	Bartram's *Travels* (1791)
1801–1809	Thomas Jefferson (third U.S. president)	Thomas Jefferson (1743–1826)	Thomas Malthus's *Essay on the Principle of Population* (1798)
1803	Louisiana Purchase; Lewis and Clark Expedition		Alexander von Humboldt's *Essays on the Geography of Plants* (1807)
1822	Jed Smith joins trapping crew to ascend the Missouri River	Jedediah Strong Smith (1799–1831) Frederick Law Olmsted (1822–1903)	
1830s	First Redemption Act passed	John James Audubon (1785–1851)	Audubon's *Birds of America* (1826–1838)
1831	First American railroads begin operation	Ralph Waldo Emerson (1803–1882)	Emerson's *Nature* (1836)
1845	Texas annexed to the United States	Francis Parkman, Jr. (1823–1893)	Parkman's *The Oregon Trail* (1849)
1849	U.S. Department of the Interior established	Henry David Thoreau (1817–1862)	Thoreau's *Walden* (1854)

Source: Adapted from Petulla, Joseph. 1977. *American Environmental History.* San Francisco: Boyd and Fraser.

on the iron age. With it came the introduction of the axe, the gun, and the wheel, intensifying the environmental impact of human activities. Second, the colonists brought a "new cast of mind"—a belief that humans could (and should) control their destiny. The first task was to bring the wilderness under control, which meant clearing forests for agricultural crops, domesticating animals for livestock production, and taming the American Indians (another form of domestication), ensuring their submission and their eventual elimination from the land. Third, the colonists brought the concept of land ownership, which helped accomplish many of their goals. Whereas Native Americans believed in the concept of common property, the European immigrants introduced fences, formal papers, wax seals, and other tools to declare ownership of property. The ultimate result

was a new land policy that forever changed human relationships toward land on the continent.

The White Indians: Daniel Boone and Jedediah Smith

At the time of the American Revolution, there were a few legendary people who helped pave the way for conservation. These were mountaineers such as Daniel Boone (1734–1820) and Jedediah Smith (1799–1831). Udall (1963) called men like them "The White Indians," for they wandered the wilderness of America as free spirits, and they had prowess and the ability to read a landscape. One could argue that these hunters and trappers were anti-conservation, since they were undisciplined and could not have cared less about their impact on animal populations. Furthermore, their explorations paved the way for westward migration and the development of new settlements. On the plus side, however, Udall (1963) argues that Daniel Boone, Jedediah Smith, Kit Carson, Jim Bridger, and other mountaineers like them helped imprint in the American psyche its love of wilderness and open space, its love of wild things, and its belief that large portions of the country should remain in public ownership for future hunters, explorers, and adventurers.

Thomas Jefferson: President and Conservationist

Thomas Jefferson (1743–1826) was not only the third president of the United States, but also a leading conservationist in his day. Although the early nineteenth century was a period of tremendous land abuse because resources then seemed limitless, there were a few individuals, like Jefferson, who called for frugal resource use. Specifically, Jefferson criticized wasteful agricultural practices, advocated soil studies, and practiced such conservation techniques as crop rotation. He was also ahead of his time when it came to landscape architecture. For example, when planning the landscaping for his estate at Monticello in 1806, he resisted radically transforming the natural landscape as was the current fashion in Europe. Rather, he designed his garden to suit the natural topography of the area and selected only indigenous plants and trees that reflected the character of the land. As pointed out by Hans Huth (1957), Jefferson laid the foundation for Frederick Law Olmsted and other landscape architects to follow. Today, particularly in the drought-prone west and southwest regions of the country, environmentalists, urban designers, and landscape architects continue to encourage the use of indigenous trees and shrubs, in this case, primarily for their water-conserving tendencies.

In the early nineteenth century, Jefferson and a number of other well-known individuals such as Darwin, Goethe, Emerson, and Thoreau were attracted to the writings of Alexander von Humboldt, who was the period's world premier man of science (Worster 1979). Although the science of ecology had yet to be declared, Humboldt's writings reflect a desire to arrive at a "holistic view" of nature—a synthesis of climatology, geology, physics, natural history, and economics. Humboldt's *Personal Narrative*—a seven-volume study of his travels in Latin America during the years 1799 and 1804—was not only a study in geography, but also a study of ecological biology, an underlying theme of modern-day environmentalism.

The Naturalists Speak for Nature

America's nineteenth century naturalists also helped stir the environmental conscious of the nation. Among the most notable were Bartram, Thoreau, Audubon, Parkman, and Emerson. The following is a brief look at these individuals and how their works or accomplishments have affected post–World War II resource management.

Bartram: The Botanist and Nature Artist. A contemporary of Thomas Jefferson and Daniel Boone was the botanist and artist William Bartram (1739–1823). Bartram is considered this country's first native-born American nature artist. His father, John Bartram, was also a famous botanist. William is most remembered for his classic book, *Travels* (1791), which is a marvelous record of wild nature on the colonial frontier and beyond. Although the book primarily focused on the botanical wonderland of the Carolinas, Georgia, and Florida, it also talked about American Indians and their harmony with the land.

Bartram explored the American wilderness as a source of aesthetic delight and spiritual enrichment, but his writings helped lay the foundation for today's naturalists, botanists, ornithologists, anthropologists, and conservationists. For example, modern-day field guides, such as Roger Tory Peterson's *A Field Guide to Birds of Eastern and Central America* (1980), lists the *Bartramia longicauda* (upland plover), a sandpiper first identified in the Carolinas by Bartram in his *Travels.* Today's anthropologists and human ecologists still refer to Bartram's writings about early Indian settlements, which include discussions of mound-building practices, comparative linguistics, musical instruments, ceremonies, and dances. Bartram's biographer, Elman (1977), also notes that Bartram was one of the first to see the importance of the biome—a concept used by today's bioregionalists, biologists, and general conservationists.

Audubon: The Bird Hunter and Painter. About the time that America's first railroads were going into operation, Haitian-born Jean Rabin (later named John James Audubon) was traveling the countryside on hunting expeditions. While today's naturalists can search and record with powerful bird scopes and cameras, Audubon first had to shoot his specimens before drawing them. Proby (1974) notes, however, that Audubon loved "blood sports," killing birds by the thousands. The birds, of course, were used for his paintings, but many were also sold to collectors to support his ventures. For this reason, some have maintained that Audubon was hardly a conservationist. Regardless, it took over 30 years of traveling, hunting, painting, and writing to produce his remarkable series of books entitled *Birds of America* (1826–1838). The volume was unusual and monumental for two major reasons. First, Audubon used freshly killed specimens, and, more important he wired the birds into lifelike positions. Previous bird artists, such as Mark Catesby and Alexander Wilson, merely used skins or dead specimens. Second, Audubon portrayed an immense number of birds, which made this work unlike any previous study.

Although Audubon did not found today's highly influential National Audubon Society, he did inspire George Grinnell (an art student of Audubon's wife), who went on to organize the society in Audubon's name. (See pp. 10–11 for further details on Grinnell.) Audubon also made significant contributions to the methods used to study birds. For example, it is believed that he was the first person to use a blind for observation purposes and the first to employ the banding of birds, a fundamental technique used in modern avian studies.

Emerson: The Philosopher, Theologian, and Poet. While Audubon and Francis Parkman (the naturalist and historian who published *The Oregon Trail* in 1849) were interested in what Udall (1963) calls the "details of specialists," Ralph Waldo Emerson (1803–1882) was more interested in the holistic picture of the environment, which today's environmentalists wish to portray and study. This theologian, philosopher, and poet began the Transcendentalist movement in America and is probably most noted for his famous work, *Nature* (1836). Although Emerson witnessed the degradation of the environment around him, he made no outright protest against resource waste during his lifetime. His contribution to the American environmental movement is found in his studies, such as *Nature*, that investigate the relationship between man, nature, and religion. Specifically, Emerson saw nature as the unifier between man and God. For further information on Emerson's philosophy, consult Sherman (1952), Rountree (1973), and McAleer (1984). One of Emerson's contemporaries and ardent followers was Henry David Thoreau.

Thoreau: The Father of the Nature Essay. To many of his contemporaries, Henry David Thoreau (1817–1862) was an eccentric and a failure. In 1854, he published *Walden*, a book that chronicled his 26-month experiment in living at Walden Pond in Concord, Massachusetts. The book made little impact at the time of its publication. In fact, it took five years to sell the 2000 copies of its first edition. Yet today,

over 200 editions later, the book is considered by many to be the single most important piece of nature writing in American literature.

Thoreau's relevance to post World War II conservation is profound. First, this "father of the nature essay" has greatly influenced the works of later naturalists. For example, Rachel Carson (of *Silent Spring* fame) was known to keep a copy of his writings by her bedside to read before going to sleep. After writing a biography about Thoreau, Joseph Wood Krutch decided to make a career change and become a nature writer. Second, Thoreau as "original preservationist" set the imaginative pattern for others interested in the preservation of natural landscapes. In 1858, a decade before Congress established its first National Park, Thoreau pleaded for "natural preserves." Today, no one who reads or writes about the wilderness or wilderness management can escape Thoreau's influence. In fact, quotations from his works have become mottos for the wilderness preservation movement. Finally, Thoreau's "experiment in simplicity" has led others today to do the same, but in the more modern and urban scene. According to a 1980 report of the prestigious Stanford Research Institute (SRI International), over 3 percent of the American public have adopted some form of the "Voluntary Simplicity" lifestyle. Specific practices may include such things as growing one's own food (organically, if possible); buying natural foods (rather than processed); reducing one's energy consumption; recycling cans, bottles, and paper; and biking to work and stores. In all cases, the emphasis is on smallness, aesthetics, independence, and self-sufficiency. For further information on Thoreau's legacy, one can consult Robert D. Richardson, Jr. (1986) and David E. Shi (1985).

THE AMERICAN CONSERVATION MOVEMENT: ITS BEGINNINGS

Influential Scientists, Explorers, and Naturalists

While Thoreau and the other early conservationists helped stir the environmental conscious of America, their writings generally had little effect on political change. Conservation became a political movement only after it had at its helm such highly political and influential individuals as Marsh, Powell, and Muir (Table 1-2).

Marsh: The Extraordinary Scientist. At the time that America was going through a grueling civil war, a Vermonter named George Perkins Marsh (1801–

TABLE 1-2

Chronology of historical events, key conservationists, important books (1862–1929)

YEAR	HISTORICAL EVENTS	KEY CONSERVATIONISTS	IMPORTANT BOOKS
1862	Department of Agriculture established; First Homestead Act passed		
1864	Yosemite Valley, California, becomes state park	George Perkins Marsh (1801–1882)	Marsh's *Man and Nature; Or, Physical Geography as Modified by Human Action* (1864)
1868	John Muir arrives in California		
1869	John Wesley Powell descends the Colorado River	John Wesley Powell (1834–1902)	Powell's *Report on the Lands of the Arid Regions of the United States* (1878)
1872	Creation of Yellowstone National Park;		
1873	Timber Culture Act		
1879	U.S. Geological Survey established		
1881	Division of Forestry created in U.S. Department of Agriculture		
1887	Hatch Act establishes agricultural experiment stations		
1891	Yosemite National Park established; Forest Reserves Act		
1892	Sierra Club organized by John Muir	John Muir (1838–1914)	
1898	Gifford Pinchot becomes first Chief Forester	Gifford Pinchot (1865–1946)	
1900	Lacey Act		
1902	Reclamation Act		
1903	Muir's four-day tour with Teddy Roosevelt	Theodore Roosevelt (1859–1919)	
1905	National Audubon Society formed; Teddy Roosevelt creates U.S. Forest Service with Gifford Pinchot first director		
1906	Antiquities Act		
1907	Teddy Roosevelt doubles forest area under protection		
1908	Teddy Roosevelt and governor's conference on conservation		Pinchot's *The Fight for Conservation* (1910)
1911	Fur Seal Treaty		Muir's *My First Summer in the Sierra* (1911); *The Yosemite* (1912)
1916	National Parks Act; Migratory bird treaty between U.S. and Great Britain; National Park Service Act		
1922	Izaac Walton League organized		
1929	Crash of 1929 leads to Great Depression		

1882) was writing a book that would revolutionize thinking on human relationships with the land. Marsh had seen Vermont change from a wild frontier to an area that had been literally stripped of its virgin forests. Marsh was angry and wanted to write something that would reach popular audiences yet be scientific enough to influence politicians. Fluent in 20 languages, Marsh had the ability to read widely and to integrate all types of information. The result was a conservation classic: *Man and Nature; Or, Physical Geography as Modified by Human Action* (1864).

Marsh's book was unique for several reasons. It was the first book to really look at the role of humans as a geologic force or as modifiers of the land. This perspective is sometimes known as *cultural determinism*. Up to this time, most scientific works maintained that the environment (particularly climate and terrain) determined human behavior and shaped society—a theory known as *environmental determinism*. Second, *Man and Nature* boldly refuted the nineteenth century belief that America could afford to wastefully exploit its natural resources. He accomplished this refutation by using his masterful skills at synthesis, combining science, history, economics, theory, and morality into his argument. Third, *Man and Nature* was so detailed and well thought out that it became a sourcebook on forestry and forest resource management policy in the early twentieth century. For this reason Lewis Mumford and others consider George Perkins Marsh the father of the conservation movement. To see how Marsh's ideas remain relevant today, see William Thomas, Jr.'s compilation *Man's Role in Changing the Face of the Earth* (1956). This is an important volume that grew out of a symposium informally called "The Marsh Festival," a gathering of over 70 scholars in celebration of the Marsh tradition.

Powell: The Explorer of the Colorado River. Five years after Marsh published *Man and Nature,* another remarkable man named John Wesley Powell (1834–1902) was about to make his mark on the American conservation movement. This self-educated scientist, explorer, politician, ethnographer, and Civil War hero became famous in 1869 for descending the unknown reaches of the Colorado River for the purpose of specimen collection, geologic inspection, map work, and general scientific observation.

Like George Perkins Marsh, Powell understood and recorded the human impact on the land. He was particularly interested in the geomorphology of the West, the role of water in landscape transformation, and the place and impact of humans on arid land-

scapes. In 1878, Powell submitted *A Report on the Lands of the Arid Region of the United States* to Carl Schurz, then secretary of the Department of the Interior. The study was more than just a report with facts and figures; it was a general land-use plan for the western half of the United States. His plan called for revising the sacred Homestead Act of 1862, which had carved up the American west into standardized packages of 160 acres without regard to watersheds, drainage basins, and other critical geographic features of the arid landscape. In order to better understand the land, Powell called for the creation of a federal agency to survey and map all U.S. lands. In 1879, the U.S. Geological Survey was created for just that purpose. Although ideas in his general plan were not accepted until much later (e.g., in the Reclamation Act of 1902), Powell remained highly respected in the scientific world. For example, he helped organize the prestigious American Association for the Advancement of Science (AAAS), and he was one of its early presidents. His influence led to the creation of the Bureau of American Ethnology, the Geological Society of America, and even the National Geographic Society, which produces *National Geographic* magazine and television specials loved by many Americans today.

Muir: The California Naturalist. About the same year that John Wesley Powell was descending the Colorado River, a young Scot named John Muir (1838–1914) was stalking plants, breaking horses, shearing sheep, and doing other odd jobs in Yosemite, California (Figure 1-3). In 1870, he also occasionally helped guide tourists through the valley. All the while he wrote, interweaving his geologic descriptions with his own interpretations of religion, science, and philosophy (Fox 1981). Unlike Emerson, who measured nature only in human terms using the Anthropocentric view of man and nature, Muir chose a "man of nature" philosophical base for his subsequent career in conservation. Muir derived this philosophy not from a formal education (though he did attend the University of Wisconsin for two years), but rather from years of direct nature observation and independent study of Thoreau's writings. In fact, according to Fox (1981), Muir often referred to those formally educated and Ph.D.'s as "professor faggots." No doubt some of the leaders of today's anti-environmental establishment organizations (e.g., Earth First! and the Greens) feel the same about the value of formal education.

Despite being an "amateur" geologist and writer, Muir's works eloquently described the experience of nature, and, more important, served as

FIGURE 1-3   John Muir. (Photo by George R. King.)

guides to finding our roots in the land around us. Although it is virtually impossible to rank Muir's works in terms of superiority, perhaps the most notable are Muir's *My First Summer in the Sierra* (1911) and *The Yosemite* (1912). Even more important than his writings were Muir's political actions, such as the founding of the Sierra Club (1892), his lobbying efforts with President Theodore Roosevelt (1903), and his battling to stop the building of Hetch Hetchy Dam. For additional information on Muir, consult Wolfe (1951), Brooks (1980), or Fleck (1985).

The Forest, Land, and Water Protectors

The period between 1890 and 1916 was particularly active in terms of discussion and legislation regarding forest, land, and water conservation. It was the time in American conservation history during which Charles Sprague Sargent (1841–1927) was fighting for forest protection, George Bucknam Dorr (1853–1944) was working to establish Acadia National Park, Frederick Law Olmsted (1822–1902) was designing what was to be Central Park in New York City and Stephen Mather (1867–1930) was making a name for himself as the first director of the National Park Service. However, the most flamboyant and controversial conservationists of this period were President Theodore Roosevelt (1859–1919) and Gifford Pinchot (1865–1946).

Theodore Roosevelt: The Most Conservation-Minded U.S. President. John Muir had a relative easy time convincing Theodore Roosevelt of the need to protect the Sierra forests, since Roosevelt was well aware of the environmental degradation that was occurring in America. As a rancher, Roosevelt had dealt with the problems of soil erosion, had seen the need to irrigate in the arid West, and had witnessed the depletion of wild animals by market hunters. Once a famous big game hunter himself, Roosevelt had eventually turned from hunting to conservation. In fact, with George Grinnell, he launched the Boone and Crockett Club—a group of dedicated hunters who were also interested in preserving big game for its own sake.

Environmentalists today still consider Theodore Roosevelt the most conservation minded of all U.S. presidents. After the famous 1903 four-day tour of Yosemite with John Muir, Roosevelt approved the completion of Yosemite National Park, created the U.S. Forest Service (1905), which is responsible for the conservation and management of our national forests, and doubled the forest area under protection (1907). As a showpiece to his last year as president in 1908, Roosevelt convened 44 state governors and hundreds of experts in the now famous Governor's Conference on Natural Resources. This conference was planned and financed by Gifford Pinchot, to whom Roosevelt also listened with much conviction.

A number of biographies have been written on Theodore Roosevelt, such as Grantham (1971), Cadenhead (1974), and, more recently, Cutright (1985).

Pinchot: The Political Forester. In addition to listening to the "intangibles" of the preservationist philosophy of John Muir, Teddy Roosevelt also paid attention to Gifford Pinchot and the other "utilitarianists"—those that spoke for material resources and jobs (Figure 1-4). Whereas Muir spoke of religion, philosophy, and proper ethical attitudes toward the land, Pinchot emphasized the scientific and practical aspects of forest management that he had learned while a student in Germany and France. Forests should be "managed" scientifically for "sustained yield" was his motto. He believed in reducing management decisions to a simple formula: Manage for the greatest good for the greatest number. Unfortunately, this philosophy had a built-in bias toward material resources that flew in the face of Muir and other preservationists who wanted such intangibles as beauty and aesthetics factored into the formula. To this day, the preservationists (Muir) and the utilitarians (Pinchot) battle for dominance.

Pinchot pushed his brand of conservation as the first director of the U.S. Forest Service after he was appointed in 1905, as a teacher of forestry at Yale University (1910–1936), and as a writer, publishing *The Flight for Conservation* (1910) and *Breaking New Ground* (1947). Pinchot is relevant to post–World War II conservation, since his basic themes are still dominant in American environmental thought. For example, in a 1984 speech at Princeton University, former Environmental Protection Agency Director William Ruckelshaus applied Pinchot's utilitarian viewpoint to a new environmental problem: the tradeoff between economic values and public health risks from hazardous substances (Ruckelshaus 1984). Today's preservationists even argue from positions within the utilitarian perspective, such as their defense of wilderness for its value to humans. In the decades following the 1960s, the avalanche of environmental legislation demonstrates the public's acceptance of Pinchot's belief that government should play a major role in environmental protection. It is also true, however, that many modern conservationists have been critical of the administrative practices of those same government agencies, in particular the practices of the U.S. Forest Service and the Bureau of Land Management. For further details about Pinchot, consult Fausold (1961), McGeary (1960), and Pinkett (1970).

FIGURE 1-4 President Theodore Roosevelt and Gifford Pinchot. (The Bettmann Archive.)

Those Who Fought for Wildlife

Between 1900 and 1935, the protection of wildlife was a major concern to many American conservationists. William T. Hornaday (1857–1937), while director of the Bronx Zoo, fought valiantly to protect North America's endangered wild animals. George Bird Grinnell (1848–1938) was active editing *Forest and Stream* (a major conservation magazine), as well as founding the National Association of Audubon Societies. Helping Grinnell was William E. Dutcher (1846–1920), who was especially important in founding New York's Audubon Society. Will H. Dilg (1867–1927), a bass fisherman and overall outdoor enthusiast, founded the Izaak Walton League, which publishes *Outdoor America*, a widely circulated conservation magazine. Willard Van Name (1872–1959), the "radical" conservationist with the American Museum of Natural History, was constantly challenging the Audubon Society and other conservation organizations to improve their methods and take greater action. And Rosalie Edge (1877–1962), also a critic of the Audubon Society, was making a name for herself as the first female conservationist to make a major impact on conservation legislation regarding wildlife regulations. A more dramatic period in conservation history, however, is the 1930s.

Conservation During the 1930s and 1940s

The Crash of 1929 led to the Great Depression in America. Droughts and dust storms wracked havoc in the West, and the country was ready for new leadership and a new phase in conservation history. In the 1920s, conservation had been primarily in the hands of business-minded Republicans. This was all to change when Franklin D. Roosevelt was elected to office. In 1933, Roosevelt appointed Democrats to the top cabinet positions, and since Democrats were to remain in office for the next 20 years, it was Democrats who primarily took the helm of the conservation movement. Leading conservationists during the 1930s and early 1940s were Franklin D. Roosevelt, Jay Norwood "Ding" Darling, Robert Marshall, and Aldo Leopold (Table 1-3).

Franklin D. Roosevelt: The New Deal President. Like his uncle Theodore, Franklin Roosevelt (1882–1945) was an advocate of conservation, with a special interest in trees, land, and water. To help prevent soil erosion due to wind, Roosevelt called for the planting of a "shelterbelt" along the 100th meridian from Texas to Canada (see Chapter 3 for further details). To help relieve unemployment and boost conservation, Roosevelt created the Civilian Conservation Corps (CCC)—an organization of over 2.5 million young men who were put to work building dams and reservoirs, planting trees, and constructing fire towers. Although their zeal sometimes offended conservationists, the overall effect of the program for the men, as well as for the land, was good. To harness an unruly river system and improve the living conditions of the region's poor farmers, Roosevelt created the Tennessee Valley Authority (TVA). The project took a regional or watershed approach to solving a major environmental problem, an approach often favored by today's conservationists. To help eliminate overgrazing in the West, Congress passed the Taylor Grazing Act of 1934, thereby dividing up 90 million acres of public rangeland into grazing districts for conservation control.

Roosevelt is also credited for combining two departments—the Bureau of Fisheries of the Commerce Department and the Biological Survey of the Agriculture Department—into today's U.S. Fish and Wildlife Service, which is now housed in the Department of

TABLE 1-3

Chronology of historical events, key conservationists, important books (1933–1948)

YEAR	HISTORICAL EVENTS	KEY CONSERVATIONISTS	IMPORTANT BOOKS
1933–1937	Drought and dust storms in the West lead to the "Dust Bowl";	Franklin D. Roosevelt (1882–1945)	
	Franklin Roosevelt's "New Deal";	Robert Marshall (1901–1939)	Marshall's article, "The Problem of the Wilderness," *Scientific Monthly* (1930)
	Civilian Conservation Corps (CCC);		
	Tennessee Valley Authority (TVA)		Marshall's *Arctic Village*, (1933); *The People's Forest* (1933)
1934	Taylor Grazing Act		
1935	Wilderness Society established		
1938	National Wildlife Federation		
1939–1945	World War II	Aldo Leopold (1886–1948)	Leopold's *Game Management* (1933)
1940	U.S. Fish and Wildlife Service established	J. N. ("Ding") Darling (1876–1962)	
1944	Soil Conservation Society of America founded		
1946	U.S. Bureau of Land Management established; Nature Conservancy established		Pinchot's *Breaking New Ground* (1947)
1948	International Union for the Conservation of Nature and Natural Resources established		Leopold's *A Sand County Almanac* (1949)

Source: Adapted from Petulla, Joseph. 1977. *American Environmental History.* San Francisco: Boyd and Fraser.

the Interior. This 1940 action, however, would not have taken place if it were not for the lobbying of such individuals as Jay Norwood "Ding" Darling and others who informed Roosevelt about the need of taking action for wildlife. Additional information on Roosevelt as a conservationist can be found in a number of sources, such as Nixon (1957), Davies (1971), and Miller (1983).

Darling: The Editorial Cartoonist. Wildlife was a low-priority issue for Roosevelt, and, consequently, he was regularly pressured by individuals such as Jay Norwood "Ding" Darling (1876–1962). Darling brought pressure to the White House through his skills as a popular editorial cartoonist for the Des Moines *Registrar*. His editorial cartoons were printed by hundreds of different newspapers across the country, thereby regularly bringing what Fox (1981) calls a "visual Will Rogers" to the breakfast tables of millions of Americans.

After years of poking fun at the administration from the outside, Darling eventually found himself on the inside facing all the problems of big bureaucracy. This transition began with his appointment to the 1933 President's Commission on Wild Life Restoration and ended one year later when he became the head of the federal Biological Survey, the predecessor to today's U.S. Fish and Wildlife Service. During his stint as director of the Biological Survey, Darling is credited with raising $8.5 million from Congress for purchasing waterfowl refuges, which was an unprecedented amount of money for the time. Sensing the jealousy aroused by his feats, Darling resigned in 1935. In 1936, Darling was to go on to become the president of the newly formed General Wild Life Federation, which was renamed the National Wildlife Federation in 1938 and became the largest and most powerful conservation organization in the country. Additional information on Darling can be obtained from Fox (1981), Brokaw (1978), and Reed and Drabelle (1984).

Marshall: Father of the Wilderness Preservation Movement. While Darling was making headway in terms of wildlife protection, a forester and explorer named Robert Marshall (1901–1939) was working on preserving America's remaining wilderness areas. Although a rugged individualist and serious hiker, Marshall was also well schooled and had excellent writing skills. By 1930, at the age of 28 years, he had completed four years of undergraduate education in forestry at New York's State College in Syracuse, a master's degree in forestry from Harvard, and a doctorate in plant physiology from Johns Hopkins University. More important, this was the year that Marshall wrote his famous article. "The Problem of the Wilderness," in *Scientific Monthly*, which Benton MacKaye (the father of the Appalachian Trail) and others have dubbed the Magna Carta of the wilderness preservation movement. Marshall's article discussed the value of the wilderness experience, the need for identifying and classifying America's remaining wilderness areas, and the need to take immediate action.

In 1933, just three years later, his books *Arctic Village* and *The People's Forest* were published. The first book recounted his 1929–1931 experience in the Koyukuk region of north central Alaska and documented his distaste for cities and the modern life. The latter book examined the exploitation and abuse of America's forests. Marshall, is best remembered, however, for being the political force that helped establish The Wilderness Society in 1935, along with cofounders Robert Sterling Yard, Benton MacKaye, Earnest C. Oberholtzer, Bernard Frank, Harvey Broome, and Aldo Leopold. Ironically, Marshall—a man who had made over 200 day hikes of 30 miles each—died of a heart attack at the age of 38 in 1939, while riding a train. For further information, Marshall (1971), Vickery (1985), and Glover (1986) provide additional insights into Marshall's character and importance to the history of conservation in America.

Leopold: The Father of Wildlife Management. One colleague of Darling and Marshall during the Roosevelt era was a man named Aldo Leopold (Figure 1-5). This Iowan, trained in the Pinchot school of forestry, went on to become what Callicot (1983, p. 329) and others have labeled "America's most distinguished conservationist." Although Leopold wrote over 300 published articles, he is most remembered for two important books: *Game Management* (1933) and *A Sand County Almanac* (1949). The books also represent the evolution of his philosophy. In his earlier work, *Game Management*, Leopold applied Pinchot's utilitarian notions of conservation to the management of wildlife. It established wildlife management as a new science, encouraging sensitive manipulation of the environment based on ecological principles. The book was so well received that the University of Wisconsin–Madison created a teaching position for him, which is how he became the first professor of wildlife management in the nation and the father of modern wildlife management.

Gradually, Leopold's ideas began to drift away from the hard-line utilitarian concepts of Pinchot. He began to realize that wildlife management was more than just sorting out the good animals from the bad

FIGURE 1-5 Aldo Leopold on his sand county farm at the Shack in 1945. (Photo by Robert McCabe; courtesy of Dr. Charles Bradley, Leopold Reserve. From Curt Meine, "The Farmer as Conservationist: Aldo Leopold on Agriculture," *Journal of Soil and Water Conservation,* vol. 42, no. 3 [May–June 1987], p. 147.)

ones, and eradicating the latter. All animals had a right to the land. There was a "land ethic" that needed to be learned, and his ideas regarding this concept culminated in his second and most famous work, *A Sand County Almanac*. In an analysis of significant books in the environmental movement, Mark Vaz (1986, pp. 56–57) recorded the feelings of some important conservationists about Leopold's book. For example, Pulitzer prize winning author Wallace Stegner knows "nothing better, purer or straighter" than Leopold's classic work. Environmental historian Donald Worster observed that "The Land Ethic," the concluding chapter in *A Sand County Almanac,* is "the clearest and most universal advice we have on how modern people can live in harmony with the Earth. The more I read it, the more convinced I am of its essential wisdom, its brilliance, and its possibilities." David Foreman, editor of the radical environmental journal *Earth First!,* has said, "*A Sand County Almanac* is not only the most important conservation book ever written, it is the most important book ever written, and the clearest way home, except for a visit to the wilderness itself." For further information about Leopold, see Wallace (1987), Meine (1987), or Tanner (1987).

ENVIRONMENTALISM: THE NEW CONSERVATION (1960–1989)

The decade of the 1950s was a relatively quiet period in the history of American conservation. Although the country was still producing conservationists (e.g.,

John D. Rockefeller, Bernard DeVoto, Joseph Wood Krutch, Charles Lindbergh, Justice William O. Douglas, Olaus J. Murie, and Jim Gabrielson), a major boost in the conservation movement did not occur until the politically turbulent 1960s (Table 1-4). It was then that a new type of conservation emerged, known as "environmentalism," which had an emphasis on the broader issue of environmental quality, in addition to just the traditional conservationist's concern about the supply of fish and wildlife for hunters and fishermen. It took political activists like David Brower, photographers like Ansel Adams and Eliot Porter, biologists like Rachel Carson, and politicians like Stewart Udall to transform conservation into the central domestic policy issue that it is today.

Sierra Club and the Exhibit Books

Brower: Muir's Reincarnate. In the 1960s, David Brower became the leader of Muir's Sierra Club, and he transformed it from the small, personal, social club for summer trips and mountain climbs into the militant activist group that it is today. In the seven years that Brower was its director, Sierra Club's membership doubled, and its conservation budget alone grew six times, from $5000 to $30,000 (Fox 1981). Much of this success was due to Brower's bold publishing program, especially the series of exhibit format photography books. Brower used the photographic genius of Ansel Adams and Eliot Porter to produce books that had an ability to "speak to others" besides the conservationists. In 1969, after some disagreements with the Sierra Club's Board of

TABLE 1-4

Chronology of historical events, key conservationists, important books (1952–1969)

YEAR	HISTORICAL EVENTS	KEY CONSERVATIONISTS	IMPORTANT BOOKS
1952	Resources for the Future established	Olaus Murie (1889–1963)	Murie's *Field Guide to Animal Tracks* (1954)
1956	"Soil bank" agricultural plan enacted; Federal water pollution control passed	Rachel Carson (1907–1963) David Brower (1912–)	Carson's *The Edge of the Sea* (1955)
1960	National Forest Multiple-use Act passed	Ansel Adams (1902–1984)	Adams's *This Is the American Earth* (1960)
1961	World Wildlife Fund established	Eliot Porter (1901–)	Porter's *In Wilderness is the Preservation of the World* (1962); Carson's *Silent Spring* (1962)
1963	Clean Air Act passed	Stewart L. Udall (1920–)	Udall's *The Quiet Crisis* (1963)
1964	National wilderness preservation system created under Wilderness Act	Jacques-Yves Cousteau (1910–) Howard Zahniser (1906–1964)	Cousteau's *The Living Sea* (1963); *World without Sun* (1964)
1965	Solid Waste Disposal Act passed; Water Quality Act passed		Glacken's *Traces on the Rhodian Shore: Nature and Culture in Western Thought* (1967)
		Roderick K. Nash (1939–)	Nash's *Wilderness and the American Mind* (1967)
1969	National Environmental Policy Act (NEPA) passed; Friends of the Earth created by David Brower	Paul R. Ehrlich (1932–) Garrett Hardin (1915–)	Ehrlich's *The Population Bomb* (1968) Hardin's "Tragedy of the Commons," *Science* (1968)

Source: Adapted from Petulla, Joseph. 1977. *American Environmental History.* San Francisco: Boyd and Fraser.

Directors, he founded his own conservation organization, Friends of the Earth. Today, he participates again with the Sierra Club, maintains his support of Friends of the Earth, continues his evangelistic "sermon" on a national lecture circuit, and overall remains a persuasive power within the conservation community. Additional information on Brower can be obtained from Kahn (1986), Wild (1986), and McPhee (1971).

Adams: The Black-and-White Wilderness Photographer. David Brower may never have become environmentally active, particularly in the Sierra Club, if it were not for the great American artist and environmentalist, Ansel Adams. The two met in the mountains when Brower was 20 and Adams was 31. They became friends, and in 1937, Adams, a Sierra Club leader since 1919, proposed that Brower accept the executive secretary position in the Sierra Club. In 1960, the Sierra Club published its first large-format exhibit book, *This Is the American Earth,* with over half of the photographs in the book by Ansel Adams. The book was a smashing success. According to California Senator Alan Cranston, the politician Adams felt closest to, "Ansel saw the West not only with his eyes, and his camera, but with his soul. In the mountains, rivers, and valleys of the West, he saw poetry, he saw truth, he saw wisdom, he saw grace" (Wilderness Society 1984, p. 2). Adams left a legacy of activism as well as art. In his later years, he worked to rid the Department of the Interior of his arch enemy, James Watt. He presented the conservation argument to President Ronald Reagan in the White House, fought to help preserve Big Sur in California, and did much, much more. In one of the last interviews before his death in 1984, Adams had said (Exterow 1984, p. 89)

. . . I wish I had gotten into the environmental work earlier because I think that's a citizen's fundamental responsibility. . . . I keep my promise of doing at least one thing a day, one thing related to the environment in some way.

Additional insights into Adam's career are found in Brower (1984) and Craine (1984).

Porter: The Color Wilderness Photographer. Whereas Ansel Adams was a master at black-and-white photography, his student, Eliot Porter, used the art of color photography in his fight for the conservation of wilderness. In 1962, Eliot Porter's spectacular photographs were displayed in the Sierra Club's second exhibit format photography book, *In Wilderness Is the Preservation of the World.* Porter's seemingly three-dimensional color plates, coupled with quotations from Thoreau and an introduction by Joseph Wood Krutch, caught the public's eye and truly launched the exhibit format book series. More important these books, brought an international reputation to the Sierra Club. Other well-known books that displayed Porter's photographic genius are *Baja California—The Geography of Hope* (1967) and *Galapagos—The Flow of Wilderness* (1968). From 1965–1971, he served on the Sierra Club Board of Directors, and, in 1967, he was awarded the Conservation Service Award from the U.S. Department of the Interior. For additional information on Porter, see Fox (1981) or the Macmillan Biographical Encyclopedia of Photographic Artists and Innovators (1983).

Public Awareness of Environmental Degradation

While the team of Brower, Adams, and Porter were "bringing the wilderness to the public" via their exhibit format books in the 1960s, it took a biologist and a U.S. Representative to awaken the country to the seriousness of the environmental degradation that it was experiencing.

Carson: The Visionary Biologist. Born at a time when women were only expected to marry and have a family, Rachel Carson's mother (Maria) encouraged her to do much more, and Rachel did just that, becoming a marine biologist and working for the Biological Survey and later for the U.S. Fish and Wildlife Service (Figure 1-6). More important, she wrote; it was her literary and visionary books that brought her fame and recognition as a leading conservationist of the day. Although her earlier works, such as *The Sea Around Us* (1951) and *The Edge of the Sea* (1955), displayed her outstanding ability to combine literary skills with scientific knowledge, she was not really recognized by conservationists until the 1962 publication of her book *Silent Spring,* which alerted the world to the dangers of pesticide contamination. Ann

FIGURE 1-6 Rachel Carson at Rosalie Edge's Hawk Mountain Sanctuary, 1945. (Photo by Shirley Briggs. Courtesy of the Rachel Carson Council, Inc.)

Zwinger, a natural history writer herself, called Carson's classic "a landmark book for courage, for information, a pivotal book for change in this country. It shows what one intelligent, caring, courageous person can do to save the world" (Vaz 1986, p. 57). As a result of the political storm caused by this book, then President John F. Kennedy called for a special study on DDT and other pesticides, which eventually resulted in the passage of over 40 bills in state legislatures across the country to monitor and regulate pesticides. Additional information about this remarkable woman can be obtained from Brooks (1972), Stroud (1985), and Gartner (1983).

Udall: The Former Secretary of the Interior. One year after Carson's book, in 1963, another book hit the market that shook America: Stewart Udall's *The Quiet Crises.* Udall warned Americans that our increasing population was stripping the country of its natural resources, that our new forms of technology were degrading the environment, and that we were running out of time to develop the necessary national policy required to correct these problems. He concluded by calling for "modern Muirs" to carry on the fight for conservation. Udall became a hero of the conservation movement during his reign as secretary of the Department of the Interior from 1961 to 1969 under the Kennedy and Johnson administrations. He oversaw the passage of the Wilderness Act, the Land and Water Conservation Fund, and the Highway Beautification Act, and he was instrumental in forming the Bureau of Outdoor Recreation to provide for long-range planning of scenic and recreation areas

(Figure 1-7). He was the recipient of numerous conservation awards, such as the Conservationist of the Year, given by the National Wildlife Federation (1964), and the Audubon Medal in 1967. Starnes (1963), Strong (1970), and Whitaker (1987) provide additional insights into Stewart Udall.

Zahniser, Cousteau, and Ehrlich. The mid- to late 1960s was also an active time for the conservationists Howard Zahniser, Jacques-Yves Cousteau, and Paul Ehrlich. Zahniser, one of the least known but influential conservationists, was busy drafting the Wilderness Act, which ultimately won him the distinction of being called the father of the 1964 Wilderness Act.

Cousteau, the famous marine explorer, filmmaker, and environmental educator, completed his books *The Living Sea* (1963) and *World Without Sun* (1964). He continues to fascinate Americans with his use of mass media to bring the frontiers of the ocean and his increasingly desperate conservation message into the American home.

Paul Ehrlich, a Stanford University professor of biology, hit Americans (and the world) hard in 1968, with the publication of *The Population Bomb.* His message was reminiscent of Thomas Malthus, in that he warned us that world population could grow to unsupportable levels and the consequences of this could prove catastrophic. Unlike Malthus, however, Ehrlich called for (1) government programs to limit population growth, and (2) "dedevelopment"—a plan for society to reduce its consumption of energy and matter. Paul Ehrlich, and coauthors Anne Ehrlich and John

FIGURE 1-7 Stewart Udall (second from left) with Howard Zahniser (far left), Robert Frost (center), Justice William O. Douglas (standing), and Chief Justice Earl Warren (far right) at the Thoreau Centennial in 1962. (Photo by Abbie Rowe/NPS; courtesy of The Wilderness Society.)

Holdren, remain prolific, with the publication of their theoretically sound and encyclopedic works *Ecoscience: Population/Resources/Environment* (1977) and *Extinction: The Causes and Consequences of the Disappearance of Species* (1981).

For additional information on these important conservationists consult Zahniser (1984) and Nash (1967) for information on Zahniser. Madsen (1986), Richards (1985), and *U.S. News and World Report* (1985) profile Cousteau. Evory and Metzger (1983) provide information on Ehrlich.

Earth Day and the Energy-Conscious Years (The 1970s)

The controversy stirred by the above writers and by others provided the impetus for Dennis Hayes and other so-called mavericks, dissidents, and cranks, to organize the first international Earth Day in 1970 (Table 1-5). The event turned out to be a smashing success, with an estimated 20 million people demonstrating their concern for the environment. It was a day of mass rallies, which included the picking up of trash alongside roadways, the cleaning up of debris in rivers, and the conducting of environmental teach-ins. The observance of Earth Day continues today in thousands of cities across the nation *and* the world.

The 1970s were also the "energy-conscious years" in America. The 1973 Arab oil embargo alerted Americans to how energy dependent we were on outside oil, and "Project Independence" was launched, which included the construction of a controversial pipeline across the Alaskan tundra (1974) and the creation of a separate Department of Energy (1977) to integrate the administration's energy policy.

It was also a time when Barry Commoner, E. F.

TABLE 1-5

Chronology of historical events, key conservationists, important books (1970–1983)

YEAR	HISTORICAL EVENTS	KEY CONSERVATIONISTS	IMPORTANT BOOKS
1970	First Earth Day; Resource Recovery Act passed; Water Quality Control Act passed		
1972	Stockholm Conference on the Human Environment	Barry Commoner (1917–)	Commoner's *The Closing Circle* (1971) Donella H. Meadow's *Limits to Growth* (1972)
1973	Arab Oil Embargo alerts nation to energy dependence on Middle East	E. F. Schumacher (1911–1977)	Schumacher's *Small Is Beautiful* (1973)
1974	Approval of Alaska Pipeline	Edward Abbey (1927–1989)	Abbey's *The Monkey Wrench Gang* (1975)
1977	Department of Energy created		Paul Ehrlich, Anne Ehrlich, and John Holdren's *Ecoscience: Population/Resources/Environment* (1977)
1980	Woman's Action for Nuclear Disarmament group founded; The Reagan years begin: environmentalists begin to fight back	Helen Caldicott (1939–) Ralph Nader (1934–)	Nader's *Who's Poisoning America* (1981)
1982	One million sign anti-Watt petition		Jonathan Schell's *The Fate of the Earth* (1982)
1983	James Watt resigns as Secretary of the Interior (October 10)	Lester Brown (1928–)	*The State of the World* series by Worldwatch Institute first published (1984)
(?)	Earth First! founded	Dave Foreman (?) Mike Roselle (1954–)	Dave Foreman's *EcoDefense: A Field Guide to Monkey-Wrenching* (1985)

Source: Adapted from Petulla, Joseph. 1977. *American Environmental History.* San Francisco: Boyd and Fraser.

Schumacher, and others were raising new questions about the types of technology that we used to maintain our relatively high standard of living.

Commoner: The Biologist Who Questioned Post-World War II Technology. In 1971, Barry Commoner, a Brooklyn-born Harvard Ph.D. in biology, published a visionary book called *The Closing Circle.* The book provided a plethora of examples of how America's technology had changed drastically after World War II from a technology using natural products to one using synthetic products (e.g., school chairs that were once made out of wood were now made from plastic; automobile tires that were once constructed from natural rubber were now made from synthetic rubber). His chief argument was that technology, not population, was the major cause of the environmental crisis. This led to the now famous public debate between Commoner and Paul Ehrlich, who argued that population was the primary culprit, not technology. Although Commoner and Ehrlich finally agreed that both technology and population affect the environment, and that no one factor was more important than another, Commoner succeeded in raising our awareness of the new types of technology that Americans are dependent upon and how these new types often do not break down or biodegrade naturally into the environment. Additional information about Commoner can be found in Fox (1981), *Forbes* (1976), and the *New York Times Magazine* (1976).

Schumacher: The Advocate of Buddhist Economics. Another critic in the 1970s, of technology achieved at the expense of environmental health, was the economist E. F. Schumacher. In his now famous *Small Is Beautiful* (1973), Schumacher argued the case for Buddhist economics—the need for simplicity and technological nonviolence. This meant using the most appropriate form of technology for a given place and society—the simplest, cheapest, and least environmentally damaging form that was available. His philosophy, consequently, called for smaller buildings, homes, and government, not for larger consolidated structures or social units; it called for decentralization, not centralization; it called for creativity, not stultification. Additional information on Schumacher can be obtained from Henderson (1978) and Locher (1979).

The Reagan Years (1980–1988)

In 1980, the environmental movement awakened to its worst nightmare: Ronald Reagan was the president and the Senate was in Republican hands (Holden 1980). While the previous administrations of Nixon, Ford, and Carter were relatively supportive of the environmental cause, the Reagan administration proved to be a major setback to the movement. In addition to James Watt, his sharp-tongued secretary of the Department of the Interior, President Reagan appointed others that had direct ties to business and industry, such as Anne Gorsuch Burford (an attorney for Rocky Mountain Bell) to head the U.S. Environmental Protection Agency (EPA), Robert F. Burford (a rancher) to direct the Bureau of Land Management (BLM), and John B. Crowell (an attorney for Georgia-Pacific) to be the assistant agriculture secretary for Natural Resources and the Environment. Environmentalists were particularly irritated when they learned in 1981 that 11 of the 15 key EPA Reagan appointees were either lobbyists, lawyers, or consultants from industries the EPA regulated. For example, the EPA's assistant administrator for air pollution, who formerly lobbied for the American Paper Institute and the Crown Zellerbach paper company to ease the enforcement of the Clean Air Act, was now in charge of enforcing the same act—thus presenting the problem of the fox watching over the chicken coop. By 1982, 10 major environmental groups accused the Reagan administration of a "wholesale giveaway" of the nation's resources by transferring public resources to private interests at "bargain-basement prices" and by easing regulations on polluters, causing public health to be jeopardized.

Even more dramatic was the public call for James Watt's resignation as secretary of the Department of the Interior. In 1982, the Sierra Club mounted a campaign demanding that Watt must go. The Sierra Club succeeded in getting over 1 million signatures on their anti-Watt petition, presenting their case to California Senator Alan Cranston on the steps of Congress. One year later, on October 10, 1983, James Watt bowed to pressure and quit. Having succeeded in ousting Watt, Sierra Club President Joe Fontaine called on the removal of other foes of the environment, such as Budget Director David Stockman, EPA chief Ann Gorsuch Burford, and James Harris, Office of Surface Mining director.

In 1984, halfway through his administration, President Reagan went on the counterattack. Speaking before the National Geographic Society, he defended his antipollution policies and condemned environmentalists for their "blind and ignorant attacks" on farmers, businesspersons, and industrialists. By now, however, Reagan was fully aware of public sentiment toward protecting the environment, and he made conciliatory statements in his State of the Union Address in 1984: ''Preservation of our environment is not a liberal or conservation challenge. It's common sense.''

Most environmental historians, however, would argue that the Reagan-Watt team did *not* use common sense, that they had abandoned the Republican principles of conservation established by Abraham Lincoln (who signed the 1864 bill setting aside Yosemite Valley as a park), Ulysses S. Grant (who in 1872 approved legislation establishing Yellowstone as the first national park), and Teddy Roosevelt (who created the first wildlife refuge and instituted the U.S. Forest Service). More recently, the passage of the Environmental Protection Policy Act, the creation of the Environmental Protection Agency, the formation of the President's Council on Environmental Quality, and the passage of the Endangered Species Act were all actions taken under Republican leadership.

Caldicott and Schell: The Antinuclear Spokespersons. In 1980, during President Reagan's first year in office, Helen Caldicott, a major leader in the antinuclear movement, founded the Woman's Action for Nuclear Disarmament Group, which in 1986 had over 20,000 members. She also cofounded the 50,000 member Physicians for Social Responsibility. Both organizations work for nuclear disarmament. They fought against President Reagan, whom they called ''the Pied Piper of Armageddon.'' More of a writer than an activist, Jonathan Schell also warned in his *The Fate of the Earth* (1982) of the threat of nuclear war. Raymond Dasmann, professor of environmental studies and well-known environmental author at the University of California at Santa Cruz, said about Schell's book that ''It made me realize that I must do more than I had been doing'' (Vaz 1986, p. 60).

Nader and Brown: Consumer Protection Advocate and Worldwatcher. Five years earlier, lawyer Ralph Nader was also warning Americans about the dangers of atomic energy (Nader 1977). Although most Americans think of Nader as America's preeminent consumer protection advocate (dating back to 1965, when he first alerted the country to the dangers of the Corvair automobile), few Americans think of him as a conservationist. Yet he has been, and continues to be, a major contributor to the environmental movement. In particular, Nader must be credited for focusing on the association between consumerism and environmentalism (Holsworth 1980). He has argued that consumerism and environmentalism are naturally linked since what one buys, uses, and con-

sumes determines our health and the contaminants that we discard into the environment (Nader 1981). Additional information on Nader can be found in Gorey (1972) and Buckhorn (1972).

Another 1980s conservationist who monitors the state of the environment is Worldwatch Institute president Lester A. Brown. Brown has been responsible for the outstanding State of the World series that has been published yearly since 1984. The series popularity is demonstrated by the use of the *State of the World 1985* issue in courses in over 170 universities across the country, and it has been translated into five languages for use abroad (Vaz 1986).

Abbey, Roselle, and Foreman: The Bad Boys! Also gaining momentum during the Reagan administration were a number of conservationists trying to put the bite back into the American environmental movement. Perceiving the 1980s environmental movement as having become too passive, they engaged in ''monkeywrenching''—a wilderness variety of industrial sabotage inspired by Edward Abbey's *The Monkey Wrench Gang* (1975). Abbey's novel was about rowdies in the Southwest who toppled billboards with chain saws, gummed up bulldozers and other construction equipment with sand and molasses in their fuel tanks, spiked trees to break sawmill saw bands, and generally drove land developers in the area crazy. Monkeywrenching was seen as taking direct action to save the wilderness from society, as opposed to the more staid approach of trying to work within the system.

Taking after Abbey's monkeywrenchers, Mike Roselle, Dave Foreman, and two others formed Earth First! (the explanation point mandatory). It is the environmental movement's most recent, most extreme, and most unpredictable organization. Its prankster/eco-guerrilla ''tribespeople'' (they prefer not to use the word *members*) use all of Abbey's monkeywrenching techniques and more. In fact, cofounder Dave Foreman sold 5000 copies of his book *EcoDefense: A Field Guide to Monkey-Wrenching* (1985), and a second edition is forthcoming. In 1986, Earth First! claimed to have 44 local groups in 16 states with 10,000 tribespeople subscribing to the group's newspaper (Setterberg 1986). Although some would write-off this bunch as being just a loosely knit group of 1960s hippies, one must remember that many conservationists (e.g., John Muir and David Brower) and conservation groups (e.g., Greenpeace) were called radical in their early period yet are now considered quite establishmentarian, or at least acceptable by society's standards.

Writer Kirkpatrick Sale has labeled the Earth

Firsters, the Deep Ecologists, and the other anti-environmental establishment groups as "The New Ecologists" since they derive their ideas and doctrines from "bioregionalism, Green politics, deep ecology, animal liberationism, ecofeminism, permaculture, steady-state economics, ecophilosophy, native spiritualism, and social ecology—and that's just for starters" (1986, p. 26). Their charges, says Sale (pp. 28-29), seem to cluster around four major themes:

1. Environmentalists are reformists, working within "the system" in ways that ultimately reinforce it instead of seeking the thoroughgoing social and political changes that are necessary to halt massive assaults on the natural world.

2. Environmentalists are basically anthropocentric, believing that the proper human purpose is to control and consume the resources of nature as wisely and safely—but as fully—as possible. They have yet to learn the ecocentric truth that nature and all its species have an intrinsic worth apart from any human designs.

3. Environmentalists have become co-opted into the world of Washington politics, playing the bureaucratic game like any other lobby, turning their backs on the grass roots support and idealism that gave the movement its initial momentum.

4. Environmentalists, finally, are not successful even on their own terms in protecting the wilderness, in stopping the onrush of industrial devastation. They are so caught up in compromise that they're actually going backward.

Sale concludes, however, that this current "split" in the environmental movement is merely the latest version of the "preservationist" vs. "conservationist" battle that began in the nineteenth century between Muir (the preservationist) and Pinchot (the conservationist).

CONCLUSION

Despite any disagreements among environmentalists, the American conservation movement is strong and growing stronger by the day. Harris polls indicate that American opinion about environmental protection and cleanup does not change with political fads, and, in fact, Americans are getting tougher and more adamant about protecting the environment. Even many of America's scientists, who traditionally thought it was unscientific to get involved in conservation politics, are now joining forces with environmental activists. For example, in a 1986 interview with the *New York Times*, Thomas E. Lovejoy, vice-president of the World Wildlife Fund in Washington, D.C., said that many biologists are now carefully scrutinizing the politics of aid agencies, such as the U.S. Agency for International Development and the World Bank, since loans to developing countries can affect land development and ultimately wildlife species. Partially as a result of their pressure, the World Bank announced in 1987 that it was creating a top-level environment department as well as implementing other actions, such as creating environmental offices in the World Bank's four regional departments (Holden 1987). Although it will take some time to bring the environment to the center of policy decisions within the strongly economically oriented World Bank, environmental scientists agree that these actions are certainly a step in the right direction. The main point here, however, is that hard-core scientists are now finding it necessary to get involved in unfamiliar turf—the social, cultural, political, legal, economic, and ethical aspects of resource management and environmental quality planning.

Other signs indicate a growing American environmental movement, such as the increasing number of, and membership in, environmental organizations (both establishment and nonestablishment oriented). The growing proliferation of environmental professional journals and specialized nature magazines and the growing number of stores that specialize in nature-related items, from colorful cards to wilderness adventure books to outdoor equipment, also indicate a growing concern with the environment.

Most important of all, however, is that environmental education (previously known as conservation education) is "making the grand leap from the narrow confines of nature centers and youth clubs to the approved curricula of America's school system" (National Wildlife Federation 1988, p. 31). Environmental Studies is now in the mainstream of the American system of education, as seen in such programs as *NatureScope* (a fourth grade environmental project), *The Class Project* (an integral, hands-on junior high school project), and personalized study projects developed by college and university professors. Furthermore, entire conservation courses are being developed in traditional college and university departments. Even more encouraging is the range of new interdisciplinary programs (e.g., environmental studies, environmental science, environmental education) and degrees (from B.A. to Ph.D) that stress the conservation and management of natural resources.

As you have just seen in this chapter, individuals can make a difference in conserving America's natural resources. The question now is how can you (like Muir, or Pinchot, or Foreman) contribute to this growing and increasingly important field? The chapters that follow will, I hope, help you answer that question. Let us begin by looking at the subject of soil.

DISCUSSION TOPICS

1. Discuss the evolution of the conservation versus preservation debate within the United States. Be sure to include the major individuals or organizations involved as well as pertinent dates.

2. Debate whether or not the North American Indian was our "First Ecologist." Include in your discussion examples from the world's remaining indigenous tribes.

3. Provide examples of how traditional (indigenous) conservation techniques can help improve our own modern systems of resource management.

4. How much power does a U.S. president have in terms of setting environmental policy? Start by doing an analysis of the presidencies of Reagan, Carter, Nixon, Franklin D. Roosevelt, and Theodore Roosevelt. How do you rate the environmental track record of the current president of the United States?

5. Who are the leading nature writers today? Discuss their backgrounds, their books, their philosophies. Are today's conservationists and environmentalists being affected by their writings? Provide examples.

6. In your opinion, who are the leading conservationists and environmentalists today? Discuss their backgrounds, their accomplishments, their philosophies, and their impact on the environmental movement.

7. Investigate the backgrounds, voting records, and major accomplishments of the current directors of the U.S. Fish and Wildlife Service, the Bureau of Land Management, the U.S. Forest Service, and the National Park Service.

8. Investigate the status of environmental education in your community at the elementary, secondary, college, and university level. How does it compare to other communities? What improvements are needed?

9. Debate whether the anti-environmental establishment groups (e.g., Earth First!) are helping or hindering the environmental movement.

10. Before continuing with this textbook, record whether or not you are considering a career in resource management, and, if so, in what particular field. After having read this textbook, record any changes in your thinking regarding this matter.

READINGS

ABBEY, EDWARD. 1975. *The Monkey Wrench Gang.* New York: Avon Books. A novel that helped stimulate the formation of the conservation group Earth First!

BARTRAM, WILLIAM. 1791. *The Travels of William Bartram.* Naturalists' edition. Edited by Francis Harper. Philadelphia: James and Johnson. Reprint, New Haven, Conn.: Yale University Press, 1958.

BROKAW, HOWARD P., ed. 1978. *Wildlife and America.* Washington, D.C.: Council on Environmental Quality. Excellent overview of wildlife history, problems, and possible management strategies.

BROOKS, PAUL. 1972. *The House of Life, Rachel Carson at Work.* Boston: Houghton Mifflin. Excellent background on this "nun of nature" and author of the classic book, *Silent Spring* (1962).

BROOKS, PAUL. 1980. *Speaking for Nature.* Boston: Houghton Mifflin. Fascinating narrative of how important the pen has been in the fight for conservation; discusses the works of naturalists from Henry David Thoreau to Rachel Carson.

BROWER, DAVID. 1984. "A Tribute to Ansel Adams," *Sierra,* July–August, vol. 69, no. 4, pp. 32–35. Excellent tribute to Ansel Adams by his long-time friend, sometime antagonist, and fellow environmentalist.

BUCKHORN, ROBERT F. 1972. *Nader: The People's Lawyer.* Englewood Cliffs, N.J.: Prentice-Hall. Excellent background on Ralph Nader's early work.

CADENHEAD, I.E. 1974. *Theodore Roosevelt: The Paradox of Progressivism.* Woodbury, N.Y.: Barren's Educational Series. Good biography.

CALLICOT, J. BAIRD. 1983. "Leopold's Land Aesthetic," *Journal of Soil and Water Conservation,* vol. 38, no. 4, pp. 329–332. Discusses Leopold's ideas regarding a "land aesthetic" (in contrast to his "land ethic") and argues that they serve as inspiration for land-use decisions today.

CARSON, RACHEL. 1955. *The Edge of the Sea.* Boston: Houghton Mifflin. Excellent example of Carson's ability to artistically blend scientific research into literary composition.

CARSON, RACHEL. 1951. *The Sea Around Us.* New York: Oxford University Press. Skillfully told story of the ocean and the ways in which it affects the lives of humans.

CARSON, RACHEL. 1962. *Silent Spring.* Boston: Houghton

Mifflin. Carson's classic work that awakened America to the problems of using pesticides such as DDT.

COMMONER, BARRY. 1971. *The Closing Circle.* New York: Knopf. The classic work that well illustrates America's post–World War II dependence on synthetic products that do not break down or biodegrade into the environment.

COUSTEAU, JACQUES-YVES. 1963. *The Living Sea.* New York: Harper & Row. Narrative describing the newest depth-exploring techniques.

COUSTEAU, JACQUES-YVES. 1964. *World Without Sun.* New York: Harper & Row. The story of the first human colony to live and work on the ocean floor.

CRAINE, KIMBER. 1984. "Ansel Adams: 1902–1984: Visions on the Frontier of Photography," *National Parks,* July–August, pp. 6–7. Short tribute to Ansel Adams.

CUTRIGHT, PAUL RUSSELL. 1985. *Theodore Roosevelt: The Making of a Conservationist.* Chicago: University of Illinois Press. Excellent study.

DAVIES, KENNETH S. 1971 *FDR, the Beckoning of Destiny.* New York: Putnam. Good discussion of Roosevelt's early political career.

EHRLICH, PAUL R. 1968. *The Population Bomb.* New York: Ballantine Books. Ehrlich's classic book about the increasing problem of overpopulation.

EHRLICH, PAUL R., ANNE H. EHRLICH, and JOHN P. HOLDREN. 1977. *Ecoscience: Population/Resources/Environment.* San Francisco: Freeman. One book of a series in biology on population resource issues in human ecology.

EHRLICH, PAUL R., and ANNE H. EHRLICH. 1981. *Extinction: The Causes and Consequences of the Disappearance of Species.* New York: Random House. Detailed survey.

ELMAN, ROBERT. 1977. *First in the Field: America's Pioneering Naturalists.* New York: Van Nostrand Reinhold. Excellent overall reference.

EVORY, ANN, and LINDA METZGER. 1983. "Paul Ehrlich." In *Contemporary Authors.* Detroit, Mich.: Gale Research, pp. 152–153. Contains brief background on this well-known population specialist.

EXTEROW, MILTON. 1984. "Ansel Adams: The Last Interview," *Art News,* Summer, pp. 76–89. The famous wilderness photographer's last interview before his death in 1984.

FAUSOLD, MARTIN L. 1961. *Gifford Pinchot: Bull Moose Progressive.* Binghamton, N.Y.: Syracuse University Press. Examination of the Progressive years through the perspective of Pinchot and his writings.

FLECK, RICHARD F. 1985. *Henry Thoreau and John Muir Among the Indians.* Hamden, Conn.: Archon Books. Good discussion of how these men experienced and perceived the wilderness.

FORBES. 1976. "A Latter Day Wizard of Oz," *Forbes,* July 1, p. 26. Discusses some of the accomplishments of environmentalist Barry Commoner.

FOREMAN, DAVE. 1985. *EcoDefense: A Field Guide to Monkey-Wrenching.* Tucson, Ariz.: Earth First!/Ludd Books. A handbook on eco-guerrilla techniques.

FOX, STEPHEN. 1981. *John Muir and His Legacy: The American Conservation Movement.* Boston: Little, Brown. Profound

analysis of the conservation movement with a focus on John Muir.

GARTNER, CAROL. 1983. *Rachel Carson.* New York: Frederick Ungar. Excellent biography of this remarkable woman.

GLOVER, JIM. 1986. "Bob Marshall: A Natural," *American Forests,* September, vol. 92, no. 9, pp. 24–26, 54–55. Personal profile of one of the most effective champions of American wilderness conservation.

GOREY, HAYS. 1972. *Nader and the Power of Everyman.* Englewood Cliffs, N.J.: Prentice-Hall. Contains a good discussion of Nader's 10 major techniques to protect the American consumer.

GRANTHAM, DEWEY W. 1971. *Theodore Roosevelt.* Englewood Cliffs, N.J.: Prentice-Hall. Good biography.

GREENWOOD, NED. 1980. "North America." In Gary A. Klee, ed., *World Systems of Traditional Resource Management,* pp. 189–216. London: Edward Arnold. Good discussion of North American Indian traditional resource management techniques.

HENDERSON, HAZEL. 1978. "The Legacy of E. F. Schumacher," *Environment,* May, vol. 20, no. 4, pp. 30–36. Edited version of Schumacher's speech at the University of Toronto.

HOLDEN, CONSTANCE. 1980. "The Reagan Years: Environmentalists Tremble," *Science,* vol. 210, no. 28, pp. 988–991. Discussion of why environmentalists feared the incoming Reagan administration.

HOLDEN, CONSTANCE. 1987. "World Bank Launches New Environmental Policy," *Science,* vol. 236, no. 4803, p. 769. Brief summary of the World Bank's apparent shift in more attention toward the conservation and environmental aspects of development projects.

HOLSWORTH, ROBERT D. 1980. *Public Interest Liberalism and the Crisis of Affluence.* Boston: G. K. Hall. Contains good discussion of the link between consumerism and environmentalism.

HUGHES, J. DONALD. 1983. *American Indian Ecology.* El Paso, Tex.: Texas Western Press. Scholarly treatment of the subject.

HUTH, HANS. 1957. *Nature and the American: Three Centuries of Changing Attitudes.* Lincoln, Nebr.: University of Nebraska Press. The background of conservation: its history, philosophy, poetry, ethics, and art.

IUCN. 1985. "Role of the Traditional Ecological Knowledge Working Group," *Tradition, Conservation, and Development,* August 1985, issue no. 3, p. 1. Occasional newsletter of the Commission on Ecology's Working Group on traditional ecological knowledge.

KAHN, JEFFERY. 1986. "Man Apart: David Brower, The Conscience of the Environmental Movement," *Image,* April 20, pp. 32–42. Highly interesting article.

KLEE, GARY A., ed. 1980. *World Systems of Traditional Resource Management.* London: Edward Arnold. Comprehensive look at indigenous systems of natural resource management.

LEOPOLD, ALDO. 1933. *Game Management.* New York: Scribner. A classic in modern wildlife management.

LEOPOLD, ALDO. 1949. *A Sand County Almanac and Sketches Here and There.* New York: Oxford University Press. Contains Leopold's classic chapter on land ethics.

LOCHER, FRANCIS CAROL. 1979. "E. F. Schumacher." In *Contemporary Authors,* vol. 81–84, pp. 497–498. Detroit, Mich.: Gale Research. Brief account of the author of *Small Is Beautiful.*

Macmillan Biographical Encyclopedia of Photographic Artists and Innovators. 1983 ed. See the section on "Porter, Eliot Furness," pp. 488–489. Brief background on this outstanding wilderness photographer.

MADSEN, AXEL. 1986. *Cousteau: An Unauthorized Biography.* New York: Beaufort Books. A good biography.

MARSH, GEORGE PERKINS. 1864. *Man and Nature; Or, Physical Geography as Modified by Human Action.* New York: Scribner. Reprinted 1965. Cambridge, Mass.: Harvard University Press. The influential classic work by the father of the American conservation movement.

MARSHALL, GEORGE. 1971. "On Bob Marshall's Landmark Article," *The Living Wilderness,* Spring, vol. 35, no. 113, p. 28. Interesting analysis of Marshall's "The Problem of the Wilderness."

MARSHALL, ROBERT. 1933. *Arctic Village.* New York: Harrison Smith and Robert Hass. Marshall's best selling book about his 1929–1931 experience in the Koyukuk region of north central Alaska.

MARSHALL, ROBERT. 1933. *The People's Forest.* New York: Harrison Smith and Robert Haas. Marshall's book about forest use and abuse in America.

MARSHALL, ROBERT. 1930. "The Problem of the Wilderness," *Scientific Monthly,* Fall, vol. 30, pp. 141–148. Classic article that helped launch the modern wilderness movement.

MCALEER, JOHN J. 1984. *Ralph Waldo Emerson: Days of Encounter.* Boston: Little, Brown. One of the latest analyses of Emerson's philosophy.

MCGEARY, M. NELSON. 1960. *Gifford Pinchot: Forester-Politician.* Princeton, N.J.: Princeton University Press. Interesting biography.

MCPHEE, JOHN. 1971. *Encounters with the Archdruid.* New York: Farrar, Strauss & Giroux. This book made archdruid David Brower a campus hero and national figure.

MEINE, CURT. 1987. "The Farmer as Conservationist: Aldo Leopold on Agriculture," *Journal of Soil and Water Conservation,* vol. 42, no. 3, pp. 144–149. Discusses how Leopold's multidisciplinary approach to farm planning is relevant today.

MILLER, NATHAN. 1983. *F.D.R.: An Intimate History.* New York: Doubleday. Good discussion of the place of the New Deal in the American political tradition.

MUIR, JOHN. 1911. *My First Summer in the Sierra.* Boston: Houghton Mifflin. Journal of Muir's travels and experiences in the Sierra.

MUIR, JOHN. 1912. *The Yosemite.* New York: Century. A descriptive guide to Yosemite National Park written by one of its founders.

NADER, RALPH. 1977. *The Menace of Atomic Energy.* New York: Norton. Nader defends renewable energy forms in preference to nuclear forms.

NADER, RALPH. 1981. *Who's Poisoning America.* San Francisco: Sierra Club Books. Nader attacks American industry and government for its careless safety standards regarding hazardous waste.

NASH, RODERICK. 1967. *Wilderness and the American Mind.* New Haven, Conn.: Yale University Press. Classic historical account of the wilderness movement in America.

NATIONAL WILDLIFE FEDERATION. 1988. "Environmental Studies Now in Mainstream," *National Wildlife,* April–May, p. 31. Brief news item indicating how environmental education has become a mainstream item in American education.

NEW YORK TIMES. 1976. "Scientist at Large," *New York Times Magazine,* November 7, sec. 6, p. 58. Highlights the perspective of Barry Commoner.

NICHOLSON, MAX. 1970. *The Environmental Revolution: A Guide for the New Masters of the World.* New York: McGraw-Hill. Contains interesting discussion of protohuman and Indian impact on the North American continent.

NIXON, EDGAR B., ed. 1957. *Franklin D. Roosevelt and Conservation.* Washington D.C.: Government Printing Office. Good discussion of the CCC and its different projects.

PETERSON, ROGER TORY. 1980. *A Field Guide to Birds of Eastern and Central North America.* Boston: Houghton Mifflin. Outstanding field guide.

PETULLA, JOSEPH. 1977. *American Environmental History.* San Francisco: Boyd and Fraser. Excellent history of the exploitation and conservation of natural resources in America.

PETULLA, JOSEPH. 1980. *American Environmentalism: Values, Tactics, Priorities.* College Station, Tex.: Texas A&M University. Petulla traces environmentalism to three traditions: the biocentric, the ecologic, and the economic.

PINCHOT, GIFFORD. 1947. *Breaking New Ground.* Seattle, Wash.: University of Washington Press. Includes Pinchot's interpretation of the Ballinger affair, which led to Pinchot being fired by President Taft. Also includes the history of forest conservation in the United States.

PINCHOT, GIFFORD. 1910. *The Fight for Conservation.* New York: Doubleday, Page. Contains the basic elements of Pinchot's views regarding conservation.

PINKETT, HAROLD T. 1970. *Gifford Pinchot: Private and Public Forester.* Urbana, Ill.: University of Illinois Press. Good biography.

PROBY, KATHRYN H. 1974. *Audubon in Florida.* Coral Gables, Fla.: University of Miami Press. Collection of Audubon's writings during a six-month stay in Florida.

REED, NATHANIEL P., and DENNIS DRABELLE. 1984. *The United States Fish and Wildlife Service.* Boulder, Colo.: Westview Press. Good history of this agency.

RICHARDS, MOSE. 1985. "Interview: Jacques Cousteau," *Calypso Log* 12 (June 1985).

RICHARDSON, ROBERT D., JR. 1986. *Thoreau: A Life of the Mind.* Berkeley, Calif.: University of California Press. Excellent biography of this most influential individual who taught so many how to live in the natural world.

ROUNTREE, THOMAS J. 1973. *Critics on Emerson.* Coral Gables, Fla.: University of Miami Press. Critical analysis of Emerson's philosophy.

RUCKELSHAUS, WILLIAM. 1984. "Risk in a Free Society." Speech at Harvard University, February 18. Ruckelshaus applies Pinchot's utilitarian concepts to trade-offs in public health hazards.

SALE, KIRKPATRICK. 1986. "The Forest For the Trees: Can Today's Environmentalists Tell the Difference," *Mother Jones,* November, pp. 25–58. Good discussion of Sale's "New Ecologists" and their seeds of discontent with the environmental establishment.

SCHELL, JONATHAN. 1982. *The Fate of the Earth.* New York: Knopf. A strong warning that the effects of a nuclear war may be irrevocable.

SCHUMACHER, E. F. 1973. *Small Is Beautiful.* New York: Perennial. Schumacher's classic book that advocates appropriate technology.

SCHWARZ, O. DOUGLAS. 1987. "Indian Rights and Environmental Ethics: Changing Perspectives, and a Modest Proposal," *Environmental Ethics,* Winter, vol. 9, pp. 291–302. Interesting discussion of today's environmentalism and Indian land ethics.

SCOTT, D. W. 1984. "The Visionary Role of Howard Zahniser," *Sierra,* May–June, vol. 69, p. 40. Interesting discussion about the "Father of the 1964 Wilderness Act."

SETTERBERG, FRED. 1986. "The Wild Bunch," *Image,* Nov. 9, pp. 20–27. Interesting article about the conservation organization called Earth First!

SHERMAN, PAUL. 1952. *Emerson's Angle of Vision: Man and Nature in American Experience.* Cambridge, Mass.: Harvard University Press. Contains excellent discussion of Emerson's views on the relationship of man, God, and nature.

SHI, DAVID. 1985. *The Simple Life: Plain Living and High Thinking in American Culture.* New York: Oxford University Press. A comprehensive history of the advocates of the simple life in American culture.

STARNES, RICHARD. 1963. "Stewart Udall and the Quiet Crisis," *Field and Stream,* vol. 68, no. 2, pp. 18, 20–23. Brief interview with this well-known secretary of the U.S. Department of the Interior.

STEGNER, WALLACE. 1981. *American Places: The Photography of Eliot Porter.* New York: Dutton. Photographic account of human and land relationships in America.

STEINHART, PETER. 1984. "Ecological Saints," *Audubon,* July, vol. 86, no. 4, pp 8–11. Discusses Indian abuses of natural resources on reservation lands.

STRONG, DOUGLAS H. 1971. *The Conservationists.* Menlo Park, Calif.: Addison–Wesley. One of the earlier histories of the American environmental movement.

STRONG, DOUGLAS H. 1970. "The Rise of American Esthetic Conservation: Muir, Mather, and Udall," *National Parks Magazine,* February, vol. 44, no. 269, pp. 4–9.

STROUD, RICHARD. 1985. *National Leaders of American Conservation.* Washington, D.C.: Smithsonian Institute Press. Excellent general reference.

TANNER, THOMAS. 1987. *Aldo Leopold: The Man and His Legacy.* Ankeny, Iowa: Soil Conservation Society. Excellent illustrated volume that recaptures the thoughts, ideas, and words of this conservation pioneer.

THOMAS, WILLIAM L., JR., ed. 1956. *Man's Role in Changing the Face of the Earth.* Chicago: University of Chicago Press. A classic work in the tradition of George Perkins Marsh.

UDALL, STEWART. 1963. *The Quiet Crisis.* New York: Holt, Rinehart & Winston. A classic book in the same league as Carson's *Silent Spring.*

U.S. NEWS & WORLD REPORT. 1985. "We Face a Catastrophe," *U.S. News & World Report,* June 24, vol. 98, no. 24, p. 68. Brief interview with Jacques Cousteau.

VAZ, MARK. 1986. "Leaves of Green," *Sierra,* May–June, pp. 56–61. Short summary of some of the most important books in the history of the American conservation movement.

VECSEY, C., and R. VENABLES. 1980. *American Indian Environments.* Syracuse, N.Y.: Syracuse University Press. Excellent discussion of indigenous peoples and their ecological awareness in North America.

VICKERY, JIM DALE. 1985. "Bob Marshall: A Hunger for Wilderness," *Sierra,* November–December, vol. 70, no. 6, pp. 59–62. Highly readable history of this amazing individual.

WALLACE, DAVID RAINS. 1987. "Sand County's Conservation Prophet," *Sierra,* vol. 72, no. 6, pp. 62–67. Discusses how today's conservationists are still finding inspiration from Aldo Leopold's writings.

WHITAKER, RALPH. 1987. "Stewart Udall: Conservationist by Heritage," *EPRI Journal,* October–November, pp. 16–21. Very interesting recent interview with this two-term Secretary of the Interior and author of *The Quiet Crisis* (1963).

WILD, PETER. 1986. *Pioneer Conservationists of Eastern America.* Missoula, Mont.: Mountain Press. Good reference.

WILDERNESS SOCIETY. 1984. "Ansel Adams 1902–1984," *Wilderness,* Summer, vol. 48, no. 165, pp. 2–3. A tribute to Adams on his death.

WILLIAMS, TED. 1986. "A Harvest of Eagles," *Audubon 86,* September, no. 5, pp. 54–58. Discusses the controversy surrounding Indian killings of bald eagles to obtain feathers for use in religious rituals.

WOLFE, LINNIE MARSH. 1951. *Son of Wilderness: The Life of John Muir.* New York: Knopf. Includes discussion of the influence of Emerson on Muir.

WORSTER, DONALD. 1979. *Nature's Economy: The Roots of Ecology.* Garden City, N.Y.: Anchor Press/Doubleday. Excellent appraisal of the antecedents leading to the contemporary ecology movement.

ZAHNISER, ED. 1984. "Howard Zahniser: Father of the Wilderness Act," *National Parks,* January–February, vol. 58, pp. 12–14. A son's tribute to his father, the constant advocate of wilderness preservation.

■2■

THE NATURE OF SOIL

Concepts of Soil
Factors Affecting Soil Formation
Soil Characteristics
The Soil Survey
Soil Classification and Distribution

*To be a successful farmer one must first know the
nature of the soil.*
Xenophon, *Oeconomicus*, 400 B.C.

Soil is one of our important yet mistreated resources. Directly or indirectly, it provides us with produce, meat, clothing (cotton and wool), timber, and many other valuable goods. Even so, many people must be reminded that soil is not "dirt" (a bothersome substance), but rather an essential resource for *survival*. Today, we are as dependent upon soils as at any time in the past.

CONCEPTS OF SOIL

The word *soil* has many meanings. Hunting and gathering societies are likely to perceive soil as the ground that supports them, the land underfoot. Agriculturalists define soil as the medium in which crops grow. Geologists perceive soil as a layer of weathered rock. To civil engineers, soil is the material that may or may not provide adequate support for buildings, bridges, and highways. Conservationists view soil as

the interface between the atmosphere and the lithosphere, seeing soil as a setting for food production, water purification, and waste disposal. Conservationists also see that soil, on occasion, darkens the sky with dust and pollutes streams with sediment. In this chapter, we shall view soil through the eyes of soil scientists (pedologists).

Modern soil science (**pedology**) defines soil as the natural surface of earth material that, as a result of weathering and the action of plants and animals, will support the growth of rooted plants. Soil contains both inorganic mineral matter and organic matter. The organic matter consists of living plants, organisms, and microorganisms as well as dead leaves and twigs and other plant remains.

Soil scientists elaborate on this definition by breaking the general concept of soil into polypedon, pedon, soil profile, soil horizon, and soil solum. They divide landscapes into **polypedons** (sometimes called *soil bodies*), which are the smallest distinctive units of the soil of a particular area—similar in appearance to the pieces of a jigsaw puzzle (Figure 2-1). Each polypedon has soil properties different from those of adjacent polypedons. For example, a polypedon of predominantly organic soil may lie adjacent to a polypedon of more highly mineralized soil.

The polypedon in turn consists of **pedons** (Figure 2-2). A pedon is the smallest volume that can be classified as a soil. As perceived by soil scientists, a pedon is hexagonal in shape and extends down from the surface to some form of **regolith** or **bedrock**. The surface area of a single pedon ranges from 1 to 10 m² (10 to 100 ft²).

The sides of the pedon reveal the **soil-profile**—a cross-sectional view that displays the characteristic layers or **soil horizons** of a particular soil type. A soil scientist may extract an entire profile to examine in the laboratory, or may study a soil profile exposed by a road cut, or may dig a deep pit to expose the soil profile at a particular location.

The real or "true" soil (**solum**) consists of the A and B horizons of the soil profile. These upper hori-

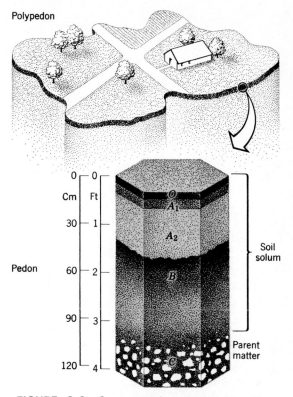

FIGURE 2-2 Concept of pedon and polypedon. Polypedons are made up of numerous interlinking pedons. (From Arthur N. Strahler and Alan H. Strahler, *Geography and Man's Environment*, p. 347. Copyright © 1977 by John Wiley & Sons, Inc.)

zons constitute the most dynamic sections of the soil profile, for it is here that the roots of living plants are active. These are also the most weathered parts of the soil profile. Beneath the solum lies the C horizon, which consists of relatively unmodified rock material that has been undisturbed by root activity. Below that lies the D horizon, known as bedrock.

In summary, the soil scientist uses the word *soil* or *solum* in a very restricted sense to mean only surface material that has certain distinctive physical, chemical, and biological qualities that permit it to support plant growth and that set it off from the infertile C and D horizons. True soil consists of both mineral and organic particles, but the underlying material usually consists only of mineral matter.

FACTORS AFFECTING SOIL FORMATION

Many processes act together to form a soil. *Soil-forming processes* are essentially processes of **weathering** that lead to the disintegration and decay of rock.

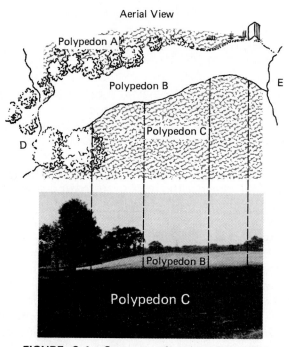

FIGURE 2-1 Concept of polypedons. Two major polypedons (landscape units) can be seen in this photograph of a southern Michigan field: polypedon B, a mineral soil; polypedon C, an organic soil. Other polypedons, such as A, D, and E, surround the visible polypedons. (Adapted from Henry D. Foth, *Fundamentals of Soil Science*, 7th ed., p. 11. Copyright © 1984 by John Wiley & Sons, Inc.)

Some weathering is the result of physical processes, such as the action of frost and changes in temperature. Some are the result of chemical processes, such as **solution** (the dissolving of a substance in a liquid), **oxidation** (the combining of a substance with oxygen), and **leaching** (the removal of soluble minerals and other materials by percolating water). Weathering may also stem from biological processes, such as the interactions of moss and lichen, tree roots, worms, moles, and rabbits.

These soil-forming processes are in turn affected by five major *soil influences*: (1) parent material, (2) climate, (3) vegetation, (4) landform, and (5) time. Although humans modify their environment and, consequently, might be considered as agents of soil formation, soil scientists traditionally have discounted their role in the genesis of soil. The human role is of far greater significance in the use and conservation of soil, topics that will be discussed in Chapter 3.

Parent Material

The nature of the **parent material** from which soil is derived has a direct effect on soil properties, particularly the properties of soils in the early stages of formation. Soils may develop from underlying consolidated rock (bedrock) or from unconsolidated earth material (regolith). In its strictest sense, however, parent material refers to weathered, unconsolidated rock material on which the soil-forming processes act to create soil. In the United States, most parent material has been carried great distances by water, glaciers, or wind before arriving at the site where the soil-forming processes begin to convert it into soil.

Bedrock. Although bedrock is not usually considered parent material itself, it may serve as a *source* of parent material. In areas where the weathering of bedrock proceeds at a greater pace than the pace at which water, wind, or other geological agents can remove the products of that weathering, thick productive soils may develop. An example is the Blue Grass region of Kentucky, where the soils have developed from limestone.

The soils of the Blue Grass region are called **residual soils**; that is, soils that have remained where they were formed. Soils developed from weathered rock materials that have been transported and deposited some distance from the original parent rock are known as **depositional soils**. Depositional soils are further classified according to the manner in which the materials from which they were derived

were transported and deposited: **alluvium** comes from materials deposited by running water, **glacial drift** comes from materials deposited by glaciers, and **loess** comes from materials deposited by wind.

Water-Deposited Sediments. Alluvial soils occur in irregular strips along streams. Large quantities of waterborne sediment are transported and deposited during floods, when erosion is most active and when the carrying capacity of streams is greatest. The deposited sediment creates distinctive landscape features, such as *flood plains* (relatively flat land bordering a stream), *natural levees* (banks built up along the edges of a stream's channel), *river terraces* (flat, horizontal shelves alongside river valleys), *alluvial fans* (fan- or cone-shaped deposits formed where a stream flows out into a level area,) and *deltas* (deposits of alluvium at the mouth of a river). Since alluvial soils are rich in nutrients and thus highly fertile, human societies around the world have long built their fields and cities on or near alluvial deposits.

Glacial-Deposited Sediments. Much of the material that forms the soil of North America and Eurasia was provided when glaciers and large ice sheets radically modified the landscape during the Ice Age. The sand, gravel, rock, and other debris deposited by glaciers are called, collectively, *glacial drift*. Once the glaciers retreated, the layer of glacial drift served as parent material for the formation of new soils.

In North America, several large glacial advances occurred during the Pleistocene period from (1,000,000 to 10,000 B.C.). From Canada, they flowed as far south as Iowa, Illinois, Indiana, and Ohio. In addition to leveling the terrain (a requirement for modern cultivation techniques), the glaciers left a landscape covered with layers of sorted and stratified clays, silts, sands, and gravels (known as *stratified drift*) and heterogeneous mixtures of rock fragments ranging from clay to boulders (known as *till*).

Glaciation also left many impediments to agriculture, such as rocks, large boulders, drumlins, eskers, and kettles. A *drumlin* is a teardrop-shaped hill of glacial till, resembling the bowl of an inverted teaspoon. Drumlins vary in size from a small mound to a hill 2 km (1.2 mi) long and 90 m (295 ft) high. An *esker* is a narrow, winding ridge consisting of stratified deposits of coarse sand and gravel. Eskers resulted from stream deposition in tunnels formed in glacial ice next to the ground surface. In Maine, there are eskers up to 150 km (93 mi) long. A *kettle* is an irregular depression in a *moraine*, a pile of drift carried or deposited by a glacier.

Although these deposits are a nuisance to farmers, they are sometimes of great economic value to city dwellers. The sands and gravels of eskers provide the aggregate used for concrete and for the base courses beneath highway pavements, and aquifers, porous earth material capable of transmitting water and consisting of thick masses of stratified drift, serve as a major source of groundwater.

Wind-Deposited or Aeolian Sediments. Wind-deposited sediments include *dune sand, loess,* and *volcanic ash.*

Dune sand is sand that has collected and drifted into low swells or steep ridges in deserts and along low-lying coasts. Many factors influence the formation of dunes, such as the strength and direction of prevailing wind, whether the surface over which the sand moves is deep sand or bare rock, the presence or absence of vegetation, and the presence or absence of groundwater at the surface. Soils derived from deposits of dune sand are of limited agricultural use. Grazing on dune sands where grass has stabilized the dunes, however, can be important, such as in the Sand Hills of Nebraska.

Loess is a deposit of yellowish to buff-colored, fine-grained sediment that has been transported by the wind to its present location. Initially, loess was probably picked up by the wind from deserts where it lay unprotected by vegetation, or, more likely, from glaciated areas that were drying out after the glacier's retreat. In the United States, loess is common in the central states, where there are particularly thick deposits in the Mississippi-Missouri river valleys. Loess was the parent material of the easily worked, well-drained soils that support much of this country's wheat and sugar beet production.

Volcanic ash is dustlike material ejected from a volcano during an eruption. Some ash falls on the surrounding land to form thick sediments from which soil develops. Some travels great distances before it settles. After the eruption of Krakatoa in the Sundra Straits in 1883, ash was carried *twice* around the world. As the ash gradually fell to Earth, it helped rejuvenate many distant soils. Recent proof of the rejuvenating ability of volcanic ash comes from Alan Goldin, a soil survey party leader with the Soil Conservation Service. In 1982, he published a report outlining the influence of volcanic ash on nearby soils from the May 18, 1980, eruption of Mount St. Helens, an active volcano in the state of Washington (Figure 2-3). Among other things, he found that the ash adds

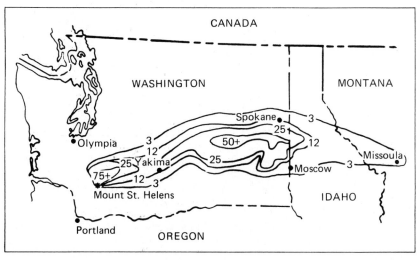

(a)

(b)

FIGURE 2-3 Mount St. Helen's eruption of May 18, 1980. (a) Distribution of ashfall, in mm. (b) Soil profile of ash and pumice deposit located about 5 km (3.1 mi) northeast of the mountain. Buried soil surface is at 70 cm (27.6 in.). Scale in feet. (From Alan Goldin, "Influence of Volcanic Ash from the May 18, 1980, Eruption of Mount St. Helens on the Properties of Soils," *Journal of Soil and Water Conservation,* vol. 37, no. 3 [May-June 1982], pp. 186, 187.)

fertilizer elements, such as potassium, calcium, magnesium, and nitrate-nitrogen to the soil.

Climate

Climate influences soil formation directly through *moisture conditions, temperature,* and *wind.* Indirectly, it influences soil development by determining the natural vegetation of a region. Consequently, there are many similarities in the distribution of climate, vegetation, and soil on Earth (Figure 2-4).

Moisture Conditions. Unless appropriate moisture conditions prevail in the soil, certain chemical and biological activities that are essential to plant growth fail to occur. Among those activities are the *dissolving* of soluble chemicals, the *ionizing* of those chemicals into positively and negatively charged particles, and the *interchanging* of complex chemical elements. These activities depend on the proper amount of rainfall, evapotranspiration (the volume evaporated *and* transpired from plants, soil, and water surfaces per unit land area), and humidity.

Too much rainfall, for example, results in the leaching of ions and *colloids*—the very fine particles of organic and inorganic matter that play a key role in

soil chemistry and plant nutrition. Colloids and other fine particles percolate downward from the A horizon of the solum and tend to accumulate in the B horizon. This accumulation of material sometimes results in what are called *hardpans*—thin stratums within or beneath the surface soil that have become relatively hard and impermeable. Hardpans are classified by the composition of the impermeable layer, for example, *ironpan* (iron salts), *limepan* (calcium carbonate), or *moorpan* (humus compounds).

Temperature. Temperature affects both chemical activity and bacterial activity within the soil. Chemical activity is generally increased by higher temperatures, reduced by cooler temperatures, and completely stopped by freezing temperatures. As a result, the parent material of tropical soils has undergone extensive chemical change, whereas the parent material of frozen tundra soils has been broken up physically but remains essentially unaltered chemically.

Temperature has a similar effect on bacterial activity. In the humid tropics, highly active bacteria consume any dead plants lying on the ground. Consequently, no layer of raw humus (undecomposed vegetative debris, such as leaves, twigs, and nuts) ac-

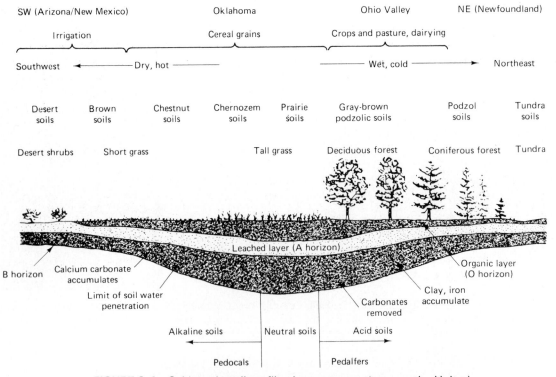

FIGURE 2-4 Schematic soil profile along a transect across the United States. (From C. B. Hunt, *Geology of Soils* [San Francisco: Freeman, 1972].)

cumulates on the surface, and little *humus* (decomposed or partly decomposed organic matter) forms within the soil. In cold continental climates, where bacterial activity is slight, both raw humus and humus are present in abundance. Temperature, of course, also has an effect on soil moisture evaporation rates.

Wind. Compared to moisture conditions and temperature, wind plays a minor role in soil formation. Still, wind does increase evaporation from the soil surface. And in arid regions it may exercise an erosive effect by removing surface soil. By depositing dust in a distant location, it may provide the parent material for a new soil. (See the discussion of the 1930s Dust Bowl in Chapter 3.)

Vegetation

Vegetation affects soil development by supplying organic debris to the soil, and secondarily, by the physical and biological effects of plant roots. Broadly speaking, natural vegetation consists of grasslands and forests (Table 2-1). Soils developed under grasslands have characteristics different from soils formed under forests. Grassland soils under comparable environmental conditions generally contain *twice* the amount of organic matter that forest soils contain. Moreover, that matter is more uniformly distributed in grassland profiles than in forest profiles. Differences between grass and forest vegetation also affect soil acidity. Grassland soils, for example, are less acid than forest soils.

As forest and grassland soils age, however, they become similar regardless of the type of vegetation under which they developed. Consequently, their implications for agriculture become less pronounced with age.

Landform

The term *landform* refers to the shape, form, and nature of the earth's land surface. It includes the *slope* (the degree of incline upward or downward), the *relief* (the variation in elevation between different points on the earth's surface), and the *aspect* (the compass direction in which slopes and other surface objects are oriented). Slope, relief, and aspect together modify soil-profile development by (1) influencing soil temperature and the moisture-holding capability of the soil, (2) influencing the rate of soil loss by erosion, and (3) directing the movement of minerals and other soil particles from one area to another.

The aspect of the surface feature affects both soil temperature and soil water. For example, north-facing slopes in the Northern Hemisphere receive less solar energy than slopes facing south. As a result, average soil temperatures on north-facing slopes are cooler, and the soil water resembles that of a moister climate, because evaporation is reduced.

Relief and drainage are intimately related. On steep slopes, where runoff is greater and water penetration is slight, the soils are thin but well drained. On gentle slopes, where erosion is slower and drainage is better, soil formation is normal. On flat lands, poor drainage results in permanently wet areas and waterlogged soil horizons. Consequently, relief and drainage have important agricultural implications, especially for tillage and crop survival. The type and amount of ground cover (e.g., grassland versus forest), of course, also affect water retention.

TABLE 2-1

The effect of vegetation on soil formation: grass versus forest

	NATURAL VEGETATION	
	GRASS = GRASSLAND SOILS	FOREST = FOREST SOILS
Organic matter		
Amount	Greater	Lesser (approximately $\frac{1}{2}$)
Uniformity of distribution with depth of profile	Greater	Lesser
Acidity and base saturation	Less acid and higher percentage base saturation	More acid and lower percentage base saturation
Rate of eluviation and leaching	Lesser	Greater
Return of alkaline earths and alkali metals to the surface vegetation	Greater	Lesser
Depth at which water is intercepted for transpiration	Lesser	Greater
Acidity of water entering the soil	Lesser	Greater
Translocation of clay from A to B horizon	Lesser	Greater
Age or development of soil	Lesser	Greater

Steep landforms retard the formation of mature soils. Hence, much of the material that might otherwise be available for soil development is lost to **mass movement**—the movement of material down a slope under the influence of *gravity*, with rainwater or snow melt usually acting as a lubricant. Consequently, soils on steep slopes have thinner solums, contain less organic matter, and exhibit less conspicuous horizons than soils on level or undulating topography.

Topography may also affect soil formation by exposing *underlying* parent material. When loess, for example, is removed by erosion, soils may develop from the underlying glacial till. Thus local topography is a direct cause of differences among soils, resulting in *associations*—soil units that occur together in characteristic patterns over a geographic region.

Time

Soils are *dynamic*. They experience constant change. Because change occurs slowly, however, people often assume that no change is taking place. Actually, soils go through a *life cycle* from parent material, to immature soil, to mature soil, to old soil. Time is a powerful influence on soil development.

Stages in Soil Development.   Soils that are just beginning to evolve from such parent material as river alluvium or glacial till are classified as *immature soils* (young soils). Because they have been subjected to the soil-forming processes for only a relatively short period, these soils have indistinct or only slightly developed horizons. Immature soils without distinct horizons are also known as **azonal** soils. Examples of azonal soils are wind-blown soils, such as sand and loess; volcanic soils evolved from ejected ash, cinder, or lava; marine soils derived from sandbanks, mudbanks, or dunes; and mountain soils. Immature soils have the following characteristics: (1) an accumulation of organic matter in the A horizon, (2) the absence of a B horizon—only the A and C horizons are present, and (3) only slight weathering, leaching, or translocation of colloids.

A *mature soil* is a soil that has developed a B horizon. At this stage, the soil has reached a greater equilibrium with its environment, the organic content in the A horizon is at its maximum, and there is a moderate accumulation of clay in the B horizon. The natural productivity of soils is highest in the immature and mature stages.

If enough time has elapsed and if climatic and biological conditions are right, a mature soil eventually develops into an *old soil*. At this stage of the life cycle, the soil horizons are most distinct, severe weathering has taken place, the amount of organic matter in the A horizon has decreased, and clay pans may have developed in the B horizon. Old soils have lost much of their fertility and natural productivity.

Time Needed for Soil Development.   How much time does it take for one inch of a mature soil to develop? It is virtually impossible to answer that question, for two main reasons: (1) soil-forming factors influence soil development at *varying rates*, and (2) the *relationship* among soil-forming factors varies from time to time. Moreover, the soil-forming factors themselves do not remain constant over time. Soil characteristics change most rapidly when the soil is young and more slowly as it ages.

The rate of development is also affected by the type of parent material and the climate. It takes longer for a soil to develop from hard rock in a cold, dry climate than it does for a soil to develop from permeable, unconsolidated material in a warm, humid climate. Even when soil scientists know the nature of the parent material, the climate conditions, and the vegetative cover, they can only give educated guesses about how long it will take for a soil to develop. Some soils have developed in humid, sandy localities within 100 to 200 years; more commonly, thousands of years are necessary for a mature soil to develop.

A more useful way to think of soil development is in terms of horizon development rather than lapsed time. According to Foth (1984), factors that accelerate soil development are warm to hot climates with high humidity; level or low topography with adequate drainage; permeable, unconsolidated material with low concentrations of lime; and forest vegetation. Soil development is slowed by such causes as cold, dry climates; steep topography; impermeable, consolidated material with high concentrations of lime; and grass vegetation.

SOIL CHARACTERISTICS

Because of the wide range of conditions under which soils evolve, soils tend to develop unique *characteristics* or *properties*. These characteristics, in turn, influence the *capability* of a given soil to support agricultural production, grassland or forest, and urban development. To maintain soil productivity, resource managers must understand the major factors that give soils their unique character: texture, structure, water porosity, aeration, biota, acidity and alkalinity, profile, color, and fertility.

Texture

Weathering breaks rock down into small particles that are classified as either gravel, sand, silt, clay, or loam (Figure 2-5). The relative *proportions* of the three major particle sizes (sand, silt, and clay) in a given soil, expressed in percentages, specify the **soil texture**. For example, in Figure 2-5, sandy loam specifies a soil made up of 65 percent sand, 20 percent silt, and 15 percent clay. A soil whose texture is made up of 40 percent sand, 42 percent silt, and 18 percent clay falls into the texture class known as **loam**. Loams are soils in which no one particle size—sand, silt, or clay—predominates.

The texture of a soil has a significant effect on the soil's cohesiveness, aeration, drainage, nutrient-holding capability, and workability (Table 2-2). Consequently, soil texture influences plant growth. Sand, for example, is made up of relatively large particles (0.05 to 1 millimeter in diameter), and the large spaces (*macropores*) between particles allow for good aeration and good drainage. But sand lacks cohesiveness. Silt (0.002 to 0.050 millimeter), on the other hand, tends to be cohesive when wet but is poor in nutrient-holding capability. Clay is very cohesive and has high nutrient-holding capability, but its small particles (less than 0.002 millimeter) provide only minute pore spaces (*micropores*). Consequently, these heavy soils are poor in aeration and drainage and are hard for farmers to work. (See page 41 for further discussion of clay colloids and plant nutrition.) Loam is the ideal soil for farming, since it contains enough clay to provide cohesiveness, water-holding capability, and ion exchange (needed for nutrient-holding capacity) and enough sand to provide infiltration, aeration, and workability.

Structure

Soil structure is the manner in which the component particles gather into groups. Soil scientists refer to these groups, which constitute secondary particles, as soil *aggregates* or *peds*.

Floccules (from the Latin *floccus,* tuft of wool) are small aggregates that result from the clustering together of colloidal particles. They arrange themselves into larger groups and behave somewhat like individual particles. *Flocculation* gives the soil a more porous quality that allows water and air to penetrate.

Soil structure is easier to identify in the B hori-

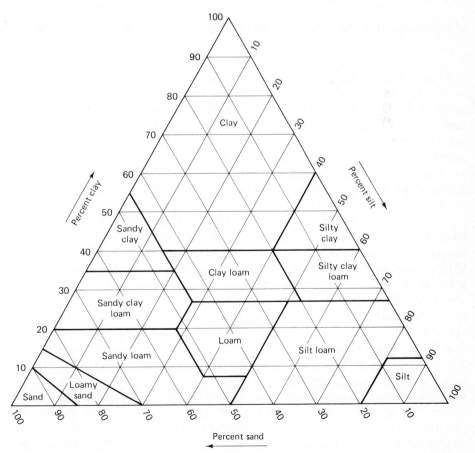

FIGURE 2-5 Soil texture classes on a triangular graph. (From Soil Survey Staff, *Soil Taxonomy,* USDA Handbook 436 [Washington, D.C.: USDA, Soil Conservation Service, 1975].)

TABLE 2-2
Soil texture

TYPE	SIZE		PLASTICITY (COHESIVENESS)	AERATION	DRAINAGE	NUTRIENTS	WORKABILITY
Gravel	Over 1mm	Gravel	None	Excellent	Excellent	Very poor	Very poor
Sand	0.05mm to 1 mm	Sand	Very little	Very good, due to *macropores* (large spaces)	Very good	Poor	Good
Silt	0.002 to 0.05mm	Silt	Slight tendency to become sticky when wet	Average	Average	Poor	Average
Clay	Under 0.002mm	Clay	Very plastic	Poor, due to *micropores* (minute pore spaces)	Very poor	High, due to absorption of positive ions of various nutrient elements	Poor
Loam	Mixture of clay (0–20%), silt (30–50%), and sand (30–50%)	Loam	Good	Good	Good	Good	Good
			Best all-around texture for agriculture				

zon than at the surface, because fine particles tend to move down from the A horizon and because the agents that give rise to structure are usually concentrated in the B horizon. The structure of the upper portion of the B horizon is more *platy* (thin, flat, horizontal peds), *blocky* (angular, equidimensional peds), or *spherodial* (granular or rounded peds) than the structure of the lower portions, which is *prismatic* (vertical, columnar peds).

Structure influences many other soil characteristics, including water-holding capacity and porosity, aeration, workability, fertility, resiliency, and susceptibility to erosion (Table 2-3). Soil structure is improved by the addition of organic matter, compost, and lime. Methods of soil management will be discussed in Chapter 3.

Soil Water and Porosity

Soil water is a dilute solution of phosphates, nitrates, sulfates, bicarbonates, and silicates of calcium, iron, potassium, sodium, and magnesium. It transports the mineral food used by plants and provides a necessary ingredient for photosynthesis and the conver-

sion of starch into sugar. It is required for plant turgidity, by which a plant maintains a shape or a position that enables it to receive sunlight. Finally, soil water is an essential component of protoplasm, which makes up 85 to 90 percent of the weight of a live plant. The water-holding capacity of a soil determines the soil's value for agriculture or for supporting natural vegetation. In specifying the water content of a field, pedologists say that the field is either *saturated* (all pore space being filled with water), at *field capacity* (pore space occupied by 50 percent water and 50 percent air), or at *permanent wilting point* (pore space occupied by 25 percent water and 75 percent air), as shown in Table 2-4.

Soil water takes three forms: gravitational water, capillary water, and hygroscopic water. **Gravitational water** is water that moves into, passes through, and drains out of the *large* pores of the soil under the forces of gravity. Gravitational water is water that is in the process of *percolating* from the soil surface to the top of the groundwater table. During heavy storms, it is gravitational water that fills the soil pores and causes fields to become saturated.

Capillary water is moisture that continues to

TABLE 2-3

Good versus poor soil structure

	GOOD STRUCTURE	POOR STRUCTURE
Feel	Spongy or crumbly; resilient and springy underfoot	Muddy and "gooey" when wet; bricklike clods when dry
Water infiltration	Abundance of pores for movement of water to root systems of crop plants	Minimum of pore spaces or chambers for water infiltration
Water-holding capacity	Medium to excellent	Poor: *arid regions*—irrigation water may not penetrate to satisfactory depths for crop production; *humid regions*—drainage problems in low-lying sites and severe water runoff and erosion in uplands
Ion-exchange capacity	Medium to excellent	Poor
Aeration	Abundance of pores for diffusion of life-sustaining oxygen	Minimum of pore spaces for diffusion of oxygen
Workability	Medium to excellent	Very difficult for farmers and urban gardeners to work
Fertility	Can promote crop or timber production	Intensive farming brings immediate deterioration (e.g., grassland and deciduous-forest biomes of America)
Susceptibility to erosion	More resistant than poorly structured soil to erosive effects of wind, rain, and runoff	Highly susceptible to erosion

TABLE 2-4

Moisture content of soil

LEVEL OF SATURATION	MICROPORES/MACROPORES	AGRICULTURAL CHARACTERISTICS
Saturated	100 percent water in pore spaces; 0 percent air content; excess water is present on field	May occur after low-lying fields have been flooded naturally (thunderstorm) or unnaturally (excessive irrigation)
Field capacity	50 percent water in pore spaces; 50 percent air content; field has been drained—no excess water	Upland crops (e.g., corn and cotton) cannot survive because of reduced oxygen content; good for growing rice
Permanent wilting point	25 percent water in pore spaces; 75 percent air content; permanent wilting point is reached when the "pull" of the plant roots for water is not sufficient to prevent permanent wilting	Often brought on by vigorously growing crops or summer droughts; agricultural crops shrivel when this point is reached
Hygroscopic coefficient	Less than 25 percent water in pore spaces; predominantly water remaining after air-drying, or water held by the soil when it is in equilibrium with atmospheric humidity	Water is held so tightly to clay particles that it is unavailable to plant roots

Note: The ideal for most plants is somewhere between field capacity and permanent wilting point.

cling to soil particles by capillary film tension after the rain stops and the field has drained. Capillary water moves through the *smaller* pores of the soil (capillary spaces) and is the most beneficial to plants. When it is abundant, it may move downward, like gravitational water. When it has been diminished by plant use or by evaporation, it may move horizontally or even upward as a result of surface tension. (See Chapter 3 for a discussion of the problem of salt development near the surface of soils.)

Hygroscopic water is a thin film of water that coats soil particles and colloids. It is unavailable to plant roots. Under very dry or drought conditions, the soil may lose all its gravitational and capillary water and be left with only hygroscopic water. Since this water does not move through the soil, it is resistant both to evaporation and to absorption by plant roots.

Soil Aeration

The gaseous content (the amount of oxygen, nitrogen, and carbon dioxide) of soils varies with the availability of pore spaces between the particles. The more water there is in the soil, the less space there is available for air. When evaporation, plant growth, or drainage depletes the water, air fills the vacated pore spaces. *Soil compaction*, resulting from long-time cropping or from the traffic of tractor tires, animal hooves, or people's shoes increases micropore space, decreases macropore space, and decreases total pore space.

The availability of pore space is vital to plant roots and other soil organisms. Most plant roots must be free to take in oxygen and give off carbon dioxide. Apple trees, for example, require a 3 percent concentration of oxygen in the soil just to exist. Most microorganisms in the soil also require a constant supply of oxygen. The soils of many marshlands, lake bottoms, and river channels do not have the necessary oxygen content for most plants; they are said to be *waterlogged*, because all their pore spaces are filled with water at the root zone. Poor aeration may impair the fertility of soil by lowering its ability to fix nitrogen. Such soils may also impair the ability of roots to absorb water and nutrients. Still, such plants as reeds are adapted to permanently waterlogged soils.

The decomposition of minerals and organic materials is also affected by the gaseous content of soil. The bright red color of many tropical soils is the result of chemical reactions that take place in the presence of air. The blue-gray colors of bog soils result from the gradual decomposition and assimilation of organic material in waterlogged swamps and other poorly drained areas where soil oxygen is largely depleted.

Soil Biota

Plants and animals, living or dead, have a definite effect on soil formation. The plant kingdom consists of *macroflora* (herbs, shrubs, and trees) and *microflora* (algae, fungi, molds, and bacteria). Similarly, the animal kingdom consists of *macrofauna* (prairie dogs, gophers, ground squirrels, moles, and badgers) and *microfauna* (protozoa, nematodes, insects, and earthworms). The soil is alive with these representatives of the biotic community.

Flora. All plants have specific functions in the formation and development of soil. The leaves, branches, trunks, and roots of various kinds of *macroflora* provide most of the organic material contained in soils, and various forms of *microflora* bring about the breakdown, decay, and subsequent recycling of the chemical constituents.

In the process of decay, *raw humus* is transformed into *humus*. Under wet, boggy conditions where the limited oxygen may prevent certain microflora from thriving, further decay may produce *peat*. This highly organic, fibrous soil is the first stage in the evolution of vegetable matter into coal. When dried, it can be used as a low-grade fuel, as it is in northern Scandinavia. Peat that decomposes further, to the point where the original plant parts cannot be identified, gives rise to a soil called *muck*.

Microflora perform other essential functions: They capture atmospheric nitrogen and forge the nitrates so vital for plant growth. Certain microorganisms produce plant hormones that maintain vigorous plant growth. Certain algae release oxygen into soil pores and serve as a source of food for other organisms.

Fauna. Animals of various sorts stir, mix, and process the soil and in so doing improve soil structure, aeration, and drainage. Protozoa and nematodes play a minor role in soil formation, but insects and earthworms play a major role. Their digestive and burrowing activities improve soil porosity, aeration, drainage, structure, and the interchange and circulation of soil nutrients.

Soil Acidity and Alkalinity

Soils range from acid to alkaline. The degree of acidity or alkalinity of a soil depends on the balance be-

TABLE 2-5
Soil acidity and alkalinity

	← INCREASING ACIDITY							INCREASING ALKALINITY →				
	← DECREASING HYDROGEN-ION CONCENTRATION							← INCREASING HYDROGEN-ION CONCENTRATION →				
pH	4.0 4.5	5.0	5.5	6.0	6.5 6.7		7.0	8.0	9.0	10.0	11.0	
Acidity	Very strongly acid	Strongly acid	Moderately acid	Slightly acid	Neutral		Weakly alkaline	Alkaline	Strongly alkaline	Excessively alkaline		
Commonly known substances		Rain (5.5)			Milk (6.7)	Blood (7.2)			Soap solution (10.0)			
Lime requirements	Lime needed except for crops requiring acid soil	Lime needed for all but acid-tolerant crops		Lime generally not required			No lime needed					
Occurrence	Rare Frequent	Very common in cultivated soils of humid climates					Common in subhumid and arid climates		Limited areas in deserts			
Great soil groups	Podzols	Gray-brown podzolic soils Tundra soils		Brown forest soils Prairie soils Latosols		Tropical black earths	Chestnut and brown soils		Black alkali soils			
Comprehensive classification system	Spodosol	Alifsol Inceptisol		Mollisol Oxisol		Mollisol		Aridisol				
Preferred soil pH of certain plants	Blueberries, citrus fruits (5.0)	Oaks (6.0)		Most crops (corn, beans, etc.) (6.5)			Basswood (8.5)		Salt grass (10.5)			

tween *hydrogen* and *hydroxyl ions:* an increase in hydrogen-ion concentration increases acidity; a decrease increases alkalinity. To measure hydrogen-ion concentration, soil scientists use the same **pH scale** used by chemists (Table 2-5).

The pH scale ranges from 0 to 14, with pH 7 denoting a balance between hydrogen ions and hydroxyl ions. Numbers 0 to 6 represent a greater dominance of hydrogen ions in the soil solution, and therefore greater soil acidity. In this lower range, hydrogen ions on the clay-humus particles displace many of the essential plant nutrients, such as calcium, potassium, and phosphorus. When rainwater,

which is already moderately to strongly acidic (pH 5.5 under normal conditions), infiltrates the soil, acidity increases. Acidity rises further as the soil water absorbs carbon dioxide from the air and acids from the products of plant decay. Higher pH numbers (8 to 14) indicate a dominance of basic ions and soil alkalinity, and therefore lower acidity. In this range, the clay-humus particles (colloids) retain most of the mineral nutrients. The chemical environment, consequently, determines whether or not the available soil nutrients will be absorbed by plant roots.

Most plants, particularly cultivated crops, grow best in soil that is mildly acidic (about pH 6.5 to 6.8).

TABLE 2-6

A hypothetical soil profile

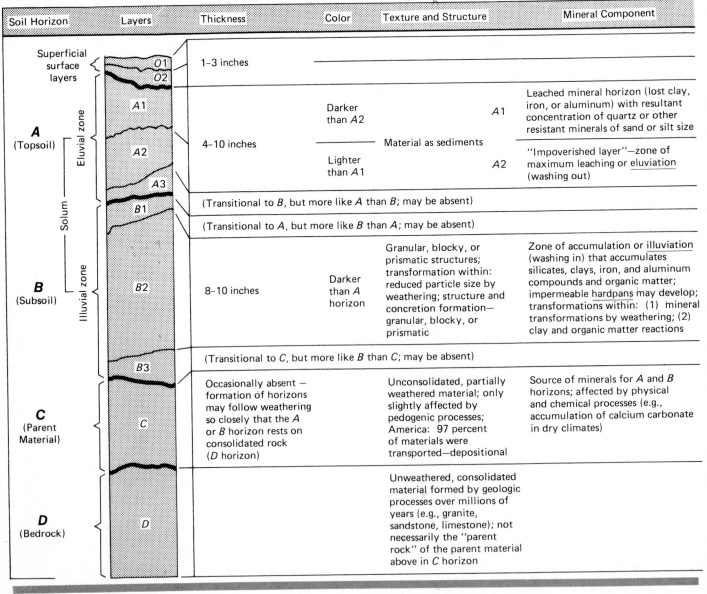

Soil Horizon	Layers	Thickness	Color	Texture and Structure	Mineral Component
Superficial surface layers	O1 / O2	1–3 inches			
A (Topsoil) / Eluvial zone / Solum	A1	4–10 inches	Darker than A2 — Material as sediments — Lighter than A1	A1 / A2	Leached mineral horizon (lost clay, iron, or aluminum) with resultant concentration of quartz or other resistant minerals of sand or silt size
	A2				"Impoverished layer"—zone of maximum leaching or eluviation (washing out)
	A3	(Transitional to B, but more like A than B; may be absent)			
B (Subsoil) / Illuvial zone	B1	(Transitional to A, but more like B than A; may be absent)			
	B2	8–10 inches	Darker than A horizon	Granular, blocky, or prismatic structures; transformation within: reduced particle size by weathering; structure and concretion formation—granular, blocky, or prismatic	Zone of accumulation or illuviation (washing in) that accumulates silicates, clays, iron, and aluminum compounds and organic matter; impermeable hardpans may develop; transformations within: (1) mineral transformations by weathering; (2) clay and organic matter reactions
	B3	(Transitional to C, but more like B than C; may be absent)			
C (Parent Material)	C	Occasionally absent — formation of horizons may follow weathering so closely that the A or B horizon rests on consolidated rock (D horizon)		Unconsolidated, partially weathered material; only slightly affected by pedogenic processes; America: 97 percent of materials were transported—depositional	Source of minerals for A and B horizons; affected by physical and chemical processes (e.g., accumulation of calcium carbonate in dry climates)
D (Bedrock)	D			Unweathered, consolidated material formed by geologic processes over millions of years (e.g., granite, sandstone, limestone); not necessarily the "parent rock" of the parent material above in C horizon	

Few plants tolerate a high degree of either acidity or alkalinity. Some, however, prefer either acidic soil (longleaf pine, blueberries, and citric fruits) or alkaline soil (basswood, maple, and salt grass). Farmers in the humid climates of the eastern United States, where high acidity creates a troublesome and costly problem, may have to add vast quantities of finely ground limestone to neutralize soil acidity. By contrast, the dry climates of the West suffer from alkaline soils. Here, farmers neutralize their soils (or get around the problem) by spreading gypsum over their fields, by flooding their fields (which washes the salts out of the surface soils), by using drip irrigation systems (which minimizes salt buildup), or by changing to salt-resistant crops.

Soil Profile

As we have seen, mature soils generally develop a distinctive vertical soil profile made up of horizontal soil horizons of differing thickness, color, texture, structure, and mineral composition. Each major horizon is the site of various exchange processes related to the biotic activity, the accumulation of organic matter, the soil water, and the gaseous content (Table 2-

Biotic Activity	Organic Material	Soil Water	Gaseous Content	
	Raw humus (undecomposed debris)			O1
	Humus (decomposed debris)			O2
Horizon with greatest amount and variety of soil organisms; root zone for most crops; organic matter from biotic activity	Horizon with greatest amount of organic matter; organic matter is accumulating or forming adjacent to the surface	Water received as precipitation, condensation, or runon; water lost by evapotranspiration and percolation	Additions of O and CO_2 from atmosphere; N, Cl, and S from atmosphere and precipitation; losses of C as CO_2 from oxidation of organic matter	A1
	Zone of leaching of organic matter			A2
				A3
				B1
Translocation within: nutrients circulated by plants; soil enmasse by animals	Little organic matter; however, receives some organic matter by percolating water from A horizon; transformation within: humification of organic matter	Translocation within: soluble salts in water	Some exchange	B2
				B3
Few organisms; consequently, unconsolidated material, rock fragments, or other mineral matter not greatly modified by living organisms, except by tree roots	Little to no organic matter	Little exchange	Little exchange	C
No organisms; unmodified rock or other material not yet changed by interactions with living organisms	None	Aquiclude—little to no penetration by soil water	No exchange	D

6). Soil horizons are of two major types: organic horizons and mineral horizons.

Organic horizons (referred to as O horizons) cover the mineral horizons. Usually, the uppermost organic horizon (O1) is composed of raw humus, and the O2 horizon, which lies beneath, is composed of humus. The processes that decompose organic material and transform it into humus in the O2 horizon are collectively termed *humification.*

Mineral horizons (referred to as A and B horizons) are made up of mostly inorganic mineral matter—grains or aggregates of sand, salt, and clay minerals, and other weathered materials. The *A horizon* ranges from 2.5 cm (1 in.) on the slopes of the Rocky Mountains to over 60 cm (2 ft) on the flat cornfields of Iowa. The A horizon has typically undergone extensive leaching, the removal of soluble salts by percolating soil water. Leaching is common in humid climates where precipitation and percolation are highest. The leached material tends to concentrate in the *B horizon.* Most crops, however, lack root systems that penetrate deep enough to reach the concentrated nutrients. The A horizon has the greatest amount of humus and biological activity; the B horizon has less of both.

The *C horizon,* which lies beneath the B horizon, is not *true soil.* Rather, it is parent material—a layer of regolith or sediment (but not bedrock) that is unconsolidated and only partially weathered. The mineral components of the A and B horizons are ultimately derived from this zone. The materials within the C horizon have usually been transported to their present site by water, ice, gravity, and wind. They are deficient in organic matter and are little affected by soil organisms, except for the roots of large trees.

The *D horizon,* which lies beneath the C horizon, consists of unweathered, consolidated bedrock, such as granite, limestone, or sandstone. This solid material is the product of such geological processes as volcanic activity and sedimentation.

Soil Color

The casual observer often notices the color of soil before noticing any of its other properties. Although the colors of soil range from white to black, the most common are shades of red, yellow, and brown. There is a definite regional gradation as one moves from the red surface soils of the southeastern United States (e.g., the Piedmont uplands of Georgia) to the brown-black soils of Illinois, Iowa, and Nebraska. Except in the tropics, soil color varies with depth and can easily be seen in a soil profile. Midlatitude forest soils, for example, have gray-brown A horizons, brown or orange-brown B horizons, and variably colored C horizons.

To the soil scientist, soil color indicates the organic and inorganic characteristics of a soil. Black in the A horizon normally means the presence of abundant organic matter and carbonates. Sometimes, however, black indicates the presence of undesirable ingredients, such as alkali in arid climates. Dark-brown and black soils are not necessarily more productive than light-colored soils. Some dark organic soils are too acidic to be productive unless they are limed; other soils may be dark because of the nature of the parent material and may be poor agricultural soils.

Red usually indicates the presence of iron oxide, good aeration, and favorable drainage. Red soils are typical of the well-drained uplands in warm, humid climates, such as that of southeastern United States. On the other hand, visitors to the Hawaiian Islands often comment on the rich red color of the soils and assume they are highly fertile. But the color is deceptive. To be productive, Hawaii's sugar cane fields must receive repeated applications of fertilizers.

White may indicate the presence of lime, sand, or gypsum. In arid climates light colors may indicate a concentration of salts and a lack of humus.

Soil color is usually related to climate, vegetation, microbial activity, and, consequently, humus content. As a result, it has certain spatial characteristics. For example, soils range from black or dark brown in cool, humid areas to light brown or gray in semi-arid steppe lands and deserts.

To measure soil color accurately, pedologists use standardized (Munsell) color books that express colors according to a letter-numeral code. That code specifies *hue* (the primary color of the soil according to the pure spectrum, associated with visible light wavelength), *value* (the degree of lightness versus darkness), and *chroma* (the pureness or saturation of the spectral color).

Soil Fertility

In addition to water and air, green plants need many essential mineral nutrients (Table 2-7). They require large quantities (greater than 500 parts per million in the plant) of **macronutrients**, such as nitrogen, phosphorus, and potassium. These macronutrients are sometimes referred to as *fertilizing elements,* since they are important components in artificial fertilizers. Plants also require **micronutrients** (also called *trace elements*), such as zinc, boron, copper, and manganese,

TABLE 2-7
Essential plant elements

MAJOR ELEMENTS FROM AIR AND WATER	MAJOR ELEMENTS FROM SOIL (MACRONUTRIENTS)	MINOR ELEMENTS FROM SOIL (MICRONUTRIENTS)
Carbon	Nitrogen	Iron
Hydrogen	Phosphorous	Zinc
Oxygen	Potassium	Manganese
	Sulfur	Copper
	Calcium	Chlorine
	Magnesium	Boron
		Molybdenum

in minute amounts (less than 50 parts per million in the plant). An oversupply of micronutrients can cause plant fatality.

In order for a soil to be fertile, these mineral nutrients must not only be present, but also present in an *available* form—that is, they must be present in *solution*. Solution is a form of weathering. Since most mineral nutrients in natural ecosystems come from rock weathering and the decomposition of organic matter, solution is essential to soil fertility.

Soil texture, structure, pH, and living organisms also affect soil fertility. Soils with a proper amount of humus and clay, for example, can retain more nutrients for plants than can sandy soils. Moreover, certain clay soils can retain more essential nutrients than others. Clay acts as a reservoir of plant nutrients.

Clay particles bind and hold chemical nutrients until the nutrients are absorbed by plants. This property is due to two traits: (1) the relatively spacious surface area of clay particles and (2) the negative electrical charge of the clay particles. The combined surface area of clay particles is very large, allowing for maximum exposure of their *negative* charge. As positive ions of such nutrient elements as potassium (K^+), calcium (Ca^+), and magnesium (Mg^+) are released by weathering or by the oxidation of organic substances, they become soluble in water, and thus become susceptible to leaching, uptake, or storage on the clay particles.

The negatively charged particles attract the positive nutrients ions, thereby rescuing and storing them for use by plants. Plant roots, in turn, give off hydrogen ions that absorb these nutrient ions from the clay particles. This exchange of various ions between a solution and a solid material is called *ion exchange*. The capacity of clay particles for ion exchange makes them a valuable component of agricultural soil.

THE SOIL SURVEY

The United States launched an inventory and survey of the nation's soils around 1900. Prompting this step were three factors: an increasing awareness of the importance of soils to society, a need to understand the underlying causes of certain agricultural problems, and a desire to foster research. The task was undertaken by state agricultural experiment stations under the direction of the U.S. Department of Agriculture.

Making the Soil Survey

Most soil maps (surveys) were done on foot in the early 1900s. Today, however, the process of mapping and surveying begins with the taking of aerial photographs of the area to be covered, usually a *county*.

FIGURE 2-6 Soil scientist recording soil type on an aerial map used in soil survey work. (Courtesy of Soil Survey Division, USDA, Soil Conservation Service.)

FIGURE 2-7 Section of soils map for Monroe County, New York. Letter symbol indicates soil name as described in accompanying report. (Courtesy of USDA, Soil Conservation Service.)

FIGURE 2-8 Soil survey reports. These reports contain soil maps, descriptions, and interpretations for various uses such as soil and water conservation. (From Frederick R. Troeh, J. A. Hobbs, and Roy L. Donahue, *Soil and Water Conservation: For Productivity and Environmental Protection* [Englewood Cliffs, N.J.: Prentice-Hall, Inc., 1980], p. 20.)

With photographs and topographic maps in hand, the soil scientist then *ground checks* the soils in the field (Figure 2-6).

Lines are then drawn around areas in which the soil is similar, called *polypedons*, and each polypedon is identified with a symbol. The same symbol is used every time the soil scientist spots that particular kind of soil (Figure 2-7). Other types of information are plotted on the photographs, such as *natural features* (streams, rock outcrops, lakes, ponds, marshes, and vegetative cover) and *cultural features* (evidence of erosion, land-use type, levees, ferries, buildings, roads, railroads, airports, churches, quarries, gravel pits, and cemeteries). The soil scientist then sends samples from the site to soil laboratories to verify texture, types and levels of nutrients, and other factors that affect farming practices or urban development.

The Published Soil Survey

The completed survey is published in two parts: (1) soil maps of the counties, and (2) descriptions of each area shown on the maps (Figure 2-8). The soil survey maps distinguish *soil types* by locality (e.g., city, river, and county) and by texture (e.g., *Pleasanton loam*, *Alamitos clay*, or *Plainfield sand*). To date, more than 70,000 such soil types have been mapped for 500 million acres of the United States. The descriptions provide information on the general nature of the county (climate, physiography, relief, and drainage); how

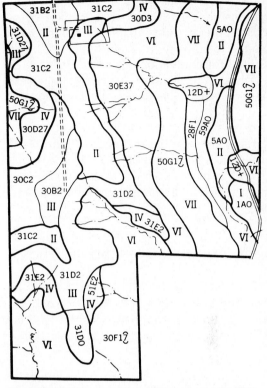

FIGURE 2-10 Land-capability map. A 200-acre dairy farm in Wisconsin. (From Henry D. Foth, *Fundamentals of Soil Science*, 7th ed., p. 246. Copyright © 1984 by John Wiley & Sons, Inc.)

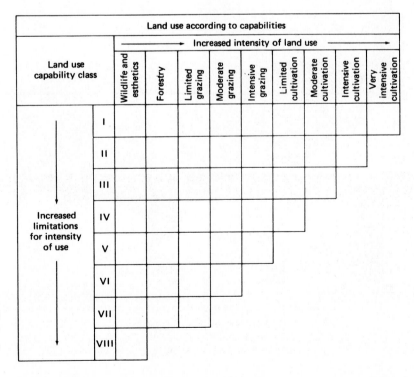

Land use according to capabilities									
Land use capability class		Wildlife and esthetics	Forestry	Limited grazing	Moderate grazing	Intensive grazing	Limited cultivation	Moderate cultivation	Intensive cultivation	Very intensive cultivation
	I									
	II									
	III									
Increased limitations for intensity of use	IV									
	V									
	VI									
	VII									
	VIII									

FIGURE 2-9 Land-capability classes. From Class I to Class VIII, choices of use become fewer and risks become greater. (Courtesy of USDA, Soil Conservation Service.)

the survey was made; the formation and classification of the soils; the best use and management of each soil unit based on the land capability classes (Classes I to IV: suited to cultivation; Classes V to VIII: generally not suited for cultivation) (Figure 2-9).

The soil survey maps are used as the basis for a variety of other maps. Scientists group and map areas according to land capability classes and produce maps (called *land capability maps*) that are useful to farmers and wildlife managers (Figure 2–10). The information is also used by engineers, city planners, foresters, land appraisers, realtors, builders, nursery owners, pipeline manufacturers, and insurance companies.

SOIL CLASSIFICATION AND DISTRIBUTION

The soil types described in the soil surveys are integrated into larger units (orders, suborders, etc.) according to their distribution over the land surfaces. The two major systems of soil classification used in

the United States are the older (1938) Great Soil Groups and the more recent (1960) Comprehensive Classification System. Both sets of terminology are still used. Although the Comprehensive Classification is now *officially* used, the older terminology lingers on.

The Great Soil Groups (1938–1960)

The Great Soil Groups system (commonly referred to as the *1938 System*) was used with a number of modifications (particularly those made in 1949) for 22 years. It uses such groupings as *tundra soils*, *prairie soils*, and *gray-brown podzolic soils*, which tend to correspond with regional climates and vegetation. Despite minor improvements, soil scientists grew increasingly aware of the system's inadequacy. For example, the system provided no means of accommodating new varieties of soil. Furthermore, scientists began to question certain assumptions the system made about the role of soil genesis (climatic and other pedogenic processes) in determining soil characteristics. During

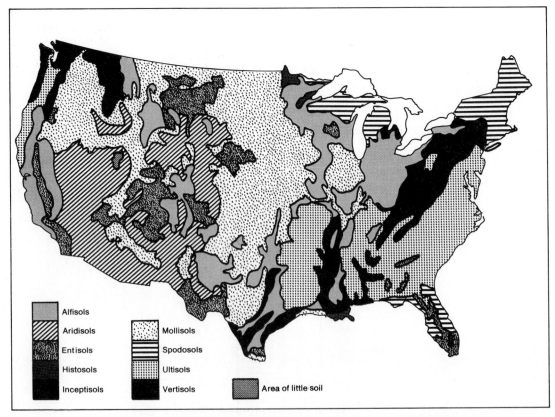

FIGURE 2-11 Soil orders of the Comprehensive Systems of 1960 for the conterminous states. (From Tom L. McKnight, *Physical Geography: A Landscape Appreciation*, 2d ed. p. 282. © 1987. Reprinted by permission of Prentice-Hall, Inc., Englewood Cliffs, N.J.)

the 1950s they began to call for a fresh approach to soil classification based on greater objectivity and quantification, especially the use of morphology as the basis of classification.

Comprehensive Soil Classification System (CSCS) (1960–Present)

In 1960 the soil survey staff of the Soil Conservation Service published a new classification system that was first known as the *Seventh Approximation* (because it was the seventh revision). After further modifications and refinement, it was officially named the *Comprehensive Soil Classification System* (CSCS). In 1975, a handbook, *Soil Taxonomy*, was published to facilitate use of the system.

The Comprehensive System differs in many ways from its predecessor. First, it is based on a hier-

archy of six levels of classification. They are listed here with the number of classes currently recognized within each category:

Orders	10
Suborders	44
Great Groups	184
Subgroups	975
Families	5,202
Series	12,156

Second, the *Soil Taxonomy* handbook defines classes in terms of soil characteristics (composition and morphology). Quantification is used as much as possible, based on morphological features than can be observed either in the field or in the laboratory, thus minimizing arbitrary or subjective classifica-

TABLE 2-8

Approximate equivalents in U.S. soil classification systems

SEVENTH APPROXIMATION ORDER	1938 SYSTEM	
	MOSTLY INCLUDED	SIGNIFICANTLY INCLUDED
Entisols	Lithosols	Alluvial soils
	Regosols	Low-humic gley soils
Vertisols	Grumusols	
Inceptisols	Ando soils	Alluvial soils
	Brown forest soils	Brown podzolic soils
	Half-bog soils	Latosols
	Sols bruns acides	Low-humic gley soils
	Tundra soils	
Aridisols	Desert soils	Brown soils
	Red desert soils	Calcisols
	Sierozems	Reddish brown soils
	Solonchak	Solonetz soils
Mollisols	Brunizems	Alluvial soils
	Chernozems	Brown soils
	Chestnut soils	Calcisols
	Reddish prairie soils	Humic gley soils
	Rendzina soils	Reddish chestnut soils
		Solonetz soils
Spodosols	Brown podzolic soils	
	Groundwater podzols	
	Podzol soils	
Alfisols	Gray-brown podzolic soils	Degraded chernozems
	Gray wooded soils	Noncalcic brown soils
	Planosols	Reddish brown soils
		Reddish chestnut soils
		Solonetz soils
Ultisols	Groundwater laterite soils	Latosols
	Humic latosols	
	Reddish brown lateritic soils	
	Red-yellow podzolic soils	
Oxisols	Laterite soils	Latosols
Histosols	Bog soils	

Source: McKnight, Tom L. 1987. *Physical Geography: A Landscape Appreciation.* 2d ed. Englewood Cliffs, N.J.: Prentice-Hall, p. 281.

tions. Third, *Soil Taxonomy* does not distinguish between zonal soils (soils associated with prevailing climate and vegetation) and intrazonal soils (soils not restricted to a latitudinal zone, e.g., peat) in the highest category–the soil *order*. Hence, it can group the soils of wet places with soils of well-drained places within the same order. Fourth, the Comprehensive System recognizes the importance of human activity in soil formation. Equal importance is given to classes of soils that obtained their characteristics from such human practices as land cultivation, crop fertilization, and waste disposal.

Finally, the Comprehensive System uses many newly established terms, such as *Entisols*, *Vertisols*, and *Inceptisols* (Table 2-8). The syllables of these terms represent the genetic elements or properties that are associated with the different soil classes. Though difficult to master at first, this *new language* has already proved useful in fieldwork and in theoretical applications (Figure 2-11).

DISCUSSION TOPICS

1. How does the soil scientist define *soil*? In what way is soil dynamic rather than static?

2. Discuss the different concepts that various economic groups have of soil. Are humans today any less dependent on soils than in the past?

3. What are the five major influences (factors) that cause soil formation? Explain with examples.

4. What is the difference between *residual soils* and *depositional soils*? How do they relate to *bedrock* and *parent material*?

5. How is time a factor in soil formation? What factors affect the maturity of soil? How much time does it take to develop 2.54 cm (1 in.) of mature soil?

6. How does soil texture influence agricultural land use?

7. How does soil structure affect plant growth?

8. When is a soil said to be *saturated*? What are the meanings of *field capacity*, *permanent wilting point*, and *hygroscopic coefficient*? What are the differences between *gravitational water*, *capillary water*, and *hygroscopic water*?

9. Why is humus important in soil development?

10. Describe the major functions of plants and animals in soil formation.

11. What is the pH scale? What does soil pH have to do with *colloids, ions, hydrogen ion concentration,* and *exchange reactions*?

12. Describe the salient characteristics of the various soil horizons. How do landform differences affect the development of the soil profile?

13. What can the soil scientist tell by observing soil color?

14. Regarding soil fertility, what is the difference between *macronutrients* and *micronutrients*? Why is *solution* important in soil fertility? What is the relationship between clay particles, *ion exchange capacity*, and soil fertility? Where does *nitrogen fixation* fit into the scheme of things? Describe the exchange reaction within the soil that facilitates plant nutrition.

15. What is the difference between the 1938 soil classification system and the Comprehensive Soil Classification System of 1960?

16. How do the factors that dominate in the development of soil relate to your local area?

READINGS

ALLAWAY, W. H. 1957. "pH, Soil Acidity, and Plant Growth." In *USDA Yearbook: Soil*, pp. 67–71. Washington, D.C.: Government Printing Office. Basic report on the importance of soil chemistry to proper plant growth.

AUTEN, JOHN T., and T. B. PLAIR. 1949. "Forests and Soils." In *USDA Yearbook: Trees*, pp. 114–119. Washington, D.C.: Government Printing Office. Early summary of the effects of forest vegetation on soil formation.

BEAR, FIRMAN E. 1964. *Chemistry of the Soil*. New York: Van Nostrand. Outstanding book on soil chemistry.

BRADY, NYLE C. 1974. *The Nature and Properties of Soils*. 8th ed. New York: Macmillan. Extremely useful book on soil characteristics.

BRIGGS, DAVID, and FRANK COURTNEY. 1985. *Agriculture and Environment: The Physical Geography of Temperate Agricultural Systems*. New York: Longman. Excellent analysis of the physical characteristics of various agricultural environments from a geographical perspective.

BUOL, S. W., F. D. HOLE, and R. J. MCCRACKEN. 1980. *Soil Genesis and Classification*. 2d ed. Ames, Iowa: Iowa State University Press. The classic treatment of pedology. No other book approaches its thoroughness. An essential reference for professionals in soil, agriculture, and land-use planning.

CLARK, FRANCIS E. 1957. "Living Organisms in the Soil." In *USDA Yearbook: Soil*, pp. 147–165. Washington, D.C.: Government Printing Office. Basic report on how plants and animals influence soil development.

COOK, R. L., and C. E. MILLAR. 1953. "Plant Nutrient Deficiencies," *Michigan Agricultural Station Special Bulletin*, vol.

353. Excellent illustration of the relationship between the chemical environment and the ability of plants to absorb nutrients.

DASMANN, R. F. 1984. *Environmental Conservation*. 5th ed. New York: Wiley. A classic introductory text in resource management.

DENT, DAVID, and ANTHONY YOUNG. 1981. *Soil Survey and Land Evaluation*. Winchester, Mass.: Allen & Unwin. Concise book describing systems of soil survey and land evaluation and the part they play in resource planning and management.

ELLIS, BOYD G. 1972. "Nutrient Cycling in Agricultural Systems." In C. L. San Clemente, ed., *Environmental Quality: Now or Never*. East Lansing, Mich.: Michigan State University, Continuing Education Service. Superb summary of the relationship between soil chemistry and the availability of plant nutrients.

FINKL, CHARLES W., JR. 1982. *Soil Classification*. New York: Van Nostrand Reinhold. Excellent history of the evolution of soil classification.

FOTH, HENRY D. 1984. *Fundamentals of Soil Science*. 7th ed. New York: Wiley. Perhaps the best introductory textbook on soils.

FOTH, HENRY D., and JOHN SCHAFER. 1980. *Soil Geography and Land Use*. New York: Wiley. Detailed textbook that takes a global and regional approach to the characterization, genesis, and classification of soils.

GARDNER, WALTER H. 1968. "How Water Moves in the Soil," *Crops and Soils*, November, pp. 7–12. Interesting article on soil water and porosity.

GOLDIN, ALAN. 1982. "Influence of Volcanic Ash from the May 18, 1980 Eruption of Mount St. Helens on the Properties of Soils," *Journal of Soil and Water Conservation*, May–June, vol. 37, no. 3, pp. 185–189. Good illustration of the effects of volcanic ash deposits on soil.

JENNY, HANS. 1941. *Factors of Soil Formation*. New York: McGraw-Hill. Important early work on the processes and influences that act together to develop soil.

LOWRANCE, RICHARD, BENJAMIN R. STINNER, and GARFIELD J. HOUSE. 1984. *Agricultural Ecosystems*. New York: Wiley. Scientific analysis of the structure and function of agricultural ecosystems.

LUKENS, JAMES R. 1982. "What's in a Survey Report For Me?" *Journal of Soil and Water Conservation*, vol. 37, no. 4, pp. 204–206. The value of soil surveys from the perspective of a Kansas farmer.

LUNDGREN, LAWRENCE. 1986. *Environmental Geology*. Englewood Cliffs, N.J.: Prentice-Hall. Excellent introductory textbook.

McKNIGHT, TOM L. 1987. *Physical Geography: A Landscape Appreciation*. 2d ed. Englewood Cliffs, N.J.: Prentice-Hall. Good introductory textbook.

MOHR, E. C. J., and F. A. VAN BAREN. 1954. *Tropical Soils*. New York: Interscience. One of the best works on the subject.

NEBEL, BERNARD J. 1981. *Environmental Science: The Way the World Works*. Englewood Cliffs, N.J.: Prentice-Hall. Good introductory textbook.

OLSON, GERALD W. 1984. *Field Guide to Soils and the Environment*. New York: Methuen. Superb introductory description of soil profiles, laboratory analyses, and soil classification.

PITTY, A. F. 1979. *Geography and Soil Properties*. London: Methuen. Excellent source material for the advanced reader.

PLASTER, EDWARD, J. 1985. *Soil Science and Management*. Albany, N.Y.: Delmar. Very good introductory textbook on soil science.

POWELL, J. C. 1983. "Progress in the U.S. Soil Survey," *Journal of Soil and Water Conservation*. September–October, vol. 38, no. 5, pp. 407–410. Good discussion of the status of modern soil surveys.

RUSSELL, M. B. 1957. "Physical Properties." In *USDA Yearbook: Soil*, pp. 31–38. Washington, D.C.: Government Printing Office. Good description of soil characteristics.

SCHALLER, FRIEDRICH. 1968. *Soil Animals*. Ann Arbor, Mich.: University of Michigan Press. One of the best books on the role of the animal kingdom (both macro- and microfauna) in soil formation.

SIMONSON, ROY W. 1968. "Concept of Soil," *Advances in Agronomy*, vol. 20, pp. 1–47. New York: Academic Press. Outstanding source on how various cultural and economic groups perceive soil resources.

SIMONSON, ROY W. 1957. "What Soils Are." In *USDA Yearbook: Soil*, pp. 17–31. Washington, D.C.: Government Printing Office. Provides standard working definition of the soil resource.

SOIL CONSERVATION SERVICE. 1977. *Classification of Soil Series in the United States*. Washington, D.C.: Soil Conservation Service, U.S. Department of Agriculture. Excellent description of the Soil Taxonomy system of soil classification.

SOIL SURVEY STAFF. 1960. *Soil Classification, A Comprehensive System*. Washington, D.C.: U.S. Department of Agriculture. At first commonly known as the U.S. Seventh Approximation of Soil Classification, then revised and later republished in 1975 as the Soil Taxonomy.

SOIL SURVEY STAFF. 1975. *Soil Taxonomy*. USDA Handbook 436. Washington, D.C.: U.S. Department of Agriculture. Current U.S. system of soil classification.

SPURWAY, C. H. 1941. "Soil Reaction (pH) Preferences of Plants," *Michigan Agricultural Station Special Bulletin*, 306. Outstanding summary.

STRAHLER, ARTHUR N. 1975. *Physical Geography*. New York: Wiley. Contains two excellent chapters on soils.

TAYLOR, STERLING A. 1957. "Use of Moisture by Plants." In *USDA Yearbook: Soil*, pp. 61–66. Washington, D.C.: Government Printing Office. Readable summary.

THORP, JAMES. 1949. "Effects of Certain Animals that Live in Soils," *Science Monthly*, vol. 42, pp. 180–191. Classic account of the role of animals in improving soil structure, aeration, and drainage.

TROEH, FREDERICK, et al. 1980. *Soil and Water Conservation:*

For Productivity and Environmental Protection. Englewood Cliffs, N.J.: Prentice-Hall. Detailed textbook on the subject.

U.S. DEPARTMENT OF AGRICULTURE. 1955. *USDA Yearbook: Water*. Washington, D.C.: Government Printing Office. Excellent government document on soil and water relationships.

WADLEIGH, C. H. 1957. "Growth of Plants." In *USDA Yearbook: Soil*, pp. 38–39. Washington, D.C.: Government Printing Office. Especially good section on soil chemistry and plant growth.

WAKSMAN, SELMAN A. 1952. *Soil Microbiology*. New York: Wiley. Very thorough analysis of how plants and animals influence soil development.

WEIL, RAY, and WYBE KROONTJE. 1984. *The Nature and Properties of Soils: A Study Guide*. New York: Macmillan. Superb study guide for teachers, students, and others interested in mastering the quantitative aspects of soils.

WILDE, S. A. 1958. *Forest Soils*. New York: Ronald. Excellent summary of the effects of forest vegetation on soil formation.

ZACK, ANNE. 1975. "Soil Surveying in Nation's Capital," *Soil Conservation*, vol. 41, pp. 12–15. Interesting article on our national soils inventory process.

■3■

SOIL RESOURCE MANAGEMENT

Soil and Civilization
Early Efforts at Soil Conservation
Soil and the Countryside
Soil and the City
Prospects for the Future

One hears a lot about the rules of good husbandry; there is only one—leave the land far better than you found it.

George Henderson,
The Farming Ladder, 1944

Human use of the land, particularly in recent times, has had a profound effect on the soils of the earth. Forestry, agriculture, grazing, and urbanization have wrought changes in erosion rates, drainage, salinity, organic matter, nutrient content, and degree of compaction. All human activities affect the soil in some way—sometimes beneficially, sometimes harmfully.

Modern agricultural practices, for example, use specialized power tools to manipulate the land—to drain swamps, to reclaim portions of continental shelves, to break up hardpans, to reshape the land for irrigation and water control, and to apply fertilizers and pesticides to the land. Management practices designed to stabilize the soil against the ravages of wind and water and to restore crop residues to the soil also tend to alter the soil, changing it from its natural state. The extraction of minerals (strip mining) and the construction of factories and commercial centers around the nation's cities often leave soils

that are little more than accumulations of barren trash. Furthermore, the relentless expansion of urban centers results in the paving over of vast tracts of prime agricultural land.

Human efforts to protect this valuable natural resource are known as **soil resource management** or **soil conservation**. Early in this century, soil resource management meant little more than an attempt to prevent soil erosion. Today, the term encompasses all measures and practices designed to improve soil conditions for the benefit of crops, grasses, trees, and human welfare.

Soil conservationists have three main goals: (1) *to prevent further damage to the soil,* (2) *to remedy damage already done,* and (3) *to ensure the highest level of productivity consistent with sustainable yield.* (Sustainable yield is the yield that a renewable resource, such as properly managed soil, can produce continuously at a given intensity of management without harming

49

the environment.) The rapid spread of urbanization has recently added a fourth goal: *to preserve existing agricultural resources by working to conserve farmland.*

To be truly effective, soil resource management requires an interdisciplinary approach that embraces pedology, agronomy, geography, geology, geomorphology, forestry, animal husbandry, engineering, and urban planning. It demands close cooperation between specialized scientists and landowners.

SOIL AND CIVILIZATION

Soil is the foundation of civilization itself. Along with water, soil is basic to human survival. Yet humans have been careless in their treatment of this essential resource. Human failure to control soil erosion, for example, has brought the downfall of many nations and continues to threaten land resources in many countries today. In *Topsoil and Civilization*, Vernon Carter and Tom Dale (1981) point out that some of our most brilliant technological achievements have paradoxically led to the destruction of the natural resources on which our very civilization is based.

The Rise and Fall of Past Civilizations

Extreme soil abuse can impair the economy of an entire nation and can contribute to the decline of a whole civilization, as may have been the case with the Sumerian and Roman civilizations.

The Sumerian Empire. In 1946, archaeologists found the earliest evidence of agriculture at the ancient village of Jarmo in the Chemchemal Valley of northern Iraq. The village was occupied about 11,000 B.C. Other prehistoric villages in the same general area date from 11,000 to 9500 B.C. Archaeological evidence from agricultural villages in the southern part of Iraq, between the Tigris and Euphrates rivers, suggests that water from those rivers was used to irrigate crops. The very word *Mesopotamia* means "the land between the rivers."

The Sumerians, who were early inhabitants of Mesopotamia, built great cities, such as Babylon, whose inhabitants depended for their food on adjacent irrigated fields. The Sumerians were the first to cultivate the soil, to invent the wheel, and to develop a system of counting based on cycles of 60, which we still use in measuring time (Troeh et al. 1980). How could such an innovative people permit their culture to perish?

According to Lowdermilk (1953), soil abuse probably brought about the downfall of this great empire. As the population grew, the rising demand for food forced farmers to cultivate land higher and higher up the hillsides surrounding the low-lying farmland. Goats and sheep overgrazed the hill pastures, and the protecting trees were cut for fuel and lumber. As a result, Mesopotamia's watersheds were denuded, causing severe erosion and erratic river flow. The irrigation canals and ditches became clogged with sediment faster than workers could remove it. As one section of irrigated land after another was abandoned, agricultural production declined. Gradually the urban populations, deprived of their food supply, abandoned the great cities.

At its height, Mesopotamia boasted a population of close to 25 million (Troeh et al. 1980). Today, a mere 4 million people make up the entire population of Iraq (the present-day country that includes ancient Mesopotamia). Babylon, at one time the strongest and most influential city on the planet, now lies entombed under erosional debris.

The Roman Empire. The Sumerian innovation of agriculture spread westward through the Middle East and Egypt to Greece, Italy, and northern Africa. Originally, the Roman Empire supported its population with food produced on fields surrounding the cities, as the Sumerians had done. Again, farmers were forced to cultivate fields farther and farther up the hillsides. The Romans felled the forests on the hillsides to clear land for farming and to provide timber for ships and buildings. As the watersheds were denuded, huge gullies developed and sediment washed into streams. Gradually, as the Romans grew preoccupied with invasions and waging wars, they neglected to remove the sediment and abandoned the irrigated fields.

As the local soils deteriorated, Rome came to rely on imported grain from outposts in northern Africa, particularly outposts in what are now Algeria, Tunisia, Egypt, and Libya. Although the soils of those regions were highly productive at the outset, they too deteriorated over the centuries. Water and wind erosion did the greatest damage. The Roman Empire collapsed under barbarian pressure in the fifth century. Later, in the sixth century, a new disaster struck the once-flourishing agricultural economy of Rome. Desert nomads invaded the African farmlands, bringing with them a pastoral, but soil-abusing, way of life. They subjected the surrounding hillsides to intensive overgrazing by goats and sheep, resulting in gigantic dust storms that eventually buried towns and cities under tons of windblown soil. El Jem, an ancient city in the modern state of Tunisia, for example, once had an amphitheater that could hold

60,000 people. In the 1930s, the area surrounding the ruins of the city had less than 5000 permanent residents. Although invasions and wars contributed to the downfall of the Roman Empire, it was soil erosion that destroyed its agricultural base (Lowdermilk 1953). Furthermore, Lester Brown (1982) notes that Libya and Algeria—once the granary of the Roman Empire—today import half of their grain from North America, whose soils are not yet degraded.

The Rise (and Fall?) of the American Empire

Today we recognize that environmental havoc brought on the demise of the Sumerian and Roman civilizations, and perhaps the ruin of other civilizations as well, such as the Mayan. As Brown (1982) points out, however, we must realize that the "economic advisers" and "decision makers" of their day may not have perceived the gradual erosion of their lands as contributing to their ultimate downfall. The cumulative environmental stresses of soil loss and sedimentation may have been so gradual that they were not aware that their food supplies and economies were being slowly undermined. Some early civilizations, including the Roman Empire, did have soil advisors. The Romans Columella, Varro, and Cato, in fact, laid the foundations for modern soil science (Coates 1981). Unfortunately, just as in ancient times, soil conservationists of today are often considered to be just "alarmists"—individuals that should be given little credence.

Despite sophisticated technology and cumulative knowledge, might the same fate befall present-day "empires," such as that of the United States, as befell Sumeria and Rome? It might, but we have certain advantages: we have the lessons of history before us; we have the technical and practical knowledge necessary to maintain and improve our soil resources; and we have the means of communicating the lessons of history to other people. But do we have the will to avoid the mistakes of the past? If not, we may find ourselves in the plight of previous empires that practiced too little soil conservation too late. Unfortunately, the history of soil conservation in the United States is not encouraging. Nevertheless, a brief look at that history will help us better understand the root cause of soil abuse: the attitudes and the consequent behaviors of farmers, ranchers, and, more recently, urbanites.

Colonial Times. America's first white settlers found a continent of vast natural wealth. The ten million Indians who occupied the North American continent at that time had made virtually no impact on the soil. They had neither horses nor cattle to overgraze and expose the soil. Neither did they have plows to overtill the land, nor axes to lay barren the forested hillsides. These were hunting and fishing peoples who practiced only swidden (slash-and-burn) agriculture. The newly arrived colonists, however, perceiving the soil as inexhaustible, planted and replanted the land along the eastern seaboard, with little regard for replacing nutrients. By 1685, some farmers had already noticed that their crop yields were declining. The New England soils had already begun to show signs of deterioration resulting from overuse and erosion. As their soils continued to deteriorate, many settlers looked for alternative sites to farm.

Settling the Public Domain. Pulling up stakes because of declining crop yields and moving west was the standard practice from 1685 to 1862. According to geographer Warren Johnson (personal correspondence), it was simply cheaper and easier to buy virgin land than to spread manure on the old. With the passage of the Homestead Act in 1862, the federal government provided an additional incentive for making such a move. The act gave homesteaders title to 160 acres of land on condition that they occupy the land and use it for five years. The federal government wished to dispose of the public domain west of the Missouri and to encourage settlement within these relatively virgin lands. Newspaper advertisements proclaiming the inexhaustible soil resources of the West helped fuel the drive for land and created the myth that there are always "more resources" just around the corner. Consequently, the Homestead Act further encouraged a philosophy of wasteful land use.

Soil Devastation of the Great Plains. The westward expansion of agriculture reached the southern Great Plains in the 1880s during a period of relatively high rainfall and lush growth. By 1890, however, the first surge of settlers had discovered that severe droughts regularly struck that region. Annual rainfall was sometimes as little as 12.7 cm (5 in.) annually, whereas at least 50.8 cm (20 in.) of annual rainfall is necessary for crop production (Owen 1985). Consequently, when the 1890 drought hit the plains and persisted for the better part of a decade, many settlers simply gave up and again turned elsewhere in their search for farmlands. The late 1890s brought a period of increased precipitation, lush vegetation growth, and resettlement, and this second wave of settlers was also hit by another severe drought in 1910.

But it was the five-year *Big Drought* from 1926 to 1931 that gave the southern Great Plains its new name, the *Dust Bowl*. The Dust Bowl experience epitomized the process of soil loss caused by drought, heat, winds, and insensitivity to the precarious soil-moisture-vegetation balance that exists in that region. Textbooks, scholarly articles, and celebrated novels, such as John Steinbeck's *The Grapes of Wrath*, record this devastating period in American history.

Careless farming practices and overstocked pastures left the prairies vulnerable to the combined assaults of drought, heat, and wind. Dust blew across the continent all the way to the Atlantic, skies grew black, drivers abandoned their cars, airplanes could not take off, and people fell victim to "dust pneumonia." An estimated loss of topsoil ranging from 5.1 to 30.5 cm (2 to 12 in.) devastated millions of acres of farmland (Dasmann 1984). Fields, fences, roads, even entire houses were buried by drifting dunes. Ruined by drought and unable to find work, farmers streamed in mass exodus from Oklahoma, Texas, and Kansas and went west to California or to the East.

Although most people associated the Dust Bowl with the Big Drought, the Great Plains continues to experience floods, droughts, nutrient depletion, and soil loss. Similar, though less disastrous, soil erosion occurred there in the mid-1950s and the early 1970s. The environmental studies professor Spencer Havlick (1974) once remarked that the farmers of this region are "the slowest learners of conservation lessons in the world."

EARLY EFFORTS AT SOIL CONSERVATION

Pre-Columbian horticulturalists in the human parts of North America did not need to practice elaborate soil conservation practices, since the small size of their fields and the limited demand for crops did not trigger accelerated erosion (Coates 1981). The white settlers, however, wasted no time in depleting the fertility of the soil and in fostering erosion to the point where they were obliged to initiate soil conservation techniques.

The Earliest Efforts

As early as 1769, George Washington was advocating farming practices that would maintain soil fertility and reduce soil erosion. He conducted experiments at Mount Vernon to determine the advisability of letting fields lie fallow, using various forms of vegetation for ground cover, and constructing check dams in gullies. By 1800, some Maryland and Virginia farmers had adopted such practices as planting grasses and legumes, contour plowing, and hillside ditching

(a primitive form of the modern terrace). By 1810, Thomas Jefferson was practicing and advocating systems of contour farming, crop rotation, and strip cropping.

In 1864, George Perkins Marsh published the first American book on the subject, *Man and Nature; Or, Physical Geography as Modified by Human Action*. Marsh's recommendations for better soil management are as valid today as they were then. Most important, his book helped stimulate government officials to recognize the seriousness of the erosion problem in America. It was another book, together with the personal crusade of one of its authors, H. H. Bennett, that aroused sufficient furor to activate the United States Congress. The publication of *Soil Erosion: A National Menace* in 1927 helped stir up public interest and governmental involvement in soil conservation. This set the stage for the soil conservation programs that were to follow. Congress immediately appropriated $160,000 to establish 10 erosion experiment stations in regions suffering from the worst erosion. Set up in 1930, these stations marked the birthplaces of official soil conservation in this country. The initial results of their research were both dramatic and startling, further convincing national leaders of the need for soil conservation.

But it was the Big Drought of 1926–1931 that truly alerted the nation to the seriousness of the problem. In 1933, the *Soil Erosion Service* (SES) was established as a temporary agency in the Department of Interior to begin remedial work on soil erosion. The SES operated 41 demonstration projects and 50 Civilian Conservation Corps camps, and it conducted the first national survey to classify types of erosion and degrees of severity. The survey revealed that productive farmland had been abandoned in many parts of the country because of extensive gullying, sheet erosion, and the consequent loss of topsoil. It estimated that the total damage caused by erosion amounted to billions of dollars annually.

A Nationwide Soil Conservation Program

Faced with this grave problem, Congress passed legislation to initiate a nationwide program of soil conservation. It established two public agencies to restore the nation's agricultural lands: the *Soil Conservation Service* (SCS), and the *Agricultural Stabilization and Conservation Service* (ASCS). The SCS, formed in 1935 as an outgrowth of the Soil Erosion Service, was charged with technical and advisory aspects; the ASCS, set up a year later, was made responsible for ensuring compliance with regulations and with making payments to landowners who followed approved conservation practices. Of these two agencies, the SCS has received the greater public attention and recognition. Although earlier federal efforts at soil conservation were under the Department of the Interior, soil-related matters (including the SCS and ASCS) were henceforth under the Department of Agriculture.

The Soil Districts. The SCS soil districts are the administrative and operating units of the Soil Conservation Service program. The districts are organized and run by elected, unsalaried board members made up of farmers and ranchers. In each district, a professional conservationist along with several aides assist farmers and ranchers in establishing and running sound conservation practices on their land. Participation is purely voluntary. Yet more than 2 million land users (covering practically all of the nation's farmlands) are now cooperators in the nearly 3000 conservation districts throughout the country (Owen 1985).

Types of Advice. The SCS assists farmers and ranchers in four ways: (1) land capability designation, (2) conservation farm plan development; (3) conservation technique application; and (4) monitoring and maintenance advice.

To create a conservation program for a farm an SCS technician first uses soil survey maps, aerial photographs, and on-site inspections to determine such land characteristics as the drainage capability, the fertility, and the potential for severe erosion. With these data, the technician then creates a *land capability map*, which identifies areas as Class I (Very Good) through Class VIII (Suitable Only for Wildlife). (See Chapter 2 for further details.) The second step is to draft a *conservation farm plan*, which indicates the best use for each acre on the farm (e.g., woodlands, croplands, pasture, or open space). Conservation strategies for protecting the land are also an essential component of each farm plan.

The third step entails the application of *conservation techniques* to the land. Here again, the SCS technician provides expertise, particularly in designing contour plowing systems, terraces, strip-cropping schemes, shelterbelts, and farm ponds. The final phase of the conservation program consists of *monitoring and maintenance*. The SCS technician helps in watching over and maintaining the new projects to assure that they function properly and that they accomplish what was intended.

Projects and Programs. The Soil Conservation Service offers several additional projects and programs for soil and water conservation. Multiple-purpose watershed projects help protect, manage, improve, and develop the water and land resources of watersheds in many communities. The SCS's *Soil and Water Conservation Needs Inventory*, which took over 20 years to develop, is a national inventory that makes it possible to compute a soil and water diagnosis for any land area in the country. Plant material centers provide various plants for erosion control.

The Soil Conservation Service also conducts snow surveys that predict the stream flow resulting from melting snow in high altitude watersheds. These surveys enable farmers to forecast the amount of water they will have available for the summer irrigation season. The *Great Plains Conservation Program* was established in 1956 to minimize the hazards brought on by the erratic climate of that region. Needed conservation programs are financed on a cost-sharing basis by the federal government. Since 1962, the SCS has also conducted *Resource Conservation and Development Projects* (RC&Ds) to speed up programs in multiple-county areas to foster economic development and environmental protection. One such project, for example, is designed to develop land and water resources for agricultural, municipal, or industrial use.

SOIL AND THE COUNTRYSIDE

There are four primary soil problems within and adjacent to the rural environment: (1) loss of topsoil to erosion; (2) loss of soil nutrients and organic matter; (3) buildup of toxic salts and chemicals; and (4) loss of lands to urbanization (resulting from road building, village expansion, and other land-consuming developments associated with economic development and population growth). The Soil Conservation Service has approved some 125 management practices to counter the first three problems. Various units of the city, county, state, and federal governments have devised techniques to cope with the fourth major problem—the disappearance of prime agricultural land near the urban fringe.

Loss of Topsoil to Erosion

Nearly $20 billion has been spent on soil conservation since the great dust storms of the 1930s, yet the erosion of croplands by wind and water remains one of the most persistent environmental problems facing the nation.

Geologic Versus Accelerated Erosion. Erosion is the wearing away of the land surface by moving water, glaciers, and wind. There are two broad categories of erosion: geologic erosion and accelerated erosion.

Geologic erosion occurs under conditions undisturbed by human activities. Consequently, it is sometimes referred to as **natural erosion**. Geologic erosion has been going on since the origin of Earth some 4.5 to 5 billion years ago. It is a relatively slow process; so slow, in fact, that in some locations soil formation may keep pace with the erosion of the surface soil. The more typical product of geologic erosion, however, has been such topographical features as mountains, valleys, and canyons. The worn-down Appalachian Mountains (once as high as the Rocky Mountains) and the deeply incised Grand Canyon (once a low channel) are dramatic examples of the action of geologic erosion.

In **accelerated erosion** human activities have speeded up the natural rate of geologic erosion. The domestication of plants and animals 10,000 to 15,000 years ago introduced a new influence on the natural landscape. Unfortunately, that influence has often been destructive, and is seen in such practices as the clearing off of vegetation, overgrazing by domesticated animals, and up-and-down slope plowing. Today, more than a billion tons of soil are washed from the surface of the United States every year. The soil conservationist is far more concerned about accelerated erosion than about geologic erosion.

Water and Wind Erosion.   Another way of classifying erosion is by the type of eroding agent.

Soil scientists recognize four types of water erosion: (1) splash erosion, (2) sheet erosion, (3) rill erosion, and (4) gully erosion.

Splash erosion (also known as **rain-drop erosion**) is caused by the splattering of small soil particles under the impact of raindrops on very wet soils. The effect of such erosion is not trivial. The large number of drops that fall during an hour of heavy downpour, each with a significant strike force, can cause extensive erosion.

Sheet erosion (also known as **sheet wash**) is erosion that gradually removes a thin, uniform layer or "sheet" of soil from a wide area. Although it may seem less spectacular than other forms of erosion, it can be very serious over time. Its effect may become apparent only after it has done extensive damage to the soil. In one case, sheet erosion washed 76.2 cm (30 in.) of soil from a sloping field within only a decade.

Rill erosion is caused when small amounts of running water come together to form rivulets that cut channels in the soil several inches deep (Figure 3-1).

FIGURE 3-1   Severe rill erosion in central California. (Photo by author.)

When sheet erosion and rill erosion act together, they can remove enormous amounts of soil from unprotected fields. By pulling a harrow over the rills, a farmer can eliminate the channels and at the same time mix subsoil with the surface layer. Left uncorrected, however, the rills may coalesce into large gullies. Rills are gullies in the making. Together, sheet and rill erosion can have quite a negative impact (Figure 3-2) on soil resources.

Gully erosion is the most spectacular form of water erosion (Figure 3-3). The running water cuts deep gashes into the land, ranging in depth from 0.30 to 0.61 m (1 to 2 ft) to as much as 23 to 30 m (75 to 100 ft) (Foth 1984). Obviously tractors cannot even cross these gullies, much less smooth them over.

Similarly, soil scientists recognize several types of wind erosion. Wind erodes the soil by lifting and removing the finer particles, nutrients, and plant residues—all of which are essential components of a productive earth. In **saltation**, the wind causes soil particles to "hop" along the ground surface. In **suspension**, the wind carries soil particles high into the air and transports them over long distances. In **surface creep**, the wind rolls particles along the surface after they have been dislodged by saltation. Foth (1984) estimates that saltation accounts for 50 to 75 percent of all wind erosion; suspension accounts for 3 to 40 percent; and surface creep accounts for 5 to 25 percent.

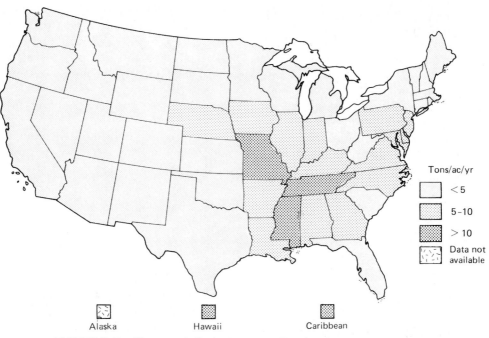

Tons/ac/yr

☐	< 5
☐	5–10
☐	> 10
☐	Data not available

Alaska   Hawaii   Caribbean

FIGURE 3-2 Sheet and rill erosion on U.S. cropland. (From Lawrence Lundgren, *Environmental Geology* [Englewood Cliffs, N.J.: Prentice-Hall, Inc., 1986], p. 74.)

Management Techniques. Several techniques are available for controlling soil erosion. *Engineering techniques* make use of tools and mechanical equipment. *Biological techniques* call for the manipulation of natural vegetation or domesticated crops. Combining the two techniques in a well-orchestrated management plan produces the best results. Among such plans are (1) tillage practices, (2) cropping systems, (3) conservation structures, and (4) related conservation practices.

The way the soil is tilled has an important influence on erosion. One practice calls for tilling the soil to form ridges, with crop residues and clods left on the surface of the soil. Variations of this practice are

FIGURE 3-3 Gully erosion near Lumpkin, Georgia. (From Frederick R. Troeh, J. A. Hobbs, and Roy L. Donahue, *Soil and Water Conservation: For Productivity and Environmental Protection* [Englewood Cliffs, N.J.: Prentice-Hall, Inc., 1980] p. 397.)

known collectively as **conservation tillage**. In **stubble mulch tillage**, the most commonly practiced form of conservation tillage, part or all of the crop residues are left on top of the ground instead of being burned or plowed under.

Since planting, cultivating, and harvesting all tend to disturb the soil, any lessening of their effects will cut down on soil loss. In **minimum tillage** the soil is plowed only to the depth needed for quick seed germination, and crop residues and ground litter are left on the surface to protect the soil. The **no-till system** carries this practice further by planting seeds directly in the existing plant cover and crop residues. No-till farming has been known to reduce soil erosion by as much as 95 percent (Miller 1988).

Both minimum and no-till farming require less labor (which lowers production costs), conserve soil moisture, furnish food and cover for wildlife, and may improve crop yields. These practices do, unfortunately, lower soil temperatures, which increases disease and pest problems. Furthermore, without the heavy application of chemicals, the organic compost and stubble of no-till fields provide an ideal environment for weed, disease, and insect pests, which tend to lower crop yields.

A third type of tillage is **contour cultivation**, which is one of the best-known engineering techniques for erosion control. In contour cultivation, plowing follows the contours of the land. Instead of tilling up and down the hillsides, as early farmers did, the farmer plows at right angles to the slope. On cotton fields in Texas, contour cultivation has reduced water runoff by as much as 65 percent (Owen 1985). Contouring is not always practical, however. In square or rectangular fields, for example, which are more suitable for straight-rowed furrows, contouring is difficult and uneconomical.

Emergency tillage is used to guard against unexpected wind erosion. Since wind erosion may set in despite previous precautions, farmers must sometimes take emergency measures to prevent soil drift. With rotary hoes, disks, or chisels, farmers can quickly roughen the soil surface to reduce wind velocity at the surface and to trap flying soil particles.

In addition to tillage practices, farmers may use a variety of *cropping systems* to minimize soil erosion. The most common cropping systems are crop rotation, strip cropping, and contour strip cropping.

Crop rotation is a biological technique in which the farmer plants a regular sequence of crops on the same land, instead of growing the same crop continuously or growing different crops in haphazard order. The farmer may rotate either **companion crops** (one crop grown with another crop) or **cover crops** (a crop grown to cover bare soil). To rotate companion crops, alfalfa, clover, or some other forage is mixed with the main crop—usually a small grain. To rotate cover crops, a quick-maturing protective *mat* crop between main crop harvests is planted to prevent the land from lying bare and vulnerable to erosion. The most common cover crops are legumes and grasses, which provide summer, winter, or perennial cover.

Crop rotation brings enormous benefits. By raising the soil-holding power of the land, it reduces soil erosion. It adds nitrogen and other nutrients to the soil. It helps maintain the supply of humus. It helps offset the development of toxic substances. It helps subdue disease and insects. And it improves the quality of crops. Unfortunately, when the selling price of a particular crop is high (as was the price of wheat in the 1970s), farmers often abandon crop rotation in order to maximize their short-term profits.

Strip cropping is another biological technique designed to control soil erosion. This method calls for crops to be arranged systematically in strips or bands. For example, strips of close-growing cover plants (such as grass and clover) may alternate with strips of regular crops (such as potatoes, corn, and cotton). When strip cropping is combined with crop rotation, a strip may be planted one year to produce a soil-exhausting crop such as corn, and the next year it may be planted to produce a soil-replenishing cover crop such as legumes (Figure 3-4). Strip cropping is often used in conjunction with contour farming, and the two practices combined can reduce erosion by 75 percent (Miller 1988).

Such *conservation structures* as terraces, terrace outlets, waterway and gully control devices, earth dams, and wind erosion barriers provide another means by which farmers can fight soil erosion.

Farmers have practiced terracing for centuries. In Peru and China, farmers still use steplike *bench terraces*, in which a narrow, level area is bounded by an almost vertical bank. Bench terraces do not lend themselves to modern farm machinery, however. The terraces currently in use are wide enough to be cultivated, seeded, and harvested with ordinary machinery. The *graded terrace*, for example, has a channel that allows runoff water to be discharged slowly into stable, vegetated areas or into specially designed outlets. Graded terraces reduce the velocity of the runoff water, produce higher crop yields, and maintain productivity by retarding soil loss.

Various *outlet, waterway,* and *gully control devices* also help control soil erosion. *Underground outlets* on terraces, for example, convey water from diversion channels through pipelines to places where it can be safely discharged. In fields, underground outlets re-

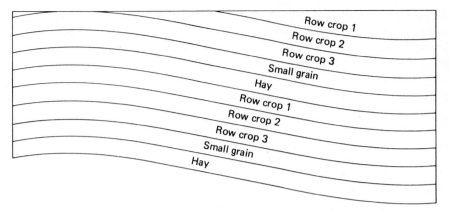

FIGURE 3-4 A contour strip cropping plan based on a five-year rotation. (From Frederick R. Troeh, J. A. Hobbs, and Roy L. Donahue, *Soil and Water Conservation: For Productivity and Environmental Protection* [Englewood Cliffs, N.J.: Prentice-Hall, Inc., 1980], p. 258.)

tard soil loss by conveying sediment to stored-water areas and by permitting only suspended material to escape. *Artificial mulches* are also useful in controlling water-induced soil erosion. Such mulches are usually made of burlap or jute, and mulch mats are made of shredded wood or paper. Synthetic mulches made of asphalt, latex, or plastic are sometimes used until vegetation can be established on a site.

Gullies can swallow up enormous portions of farmlands. For example, part of a gully on a farm near Lumpkin, Georgia, was neglected for over 100 years. By 1980, it had become several miles long and 15–60 m (49–196 ft) deep. It covered over 40,000 ha (99,000 acres) (Troeh et al. 1980). *Check dams* of broken rock (rip-rap), piled-up brush, stacked logs, or woven-wire baskets (gabions) are effective in stabilizing even extensive gullies. Once water runoff has been slowed by these means, the soil can be further stabilized by planting growing vines, shrubs, and trees such as willows. In addition to conserving soil, gully reclamation enhances wildlife by providing additional cover, food, and breeding sites.

Earthen dams, another type of conservation structure, are used to trap sediment and retard gully erosion. They are also used to provide a waterfront for wildlife and human recreation, to minimize flood damage, and to store water for irrigation, livestock, municipal, and household use. In Washita Basin, Oklahoma, a series of earthen dams reduced sediment loss from 61 to 48 percent (Coates 1981).

Wind erosion barriers are yet another form of conservation structure. Windbreaks and shelterbelts are groups of trees and shrubs planted at right angles to the prevailing wind. **Windbreaks** are usually small groups of trees and shrubs intended to protect livestock and buildings. **Shelterbelts** are larger groups of trees intended to protect fields. By moderating the wind, windbreaks and shelterbelts reduce wind erosion, trap dust and snow, reduce evaporation, con-

serve snow cover on fields for insulation and spring moisture supply, increase the relative humidity, ameliorate the environment for livestock and wildlife, reduce fuel costs in heating and cooling a home, and generally enhance the environment.

In the 1930s, in a vigorous effort to prevent future soil catastrophes, the federal government authorized the Civilian Conservation Corps (CCC) to plant 32,000 km (19,884 mi) of shelterbelts with more than 218 million trees on 30,000 farms of the Great Plains. Despite the effectiveness of shelterbelts in controlling soil erosion and increasing crop yields, farmers have recently been removing them to increase acreage for crop production. By 1974, for example, Oklahoma alone had removed 20 percent of its shelterbelts (Coates 1981).

Woven mats, wooden fences, and sand-filled burlap sacks are temporary, yet less expensive and useful conservation structures that help check wind erosion. Grasses, reeds, and crop stalks, for example, are sometimes woven into protective mats. Snow fences can be used to stop snow from drifting onto highways, airport runways, and other critical areas. They can also be stretched across dune crests, and when the wind blows under and over the fence, the sand is funneled down the leeward side instead of being blown away. In the early fight against encroaching dunes on the Great Plains, sand-filled burlap sacks were placed along the dune crests to retard wind erosion.

Clearly, proper soil management calls for a combination of the techniques that are directly related to agricultural production, such as tillage practices, cropping systems, and conservation structures. It also calls for *related conservation practices*, including good management of forests, grasslands, and water resources. If the forest lands surrounding farms are denuded, precipitation will accelerate soil erosion, increase seasonal flooding, and advance siltation. If rangelands are overgrazed, the soil-holding vegetation will vanish and the impact of animals' hooves will compact the soil. Aeration and infiltration will be impaired and desertification may develop and spread. Faulty irrigation projects may produce waterlogging, salinization, and alkalinization.

Loss of Soil Nutrients

Closely related to soil erosion is the depletion of soil nutrients. Intensive crop production, accelerated erosion, the application of pesticides, and the use of heavy machinery all serve to increase the rate of depletion. As a result, crop yields level off or fall, and the soil becomes more susceptible to erosion. In the 1970s, the depletion of soil nutrients quickened even at a time of rising interest in grain production for export, in the use of crops and crop residues as energy sources, and during efforts to preserve prime agricultural lands.

Causes of Soil Depletion.   Prior to colonization, America's vast prairies and deciduous and coniferous forests had been little touched by human activity. For thousands of years, plants had been absorbing life-sustaining nutrients from the soil and then, after death, these plants had returned the nutrients to the earth. The waste products and the decaying bodies of untold numbers of birds and other animals also helped maintain soil fertility. Millennia after millennia, the normal flow of soil nutrients had gone on without disruption.

With the introduction of intensive European methods of crop production, however, all that changed. The natural nutrient cycle gave way to a linear pattern: Nutrients were channeled to animal or plant crops, then consumed by humans, and then transformed into excrement that was flushed into cesspools, septic tanks, lakes, rivers, and oceans. Our agricultural soils are now commonly deficient in such macronutrients as nitrogen, phosphorus, and potassium; they are also deficient in such micronutrients as boron and molybdenum. Only occasionally do farmers entirely replace the kinds and the amounts of all the nutrients their crops need for best growth results. Consequently, soils are wearing out and are often abandoned after their depletion has reached a critical level.

Accelerated erosion has also taken a heavy toll on soil fertility. A century ago, Iowa, with some of the richest corn and soybean land in the world, had 30 to 41 cm (12 to 16 in.) of topsoil. Today most areas of Iowa are left with only 15 to 20 cm (6 to 8 in.) of topsoil, in some areas even less. Iowa is losing 1 in. of topsoil every 12 years. If steps are not taken to check erosion on the more susceptible cropland, all the topsoil will be gone in less than a century.

Wind and water erosion grew increasingly serious in Iowa during the late 1970s and early 1980s, when farmers began planting a record number of acres. To be eligible for price-support programs, midwestern farmers were once required to set aside a specified percentage of their cropland each year. They chose to set aside their poorest lands—lands that should never have been farmed in the first place. When those restrictions were lifted in 1974, at a time when wheat prices were high, many farmers who had been fallowing half their land each year returned to "fence-to-fence" farming.

We know little about the long-range effects of pesticides on soil fertility. Yet there is a mounting suspicion that such pesticides as aldrin, chlordane, toxaphene, endrin, and DDT remain in the soil for long periods of time and may ultimately impair soil fertility. We do know that pesticides, especially insecticides, affect soil organisms ranging in size from earthworms to protozoa. Might these chemical poisons also be acting on nitrogen-fixing and nitrification bacteria? If so, soil fertility will surely be impaired.

Urgency of Restoring Soil Fertility.   The most obvious reason to restore soil fertility is to increase crop yields, that is, the *quantity* of crops produced. A less apparent reason is to maintain the nutritional value of crops, that is, their *quality*. Soil fertility has a direct effect on nutrition, and high crop yields are not necessarily related to high nutrient content in the foods produced. A farmer who increases his yield by using large quantities of inorganic nitrate fertilizers may be disguising a steady decline in soil fertility. A high carbohydrate yield per acre may entail a reduced yield of vitamins, proteins, and essential minerals in the final product. The farmer is increasing *calories* in the food, but not nutrients. Unless we adopt conservation practices that produce high-quality food, the consequence will be a decline in human health and vitality, and, conceivably, an increase in diseases related to nutrient deficiency.

Means of Restoring Fertility.   Many of the methods used to retard soil erosion also serve to restore soil fertility. Cover crops, for example, not only protect the soil from excessive rainfall but also enrich the soil. Specifically, soil fertility can be restored by three major methods: (1) the use of organic fertilizers such as animal manure, human manure (used for centuries in many parts of the world), legumes, and green manure, (2) the use of inorganic fertilizers such

TABLE 3-1

Soil benefits from using organic fertilizers

SOIL CHARACTERISTICS	SOIL BENEFITS
Soil structure	Improved soil structure
Soil water and porosity	Increased water absorption and retention capability; thus, reduced soil erosion
Soil aeration	Increased pore space and aeration around root zones; hence, facilitated seedling growth
Soil biota	Improved medium for the growth and reproduction of soil bacteria (the necessary ingredient for nitrification)
Soil acidity and alkalinity	Prevents sudden shifts in soil pH; important since most plants require a constant pH level
Soil fertility	Helps prevent the leaching of soil nutrients by providing *chelating agents*—compounds that chemically hold nutrient minerals (e.g., calcium, phosphorous, potassium, magnesium) in the topsoil

as nitrogen fertilizers and complete fertilizers, and (3) crop rotation.

Organic fertilizers have long been used to improve soil fertility, with impressive results (Table 3-1). For centuries farmers have recognized that barnyard or stable manure is an excellent soil-builder and fertilizer. Animal manure may be either spread on the soil green or stored for later application. Cow manure, for example, contains large quantities of nitrogen, potash, and phosphoric acid—all essential soil nutrients.

The application of manure also reduces soil loss and increases the soil's nutrient exchange capacity (like clay, humus anions hold cations). In Iowa, for example, an application of 6.4 tons/hectare reduced annual soil loss from 8.9 tons/hectare to 1.9 tons/hectare (Coates 1981). Similar successes have been recorded in other states.

Early American farmers also recognized that planting legumes every second or third year would restore fertility. Although alfalfa is the favorite legume of present-day farmers, other species can be used, including sweet or red clover, cowpeas, soybeans, and vetch. Legumes perform a distinctive service: They enrich the soil with nitrogen from the atmosphere.

As farms became mechanized, tractors and other machinery gradually displaced draft animals, and as a consequence an important source of manure vanished. To compensate for that loss, farmers have turned to the practice of **green manuring**. Plowing under legumes or grass crops while they are still green adds organic matter and nutrients to the soil (Table 3-2), regenerates the humus, maintains topsoil structure, improves soil **tilth** (the physical condition of the soil), increases yields, and reduces erosion. Farmers also plow under various organic wastes, including leaves, straw from threshed grain, and compost from household garbage.

More unusual forms of organic waste used to restore soil fertility are sewage sludge (the semiliquid matter remaining after sewage treatment); waste from food processing plants; dried animal blood, flesh, and bones from canneries and slaughterhouses, and guano (the nutrient-rich excrement of birds). For years a plant in Milwaukee, Wisconsin, has marketed a product known as Milorganite, a packaged fertilizer made from sewage sludge with the addition of lime to adjust the pH factor. Milorganite has been plowed into farmlands and reclaimed strip-mine areas. Since it is relatively expensive, how-

TABLE 3-2

Average composition of legumes and grasses

PLANT	PERCENTAGE COMPOSITION			
	NITROGEN	POTASSIUM	CALCIUM	MAGNESIUM
Grasses	0.99	1.54	0.33	0.21
Legumes	2.38	1.13	1.47	0.38

Source: Foth, Henry D. 1984. *Fundamentals of Soil Science.* 7th ed. New York: Wiley, p. 357.

ever, it is generally used just for backyard purposes. Sludge may also be piped, injected into the subsurface, or sprayed directly onto the farmland, although this practice has met with limited acceptance in the United States. Sludge is rich in nitrogen and phosphorus; however, it often contains toxic heavy metals as well, so its use must be carefully monitored.

Early in the century as tractors began to replace horses and oxen on the nation's farms, inorganic nitrogen fertilizers and complete fertilizers (commercial mixtures containing stated proportions of phosphorus, nitrogen, potassium, and trace elements) came into widespread use. These new fertilizers were easier to use than organic fertilizers, they increased crop yields, and they were cost-effective. By adding nutrients (particularly nitrogen) to the soil, they made it possible for a field to be used every year instead of every second or third year. Moreover, unlike many organic fertilizers, they contain the mineral nutrients needed by certain high-yield crops.

Inorganic fertilizers alone, however, cannot sustain the long-term fertility of farmland. They must be supplemented by organic matter to provide a proper balance and maintain good soil structure. The lack of organic matter leads to various forms of soil deterioration: (1) soil organisms die of starvation as they gradually consume and exhaust the residual humus; (2) as a result of organism decline, the chemical and physical properties of the soil that depend on the presence of those organisms and on the presence of humus ultimately deteriorate; (3) the water-holding and ion-exchange capacity of the soil declines; and (4) the soil hardens and becomes unworkable. Moreover, the exclusive use of inorganic fertilizers leads to a vicious circle in which heavier and heavier applications are required to achieve results as time passes. Once the soil has been degraded, however, additional applications may do little to foster plant growth. Furthermore, much of the fertilizer is washed into waterways and lakes, creating eutrophication and further pollution.

In summary, both organic and inorganic fertilizers are needed for sustained crop production, but both have disadvantages as well as advantages. Good soil management requires an understanding of their respective roles in sustaining soil fertility.

Demands on soil fertility are reduced by crop rotation (Troeh et al. 1980). In *sequential cropping* two or more crops are grown each year in sequence on the same land. In *intercropping* two or more crops are grown on the same field at the same time. Both practices help maintain soil fertility and at the same time protect the land from erosion. For example, coffee trees and banana trees are intercropped with each other, as well as with annual crops. The large leaves of the tall banana trees shield the shorter coffee trees from the sun and wind and protect the soil from heavy rains. Sequential cropping and intercropping provide continuous soil cover and help control erosion, plant diseases, and insects. Both practices are common in tropical areas where individual families intensively use small holdings. This **polyculture** (multiple-crop) agriculture produces a more varied and nutritious diet than does **monoculture** (single-crop) agriculture.

Unfortunately, the widespread use of inorganic fertilizers in this country and in developing countries has influenced farmers to change from polyculture to monoculture. The long-term consequences of this shift will be rising soil erosion and declining soil fertility.

Build-Up of Toxic Salts and Chemicals

The poisoning of the soil by salts, acid rain, and chemicals may be an even more serious problem than the loss of topsoil and the depletion of nutrients. Soil pollution has recently become a severe threat to effective soil management in the United States.

Toxic Salts.   Since many farms lack sufficient water for crop production, they often channel or pipe water in from outside sources, or from the ground. This water contains varying amounts of soluble salts that may in time accumulate in the soil. The resulting **salinization** may eventually leave the land worthless for agriculture. Salinization produces two major types of impaired soil: saline soils and sodic soils. *Saline* soils contain soluble salt in sufficient quantities to impair plant growth. *Sodic* soils contain exchangeable sodium in sufficient quantities to impair plant growth and to alter soil properties. A high concentration of such neutral salts as sodium chloride and sodium sulfate has several deleterious effects: It interferes with the water-absorption capacity of plants, raises the wilting coefficient of soils, creates nutritional deficiencies, and, by bringing about the deflocculation of colloids, leads to a breakdown of soil structure and a reduction in aeration. Over 8 million acres in the western United States have experienced reduced crop yields resulting from improper irrigation and consequent salinization.

Certain management techniques can be used to prevent or even to reverse salinization. For example, drainage systems can be installed to draw off excess water that contains dissolved salts and maintain or reestablish a net downward flow of water (Figure 3-5). The cost of installing such systems is high, however,

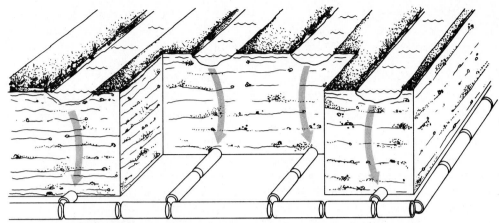

FIGURE 3-5 Subsurface drainage. One means of avoiding salt buildup in soil resulting from improper irrigation and drainage is the construction of underground drainage systems. (From Bernard J. Nebel, *Environmental Science: The Way the World Works* [Englewood Cliffs, N.J.: Prentice-Hall, Inc., 1981], p. 198.)

and is generally done only in areas where the land value is high enough to justify the expense (e.g., Imperial Valley, California).

A less expensive alternative is center pivot irrigation, in which water is pumped from a central well and is applied to the field by means of a sprinkler system that pivots around the well. Because the system maintains a downward drainage of ground water, the soils are well-drained, thus preventing salinization. Center pivot irrigation has certain drawbacks, however: Much of the water is lost to evaporation and transpiration, the pump requires a large expenditure of energy, and there is a slow buildup of salinity in the water. Another way of coping with salinization is through the selective breeding of salt-tolerant plants. This approach, however, makes no attempt to prevent or reverse salinization, instead accepting it as a necessary evil in irrigating arid lands.

Acid Rain. Another source of soil contamination is the acid that falls to the earth in rain, a phenomenon known as **acid rain**. In a 1973 survey, pH readings as low as 3.5 were reported for Chicago, New York, Cleveland, Boston, and Los Angeles (Figure 3-6). Recall that normal rainfall has a pH of about 5.7 and that lower readings indicate more acidic conditions. Soils contaminated by acid undergo various undesirable change, including the accelerated leaching of such trace elements as manganese and aluminum, the atrophy of organisms that break down forest-floor litter, and the reduction of nitrogen content.

The effect of acid rain on plant growth is already

apparent. Acid rain has almost certainly retarded forest growth in the northeastern United States, in Sweden, and in the Black Forest of Germany. One way of coping temporarily with the effects of acid rain is to apply substantial amounts of lime to the soil, a practice farmers have long used to correct pH imbalances resulting from natural causes. However, adding lime on a global basis would be impractical and would only postpone the inevitable. If the incidence of acid rain continues unabated, vast tracts of sensitive soils will slowly decline in fertility until their productivity fails.

Agricultural Chemicals. Thousands of chemicals are used in this country to produce and process foods. Those that occasion the greatest environmental concern are synthetic fertilizers and pesticides, nitrates and nitrites used as food preservatives, and various growth stimulants.

Fertilizers and pesticides have the most direct effect on the soil. Millions of tons of inorganic fertilizers (nitrogen, phosphorus, and potassium) are applied to soils around the world every year, and the rate of their use is increasing. Since 1950, U.S. farmers have boosted their use of these chemicals sixteenfold (Owen 1985). Although inorganic fertilizers do increase crop production, their excessive use creates three environmental problems: (1) it produces water pollution, (2) it leads to denitrification in the ozone layer of the atmosphere, and (3) it is harmful to soil organisms. In the short term, the nitrogen contained in inorganic fertilizers speeds up the decomposition of plant residues in the soil. In the long term, how-

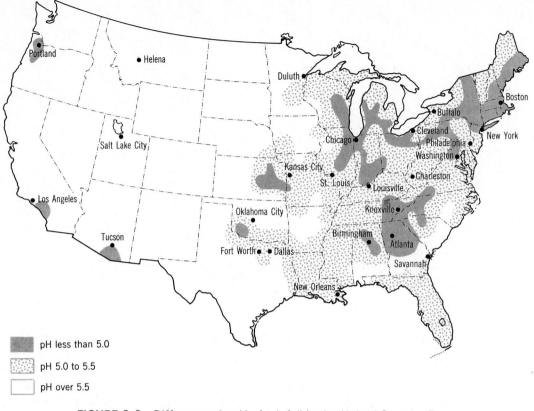

pH less than 5.0

pH 5.0 to 5.5

pH over 5.5

FIGURE 3-6   Differences in pH of rainfall in the United States. (From A. E. Klein, ''Acid Rain in the U.S.,'' *Science Teacher*, May 1974, p. 38.)

ever, heavy use and heavy concentrations of chemical fertilizers have been known to dehydrate and kill microbial populations.

Insects, molds, bacteria, and rodents reduce the world's potential food production by at least *one-half*, and clearly there is a need for effective pest control. During recent years, farmers have increasingly relied on a variety of pesticides to kill insects, weeds, fungi, and other organisms. **Pesticides** include the entire range of chemicals used to kill organisms that humans consider undesirable. Specifically, **insecticides** kill insects; **herbicides** kill plants; **fungicides** kill fungi; and **rodenticides** kill gophers, rats, and mice. Other poisons have been developed to control other pests.

Despite elaborate tests designed to demonstrate that pesticides do not harm the environment, the use of pesticides creates very real problems, mainly:

1. the elimination of natural predators that prey on existing pests;
2. the emergence of new pests formerly kept under control by the natural predators;
3. the evolution of genetic resistance of chemi-

cal poisons, which leads to heavier and heavier applications and eventually to the development of new, more toxic chemicals;
4. the simplification of the ecosystem through the disruption of the food chain and the disturbance of the predator-prey balances;
5. the development of local and regional contamination as wind and water carry the chemicals;
6. the development of biological magnification, that is, the concentration of such substances as DDT and dieldrin in successively higher levels of the food chain; and
7. human illness and death, from the careless handling of highly toxic pesticides and from long-term exposure to low levels of pesticides.

The effect of pesticides on soil is related to their chemical *persistence*—that is, the length of time they remain in the soil or on crops after they are applied. Sunlight and bacteria do not break down such *persistent pesticides* as the chlorinated hydrocarbons (e.g., DDT, DDE, DDD, aldrin, dieldrin, kepone) or those that contain arsenic, lead, or mercury. Their persistence in the soil ranges from 2 to 15 years. Furthermore, when a farmer applies them year after year, their concentration builds up in the soil. In orchards repeatedly sprayed with lead arsenate, for example, the pesticide buildup may eventually kill the trees. Fortunately, several of the above-mentioned persistent pesticides are now banned by the U.S. Environmental Protection Agency.

Secondary contamination also contributes to the persistence of pesticides. DDT, for example, adheres to soil particles long after it has been applied and may be carried for great distances by dust storms. The contaminated soil particles settle on pastures, croplands, and gardens that have never been treated with pesticides.

Pesticides have a significant impact on soil organisms ranging from earthworms to protozoa. That impact depends on how toxic the pesticides are, their persistence, and how thoroughly they are mixed into the soil. Fortunately, however, soil organisms normally adjust to the effects of applied chemicals and repopulate the soil within a few months. Consequently, the ecological effects of chemical pollution are probably less serious than those of water pollution.

Fortunately, research is underway to develop alternatives to pesticides. Before the development of synthetic pesticides, farmers used such *cultural controls* as crop rotation, strip cropping, field fallowing (using strips of uncultivated land), and debris removal (removing potential breeding places for insects) to curtail insect infestation. All of the above cultural controls modify the crop ecosystem to hinder pest species. Some farmers are now taking a second look at those familiar practices. Other alternatives are *biological control* (the reintroduction or development of new natural predators, parasites, and pathogens to combat specific insects), *attractants* (the use of sex attractant chemicals, light, or sound to lure pests into toxic traps or to upset their mating process), *sterilization* (the use of radiation or chemicals to sterilize the male of the insect pest species), *hormones* (the use of insect hormones to prevent pest insects from reaching maturity or reproducing), and *resistant crop varieties* (the breeding of plants that are resistant to diseases, insects, and fungi). Each technique, of course, has its own set of advantages and disadvantages in terms of pest control, economic cost, and environmental impact.

A more promising approach to pest control is **integrated pest management** (IPM). This is an ecological approach that sees each crop and the pests associated with it as an ecological system. It calls for a control program that combines cultural, biological, and chemical methods in a specified sequence. It emphasizes the control of pests rather than their total elimination, careful field monitoring, and the use of different pesticides at different times to avoid the emergence of genetic resistance. Dozens of successful control programs illustrate that IPM can control pests without the use of conventional insecticides while maintaining high yields at reduced costs.

IPM is an extremely complex system, however, that requires expert knowledge about each situation. Farmers must engage and pay for expert consultants to analyze the particular problem at hand. Moreover, procedures developed for one area may not be applicable to other areas with slightly different growing conditions. The initial costs of using IPM are typically higher than the costs of using pesticides alone.

Loss of Land to Urbanization

The agricultural soils of the United States are rapidly being paved over. Every day, four square miles of our *prime* farm lands are being shifted to nonagricultural uses. That comes to 1 million acres each year, the equivalent of *a half-mile strip of land stretching from New York to California!* We have been losing farmland—some of our best farmland—at this rate since 1945.

Prime farmland is flat or gently rolling land, rich in fertility, and susceptible to little or no soil erosion. It is our most energy-efficient land for producing the greatest quantities of food, feed, fiber, and forage with the lowest expenditures of fuel, fertilizer, and labor. It is land that assures high productivity along with the least degradation of the environment.

We are also losing another 2 million acres of farmland of lesser quality every year. Three hundred and twenty acres of such land (a half-section) are lost every hour of the day (Fields 1980).

Reason for the Loss. The primary thief of this farmland is urbanization. Decade after decade, our cities have grown by devouring the land around them. Cities tend to first expand onto flat land that is free of dense vegetation. That land, of course, is often prime farmland. As cities expand, so do highways, factories, and shopping centers.

In the absence of responsible planning, urban sprawl moves haphazardly. As it leap-frogs across the countryside it affects even farmland that has not itself been preempted. The farmers who survive must somehow cope with the hostility of suburbanites, vandalism, the depletion of groundwater, and increased costs of tillage.

Profitable farming on these checkerboardlike acres, surrounded by urban sprawl, becomes difficult, if not impossible. Thus, "bad economics" is the second major cause of farmland loss. Fresh fruits and vegetables once sold to local communities must be transported at great expense to market centers; farmers must travel greater distances to obtain seed and equipment; and farm labor grows scarcer and more costly as workers are attracted to higher-paying city jobs. The remaining parcels of farmland may be too small to be cultivated economically. Farmers may be unable to afford efficient technology and a viable transportation, marketing, and supply system.

As the price of land soars, farmers are faced with higher property taxes and legal and economic headaches. Unless they are protected by tax deferments and other relief, they are driven out of business.

Finally, governmental agencies add to the problem by fostering programs that encourage land conversion. For example, the U.S. Department of Transportation helps finance highways that slice across agricultural land and that encourages industrial and rural development; the USDA's Farmer's Home Administration finances rural housing; and even the U.S. Environmental Protection Agency—an agency dedicated to the conservation of resources—finances sewerage facilities in rural areas that encourage growth that would have otherwise been confined to the cities. As long as conflicting federal policies spur such economic programs, prime farmland will continue to disappear at an accelerating rate.

Need for Farmland Preservation.   Farmers and nonfarmers alike have reason to be concerned about this loss of agricultural land. Farmlands give an area its aesthetic character by providing a visual and topographical boundary that bestows on city dwellers a sense of place. Rural landscapes rest the eye, refresh the spirit, and provide recreation for the weary urbanite. Farmlands are a *greenbelt* around the city—something that is expensive and difficult to create through legislation and various land-use controls.

But farms do more than provide scenery. Farming is an important component of the nation's economic base. It employs hundreds of thousands of people and produces billions of dollars in revenue. In Ohio alone, nearly a million acres of cropland were converted to other uses between 1967 and 1977. Had they not been taken out of production, they would have produced more than $230 million a year in wheat, hay, soybeans, fruits, and vegetables (Fields 1980). Many political scientists believe that the United States may be on the verge of losing its position of world leadership as a result, in part, of its loss of agricultural land. On the other hand, economists and others argue that these converted lands now produce

higher incomes from nonfarm uses (e.g., as rental income properties).

Farmlands also have environmental significance. By absorbing rainwater they reduce flooding and replenish the water table. Someday, farms may even help solve urban sewage problems by using treated wastewater for irrigation. Furthermore, the shift from prime farmland to nonprime farmland is costly to the environment: It increases erosion and sedimentation; it impairs water quality; and it destroys the habitat of wildlife.

Most important of all, farmland is a precious productive resource that the United States can no longer afford to squander. We need all our best agricultural land for increased crop production. According to the National Agricultural Lands Study, U.S. farmers will have to plant between 84 and 143 million additional acres by 2000 in order to meet the anticipated domestic and foreign demand for food. Per acre yields cannot keep pace with the world's rising need for food. Although world food output has more than doubled since 1950, that gain has brought with it increased soil erosion. According to Lester Brown (1982), approximately one-third of the global cropland is losing soil at a rate that will undermine its long-term productivity. As the productivity curve levels off, it will be very important to keep land in production. And, as the costs of transporting and storing food rises, it will be crucial to preserve productive farmland near urban centers. Some way must be found to direct urban development to less productive areas and to save our irreplaceable prime farmland from further encroachment.

We are beset by still other problems in our efforts to preserve our agricultural lands. Modern agriculture in the United States is highly energy-dependent, yet our oil and natural gas supplies are precarious. Overgrazing, the clear-cutting of forests, and strip-mining have brought floods and sedimentation to thousands of farmland acres. Heavy farmland machinery compacts the soil and reduces aeration and the water-holding capacity of the soil, thereby curtailing crop yields. Atmospheric pollutants are changing global temperatures and regional growing seasons. Preserving our existing farmlands will serve as a safety net against the consequences of these mounting problems.

Finally, farmlands represent a valuable part of our cultural heritage. Country living nourishes both the stomach and the spirit of millions of Americans, strengthening their sense of what makes life worthwhile. Wendell Berry, author of *The Unsettling of America: Culture and Agriculture* (1978), and others have begun to explore the relationship between spiritual, environmental, and economic productivity of farmland culture in America.

Techniques for Preserving Farmland. Various governmental and private organizations have sought to check the loss of farmland by techniques ranging from simple tax relief to complex programs designed to coordinate farmland preservation with public services and facilities. One of the most common techniques is known as *preferential assessment.* Under this plan, land is taxed at its agricultural value, regardless of its market value for residential or industrial uses. Normally, the farmer is required to use the property only for agricultural purposes for a specific length of time. If the land is put to nonagricultural use during that period, deferred taxes must be paid. Unfortunately, preferential assessment often provides tax relief to landowners who have never farmed, reduces local tax bases, and rarely saves farmland in rapidly urbanizing areas where land values are highest.

The *transfer of development rights* is another method of steering development to a specific area of a community and minimizing the impairment of prime agricultural land. With this approach, the community first identifies a *preservation zone* in which development will not be allowed and a *transfer zone* in which it will be allowed. Landowners within the preservation zone are issued certificates of development rights. By purchasing those certificates from the landowners, developers can shift the rights to the transfer zone, where they can build at a higher density than normal zoning laws would allow. This technique has proved to be overly complex and often produces inconsistencies in zoning and land-use standards.

Relief from inheritance and estate taxes, agricultural districting, the delineating of urban limit lines, and community land trusts are innovative methods that have met with some success across the country, especially in Wisconsin, Oregon, California, Iowa, and Michigan. Yet they are too often marked by loopholes, inequities, and a general failure to preserve prime agricultural lands against the onslaught of urban encroachment.

According to Charles E. Little (1981, p. 2), president of the American Land Forum, few farmland-protection programs have been instituted thus far:

- Fifteen states produce 86 percent of our wheat, but only one, California, has even come close to adopting a farmland-protection program.
- Fifteen states produce 91 percent of our corn, but only one, Wisconsin, has a farmland-protection program.
- Fifteen states produce 92 percent of our soybeans, but none has a farmland-protection program.

SOIL AND THE CITY

Soil problems affect urban dwellers as well as rural dwellers, and yet city dwellers and suburbanites seem to have insulated themselves from the earth. Soil is something to be bought in plastic bags or to be dumped on their driveway. Few Americans have ever heard of soil profiles, sheet erosion, or soil resources as part of a life-support system. Nevertheless, city dwellers have altered the shape, distribution, and quality of the soil in numerous ways, primarily through activities at mining and construction sites, landfill sites, and home sites.

Soil Problems at Mining and Development Projects

Effects of Surface Mining Activities. Urbanites derive many benefits from the production of surface-mined minerals. Coal and uranium, metals, mined nutrients (such as phosphate rock), clay, sand, gravel, and stone are all essential to the material culture of our urban civilization. Furthermore, the economic and social wellbeing of the United States depends on a supply of minerals and fossil fuels.

Surface mining affects the quality of other resources, however, including soil, water, air, and animal and plant life. The runoff and sediment from mines impairs water quality, surface and underground drainage, fish and wildlife habitats, and traditional land-use patterns. Furthermore, mining activities break the migration routes of animals, preempt water rights for power generation, and pollute the atmosphere with fumes and dust. Abandoned surface mines leave a scarred earth, barren testimony to the activities of the departed operators.

Land reclamation is often used to counteract the effects of surface mining. An important part of reclamation is separately removing and storing the topsoil layer before mining is started, so it is not just mixed in with the rest of the overburden and lost. This method sometimes succeeds, but its results are usually disappointing. On steep mountainsides, land reclamation is simply not feasible. The Soil Conservation Society of America estimates that two-thirds of the 2.3 million ha (5.7 million acres) of U.S. land surface-mined through 1977 are in need of reclamation. The remaining one-third has been reclaimed through natural seeding or through other efforts by landowners and mine operators.

Soil Problems at Development Projects. At the construction sites of roads, highways, and subdivisions, soil erosion is often excessive. Contractors may grade more land than is actually needed or may fail to plant a temporary grass cover over graded areas prior to construction. A variety of erosion-control measures might be put to use at construction sites: planting fast-growing plants such as millet, oats, and rye; reseeding steep road cuts with a hydroseeder; and constructing asphalt-paved aprons, drop chutes, and catch basins to intercept runoff water and trap its load of sediment.

In building suburban developments, contractors often take the easy way out, scraping off the vegetation and topsoil and leaving only a clayey subsoil. Once they get the houses near completion, they lay a thin layer of imported topsoil over the B horizon to cover up the clay or to mask a landfill. Some unscrupulous contractors even scoop up the topsoil and sell it to a landscaper, who, in turn, sells it back to the homeowner. Such practices create imbalances in surface drainage and groundwater recharge and cause other soil-related problems. Communities can discourage such practices by enacting ordinances requiring developers to guarantee that they will take erosion-control measures as a condition of their winning approval of their plans.

Soil Problems at Refuse Areas

Urban dwellers, perhaps unwittingly, influence soil resources by dumping their solid and liquid wastes into natural or artificial depressions. Everything gets dumped—garbage, rubbish, ashes, street sweepings, dead plants and animals, and industrial wastes. Ninety percent of this refuse goes into land disposal sites, of which only 6 percent are classified as **sanitary landfills**. These are landfills where the refuse is covered with soil every day, where the burning of refuse is not allowed, and where clay or some other impermeable material blocks the seepage of potentially toxic chemicals into the water table.

For highly toxic materials, special sites must be used. In California, for example, the semiconductor, electroplating, pharmaceutical, explosive material, chemical, and other industries produce hazardous wastes that contain acids, caustic chemicals, solvents, and such heavy metals as chromium, copper, lead, gold, silver, and zinc. These wastes are too toxic to be handled by biological sewage-treatment plants and are poisonous to many aquatic organisms. Con-

sequently, these wastes are deposited in sealed, theoretically impervious pits or lagoons and are then incinerated or chemically treated to render them inert. Many industries, however, illegally dump toxic wastes to avoid the cost of proper disposal.

When waste products are dumped directly into the soil, several factors must be considered: (1) the ability of the soil to assimilate the waste, (2) whether or not the wastes contain nutrients or heavy metals, and (3) whether or not the vegetation in the disposal area can utilize whatever nutrients are present. SCS soil surveys contain soil maps and descriptions of soil properties that affect waste disposal. This information enables soil scientists to determine if an area is suitable for a septic tank absorption field, a sewage lagoon, a sanitary landfill, or a hazardous waste disposal site.

Soil and the Suburban Resident

Prudent citizens avoid building their houses on certain kinds of clayey soils, because they know that the foundation may shift or settle unevenly, and that the walls, plaster, and foundation may crack. Clays that expand as they absorb water and shrink as they dry can move a house several inches up and down. *Soil slippage*—the downslope movement of a saturated layer of surface soil underlain by impervious rock—may cause even greater damage.

Homebuilders can use several techniques to control soil erosion as the house is being built. These techniques, all of them familiar to farmers, include the use of protective grasses and mulches, the building of sediment traps, and the construction of diversion ditches.

In caring for suburban vegetable and flower gardens, the homeowner can scale down many of the soil-management practices used on farms. Unfortunately, however, many amateur gardeners believe that they should work the soil vigorously. In their zeal, they impair soil structure, hasten water loss and the oxidation of humus, and expose the soil to splash erosion. Clearing a garden of all organic debris is particularly harmful, especially in the winter months when rainfall and runoff are at a maximum. The soil would be better off if the gardener were to practice minimum tillage.

Many suburbanites are unaware that when they carry their bags of grass clippings out to the curb for pickup, they are fostering soil erosion. What they are doing is exporting soil nutrients to the local dump. A better practice is to leave the grass clippings on the lawn or to compost them for later use on the lawn or a flower bed. Such practices as minimum tillage, composting, and other rural techniques would also curtail the suburban gardener's indiscriminate use of insecticides, herbicides, and other synthetic chemicals.

PROSPECTS FOR THE FUTURE

The assault on our soil resources is greater today than in the past. Erosion is taking an enormous toll; over a third of our topsoil has been lost in the last 200 years. Efforts to conserve the soil since the days of the Dust Bowl have not slowed the rate of erosion appreciably. From 1969 to 1979, for example, 6.9 million hectares (17 million acres) of agricultural land have been lost to highways, reservoirs, subdivisions, shopping centers and parking lots. During that same decade, there became 900 million more hungry mouths to feed worldwide, and the pressure on farmlands to produce will certainly grow. To make matters worse, Americans are now moving back to rural areas, intensifying the demand for housing sites.

Positive Signs and Success Stories

There is some reason for cautious optimism in soil resource management mainly in the areas of (1) farmland preservation, (2) erosion control, (3) low-input agriculture, and (4) basic research.

1. *Americans want farmland protected.* Although farmlands are being converted to nonagricultural uses at an alarming rate, a 1980 Harris Poll for the U.S. Department of Agriculture revealed that many Americans want prime farmlands protected. They rated the loss of good farmland as a "very serious" problem, and by a seven-to-one margin they were willing to accept federal action to protect farmland from erosion. Of course, the actual landowners would probably feel quite differently about the prospect of federal intervention.

An impressive number of state and regional experiments have already been launched to save agricultural land: Some 40 states tax agricultural land at a lower rate than adjacent commercial land. One innovative and controversial project is the POS (People for Open Space) Farmlands Conservation Project. After two years of research, the POS Project published in 1980 a report on the past treatment, the present-day status, and the future outlook for farmlands in the San Francisco Bay region. It revealed that farmers and ranchers in the nine Bay Area counties produce more than any one of 13 states in the nation, and that most of the area's 1600 commercial farms are medium-sized, family-run farms. Furthermore, the 5

million people in this fifth largest metropolitan region in the United States receive the freshest produce at very low transportation and storage costs. In 1980, Bay Area farms sold over $800 million worth of goods, providing jobs for about 100,000 workers—all this despite the loss of over 23,000 acres of Bay Area cropland and grazing land every year, primarily to residential developments.

To slow the rate of land conversion, POS proposed a three-step program: (1) the creation of a temporary Agricultural Land Commission, (2) the preparation of a detailed plan for the preservation of farmland, and (3) the submission of that plan to the voters of the nine counties. Although the POS Strategy for keeping agriculture alive in the Bay Area fell before the powerful forces marshalled by the building industry, the organization continues to search for ways to carry out the public will. Remembering that the citizens of the Bay Area united in the early 1970s to clean up San Francisco Bay, POS hopes to rally northern Californians to defend their farmbelt.

Another encouraging sign is the recently completed National Agricultural Lands Study, the first comprehensive analysis of farmland conversion by the federal government. Prepared by the U.S. Department of Agriculture, the Council on Environmental Quality, and other federal agencies, this report found that, for the first time in American history, the end of our cropland "frontier" is in sight. No longer is the nation's farmland an unlimited resource. According to this report, the United States has a cropland "bank" totaling 540 million acres, 413 million of which were being used for crops in 1977. The other 127 million acres are "reserve" acres that can be economically used to grow grain, vegetables, fruits, nuts, and other products. The remaining 820 million acres of nonurban land (range, pasture, and forest) have little or no agricultural potential in the foreseeable future. (These figures do not include federally owned land, since little of that land has crop potential.)

Some farmers are themselves experimenting with innovative ways to make their farms more economically viable. Veale Tract Farms in Contra Costa County, California, is experimenting with recoverable resources, those that can be used as *soil amendments* (any substance such as lime, used to alter the properties of a soil), as fertilizers, or as recycled industrial material. Since 1975, they have been recycling wallboard, sheetrock (gypsum aids in the leaching of toxic salts), paper pulp effluent, sawdust, and woodchips (valued for their organic matter), lime sludge (used for pH control and soil structure), and many other materials (Figure 3-7).

FIGURE 3-7 From waste to resource. (upper) A northern California farming operation that uses industrial wastes as a soil additive. (lower) Piles of industrial wastes (e.g., crushed wallboard, paper pulp effluent, sawdust/wood chips) used as soil additives. (Photos by author.)

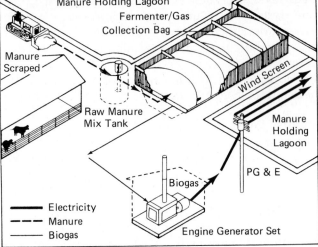

FIGURE 3-8 From cow manure to electricity. (upper) A methane digester bag next to a milking barn on a central California dairy farm. (Photo by author.) (lower) A diagram of Marindale Dairy's methane digester system. (From *Northern California Sun*, vol. 10, no. 5 [September–October 1984], p. 13.)

Although it is a time-consuming process to search out usable by-products and to clear their use with various governmental agencies, the outlook for such recovery operations is promising. As the cost of disposing unwanted materials arise, it becomes more and more economical for industrialists and farmers to give serious attention to resource recovery.

Dairy farmers are also experimenting with ways to make their operations more cost-effective. One way is to convert cow manure into an energy source for generating electricity. With a methane digester and a power generator, dairy farmers can produce all the electricity they need for their dairy and household requirements. They can also sell surplus power to the local utility company, thereby earning a marginal profit (Figure 3-8).

2. *Some successes in erosion control.* There is also some good news on the erosion front. Farmers on 10 percent of American farmlands have shifted from plowing practices that hasten erosion to minimum tillage techniques that halt soil loss. As we have seen, however, there is a tradeoff here: Minimum tillage requires large amounts of chemical herbicides, which contribute to pollute runoff. Recent scientific and technological advances are making new systems available for controlling soil erosion and for reclaiming marginal land. For example, newly designed furrow systems reduce water runoff appreciably. Grasses that withstand drought have been developed to hold soil in place, and improved cropping sequences are being devised. A particularly promising new approach to soil erosion is known as *slotting fields*. Slotting hilly fields with straw-filled trenches spaced 5.5 to 7.3 m (18 to 24 ft) apart permits water to drop into the soil profile even when the surface is puddled or frozen. This technique dramatically reduces erosion and also increases the amount of water available for crops.

Several erosion control and stormwater management projects are being undertaken, such as the Gateway Hills Planned Unit Development (PUD) in Ames, Iowa. In this mixed development of single-family residences, townhouses, and garden apartments, lots are designed to slope away from the street and are equipped with individual soil detention areas. These areas trap many of the pollutants generated on the lot, such as sediments, grass clippings, and fertilizers. The Gateway Hills project is an impressive demonstration of what can be done to retard soil erosion.

Finally, the Agricultural Conservation Program of the SCS is stepping up its effort to advance agricultural conservation. The SCS program now stresses that farmers can *increase production* through following good conservation practices, minimizing their use of irrigation water and preserving wetlands for wildlife. By doing so, farmers can reduce erosion, curb water pollution, and achieve greater self-sufficiency in their use of energy.

3. *Heightened interest in low-input agriculture.* Although no one has come up with a way to prevent pesticides from washing down into the soil and into the nation's waterways, integrated pest management (IPM) promises to minimize the pesticide problem. Since 1950, dozens of integrated programs have been launched with great success. Many of them have reduced the use of insecticides by 50 to 75 percent while increasing crop yields and reducing overall costs. It seems likely that IPM will prove more effective in controlling pests than are today's pesticides—and with less harmful effects on natural ecosystems and human health.

Evidence also suggests that organic farming, which incorporates certain features of IPM, may prove more efficient than farming techniques that use chemical pesticides and fertilizers. In 1980, a USDA study team reported that organic farms generally use less energy than conventional farms and are only slightly more labor intensive. They have crop yields that are neither superior nor inferior to those of conventional farms, and they are economically competitive when the long-term costs of correcting soil erosion and water pollution are taken into account.

Soil researchers are also experimenting with *soil innoculents* to repair the damage brought on by surface mining. The Chicago-based Bionomics Research Corporation, for example, claims to have developed a soil innoculent that can transform areas spoiled by strip mining back into healthy, pollution-free cropland at less than the cost of sludge and commercial nitrogen fertilizers. The aerial application of the product, known as 628-plus, is advertised as being able to reintroduce microorganisms into sterile soil. Coal companies are interested in this product because it is cost-effective, costing about $97 per acre compared to the $1500 to $4000 per acre that traditional reclamation techniques cost. Extensive experimentation and field analysis will be required before firm conclusions can be drawn about the effectiveness of this new product.

4. *Basic research.* By using laser beams in grade control, researchers have devised more efficient ways of leveling land and placing drain tiles. The use of neutron probe devices now enables soil scientists to measure soil density, and soil water without disturbing the soil. Basic research on the nucleotide sequence in RNA molecules has suggested methods of controlling protein synthesis to improve the quantity and quality of proteins. Plant geneticists at dozens of university and private laboratories are working to develop new plants that will be resistant to diseases and insects, that will survive drought and high winds, and that will grow without fertilizers or pesticides.

Basic research is also being done on remote sensing devices to develop crop yield models and to measure plant stress under various field conditions. (Some critics contend, however, that remote sensing wastes more energy and creates more pollution than it is worth.) Newly developed computer programs make it possible to store data on soil and crop growth for decision making by individual farmers and in programing by public and private agencies.

We may be witnessing the birth of a third agricultural revolution. The first began 10,000 to 15,000 years ago when hunting and gathering cultures began to cultivate plants. The second, popularly known as the *Green Revolution*, peaked in the 1960s. Concentrating on traditional plant breeding, agriculturalists developed with painstaking cross-pollination new strains of corn, rice, and wheat over the past 20 years. The introduction of those new strains into the Third World, along with chemical fertilizers, resulted in dramatic increases in yields. By 1967, for example, Mexico had tripled its corn production; between 1965 and 1967, India's grain harvest grew by 50 percent. But the techniques of this second revolution proved to be very expensive. Relatively few Third World farmers could afford the chemicals, machinery, and hybrid seeds needed to grow the new crops, and the use of synthetic chemicals and heavy machinery aggravated existing soil resource problems. Still, the Green Revolution triggered the new major revolution in agriculture.

The scientists spearheading this latest agricultural revolution speak in terms of *recombinant DNA, cell culture, tissue culture,* and *protoplast fusion.* They are searching for plants that can resist pollution and can generate their own fertilizers, and for faster-growing chickens and more prolific pigs. Plant geneticists, for example, hope to equip plants that depend on heavy fertilization, such as corn, with the nitrogen-producing capacity of peas and beans, which in a sense will allow the plants to fertilize themselves. Such crops would save farmers enormous amounts of time, money, and energy, and would rescue soil from damaging applications of synthetic fertilizers. By devising *custom-designed* crops to meet such emergencies as insect or disease contamination, drought, soil salinization, and temperature stress, genetic engineers may some day reduce farmers' dependence on pesticides, irrigation water, and fossil fuels.

This latest agricultural revolution is still in its infancy, and no one can yet predict its success or what its environmental side effects will be.

Action for Soil

Conservation is a valid concern of both city dwellers and farmers. We all depend on soil for our food and for many other products. You can participate personally in the conservation effort, by adjusting your own soil-related habits or by choosing a career in soil science.

1. *Adjust your soil-related habits.* The place to begin is at home. Here are some activities that help conserve soil:

- *Use part of your backyard for a vegetable garden.* Growing some of your own food will ease the strain, however slightly, on the nation's agricultural lands, as did the Victory Gardens of World War II.
- *Practice organic gardening.* Use many of the scaled-down soil conservation practices we mentioned earlier, and avoid using pesticides.
- *Practice soil-conscious landscaping.* Leave grass clippings on the lawn to cut down on the need for fertilizers; use compost and other natural fertilizers to add nutrients to flower beds; avoid chemical pesticides.

- *Do not insist on blemish-free, insect-free produce.* ''Perfect'' fruit and vegetables require the intensive use of pesticides.

2. *Support soil conservation programs.* You can lend your support on three fronts: political action for the preservation of prime agricultural land; the movement for improved regulation of pesticides; and the reclamation of surface mines.

It is critical that prime agricultural lands be protected. Here are some guidelines, abbreviated from Robert Coughlin's 1981 report, for you to follow:

- *Seek a comprehensive growth management system designed to protect farmland and to guide urban growth.* Such systems are more effective and durable than efforts to protect individual or isolated pieces of land.
- *Seek multifaceted farmland protection programs.* Such programs address several of the causes of farmland conversion, including rising real-estate property taxes and inflated offering prices for farmland.
- *Encourage your state to declare its commitment to the protection of agricultural land.* Such declarations will provide political and legal support for local efforts.
- *Vote for able, dedicated, and politically astute advocates of farmland protection.* Poor leadership leads to ineffective programs or to no program at all.
- *Require that farmland protection programs go beyond mere land-use controls.* Farmers must have access to adequate credit, labor, suppliers, and support businesses and facilities.

Regulating pesticides is a matter of human health as well as soil survival. Here are some recommendations for achieving improved regulation of pesticide use:

- *Call for a new system for establishing pesticide residue tolerances.* The U.S. Environmental Protection Agency currently calculates average consumption of a given fruit or vegetable by dividing the total national production by the population of the country. According to that method of calculation, the average consumer eats one avocado and three plums a year. Such figures have no relevance to the amount of produce and pesticides actually consumed. A more accurate method would be to base residue limits on the maximum quantity of a given fruit or vegetable that an individual can reasonably be expected to eat in the course of a year.

- *Call for clinical and epidemiological research on the health effects of pesticide exposure.* Insist that all tests be carried out by laboratories independent of the pesticide industry. Until we know the long-term health effects of pesticides—for example, their effects on the incidence of cancer, sterility, and birth defects—policy making will never get beyond unproductive debates.

- *Call for the elimination of provisional registration of toxic pesticides.* Several state governments currently permit the registration and sale of toxic pesticides for as long as three years before thorough laboratory studies have been completed. Meanwhile, workers, consumers, and the soil are exposed to chemicals whose long-term effects are virtually unknown.

- *Insist that states require users of pesticides to consider nonchemical alternatives.* Growers seeking a permit to apply a pesticide should be required to list the nonchemical pest control methods they considered and to indicate why they rejected them. This requirement would enable county agricultural commissioners to make more intelligent decisions about issuing permits and would encourage growers and licensed pest control advisors (90 percent of whom are employees of pesticide manufacturers or applicators) to learn more about alternative pest control methods.

- *Encourage state legislators to create an independent fund for pesticide research.* University faculty members who do research on pesticides tend to rely heavily on grants from companies that produce pesticides, which may explain why they spend so much energy demonstrating the benefits of pesticides. Legislators should consider the creation of an unbiased independent fund for financing pesticide research, possibly financed by a tax on the pesticide industry.

- *Encourage state legislators to remove pesticide regulation from state departments of agriculture.* State departments of agriculture must decide whether to play pesticide regulator or to promote agriculture. This is clearly a conflict of interests. After all, the U.S. Congress created the EPA to take pesticide regulation away from the USDA to avoid such a conflict. To avoid creating a new layer of bureaucracy, regulatory power could be transferred to existing state departments that deal with health and welfare.

- *Urge that governments, dealers, and consumers reexamine their standards of produce quality.* As much as 20 percent of pesticides are applied not to prevent pests from doing serious damage to produce but to ensure that it will be cosmetically "perfect." Fruits and vegetables cannot be both absolutely pest-free and absolutely pesticide-free. Government standards on the cosmetic quality of produce should be eased.

- *Insist that the Federal Insecticide, Fungicide, and Rodenticide Act (FIFRA) passed in 1972 and amended in 1975 and 1980, be strengthened, not weakened.* This law permits states to set their own standards for the sale and use of federally registered pesticides as long as those standards are at least as strict as federal regulations demand. Agrichemical lobbies are trying to get FIFRA amended to prevent states from setting stricter controls than the federal ones. The residents of leading agricultural states, such as California, need extra protection because they run a greater-than-average risk of pesticide exposure.

- *Call for a corps of licensed pest management advisers independent of the pesticide industry.* Such advisers would provide free information on alternatives to pesticides in order to counteract the free but biased information provided by pesticide sales representatives.

- *Demand that citizens have access to safety data on any registered or proposed pesticide.*

- *Insist that the EPA eliminate unnecessary delays in assessing the safety of pesticides.* Lengthy administrative procedures need to be streamlined so that pesticides deemed harmful can be denied registration without delay.

- *Call for restrictions or prohibitions on the export to other nations of pesticides that are either unregistered or banned in the United States.* Exporting harmful pesticides to other countries is not only morally questionable, it is counterproductive, since many of those same pesticides come back home by way of wind and rain, and in imported fish, rice, coffee, and bananas.

The Soil Conservation Society of America has established a number of principles and actions in relation to the reclamation of surface mines. In brief, they recommend the following:

- *Support research and development in land reclamation technology.* Each site to be reclaimed has its own special problems. For each site, specific information and techniques are required for reconstructing the soil profile, for using plant species that are right for the site, and for applying appropriate water conservation technology. Further research is also needed on the nature of spoils.

- *Encourage better planning before mining.* Inventories of soil, water, overburden, plant communities, wildlife, and other natural resources must be made prior to mining if proper land restoration is expected.
- *Encourage the conservation and the recycling of existing minerals.* Land disturbance can be minimized if industry extracts the maximum amount of the mineral once a site has been opened to mining, and if both the public and industry reuse (recycle) minerals as much as possible.
- *Encourage public awareness of the cost of mining and reclamation.* Consumers must understand that reclamation is a part of the mining operation and that the cost will ultimately come down to them. Willingness to pay this extra

cost is a prerequisite to land reclamation and soil resource conservation.

- *Insist that legislators keep reclamation laws current.* Legislation is an important impetus to reclamation and must keep pace with the latest technology.
- *Require local input into mine planning and land-use decisions.* Local citizens can best assess the impact of mining on unique and natural areas, farmland, and water resources within their region.
- *Insist that the Surface Mining Control and Reclamation Act of 1977 be strengthened, not weakened or declared unconstitutional.*

3. *Become a member of a soil organization.* To keep abreast of new and recurring soil problems and alternative solutions, consider joining one of the private, nonprofit scientific and educational organizations concerned with soil conservation. The Soil Conservation Society of America, for example, provides its members with information and guidelines on land and water conservation problems. Membership in

TABLE 3-3

Careers in soil

TITLE	DESCRIPTION	QUALIFICATIONS
Soil scientist	Collects information about the soil through direct field examination; records information on maps and field notes for use by soil conservationists, urban planners, and technical specialists in other fields	College degree in soil science or closely related field
Soil conservationist	Uses the information collected by soil scientists and other specialists to help local people prepare conservation development plans; gives on-site technical assistance in conservation improvements	College degree with major in soil conservation, geography, environmental studies, or closely related natural resource management field
Conservation technician	Helps professional conservationists prepare conservation farm plans	Experience in conservation farming through farm or ranch background
Agronomist	Provides technical guidance on agronomic problems (soil management, weed control, crop production, tillage) to SCS employees, landowners, and operators who need information on food, feed, and fiber production	College degree with major in agronomy or closely related field
Range conservationist	Determines the potential of land for producing forage from native plant communities for livestock, wildlife, and recreation; works with ranchers and other range users to prepare conservation plans	College degree with major in range management or range conservation
Plant materials specialist	Field tests selected plants for such specialized uses as ground cover, forage, pond margins, and wind barriers; determines physical and cultural requirements for proper management	College degree with major in agronomy, range conservation, or other plant science
Woodland conservationist	Evaluates soil-tree relationships and determines woodland conservation practices in relation to specific soil or site conditions	College degree with major in forestry
Geologist	Investigates and interprets surface and subsurface conditions in relation to planning (design and construction), groundwater (supply, management, recharge), and sediment (yield, sources, damage, control)	College degree with major in geology

such organizations will put you in touch with a variety of professionals and laypersons in decision-making positions.

4. *Become a soil conservation volunteer.* The U.S. Department of Agriculture is looking for volunteers to help protect soil and water resources. Authorized by Congress in the Agriculture and Food Act of 1981, this program needs people who will volunteer their time and talents to help the U.S. Soil Conservation Service and local soil and water conservation districts. Volunteers engage in varied activities, including field surveys, soil analyses, and the design of conservation projects.

5. *Consider a career in soil science.* Professional soil resource managers are trained in such fields as soil science, agronomy, range conservation, geography, geology, environmental studies, landscape design, wildlife management, forestry, botany, and plant materials testing (Table 3-3). Hydraulic, drainage, agricultural, irrigation, and civil engineers also do work related to soil resource management and land use.

Traditionally, a college degree in the physical or natural sciences was required for a career in soil conservation. Today, however, students have a variety of electives available that were not formerly offered as a preparation for soil resource management positions. For example, environmental studies programs and some geography departments offer courses in environmental assessment, impact analysis, soil geography, meteorology, biogeography, and systems analysis that pertain directly to soil conservation.

Federal agencies, such as the U.S. Soil Conservation Service, employ the largest number of soil conservationists and other soil specialists. Most state departments of natural resources also employ soil specialists, as do regional planning and river basin commissions. Growing opportunities for soil professionals are opening up in private industries that depend on the use and management of soil and related resources. Commercial timber producers, surface mining companies, oil companies, building contractors, and the operators of large farms and ranches frequently employ soil specialists. Other opportunities exist in private conservation organizations interested in preserving agricultural land or open space. In whatever capacity, soil professionals help rectify soil abuses and are instrumental in preserving and increasing the productive capacity of the soil.

DISCUSSION TOPICS

1. Define *soil resource management* and explain its three primary goals. Recently, a fourth goal has been added. Name and explain.

2. Explain the role of soil deterioration and sedimentation in the decline of early civilizations. Debate whether the U.S. "empire" will succumb to the same forces that depleted the soil in other civilizations. What action must be taken if the United States is not to succumb?

3. How did the Homestead Act of 1862 influence American attitudes toward their soil resources? Can you think of recent federal legislation that has had either a positive or a negative influence on our attitudes toward soil? State legislation? Local legislation?

4. Debate whether present-day soil loss is propelling the United States toward another Dust Bowl. Why is it that farmers quickly forget past lessons? What economic, political, social, and cultural forces come into play?

5. Summarize early American soil conservation efforts.

6. What are the principal responsibilities of the Soil Conservation Service? What is a Soil District and how does it function? What is the difference between a land capability map and a conservation farm plan? Why have SCS conservation officers not played a more active political role in urging soil conservation? Should they?

7. What is a soil survey? What can the user expect to find in a soil survey report? How are soil surveys useful in transportation planning, urban planning, house construction, and wildlife resource management?

8. Why is accelerated erosion more serious than geologic erosion? Are there examples of accelerated erosion around your neighborhood? If so, provide examples.

9. How do the following soil characteristics affect the erodibility of soil: soil structure, soil texture, organic matter content, and moisture content?

10. List and explain the differences between the four major types of water erosion. Explain how runoff depth, land slope, and surface condition affect the erosiveness of running water. Discuss the influence of soil structure on the amount of soil lost by splash erosion and runoff water. In what ways does vegetation reduce soil loss caused by water erosion?

11. Contrast engineering approaches and biological approaches to soil management. In what particular cases would one approach be better than the other?

12. Discuss the four major types of tillage practices used in soil conservation. What are their advantages and disadvantages?

13. What are conservation structures and how do they conserve soil resources? Why are U.S. farmers removing millions of trees in shelterbelts that the Civilian Conservation Corps planted in the 1930s?

14. What are the major causes of nutrient loss in soils? What is the difference between a companion crop, a cover crop, and a green manure crop? Under what conditions would you choose one crop over the other? Why do many farmers prefer to plow crop residues under rather than leave them on the surface?

15. Describe how toxic salts, acid rain, and agricultural chemicals affect the soil. What can farmers and urbanites do to lessen this problem?

16. List the advantages and disadvantages of alternatives to using synthetic chemicals to control agricultural pests. Why did U.S. farmers abandon the use of cultural controls after World War II?

17. What is the difference between monoculture and polyculture farming? Why do U.S. farmers prefer monoculture farming? Debate whether it is possible or desirable for U.S. farmers to switch to polyculture farming. What is the relationship between polyculture farming and Integrated Pest Management?

18. What are the reasons for the loss of prime agricultural lands or urbanization? Why should a factory worker living in an apartment or a college student living in a dormitory be concerned about the loss of farmland? Discuss the pros and cons of the various techniques for preserving farmland from urban encroachment. In your opinion, what will it take to preserve prime agricultural land in this country?

19. Why is it often difficult and sometimes impossible to reclaim mine-spoiled lands?

20. Discuss the various actions that one can personally take to conserve soil resources. To what degree do you think you might get involved? What will your first step be?

READINGS

ALLAWAY, W. H. 1975. *The Effect of Soils and Fertilizers on Human and Animal Nutrition*. Agriculture Information Bulletin No. 378. Washington, D.C.: Agricultural Research Service and Soil Conservation Service, U.S. Department of Agriculture. Excellent technical report, which argues that high crop yields are not necessarily a consequence of high nutrient content.

ALLEN, PATRICIA, and DEBRA VAN DUSEN, eds. 1987. *Comparative Farming Systems*. New York: Guilford Press. A very good collection of original case studies. The book attempts to integrate the environmental, technological, and socioeconomic characteristics of soil resource management.

ALTIERI, MIGUEL A., et al. 1987. *Agroecology: The Scientific Basis of Sustainable Agriculture*. Boulder, Colo.: Westview Press. A pioneer book on the ecological approach to agriculture. A must for anyone interested in sustainable agriculture.

AMERICAN FARMLAND TRUST. 1984. *Soil Conservation in America*. Washington, D.C.: American Farmland Trust. Calls for important changes in federal programs that support crop prices and farm incomes, and in soil conservation.

BATIE, SANDRA S. 1983. *Soil Erosion: Crisis in America's Croplands?* Washington, D.C.: The Conservation Foundation. Analysis of soils, terrain, weather, and other factors affecting erosion, with suggestions for erosion control.

BATIE, SANDRA S., and ROBERT G. HEALY, eds. 1980. *The Future of American Agriculture as a Strategic Resource*. Washington, D.C.: The Conservation Foundation. Good defense of farmland protection.

BENNETT, H. H., and W. R. CHAPLINE. 1927. *Soil Erosion: A National Menace*. Washington, D.C.: U.S. Department of Agriculture. A classic in soil literature.

BERRY, WENDELL. 1978. *The Unsettling of America: Culture and Agriculture*. New York: Avon Books. Outstanding study of the relationship between the spiritual and environmental and the economic productivity of traditional small-scale, diverse farming methods as compared with modern agribusiness.

BROWN, LESTER R. 1982. "Soils and Civilization," *Audubon*, January, vol. 84, no. 1, pp. 18–24. A reminder that soil is the foundation of civilization as well as agriculture.

BROWN, LESTER R., et al. 1987. *The State of the World 1987*. New York: Norton. Contains excellent chapter on sustaining world agriculture.

BROWN, LESTER R. 1978. "The Worldwide Loss of Cropland." In *Worldwatch Paper 24*. Washington, D.C.: Worldwatch Institute. Good summary by respected cropland specialist.

CARTER, LUTHER J. 1980. "Organic Farming Becomes Legitimate," *Science*, July, vol. 209, pp. 254–256. Timely discussion of the increased recognition of the importance of organic farming by modern farmers.

CARTER, LUTHER J. 1977. "Soil Erosion: The Problem Persists Despite the Billions Spent on It," *Science*, April, vol. 196, pp. 409–411. Detailed summary of America's soil conservation successes and failures.

CARTER, VERNON GILL, and TOM DALE. 1981. *Topsoil and Civilization*. Norman, Okla.: University of Oklahoma Press. Important book on the subject of declining empires and the associated soil abuse.

COATES, DONALD R. 1981. *Environmental Geology*. New York: Wiley. Very good introductory textbook on environmental geology.

COMMITTEE ON CONSERVATION NEEDS AND OPPORTUNITIES. 1986. *Soil Conservation: Assessing the National Resources Inventory*. Vols. 1 and 2. Washington, D.C.: National Academy Press. Important report.

COOK, R. L., and BOYD G. ELLIS. 1988. *Soil Management: A World View of Conservation and Management*. New York:

Wiley. Broad coverage of world soil characteristics, food problems, and production in developing countries.

COUGHLIN, ROBERT E., et al. 1981. *The Protection of Farmland: A Reference Guidebook for State and Local Governments/Executive Summary.* A Report to the National Agricultural Lands Study from the Regional Science Research Institute. Washington, D.C.: Government Printing Office. Superb summary of various tactics that state and local groups have used to protect farmland.

COUNCIL ON ENVIRONMENTAL QUALITY AND THE DEPARTMENT OF STATE. 1982. *The Global 2000 Report to the President.* New York: Penguin. Important document that puts soil problems in a global perspective.

COUNCIL ON ENVIRONMENTAL QUALITY. 1973. *Integrated Pest Management.* Washington, D.C.: Government Printing Office. Good summary of this alternative to the use of synthetic pesticides.

COX, GEORGE W., and MICHAEL D. ATKINS. 1979. *Agricultural Ecology: An Analysis of World Food Production Systems.* San Francisco: Freeman. Outstanding discussion of the ecological and historical context of agriculture, the dynamics of agroecosystems, and the future prospects for agriculture.

DASMANN, RAYMOND. 1984. *Environmental Conservation.* 5th ed. New York: Wiley. Excellent introductory textbook on environmental studies.

EDWARDS, C. A. 1969. "Soil Pollutants and Soil Animals," *Scientific American,* vol. 220, pp. 89–99. Excellent discussion of the effects of pesticide toxicity and chemical persistence on soil animals.

ENTOMOLOGICAL SOCIETY OF AMERICA. 1975. *Integrated Pest Management: Rationale, Potential, Needs, and Implementation.* Washington, D.C.: Entomological Society of America. Comprehensive overview of IPM as an alternative to modern pest management.

FIELDS, SHIRLEY. 1980. *Where Have all the Fields Gone?* Washington, D.C.: National Agricultural Lands Survey. Useful pamphlet.

FLETCHER, W. WENDELL, and CHARLES E. LITTLE. 1982. *The American Cropland Crisis.* Bethesda, Md.: American Land Forum. Strategies to protect U.S. farmland.

FOTH, HENRY D. 1984. *Fundamentals of Soil Science.* 7th ed. New York: Wiley. Perhaps the best basic textbook on soils.

FOTH, HENRY D., and JOHN W. SCHAFER. 1980. *Soil Geography and Land Use.* New York: Wiley. Textbook with a worldwide perspective; takes a regional approach to the characterization, genesis, and classification of soils.

GERSHUNY, GRACE, and JOSEPH SMILLIE. 1986. *The Soul of Soil: A Guide to Ecological Soil Management.* St. Johnsbury, Vt.: Gaia Services. Good introduction to sustainable agriculture.

GUSTAFSON, A. F. 1937. *Conservation of Soil.* New York: McGraw-Hill. Contrasts the soil practices of the pre-Columbian North American horticulturalists with the soil practices of the colonists.

HAVLICK, SPENCER. 1974. *The Urban Organism.* New York: Macmillan. General resource management textbook with good chapter on soils from an urban perspective.

JACKSON, WES, et al., eds. 1984. *Meeting the Expectations of the Land.* San Francisco: North Point Press. Contains outstanding essays in sustainable agriculture and stewardship.

JACKSON, WES. 1980. *New Roots for Agriculture.* San Francisco: Friends of the Earth. Proposes alternatives to modern industrialized agriculture.

LIKENS, GENE E., and F. HERBERT BORMANN. 1974. "Acid Rain: A Serious Regional Environmental Problem," *Science,* vol. 184, pp. 1176–1197. Excellent summary of this serious problem.

LITTLE, CHARLES. 1981. "Farmland and the Economy," *The Other Side,* Summer, no. 23, pp. 1–2. Brief new idea related to our vanishing farmlands.

LITTLE, CHARLES. 1979. "Farmland and the Future." In Max Schneph, ed., *Farmland, Food, and the Future,* pp. 123–127. Ankeny, Iowa: Soil Conservation Society of America. Thought-provoking statement regarding the seriousness of our soil problems in America.

LOWDERMILK, W. C. 1953. *Conquest of the Land Through Seven Thousand Years.* USDA-SCS Agricultural Information Bulletin #99. Washington, D.C.: U.S. Department of Agriculture. One of the best analyses of fallen civilizations and the associated soil degradation.

LOWRANCE, RICHARD, et al. 1984. *Agricultural Ecosystems: Unifying Concepts.* New York: Wiley. The study of farmland as an ecosystem.

LUNDGREN, LAWRENCE. 1986. *Environmental Geology.* Englewood Cliffs, N.J.: Prentice-Hall. Excellent introductory textbook.

MARSH, GEORGE PERKINS. 1864. *Man and Nature; Or, Physical Geography as Modified by Human Action.* New York: Scribner. Reprinted 1964. Cambridge, Mass.: Harvard University Press. Classic book by a geographer about the human impact on land.

McDONALD, ANGUS. 1941. "Early American Soil Conservationists," *Miscellaneous Pub. No. 1449.* Washington, D.C.: U.S. Department of Agriculture. Interesting account of American colonial conservation efforts.

MILLER, G. TYLER. 1988. *Living in the Environment.* 5th ed. Belmont, Calif.: Wadsworth. Outstanding introductory textbook on environmental studies.

MORGAN, R. P. C., ed. 1981. *Soil Conservation: Problems and Prospects.* New York: Wiley. Selected readings on soil conservation.

NEBEL, BERNARD J. 1981. *Environmental Science: The Way the World Works.* Englewood Cliffs, N.J.: Prentice-Hall. Contains a good chapter on soils.

OELHAF, ROBERT C. 1978. *Organic Agriculture: Economic and Ecological Comparisons with Conventional Methods.* New York: Halsted Press. Detailed analysis of the subject by an experienced economist; compares conventional and organic systems of agriculture.

OLMERT, MICHAEL. 1982. "Genes and Viruses are Harnessed on a Farm Tended by Scientists," *Smithsonian,*

March, vol. 12, no. 12, pp. 54–63. Interesting account of pioneering efforts at genetic engineering for "super" plant development.

OLSON, GERALD W. 1981. *Soil and the Environment: A Guide to Soil Surveys and their Application*. New York: Chapman and Hall. Superb geographical account of soil surveys and their applications in improving soil utilization.

OWEN, OLIVER. 1985. *Natural Resource Conservation*. 4th ed. New York: Macmillan. An excellent introductory textbook in natural resource management for those interested in the ecological approach.

PHILLIPS, RONALD E., and SHIRLEY H. PHILLIPS. 1984. *No-Tillage Agriculture: Principles and Practices*. New York: Van Nostrand Reinhold. Excellent review of research findings and practical knowledge on this timely topic.

POINCELOT, RAYMOND P. 1986. *Toward a More Sustainable Agriculture*. Westport, Conn.: AVI. Perhaps the best technical introductory textbook on sustainable agriculture.

POS (PEOPLE FOR OPEN SPACE). 1980. *Endangered Harvest: The Future of Bay Area Farmland*. San Francisco: POS. Effective argument for farmland preservation in the San Franciso Bay region.

RISSER, JAMES. 1981. "A Renewed Threat of Soil Erosion: It's Worse than the Dust Bowl," *Smithsonian*, March, vol. 11, no. 12, pp. 120–131. Readable account of soil erosion problems in America.

SAMPSON, R. NEIL. 1985. *For Love of the Land*. League City, Tex.: National Association of Conservation Districts. A history of the National Association of Conservation Districts.

SCHNEPF, MAX., ed. 1979. *Farmland, Food, and the Future*. Ankeny, Iowa: Soil Conservation Society of America. Culmination of what the SCSA refers to as its agricultural land retention book project.

SCHWAB, GLENN O., et al. *Soil and Water Conservation Engineering*. New York: Wiley. Engineering approach to soil conservation.

SOIL CONSERVATION SOCIETY OF AMERICA. 1977. *Conservation Tillage: Problems and Potential*. Ankeny, Iowa: Soil Conservation Society of America. Detailed overview.

SOIL CONSERVATION SOCIETY OF AMERICA. 1979. *Soil Conservation Policies: An Assessment*. Ankeny, Iowa: Soil Conservation Society of America. Historical analysis of American soil conservation policy.

SOPHEN, C. D., and J. V. BAIRD. 1982. *Soils and Soil Management*. Reston, Va.: Reston. Excellent introductory text on soils.

STEINBECK, JOHN. 1967. *The Grapes of Wrath*. New York: Viking. First printed by Viking in 1939. Classic novel of the Dust Bowl era.

STEINER, FREDERICK. 1980. *Ecological Planning for Farmland Preservation*. Pullman, Wash.: Student Book Corporation, Washington State University. A case study using Ian McHarg's ecological approach to land-use planning and farmlands preservation.

TROEH, FREDERICK, et al. 1980. *Soil and Water Conservation: For Productivity and Environmental Protection*. Englewood Cliffs, N.J.: Prentice-Hall. Excellent textbook on soil resource management.

TURNER, B. L., II, and STEPHEN B. BRUSH, eds. 1987. *Comparative Farming Systems*. New York: Guilford Press. A very good collection of original case studies. The book attempts to integrate environmental, technological, and socioeconomic characteristics of soil management.

USDA STUDY TEAM ON ORGANIC FARMING. 1980. *Report and Recommendations on Organic Farming*. Washington, D.C.: U.S. Department of Agriculture. Pros and cons of incorporating organic farming techniques into modern systems of agriculture.

WOODRUFF, ARCHIBALD M., ed. 1980. *The Farm and the City: Rivals or Allies?* Englewood Cliffs, N.J.: Prentice-Hall. Explores the process and implications of our disappearing farmland and seeks to answer important related questions.

4

WATER RESOURCES

A river is more than an amenity—it is a treasure.
Oliver Wendell Holmes

INTRODUCTION

Water sets Earth apart from all other known planets. It is one of the simplest substances known to humans—two molecules of hydrogen and one of oxygen—yet it is one of the most important. Every living thing depends upon it. In fact, plants and animal life are mostly water. For example, the human body is 65 to 70 percent water; the average person containing about 50 quarts or, roughly, 100 pounds of water.

Moreover, Earth's ecosystems could not function without water. Water is necessary in the process of photosynthesis; in the dissolving and transporting of nutrients from the soil to plants, fish, wildlife, and humans; in the conducting of heat; and in the carrying off of waste—all of which are necessary for life to continue.

Furthermore, water is a determining factor in local weather conditions and world climate patterns. Not only do humans require it for various bodily functions—water being the medium in which all bio-

chemical reactions take place—they need it for daily living—for bathing, gardening, agricultural production, food processing, manufacturing, transportation, power generation, aquatic-related recreation, waste disposal, and a host of other human activities. Water is the basic chemical of life; it sustains the planet and life cannot exist without it.

Water is so necessary and abundant that Earth is sometimes known as "the watery planet." Some have estimated Earth's total water supply as 369 quintillion gallons, or if written out, 369,820, 250,000,000,000,000 gallons. Approximately 70 percent of the globe is covered with oceans and seas, with an additionally high percentage covered by lakes, ponds, rivers, streams, swamps, and marshes. Yet despite a global supply numbered in quintillions, we are increasingly learning that water is a declining resource that must be conserved. Water is neither created nor destroyed in the global sense--the total quantity of water available is fixed. However, it is the *usable supply*—water of adequate quality and quantity—of water that has scientists and regional planners concerned.

Despite the fact that we cannot live without it, we continue to overuse, misuse, and abuse this previous resource. In many regions of the United States our groundwater resources are being depleted. Many of our streams, rivers, and lakes are being contaminated by agricultural runoff, inadequate sewage treatment, and illegal, hazardous waste dumps. Much of this is a result of wasteful consumption and poor management.

Before focusing on water resource management (Chapter 5), students must first have an understanding of the basic principles of surface water and groundwater hydrology—the subject of this chapter. We first examine the *natural hydrologic cycle*, that is, the global water cycle as it would exist without human intervention. Important hydrological concepts and terminology will be introduced. Major natural water problems, such as the unequal spatial distribution of water occurrence, will also be discussed. The second half of this chapter will focus on the *cultural hydrologic cycle*—the global water cycle as now altered by human interferences in the landscape, such as dams, reservoirs, agricultural fields, roads and highways, and, above all, the human activities that lead to water contamination.

THE HYDROLOGIC CYCLE

All the rivers run into the sea; yet the sea is not full; unto the place from whence the rivers come, thither they return again. (Ecclesiastes)

Our freshwater resources are classified as either surface water, soil water, or groundwater. **Surface water** is water that is exposed to the atmosphere and can be either flowing or ponded. This is the type of water that most concerns water resource managers or planners. Of particular concern to agriculturalists and plant ecologists is **soil water**, for it is the water held within the first few feet of the surface and is crucial for proper plant growth. **Groundwater**, also known as *phreatic water* or *subsurface water*, is that water contained in the soil, subsoil, and underlying rocks above an impermeable layer. Geologists have a particular interest in this type of water. The science that deals with the distribution and circulation of these three types of water is called **hydrology**.

The Natural Hydrologic Cycle

The **hydrologic (water) cycle** is a natural system of water movement—an endless interchange of water between the sea, air, and land (Figure 4-1). Driven by

energy from the sun, the process collects, purifies, and distributes water around the globe in either its vapor, liquid, or solid state. Since 97 percent of terrestrial water is in the ocean, the hydrologic cycle desalts (through solar evaporation) and transfers (through wind systems) this ocean water source great distances to the land in a form that is usable by terrestrial plants and animals, including humans. Although rainwater may pick up some natural or human-caused contaminants as it falls, the water undergoes a natural filter process as it passes through the soil on its way to groundwater reservoirs. Although considered a closed system on a worldwide basis (recall that the total amount of water is fixed), there are many open-ended subcycles that affect water supply and demand—all which are a concern of hydrologists and water resource managers.

There are five major components of the hydrologic cycle: precipitation, infiltration, evaporation, transpiration, and runoff. Each of these components of the hydrologic equation must be studied in order to understand the variability of water supply.

Precipitation.   All forms of falling moisture, including drizzle, rain, snow, sleet, and hail, come under the general term of **precipitation**. Consequently, it is one of the most important stages of the hydrologic cycle. As a whole, the conterminous United States receives an average 76.2 cm (30 in.) annual precipitation per year, of which 55.9 cm (22 in.) is lost through evapotranspiration and 20 cm (8 in.) is lost to runoff (Satterlund 1972).

Rainfall varies from place to place, depending upon latitude, altitude, slope, orientation, and wind direction. On a global scale, for example, portions of the Atacama Desert in Chile have received no rainfall during historic times; by contrast, parts of northern India have experienced over 2600 cm (1024 in.) of rainfall in just 12 months (Griggs and Gilchrist 1977). Within the conterminous United States, the U.S. Geological Survey records indicate extremes in annual precipitation ranging from less than 12.7 cm (5 in.) in the Southwest to more than 508 cm (200 in.) on the Olympic Peninsula of Washington (Figure 4-2).

Even more striking contrasts are noted where moisture-laden winds regularly blow across mountain ranges. As moist air is deflected upward, it cools and moisture is precipitated on the westward slopes (the slopes facing the wind). As the air descends the leeward slopes on the other side, it warms and becomes drier. Consequently, the leeward sides of mountain systems have minimal rainfall and are often deserts. Many of the world's most severe deserts are caused by this **rainshadow** effect. For exam-

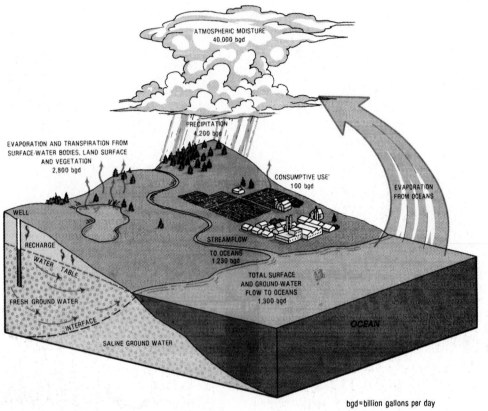

bgd=billion gallons per day

FIGURE 4-1 Schematic diagram of the hydrologic cycle. (From U.S. Geological Survey, *National Water Summary for 1983: Hydrologic Events and Issues,* U.S. Geological Survey Water-Supply Paper 2250, 1984, p. 9.)

ple, Death Valley, California, which is on the leeward (rainshadow) side of the Sierra Nevada Range has an average annual rainfall of only 4.3 cm (1.7 in.), whereas on the other side of the Sierra Nevada (the windward side), the average annual precipitation ranges from 356 cm (140 in.) to 381 cm (150 in.) (Kormondy 1976). Mount Waialeale on the island of Kauai in Hawaii is possibly the wettest spot on Earth, with an annual rainfall of 1168 cm (460 in.)—but this is only on the northeast slopes of the mountain, which receive moisture from the northeast trade winds. On the leeward side, by contrast, average annual rainfall is 46 cm (18 in.). Obviously, the spatial distribution of precipitation is an important factor to be considered by regional water planners.

Infiltration. As rain falls, a certain percentage of it is first *intercepted* by vegetation before striking and entering the soil surface. This process, where water droplets are held by the foliage, twigs, and branches of trees or by shrubs, is known as **interception**. The amount of precipitation that adheres to vegetation, known as *interception storage*, will remain in this state until it is eventually evaporated and re-

turned to the atmosphere. The quantity of precipitation and the type of vegetation determines the amount of water actually intercepted. For example, in a study of Norway spruce and beech forests in West Germany, Eidmann (1959) noted that summer interception by spruce (over a three year period) decreased from 82 percent to 24 percent of the total rainfall as the amount of rainfall increased from 1 mm (0.04 in.) to more than 20 mm (0.79 in.). For the same range of rainfall, summer interception by beech decreased from 72 percent to 18 percent of the total rainfall. Since interception affects the amount of precipitation reaching the ground, the distribution of precipitation over the soil surface, and ultimately the amount and timing of the water that becomes streamflow, hydrologists and water resource planners have a direct interest in the importance of interception and its relationship to their "water losses" in the hydrologic cycle.

Another form of water loss in the hydrologic cycle is through a process known as **detention**, or depression storage. This occurs when precipitation is temporarily *detained* in irregularities (depressions) on the ground surface. Simple mud puddles or ruts in a

AVERAGE ANNUAL PRECIPITATION

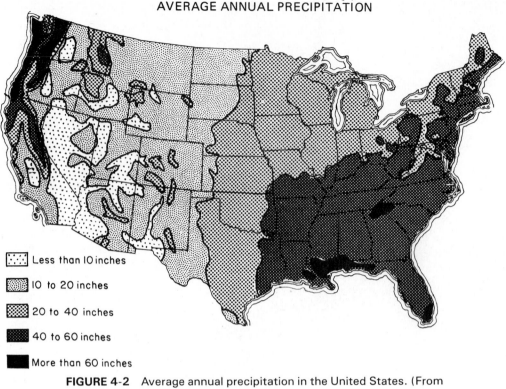

Less than 10 inches

10 to 20 inches

20 to 40 inches

40 to 60 inches

More than 60 inches

FIGURE 4-2 Average annual precipitation in the United States. (From Ruben L. Parson, *Conserving American Resources*, 3d ed. [Englewood Cliffs, N.J.: Prentice-Hall, Inc., 1972], p. 94.)

road are examples of detention (Figure 4-3). Only after depression storage is exceeded will surface runoff occur.

If not intercepted by vegetation or detained in surface depressions, precipitation will *infiltrate* the soil—a process known as **infiltration**. Specifically, infiltration refers to the process by which water *enters* the soil from the point of impact and percolates through the upper layers of the ground. The rate of infiltration is affected by such things as precipitation type and intensity, the friability or compactness of the surface (often determined by good or bad land use or management practices), the texture and porosity of the soil, the ground slope, the vegetation cover, and the existing moisture content of the soil.

Of particular importance is **infiltration capacity**, which is the maximum rate at which soil can absorb falling rain or melting snow. When rainfall occurs after a long dry period, infiltration into the soil is relatively rapid. As the soil interstices are filled, however, the rate of infiltration declines. Furthermore, porous sandy soils have a greater infiltration capacity than tighter clay soils. Wiesner (1970), for example, recorded infiltration rates at 0.75–1.00 in. per hour in course sand, 0.50 in. per hour in fine sandy loams, and 0.30 in. per hour in clay loam. However, these

were soils with good soil structure. Similar soil types with poor soil structure came in with lower infiltration rates, 0.50 in., 0.30 in., 0.25 in., respectively. If infiltration capacity is exceeded, surface runoff will occur. Much attention has been given to infiltration capacity by water resource managers, and rightfully so, since those factors that influence infiltration capacity are readily modified by humans.

Evaporation. Water resource managers have less control over another aspect of the hydrologic cycle—evaporation. **Evaporation** can be defined as the physical process by which a liquid is changed to a vapor or gas. The rate of evaporation is determined by such factors as air temperature, wind velocity, vapor pressure, and the nature of the ground surface. As one might suspect, the largest source of atmospheric water vapor comes from the world's oceans.

Over half of the precipitation that falls on the United States is returned to the atmosphere by evaporation (Water Resources Council 1978). During dry periods, a good portion of that evaporation comes from large bodies of water such as lakes and reservoirs. Average annual evaporation from lakes in the United States range from 51 cm (20 in.) per year in the cool, humid northeast to 203 cm (80 in.) per year

FIGURE 4-3 Detention in Kauai, Hawaii. (Photo by author.)

in the hot, dry southwest. Water resource managers require accurate estimates of evaporation for a number of reasons, such as calculating the storage capacity of reservoirs or planning additional surface water storage capacity for dams.

Transpiration. One aspect of the hydrologic cycle that resource managers have even less control over is transpiration. **Transpiration** is the photosynthetic and physiological process by which water vapor escapes from living plants (principally through the minute pores or *stomata* of the surface of leaves) and enters the atmosphere. For example, Kormondy (1976) reported that single mature oak tree is capable of transpiring 379 L (100 gal) per day or approximately 151,416 L (40,000 gal) annually.

In the past, hydrologists, engineers, and others have measured water loss from the land in terms of both evaporation and transpiration, called **evapotranspiration**. Here, they attempted to measure the combined volume of water evaporated and transpired from water bodies, land surface, and plant tissues. However, the measurement process proved extremely difficult, and consequently, was full of flaws. More recently, scientists have attempted to measure water loss in terms of potential evapotranspiration, which is a theoretical value based almost entirely on the climatic factors of radiation, wind, and humidity. Mather (1984) has defined *potential evapotranspiration* as ''the water loss from a vegetation cover that never

suffers from a lack of water.'' Using statistics on precipitation and potential evapotranspiration, Satterlund (1972) illustrates *water surplus* (where precipitation exceeds potential evapotranspiration) as compared with *water deficit* (where potential evapotranspiration exceeds precipitation) regions within the United States. Regional extremes in water availability are noted, from a water surplus of over 102 cm (40 in.) annually in the coastal regions of Oregon and Washington and central Washington to an annual water deficit of more than 102 cm (40 in.) in southwestern Arizona. According to Satterlund's analysis, the country can clearly be divided between the *haves* and the *have nots*, as far as water supply is concerned. East of the 96th meridian, there is generally a water surplus. Here, water is available to regularly supply groundwater aquifers, runoff, and streamflow. West of the 96th meridian, one generally finds a water deficit. It is a region of only sporadic streamflow. Only in the coastal regions and higher mountains of the Pacific Northwest does one find water surplus lands west of the Pecos.

Runoff. The fifth and final major component of the hydrologic cycle is **runoff**—the downward movement of surplus rainfall or snowmelt towards the oceans. Hydrologists, engineers, and other water resource managers have an interest in all the factors that affect runoff, including the duration and intensity of precipitation, the nature of topography and geology, the amount and type of vegetation in the watershed, and the rate of evapotranspiration. Satterlund (1972) identifies four primary types of runoff: (1) channel interception; (2) overland flow; (3) throughflow; and (4) groundwater flow. These various types of runoff are based on routes by which the runoff gets to the sea.

Channel interception refers to precipitation that has fallen directly into a creek, stream, or river. Channel interception is really only significant in areas where there are large bodies of water in relation to land area, such as in the Great Lakes states.

Substantially more significant is **overland flow**, which is commonly called *surface runoff*. Here, hydrologists are referring to precipitation that does not infiltrate the soil, but rather flows over the surface until it reaches a creek, stream, or river channel. Since vegetation cover vastly affects infiltration rate, it is understandable that humid regions with lush vegetation experience relatively little overland flow as compared with semiarid areas that have sparse vegetation. According to Mather (1984), typical velocities for overland flow (where conditions for overland flow exist) would be in the order of 200 to 300 m (656 to 984 ft) per hour. Consequently, overland flow quickly reaches various water channels. Natural drainage patterns within a region make up a drainage or catchment basin called a **watershed**—the entire land surface or *gathering ground* of a single river system.

Excess rainfall also moves towards (feeds) stream channels in another fashion called **throughflow**, or *interflow*. Here, precipitation infiltrates the upper soil layers, reaches an impermeable layer, then moves *laterally* until it reaches a stream channel or until it returns to the surface at some point downslope from its point of infiltration. In other words, these are waters that are moving laterally *below* the ground surface but *above* the water table. In comparison to overland flow velocities, throughflow velocities are quite a bit slower—as slow as 20 to 30 cm (8 to 12 in.) per hour (Mather 1984).

A final type of runoff is **groundwater flow**, also called **base flow**. This refers to underground drainage that is discharged into a stream channel as *spring* or *seepage* water. This type of drainage occurs in the *lower* soil layers, as opposed to throughflow, which occurs in the upper soil layers. To further explain groundwater flow and how it interrelates with the other forms of runoff, we first need to look at the various components of the entire groundwater system.

The Groundwater System.   Ninety-five percent of the world's supply of fresh water comes from underground reservoirs, called *groundwater*. With the exception of a few isolated cases, groundwater is not in the form of underground streams or pools, but rather it is contained within the interstices of porous and permeable subsurface geological formations. Specifically, subsurface water can be divided into two major zones: (1) the zone of aeration, and (2) the zone of saturation (Figure 4-4).

In the uppermost band, the **zone of aeration**, the spaces between the soil particles and rock are filled partly with water and partly with air. This zone normally has three distinct layers—the soil water belt, the intermediate belt, and the capillary fringe. The soil water belt extends to the depth of the root zone. Consequently, most plants receive their moisture from this zone. As might be suspected, it is a zone of marked fluctuations in water availability; sudden heavy rains, for example, can temporarily saturate this layer. On the other hand, most of the moisture in this belt is lost to the atmosphere through evaporation and transpiration. Hydrologists measure the amount of moisture in the soil belt in terms of field capacity and wilting point. An area is said to be at **field capacity** when all *gravity water* (water pulled

downward by gravity) has been drained after the cessation of rainfall and the remaining *capillary water* (water held to individual soil particles by surface tension) is still sufficient to provide the needs of growing plants. Field capacity is usually expressed as a percentage of the oven-dry weight of the soil.

Under drought conditions, evapotranspiration may reduce field capacity to a degree where plants begin to wilt, known as **wilting point**. This is a measure of soil moisture most often used by botanists and agriculturalists. Specifically, it is the soil moisture condition where plants wilt and fail to recover their turgidity. Except in very dry regions, moisture within the *intermediate layer* of the zone of aeration remains at field capacity. This moisture, however, is out of reach of most plant roots. Below the intermediate layer is the **capillary fringe**, where capillary water is moved *upward* from the zone of saturation into the intermediate layer, much like kerosene rises on a lamp wick. This zone may range from 1 cm (0.39 in.) thick in coarse sand or fine gravel with large pore spaces to 1 m (3.3 ft) thick in silty material. The smaller the pore spaces, the higher the capillary rise (Strahler and Strahler 1978). The few plant roots that reach this zone have an almost limitless supply of water to transpire.

The **percolation** of moisture down through the zone of aeration (the *vadose zone*) accumulates above an impermeable layer of what is known as the **zone of saturation**, or the *true groundwater* zone. In this lowermost band, the rock or soil pores are completely filled with water under hydrostatic pressure. The upper surface of this groundwater reservoir is called the **water table**. To tap groundwater resources, wells must be dug that pass through the capillary fringe (which is an undependable source of water) and the water table into the zone of saturation.

Water tables have many interesting characteristics. First, they generally follow the surface profile of the ground, except that the water table's gradients are somewhat flattened out. Second, they may be found a mile deep, or they may be at or near the ground surface in the form of springs, marshes, swamps, or lakes. Third, the water table level is not static—it fluctuates with the seasons (Figure 4-5). During rainy periods when recharge exceeds the discharge, the level of the water table will rise; likewise, during drought periods, when discharge exceeds recharge, the level of the water table will fall. Consequently, wells must be dug deep enough to allow for normal seasonal fluctuations in the water table level. In most areas, the water table is found at less than 30 m (100 ft) below the ground surface (Moran et al.

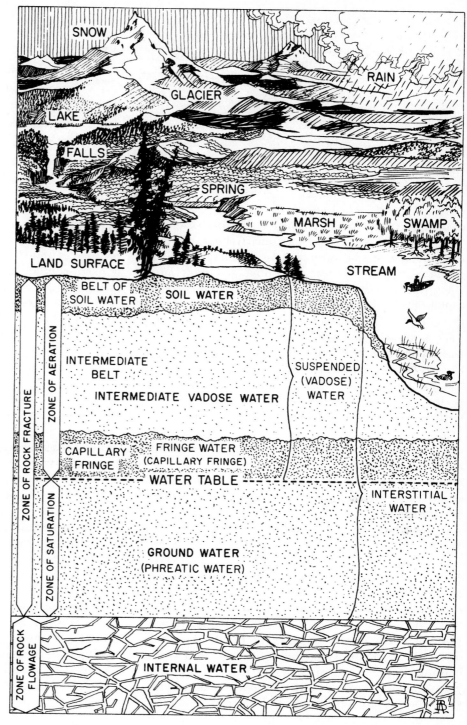

FIGURE 4-4 Vertical distribution of subsurface water. (From Ruben L. Parson, *Conserving American Resources*, 3d ed. [Englewood Cliffs, N.J.: Prentice-Hall, Inc., 1972], p. 96.)

1986). In arid regions, however, wells must usually be dug several hundred meters deep to reach the water table level.

Water tables also influence the rate of groundwater flow. Both groundwater and surface water normally flow from high to low points, but groundwater flows according to the shape of the water table, whereas surface water flows according to the shape of the land. In both cases, the steeper the slope, the faster the water will generally flow. However, groundwater flow is also affected by the **permeability** of the rock or sediment, that is, its capacity for transmitting a fluid through its pores. Consequently, the degree of permeability is determined by the volume

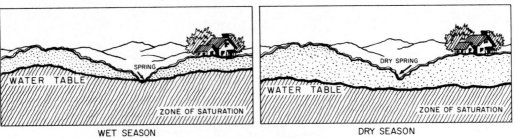

FIGURE 4-5 The seasonal variation of the water table. (From Ruben
L. Parson, *Conserving American Resources*, 3d ed. [Englewood Cliffs,
N.J.; Prentice-Hall, Inc., 1972], p. 100.)

of pore or void space (porosity) in the rock or other material as well as by the interconnections (as related to grain size, shape, arrangement of cementation or solution) between pores. According to Griggs and Gilchrist (1977), porosity may range from 5 to 10 percent for lithified sedimentary rock (e.g., shale or limestone) to 35 to 50 percent for unconsolidated material, such as alluvial sands and gravel. Griggs and Gilchrist also point out that highly porous materials do not necessarily guarantee high permeability; pore spaces must also be relatively large and interconnected to allow flow. Clay has a high porosity, between 45 to 55 percent. However, its pore spaces are too small and unconnected for the easy transmission of water. Sands, on the other hand, have a lower porosity than clay but normally have a higher permeability because of the larger and more connected spaces between the sand particles (Griggs and Gilchrist 1977).

Groundwater flows through these permeable layers towards various points of discharge, such as springs, marshes, streams, rivers, lakes, and seas. The rate of movement is extremely slow, on the order of 1.5 m (5 ft) per day to a few feet per year (Viessman and Welty 1985). Moran and colleagues (1986) have put a typical flow rate as high as 15 m (50 ft) per year. There is no question, however, that the rate and direction of groundwater flow will vary widely according to place and season. For example, during heavy channel flow, a stream may *feed* or recharge the groundwater table. In this case, the stream would be classified a *losing stream*. By contrast, during periods of minimum channel flow, the groundwater flow may help recharge the stream flow. In the latter case, the stream would be called a *gaining stream*.

The geologic formation in which water flows to streams and other points of discharge are called **aquifers** (Latin for *water bearing*). These are underground layers of porous rock material, gravel, and sand that are capable of transmitting water through their pores at a rate *sufficient* (economical to use and

develop) for human water supply purposes. In general, layers of sand and gravel make the best aquifers because of their relatively high permeability. Chalk (e.g., in southeastern England) and sandstone (e.g., in the eastern flanks of the American Rockies) also make good aquifers. There are two types of aquifers: unconfined aquifers and confined aquifers (Figure 4-6). In an unconfined aquifer, the water table is free to rise through permeable material and, consequently, is not restricted by an **aquiclude** (sometimes called *aquitard*)—an impermeable layer such as granite, clay, or shale. By contrast, a *confined aquifer* has an aquiclude that overlies it. This is important to understand when tapping groundwater resources. For example, if a well is drilled to an unconfined aquifer, the water will rise to the level of the water table. However, if a well is drilled to a confined aquifer (the well then being located below the water recharge area), hydrostatic pressure will force the water to flow up out of the ground. This type of well is called an *artesian well*.

In addition to their function as a pipeline or transmitting device, aquifers have two other functions: They serve as natural filters and reservoirs. As groundwater moves through water-bearing formations, disease-causing microorganisms and particulates that contain toxic compounds are trapped by such processes as *adsorption adhesion* (the attachment of certain impurities to soil particles) and by *ion exchange*. As we will see later, however, the process is not perfect, especially when dealing with the highly toxic pollutants introduced by humans. Groundwater may also dissolve and carry along various molecules and ions gathered from material through which it passed, a process known as *leaching*. These leached materials may either be highly desirable (e.g., in sulfur springs, where groundwater leaches sulfur-containing materials to make good-tasting water), a nuisance (e.g., in springs that have iron as ferrous hydroxide, which colors the water brown; or calcium carbonate, which produces hydrogen sulphide, pro-

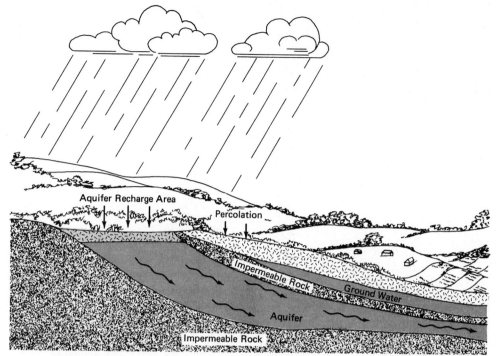

FIGURE 4-6 The groundwater system: aquifers versus aquicludes. (From Bernard J. Nebel, *Environmental Science: The Way the World Works* [Englewood Cliffs, N.J.: Prentice-Hall, Inc., 1981], p. 214.)

ducing a rotten-egg odor), or a danger to human health (e.g., in the poisonous springs of the Southwest, where groundwater leaches arsenic materials).

Twenty percent of the U.S. water supply comes from the country's aquifers (Griggs and Gilchrist 1977). They serve as great natural storage reservoirs of groundwater to be used for irrigation, industry, and drinking. Aquifers can be found in most (but not all) areas within the United States (Figure 4-7). In the United States, aquifers can generally be classified as (1) watercourse aquifers, (2) unconsolidated aquifers, (3) consolidated rock aquifers, and (4) combination aquifers. *Watercourse aquifers* are highly productive aquifers made up of unconsolidated sands and gravels found along watercourses and in floodplains, alluvial valleys, or coastal plains. Examples of this type of aquifer can be found in the East, in the Midwest, and in California's Central Valley. *Unconsolidated aquifers*, mostly sand and gravel, are predominant along the eastern and southeastern coastal regions. The largest and most famous unconsolidated aquifer in the United States is the Ogallala aquifer; it covers 582,705 km² (225,000 mi²), extending over eight states from Nebraska to Texas. It is estimated that this one aquifer contains as much as 2.5 million billion L (650 trillion gal) of groundwater (Owen 1985). *Consolidated rock aquifers* are generally formed

of volcanic rock (e.g., in large portions of Oregon and Washington in the Northwest) or of sandstone and limestone (e.g., in central Tennessee and the Shenandoah Valley of Virginia). Finally, overlying productive rock aquifers, one can often find *combination aquifers* made of sand and gravel. As you can see in Figure 4-7, the mountain regions and the arid West conspicuously lack many aquifers. Here, the groundwater is either too little or too brackish.

The United States also has thousands of smaller, less productive aquifers that are important for local water supplies. These *mini* aquifers are perched above the main water table line, providing independent and isolated sources of water called **perched water tables** (Figure 4-8). The mini aquifer is separated from the main water table by an aquiclude; the impermeable layer, in this case, is usually clay. Naturally, wells that tap perched water tables have a relative limited supply of groundwater.

The Cultural Hydrologic Cycle

Humans have drastically altered the natural hydrologic cycle by such activities as harvesting forests, creating agricultural fields, constructing dams and reservoirs, digging wells, diverting and channelizing streams, building storm sewers, and paving surfaces

GROUNDWATER AREAS IN THE UNITED STATES

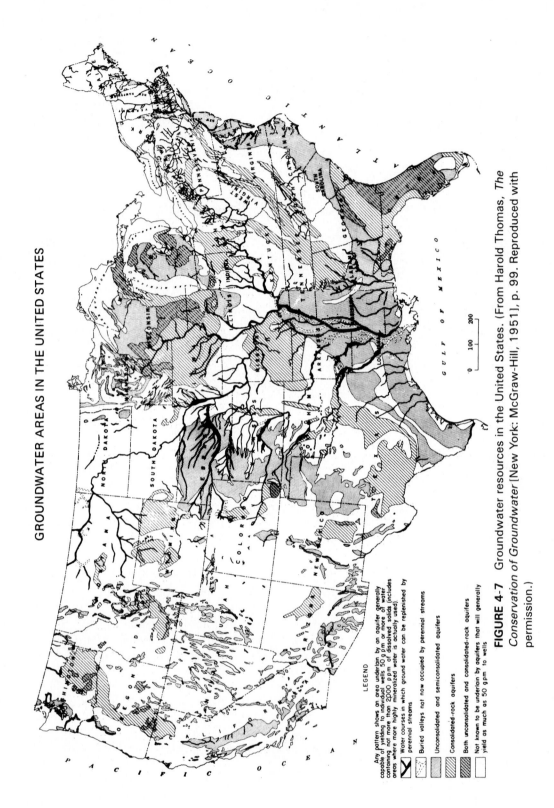

LEGEND

Any pattern shows an area underlain by an aquifer generally capable of yielding to individual wells 50 g pm or more of water containing not more than 2,000 p p m of dissolved solids (includes areas where more highly mineralized water is actually used)

Water courses in which ground water can be replenished by perennial streams

Buried valleys not now occupied by perennial streams

Unconsolidated and semiconsolidated aquifers

Consolidated-rock aquifers

Both unconsolidated and consolidated-rock aquifers

Not known to be underlain by aquifers that will generally yield as much as 50 g pm to wells

0   100   200

FIGURE 4-7 Groundwater resources in the United States. (From Harold Thomas, *The Conservation of Groundwater* [New York: McGraw-Hill, 1951], p. 99. Reproduced with permission.)

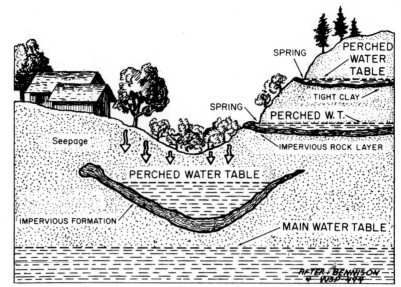

FIGURE 4-8 A perched water table. (From Ruben L. Parson, *Conserving American Resources,* 3d ed. [Englewood Cliffs, N.J.: Prentice-Hall, Inc., 1972], p. 101.)

for highways and parking areas. All these activities, and more, have an effect on the components of the natural hydrologic cycle to the point that it really must now be called the *cultural hydrologic cycle.* We now turn to the more obvious hydrologic implications of human land use.

Altered Precipitation Rates. The creation of cities has altered the occurrences and rates of precipitation within metropolitan districts, particularly downwind of city centers. Overall, urban complexes increase precipitation rates as a result of increased particulate matter in the air from the burning of fuels and waste, increased water vapor in the atmosphere from combustion sources, and higher temperatures that intensify thermal convections. For example, Changnon (1968) noted that city precipitation rates at Chicago, St. Louis, and Champaign-Urbana, Illinois, and Tulsa, Oklahoma, were 5 to 8 percent higher than the average of nearby rural districts. In fact, at La Porte, Indiana, an area downwind of the giant Chicago-Gary, Indiana, urban complex, precipitation was as much as 31 percent higher than in adjacent areas. Although the effects of cities on precipitation rates are difficult to determine, the scientists often disagree as to the exact figures of altered precipitation rates per city, there is no question that urbanization drastically alters what would otherwise be the normal amount and distribution of rainfall within a particular region.

Altered Transpiration and Evapotranspiration Rates. Human settlements and their associated environs have also altered the transpiration and evapotranspiration components of the natural hydrologic cycle. For example, the clearing of a field for agricultural purposes alters the vegetation cover (the number and types of plants) and the related soil moisture. Moran and colleagues (1986) have noted that a single hectare (2.5 acres) of growing corn normally transpires 35,000 L (9246 gal) of water each day. Since different crops have different transpiration and evapotranspiration rates, understanding the consumptive use of water by crops is of great value to water resource managers when determining irrigation water requirements.

Altered Infiltration Rates. As humans settle into a region and over the land with such impermeable surfaces as streets, sidewalks, parking lots, and roofs, the amount of water infiltration is greatly reduced. In one study (Leopold 1968), large suburban parcels of 1336 m² (about 0.33 acre) had a 25 percent impervious area, whereas smaller suburban parcels (486 m², about 0.12 acre) had as much as 80 percent of its area impervious to infiltration. In some areas, such as from Portland, Maine, to Richmond, Virginia, there is an almost continuous cover of concrete. Here, and in similar areas, even the hinterlands cannot provide natural flows to all for all purposes (Satterlund 1972).

Altered Overland Flow and Runoff. Reduced infiltration also results in increased overland flow and runoff from the urbanized area. This generally appears in the form of either (1) changes in peak flow characteristics or (2) increased flooding.

Peak flow periods are altered by the creation of impermeable surfaces and the building of storm sewers, which together reduce runoff travel time to stream channels. Consequently, creeks and streams that characteristically had modest, continuous flow are now transformed into riverine systems that have dramatic surges that correspond to periods of torrential rainfall (Figure 4-9). For example, Van Sickle (1969) has plotted the changes in peak stream flow resulting from development on Brays Bayou in Houston, Texas. Van Sickle discovered that peak stream flow increased from 1300 ft³ before development in the year 1941 to 2300 ft³ during development in 1953, to 4700 ft³ after development in 1960.

As one might expect, the introduction of torrential peak flows increases the possibility of flooding—one of the few times when the general public is consciously aware of water resources. (Periods of drought, of course, also get the public thinking about water.) A **flood** can be defined as a period when runoff cannot be contained within the banks of a river channel. Using data of past river flows, hydrologists and water resource managers determine *flood frequency*—the number of times per year, per 50 years, and per 100 years that the flooding of a particular area may be anticipated. Such statistics, however, can be misleading since human interference in the hydrologic cycle (e.g., storm sewers, stream channelization, levee building) has drastically altered precipitation, evapotranspiration, and water runoff relationships. According to Mather (1984), rivers that would normally have flood stages every 100 years may now actually have them every 10 years as a result of human-made changes in the local watershed.

There are numerous natural and human induced causes of flooding. Under the category of *natural* causes, *excess precipitation* creates the majority of floods. In parts of the country with heavy snowfall, particularly the Midwest and Far West, abnormally rapid melting of snow—*snowmelt*—can cause rivers to overflow their banks. Downstream areas far removed from the actual snowmelt (e.g., the lower Mississippi River) often receive the brunt of the flooding. In Alaska, Canada, and other northern climates where river ice creates *ice dams* (where river flow is restricted behind dams of ice), the sudden breakup of these ice dams will cause downstream flooding. Like ice dams, *landslides* can also restrict normal river flow, and the sudden breaching of that barrier can also create floods.

As indicated earlier, *cultural* practices such as paving and storm sewer construction increase the likelihood of flooding. It has been estimated that the very process of urbanization increases the mean annual flood by as much as six times (Leopold 1968). Other forms of human activity that increase the likelihood of flooding include deforestation, overgrazing, stream channelization, the construction of faulty dams, surface and strip mining (causing excess sediment to clog channels and disrupt flood peaks), and weather modification through cloud seeding.

The expansion of human settlements onto a river's floodplain invites disaster. One must remember that rivers gradually develop a **floodplain**—a narrow strip of land bordering both sides of a river. A river is a dynamic system, constantly depositing sediment on different banks, changing course, and ''flexing its presence'' within its floodplain. A river and its floodplain are one unit; the river ''owns'' its floodplain. Often ignoring this fact, urban developers encroach on the river's floodplain. Schneider and Goddard

(a)　　　　　　　　　　　　　　　　　　(b)

FIGURE 4-9 Streams with sharply fluctuating flow—one effect of urban development on nearby water systems. (a) Minimal runoff; (b) high surge of runoff. (Photos by author.)

(1973) studied the extent of development on some urban floodplains and found some startling figures. For example, 53.3 percent of the floodplains in Charleston, South Carolina, were found to be covered with buildings, parking lots, and other forms of urbanization. Even higher percentages of floodplain development were found in Denver, Colorado (62.2 percent); Harrisburg, Pennsylvania (83.5 percent); and Phoenix, Arizona (89.2 percent).

The stage is also set for disaster when various flood protection devices such as levees—devices that give the illusion of safety and invite surrounding development—are overtopped by extremely heavy rains. In February 1986, for example, heavy losses due to flooding occurred in agricultural areas, towns, and cities throughout northern California. Hardest hit was the Sacramento and San Joaquin delta region. Formed by the confluence of the Sacramento and San Joaquin rivers, the delta region is a monument to a long and expensive struggle to control floodwaters coming from two directions. Levees have been built since Gold Rush days, when farmers first discovered the riches to be from the delta's deep peat soils. Today, over 283,290 ha (700,000 acres) of swamplands have been transformed into 60 islands, separated by a lacework of 1127 km (700 mi) of interconnecting waterways. Ringing the islands are more than 1770 km (1100 mi) of levees, which are mostly made up of soil dredged from the former marshlands. One of the problems is that the levees continue to compress with time, requiring constant addition of more material on top. Prior to an 1884 court injunction, the discharge of hydraulic mining debris from gold mining operations in the Sierra Nevadas sent massive amounts of debris toward the delta, clogging channels, and forcing dikes to be raised. Although hydraulic mining has stopped, the delta's problems continue. As the islands dry out, the soft soil subsides, thereby lowering some island farmlands to as much as 6 m (20 ft) below sea level and further intensifying the likelihood of flooding. In 1986, the California State Water Resources Department estimated that it would cost a minimum of $1 billion to properly repair the crumbling levee system, taking from 10 to 20 years to complete the reconstruction.

Altered Groundwater Supplies. Human activities also disrupt the groundwater component of the hydrologic cycle. In regions where there is a shortage of surface waters, *overdraft*, or excessive groundwater withdrawal, is a major problem. If continued, the aquifer may eventually be damaged by either *saltwater intrusion* (the contamination of groundwater with saltwater) or *ground subsidence*, the sinking of the land as groundwater is withdrawn. We will now take a closer look at each of these major problems associated with humans and groundwater.

Groundwater withdrawal is extremely important in the United States, particularly in the arid and semiarid regions of the country (Figure 4-10). In 1980, California withdrew the greatest amounts of groundwater per day (14,500 million gallons [Mgal]), followed by Texas (9700 Mgal), Nebraska (7100 Mgal), Idaho (6300 Mgal), and Kansas (5600 Mgal) (Heath 1985). Unfortunately, the aquifers in these states, as well as in others, are experiencing **overdraft,** defined as the conventional lowering of the water table due to excessive withdrawal. Consequently, it can be said these states are *mining* the groundwater—the practice of withdrawing it at a rate in excess of the recharge rate from annual precipitation and limited stream flow. In the United States, the greatest ''miner'' of all is irrigated agriculture, which accounts for approximately 68 percent of groundwater withdrawals (Moran et al. 1986).

When groundwater is pumped at a rate faster than it can percolate laterally through the aquifer, the surrounding water table is lowered in the shape of a conical surface, called the **cone of depression**. The height of the cone of depression is referred to as **drawdown**. When wells are spaced in relatively close proximity to each other, and pumping is excessive, overlapping or *compound drawdown* occurs. Consequently, excessive pumping by one farmer on his property may cause his neighbor's well to run dry. Continued overdraft can have several negative environmental effects. First, water table ponds and bogs (aquatic habitats that are dependent upon continued surface exposure of the water table and that sustain stable communities of plants and animals) are disrupted. Second, stream flows of streams that are sustained by groundwater seepage are curtailed. And, third, water quality is damaged when reduced stream flow allows pollutants to be more highly concentrated, and consequently, more harmful. One location where the water reservoir is being depleted, and consequently groundwater mining is occurring, is at Evangeline aquifer in the Houston, Texas, area. Once again the culprit is irrigated agriculture.

It is the Ogallala aquifer, however, that one hears the most about, for it is a California-sized aquifer—a water-laden sand, silt, and gravel deposit that stretches from northern Texas to South Dakota (Figure 4-11). It ranges in thickness from 366 m (1200 ft) in Nebraska, where two-thirds of the state's waters lie, to just a few inches in parts of Texas. Although the Ogallala aquifer contains about as much water as Lake Michigan, its annual overdraft approximates the annual flow of the Colorado River (Miller 1985). Griggs and Gilchrist (1977) note that the num-

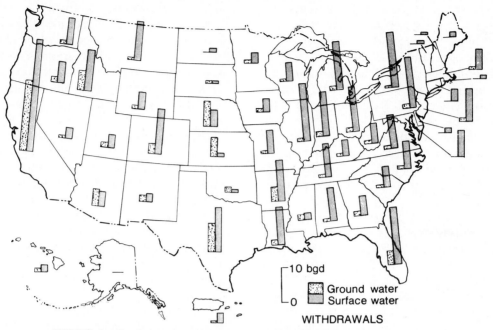

FIGURE 4-10 Groundwater and surface-water withdrawals in 1980 for the United States. (From Lawrence Lundgren, *Environmental Geology* [Englewood Cliffs, N.J.: Prentice-Hall, Inc., 1986], p. 117.)

ber of irrigation wells in the Ogallala region has increased from fewer than 300 in 1935 to 44,000 in 1960, transforming the area into a multibillion-dollar-a-year agricultural center. In Lubbock, Texas, alone, the rate of withdrawal is *50 times* the natural rate of aquifer recharge (Moran et al. 1986). As the water table declines, the cost of pumping water from greater depths increases, thus forcing farmers to abandon irrigation agriculture—a process that has already begun within the region of the Ogallala. For example, in Nebraska, Kansas, Oklahoma, Colorado, and Texas, 80,940 ha (200,000 acres) of corn-producing lands were taken out of use between the years of 1977 and 1980 because of water shortages (Chiras 1985). Overdraft is occurring in other areas as well, such as in California's San Joaquin Valley, in western Kansas, along the Colorado-Nebraska border, and in Savannah, Georgia.

One of the most bizarre effects of groundwater overdraft is *ground subsidence*—a sinking of the land (Figure 4-12). Since groundwater fills pores in the soil and thus helps support the immense weight of the earth above, the gradual removal of this water causes the soil to compact and subside. In recent years, dramatic examples of subsidence have occurred southeast of Phoenix, Arizona, where approximately 310 km² (120 mi²) of land sunk more than 2 m (7 ft) because of groundwater overdraft (Moran et al. 1986).

So prevalent is subsidence in Arizona that "Subsidence Area" road markers are now appearing across the landscape—a "sign" of groundwater depletion. In the San Joaquin Valley in California, pipelines, railroads, highways, factories, and canals have been damaged by subsidence. According to Moran and his colleagues (1986), 30 percent of the San Joaquin Valley has subsided by at least 0.3 m (1 ft).

When groundwater overdraft occurs in areas underlain with limestone, one of the more severe types of subsidence, a **sinkhole**, may develop. In this case, the withdrawal of groundwater causes the roof of an underground limestone cavern to collapse, thus gobbling up whatever is on the land surface above, including agricultural fields, houses, and cars. Chiras (1985) noted that recently in Florida, groundwater overdraft resulted in sinkholes measuring 100 m (330 ft) across and 50 m (165 ft) deep. Sinkhole formation is prevalent in the southeastern United States, since it is here that one can find numerous ancient beds of underlying limestone that have been leached. (Leaching is necessary for the formation of the underground caverns that collapse.) It has been estimated that there are 4000 sinkholes in Alabama alone (Nebel 1981).

In summary, the natural hydrologic cycle has been altered by excessive groundwater withdrawal, which often results in saltwater intrusion or land sub-

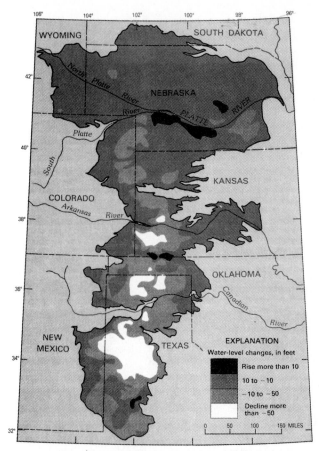

FIGURE 4-11   Changes in water level in 1980 in the Ogallala aquifer. (From U.S. Geological Survey, *United States Geological Survey Yearbook, Fiscal Year 1982*, 1983.)

sidence. Further groundwater depletion will lead to serious environmental and economic consequences. One of the most serious forms of environmental damage is brought about by water contamination, which is the subject of the final section of this chapter.

WATER POLLUTION

Water pollution can be defined as the addition of *harmful* (e.g., toxic wastes) or *objectionable* (e.g., sediment) materials to water causing an alteration of water quality. *Water quality* is a relative term, since water too polluted for one use may still be suitable for another use. For example, water not suited for drinking may be suitable for industrial use, fishing, sailing, or hydropower. According to the President's Council on Environmental Quality (CEQ), the quality of our nation's water continues to deteriorate (CEQ 1981). Because the government establishes specified water quality standards and local water districts test for contaminants, Americans have generally taken safe drinking water for granted. But recently, with new testing techniques, which permit scientists to determine very low levels of toxicity, the quality of the nation's water supply is being reassessed. Furthermore, the public is beginning to learn that local water districts do not test for many of the carcinogens and other dangerous chemicals that now exist in our waters. The largest area of serious water pollution in the United States continues to be in the heavily populated, industrial Northeast (Figure 4-13).

Pollutants come from a variety of natural and human sources. Scientists usually classify these wa-

FIGURE 4-12   Land subsidence due to the extraction of groundwater or oil. (Courtesy of USDA, Soil Conservation Service.)

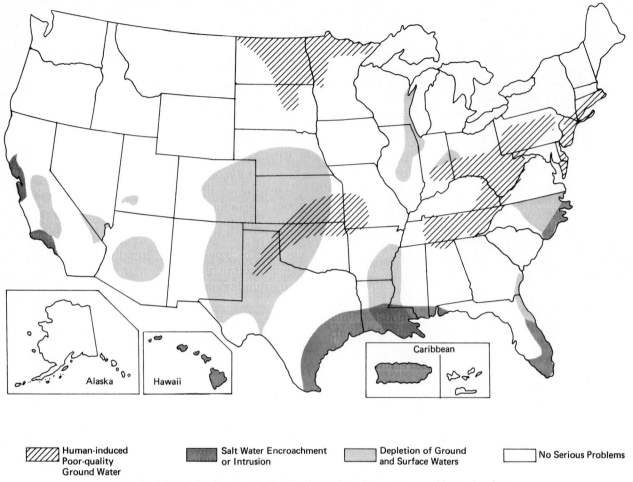

| Human-induced Poor-quality Ground Water | Salt Water Encroachment or Intrusion | Depletion of Ground and Surface Waters | No Serious Problems |

FIGURE 4-13 Regional distribution of major water problems in the United States. (From U.S. Water Resources Council.)

ter pollutants as either *point source* or *nonpoint source*. **Point source** pollutants are those that have a highly defined origin, such as a factory or a municipal sewerage outfall (e.g., a pipe, ditch, or tunnel). Offshore oil well blowouts and oil tanker accidents would also be classified as point source pollutants. All are clearly discernible in terms of origin.

By contrast, a **nonpoint source** (or *runoff*) pollutant arises from an ill-defined and diffuse source, such as the runoff from agricultural fields, construction sites, forest fires, logging operations, abandoned coal mines, streets, and parking lots. Here, pollution arises from large or broad areas rather than from discrete points. Consequently, it is the more difficult type of pollution to manage. The National Wildlife Federation (NWF) claims that nonpoint source pollution, sometimes known as *contaminated runoff*, accounts for more than 50 percent of our water pollution. In Pennsylvania alone, the NWF claims, over 3219 km (2000 mi) of streams are either acidic or iron-stained as a result of runoff from abandoned mines

(NWF 1985). Viessman and Welty (1985) noted that in 1976, nonpoint sources contributed from 65 to 75 percent of the nitrogen and phosphorous loadings into water bodies in the United States. They further note that urban runoff contributed from 80 to 90 percent of the petroleum discharges into our nation's harbor areas.

Although they are not mutually exclusive, and are often combined, the major water pollutants can be grouped according to the following nine categories: (1) sediment, (2) disease-causing agents, (3) oxygen-demanding wastes, (4) plant nutrients, (5) inorganic chemicals, (6) organic chemicals, (7) synthetic chemicals, (8) radioactive wastes, and (9) heat. We will now briefly look at each of these major types of water pollutants.

Sediment

The dominant pollution problem in many of our streams and rivers arises from inorganic particulates known as **sediment**. Specifically, sediment refers to mineral and rock fragments ranging in size from coarse sand particles to fine silt and clay, and to even finer colloidal particles (see Chapter 2 for further details). Sediment ranks high as a nonpoint pollutant. For example in 1979, the President's Council on Environmental Quality noted that sediment flows from nonpoint sources was 360 times greater than from industrial and municipal outfalls. According to Owen (1985), our nation's aquatic ecosystem annually receives 1 billion tons of sediment. Much of this comes from a *natural* erosion process. For example, Viessman and Welty (1985) note that the undistributed southern pine forests of the Coastal Plain produce 200 to 300 tons of sediment per square mile annually. However, *accelerated erosion* (human-induced erosion) has greatly increased the sediment loads of many streams, lakes, and reservoirs. For example, Moran and his associates (1986, p. 231) report that construction sites "contribute 10 times more sediment per unit of area than cultivated land, 200 times more than undisturbed grassland, and 2000 times more than undisturbed forest land." Other forms of human-induced erosion would include poor farming practices, deforestation, channelization works, and off-road vehicle use. Changes in land use clearly have a direct bearing on sediment yield and profoundly impact local and regional ecosystems.

The effects of excessive sediment load are both environmental and economic. Sediment damages turbines and pumps, and excessive sediment loads result in *reduced reservoir and lake capacity*. All lakes and reservoirs (Figure 4-14) gradually fill with sediment, but humans accelerate the process through their negligent land-use practices. As reservoirs and lakes fill with sediment, their ability to store drinking water, irrigation water, water for electricity generation, and so on declines. Simply stated, the lifespan of these water bodies, and their associated use, rapidly declines with accelerated sedimentation. Accelerated erosion and sedimentation also results in *silt-polluted drinking water*, which is expensive to filter before human consumption can take place.

Reduced stream channel capacity is also a consequence of accelerated sedimentation. When rivers become clogged, irrigation systems are disrupted, barge and ship transportation becomes tenuous, if not dangerous, and harbors require dredging, an expensive and time-consuming endeavor. As beds of aquatic vegetation are blanketed with silt, *extensive fishkills* may result. Sediment-laden water reduces light penetration, which is a requirement for photosynthesis to take place. Without sunlight, algae and the other plants that provide the base for aquatic life would die. Sediment also directly kills stream bottom organisms by clogging their gills. (See Chapter 11 for further details.) If sedimentation continues to the point that the elevation of the channel bed is raised, *increased flooding* may occur. Finally, sediment particles absorb many contaminants, such as pesticides, toxic metals, and radionuclides. Consequently, with increased sediment load comes increased toxic flow of pollutants within and surrounding the riverine system.

Disease-Causing Agents

In addition to sediment, water can also transmit **pathogens**—disease-producing organisms, such as bacteria, viruses, parasitic worms, and protozoa (unicellular animals). These organisms can result in such dreaded diseases as cholera, typhoid fever, infectious hepatitis, and amoebic dysentery. Most of these dis-

FIGURE 4-14 Silt deposits—a death blow to dams and reservoirs. (Courtesy of USDA Soil Conservation Service.)

eases occur in the underdeveloped Third World countries of Asia, Africa, and Latin America.

In the United States, such waterborne diseases have been dramatically reduced because of the practice of **chlorination**—the application of chlorine to drinking water, sewage, and industrial waste. This practice, however, has its drawbacks, which will be discussed in the following chapter on water resource management. Furthermore, this practice is not foolproof, since outbreaks of waterborne diseases in the United States still occur. For example, between 1971 and 1974, there were 16,950 cases of waterborne infectious diseases in the United States (National Research Council 1977). In 1985, the National Wildlife Federation reported that two University of Missouri civil engineers, who had analyzed samples from 83 water treatment plants in the state, had found that the federal Environmental Protection Agency's water quality standards miss up to 99 percent of the bacteria in drinking water. The scientists argued that the EPA is wrong when it assumes that removing solid particles from water reduces bacterial content. Their research indicates that bacteria are present as single cells, unattached to other particles. One thing is certain: Detecting pathogens in water is extremely difficult, time-consuming, and costly.

Oxygen-Demanding Wastes

A third type of water pollution occurs when high concentrations of biodegradable organic matter enter a water body. Organic wastes, such as sewage from dairies, cheese factories, canneries, meatpacking plants, and bakeries, decompose in the water. Respiration by the decomposers (mostly bacteria) reduces the amount of dissolved oxygen in surface water. The quantity of dissolved oxygen required by decomposers to break down organic wastes in a given volume of water is known as **biochemical oxygen demand** (BOD), or biological oxygen demand. Scientists use BOD as a measure of the level of organic contamination in wastewater. For example, Owen (1985) notes that each flush of your toilet carries approximately 250 parts per million (ppm) of BOD. By comparison, canneries and cheese factories have BOD levels ranging from 5000 to 15,000 ppm.

Since most aquatic organisms require dissolved oxygen for survival, a reduction in the **dissolved oxygen content**, or DO content, in a stream, river, or lake can drastically affect fish populations. When BOD levels cause DO to fall below 5 ppm, the water body is considered *seriously polluted*; DO levels below 4 ppm are considered *gravely polluted* (Miller 1986). In recent years, for example, the discharge of sewage

into the Potomac River near Washington, D.C., has reduced DO levels *below one ppm*, resulting in extensive fishkills during spring spawning migration (Southwick 1976). In 1984 alone, there were several incidences of fishkills (USGS 1985), most of which were probably a result of reduced DO levels. For example, in northwestern Indiana, drainage from an area spray-irrigated with swine waste killed about 21,000 fish; in northeastern Florida, discharges from food-processing operations killed approximately 480,000 fish.

Plant Nutrients

Natural Eutrophication. Nutritional pollutants are also a source of water pollution. For example, overland flow and tributary streams bring nutrients to lakes that cause them to eventually "die"—that is, the lakes slowly evolve into marshes and gradually disappear altogether. This natural aging process, called **eutrophication** or *natural eutrophication*, normally takes thousands of years.

In the early stage of life, lakes are deep, cold, clear, and have little biological life. Since they have a relatively low supply of nutrients, plankton and rooted vegetation are scarce. Characteristic fish within these **oligotrophic** (nutrient poor) lakes are trout and whitefish. Lake Superior and the Finger Lakes of New York fall into this category of lakes. As time passes, additional nutrients are washed into a lake causing it to be more shallow and biologically productive. Lake Ontario is characteristic of this **mesotrophic** or transition stage. Finally, as nutrients continue to flow in, phytoplankton and other aquatic vegetation multiply, providing more food for herbivorous organisms. As these organisms die, further nutrients are added to the lake. Eventually, the lake begins to take on undesirable characteristics. For example, Lake Erie is at this **eutrophic** (nutrient rich) stage. Characteristically, eutrophic lakes are shallow, warm, and have an abundance of plankton and rooted vegetation. Furthermore, there are excessive amounts of plant nutrients, such as nitrates and phosphates. Carp, sunfish, and yellow perch would be the fish typically found in a eutrophic lake.

Cultural Eutrophication. Just as there is a distinction between the natural hydrologic cycle and the cultural hydrological cycle, there is a similar distinction between natural eutrophication and **cultural eutrophication**, the latter referring to a *speedup* or *acceleration* of the enrichment (aging) process of a water body. In other words, humans increase the rate at which water bodies "die" by polluting water bodies with their agricultural, industrial, and urban wastes. For example, Lake Erie has aged 15,000 years in the 25 years between 1950 and 1975 (Owen 1985). According to Owen (1985), nitrogen and phosphorus are the most significant nutritional pollutants added to our nation's water, with 75 to 80 percent coming from human activities.

Specific sources of cultural eutrophication are numerous, but they can generally be grouped into four major categories: (1) farmland fertilizers, (2) animal wastes, (3) domestic sewage, and (4) urban runoff. *Farmland fertilizers* rich in nitrates and phosphates are a significant contributor to nutrient runoff and cultural eutrophication. Although there is not too much difference between properly managed farmlands and natural areas in terms of nutrient runoff, there is a major difference found between the two areas in heavily farmed areas, such as the Central Valley of California. For example, Moran and his associates (1986) note that the farmlands in this region characteristically have drainage conditions that promote runoff and erosion. Nitrate concentrations in water from highly fertilized irrigated fields approach 50 parts per million. *Animal wastes* from feedlots are an important source of plant nutrients, and the problem is increasing as we crowd more and more livestock into feedlots rather than grazing them on open range. In 1984, 4400 fish died in a tributary of the Susquehanna River, near Liverpool, Pennsylvania. The cause was runoff from a hog-manure lot (USGS 1985). *Domestic sewage* contains human waste and household detergents that are not thoroughly cleaned by modern water treatment plants. Consequently, 50 percent of the nitrogen and 70 percent of the phosphorus from domestic sewage actually ends up in our streams, rivers, and bays (Owen 1985). Finally, *urban runoff* is a significant nonpoint source of plant nutrients. Here, nitrogen and phosphorus are added to water bodies from such sources as lawn fertilizers, urine and feces from domesticated pets, leaf litter, and cleaning agents used to clean driveways, automobiles, and other surfaces.

Adverse effects of nutrient pollution are numerous. One of the first signs of nutrient pollution is the formation of *algal blooms*, the proliferation of algae on the surface of streams, ponds, or lakes. Lake Tahoe, located on the northern California-Nevada border, is a lake slowly turning green. For 2 million years, this Sierra Nevada lake was deep, cold, and crystal clear. A recent building frenzy has brought roads, houses, shopping centers, casinos, and tourists to this once isolated mountain community. According to a University of California Tahoe Research Group, uncontrolled development since 1960 has destroyed 75 per-

cent of the marsh areas, 50 percent of the meadows, and 33 percent of the stream bank areas in the 500-square-mile basin. With these *buffer areas* removed, nutrient rich sediment now enters the lake unfiltered. The nutrients spawn algae. As developers, property owners, legislators, and conservationists grapple with these problems, the *greening* of Lake Tahoe continues. As water bodies become green "pea soup," aesthetic and recreational values decline. Furthermore, water quality is impaired: The water takes on an unpleasant odor and becomes foul tasting. Eventually, dissolved oxygen levels decline, aquatic organisms change from clean water organisms to organisms and fish that can tolerate low-oxygen levels. Fishkills will then occur, and, ultimately, the water body fills in and becomes *extinct*.

Inorganic Materials

Our nation's water resources are also polluted by inorganic materials, which include salts, acids, and heavy metals (e.g., mercury and lead). More recently, trace elements (e.g., selenium) have become a concern to water resource managers.

Salts. As has been shown earlier, one means by which salt contaminates aquifers is through saltwater intrusion. This problem is particularly acute along coastal zones. In northern cities where salt is used to melt snow on winter roads, street drainage increases the salinity of water supplies. In 1984, for example, the National Wildlife Federation reported that 500,000 tons of salt were spread on roads each year in New England; 200,000 tons per year were applied in Massachusetts alone. As a result, the contaminant levels in water supplies in Massachusetts have exceeded the state's maximum allowable level, thereby forcing many wells to be shut down.

In the southwestern part of the country, rivers pick up salt while flowing over highly saline soils and from return-flow irrigation water; they also pick up salt from salt springs. For example, the Colorado River has a major salt pollution program, and its increasing salinity is now threatening fisheries, agriculture, and domestic water supplies. The river's salinity problem is further aggravated by increased use of the relatively pure water of the upper river basin. With less pure water available for diluting the river's salt load, downstream areas have higher salinity. Kneese (1982) found that the Colorado River's headwaters in Colorado had only 50 ppm of inorganic salts, as compared with 870 ppm in the downstream areas of the Imperial Valley in California. Although the water in the Imperial Valley is still usable, it adversely affects crops and corrodes water conveyance facilities.

Acids. Acids contaminate our water supplies, coming from both point (e.g., acid spills) and non-point (e.g., acid rain) sources. On April 29, 1984, for example, 2461 liters (650 gal) of sulfuric acid spilled into the James River, south of Richmond, Virginia, from a defective heat exchanger at a chemical plant (USGS 1985). Similar incidences occur across the country on a regular basis.

Acid precipitation, a nonpoint source pollutant, is far more difficult to control. It is caused primarily by sulfur dioxide emissions from the country's numerous coal-burning industries and power plants; nitrogen oxides from automobile exhaust further intensifies the problem. This invisible and inconspicuous pollutant damages forests, crops, soil fertility, lakes, fish, and even structures, such as Europe's 1000-year-old stained glass cathedral windows. According to some 1985 maps prepared by the federal Environmental Protection Agency (EPA), more than 50 percent of the total lake area in New England and New York, and some 300,000 acres of lakes in the upper Midwest, are "vulnerable" to acid rain damage. The lakes simply lack the alkaline substances that can neutralize acids. Consequently, thousands of lakes and streams in North America are already dead. Acid rain can also leach toxic metals into water supplies. In 1984, for example, Minnesota health officials warned residents to limit the consumption of fish from the state's lakes because acid rain had aggravated mercury contamination in fish.

Once confined to New England, acid rain now threatens the rest of the country, from Florida to California. The problem of acid rain worsens every day. According to a 1984 National Wildlife Federation report, Virginia's summer rainfall in 1983 was twice as acidic as in 1982; rainfall in the Houston-Galveston area of Texas was 400 times as acidic as natural rain; and fog in some parts of California was acidic enough to burn the eyes and throat.

In 1985, the prestigious World Resources Institute in Washington, D.C., released what is reported to be the first comprehensive look at the problem of acid rain in the American West. Compiled by a group of California researchers, the report found increasing levels of acidity in the rain, snow, fog, and air in the West. Whereas the eastern United States is in the third stage of acid-induced damage, involving biological damage, with dying lakes, forest, and fish, the West is at the beginning of the second stage, involving chemical changes in surface and groundwater that result from rising acid levels. (The first stage is merely the observation of acidic rainfall.) The report also noted that even though acid levels in the East are 10 times higher than in the West, ecology in the West is more vulnerable to acid rain because it is less able to neutralize it. Soil covers that act as acid buffers are much thinner in the West than in the East. Furthermore, the large amounts of snowmelt or summer rainfall can often overcome a waterway's ability to neutralize acidity. Finally, the World Resources Institute report concluded that unless immediate action is taken to minimize acid precipitation, acid-induced damage in ecologically sensitive areas of the West could someday equal what has already happened in the eastern United States.

United States–manufactured acid rain is also floating across the northern border into Canada, outraging our northern neighbors. According to a 1984 Canadian Wildlife Federation report, 2000 to 4000 lakes in central Ontario are so acidified that they no longer support trout and bass. Furthermore, Canadian scientists predict that within 20 years an additional 48,000 lakes will be acidic and barren of fish. Until recently, the U.S. government has done nothing but provide funds for further research, a policy which Canadians and U.S. conservation organizations have seen as stonewalling, rather than as positive action.

Heavy Metals. **Heavy metals** are also highly toxic contaminants in our water systems. Heavy metals include such metallic elements as mercury, lead, chromium, cadmium, and arsenic. Characteristics of heavy metals are (1) high molecular weights (a specific gravity of 5.0 or over), (2) high toxicity to plants and animals in relatively low concentrations, and (3) a tendency to accumulate in the food chain. Perhaps the most famous case of water pollution by a heavy metal occurred in the early 1950s when mercury poisoned Minamata Bay in Japan. For decades, the Chisso Corporation, a nearby chemical plant, released mercuic chloride in its industrial waste waters. Certain microorganisms in the bay converted the mercuic chloride into methyl mercury, an even more toxic compound that easily moves through the food chain, accumulating at higher trophic levels. The local fishermen and their families unknowingly consumed highly toxic fish, and hundreds of them became gravely ill, mentally retarded, and paralyzed. Many died.

Lead contamination is also a serious heavy metal problem in many countries. Some years ago, in another area of Japan, farmers were using water from a river downstream from a sulfide mine to irrigate their rice paddies. This water contained high amounts of lead. The result was serious illness and a number of deaths (Kitagishi and Yamane 1981). Private testing firms have also discovered lead in tap water in various regions of the United States. The lead is believed to be leached from the very pipes that transmit the water to your home or dwelling. According to a 1985 National Wildlife Federation report, the levels were below the current EPA standard for lead in drinking water, but caution was in order since British researchers were also finding surprising lead concentrations in their country's tap water.

Trace Elements. **Trace elements**, or micronutrients, are chemical elements that are necessary for the normal growth of plants. They are only needed, however, in extremely small amounts, in amounts usually less than 1 part per billion (ppb). Common examples of trace elements are iron, manganese, zinc, boron, copper, and chlorine. One trace element that has received much publicity recently is selenium. Selenium is present in the soils and groundwater of many regions within the United States. This naturally occurring, nonmetallic element is believed to be essential for human and animal nutrition at minute levels (40 ppb; 0.040 mg/L); however, at higher levels of concentration (4000 ppb; 4.0 mg/L), it can prove fatal (Lakin 1973).

In 1982, the U.S. Fish and Wildlife Service discovered abnormally high levels of selenium in the fish at Kesterson National Wildlife Refuge between Los Banos and Merced, California. Selenium levels there were 100 times the levels in fish from an adjacent state wildlife area (U.S. Bureau of Reclamation 1984). It was later found that agricultural drainage water that flows into the wetland refuge had picked up selenium from sedimentary deposits along the west side of the San Joaquin Valley. Selenium concentrations from the farm drainage system were as high as 4200 ppb or 4.2 mg/L (Presser and Barnes 1984). Deformities and a high mortality rate among stilts, grebes, coots, ducks, and other forms of wildlife at Kesterson resulting from selenium poisoning continue to be major management problems (Deverel 1985). (See Chapter 12 for further information on trace elements.)

Organic Chemicals

Trace organic compounds also bioaccumulate though food chains and can, therefore, prove harmful to the environment and humans. Since the types and sources of organic compounds are more diverse than inorganic chemicals, managing these toxic compounds is extremely difficult. In this category fall the synthetic organic chemicals (SOCs), which are human-made chemicals containing carbon. The SOCs include the pesticides and all of the other petroleum by-products such as refined oil, gasoline, and industrial solvents.

Pesticides. Moran and his associates (1986) have noted that pesticide contamination is one of our greatest concerns, since there are some 1800 different toxic chemicals used as active ingredients in pesticides, and since these chemicals, when combined with each other in various ways, can make more than 40,000 different pesticide formulas. One class of pesticides, the *chlorinated hydrocarbons*, form a particularly great threat to the environment, so much so, in fact, that the Environmental Protection Agency (EPA) only allows their use on an "emergency basis." Examples of these highly dangerous pesticides are DDT, dieldrin, heptachlor, aldrin, toxaphene, and chlordane. Although there is some evidence that concentrations of chlorinated hydrocarbon insecticides (including DDT, chlordane, and dieldrin) are declining in U.S. rivers since the mid-1970s (Gilliom 1985), improved monitoring and analytical techniques may find the trend to be quite the contrary.

Oil. On March 19, 1984, on the Columbia River north of Portland, Oregon, an oil tanker ran aground, spilling more than 567,810 L (150,000 gal) of heating oil into the river (USGS 1985). Even more dramatic was the grounding of the supertanker *Amoco Cadiz* on March 16, 1978. The giant oil tanker ran aground on the northwest coast of France, spilling an estimated 248 million L (65.5 million gal) of crude oil, thereby creating ecological and economic havoc for thousands of miles. More recently, on March 24, 1989, the *Exxon Valdez* tanker spilled 41 million L (11 million gal) of crude oil 40 km (25 mi) from the southern end of the Trans-Alaska Pipeline. Moran and his colleagues (1986) note that although they are spectacular, these oil spills only account for 20 percent of the estimated 3.6 million metric tons of oil that enters our oceans each year. Regardless of whether the oil comes from natural seepage, tanker accidents, or from purposeful dumping, the oil and grease are a type of organic compound detrimental to our nation's and the world's water supplies.

PCBs. Polychlorinated biphenyls (PCBs) are another highly toxic synthetic organic chemical that have been found in our nation's water supply. These fire-resistant chemicals have been used as insulating materials in a number of items, such as electric transformers and hydraulic fluids. Furthermore, PCBs have sometimes been used in the manufacture of paper and plastics. Although the manufacture of PCBs has been banned since 1977, they continue to plague the country. One of the most common means by which PCBs contaminate our water resources is through leakage from electrical transformers. For example, on April 6, 1984, at Groton, Connecticut, a transformer leaked 38 L (10 gal) of PCBs into the Thames River (USGS 1985). Aquatic ecosystems can also be contaminated by PCB-laden dust (resulting from the burning of paper or plastics containing PCBs), PCBs in runoff from accidental spills, or PCBs in leakage from industrial waste disposal ponds or lagoons. As with any other extremely toxic chemical, such as dioxin, the natural concentration mechanism of bioaccumulation is at work, and PCBs can severely contaminate food supplies, particularly freshwater and marine fisheries.

Industrial Solvents. In May 1986, residents within Santa Clara County, California, were shocked to learn that a synthetic organic chemical known as trichloroethylene (TCE) may have reached lower-level drinking water aquifers. Previously, residents were informed with glossy brochures, which accompanied their monthly water bill, that they need not be concerned about leaking waste storage tanks, since they only contaminated surface aquifers that were not used for drinking water. However, in the process of continued monitoring of groundwater contamination, local engineers discovered that concentrations of TCE—a cleaning solvent frequently used by the ''Silicon Valley'' electronic industries—had been found as deep as 152 m (500 ft). Hydrologists believe that the chemicals spread from the upper-level aquifers by entering the corroded casings of abandoned agricultural wells and by then dropping to a lower drinking water aquifer. Although there is as yet no evidence that TCE has reached any drinking water wells, local residents and officials are very concerned since the National Cancer Institute has concluded that this particular chemical is a liver carcinogen in mice. It has also been known to affect the central nervous system, the respiratory system, and the cardiovascular system.

Detergents. Though much less hazardous than PCB, dioxin, or TCE, household detergent also contaminates our nation's water supplies with synthetic organic chemicals, such as sodium tripolyphosphate. Since sewage treatment plants do not remove phosphates, the chemicals travel virtually intact from the household or industrial washing machine through the treatment plant to the nearest lake or bay. Some regions have banned the use of phosphate detergents, but in those regions that have no such ban, 30 to 70 percent of the phosphate in wastewater is from detergents (Miller 1986).

Radioactivity

Of increasing public concern is the addition of radioactive materials to the water. Mining or industrial operations that process radioactive ores can cause radioactive water pollution. Radioactive water contamination can also occur from the testing and using of nuclear weapons, the development of leaks in nuclear power plants, the accidental spillage that may occur during the transport of radioactive material, the use of radioactive isotopes in hospitals and research laboratories, the processing of radioactive materials and wastes, and the use of inadequate facilities for long term storage.

The Soviet Record. It was in April 1986 that people around the world turned on their radios and television sets to learn of the Chernobyl nuclear power plant disaster near Kiev, a heretofore unknown city within the Ukrainian Republic of the Soviet Union. Although the immediate focus was on the movement of the massive radioactive cloud produced by the disaster, scientists around the world began to question the effect of such a disaster on the region's surface and groundwater supplies, as well as on its agricultural fields. Of course, studies will need to be done to determine the short- and long-term effects on the environment. This was not the Soviet Union's first nuclear disaster. An accident in the late 1950s near Chelyabinsk, in the Ural Mountains, spread radioactive material over as much as 2590 km^2 (1000 mi^2), forcing the evacuation of several towns and villages.

The U.S. Record. Although the U.S. government likes to point its finger at the Soviet Union, claiming that it does not have adequate safety measures at its nuclear facilities, the United States has a long record of major nuclear accidents. Nuclear accidents have occurred in 1961 at an experimental reactor in Idaho Falls, Idaho; in 1966 at the Enrico Fermi experimental breeder reactor near Detroit, Michigan; in 1975 at the Browns Ferry reactor in Decatur, Alabama; in 1979 at the Three Mile Island reactor outside Harrisburg, Pennsylvania, and at the nuclear fuel plant near Erwin, Tennessee; in 1982 at the Ginna plant near Rochester, N.Y.; in 1985 at the Davis

Bessee plant near Oak Harbor, Ohio; and in 1986 at the Kerr-McGee plant at Gore, Oklahoma. In addition to specific incidences, radiation leaks have occurred over long periods of time, such as the 16 major leaks that occurred between 1958 and 1973 at a nuclear processing facility at Hanford, Washington (Moran et al. 1986). In 1985, the Sacramento Municipal Utility District, in California, admitted that for four years it had discharged cesium (a radioactive by-product of uranium fission) from its Rancho Seco nuclear power plant into a nearby creek, which eventually feeds into the Sacramento–San Joaquin River Delta. Representatives of the municipal utility district attributed the discharge to a "calculating error" and were "confident" that public health was not endangered. They did admit, however, that the level of radioactive wastewater was higher than the federal Nuclear Regulatory Commission's guidelines permit.

In 1985, the citizens of Florida learned that parts of their state had groundwater contaminated with radium—a result of the processing of phosphate deposits, which are often rich in uranium. Furthermore, medical researchers found a strong correlation within the state between areas with radium-tainted groundwater and above-average rates of leukemia. Although the researchers stopped short of making a cause-and-effect connection in the Florida study until further research is conducted, their study raised additional questions regarding the cleanliness of the nuclear industry.

Heat

The last major type of water pollution is *heat* or **thermal pollution**. This term refers to human activities that change the natural temperatures of water bodies, thereby disrupting the natural life processes of aquatic plants and animals. For example, the removal of overhanging trees and shrubs that shade streams can increase the annual maximum stream temperature from 14°C to 30°C (57°F to 86°F). Most researchers, however, use the term *thermal pollution* to refer to the discharge of water heat (warmer water) from power and industrial plants. A *thermal plume*, which is a zone of heated water mixing with cooler water, can often be found downstream from the industrial outfall of hot water.

Temperatures of a thermal plume generally range from 10°C to 20°C (50°F to 68°F) (Cutter et al. 1985), which is sufficient to cause a number of disruptions in aquatic ecosystems. For example, as water temperature increases, the amount of oxygen that can be dissolved in water *decreases*. Unfortunately, this occurs at the same time that fish, clams, oysters, and other aquatic organisms need more dissolved oxygen; that is, increased water temperatures mean increased body temperatures of these organisms that increase their respiration rates and their need for more dissolved oxygen. Obviously, having less dissolved oxygen at a time when more is needed places a great stress on aquatic organisms.

Thermal pollution can also cause a *disruption in reproduction*. Most fish are highly sensitive to changes in water temperature and a significant change may disrupt spawning cycles. For example, trout, northern pike, and walleye will not spawn at temperatures greater than 9°C (48.2°F) (Cutter et al. 1985). Heated water may also result in an *encroachment of undesirable organisms*. For example, many desirable game fish, which cannot tolerate warm waters, may be replaced with organisms that survive well in higher temperatures, such as carp and other undesirable species. As water temperatures increase, there is also a greater likelihood of *increased diseases* within aquatic organisms. For example, Owen (1985) notes that the bacteria *Chondroccus* can more easily penetrate the bodies of fish at temperatures greater than 15.5°C (60°F). As might be suspected, thermal pollution may also result in *changes in nutrient cycling*, resulting in the acceleration of the eutrophication process. (See the earlier section in the chapter on nutrient pollution.) *Thermal shock*, or direct mortality, is the final major consequence of thermal pollution. This occurs when there is a sudden warming of the water body when a power plant starts up abruptly, or a sudden cooling when it shuts down quickly. For example, Owen (1985) notes that lake trout will perish if temperatures go higher than 10°C (50°F).

Although many scientists see waste heat as a form of water pollution, others are beginning to see it as a new resource. The various possibilities of turning harmful thermal pollution into beneficial *thermal enrichment* will be discussed in the following chapter on water resource management.

CONCLUSION

Our nation's water problems are varied and complex. They include inadequate surface water supplies, the overdrafting of groundwater, flooding, sedimentation, and the pollution and degradation of drinking water. The multiplicity and complexity of these water problems present a major challenge to water resource managers. Finding solutions to these problems is not just an academic question, but one involving human survival itself.

DISCUSSION TOPICS

1. Check your morning newspaper and clip out those articles related to water resources. What water issues are paramount in your local community? In the nation? In the world?

2. How has water played an important role in the historical development of your region?

3. What is the hydrologic cycle? List and describe its five major components. From what component or reservoir does your community receive its water supply? Who are the biggest users of water in your region? Agriculture? Industry? Domestic users? Is water ever ''lost'' from this hydrologic cycle?

4. Make a diagram of the hydrologic cycle. With flow arrows, indicate how water gets to your faucet and back to the ocean. Discuss the many ways that you directly or indirectly use water every day. How are your community leaders presently trying to modify the hydrologic cycle for flood prevention or for increased water supply? Does your local utility company have hydrologic power plants?

5. Name several ways in which you see water being wasted in your community. Could water use be reduced without a major change in lifestyle? Debate this last question with fellow students.

6. How has development in your community altered the natural hydrologic cycle? In your opinion which forms of development were necessary? Which were not necessary? What effect has development in your community had on infiltration rates, stream flow, the frequency of flooding, streambank erosion, and sedimentation?

7. What is the average precipitation in your region? How do average precipitation figures for your city differ from nearby rural communities? Is average precipitation a good measure of the water actually available for human use?

8. What is rainshadow? Is there an example of a rainshadow effect near your local community? If so, can you observe a difference in human adjustment or adaptation to this phenomenon?

9. Discuss infiltration as it relates to interception, detention, and infiltration capacity. Pick three examples of city blocks and determine the percentage of paved surfaces. Obtain historical and present-day records of groundwater levels and discuss your conclusions regarding infiltration rates and urbanization.

10. What is the difference between evaporation, transpiration, evapotranspiration, and potential evapotranspiration? How do evaporation figures for your region differ from the figures for the nation as a whole? Is evaporation a serious problem in your region?

11. List and discuss the four major types of runoff. Discuss the relationship of runoff to surface topography and soil horizons.

12. Draw a diagram of the major components of the groundwater system, including the soil water belt, the zone of aeration, the capillary fringe, and the water table, and the zone of saturation. Identify aquifers and aquicludes and the location of the *true* groundwater.

13. Discuss the relationship between field capacity and wilting point.

14. Draw a diagram that illustrates a regular spring as compared with an artesion well. Using your diagram, discuss the necessary components of an artesian well.

15. What is the difference between a perched water table and a standard water table? Describe problems associated with drilling wells for groundwater.

16. Using a sheet of tracing paper or clear plastic, draw an overlay of the cultural hydrologic cycle on top of the natural hydrologic cycle. Using your diagram as an illustration, discuss the various ways that humans have altered the rate of precipitation, transpiration, evapotranspiration, infiltration, and runoff.

17. Why does a river ''own'' its floodplain? Has your city, or a city nearby, developed upon a floodplain? What have been the consequences of this development on the overall drainage system? On riverine ecology? On wildlife? On aesthetics?

18. Is there overexploitation of groundwater resources in your region? If so, how have water table levels changed in the last ten years? Who are the greatest users? Discuss the ecological, economic, and social problems that can occur with the continued ''mining'' of groundwater.

19. Is the groundwater in your region being polluted? If so, is it occurring from point or nonpoint sources or from both? Be specific.

20. Are there natural factors, such as rock or soil types, that contaminate groundwater in your region? Discuss the negative ramifications of each.

21. What types of pollutants still remain in your domestic wastewater *after* it passes through your local sewage treatment plant? In turn, where does this wastewater go and what negative effects might it cause in the environment?

22. Describe the various causes of ground subsidence. Be sure to describe the term *sinkhole*.

23. Discuss the relationship between biochemical oxygen demand (BOD) and dissolved oxygen content (DO) as they relate to a stream receiving organic wastes.

24. What is the difference between natural and cultural eutrophication? Using the aging of a lake as an example, discuss the terms *oligotrophic*, *mesotrophic*, and *eutrophic*. At what stage of eutrophication are the lakes in your region? Are they undergoing natural or cultural eutrophication? If cultural eutrophication is occurring, be specific as to the types of nutrients being added to the lakes.

25. Each state in the United States has regional character-

istics pertaining to major water issues (e.g., southern California has water shortages, central California has groundwater contamination, and northern California has flooding). What are the major regional water problems within your state?

26. What are the major organic chemical groundwater contaminates in your local region? Pesticides? Oil? PCBs? Industrial solvents? Be specific as to the type and its source.

27. Discuss organic chemicals in relationship to what we know about bioaccumulation.

28. Are your local streams, rivers, or bays being affected by thermal pollution? If so, has there been any evi-

dence in your area of general aquatic stress or actual fishkill?

29. Since the publication of this book, what new information have American and Soviet scientists learned about the surface and groundwater contamination around the site of the Chernobyl nuclear plant disaster? Is there any new evidence as to the distance traveled by its radioactive waters? What about the health effects of radioactive water in the region?

30. Debate the question: Is the nuclear industry (American or Soviet) as clean as if often claims to be in utility brochures and in television commercials? Relate your discussion to the issue of water quality.

READINGS

BERRY, BRIAN, and FRANK E. HORTAN. 1974. *Urban Environmental Management: Planning for Pollution Control.* Englewood Cliffs, N.J.: Prentice-Hall. A good resource management reference with emphasis on urban spatial analysis and interdisciplinary synthesis.

BOTKIN, DANIEL B., and EDWARD A. KELLER. 1982. *Environmental Studies: The Earth as a Living Planet.* Columbus, Ohio: Merrill. Basic introductory university textbook for environmental studies.

CHANGNON, S. A. 1968. "Recent Studies of Urban Effects on Precipitation in the United States." Paper presented at the W.M.O. Symposium on Urban Climates and Building Climatology, Brussels, Belgium.

CHIRAS, DANIEL D. 1985. *Environmental Science: A Framework for Decision Making.* Menlo Park, Calif.: Benjamin/Cummings. A basic university textbook in environmental studies that stresses a holistic overview of critical environmental issues. The book includes both a social science as well as a science perspective.

CHORLEY, R. J., ed. 1969. *Water, Earth, and Man.* London: Methuen. Classic water resource management textbook.

COATES, DONALD R. 1981. *Environmental Geology.* New York: Wiley. Excellent university textbook on the importance of geology to environmental issues.

COUNCIL ON ENVIRONMENTAL QUALITY. 1981. *Twelfth Annual Report.* Washington, D.C.: Government Printing Office.

CUTTER, SUSAN L., et al. 1985. *Exploitation, Conservation, Preservation: A Geographic Perspective on Natural Resource Use.* Totowa, N.J.: Rowman and Allanheld. A spatial approach to resource management.

DASMANN, RAYMOND F. 1984. *Environmental Conservation.* 5th ed. New York: Wiley. A widely read introductory textbook on conservation written by a well-known ecologist.

DEVEREL, STEVEN. 1985. "Selenium in the San Joaquin Valley of California." In *National Water Summary 1984.* USGS Water-Supply Paper 2275, pp. 45–46. Washington, D.C.: Government Printing Office. Excellent summary.

EIDMANN, F. E. 1959. "Die interception in buchen-und Fichtenbestanden." *C. R. Ass. Int. Hydrologie Sci. Hannover*

Symp., vol. 1, pp. 5–25. Good discussion of interception storage in West Germany.

GILLIOM, ROBERT J. 1985. "Pesticides in Rivers of the United States." In *National Water Summary 1984.* USGS Water-Supply Paper 2275, pp. 85–92. Washington, D.C.: Government Printing Office. Excellent summary.

GRIGG, NEIL S. 1985. *Water Resources Planning.* New York: McGraw-Hill. Water resources from a planning perspective.

GRIGGS, GARY B., and JOHN A. GILCHRIST. 1977. *The Earth and Land Use Planning.* North Scituate, Mass.: Duxbury Press. Excellent text on environmental geology.

HEATH, RALPH C. 1985. "Introduction to State Summaries of Ground-Water Resources." In *National Water Summary 1984.* USGS Water-Supply Paper 2275, pp. 118–121. Washington, D.C.: Government Printing Office.

KITAGISHI, K., and J. YAMANE, eds., 1981. *Heavy Metal Pollution in Soils of Japan.* Tokyo: Japan Science Society Press. Good summary.

KNEESE, ALLEN V. 1982. "Salinity in the Colorado River," *Resources,* July, no. 70, pp. 8–10. Interesting discussion of the negotiation between the United States and Mexico over the salinity problem of the Colorado River.

KORMONDY, EDWARD J. 1976. *Concepts of Ecology.* 2d ed. Englewood Cliffs, N.J.: Prentice-Hall. Good discussion of the role of transpiration in the hydrologic cycle. Basic ecology textbook.

LAKIN, H. W. 1973. "Selenium in our Environment." In E. L. Kothny, ed., *Trace Elements in the Environment,* pp. 76–111. Washington, D.C.: American Chemical Society, Advances in Chemistry Series 123. Good summary.

LEOPOLD, LUNA B. 1968. "Hydrology for Urban Land Planning—A Guidebook on the Hydrologic Effects of Urban Land Use." In *U.S. Geologic Survey Circular 554,* p. 5. Washington, D.C.: Government Printing Office. Includes good discussion of changing infiltration rates with urbanization.

LUNDGREN, LAWRENCE. 1986. *Environmental Geology.* Englewood Cliffs, N.J.: Prentice-Hall. Contains good chapter on water resources.

MATHER, JOHN R. 1984. *Water Resources: Distribution, Use and Management*. New York: Wiley. Detailed introductory textbook on water resource management, with an emphasis on the incorporation of concepts from physical, human, and cultural geography.

McKNIGHT, TOM L. 1987. *Physical Geography: A Landscape Appreciation*. 2d ed. Englewood Cliffs, N.J.: Prentice-Hall. Contains good chapters on the hydrosphere.

MEADE, ROBERT H., and RANDOLPH S. PARKER. 1985. "Sediment in Rivers of the United States." In *National Water Summary 1984*. USGS Water-Supply Paper 2275, pp. 49–60. Washington, D.C.: Government Printing Office. Excellent summary.

MILLER, G. TYLER. 1986. *Environmental Science: An Introduction*. Belmont, Calif.: Wadsworth. Basically Miller's *Living in the Environment* (1985) textbook minus the chapters on economics, politics, and ethics.

MILLER, G. TYLER. 1985. *Living in the Environment*. 4th ed. Belmont, Calif.: Wadsworth. Perhaps the best introductory textbook in environmental studies.

MORAN, JOSEPH M., MICHAEL D. MORGAN, and JAMES H. WIERSMA. 1986. *Introduction to Environmental Science*. 2d ed. New York: Freeman. Excellent general environmental science text, which stresses scientific principles and the natural functioning of the environment.

NATIONAL RESEARCH COUNCIL. 1977. *Drinking Water and Health*. Washington, D.C.: Government Printing Office. An important early report on U.S. water quality.

NATIONAL WILDLIFE FEDERATION. 1985. *Conservation News*, February 25, vol. 3, no. 2. A NWF newsletter.

NEBEL, BERNARD J. 1981. *Environmental Science: The Way the World Works*. Englewood Cliffs, N.J.: Prentice-Hall. Good chapter on human activities as they relate to the water cycle.

OWEN, OLIVER S. 1985. *Natural Resource Conservation: An Ecological Approach*. 4th ed. New York: Macmillan. Contains two good chapters on water resources from a biological perspective.

PARSON, RUBEN L. 1972. *Conserving American Resources*. 3d ed. Englewood Cliffs, N.J.: Prentice-Hall. Classic resource management text.

POSTEL, SANDRA. 1984. *Water: Rethinking Management in an Age of Scarcity*. Worldwatch Paper 62. Washington, D.C.: Worldwatch Institute. A global perspective on water problems and their management.

PRESSER, T. S., and IVAN BARNES. 1984. *Selenium Concentrations in Waters Tributary to and in the Vicinity of Kesterson National Wildlife Refuge, Fresno and Merced Counties, California*. U.S. Geological Survey Water Resources Investigations Report 84-4122. Washington, D.C.: U.S. Geological Survey. Scientific report on selenium concentrations in a California wildlife refuge.

SATTERLUND, D. R. 1972. *Wildland Watershed Management*. New York: Ronald Press. Key water resources text stressing the importance of proper watershed management.

SCHNEIDER, WILLIAM J., and JAMES E. GODDARD. 1973. "Extent and Development of Urban Floodplains." In *U.S. Geological Survey Circular 6001-J*, p. 12. Washington, D.C.: Government Printing Office. Good summary.

SOUTHWICK, CHARLES H. 1976. *Ecology and the Quality of Our Environment*. 2d ed. New York: Van Nostrand. Includes good discussion of dissolved oxygen content.

SPIRN, ANNE WHISTON. 1984. *The Granite Garden: Urban Nature and Human Design*. New York: Basic Books. A refreshing insight into the health of the city, from the perspective of a landscape architect and environmental planner.

STENOGL, RICHARD. 1982. "Ebbing of the Ogallala: The Great Watering Hole Beneath the Great Plains is Going Dry," *New York Times Magazine*, May 10, 1982, pp. 98–99. Interesting discussion of groundwater overdraft.

STRAHLER, ARTHUR N., and ALAN H. STRAHLER. 1973. *Environmental Geoscience: Interaction between Natural Systems and Man*. Santa Barbara, Calif.: Hamilton. Includes good chapter on the groundwater system.

STRAHLER, ARTHUR N., and ALAN H. STRAHLER. 1977. *Geography and Man's Environment*. New York: Wiley. Excellent physical geography textbook that interweaves environmental problems and issues with the principles of science.

STRAHLER, ARTHUR N., and ALAN H. STRAHLER. 1978. *Modern Physical Geography*. New York: Wiley. Includes good chapter on surface and groundwater.

TROEH, FREDERICK, et al. 1980. *Soil and Water Conservation for Productivity and Environmental Protection*. Englewood Cliffs, N.J.: Prentice-Hall. Detailed textbook on the subject.

U.S. BUREAU OF RECLAMATION. 1984. *Information on Kesterson and Waterfowl*. U.S. Bureau of Reclamation Information Bulletin No. 2. Washington, D.C.: Government Printing Office. Useful update on the problems at Kesterton.

U.S. GEOLOGICAL SURVEY. 1985. *National Water Summary 1984*. USGS Water-Supply Paper 2275. Washington, D.C.: Government Printing Office. Hydrologic events; selected water quality trends; groundwater resources.

VAN SICKLE, DONALD. 1969. "Experience with the Evaluation of Urban Effects for Drainage." In W. Moore and C. Morgan, eds., *Effects of Watershed Changes on Stream Flow*, pp. 229–254. Austin, Tex.: University of Texas Press. Interesting study of the effects of urbanization on stream discharge.

VIESSMAN, WARREN, JR., and CLAIRE WELTY. 1985. *Water Management: Technology and Institutions*. New York: Harper & Row. Engineering designs and objectives as they relate to human and environmental factors concerning water management.

WATER RESOURCES COUNCIL. 1978. *The Nation's Water Resources: 1975–2000*. Washington, D.C.: Government Printing Office. Important government document on U.S. water resources.

WIESNER, C. J. 1970. *Climate, Irrigation, and Agriculture*. Sydney, Australia: Angus and Robertson. Includes good statistics on infiltration rates.

WATER RESOURCE MANAGEMENT

Introduction
Major Water Management Methods
Prospects for the Future
Action for Water

I want to say to you, there is not sufficient water to supply these lands.

John Wesley Powell,
Nineteenth Century Explorer

INTRODUCTION

Chapter 4 described the water cycles that exist within nature and how humans have altered those systems. This chapter will focus on **water resource management,** that is, the various methods by which humans attempt to get the right amount and the right quality of water for a particular use at a particular time. We will begin by looking at the major methods for managing water resources. After evaluating these various techniques, and mentioning some real success stories in water management, we will conclude with several ways in which you can personally get involved in helping our nation better manage its water resources. Before proceeding, however, it is first necessary to understand the different types of water resource management and the major agencies that do the managing.

Major Subfields of Water Resource Management

There are three separate, but interrelated, subfields of water resource management: (1) watershed management, (2) floodplain management, and (3) groundwater management. In each case, resource managers attempt to plan *holistically* for the area in question.

Watershed Management. **Watershed management** deals primarily with a particular watershed—its use, regulation, and treatment of water. Its primary objective is to improve the ability of the land *to hold water in place.* Techniques for accomplishing this objective range from reforestation (including the reseeding of denuded areas), to the terracing of slopes, to altering farming techniques (e.g., promoting contour plowing, strip cropping, and the use of cover crops). For example, watershed managers have struggled for years to control stream discharge and flooding in the watershed of the Middle Colorado River in Texas.

Floodplain Management. By contrast, the floodplain is the focus of **floodplain management.** Here, resource managers try to develop a comprehensive plan for either the preservation of a floodplain in its natural state or the wise use of a developed floodplain. Management techniques include water control projects (e.g., dams, levees, channel modificatons), land treatment (to retain precipitation), land-use regulations, public open space acquisition, flood insurance, and the establishment of warning systems. Without adequate floodplain regulations, for example, the U.S. Water Resources Council (1978) estimates that by the year 2000 flood damage within our major cities could increase by 38 percent.

Groundwater Management. The third and final subfield of water resource management is **groundwater management.** Here, resource managers attempt to manage the quantity and quality of our nation's economically accessible groundwater resources. They deal with such problems as groundwater mining, saltwater intrusion, salinization, land subsidence, and groundwater contamination. Management techniques range from using wells, pumps, and irrigation systems to tap unused groundwater, to enforcing regulations regarding groundwater withdrawal, to constructing recharge ponds, to flushing contaminated aquifers (although the methods to do this are usually inadequate). Of the three subfields of water resource management, groundwater management is perhaps the most difficult. For example, cleaning up a contaminated groundwater aquifer is virtually impossible with current technology. The polluted water within that aquifer will remain unusable for hundreds to thousands of years.

Principal Managing Agencies

There are numerous federal agencies in the United States that deal with water resource management. Agencies that deal primarily with *water supply* are the U.S. Army Corps of Engineers (CE), the U.S. Bureau of Reclamation (USBR), the Soil Conservation Service (SCS), and the Tennessee Valley Authority (TVA). The federal agency that primarily handles *water quality* issues in the United States is the Environmental Protection Agency (EPA). In addition to those listed

above, there are a number of other federal agencies that are active in water resource planning, development, and management. For example, the U.S. Geological Survey (USGS) has gathered water data for the nation since 1888. In addition to maintaining a nationwide system of stream-gauging stations, it also has a nationwide system of surface water and groundwater quality sampling sites. The data gathered by USGS scientists are compiled for such uses as hydrologic appraisals, environmental impact assessments, and energy-related studies. Furthermore, to help organize water information for water resource managers, as well as to increase public understanding of the nature, geographic distribution, magnitude, and trends of the nation's water resources, the USGS has established the National Water Summary Program. As part of this program, the USGS produces annual reports on the status of water resources in this country.

Water agencies also exist at the state and local level. In California, for example, the California Department of Water Resources is the state's principal water agency. Its primary role is to conduct investigations, collect data, and provide advice and technical support to local agencies, such as to the Santa Clara Water District in Santa Clara Valley ("Silicon Valley"). Whereas the State Water Resources Control Board and nine regional boards establish and enforce standards for groundwater quality, the Department of Health Services actually monitors the quality of drinking water supplies. As with the other states, one of the major problems in water resource management in California is the lack of coordination (and often cooperation) between federal, state, and local agencies. Numerous examples will be provided as this chapter evolves.

MAJOR WATER MANAGEMENT METHODS

Water management methods usually fall within one of two categories: structural methods or nonstructural methods (Table 5-1). *Structural methods*, commonly referred to as the "hard path," are generally associated with large engineering projects, such as dams, canals, and irrigation systems. These highly capital-intensive constructions generally have a wide range of environmental impacts. By contrast, *nonstructural methods*, the so-called "soft path," emphasize designing social, cultural, economic, legal, and even biological techniques for proper water management. Examples under this category include environmental education media projects to encourage volun-

TABLE 5-1

Major methods for managing water resources

METHOD	PRIMARY PURPOSE
Structural methods	
Dams	To create lake reservoirs for water storage, hydropower, recreation, and flood control
Interbasin transfers	To transport water from one region to another
Channelization	To improve river flow and minimize flooding
Recharge ponds	To recharge (augment) or replace groundwater supplies
Desalination plants	To desalt brackish water and seawater
Water harvesting	To collect all possible water that falls as rain on an area
Wastewater treatment plants	To partially cleanse water before returning it to the sea
Nonstructural methods	
Nonstructural approaches to wastewater treatment, such as the use of aquaculture or wastewater renovation and conservation cycle	To partially cleanse water in a more natural way—a way that uses nature's own cleansing mechanisms
Conservation	To redesign the farm, industry, and the home so that they use less water and are more efficient
Weather modification	To alter weather systems to bring precipitation to water shortage regions
Towing icebergs	To transport freshwater icebergs from the Antarctic to arid regions

tary water conservation, the creation of economic incentives to encourage wastewater recycling, and compulsory water conservation when necessary. A discussion of the advantages and disadvantages of the different types of water management methods follows.

Structural Methods

Dams. Perhaps the most controversial structural method of water resource management is the construction of dams. For almost every advantage, there are at least two or three disadvantages (Table 5-2). Yet, this country has long favored this method of managing water resources. In 1981, the United States had 49,422 large dams, of which 1400 impounded major reservoirs (Coates 1981). Although the construction of dams is steeped in controversy, Coates further notes that dams continue to be constructed at a rate of five each day, many of which are for private real estate developers. Most of the larger dams are of two major types—gravity dams or arch dams. Whereas gravity dams rely principally on their weight to hold back the impounded water, arch dams depend primarily on cantilever action to withstand the water pressure. Of the two types, gravity dams

are more common since only they can span wide streams.

One obvious benefit of dams and reservoirs is *water storage*. Dams collect precipitation and runoff during wet periods and store it for drier periods, thereby allowing a steady, dependable source of water for agriculture, industries, and municipalities. Consequently, dams allow more lands to be farmed, more industries to grow, and urban and rural populations to increase.

With water storage, however, comes a number of drawbacks. In drought-prone areas, for example, water storage creates a false sense of security about the abundance of water that leads to overdependency on the water storage and wastefulness of water resources. There are *limitations to the size of reservoirs*, and the water stored is equivalent only to the total river flow during the time it takes to fill the reservoir. If demand is high, this supply may only last a few years. With water storage also comes another negative drawback: *back seepage*. Lake Powell, Utah, for example, is a reservoir notorious for the amount of water that is lost along the banks through seepage. Even greater amounts of water are lost from reservoirs through *evaporation*. The reservoir behind Egypt's Aswan Dam annually looses 10 percent of its total water

TABLE 5-2
Dams: advantages and disadvantages

ADVANTAGES	DISADVANTAGES
Water storage	Limitations to the size of reservoirs
	Bank seepage
	Evaporation
	Breeding ground for diseases
	Raised water table levels
	Salt buildup
Flood control	Encourages development below dams
	Siltation
	Eliminates floodwaters that fertilize downstream agricultural fields
	Loss of sand from beaches
Power production	High capital investment
Improved navigation	Inhibits spawning migrations
	Loss of wild rivers
	Death or changes in river organisms
	Saltwater intrusion at river mouths
	Destruction of wilderness and open space
	Loss of wildlife and wildlife habitats
Job opportunities	Displacement of people from their homelands
	Cultural disruption
National pride	Self-perpetuating feedback cycle

supply to evaporation (Chiras 1985). In the dry American Southwest, evaporation can account for the loss of the top 3 m (10 ft) of reservoir levels (Coates 1981). Lake Mead, on the Nevada-Arizona border, for example annually losses 2 m (7 ft) to evaporation. Owen (1985) also notes that of the 1250 large western reservoirs in the United States, 6 million acre-feet are lost each year, which represents enough water to supply the domestic needs of 50 million people for one year. Evapotranspiration from vegetation on the edges of reservoirs also accounts for water losses. Of the inflow into a reservoir, 1 percent is lost to seepage, 2 to 20 percent is lost to transpiration (5 percent is the average), and 2 to 3 percent is lost by evaporation directly from the reservoir's surface (Mather 1984). Consequently, the general average loss is 8 percent, though it can reach as high as 25 percent. Techniques exist for minimizing evaporation from reservoir surface waters, such as putting a film of hexadecanol over the surface, but such practices are often costly, labor intensive, and ecologically damaging to aquatic organisms and wildlife.

Stored water also provides a *breeding ground for diseases*. For example, Walton (1981) notes that the construction of the Kariba Dam on the Zambezi River in Africa resulted in a 58 percent increase in the incidences of schistosomiasis—a debilitating, sometimes fatal, disease carried by snails. The snails require a constant supply of water; a requirement met by the creation of a reservoir. Although the construction of

the Aswan High Dam in Egypt has yet to cause the 60 percent increase in the incidence of schistosomiasis as originally predicted by some researchers, schistosomiasis remains a very serious problem in the region. Roundworm (*Ascaris*), hookworm (*Ancylostoma*), and amoebas (*Entamoebas*) that cause dysentery are other common intestinal parasites that are transmitted via stored water (Walton 1981).

Water stored within reservoirs can also lead to *raised water table levels* to the point that adjacent land is susceptible to *salt buildup*, which can seriously affect soil fertility. This is particularly a problem in areas where the water table is naturally high—such as in the Nile Delta region (Walton 1981). Countermeasures, such as pumping groundwater to lower the water table or installing tile drains in irrigated areas, are expensive. Scientists also maintain that even the sheer weight of the water in a reservoir is great enough to cause possibly adverse geologic effects, such as landslides and even earthquakes.

On the more positive side, however, dams are helpful in *flood control* by storing excess water during rainy periods and gradually releasing water during periods of drought. According to Cutter and her associates (1985), floods account for more property damage in the United States than any other hazard, with annual damages in the billions. Dams are only one technique, however, for controlling flood waters. Protecting the watershed—that vegetational "sponge" that restrains the downhill rush of water—

is an extremely effective technique. Periodic dredging of sediment from channels, thus keeping them free and clear for easy water flow, also decreases the probability of flood occurrence. Although the construction of levees (dikes constructed of stone, mortar, earth, or sand bags) can temporarily prevent flooding, it can also lead to more devastating flood damage at a later date. Furthermore, this traditional structural approach—the building of more and more dams, levees, and the dredging of channels—also exacerbates the problem of causing faster and more devastating floods downstream (Mather 1984).

However, there are "softer paths" or nonstructural approaches to flood control, such as using land-use zoning regulations to keep cities from building on floodplains, using floodproofing techniques for buildings and homes, purchasing flood insurance, planning evacuation and relocation procedures, and installing various warning systems. Citizens, for example, can be warned that they live in a flood-prone area, and be instructed to take the necessary precautions. Just as meteorologists attempt to predict the likelihood of an advancing tornado for the purpose of providing advance warning to affected residents, the U.S. Geological Survey now sends out surveyors to measure the extent of snowpack in many western mountains for the specific purpose of predicting possible flood occurrence.

While dams are often built and defended for their ability to control floods, dams, like levees, can give a false sense of security that *encourages development below dams*, often on floodplains. Using dams for flood control or prevention is also only a temporary measure since all dams eventually "die" from *siltation*. As the reservoir above the dam traps the sediment carried by rivers, its storage capacity is gradually reduced, and eventually the river creates a waterfall over the dam, thereby reclaiming its right to flow unhampered. On the Indus River in Pakistan, the Tarbela Dam was completed in 1975 and was reported to be the world's largest earth and rockfill dam. Because of upstream soil erosion, however, engineers now estimate that this $1.3 billion project that took nine years to build could be filled with sediment and rendered useless within 20 years (Chiras 1985). In Columbia, the Anchicaya Dam was completed in 1955, yet 21 months later it was 25 percent filled with sediment (Coates 1981). In the United States, over 2000 reservoirs are clogged with sediment (Chiras 1985), and according to a 1941 study, 39 percent of the nation's reservoirs have less than a 50-year life (Coates 1981). California's Mono Reservoir, for example, was constructed to be a permanent source of water for Santa Barbara. Within only 20 years, the reservoir filled with sediment (Owen 1985). A system of sediment traps to filter out sediment before it reaches the main reservoir, such as exists at Imperial Dam on the lower Colorado River, is one means to try to minimize the problem of sediment buildup, but the system is costly, as is the continual dredging of the reservoir itself.

Also on the minus side, dams *eliminate floodwaters that fertilize downstream agricultural fields*. For example, the reservoir behind Aswan Dam now traps 13 million m^3 of nutrient-rich sediment that Egyptian farmers had depended on for more than 5000 years to fertilize their fields. According to Coates (1981), the trapped silt had supplied about 22 percent of the needed plant nutrients to the floodplain and delta region, which must now be supplied by 2 million tons annually of synthetic fertilizers, which are costly, energy inefficient, and ecologically harmful. Since many coastal areas are dependent upon sand nourishment from rivers, dams also cause a *loss of sand from beaches*, which often leads to intensified shoreline erosion (Figure 5-1). For example, numerous dams have been built on the Brazos River in Texas, resulting in a 71 percent decrease in the suspended load of the river. The sand discharge at the coast where the river empties into the Gulf of Mexico is five to nine times less than was normal (without impoundment) (Coates 1981). Lowered sediment discharges is a particular problem in the coastal states of California, Oregon, and Washington, where it has intensified problems in beach erosion.

Power production, of course, is a major benefit of hydroelectric dams. Ever since the world's first hydroelectic power plant was built in Appleton, Wisconsin, in 1882, people have recognized hydroelectric dams as a technique for energy production based on a renewable resource (flowing water) and a technique that does not create air or water pollution. In the United States today, hydropower accounts for approximately 14 percent of the nation's electrical capacity (Viessman and Welty 1985). Since the energy crisis of the 1970s, there has been a renewed interest in this non–fuel-consuming, nonpolluting form of energy production; in particular there has been interest in the constructon of small hydropower units on minor rivers and tributaries. Hydropower, however, has its drawbacks. The larger dams require *high capital investment*, and their overall economic benefits are a hotly debated issue. During the Carter administration, for example, one proposal called for a Hillsdale Dam in Kansas, costing an estimated $55.7 million. The proposed project was intended to protect 2800 ha (6919 acres) of farmland from flooding, but the same reservoir would have flooded 5600 ha (13,837 acres)

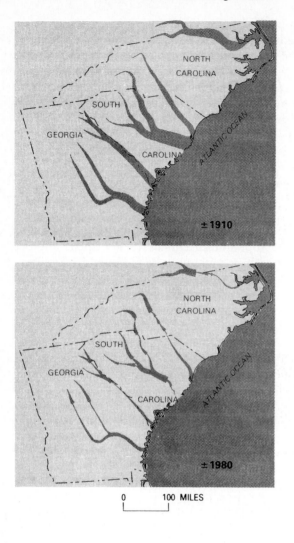

EXPLANATION

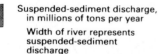

Suspended-sediment discharge,
in millions of tons per year

Width of river represents
suspended-sediment
discharge

FIGURE 5-1 Average suspended-sediment discharges of major rivers in Georgia and the Carolinas during two periods, about 1910 and about 1980. (From U.S. Geological Survey, *National Water Summary 1984: Hydrologic Events, Selected Water-Quality Trends and Groundwater Resources,* U.S. Geological Survey Water-Supply Paper 2275, 1985, p. 56.)

of already productive upstream farmlands (Coates 1981). Although this project was eventually dropped, the history of water development in this country is riddled with water projects with questionable economic benefits.

Our nation's rivers have long been used as transportation links between places, and one can often hear the claim that dams provide *improved navigation.* In some cases, this is true, such as on the Missouri River where releases from reservoirs are purposely made for the maintenance of navigation. In most cases, however, water does not have to be released from reservoirs to maintain navigation (Mather 1984). Mather does admit, however, that releases from reservoirs for other purposes will naturally help navigation during periods of low flow. Of course, if you happen to be a *fish,* your navigation has not been improved, since dams often *inhibit spawning migrations* for fish, such as salmon. Although fish ladders are sometimes constructed to theoretically enable fish to cross dams and continue on their migration path, the ladders are far from 100 percent effective. Navigation also is not improved for the whitewater rafter. The *loss of wild rivers* is a negative consequence of dams, destroying opportunities for such river recreation as wilderness rafting, kayaking, and canoeing. Interest in preserving our nation's wild rivers is increasing, particularly since Congress passed in 1968 the Wild and Scenic Rivers Act to protect the last vestiges of wild rivers in this country. New dam projects always bring out the special interest groups, as was seen in the battle over the inclusion of the Tuolumne River, which drains part of the Sierra Nevada Mountains in central California. (See Chapter 10 for further details on the Tuolumne River controversy.) In 1986, the nation's environmentalists cheered the decision of Maine's Great Northern Paper Company to abandon plans for construction of the so-called Big A dam on the scenic West Branch of the Penobscot River. According to the National Wildlife Federation, the Natural Resources Council of Maine, and other conservation groups, the project would have destroyed not only a unique landlocked salmon fishery, but also a popular scenic gorge and the most challenging stretch of whitewater for rafters in the Northeast.

Stabilizing river flow, whether for flood control, hydropower production, or improved navigation, also brings about a number of ecological changes within the river, sometimes resulting in *changes in river organisms or in their death.* Water from reservoirs is altered in a number of ways; pH levels, levels of dissolved solids, and water temperature may be changed. For example, the construction of the Aswan Dam in Egypt resulted in a reduction in algal growth at the mouth of the Nile, which in turn, effectively killed off the country's sardine fishing industry. With the food web altered, the sardines simply changed their migration patterns. According to Chiras (1985), Egypt's annual sardine catch dropped from 16,000 metric tons (18,000 tons) to 450 metric tons (500 tons).

In the United States, the snail darter (a member of the perch family) was severely affected by the construction of the TVA's Tellico Dam. (See Chapter 8 for further details on the snail darter story.)

Estuaries are particularly vulnerable to ecological changes resulting from dam construction. Estuaries are zones at a river's mouth where freshwater and salt water mix. Aquatic organisms are "highly salt sensitive," meaning that they are adapted to particular salt concentrations within the estuary. When humans restrict the natural river flow with their dams and associated reservoirs, salt water intrudes farther up the river mouth, altering the entire estuary ecosystem. For example, reduced freshwater flow from the heavily impounded Colorado River is altering the estuarine ecosystems of the entire northern end of the Gulf of California (Nebel 1981). Consequently *saltwater intrusion at river mouths* is another negative aspect of dams.

In addition to the advantages of providing a dependable water reserve, hydroelectric power, and improved navigation, dams and reservoirs can be a new source of water recreation, ranging from power boating and water skiing, to sailing, to freshwater fishing. However, there are several tradeoffs. Not only are other forms of water recreation minimized or eliminated (e.g., whitewater rafting, kayaking, or wilderness canoeing), but there is a general *destruction of wilderness and open space.* Cutter and associates (1985) estimate that nearly 8 million ha (19 million acres) of U.S. land are now covered with reservoirs and regulated lakes. Although some of this area was under water before reservoir development (e.g., a stream channel), most of it was forest lands, wetlands, and other forms of open space that were available for recreation. Perhaps the two most famous examples of inundated open space due to dams are the O'Shaughnessy (Hetch Hetchy) Dam (Figure 5-2) in Yosemite National Park, which inundated what John Muir and others labeled a "Little Yosemite," and Glen Canyon Dam in Arizona, which inundated a portion of the Colorado River considered by many to be as spectacular as the Grand Canyon. Environmentalists argued that untold opportunities for solitude and other wilderness experiences (the soft path) were traded off for power boats and jet skis—the energy consuming, air- and water-polluting hard path. (See Chapter 10 for further details on recreation.)

Accompanying the loss of wilderness and open space is a *loss of wildlife and wildlife habitats.* Certain wildlife species only exist in particular habitats, and, if these areas are inundated with water, the animals either migrate to adjacent territories where they must compete with other animals or they die. For example,

FIGURE 5-2 O'Shaughnessy Dam and Reservoir in Hetch Hetchy Valley, California—the damming of John Muir's "Little Yosemite." (Photo by author.)

reservoirs often destroy the habitat of bighorn sheep, black bear, and other animals. Chiras (1985) notes that wildlife biologists predict that 50 percent of the bighorn sheep in the region of one dam in Waterton Canyon near Denver, Colorado, will eventually perish. (See Chapter 8 for further details on animal territoriality and migration.)

Although dam construction certainly provides increased *job opportunities* for some, others not only lose their jobs but also their homes and patterns of livelihood. In addition to inundating wilderness areas and wildlife habitat, reservoirs often inundate farmlands, villages, and even entire towns, resulting in a *displacement of people from their homelands.* For example, Pakistan's Tarbela Dam displaced 85,000 people (Chiras 1985), Ivory Coast's Kossov Dam created 80,000 refugees, and Egypt's Aswan Dam displaced 100,000, as did the Lake Volta Dam in Ghana (Coates 1981). Of the 100,000 people who lost their jobs and became refugees as a result of Egypt's Aswan Dam, 45,000 were Nubian villagers—a culturally distinct Negroid people who have lived along the Nile River for centuries. According to Walton (1981), this is not the first time that the Nubians have experienced *cultural disruption* or changes in their patterns of livelihood. Their cultural ways were significantly disrupted with the first Aswan Dam built in 1902, its razing in 1912, and its reconstruction again in 1932.

Finally, a generally unspoken reason for contructing a dam (especially a giant-sized one) is for *national pride.* Many political leaders like to leave "monuments" to their presence in office. For example, what better monument for President Hoover than a 221 m (726 ft) high, 6.5-million ton concrete superdam that can control rivers, prevent flooding, and provide irrigation water and cheap electrical power to thousands of people? And if Hoover Dam's impounded river creates the largest reservoir in the world, Lake Mead, what could be a better symbol of a country's power? Just as corporations like to build the tallest building within a city to boost the corporate image, presidents, governors, and various legislators like to build superdams to boost state and national pride.

In 1985, the Chinese government, aided by the U.S. Bureau of Reclamation, announced plans to construct the largest hydroelectric project in history. The proposed Three Gorges Dam would be located on the Yangtze River, standing nearly twice as tall as Egypt's Aswan Dam and having six times more generating capacity. The project would force the resettlement of 2 million people and destroy 40,470 ha (100,000 acres) of farmland in the world's most populous and agriculturally productive river basin. Wildlife biologists predict that endangered species, such as the Yangtze crocodile and the Chinese sturgeon, would be threatened. For the above reasons and more, there is strong opposition to this proposal by both American and Chinese scientists and environmentalists. Even if analysis shows that less expensive, less harmful, and better alternatives are available, the political reason for the dam may prevail. With all the drawbacks to dam construction, one wonders if there are not more culturally, economically, and ecologically acceptable ways of obtaining national pride and world recognition.

If the Three Gorges Dam is built, it will only be the beginning of a *self-perpetuating feedback cycle*. Every dam built requires the construction of additional dams, either upstream or downstream, to counter the negative consequences of the original dam. It is somewhat analogous to the vicious cycle of the nuclear arms race: If one country builds more arms, its adversary must counter with more arms; if one dam is built, engineers must counter the negative effects of the first by building a second. The history of the damming of the Colorado River is a case in point. The process began in the 1930s when engineers built the first major "control" on the Colorado River: Hoover Dam. Ever since then, dam after dam has been constructed on the river, partially for the purpose of correcting the negative ramifications of the first dam. Dams now obstruct much of the river's 2414 km (1500 mi) course (Figure 5-3). In 1983, former Department of Interior Secretary James Watt claimed that the Glen Canyon Dam had tamed the waters of the Colorado. Within days, however, the river refuted Watt's remarks, resulting in the awesome Colorado River flood of 1983 (Morris 1985).

In summation, dam construction projects present a difficult human dilemma in which numerous positive benefits are pitted against a multitude of negative effects. It must be remembered that Hoover Dam, for example, generates nearly 2.5 million kilowatt hours of electricity each year, provides billions of dollars of utility-derived revenues for the federal government, and allows restaurants in New York City to serve lettuce watered by Rocky Mountain snowmelt, the lettuce having been grown on the floor of the Great American Desert. In the 1980s, at the same time that there was growing anti–dam-building sentiment among the general public (Viessman and Welty 1985), the Reagan administration was calling for nine new dam-building starts, including the controversial Randleman Dam in North Carolina and the Strube Dam in Oregon. Environmentalists are asking: Are these projects the best alternative methods available for water resource development, or are they merely outmoded approaches and more water works boondoggles? Furthermore, can this country ecologically afford to grow lettuce and other crops in deserts and other drought-prone areas?

Interbasin Transfers. Structural methods of water resource management often associated with dams are *interbasin transfers*, or *interbasin diversions*. **Interbasin transfers** are structures (canals, aqueducts, or giant pipes) that transfer water from one drainage basin to another. In some cases water is transferred to arid rural areas that require irrigation for agriculture. By 1977, for example, the United States had 314 irrigation canals with a combined total length of approximately 9656 km (6000 mi) (Bureau of Reclamation 1977). In other cases, water is transferred to cities (e.g., Los Angeles, Phoenix, Denver, and New York) for growing domestic consumption. In almost all cases, the interbasin transfer projects are highly controversial and are often condemned on environmental grounds.

The United States has been dependent for years on interbasin transfer projects. For example, California has long been victimized by water shortages and has historically used interbasin transfer projects to at least partially solve its water problems. California's Owens Valley Project was one of the earliest large scale interbasin transfer projects in the United States. Its eventual outcome produced an aqueduct that transported water from Owens Valley on the eastern side of the Sierra Nevada mountains to the former desert region called Los Angeles. In 1924, the city of San Francisco won its battle against John Muir, the preservationist who wanted to prevent the flooding of Hetch Hetchy Canyon in Yosemite National Park.

FIGURE 5-3 The damming of the Colorado River. (From Roger Morris, ''It was a Dam Disaster,'' *National Wildlife,* October–November 1985, p. 47.)

With the approval of the Hetch Hechy Project, John Muir's ''Little Yosemite'' was flooded, and an aqueduct was built to transfer the impounded water to San Francisco.

In addition to projects that provide a specific city with additional water supplies, interbasin transfers have been designed in California to transport water from northern California to numerous cities and farmlands in central and southern California. The California Water Project (CWP), sometimes called the State Water Project (SWP), is such an interbasin transfer scheme. It is reported to be the most complex and expensive interbasin transfer project in the world; it includes 1102 km (685 mi) of canals and pipelines that are connected to 21 dams and 22 pumping stations (Owen 1985). Although its aim is hydropower production, flood control, recreational facilities, and irrigation, its primary function is the latter—supplying irrigation water to farmlands in the San Joaquin Valley and to southern California. Despite numerous benefits, particularly irrigation and power production, critics often cite the state's associated losses in scenic beauty, wild rivers, and fish and wildlife habitat.

There are existing interbasin projects in other states as well. In Colorado, for example, Mather (1984) notes that interbasin transfers bring more than 50 percent of Denver's water supply from watersheds on the western slopes of the Rocky Mountains. He also notes that interbasin transfers are not just confined to the drier portions of the country. New York, for example, receives over 50 percent of its total water supply via an interbasin transfer from the Delaware River, over the continual objections of the State of New Jersey.

In 1985, the Central Arizona Project was scheduled to be completed. Though not truly an interbasin transfer, this similarly massive and expensive water diversion scheme is intended to take water from the lower Colorado River basin (at Parker Dam) and pump it 400 km (249 mi) horizontally and 600 m (1969 ft) vertically to the rapidly expanding urban and rural communities around Tucson and Phoenix (Cutter et al. 1985). Perhaps the most controversial aspect of this project is that it is taking water away from the Colorado River—water that has been already allocated for use elsewhere. Once the Central Arizona Project is fully completed, Los Angeles and other cities in southern California that currently use Colorado River water will have to withdraw less water from the Colorado River.

One of the most controversial projects currently under construction is the Garrison Diversion Irrigation Project in North Dakota. Although the project was originally authorized in 1944 to channel Missouri River water to irrigate 101,175 ha (250,000 acres) of North Dakota farmland, as of 1984 the project was only 25 percent complete. Critics have delayed the process, contending that the massive $1.3 billion project would drain or flood some 28,329 ha (70,000 acres) of prime waterfowl breeding grounds with its latticework of canals and irrigation works. The project has even angered the Canadian government, since excess irrigation water would return to Canada via the Red River of the North, which flows into Manitoba's Lake Winnipeg and eventually into Hudson Bay. The Canadian government fears that water from this project, with its pollution and unwanted species of fish, could threaten Manitoba's multimillion-dollar fishing industry. In 1986, after years of negotiation, an historic compromise was made between North Dakota officials and environmental groups that led

House and Senate negotiators to approve a scaled-down version of the project. In brief, the compromise plan (1) cuts by half the number of acres to be irrigated, (2) requires the U.S. Bureau of Reclamation to restore or protect an acre of wildlife habitat for every acre destroyed, and (3) authorizes construction, with federal aid, of water supply facilities to help meet the area's water needs.

Interbasin transfers are also used to get rid of excess water. In June 1986, for example, the rising Great Salt Lake in Utah burst an earthen dike and threatened to surge toward an interstate highway and Union Pacific Railroad tracks. It was the consequence of the previous four winters in which rainfall and snowfall had been more than twice as much as usual, adding 3.7 m (12 ft) to the lake's depth. By 1986, the lake sprawled across the desert, growing from 404,700 ha (1 million acres) in 1982 to 607,050 ha (1.5 million acres) in 1986. Local citizens described the lake as "a bathtub with a dripping faucet and no drain," since its only outlet is evaporation. This also explains why excess water in Great Salt Lake cannot be used for other purposes—it is simply too salty. After eons of stagnation, the lake, which ranges from 5 percent to 15 percent salinity, is saltier than the ocean, which is 3.5 percent salt. To cope with this seemingly unusable water, Utah officials designed The Great Salt Lake Project—a $55 million scheme to create a 1295 km^2 (500 mi^2) lake, which would be bigger than San Francisco Bay. The plan calls for a newly constructed pumping station to hoist the excess lake water into a new 7.2 km (4.5 mi) canal that will transfer the water 48 km (30 mi) to a nearly flat plain known as the West Desert, which is currently used only as a military bombing range. Here the water will theoretically spread into a huge, shallow lake. According to project engineers, Utah's "Second Great Salt Lake" will be 2.1 m (7 ft) deep at its greatest depth, 80 km (50 mi) long, and 16 km (10 mi) wide. Despite its immense size (one-fifth the size of Great Salt Lake), engineers predict the newly created lake would only reduce the level of Great Salt Lake by 33 cm (13 in.) the first year (as it is filling), and by just 18 cm (7 in.) of any excess Great Salt Lake water that accumulates in each additional year. In theory, the water of the newly created lake is supposed to evaporate at a faster rate than the rate of inflow will add water to the new lake.

Some day water diversion projects may even be used to help many nations deal with the projected global rise in sea level. According to a 1986 National Wildlife Federation report, two New York city professors of geology maintain, for example, that it might be easier and less costly to divert rising seawaters to inland seas and other natural basins, such as the Rocky Mountain Trench in the Canadian Rockies, than to hold back the sea from coastal areas. However, these same scientists also note that surface storage space would probably run out by the middle of the next century, forcing areas to turn to alternative disposal methods, such as subsurface storage or the conversion of seawater into hydrogen fuel.

In addition to the many existing interbasin transfers, as well as those that are currently under construction, there are also many "dreams" of giant-sized water diversion projects, such as the Ogallala

Project. As mentioned in the previous chapter, the enormous Ogallala aquifer in the High Plains states is rapidly being depleted. To help solve this problem, the Army Corps of Engineers has proposed building four separate canals to transfer water from several rivers in the east to the High Plains states (Figure 5-4). The Army Corps of Engineers calculates the cost of the transferred water to be $320 to $880 per acre-foot at projected energy prices (High Plains Associates 1982). According to Allen V. Kneese (1984), senior fellow in Resources for the Future's Quality of the Environment Division, these costs only include the

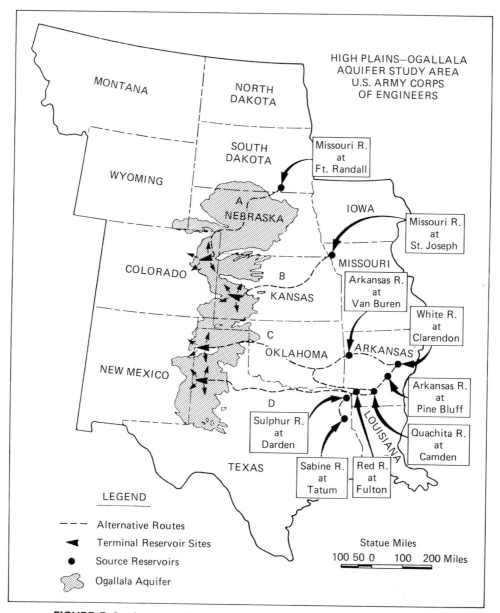

FIGURE 5-4 A water diversion scheme by the U.S. Army Corps of Engineers to save the Ogallala aquifer. (From Allen V. Kneese, "High Plains, Low Water," *Resources*, Fall 1984, p. 9.)

cost of bringing water to a terminal storage reservoir. If distribution costs were included, the actual price of the water per acre foot might double, costing nearly 10 times the amount that farmers in the area currently pay to irrigate their fields. Why would local farmers even consider a scheme that they could not possibly afford? According to Kneese, the answer is that they do not believe they would really have to end up paying for the water; that is, someone else would pick up the bill. In addition to what Kneese and others consider to be outrageous monetary costs, there is a tremendous environmental impact of such a project.

One of the most grandiose interbasin transfer schemes was proposed by the Ralph M. Parsons Company in 1964. This staggering transfer scheme, known as the North American Water and Power Alliance (NAWAPA), calls for the transfer of surplus water from Alaskan and Canadian rivers to other regions within Canada, to 33 states in the United States, to the Great Lakes region, and to three states in Mexico. This $100 billion plus project would require a dam taller than the Empire State Building, 15 reservoirs that would be larger than Lake Mead behind Hoover Dam, one water storage area 16 times greater than Lake Mead, many other facilities, and up to 20 years of construction time. As one can imagine, there would be a tangled web of interstate, federal-state, and international regulations to satisfy. Environmentalists would be up in arms, since the project would flood miles of pristine wilderness, crucial wildlife habitats, and prime agricultural soils. Mather (1984) makes the interesting observation that such a gargantuan project just might trap us into a form of hydraulic civilization as theorized by K. A. Wittfogel in his well-known article, ''The Hydraulic Civilizations'' (Wittfogel 1956). With tremendous amounts of money and labor locked into the system in order to keep it operating, Mather concludes that we may end up with some of the same consequences as experienced by China, India, Egypt, and other great hydraulic civilizations of the past.

The Soviet Union is also proposing similar grandiose interbasin transfer plans, in this case to *reverse* the direction of its northern rivers so that they would flow southward through parched farmland in the southern Soviet Union. According to the Soviets, their Soviet River Diversion Project is a multibillion-dollar scheme to correct what they refer to as the ''blunders of nature''—that only 16 percent of the annual flow of the country's rivers goes to the southern and central areas, where 85 percent of the population is concentrated and where 80 percent of the industrial production takes place (Figure 5-5). Specifically, the project has two stages: (1) The Volga Plan, and (2)

The Siberian Plan. The Volga Plan, which some believe is already under construction, is intended to annually divert 5.8 cubic kilometers of water from Sukhona River and Lacha, Vozhe, and Kubenskoye lakes, by means of canals, pumping stations, and channels into the Sheksna River, then into a reservoir, and eventually into the Volga River. The project, which is expected to be completed in 1990, is supposed to supply water for new irrigation projects in southern Russia, in the Ukraine, in the Caucasus, and in Moldavia. Consequently, the plan would affect only the European part of the Soviet Union.

The Siberian Plan, the more ambitious second stage, would divert rivers from northern Siberia to Soviet Central Asia and Kazakhstan. The plan is a massive scheme designed to annually divert 27 cubic kilometers of water from the Ob and Irtysh rivers in the north, via a 2414 km (1500 mi) canal, to the Aral Sea in the south. This $100 billion plus project would entail building 25 large dams and an untold number of channels and pumping stations, and it would take a half century to build. In theory, it would transfer enough water to irrigate an area larger than the state of California. On the negative side, entire villages and towns in the north would be inundated with water, thereby displacing tens of thousands of people.

Aside from the social and economic costs, scientists are concerned about the possible negative environmental consequences of these projects. Will this massive rechanneling of water alter the climate and ecosytsems of Siberia and Central Asia? Since the infusion of freshwater from Siberia's rivers builds up the polar icecap, will the deprivation of this freshwater cause the polar icecap to recede, thereby affecting the entire weather pattern of the Northern Hemisphere? Or, as some have theorized, will the river diversion scheme actually reduce rainfall in parts of the Soviet Union, which would be an ironic outcome of the water diversion scheme? And, of course, there are also questions about the effects of altering the salinity of the Baltic Sea into which the northern rivers presently drain, and about the effects of tampering with the ecology of the Azov and Caspian seas. Most certainly fisheries and the Soviet fishing industries will be affected. Like the United States' proposed NAWAPA project, this project will be a difficult beast to manage or to kill once it is operative. As more and more nations move in the direction of constructing these massive water schemes, there may be a rise in the number of Wittfogel's hydraulic civilizations!

Channelization. A third structural method of water resource management, and one that is also highly controversial, is **channelization**—the mechan-

PRESENT

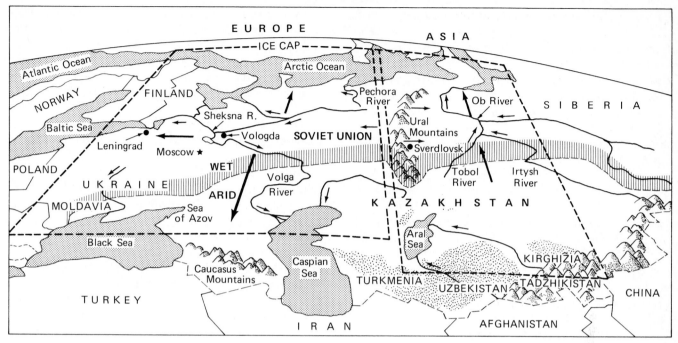

(b)

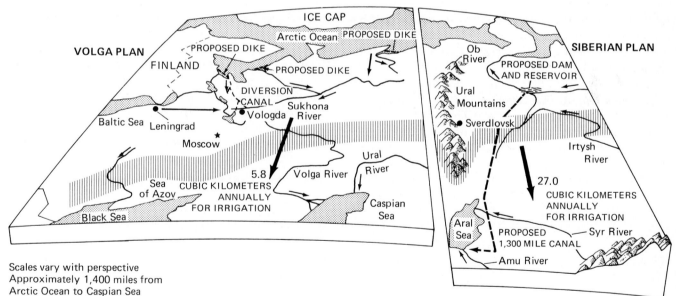

Scales vary with perspective
Approximately 1,400 miles from
Arctic Ocean to Caspian Sea

FIGURE 5-5 **(a)** The present flow of rivers in the Soviet Union; **(b)** the Volga Plan and the Siberian Plan to reverse river flow. (From *Christian Science Monitor,* January 16, 1985. Courtesy of the artist, William Palmstrom.)

ical process by which streams are straightened and deepened to control the velocity of runoff and flooding, and to improve navigation. The technique usually entails the removal of shrubs and trees up to 30 m (100 ft) from the banks of the river, with the denuded area then planted with a cover crop. Bulldozers deepen and straighten the channel, essentially converting it from *a living river* to *a functional water-filled ditch*. River channels may also be realigned into smooth, sweeping curves that are lined with rock and cement. According to a report prepared for the President's Council on Environmental Quality, the past century and a half has seen more than 321,869 km (200,000 mi) of waterways channelized in the United States, of which 54,716 km (34,000 mi) were channelized between 1940 and 1970 (Arthur D. Little, Inc., 1973). The U.S. Soil Conservation Service and the Army Corps of Engineers have been the principal advocates of channelization.

There are some standard benefits and drawbacks to channelization as seen in Table 5-3. *Improved flood control* is often hailed as the number one benefit of channelization, but effective flood control is often only achieved directly on either side of the channelized portion of the stream. Like the construction of new freeways to relieve traffic congestion, channelization simply pushes the problem of too much water elsewhere, in this case, downstream. Hence increased downstream flooding and increased downstream sedimentation are associated drawbacks of channelization.

On the more positive side, channelization is an effective technique for *land drainage*. However, in the case of the 53 million ha (130 million acres) of wetlands that have been drained by channelization in the United States, there has been little thought given to

sound conservation practices (Arthur D. Little, Inc., 1973) and to the *loss of wildlife habitat*. With the scraping away of riparian habitat, food and cover for such river-dwelling organisms as otters, racoons, and bears are eliminated. The alternative for these animals is migration (if other adjacent habitat is available) or death. Because of channelization (and other drainage techniques), the nation's original 51 million ha (127 million acres) of wetlands have been reduced to only 30 million ha (74 million acres), with just 9 million ha (22 million acres) considered to be in good condition (Mather 1984). (See Chapters 8 and 9 for further information regarding wetlands and wildlife.)

Upstream *erosion control* is often cited as a benefit of channelization. Once again, however, other areas suffer as a consequence, for with the stabilizing effect of the riparian habitat removed, there is *increased bank erosion*. With rivers that have been lined with concrete, the increase velocity of the river flow erodes streambanks further downstream, causing entire banks to slump into the channel. With the riparian habitat removed, there is also a *loss of timber reserves*—wood already being a natural resource in short supply. With a river's overhanging trees removed, there is less leaf litter, and, consequently, *reduced stream enrichment*. The elimination of overhanging trees and leaf litter causes *decreased fish food*, since numerous insects and leaves fall from tree canopies into rivers. With their diet altered, the average size and weight of fish is reduced (Tarplee et al. 1971), as well as the actual numbers of fish, within channelized portions of a river (Jahn and Trefethen 1973). Furthermore, the removal of overarching trees, which formerly filtered incoming solar energy, causes *increased water temperatures*, thereby placing an additional strain on aquatic organisms.

TABLE 5-3

Major advantages and disadvantages of channelization

ADVANTAGES	DISADVANTAGES
Improved flood control (adjacent to channel)	Increased flooding (downstream from channel)
	Increased downstream sedimentation
Land drainage	Loss of wildlife habitat
Erosion control (adjacent to channel)	Increased bank erosion (downstream from channel)
	Loss of timber reserves
	Reduced stream enrichment
	Decreased fish food
	Increased water temperatures
Improved navigation	Irregular stream flow
	Lowered water tables
	Saltwater intrusion
Small recreational lakes for recreation and wildlife	Loss of recreational activities
	Loss of aesthetics

Channelization can provide *improved navigation,* since the process most often deepens, widens, and straightens the water body, thereby creating an obstacle free path for watercraft. The drawback, however, is that natural (unmodified) streams that characteristically have constant flow the year around can now become completely dry during periods of summer drought. The effect of this *irregular stream flow* on fish and other forms of aquatic life is obvious. Of course, with a low or curtailed flow of water within the streambed comes the additional drawback of a *lowered water table* and *salt water intrusion* at the river mouth. As a consequence wells go dry and coastal aquifers get contaminated, further straining domestic, agricultural, and industrial water needs.

Finally, there is the question of recreation opportunities related to channelization. Owen (1985) notes that *small recreational lakes* are sometimes constructed by the Soil Conservation Service in association with the channelized river, and that these lakes provide certain benefits in terms of wildlife habitat and recreation. At the same time, however, there is also a *loss of recreation activities,* since the elimination of riparian habitat also changed, minimized, or eliminated the opportunity to hunt, bird watch, hike, or search for wildflowers along the natural river. Closely associated with this, of course, is the *loss of aesthetics*— an eroded ditch (an open storm drain?) or a concrete-lined channel (a river freeway?) simply is not the same as a picturesque meandering stream.

In view of the high number of negative environmental impacts associated with it, channelization has been coming under closer scrutiny in recent years. For example, critics are beginning to question channelization's primary benefit—flood prevention—since other ''softer path'' solutions are available. They cite storm management techniques that are founded on the less ecologically disruptive philosophy of *holding and draining* as opposed to the philosophy of channelization, which calls for *diverting and flushing away*. The Soil Conservation Service already has plans for channelizing an additional 9000 watersheds by the year 2000 (Owen 1985). Certainly, the feasibility of alternative techniques should be further explored before additional watersheds are destroyed by channelization.

Recharge Ponds. An engineering technique that is far less controversial then dam building or channelization is the construction of *recharge ponds*. Although an ancient technique, this most common method of spreading water, utilizes dikes and basins into which water arrives either by natural stream flow, by diversions from dams, or by channelized streams. Within the basins, the captured water is al-

lowed to percolate into the substrate where the water is free from evaporation. The primary purpose of constructing recharge ponds is to increase groundwater supplies, and the system is quite effective. For example, at the Saticoy spreading field in Santa Clara Valley, California, water tables have been raised from 24 m (79 ft) below the gound surface to just 3 m (10 ft) below the surface (Coates 1981).

Recharge ponds also come with a number of fringe benefits, which include (1) the prevention of saltwater intrusion into coastal aquifers, (2) the control of land subsidence due to excessive oil and groundwater withdrawal, (3) the increase in food and cover for wildlife, particularly avifauna, and (4) the increase in recreational opportunities (Figure 5-6).

Desalination Plants. A structural method of water resource management that initially sounds very appealing is **desalination**—the reduction or removal of salts from ocean water or brackish (slightly salty) inland water. What is unique and attractive about this particular method is that it does not just take water from one region and put it in another (as do dams and channelization) or transfer water from the surface of the ground to the subsurface level (as do recharge ponds) or make more efficient uses of existing water (as is done in conservation, which will be discussed), but rather desalination attempts to develop a whole new supply of fresh water from a previously unusable source. For example, the process can take seawater, which contains 35,000 ppm of dissolved salts and convert it into water suitable for irrigation (700 ppm of dissolved salts) and even drinking water (500 ppm of dissolved salts) (Moran et al. 1986).

Mather (1984) has outlined three general methods of desalination: (1) processes using a phase change in water, (2) processes using membranes, and (3) processes using ion exchange. Under the first category, *distillation* (evaporation) is the most common practice. It is a simple, but slow, process wherein seawater or brackish water is heated and evaporated, leaving behind the salts and minerals. This is nature's own way of providing fresh water for precipitation. The second general method of desalination entails passing saltwater through semipermeable membranes that allow water to flow through but not salts and minerals. Of the two major techniques using membranes, *electrodialysis* and *reverse osmosis,* the latter is the most commonly used. The third method of desalinization, ion exchange, is the most sophisticated. Here seawater passes through a cation exchange resin, where sodium and magnesium ions are exchanged with hydrogen ions in the resin. Then the water, now high in hydrogen ion content, is passed

(a)

(b)

FIGURE 5-6 Multiple use of a recharge pond, Lake Alamitos, California. (a) Water collected from nearby creeks is temporarily retained in a recharge pond. (b) In the summer, the pond is used for wind surfing and other water sports. (Photos by author.)

through an anion exchange resin, where sulfate and chloride ions exchange with the hydroxide ions. By then combining the hydroxide ions with the hydrogen ions, water molecules free of dissolved materials are formed. Of the 800 or more desalination plants in operation around the world, 93 percent use the phase change of water process, 6 percent use the membrane process, and less than 1 percent use the ion exchange process (Mather 1984).

There are over 100 desalination plants in the United States, with many of these facilities in the coastal cities of Florida, California, Texas, and the Northeast. Yet, in 1985, desalination provided only 0.4 percent of America's water needs (Miller 1986). What is holding desalination back? There are two primary reasons: (1) economics, and (2) ecological impacts. Because of energy requirements, water from desalination plants costs 4 to 6 times as much as tap water. Part of the problem is that desalinated water has a *place value;* that is, the further it must be transported inland and uphill from the coastal plant at sea level, the more costly the water becomes. Although improved technologies have brought the cost of desalinated water down (e.g., in 1951 it cost $7 per 1000 gal; in 1971 it cost $1 per 1000 gal), a change in energy costs can adversely affect these accomplishments (Viessman and Welty 1985). For the time being, the economic factor restricts the use of desalinated water to domestic purposes only. Desalinated water for irrigation, our prime water use, is economically out of the question. The second reason that desalination is not being pursued is because of the possibility of adverse environmental impacts. The principal problem has to do with the waste byproduct of desalination.

For example, 2000 tons of brine waste will be generated for every 3.8 million L (1 million gal) of fresh water (Viessman and Welty 1985). What is to be done with these mountains of salt? Disposal at sea would increase salt concentrations near the coast and threaten wildlife and fisheries, particularly within estuarine habitats and inshore from the continental shelf. Inland disposal methods are numerous, but they all have associated costs and environmental problems. For example, evaporation ponds could be used, but how many would have to be built, how much open space would be lost, and what about adverse effects on the groundwater? The waste could be liquified and transported by pipe, but piped to where? Deep injection wells could be used, but what about the effects on groundwater aquifers? The dry salt could be centrally stockpiled and some of it marketed, but most of it would eventually require disposal.

Despite economic and environmental drawbacks, there are those who see desalination as having a future in the United States, particularly in the northern central states and in the Southwest, where desalination has the potential of competing with other forms of water resource management. Although an important process, it should not be concluded that desalination can be practical in all situations.

Water Harvesting. Another technique, which is not practiced in the United States but which does have some potential, is *water harvesting* or *rainwater harvesting.* This is simply the technique of collecting all the water that falls as rain on a given area, rather than diverting water from rivers or tapping water from underground aquifers. Water harvesting is an ancient technique. For example, traditional societies in the dry areas of the Near East, Southern Asia, and Central America have used such simple water harvesting techniques as ditches, low berms on hillsides, and underground cisterns to capture rainwater (Cutter et al. 1985). A modern, yet still simple, version of water harvesting is used in the Truk Islands in Micronesia. Rather than the traditional thatch roof made of pandanus leaves, the Trukese are now using sheets of corrugated tin with gutters to capture rainwater. Rainwater in the gutter flows to an old metal oil drum, which acts as a catchment basin. This water harvesting system is quite efficient, despite the many drawbacks of using corrugated tin, such as a severe noise problem during tropical downpours (the inhabitants can barely hear each other speak) and sweltering room temperatures (in the tropical heat, the "tin boxes" do not "breathe" as well as the traditional bamboo houses with thatched roofs).

Western hydroengineers and geologists are also experimenting with various high-tech materials and methods for making soil surfaces shed water more easily. For example, the U.S. Geological Survey is exploring the idea of coating a portion of a desert floor with asphalt. The notion is that rainwater will strike this impervious surface, then flow into a specially designed cistern that holds the water for later use. A similar concept is already being widely used in Western Australia, where three small towns augment their water supplies by using 240 ha (593 acres) of asphalt-concrete water harvesting areas (Kellsall 1962). Rather than using asphalt, Fink and associates (1973) have experimented with a granulated paraffin wax as a soil sealant. They found that wax-treated plots captured 90 percent of the runoff as opposed to untreated plots that capture only 30 percent of the runoff. Water-harvesting experiments have also been made with other materials, such as silicones, latexes, butyl rubber, metal foil, plastic sheets, and chemicals that break down soil particles and thus seal soil pores and cracks.

As one can imagine, there are many limitations to these various water harvesting schemes. First, none will work if installed in low or no rainfall areas. Mather (1984) maintains that water harvesting is really only feasible in areas with an average rainfall of at least 5 to 8 cm (2 to 3 in.) annually. Second, most water harvesting schemes have limited lifetimes and must be renewed, just as asphalt roads crack and must be periodically rebuilt. Last, the latest high-tech harvesting schemes raise all kinds of environmental impact questions, such as what will be the long-term

implications of applying chemical additives to the soil? What will be the effects on groundwater? What will be the effects on wildlife?

Perhaps a less environmentally harmful approach would be for architects to design American homes to capture water in a way similar to the Trukese method. American homes with Spanish tile roofs and gutters already capture water. If engineers can design complicated dams and water diversion projects, they can certainly design small catchment basins that would be aesthetically pleasing to the American homeowner. If the water collected could not somehow be brought up to current water quality standards, the water could still be used for home irrigation of lawns, shrubs, and gardens, or for washing cars and watering indoor plants, thus slowing down the need for additional dams, water diversion projects, and so on. In addition to passively designed solar homes (energy conservation) and backyard gardens (soil conservation), the benefits of *decentralization* can be applied to our water resources by the individual homeowner.

Wastewater Treatment Plants. Civilizations have long struggled with what to do with their liquid wastes. In many underdeveloped countries (as well as in some poverty-stricken areas within developed countries, including the United States) backyard outhouses are still located over streams (Figure 5-7),

FIGURE 5-7 Palauan children standing by an "over-the-river" outhouse. (Photo by author.)

which can cause an outbreak of waterborne disease. In developed countries, rural areas generally use either artificial lagoons or septic tanks for degrading human wastes, and cities are most often serviced by one of three types of conventional sewage treatment plants: primary, secondary, or tertiary. In the United States, 24 percent of our liquid wastes receive primary treatment, 70 percent receive secondary treatment, 1 percent receive tertiary treatment, and 5 percent receive no treatment, the untreated waste simply being discharged into waterways (Owen 1985). We will now briefly examine the three conventional systems of wastewater treatment.

Primary treatment is the first stage of wastewater treatment. It is a method by which floating debris and solids are *mechanically* removed by screening and sedimentation. The plant receives both domestic sewage (e.g., human urine and feces, and anything and everything that people flush down toilets and stuff down home garbage disposal units) as well as urban runoff (e.g., animal urine and feces, sediment, leaves, and everything that floats down city sewerage systems, including rats). Unfortunately, the primary process only removes 60 percent of the suspended solids and 35 percent of the BOD before they are discharged into the sea (Moran et al. 1986).

Secondary treatment goes beyond the primary stage, using bacteria to further consume the organic wastes. Consequently this stage is a *biological* process, with the bacterial degradation taking place in an aeration tank. Secondary plants use either a system of *trickling filters*, where sewage is sprayed over a bed of bacteria-covered stones, or a system of *activated sludge* where the sewage undergoes aeration to further aid bacterial degradation. On the positive side, secondary treatment removes 90 percent of suspended solids and 90 percent of the BOD (Moran et al. 1986). On the negative side, however, many of the substances that aggravate water pollution problems have only been partially removed. For example, the process leaves behind 30 percent of most synthetic organic compounds, 50 percent of the nitrogen, 70 percent of the phosphorus, and nearly 100 percent of persistent organic substances. As a result, secondary treatment does *not* alleviate the causes of cultural eutrophication, pesticide contamination, and radioactive isotopes in our waterways (Miller 1986).

A third class of wastewater treatment, **tertiary treatment,** is the most sophisticated technique presently available. Unfortunately, it is also the most expensive. Compared with secondary treatment plants, tertiary systems are twice as expensive to build and four times as expensive to operate—the main reason that only 1 percent of U.S. liquid wastes are proc-

essed by tertiary treatment plants. Tertiary treatment is really a variety of mechanical and biological procedures, depending upon an area's primary needs. If suspended solids and phosphates are the primary problem, then a form of tertiary treatment called *precipitation* is used in which lime (calcium oxide) is added to the sewage to aid the settling process. *Adsorption*, a process that uses activated carbon, is the prescribed tertiary treatment for removing dissolved organic compounds. A third process, *reverse osmosis* or *electrodialysis*, is used to help reduce organic and inorganic substances. If all U.S. liquid wastes underwent these three processes at tertiary treatment plants, our waterways would be in very good to excellent condition.

Tertiary treatment can also be done in an aesthetic way, substituting waterfalls and sculpted channels for the relatively unattractive buildings and grounds of a primary or secondary plant facility. For example, at Bishop's Lodge resort in New Mexico, an artificial system of waterfalls and sculpted channels was designed to not only provide tertiary treatment of wastewater but also to do so in an attractive manner. Part of the tertiary process is done in a treatment plant that is hidden from view by creative earth mounding and landscaping. The remaining part of the process is provided by the ''seven magic pools''— a gravity system of channels, pools, and waterfalls that cascades the water down 30 m (100 ft) to the resort's entrance, thereby providing further tertiary treatment by aerating the wastewater and exposing it to sunlight (Burgh 1982). Whereas Bishop's Lodge used to use 37,854 L (10,000 gal) of groundwater per day to irrigate its lawns (one-third of its total daily consumption), the lodge now uses only tertiary treated waters. According to Anne Spirn (1984), a Harvard professor of landscape architecture and environmental planning, this is an example of how cities can blend waste treatment with urban beautification.

Regardless of which of the previous three processes are used, wastewater must also undergo disinfection. **Disinfection** can be defined as any chemical or physical process that will destroy disease-causing bacteria which may have survived the earlier treatment steps. In most parts of the world, chlorine is used to disinfect sewage treatment effluent. The practice of using chlorine, however, has recently come under attack. Scientists have discovered that chlorine can combine with organic compounds in the water to form chlororganic compounds, such as carbon tetrachloride and chloroform, both of which are known carcinogens. This discovery has led scientists and policymakers to explore alternative methods of disinfection, such as using activated carbon filters, other types of disinfectants (e.g., chlorine dioxide or ozone), or mechanical techniques (e.g., ultrasonic energy). The drawback, however, is that these other methods are considerably more expensive than chlorination. For example, Moran and associates (1986) estimate that the activated carbon process would add an additional $7 to $30 annually to an average household's water bill. Policymakers will eventually have to weigh the risk of the continued use of chlorine as a disinfectant versus the higher cost of the alternative methods.

Another problem associated with primary, secondary, and tertiary treatment plants is sludge disposal. **Sludge** is the combination of liquid and solid waste that remains after sewage treatment. In 1980, this country's sludge was disposed of by using landfills (40 percent), by incineration (25 percent), by using on agricultural lands (20 percent), and by using ocean dumping (15 percent) (Moran et al. 1986). Disposing of sludge by application to agricultural lands makes the most sense, since sludge contains high levels of nitrogen and phosphorus and because its water-retention capacity makes it a good soil conditioner. (See Chapter 3 for further details.) Care must be taken, however, not to apply sludge that contains heavy metals or organic chemicals, particularly PCBs. Whether or not sludge contains these troublesome compounds is determined by the types of industrial plants that feed wastewater to the sewage treatment plant. Incineration and ocean dumping are the least ecologically sound alternatives of sludge disposal, since they both pollute the environment, the first one pollutes the air, the second contaminates the ocean. (For details on ocean dumping and its affect on marine life, see Chapter 12.) Some treatment plants are already using anaerobic bacteria to digest sludge, thereby producing methane gas for sale as a commercial fuel source. Since sludge even has nutritive value, scientists are even exploring the possibilities of sludge as a poultry or cattle feed supplement.

Nonstructural Methods

In addition to the conventional structural approaches to water resource management, there is a new array of highly innovative nonstructural or soft path approaches that are being increasingly explored. We will start by looking at some of the nonstructural approaches to wastewater treatment.

Nonstructural Approaches to Wastewater Treatment. A number of scientists and social scientists, such as anthropologist John H. Bodley (1985), have

suggested that the answer to many of our environmental problems lies in the *paraprimitive solution,* meaning that one should combine the best aspects of two different worlds—the primitive and the modern world. Taking the ancient Chinese technique of using aquaculture for sewage disposal (in some reports, latrines were literally built over the fish ponds) and combining it with modern systems of sanitation control is an excellent example of a para-primitive solution to an environmental problem. The technique of *aquaculture for wastewater treatment* is currently being used by the 20,000 residents of the city of Arcata in northern California. Here, the city's wastewater is fed through standard primary and secondary treatment plants. What is different, however, is that their secondary plant has oxidation ponds that provide water for Pacific salmon fingerlings. The sewage provides such nutrients as nitrogen, phosphorus, and trace elements to the phytoplankton within the ponds, which, in turn, aids fish growth. Eventually, the young pond-raised salmon are released into streams and into Humboldt Bay, where they remain until they later migrate upstream to spawn. The primary benefit of aquaculture as a form of *advanced biological tertiary treatment* is that it eliminates the need for chlorination or other methods of disinfection (Allen and Carpenter 1977). Aquaculture, however, can only be used in conjunction with conventional sewage treatment plants, such as in Arcata, that process only home and nontoxic industrial wastes. (See Chapter 12 for a further discussion of aquaculture.)

The *wastewater renovation and conservation cycle* is a phrase sometimes used to describe another nonstructural approach to wastewater treatment (Figure 5-8). In this case, land is used as a natural physical and biological filter for tertiary treatment. After undergoing primary and secondary treatment, the wastewater is applied to crops via sprinklers or directly to forest lands. The wastewater then percolates through the soil, undergoing a natural purification process. Gradually the groundwater is recharged, and it is reused again for agricultural, industrial, or domestic purposes (Parizek and Myers 1968). An example of this type of wastewater recycling system is currently in operation near Muskegon and Whitehall, Michigan. According to Botkin and Keller (1982), the system removes most of the worst pollutants, including heavy metals.

Wastewater and park landscapes is another soft path approach to wastewater treatment. In Mt. Clemens, Michigan, for example, the city designed a new sewerage overflow treatment facility on a former sanitary landfill site (Mahida and DeDecker 1975). The system consists of three small lakes and a park.

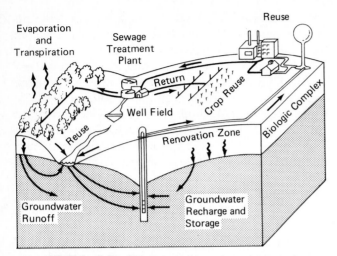

FIGURE 5-8 Waste-water renovation and conservation cycle. (From Daniel B. Botkin and Edward A. Keller, *Environmental Studies: The Earth as a Living Planet* [Columbus, Ohio: Merrill, 1982], p. 217. Reprinted by permission of the publisher.)

Sewerage overflow enters the first lake and remains there until it is partially treated in a treatment facility. The water is then released for aeration in the second lake. Eventually, the treated effluent reaches the third lake, where it is safe enough to be used for boating, fishing, and irrigating the park's landscape. According to Spirn (1984), the park would be more of a success story if it were not for funding problems. Nevertheless, as traditional chemical methods for advanced tertiary treatment become too costly, natural treatment systems will likely become more attractive (Bastian 1982).

Finally, experiments are also being made with *wastewater and wetlands*. Projects using natural or con-structed wetlands are presently underway in Arcata, California (Weireter 1982), and Austin, Texas (Spirn 1984). In addition to being potential recreational sites, these wetlands also serve as wildlife habitats. As one might expect, however, the wetlands approach to wastewater treatment requires lots of land and can only handle sewage that is not heavily contaminated with toxic pollutants.

Conservation. Historically, water resource management has focused on water development—the building of dams, reservoirs, and water diversion projects to get more water supplies. Today, water specialists are becoming increasingly interested in the ''less is more'' approach, that is, water conservation. According to Postel (1985), several factors have collectively caused this interest: (1) serious effects of surface and groundwater overdraft, (2) the high capital expenditures associated with traditional structural approaches to increasing water supply, including high pumping costs, and (3) the associated ecological drawbacks of conventional methods. Since 30 to 50 percent of the water used in the United States is unnecessarily wasted (Miller 1986), conservation is a viable means by which to cut waste and get more production out of existing water supplies. We will now look at various ways to conserve water within agriculture, the city, industry, and the home.

There are numerous techniques that farmers can use to conserve water, such as using good soil management practices, controlling water losses during transportation, and using new cropping patterns (Table 5-4). Such *good soil management practices* as terracing, contour tillage, and mulching conserve water as well as minimize soil erosion. (See Chapter 3 for further details.)

TABLE 5-4

Major methods of conserving water on the farm

METHOD	EXAMPLE
Good soil management practices	The use of terracing and contour tillage in Kauai, Hawaii
Efficient irrigation methods	The use of computers and drip (trickle) irrigation in Arizona
Good systems management	Precise water application scheduling in Davis, California
Control of losses in water transit	The use of plastic or cement to line canals to minimize seepage
Increased use of reclaimed water	The use of treated municipal wastewater for irrigation in the semiarid Southwest
New cropping patterns	The practice of dryland farming by organic farmers in Santa Cruz, California
Altering the crops grown	The reintroduction of the tepary, a drought-resistant legume, to Arizona

Since irrigation places the greatest demand on water in this country—up to 80 percent of water used in the West (Moran et al. 1986)—choosing the most *efficient irrigation methods* is critical to water conservation on the farm. There are basically three types of irrigation systems: (1) gravity systems, (2) sprinkler systems, and (3) drip (trickle) irrigation systems. Each system has its own advantages, disadvantages, and levels of efficiency.

Gravity systems (also known as surface systems) are the oldest form of irrigation, dating back 5000 years (Postel 1985). Gravity systems are of two types: furrow irrigation or flood irrigation. Furrow irrigation uses canals and small channels to bring water to parallel furrows on gently sloping fields. In this system, irrigation water flows under the force of gravity, seeping into the soil as it disperses among the furrows. Whereas furrow irrigation is used for row crops, flood irrigation is used for rice and other close-growing field crops. The latter involves the flooding of an entire field that has been surrounded by small levees (Figure 5-9). Of the two systems, flood irrigation is the least efficient, since it is extremely difficult to control water flow (Viessman and Welty 1985). Despite the fact that gravity systems are the least expensive and most common irrigation method, they are less than 50 percent efficient, with half of the water applied to the field being lost to evaporation and runoff (Postel 1985). However, methods exist to improve gravity systems, such as leveling the land to even out water distribution, and the construction of ponds to collect and store runoff water for reuse. A new technique to improve gravity systems, called *surge irriga-*

tion, appears to hold much promise. This technique uses timing devices to release water at specific intervals rather than the traditional continual stream of water. According to Postel (1985), field tests indicate that the surge technique can reduce water and energy use by 10 to 40 percent.

Sprinkler systems became popular in the United States in the 1960s, particularly on hilly and marginally useful lands unsuitable for gravity methods. In 1985, sprinkler systems were used on 35 to 40 percent of U.S. irrigated lands. Typically, they irrigate more uniformly than gravity systems, giving them a higher (70 percent) efficiency rating (Postel 1985). Of the three basic types of sprinkler systems, (1) tow-line irrigation sprinklers, (2) traveling sprinklers, and (3) center pivot sprinklers, the last is the most common design. With center pivot systems, a horizontal sprinkler arm rotates continually around a pivot point. Center pivot systems are driven by electricity, water, or oil hydraulic drive, and they have varying levels of efficiency. Causes of differences in efficiencies range from farmer modifications of the unit, to lack of maintenance, to design problems (Hanson and Lancaster 1986). Sprinkler systems, including center pivot systems, can be made more efficient through a technique known as Low Energy Precision Application (LEPA). Whereas unmodifed sprinklers spray water high into the air, which exacerbates the problem of evaporation in windy, dry areas, the LEPA method uses *drop tubes* that extend vertically from the sprinkler arm to deliver water closer to the crops. When used in conjunction with other land conservation practices, LEPA can bring irrigation efficiencies up to 98 percent (Postel

(a)

(b)

FIGURE 5-9 Flood irrigation. (a) Overview of Hanelei Valley on Kauai, Hawaii. Note the large cleared and flooded agricultural patches to the right of the Hanelei River. (b) Hawaiian farmers harvesting taro in the same flooded patches shown in (a). (Photos by author.)

1985). LEPA irrigation is already being used by many farmers in northwestern Texas.

Drip irrigation systems, or trickle irrigation, is the most efficient of all three systems, with efficiency ratings as high as 90 to 95 percent (Chiras 1985). Drip irrigation is the most common of the *microirrigation techniques,* which is a collective name for a group of water-saving irrigation techniques. Specifically, drip irrigation involves a network of porous or perforated black plastic piping installed on or below the soil surface (Figure 5-10). It is extremely efficient because it delivers water directly to the crops' roots, thereby minimizing evaporation and runoff losses. Drip irrigation has several other advantages:

1. Crop yields are higher due to the constant flow of water, which allows plants to grow without stress. For example, Anon (1983) and O'Dell (1983) report that pepper and tomato crops had up to 40 percent larger yields under drip irrigation, and Coates (1981) reports that tomato production yields with drip irrigation under optimal conditions can be 163 percent greater than normal.

2. Drip irrigation is better suited for using brackish water, since the constant flow of moisture at the root zone helps prevent salinization (Shoji 1977). According to Coates (1981), salt content within the water can be as much as three times higher than in water used for other irrigation methods.

3. Less fuel and fertilizers are required.

4. Drip irrigation can be used on steep terrain, since runoff and related soil erosion are less of a problem.

5. Less labor and herbicides are required, since drip irrigation minimizes weed growth.

6. Drip irrigation is well adapted to greenhouse production.

7. Drip irrigation systems can be easily computerized. For example, computerized systems can now be found in Hawaii, California, Arizona, and Florida (Stout 1984).

The primary drawback to drip irrigation is the cost. Although researchers agree that capital expenditures are relatively high, their figures do not always agree. For example, Poincelot (1986) estimates costs from $1235 to $1729 per ha ($500 to $700 per acre), while others such as Postel (1985) estimate capital expenditures even higher, from $2200 to $3500 per ha ($890 to $1416 per acre). Regardless of which set of figures is most representative, this is money that most farmers do not have. Another drawback is that drip irrigation systems characteristically require high maintenance. Artificial deposits (e.g., chemical deposits from soluble fertilizers) and natural contaminants (e.g., soil particles, algae, and mineral salts) often clog the emitters. The plastic lines of drip irrigation are also vulnerable to attack by animals, such as worms, rabbits, and even coyotes.

Despite these drawbacks, Americans are becom-

(a)

(b)

FIGURE 5-10 Drip irrigation. (a) Use of drip irrigation in sugar cane fields of Kauai, Hawaii. Water is brought to the fields by large plastic pipes (left) and first passed through large filters (center) to minimize clogging of the small black pipe (not shown). (b) Organic farmer adjusting drip irrigation pipe on his farm in Santa Cruz, California. (Photos by author.)

ing increasingly interested in this method of conservation irrigation. Postel (1985) reports that the use of drip irrigation has greatly expanded over the last decade, from 29,000 ha (71,658 acres) in 1974 to more than 226,000 ha (558,438 acres) in 1983. California pioneered its use in the United States in the 1960s (Coates 1981) and remains the leading state in drip irrigation, accounting for nearly half the U.S. total (Postel 1985). In California it is practiced on some 123,484 ha (305,120 acres) (Poincelot 1986). There is little doubt that the use of drip irrigation will further increase as arid and semiarid regions cope with declining surface and groundwater supplies.

Once the proper irrigation method is selected, *good systems management* is required to keep the system properly maintained and operating. Although what constitutes good systems management varies from farm to farm, what it generally entails is the precise determination of a *water application schedule*—deciding how much water plants need and at what time during their growth. Simply put, proper scheduling cuts out unnecessary water application and improves irrigation efficiency. Viessman and Welty (1985) note that soil moisture detection devices to estimate the moisture content of their fields are available to farmers with limited financial resources. They note that farmers with greater financial resources can employ computers to further interpret soil moisture data. With additional data, such as rates of evapotranspiration and rainfall, farmers can maintain a water budget, using computer printouts to inform them when crops need more water (Hiler and Howell 1983). In addition to estimating water requirements, good systems management also entails the precise estimate of leaching requirements. If too much water is applied, water is wasted and drainage problems increase. But if too little water is applied, there may not be enough water for leaching to prevent salt from accumulating in the root zone. Deciding the leaching requirement to achieve a balance between salt buildup and drainage amounts is no easy task. Fortunately, training in the balancing of these factors is now available to growers through various government agencies, water districts, and universities (Postel 1985).

Another conservation technique for agricultural areas is to *control the losses of water in transit.* Less than half of the water delivered to farms for irrigation purposes ever reaches the crops (U.S. GAO 1976); most of the water loss is through seepage. Water conveyance efficiency can be increased by using cement or plastic-lined ditches. Better yet, the use of closed pipes has the additional advantage of reducing losses by evaporation.

Growers can also conserve water through *in-creased use of reclaimed water.* This is a particularly viable option for farmers in the semiarid Southwest where water is in short supply. For example, in 1971, irrigators in the Southwest used most of the 503 billion L (133 billion gal) of municipal wastewater available to that region (Viessman and Welty 1985). As natural water supplies decline, wastewater reuse on the farm is likely to become a more recognized option to farmers.

The creation of *new cropping patterns* is another type of water conservation available to farmers. One specific method is **dryland farming** (sometimes called *rain-fed farming)*, which refers to traditional farming without the use of irrigation. With this method, farmers practice the ancient technique of using stored soil water for crop production, which requires a summer fallow period during which rainwater accumulates in the root zone. Since rainfall is unpredictable, dryland farming is naturally a risky business. There are other drawbacks as well. First, the required summer fallow period takes land out of production for several months. According to Poincelot (1986), a 60 percent loss in yield would occur in the Great Plains if it reverted to dryland farming. Other researchers, however, have found evidence to suggest that declines would not be so severe. For example, Loomis (1983) found that under well-planned crop-fallow rotations, yields can sometimes increase so dramatically as to more than compensate for the fewer number of harvests. Other drawbacks include saline seeps and wind erosion during fallow periods and poorer response of traditional crops, such as corn. Approximately 15 million ha (37 million acres) of cropland are currently under summer fallow in the United States (Poincelot 1986), with most of the dryland farming occuring in the northern and central Great Plains, where farmers have been successful at trapping 30 to 40 percent of the precipitation (Troeh et al. 1980).

Another conservation method closely related to dryland farming is **runoff agriculture.** This is a form of water harvesting wherein rainwater is captured and diverted to croplands located in an otherwise hostile environment. One technique is to strategically place stone barriers across intermittent stream channels. When the rain comes, water within the stream is diverted to adjacent croplands (Figure 5-11). A variant of runoff agriculture is **micro-catchment farming,** where the croplands are divided into small basins, ranging from 10 m² (108 ft²) to 1000 m² (10,764 ft²) (Mather 1984). The basins are designed so that water falling within them will drain towards the planted vegetation (Figure 5-12). Runoff agriculture is an ancient technique widely used throughout the Middle East, South Asia, and the American Southwest. If

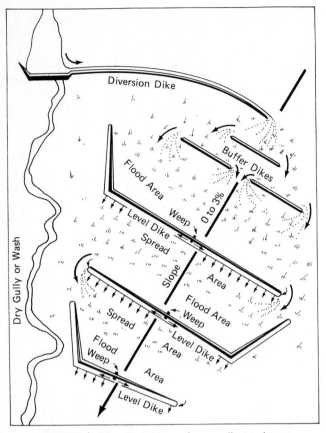

FIGURE 5-11 One type of spreading scheme for runoff agriculture. (From John R. Mather, *Water Resources: Distribution, Use and Management*, p. 240. Copyright © 1984 by John Wiley & Sons, Inc.)

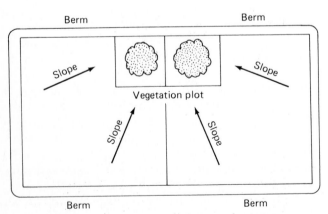

FIGURE 5-12 Microcatchment farming. (From John R. Mather, *Water Resources: Distribution, Use and Management*, p. 242. Copyright © 1984 by John Wiley & Sons, Inc.)

these ancient concepts are combined with modern knowledge of precipitation patterns and crop requirements, new forms of runoff agriculture could be developed to increase dryland production and minimize the risks of dryland farming (National Academy of Sciences 1974).

Farmers can also conserve water by *altering the crops grown*. Interest is growing, for example, in breeding and growing *drought-resistant crops*. Poincelot (1986) reminds us that Indians within the American Southwest grew crops before the advent of irrigation. However, these drought-resistant crops were lost or neglected as irrigators transferred water to the drylands and deserts. Scientists are now trying to bring back some of these old crops through plant breeding, as seen in the efforts to revive tepary (*Phaseolus acutifolius*), a legume once grown by Arizona Indians (Nabhan 1983). Since tepary yields actually *decline* with irrigation, the plant simply disappeared with the introduction of irrigation (Poincelot 1986).

Growing *salt-tolerant crops* may be a partial answer to crop production in regions where irrigation waters are becoming saline. Since some crops can tolerate salt more than others, the theory is to match the existing salinity condition with the proper type of vegetation. Scientists are also experimenting with breeding plants for salt tolerance. For example, Epstein and associates (1980) note the successes with tomatoes, wheat, and barley—the three crops that have been bred for salt tolerance. While some researchers see the development of salt-tolerant crops as a "promising avenue for reducing freshwater requirements in arid lands" (Viessman and Welty 1985, p. 25), others such as Poincelot (1986, p. 180) only see it as a "last resort for failed areas of irrigation."

Finally, water shortages may gradually force farmers to shift to *new crop varieties*, such as amaranth—an ancient plant that produces an edible cereal-like grain. According to Postel (1985), over 20 U.S. farmers are experimenting with this hearty, drought-resistant crop; some are hoping it will be a viable substitute for their traditional crop of water-consuming sorghum. However, further research is necessary to get around the problems of relatively high planting costs and comparatively low yields before amaranth becomes a common cereal in the High Plains (National Research Council 1984).

In summary, there are a myriad of technologies and practices available to today's farmer. The technique or combination of techniques used will be site-specific and determined by local economics and politics. According to Postel (1985), farmers could cut water use by 10 to 40 percent without any appreciable drop in crop production. She further points out that with better water management on the farm comes the added benefits of reduced soil erosion and a smaller amount of soil that becomes waterlogged. One merely has to look at Israel for an example of the benefits of water conservation. Using many of the conservation techniques discussed above, Israel amazingly decreased water waste from 83 percent in 1950 to a mere 5 percent in 1980 (Miller 1986). There are many water conservation lessons to be learned from studying Israel and other arid and semiarid nations that have long struggled with water deficits.

In recent years, industry has made major strides in conserving water. It has used water conservation techniques ranging from the elimination of wasteful water practices to the recycling and reuse of water and the total elimination of water in many aspects of the manufacturing process (Table 5-5). We will now briefly discuss the six major methods of conserving water within industry.

The *elimination of wasteful or unnecessary practices* is perhaps the most expedient method of conserving water in industry. For example, water pipes can be carefully monitored for leaks and repaired, water control flow values can be installed, and alternative means can be found to transport vegetables and other products within industries. Since only 2 percent of the water used in industry requires potable water (Miller 1985), industries are already making additional strides through the *recycling of water*, that is, the use of water over and over again within a given factory. For example, just four industries (the paper,

chemical, petroleum, and primary metal industries) consume 80 percent of all water used in U.S. manufacturing (Postel 1985), yet all are steadily increasing their rate of water recycling. Numerous success stories in water recycling exist, such as in Israel (Rakosh 1978), in Sweden (Swedish Preparatory Committee 1977), in the Soviet Union (Belichenko and Dolgopolova 1984), and in the United States (Hamilton 1984, Antosiak and Job 1981).

Associated with water recycling is a third water conservation technique wherein industries *use different water qualities for different stages of production*. This conservation strategy reserves potable water for industrial processes that require the cleanest water, slightly polluted water for stages that do not require high-quality water, and even more polluted water for industrial processes that can use highly contaminated water. As Mather (1984) notes, this *stepwise reuse* conservation scheme can be built into new factories at a reasonable cost, but the cost of retrofitting an older plant with the appropriate interlinking maze of water pipes may be prohibitive.

Industries are also finding that they can conserve water by increasing their *use of treated wastewater from municipalities*. In 1971, for example, 144 municipalities in the United States supplied treated wastewater to local industries. Of the total 541 billion L (143 billion gal) of sewage effluent utilized, reuse was divided as follows: irrigation (50 percent), industry (37 percent), groundwater recharge (11 percent) and recreation (2 percent) (Schmidt et al. 1973). Of the 37 percent, or 202.5 billion L (53.5 billion gal) used for

TABLE 5-5

Major methods of water conservation in industry

METHOD	EXAMPLE
Elimination of wasteful or unnecessary practices	Eliminating leaks Turning off unused waterlines Installing water control valves
Recycling of water	Reuse of water over and over again in oil refineries, pulp and paper mills, and chemical plants
Use of different water qualities for different stages of production	Potable water is used for one step in an industrial process Slightly contaminated water is used for another process that does not require the cleanest possible water
Use of treated wastewater from municipalities	The replacement of potable water with treated or saline water in a steel plant for cooling purposes
Reuse of wastewater *treated within* the factory	A chemical plant that treats and reuses its own wastewater
Elimination of the use of water	The on-site transportation of vegetables and other products without the use of water

industrial purposes, one customer—the Bethlehem Steel Company plant in Sparrows Point, Maryland—used 166.5 billion L (44 billion gal). According to this same 1971 survey, only 15 industrial plants in the United States were using municipal wastewater. Two-thirds of the reclaimed water was being used for cooling purposes, with the remaining water being used for boiling feed and manufacturing processes. Rather than use treated wastewater from municipalities, some industries have begun to *reuse wastewater treated within the factory* itself. In other words, each factory has its own self-contained water treatment facility. Water is used, treated, then reused, all within the same facility. As Mather (1984) notes, however, most of these industries were forced by local governments to treat their wastewater before releasing it into city sewers or nearby streams.

Even some office buildings are now being constructed with built-in water treatment facilities. For example, Mitsubishi's 60-story office building in Tokyo, Japan, purifies and recycles all the building's wastewater (Chiras 1985). Perhaps one day water treatment will be decentralized, with each industrial plant, office building, or residential home having its own fully automated recycling system. Until then, however, a final water conservation tactic might involve the *elimination of the use of water* whenever and wherever possible. For example, the substitution of dry cooling towers for the traditional wet cooling towers in steam-operated electric power plants could cut water consumption by one-fourth (Chiras 1985).

As one can see, there are a variety of ways in which industry can conserve water. Some researchers, such as Mather (1984), maintain that industry will have the greatest success in conservation of all the water users, with a further reduction in freshwater needs by industry in the next two decades.

Cities will face severe water demands for their sprawling suburbs, thirsty lawns, swimming pools, and other water-intensive uses if conservation measures are not enacted. Cities in the West will especially need to establish conservation measures, since their residential use of water is typically 50 percent greater than in the East. There is no question that conservation within cities is effective. In Tucson, Arizona, for example, per capita use is 40 percent less than in nearby Phoenix because of Tucson's conservation efforts (Postel 1985). There are a number of alternative ways through which cities can achieve remarkable water savings through conservation (Table 5-6). These methods are briefly discussed below.

Detecting and eliminating leaks, whether they be from leaky water mains, pipes, faucets, or toilets, is a cost-effective conservation technique that cities can undertake. The loss of water through leaks is a serious problem. According to a leakage survey of 379 U.S. cities, 10 percent (approximately 40 cities) had unaccounted for losses of water that were greater than 25 percent of water pumped (Seidel and Bauman 1957). In Boston, it is estimated that leaks from decaying water mains account for as much as 50 percent of all the water pumped into the city (Miller

TABLE 5-6

Major methods of conserving water in the city

METHOD	EXAMPLE
Detecting and eliminating leaks	Repairing Boston's notorious leaky water mains
Reuse	The use of reclaimed wastewater for park landscapes and home lawns in parts of California
Mandatory water restrictions	Hawaii's restrictions on lawn-watering during drought years
Higher water rates	Tucson's imposed increases in water prices for conservation purposes
Metering	The installation of meters to monitor water use in Boulder, Colorado
Developing plumbing codes	Plumbing codes that require the use of water-conserving 6-liter toilets in Scandinavia
Water-conserving landscaping	The use of native plants in park design in Philadelphia
Conservation education	The use of the news media to promote the use of low-flow showerheads and other water-conserving devices in California
Improved management techniques	England's regional approach to water management

1985). Repairing these systems, which will eventually have to be done anyway, could help delay, and in some cases avoid the need for water development projects.

Increasing the *reuse* of renovated municipal water supplies is also a viable conservation technique. In Israel, all new water demands are met by treating and reusing wastewater. In 1980, 4 percent of Israel's total water needs were met with treated wastewater. It is projected that by the year 2000 this same figure will be 16 percent (Selbst 1985). By contrast, only 0.2 percent of the total annual water use in the United States is met by the reuse of reclaimed wastewater (Postel 1985). Despite federal water quality laws that encourage reuse, most urban communities choose the conventional *treat and dispose* method. Of the 536 reuse projects in operation in the United States in the late 1970s, 60 percent supplied water for irrigation (landscapes, parks, crops) and 30 percent supplied water for industry (processing and cooling), with the remainder supplying water for recharging the groundwater and recreation (Culp et al. 1979). California leads the nation in the number of reuse projects, with 380 individual sites supplied with reclaimed water—collectively providing a volume of water equal to the annual household demands of 1 million people (Crook 1985). Experiments are even underway that use reclaimed wastewater for drinking purposes. In 1985, for example, El Paso, Texas, began injecting highly treated wastewater into an aquifer used for public drinking water. Years of careful monitoring and analysis will determine if this first-in-the-nation experiment will prove useful as a water conserving technique (Texas Water Resources Institute and the Texas Agricultural Experiment Station 1984).

Mandatory water restrictions are effective conservation techniques, though generally they are used only as short-term measures during particularly dry periods. In 1984, for example, after a year and a half of record dry weather, Oahu (Hawaii's most populous island) was placed under mandatory water restrictions. All residents and businesses, including hotels and military facilities, were required to conserve water. Some of the restrictions imposed by the Honolulu Board of Water Supply were as follows: (1) an even-odd digit address system was created to regulate lawn-watering, which was allowed only between 6 P.M. and 9 P.M.; (2) agriculturalists were required to cut irrigation by 25 percent; and (3) domestic, industrial, and commercial users were required to cut back by 10 percent. Violaters were fined, had flow restrictors placed on their water lines, or had their water supplies totally cut off. Repeat offenders could expect

a $1000 maximum fine and a year in prison. Sometimes, these temporary measures have been made permanent policy within cities, such as the restrictions on lawn-watering in Tucson, Arizona.

There is no question that *higher water rates* is an effective conservation tool, particularly in the drier regions of the country. In some areas of the country, however, water is so cheap that water companies could triple the price and domestic demand would not be appreciably reduced (Mather 1984). Overall, however, the charging of high rates is a conservation strategy worth pursuing. In Tucson, Arizona, for example, water use dropped dramatically with the imposition of severe increases in water prices (Postel 1985).

Substantial water savings can also be made through *metering*. Most U.S. cities meter their water with payment based on the amount used. In some cities, such as New York City, individual users pay a flat rate, which does not encourage conservation. According to D'Angelo (1964), New York City could reduce average daily consumption by 10 percent if individual use were metered. Other studies have indicated that the installation of meters have typically reduced per capita demand by 20 to 40 percent (Baumann and Dworkin 1978). When Boulder, Colorado, went from 5 percent to 100 percent metering, it experienced a 40 percent drop in demand (Hanke and Flack 1968). Although there is a general tendency for demand to creep up after the immediate impact of metering, usage does not return to premetered levels (Mather 1984).

Developing plumbing codes that require the installation of water-saving devices can reduce domestic water consumption by 20 percent or more (Viessman and Welty 1985). The biggest water user in the U.S. home is the toilet, turning 19 L (5 gal) of potable water into wastewater with each flush (Postel 1985). Other countries use much more efficient toilets, such as West Germany, which uses 9-liter toilets (World Environment Report 1984) and Scandinavia, which uses 6-liter toilets (Siegrist 1983). According to the California Office of Water Conservation (1985), a 1985 bill was introduced into the California legislature that would require that all toilets installed in new construction be designed to use 5.7 L (1.5 gal) of water per flush, which is less than 50 percent of the current California limit and 70 percent less than most toilets use in the East. Plumbing codes could also be revised to allow the use of waterless toilets. These odorless toilets use bacteria to degrade human and kitchen wastes into a rich organic supplement for backyard gardens. In addition to cutting household water use by 25 percent, the use of waterless toilets would help reduce the wastewater stream to sewage treatment plants and, eventually, to our lakes, bays, and streams (Chiras 1985). Other savings can be made by enacting plumbing codes requiring low-flow or flow-limiting showerheads and faucets and by setting water appliance efficiency standards on such items as clothes washers and dishwashers.

Since lawn and garden watering accounts for 40 to 50 percent of residential water use (Postel 1985), the use of *water conserving landscaping*, or *desert landscaping*, can help curtail this consumption. For example, the promotion of desert landscaping in Tucson, Arizona, largely altered outdoor water use patterns to the point that the year-round average demand fell by 27 percent. Curbing outdoor use through the use of water-conserving landscaping is also being promoted in the state of California, in the Colorado cities of Denver, Fort Collins, and Aurora, and in San Antonio and Austin, Texas (Postel 1985). Cities are also experimenting in park design by using native plants, such as at Chestnut Park in downtown Philadelphia. Here, the park's native plants thrive without the use of irrigation (Spirn 1984). As Rondon (1980) and others have illustrated, there are many aesthetically pleasing options within water-conserving landscaping. If a household cannot afford (or does not want) to replace its "out of place oasis vegetation," it can reduce its water use by installing one of many drip irrigation systems that are currently on the market. *Conservation education* is necessary to gain the public support for almost any water-conserving technique or policy change. For example, it is natural for consumers to be skeptical at the notion of drinking water that has been reclaimed by a sewage treatment plant. They must be educated to understand that reclaimed sewage water may be even purer than the treated water that they have been receiving from a river or reservoir (Mather 1984). Homeowners also have to be educated to water their lawns and gardens with *gray water*, that is, water that has been used for showers and washing. Where U.S. homeowners have set up a separate system for gray water, they have cut average domestic water use by more than 50 percent (Miller 1986). Educational campaigns promoted through television, radio, newspapers, and newsletters from local water districts can also help educate consumers as to the proper showerhead to purchase, the benefits and drawbacks of sprinklers as compared with drip irrigation systems, and so on.

Improved management techniques can also conserve water within the city. For example, the Washington, D.C., metropolitan area was recently facing a 30 percent shortfall in water supplies. Rather than take the structural approach of building new dams and reservoirs, the city chose a combination of creative approaches. In addition to using some of the techniques discussed above, city officials created new institutional arrangements to more efficiently handle water delivery, sought improved hydrologic forecasting, and made reallocations from the flood storage capacity to the water supply (U.S. Geological Survey 1984). We can also look to England and Wales for examples of improved water management. There, a regionalized approach to water management is practiced. Rather than base water decisions on artificial political boundaries, actual watershed boundaries are used (Miller 1985). Regardless of the mix of water conservation techniques practiced, conservation is a key to relieving the strain on existing municipal water systems.

Weather Modification. Cloud-seeding is another nonstructural approach to water resource management. In this case, scientists use the high-tech wizardry of computers, weather satellites, radar, and other gear to target storm clouds that are well-suited for seeding. Specially designed airplanes or mountaintop generators actually seed the clouds. In most cases, researchers have used crystals of silver iodide, which seems to be the most effective cloud-seeding chemical. Dry ice pellets, salt crystals, and even clay particles have been used. The theory is that these particles serve as condensation nuclei around which small water droplets or ice particles can form.

According to Miller (1986), cloud-seeding has taken place in 23 states, covering 7 percent of the U.S. land area. For example, the Desert Research Institute in Reno, Nevada, routinely seeds storms on the west side of the Sierra crest in California. The state-funded institute uses four electronically activated, ground-based generators on mountaintops at an elevation of about 2286 m (7500 ft). The generators release silver iodide smoke into clouds west of the Truckee-Tahoe region. Since the ice crystals take 20 to 30 minutes to form after seeding, the clouds usually drift 32 km (20 mi) eastward beyond the Sierra crest toward Lake Tahoe, dumping their heavy load on the Truckee River watershed that feeds western Nevada. The Truckee River then carries the water to the burgeoning (and thirsty) Reno-Sparks area, the intended destination site. Using aircraft, the institute also seeds the Carson River watershed, about 64 km (40 mi) south of Reno, and the Walker River watershed, about 161 km (100 mi) south of Reno. Researchers at the Institute maintain that their cloud-seeding operations boost the amount of snowfall in the eastern Sierra Range around Lake Tahoe by up to 16 percent.

Many questions remain regarding cloud-seeding as a technique in water resource management. For example, just how effective is cloud-seeding? Proponents will claim that cloud-seeding can result in precipitation increases between 15 and 20 percent, yet, in many cases, cloud-seeding has had absolutely no effect. After 40 years of experimentation with cloud-seeding, we still have no real evidence as to just how much precipitation is produced (Chiras 1985). Then there is the question of using a technology that may not really work in the driest regions of the country, where water is most needed. Remember, dry regions have few clouds and clouds are a prerequisite to cloud-seeding. If a cloud-seeding operation is successful, then there is the problem of having a lack of control over the rainwater's distribution. Additional rainfall may be a blessing to a cattle rancher but simultaneously cause disaster in his neighbor's fruit orchard. Then, of course, there is the related question of whether cloud-seeding merely "steals" water from one region and gives it to another, thereby leaving the latter with a deficit. Such questions open a Pandora's box of possible legal disputes and lawsuits between adjacent regions, states, and countries. Just who owns the moisture in a cloud?

Furthermore, what types of environmental havoc may result from widespread cloud-seeding efforts? For example, Miller (1986) warns that intensified cloud-seeding operations may change regional and even global weather patterns. In the Lake Tahoe region, critics of cloud-seeding maintain that these operations have intensified the danger of avalanches and flooding. Furthermore, they do not like having to pay for the additional cost of snow removal from roads and highways. In addition, critics have other concerns: increased driving hazards, increased road damage from heavy snowfall, more damage to private property, greater snow loads on buildings, higher heating bills, more extensive soil erosion, and more interruptions of utility and communication services. Critics contend that heavier snowfalls from cloud-seeding stifle plant growth or disrupt birds, rodents, and other mammals (including big game). There is also some scientific evidence linking minor changes in plant and animal communities with altered climatic conditions resulting from cloud-seeding operations (Cooper and Jolly 1969).

Finally, will the deposition of silver iodide and other cloud-seeding chemicals adversely affect food webs, wildlife, and ultimately human health? According to Mather (1984), one cloud-seeding project in the upper Colorado River Basin would release nearly 3629 kg (8000 lb) of silver iodide each winter. Since sunlight causes silver iodide to break down to form metallic silver and iodine, Mather wonders whether insoluable silver might enter into food chains and concentrate at dangerous levels in higher life forms. This leads Mather to conclude that, although seemingly not dangerous at current use levels, silver iodide may become a serious pollutant if cloud-seeding becomes widely practiced in this country.

Towing Icebergs. Looming in the fog, mammoth floating icebergs are a menace to shipping—recall the Titanic, the so-called unsinkable passenger liner that collided with an iceberg in the dead of night in April 1912. However, scientists also recognize that these broken away sections of glaciers contain billions of gallons of fresh drinking water. Today, engineers and glaciologists are plotting various schemes to tap this frozen resource. In 1977, for example, the Saudi Arabian government requested a French engineering firm to devise a plan to tow huge icebergs 12,070 km (7500 mi) from Antarctica to the Red Sea port of Jidda (Figure 5-13). U.S. interest in "berg water" was further sparked with the convening of the First International Conference and Workshop on Iceberg Utilization, which was held at Iowa State University in Ames, Iowa, in 1978 (Husseiny 1978).

The whole notion of towing flat tablelike icebergs from Antarctica to dry coastal regions, such as Saudi Arabia, southern California, Australia, and Chile, has a certain appeal. Proponents argue that the concept of towing icebergs for a freshwater resource is not new, noting that it was done on a small scale between 1890 and 1900 in South America. Specifically, small icebergs were towed from Laguna San Rafael, Chile, to as far north as Callao, Peru, a distance of 3850 km (2393 mi) (Coates 1981). Proponents also argue that icebergs will allow drier regions, such as southern California, to reduce their withdrawals of surface and groundwater supplies, thereby conserving their precious water resource. Furthermore, they maintain that using berg water makes practical use of a resource that would otherwise be wasted. Finally, towing icebergs, in their estimation, would create less environmental havoc than other strategies for bringing water to a region, such as the construction of dams and water diversion projects.

The dream of towing icebergs, however, has some real problems. First, is the lack of technological know-how needed for the transport of such a large volume of frozen water. According to Mather (1984),

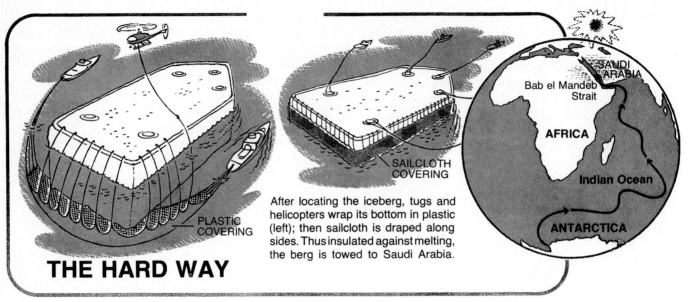

THE HARD WAY

PLASTIC COVERING

SAILCLOTH COVERING

After locating the iceberg, tugs and helicopters wrap its bottom in plastic (left); then sailcloth is draped along sides. Thus insulated against melting, the berg is towed to Saudi Arabia.

SAUDI ARABIA

Bab el Mandeb Strait

AFRICA

Indian Ocean

ANTARCTICA

FIGURE 5-13 Iceberg towing scheme. (From "The Iceberg Cometh," *Newsweek*, July 4, 1977, p. 2. Courtesy of the artist, Harry Carter.)

a large iceberg would be one that is 2.8 km (1.7 mi) wide, 11.2 km (7 mi) long and 250 m (820 ft) thick, which is approximately equivalent to the water volume contained in Shasta Reservoir in northern California. The Ames conference concluded that the optimum iceberg would be 305 m (1000 ft) wide, 1.6 km (1 mi) long, and 274 m (900 ft) thick. How does one wrap and tow an object this large? Furthermore, the slowness of transport presents a problem. Traveling at an estimated speed of 1 knot, it might take six months to reach Chile or Australia and nine months to reach Saudi Arabia (Husseiny 1978). During that time, much water loss would occur through evaporation and melting. International shipping lanes will also be temporarily blocked, particularly if present plans of having "trains" of these icebergs were put into effect. Additional shipping hazards could occur if an iceberg accidentally broke loose from the "ice train." Since no nation owns Antarctica, legal disputes are also bound to arise over the ownership of the ice.

As with cloud-seeding, icebergs towed out of their natural place could cause serious ecological disruptions. Placing such a large cold mass within semitropical waters will no doubt have an effect on fish reproduction and migration patterns. The introduction of such a large cold mass within coastal waters may also bring adverse climatic changes to the region.

Assuming that all the previous questions were resolved, what about the financial cost of such a venture. The Ames conference estimated that wrapping and transporting their "optimum-size berg" would require an initial outlay of $130 million—$30 million to manufacture the plastic cover to shield the iceberg and $100 million for research funds to work out the engineering details. Of course, there would also be the enormous cost for fuel to tow the icebergs, as well as distribution costs once the iceberg had reached its destination. Some researchers, however, find that towing icebergs can be economically feasible. For example, the Rand Corporation projected that if icebergs were towed to California, iceberg water would cost only $30 per acre-foot, as compared with the cost of aqueduct water ($65) or desalinized seawater ($100) (Coates 1981). Certainly, interest in iceberg towing will increase as water scarcity continues and related technologies improve.

PROSPECTS FOR THE FUTURE

In *The Nation's Water Resources: 1975–2000*, the U.S. Water Resources Council (1978) identifies 10 critical water resource problems facing the United States in the next several decades, including inadequate surface water supply, pollution of surface water, overpumping of groundwater supplies, groundwater pollution, decreased drinking water quality, erosion, and sedimentation. Solving these problems and others will require a creative combination of structural and nonstructural approaches to water management.

Positive Signs and Success Stories

Despite the serious water problems facing the nation, these problems *are* being solved in various parts of the country. The following will review just a few of the many positive trends and success stories that should give us reason for hope:

1. *Heightened interest in nonstructural approaches.* One of the most encouraging signs is that massive structural projects are no longer seen as the only way to solving the nation's water problems. For example, it has been nearly a decade since Congress has passed an omnibus water bill funding new projects by the Army Corps of Engineers. Partially because of the economic belt-tightening mood of the country, and partially because of the prospect of environmental damage, large, unnecessary, and potentially environmentally damaging water projects have recently come under much criticism. This is not to say that structural approaches are no longer needed, it simply means that nonstructural approaches are becoming more attractive.

2. *Increased interest in water conservation.* One nonstructural approach that has received much attention is water conservation. For example, Tucson, Arizona, has developed a "desert mentality," thereby dropping the "oasis mentality" of its sister city, Phoenix. Tucson came to recognize that it is located in a desert biome and, therefore, should look like one, rather than attempting to maintain an artificial water-consuming landscape of thick lawns, mulberry trees, and towering green hedges, such as is the practice in Phoenix. According to a 1984 National Wildlife report, Tucson's various conservation measures (e.g., higher water rates and restrictions on landscape watering) have lowered water consumption to 606 L (160 gal) per person per day. In Phoenix, just 161 km (100 mi) away, average use is 984 L (260 gal) per person per day, with some of the suburban communities awash in as much as 3785 L (1000 gal) of water per person per day.

3. *Creative nonstructural approaches to flood control and stormwater runoff.* In the last several years, there has been a profusion of highly innovative approaches to flood control. The flood control management plan developed for the Charles River watershed (the most densely populated river basin in New England) is a case in point (Spirn 1984). Rather than build an upstream flood-control dam that would cost $100 million, the U.S. Army Corps of Engineers decided that the use of adjacent wetlands was the most effective method of managing and storing floodwaters in the region. Specifically, the Corps se-

lected 17 natural storage areas from among 8094 ha (20,000 acres) of wetlands along the Charles River. Using the $10 million appropriated by Congress, the Corps made its first purchase in 1977. Although owned by the Corps, the wetlands are now managed as wildlife refuges by the Massachusetts Division of Fisheries and Wildlife (Notardonato and Doyle 1979).

4. *New towns are being built with natural drainage systems.* Some developers are now beginning to design new towns that work with (rather than against) the forces of nature (Spirn 1984). For example, developers decided to use a *natural drainage system* in the new town of Woodlands, Texas, rather than the conventional storm drainage system. The natural system utilizes undisturbed floodplains to accommodate runoff and well-drained soils to soak up rainfall. An added benefit is that the process recharges the aquifers of Woodlands as well as the neighboring city of Houston.

5. *Stricter guidelines for major water projects.* When conventional structural water projects are given approval, many must now adhere to stricter guidelines than in the past. In 1984, for example, two high-level courts ruled that the Federal Energy Regulatory Commission (FERC) must pay more attention to the environment in issuing licenses for hydroelectric projects. In the first case, the Supreme Court ruled that federal agencies, such as the U.S. Forest Service, have the right to impose environmental conditions on new hydro projects on federal lands. In the second case, a federal appeals court in Seattle, Washington, determined that FERC must consider environmental considerations before licensing even small dam projects. FERC was trying to eliminate its own environmental review of hydroelectric projects of less than 5 megawatts, as well as prevent state and federal agencies from imposing terms designed to protect wildlife and habitat. In 1985, the U.S. Congress imposed strict guidelines on major water projects undertaken by the U.S. Army Corps of Engineers and the Bureau of Reclamation. In most cases, projects could not proceed without first working out environmental issues. The restrictions, contained in the 1986 funding bills, apply to some of the largest and most controversial water projects, such as the Bonneville Unit Diverson Project in Utah, the Narrows Dam in Colorado, and the Garrison Diverson Project in North Dakota.

6. *Rivers, seas, and bays are being cleaned up.* There have been a number of success stories in the cleanup of waterways. The Thames River in England has made a remarkable comeback after centuries of contamination from the dumping London's sewage.

An improvement in water treatment has now allowed the return of a number of species of fish to the river (Botkin and Keller 1982). Although the Mediterranean Sea is not cleaner than it was 10 years ago, international efforts have dramatically slowed down the rate of contamination (Greenberg 1985). Like the Mediterranean Sea, San Francisco Bay in California was once considered a "cesspool." But today, despite recent concern about increasing contamination, the Bay is still cleaner than it was 20 years ago. To the north, Oregon's Willamette River was also extremely contaminated a decade ago. But today, thanks to cooperative efforts between municipalities, business, and industry, the river is now suitable for recreation.

One of the more interesting cases in river cleanup is Denver's transformation of a 16 km (10 mi) stretch of the South Platte River from "a rubble-strewn, filthy, open sewer, lined by garbage and derelict land, into a landscaped park for water sports, public gatherings, bicycling and hiking, and nature study" (Spirn 1984, p. 158). The Denver Greenway (also called the Platte River Greenway) links 18 parks covering 182 ha (450 acres), making it the city's largest single park. Once an eyesore and health hazard, the Platte River now serves as an urban focal point for canoeing, kayaking, rafting, and slalom runs. Detailed descriptions of the Denver Greenway Project can be obtained from Shoemaker and Stevens (1981), Searn (1980), and Wright and Taggart (1976).

7. Past mistakes are being reversed. In some cases, even faulty multimillion-dollar water projects are being dismantled in order to restore the natural environment. According to a 1984 National Wildlife Federation report, for example, the state of Florida is in the process of restoring a stretch of the Kissimmee River to its natural state. Why? Approximately 22 years ago, the U.S. Army Corps of engineers built a 84 km (52 mi) flood control channel through the meandering Kissimmee River. At the time it seemed a good idea, but in 1984, it was nothing more than a "dirty ditch," with 8094 ha (20,000 acres) of marshland dried up; eagles, ospreys, and waterfowl were virtually gone, and the ecology of the Everglades to the south was disrupted. Some $65 million will be required to undo the damage and once again allow water into the former Kissimmee riverbed.

8. Collection programs for toxic wastes are being developed. Cities and counties are also beginning to tackle one of the more hidden water pollution problems—the tons of hazardous pesticides, cleaners, solvents, and paints that are dumped from household garages and basements. According to a 1985 estimate by a regional government office in Seattle,

Washington, there were more than 45,360 kg (100,000 pounds) of the banned pesticide DDT stored in homes in the metropolitan area alone. One can only imagine how much DDT had already been washed down driveways into the city sewerage system or placed in garbage cans for dumping at landfills! The National Wildlife Federation notes that cities and counties in some 25 states are now organizing collection programs, though in 1985, Seattle was the only city with permanent collection points where residents can safely dispose of toxic wastes the year around.

9. Improvements in water quality. In its 1984 National Water Quality Inventory, the U.S. Environmental Protection Agency noted that 36 states reported improvements in water quality resulting from new wastewater plants. This led William Ruckelshaus, former EPA administrator, to claim that this was evidence that the basic approach of the Clean Water Act was working. However, the same report noted that pollution from municipal, industrial, and nonpoint sources continues to cause problems nationwide.

10. New horizons in water research. Scientists are exploring a variety of new research frontiers. For example, the SCSA (Soil Conservation Society of America) reported that Cornell University initiated in 1985 a nationwide research plan called the Groundwater Quality Program. Its primary purpose is to explore methods of minimizing agriculture's contribution to groundwater contamination. Innovative experiments in sewage treatment are also taking place.

In San Diego, California, for example, the city's water department has been experimenting with an aquaculture plant that, at least theoretically, will provide potable water from treated sewage. San Diego's water officials anticipate that within a few years, the water department will have a new set of odorless aquaculture ponds within pristine Balboa Park, which will be capable of producing 379 million L (100 million gal) of drinkable water daily. Since that is 40 percent of the city's daily consumption, such a treatment plant, if it proves to be economically and environmentally sound, will make a major contribution to the water supply of San Diego.

11. Innovative methods in monitoring water quality. Countries around the world are paying more attention to water quality and, in some cases, are developing new methods for monitoring water quality. For example, the German cities of Goeggingen, Würzburg, and Ulm are now using electric West African elephant-trunk fish to monitor the quality of their drinking water. This particular species of fish emits hundreds of electrical signals each minute to mark their territory and to navigate. In even slightly contaminated water, however, the number of impulses plummets. Technicians have installed an automatic alarm system in which a buzzer is triggered when the number of electrical signals drops to a particular level. When the alarm goes off, technicians are alerted to test the water for various chemicals. This method is similar to the practice of using canaries to test air quality in coal mines.

12. *New technologies to stretch water supplies.* Finally, there is a plethora of new techniques being developed to stretch existing water supplies. For example, farmers can use lasers to accurately level fields so that water placed on the land is evenly distributed. Computer programs are available for automatically calculating water amounts and the optimum times for irrigating specific crops in different soil types. In 1986, the University of California at Davis was in the process of establishing a statewide computer network for the region's growers. Its purpose would be to provide custom-tailored irrigation. Furthermore, electronic and neutron sensors have been developed that can not only determine the moisture and salt content of fields but also the water content in plant leaves.

ACTION FOR WATER

Despite the many positive signs and success stories, our nation's water problems are not going to be resolved unless individual citizens become directly involved in one or more aspects of water management. Here is how you can personally make a difference:

1. *Practice home water conservation.* The U.S. Environmental Protection Agency recommends a number of ways that you can conserve water within your own home. In addition to the techniques for saving large amounts of water in the home (Table 5-7), moderate savings can be made by using your dishwater efficiently (or, better yet, not at all), repairing any leaks in toilets and faucets, insulating hot water pipes to reduce *come up time* (the time needed for hot water to reach the faucet), and not wasting cold water when filling a bathtub or sink. Small, but nevertheless significant savings, can be made by such techniques as not letting the bathroom sink water run while shaving or brushing teeth, using less (or recycled) water for household cleaning, thawing frozen foods and ice trays with air rather than with hot water, keeping a bottle of drinking water in the refrigera-

tor rather than wasting tap water while waiting for it to get cold, discouraging waiters from bringing water to your restaurant table, and using a compost pile rather than a garbage disposal. Additional ideas for water conservation within the home can be obtained from your county water district office or your state department of water resources.

2. *Call for improved laws to protect watersheds from abuse.* The U.S. Soil Conservation Service manages over 13,000 small watersheds, 61 percent of which have serious erosion and flooding problems (Chiras 1985). Larger watersheds are managed by such federal agencies as the Bureau of Reclamation, the U.S. Army Corps of Engineers, and the Tennessee Valley Authority. Inform your legislators if these agencies are not properly managing watersheds to prevent deforestation, overgrazing, and other practices that degrade water quality.

3. *Take water resource offenders to court.* If necessary, meet with neighbors that are equally concerned about a local water abuse problem and take the offending business, industry, institution, or agency to court. You just might win a multimillion dollar lawsuit! On July 3, 1986, for example, Fairchild Semiconductor Corporation announced that it and several other companies, including prestigious International Business Machines (IBM), had agreed to pay a multimillion dollar sum to 530 residents of a south San Jose, California, neighborhood as required under a legal settlement of a lawsuit. The residents claimed they were injured by the chemical contamination of their drinking water supply in the early 1980s. The lawsuit arose out of a 1981 discovery of toxic industrial solvents in the soil at the Fairchild plant in south San Jose near the Los Paseos neighborhood. The final outcome can really be credited to the efforts of one woman, Lorraine Ross, who for five years worked with the Great Oaks Water Company and the state Department of Health Services, pushing and pushing until officials agreed to study the community. There is no question that her actions made a difference. Today, other businesses and industry are more alert, fearing that they, too, may be seriously fined for past or present water abuses.

4. *Insist upon comprehensive, integrative efforts at water management.* Water problems will never be resolved if "the left hand doesn't know what the right hand is doing." City officials need to coordinate the activities of urban planners, developers, water resource managers, and other groups that have an effect on the flow, distribution, and quality of water within a region. Specifically, there

TABLE 5-7

Techniques for substantial water savings in the home

CATEGORY	SPECIFICS
Toilet	
Flush less often	Flush only feces, urine, and toilet paper. Use waste container for tissues, trash, hair, paper towels, paper diapers, etc. Be sure not to flush more often than necessary.
Add bottles to tank	Use plastic bottles filled with water and weighted with pebbles to displace water in tank. Be sure not to obstruct float. Do not use bricks. They may flake and clog tubes and valves and, if dropped, could crack tank.
Shower	
Shorter, lighter showers	Turn off water while soaping up. See how light a spray you can wash with. Less than 5 minutes for a shower is adequate. Any longer comes under the heading of recreation.
Bathtub	
Do not overfill tub	A full tub holds 189 L (50 gal) or more. You can bathe adequately with one quarter as much.
Do not waste cold water	Stopper tub before turning on water. Initial cold water can be warmed by adding hot water later. Bathe small kids together. Consider recycling bath water (if not too dirty) for heavy cleaning jobs.
Washing machine	
Wash efficiently	Use load selector for large or small loads if there is one. Otherwise, wash only full loads. Use cold water. You will not save water, but you will save energy and money. Try using less detergent.
Buy a water saver	When you buy a new machine, select the one that uses the least water per pound of wash. Get a suds-saver attachment. Be sure to check energy consumption. Buy machine that uses less water and energy.
Utility sink	
Hand wash efficiently	Soak well with smallest possible quantity of low-sudsing detergent. Save rinse water for next wash. Just add soap. Presoak very dirty items overnight.
Lawn, garden	
Make every watering count	Water slowly, thoroughly, and as infrequently as possible. Water at night to minimize evaporation. Keep a close watch on wind shifts while using sprinklers. Aerate lawn.
Practice water-saving horticulture	Select hardy species that do not need as much water. (Try native plants.) Mulch heavily. Let grass grow higher in dry weather—saves burning and saves water.
Backyard pool	
Prevent evaporation and splashing	Cover when not in use to prevent evaporation and to keep clean. Do not fill up high—water splashes easily. Recycle wading pool water for plants, shrubs, and lawn.
Driveway or street	
Wash car sensibly	Wash in sections, rinse with short spurts from hose. If you need to wash often, use a car wash that recycles water.

Source: Adapted from U.S. Environmental Protection Agency. 1977. *Water Wheel: Your Guide to Home Water Conservation.* Washington, D.C.: Environmental Protection Agency.

must be a holistic approach to flood control, storm drainage, water supply, waste disposal, sewage treatment, and water conservation. Spirn (1984) provides a comprehensive list of considerations for every city.

5. *Encourage international cooperation on water pollution control.* Many water problems, such as acid rain, require international cooperation. Send letters or mailgrams to your senators and representatives, letting them know that you care about acid rain and other water problems. Better yet, call their offices and visit them when they return home. Let them know that you support international cooperation and legislation to abate these problems.

6. *Call for increased research in water pollution.* One of the barriers to water reuse is a lack of knowledge about the health effects of various pollutants. Although much is known about how to reduce bacteria in wastewater, much is still unknown about heavy metals, organic chemicals, and even viruses in water. Support research that investigates these and other water-related problems.

7. *Volunteer for river revivals, acid rain watches, and other water-related projects.* A number of cities now have *river revivals*, which are concerted efforts by conservationists to rid urban waterways of discarded and disfiguring junk. For more than 12 years, for example, San Jose conservationists and interested citizens have loaned their support toward a cleanup of the Guadalupe River, which runs through downtown San Jose, California. Hundreds of volunteers regularly have showed up to pull obstacles, such as shopping carts, from the river and to restore hiking trails along the river banks. According to Lilyann Brannon, president of United New Conservationists, a local conservation organization, their efforts have helped protect the most historic stretch of the most historic river in the state of California. Furthermore, their efforts have no doubt helped bring public attention to the river, for, in 1986, the city of San Jose established elaborate plans to restore and upgrade the river. These plans are similar in concept to the preservation of the Platte River in Denver, Colorado.

Some states are also organizing *acid rain watches* in which you can participate. For example, the Michigan United Conservation Clubs (MUCC), a National Wildlife Federation affiliate, launched an acid rain watch to inform the public about the impact of acid rain. A major activity of the watch is to provide weekly reports to the news media that describe the acidity of the rain and snow falling throughout the state. The professors of meteorology on your campus will probably know if your local area has such an organization.

8. *Demand that university curricula include nonstructural approaches to water management.* Make sure the professors in charge of your university curricula include courses on water resource management, water policy analysis, groundwater restoration, and water resource law. If departmental budgets and faculty time cannot support the creation of separate courses on these subjects, then request that individual faculty members incorporate aspects of water resource management into their existing courses. For example, one reason for the slow shift to water reuse in this country is that the sanitary engineering curricula offered at universities has made only modest efforts at teaching water reuse methods (Thomas 1985). You can help push professors in the right direction. Without this information being taught, water managers and consultants will be reluctant to plan, design, and implement alternative water management schemes.

9. *Choose a career in water resource management.* Finally, you can choose a professional career in some aspect of water resources or water resource management. Today, opportunities for various kinds of water experts are outstanding. Opportunities exist for *specialists*—the so-called hard scientists (geologists, geochemists, geophysicists, hydrologists, and civil engineers), as well as for *generalists*—those individuals with an interdisciplinary background in environmental science or environmental planning and policy. Graduates with backgrounds in solid and hazardous waste disposal, environmental impact analysis, and environmental risk assessment have a special advantage. Many large businesses and industries, such as Fairchild Semiconductor and IBM, now have environmental planning divisions that are set up for the express purpose of dealing with municipal, state, and federal guidelines on water quality. No longer can one successfully run a business (at least for the long term) without having an understanding of water economics, water policy, and water law.

DISCUSSION TOPICS

1. Define *water resource management*. Explain how its three subfields interrelate.
2. Using a topographic map, identify the various watersheds within your local area. Who are the watershed managers within these areas? Discuss any on-going projects to reduce or control sedimentation and pollu-

tion from point and nonpoint sources. What recommendations would you make for further improving the watershed?

3. What are the principal managing agencies for floodplain and groundwater management in your local area? Are there any conflicts of interest between these agencies that are currently being discussed in the news media? If so, debate the issues.

4. Debate the proposition: There is no such thing as a "soft path" approach to water management.

5. Is a new dam currently being planned for your area? If so, debate the pros and cons that relate to its creation. Be sure to discuss the economic benefits versus environmental trade-offs. If the dam is not built, what alternatives exist to maintain an adequate water supply for your community?

6. Are there any existing dams in your local area that are particularly controversial? Do the dams fill an actual need? Are they reliable and safe? Debate these issues.

7. You are at an open forum at your university and you hear someone say, "All dams are bad and all new projects should be scrapped." If you don't agree, what would be your rebuttal? Explain in your rebuttal how you weigh the benefits and drawbacks to dam construction.

8. How dependable is your community's water supply for the next 10, 25, and 50 years? How do water resource managers project a community's future water needs? Discuss possible fallacies in their assumptions and models.

9. What are interbasin transfers? In terms of water supply, should the *have nots* be allowed to take water from the *haves*? Debate this issue, using California as the battleground.

10. How has channelization been used in your area? What have been its ecological effects? Are any new projects being proposed? If so, do an environmental impact statement as a class assignment.

11. Locate, map, and photograph the recharge ponds in your community. Design plans for the possible multiple use of these ponds.

12. Discuss the economic and ecological drawbacks to desalination plants. If there is a desalination plant near your university, request that your instructor arrange a tour of the facility.

13. What is water harvesting? Differentiate between rainfall harvesting and runoff agriculture. Visit those areas in your community that use these dryland farming techniques.

14. Explain how the existence of primary and secondary wastewater treatment plants in a community can hasten cultural eutrophication. How can this problem be remedied?

15. Draw a map that illustrates the inflow of water into your house, including dams, water diversion projects, and filtration plants. Show the outflow of wastes from your house, including the sewerage lines, treatment plants, and the ultimate destination of the wastewater.

16. What type of sewage treatment plant services your region? Using information gathered on the plant, including on-site interviews, determine if the plant is adequately cleaning the wastewater.

17. Is your community aware of the potential danger of using chlorine as a disinfectant in secondary treatment? If so, is your water district office actively pursuing viable alternatives to chlorination?

18. Check your monthly water bill for literature from your local water supplier. Can you identify any half-truths in what they are telling you, particularly about toxic substances in the water? In class, debate the water company's assumptions and their use of statistics.

19. What happens to the sewage sludge from your treatment plant? Is it being used as a soil supplement, or is it being disposed of in the traditional manner? Is your community considering any innovative methods of converting this "waste" into a resource?

20. Design a system of wastewater renovation and a water conservation cycle for your community. Be sure to incorporate the use of park landscapes and wetlands into your scheme.

21. What types of water conservation strategies are farmers using within your region? Which water conserving strategies discussed in the text are not being used? Why not?

22. Visit a farm within your region. Calculate the water savings and pay-back period if the farmer were to install drip irrigation.

23. What are the major industries within your community? How are they conserving water? What measures are they taking to prevent groundwater contamination? Have any of them been fined for illegal dumping? If so, do you consider their fines severe enough?

24. Would you be willing to pay higher water rates for water conservation? How would you feel about having mandatory water restrictors placed on your house? What would be the economic and environmental effects of higher water prices in your region?

25. Design a water conservation plan for your home. Measure its effectiveness by taking water meter readings and regularly inspecting your water bill (most bills include monthly comparisons of water usage).

26. Design a water conservation plan for your college or university. Submit the plan to the appropriate officials on campus. Work with officials to get the plan implemented.

27. Using data on power trends from your local power company and water trends from your local water company for the same time period, note and discuss any similarities and differences between the two trends. How are they interrelated?

28. Is cloud-seeding done in your region? If so, discuss the benefits and any drawbacks that it has brought. What long-term environmental problems might it create?

29. What advantages and disadvantages does the towing of icebergs have over cloud-seeding as a water man-

agement tool? If you live within a coastal state, discuss the possible ecological ramifications of a medium-sized iceberg within your coastal waters.

30. If you were to become a water resource manager, what

field would you most like to pursue? Why did you choose this subfield over another? Pursue an internship with the manager of your choice.

READINGS

ALLEN, G. H., and R. L. CARPENTER. 1977. ''The Cultivation of Fish with Emphasis on Salmonids in Municipal Wastewater Lagoons as an Available Protein Source for Human Beings.'' In F. M. D'Itri, ed., *Wastewater Renovation and Reuse*, pp. 479–549. New York: Marcel Dekker. Informative discussion of aquaculture and wastewater treatment.

AMERICAN FARMLAND TRUST. 1986. *Eroding Choices Emerging Issues*. San Francisco: American Farmland Trust. Good evaluation of California's agricultural land resources and problems, including alternative options.

ANON. 1983. ''Higher Yields with Less Water,'' *American Vegetable Grower*, April, p. 49. Useful statistics on drip irrigation and crop yields.

ANTOSIAK, LEONARD B., and CHARLES A. JOB. 1981. ''Industrial Water Conservation Within the Great Lakes Region: An Overview,'' *Journal AWWA*, January, pp. 9–12. Good description of water recycling schemes in Great Lake industry.

ARTHUR D. LITTLE, INC. 1973. *Report on Channel Modification*. Vol. 1. Washington, D.C.: Council on Environmental Quality. Useful statistics on the number of channelized waterways in the United States.

BASTIAN, ROBERT K. 1982. ''Natural Treatment Systems in Wastewater Treatment and Sludge Management,'' *Civil Engineering*, May, pp. 62–67. Comprehensive review of natural treatment systems.

BAUMANN, D. D., and D. DWORKIN. 1978. ''Water Resources for Our Cities,'' *American Association of Geographers Resource Paper #78-2*. Includes good discussion of water conservation through metering.

BELICHENKO, YU P., and T. L. DOLGOPOLOVA. 1984. ''Creation of Closed Water Management Systems at Industrial Enterprises,'' *Water Resources*, July. Translated from original article in *Vodnye Resursy*, January 1982. Interesting discussion of water recycling at six oil refineries in the Soviet Union.

BERRY, BRIAN, and F. E. HORTON. 1974. *Urban Environmental Management: Planning for Pollution Control*. Englewood Cliffs, N.J.: Prentice-Hall. Key water resource management textbook.

BODLEY, JOHN H. 1985. *Anthropology and Contemporary Human Problems*. 2d ed. Palo Alto, Calif.: Mayfield. Discusses the concept of the *para-primitive* solution to environmental problems.

BOTKIN, DANIEL B., and EDWARD A. KELLER. 1982. *Environmental Studies: The Earth as a Living Planet*. Columbus, Ohio: Merrill. Basic introductory university textbook for environmental studies.

BUREAU OF RECLAMATION. 1977. *Carriage Facilities—Canals*. Denver, Colo.: U.S. Department of the Interior. Includes statistics on the number of irrigation canals in the United States.

BURGH, JOHN. 1982. ''Saving Water Scenically,'' *Water Engineering and Management*, March, pp. 46–47. Detailed discussion of an innovative tertiary treatment facility near Santa Fe, New Mexico.

CALIFORNIA OFFICE OF WATER CONSERVATION. 1985. *Water Conservation News*, June. Includes California's efforts at legislating minimum-flow plumbing fixtures.

CHIRAS, DANIEL D. 1985. *Environmental Science: A Framework for Decision Making*. Menlo Park, Calif.: Benjamin/Cummings. A basic university textbook in environmental studies.

COATES, DONALD R. 1981. *Environmental Geology*. New York: Wiley. Excellent university textbook on the importance of geology to environmental issues, including water resources.

COOPER, C. F., and W. C. JOLLY. 1969. *Ecological Effects of Weather Modification: A Problem of Analysis*. Report on Contract 14-06-D-6576. University of Michigan, School of Natural Resources. Washington, D.C.: U.S. Department of Interior, Bureau of Reclamation, Office of Atmospheric Water Research. Excellent discussion of the ecological effects of cloud-seeding.

COUNCIL ON ENVIRONMENTAL QUALITY. 1984. *Environmental Quality 1984*. Washington, D.C.: Government Printing Office. Fifteenth annual report of the President's Council on Environmental Quality.

CROOK, JAMES. 1985. ''Water Reuse in California.'' In *Future of Water Reuse: Proceedings of the Water Reuse Symposium III*. Vol. 1, pp. 153–178. Denver, Colo.: AWWA Research Foundation. Good summary.

CULP, R., et al. 1979. *Water Reuse and Recycling: Evaluation of Needs and Potential*. Vol. 1. Washington, D.C.: U.S. Department of the Interior. Good summary of uses of wastewater in the United States.

CUTTER, SUSAN L., et al. 1985. *Exploitation, Conservation, Preservation: A Geographic Perspective on Natural Resource Use*. Totowa, N.J.: Rowman and Allanheld. A spatial approach to resource management.

D'ANGELO, A. 1964. ''Report on Universal Metering'' to Honorable Robert F. Wagner, Mayor of New York City, October 7. Interesting statistics on water savings if New York City metered its water.

EPSTEIN, E., et al. 1980. Saline Culture of Crops: A Genetic Approach,'' *Science*, April, pp. 399–404. Detailed discussion of the advances made in genetically engineered salt-tolerant crops.

FINK, D. W., et al. 1973. "Wax Treated Soils for Harvesting Water," *Journal of Range Management*, November, pp. 396–398. Includes useful statistics on the efficiency of water-conserving wax-treated plots.

GOODMAN, ALVIN S. 1984. *Principles of Water Resources Planning.* Englewood Cliffs, N.J.: Prentice-Hall. Excellent general text.

GORDON, WENDY. 1984. *A Citizen's Handbook on Groundwater Protection.* New York: Natural Resources Defense Council. A good reference for citizens, community groups, and government officials interested in protecting groundwater resources.

GREENBERG, DANIEL. 1985. "Diplomat of Troubled Waters," *International Wildlife*, May–June, pp. 40–43. Discusses Stephan Keckes's successful efforts at helping clean up the Mediterranean Sea.

HAMILTON, ROBERT A. 1984. "What Will We Do When the Well Runs Dry?" *Harvard Business Review*, November–December, pp. 28–31, 36–40. Good summary of water recycling at Armco plant in Texas.

HANKE, S. H., and J. E. FLACK. 1968. "Effects of Metering Urban Water," *Journal of American Water Works Association*, December, pp. 1359–1366. Good summary.

HANSON, BLAINE R., and DONALD L. LANCASTER. 1986. "Evaluation of Center-Pivot Sprinkler Systems," *California Agriculture*, May–June, pp. 24–26. Evaluation of three center-pivot sprinkler systems of different design to determine their performance characteristics.

HEATH, R. C. 1984. *Ground-Water Regions of the United States.* Washington, D.C.: Government Printing Office. Excellent summary.

HIGH PLAINS ASSOCIATES. 1982. *Six-State High Plains—Ogallala Aquifer Regional Resources Study.* A report to the U.S. Department of Commerce and the High Plains Study Council. Austin, Tex.: High Plains Associates. Important study outlining water management strategies for the High Plains states that are depleting the Ogallala aquifer.

HILER, EDWARD A., and TERRY A. HOWELL. 1983. "Irrigation Options to Avoid Critical Stress: An Overview." In H. M. Taylor et al., *Limitations to Efficient Water Use in Crop Production*, pp. 479–497. Madison, Wis.: American Society of Agronomy. Includes discussion of the use of computers to manage water for irrigation better.

HUSSEINY, A. A., ed. 1978. *Iceberg Utilization.* New York: Pergamon Press. Important book on the potential of using icebergs as a water source.

JAHN, L. R., and J. B. TREFETHEN. 1973. "Placing Channel Modifications in Perspective," *Proceedings of the National Symposium on Watersheds in Transition*, pp. 15–21. Minneapolis, Minn.: American Water Resources Association. Good discussion of the effects of channelization on fish populations.

KELLSALL, K. J. 1962. *Construction of Bituminous Surfaces for Water Supply Catchment Areas in Western Australia.* Perth, Australia: Public Works Department. Mimeographed. Discussion of Australia's successes at water harvesting.

KNEESE, ALLEN V. 1984. "High Plains, Low Water," *Resources*, Fall, pp. 7–9. Brief, but interesting discussion of the current management strategies for solving the Ogallala aquifer overdraft problem.

LOOMIS, ROBERT S. 1983. "Crop Manipulations for Efficient Use of Water: An Overview." In H. M. Taylor et al. *Limitations of Efficient Water Use in Crop Production.* Madison, Wis.: American Society of Agronomy. Good statistics on crop yields under dryland farming.

MAHIDA, VIJAYSINH U., and FRANK J. DeDECKER. 1975. *Multi-Purpose Combined Sewer Overflow Treatment Facility, Mount Clemens, Michigan.* Cincinnati, Ohio: U. S. Environmental Protection Agency. Interesting discussion of how Mount Clemens combined wastewater treatment with park landscaping.

MATHER, JOHN R. 1984. *Water Resources: Distribution, Use and Management.* New York: Wiley. Superb introductory textbook on water resource management, with an emphasis on the incorporation of concepts from physical, human, and cultural geography.

MATTHEW, OLEN PAUL. 1984. *Water Resources, Geography and Law.* Washington, D.C.: Association of American Geographers. Excellent description of the ways in which law interacts with natural and cultural processes related to water resources.

MILLER, G. TYLER. 1986. *Environmental Science: An Introduction.* Belmont, Calif.: Wadsworth. Basically Miller's *Living in the Environment* (1985) textbook minus the chapters on economics, politics, and ethics.

MILLER, G. TYLER. 1985. *Living in the Environment.* 4th ed. Belmont, Calif.: Wadsworth. Perhaps the best introductory textbook in environmental studies.

MORAN, JOSEPH M., et al. 1986. *Introduction to Environmental Science.* 2d ed. New York: Freeman. Excellent introductory environmental science text, which stresses scientific principles and the natural functioning of the environment.

MORRIS, ROGER. 1985. "It was a Dam Disaster," *National Wildlife*, October–November, pp. 43–47. Informative discussion of the Colorado River flood of 1983.

NABHAN, G. P., ed. 1983. "The Desert Tepary as a Food Resource," *Desert Plants*, Spring, pp. 1–64. Interesting discussion of reviving ancient drought-resistant crops, such as the tepary, for dryland farming.

NATIONAL ACADEMY OF SCIENCES. 1984. *Groundwater Contamination.* Washington, D.C.: National Academy Press. Excellent overview.

NATIONAL ACADEMY OF SCIENCES. 1974. *More Water for Arid Lands: Promising Technologies and Research Opportunities.* Washington, D.C.: National Academy of Sciences. Good overview of the ancient practice of runoff agriculture and its potential for modern application.

NATIONAL RESEARCH COUNCIL. 1984. *Amaranth: Modern Prospects for an Ancient Crop.* Washington, D.C.: National Academy Press. Good discussion of the prospects of amaranth as a crop for dryland farming.

NEBEL, BERNARD J. 1981. *Environmental Science: The Way the World Works.* Englewood Cliffs, N.J.: Prentice-Hall. Basic introductory textbook to environmental science.

NOTARDONATO, FRANK, and ARTHUR F. DOYLE. 1979. "Corps Takes New Approach to Flood Control," *Civil Engineering*, June, p. 66. Good discussion of the use of wetlands for flood control management in New England.

O'DELL, C. 1983. "Trickle Did the Trick," *American Vegetable Grower*, June, p. 56. Useful statistics on drip irrigation and crop yields.

OWEN, OLIVER S. 1985. *Natural Resource Conservation: An Ecological Approach*. 4th ed. New York: Macmillan. Contains two good chapters on water resources from a biological perspective.

PARIZEK, R. R., and E. A. MYERS. 1968. "Recharge of Groundwater from Renovated Sewage Effluent by Spray Irrigation." In *Proceedings of the Fourth American Water Resources Conference*, pp. 425–443. Useful information regarding wastewater renovation and conservation cycle.

POINCELOT, RAYMOND P. 1986. *Toward a More Sustainable Agriculture*. Westport, Conn.: AVI. Includes excellent chapter on water conservation strategies for agriculture.

POSTEL, SANDRA. 1985. *Conserving Water: The Untapped Alternative*. Worldwatch Paper 67. Washington, D.C.: Worldwatch Institute. Excellent summary.

POSTEL, SANDRA. 1986. "Increasing Water Efficiency." In Lester Brown, ed., *State of the World 1986*, pp. 40–61. New York: Norton. Basically a condensed version of Postel's *Conserving Water: The Untapped Alternative*.

POSTEL, SANDRA. 1985. "Managing Freshwater Supplies." In Lester Brown, ed., *State of the World 1985*, pp. 42–72. New York: Norton. Global discussion of water resource management.

POSTEL, SANDRA. 1984. *Water: Rethinking Management in an Age of Scarcity*. Washington, D.C.: Worldwatch Institute. Excellent overview.

RAKOSH, L. 1978. "Water Reuse in the American Israeli Paper Mills, Hadera." In *Israqua '78*. Tel Aviv: Israel Centre of Waterworks Appliances. Good discussion of water recycling in an Israeli paper mill.

RONDON, JOANNE. 1980. *Landscaping For Water Conservation in a Semiarid Environment*. Aurora, Colo.: Department of Utilities. Detailed handbook and guide to water-conserving landscaping in semiarid regions.

SCHMIDT, C. J., et al. 1973. "A Survey of Industrial Use of Municipal Wastewater," In L. K. Cecil, ed., *Complete Water Reuse: Industry's Opportunity*. New York: American Institute of Chemical Engineers. Papers presented at the National Conference on Complete Water Reuse sponsored by the American Institute of Chemical Engineers, April 23–27.

SEARN, ROBERT M. 1980. "Denver Tames the Unruly Platte: A Ten-Mile River Greenway," *Landscape Architecture*, July, pp. 382–386. An article by the landscape architecture consultant to the Denver Greenway Project.

SEIDEL, H. F., and E. R. BAUMANN. 1957. "A Statistical Analysis of Water Works Data for 1955 Data," *Journal of American Water Works Association*, December, pp. 1531–1566. Analysis of U.S. cities and water leaks.

SELBST. 1985. "Water Management in Israel." *Future of Water Reuse: Proceedings of the Water Reuse Symposium*. Vol. 1. Denver, Colo.: AWWA Research Foundation. Wastewater treatment in Israel.

SHOEMAKER, JOE, and LEONARD STEVENS. 1981. *Returning the Platte to the People*. Denver, Colo.: Greenway Foundation. A book written by the chairman of the Platte River Development Committee.

SHOJI, KOBE. 1977. "Drip Irrigation," *Scientific American*, November, pp. 62–68. Background and basic features of drip irrigation.

SIEGRIST, ROBERT L. 1983. "Minimum-Flow Plumbing Fixtures," *Journal AWWA*, July, pp. 342–347. Efficient toilets in Scandinavia.

SPIRN, ANNE W. 1984. *The Granite Garden: Urban Nature and Human Design*. New York: Basic Books. Contains excellent chapters on water resource management within urban areas.

STOUT, G. L. 1984. "How You Can Computerize Drip Irrigation," *American Vegetable Grower*, February, pp. 14–15. Interesting discussion of the use of computers with drip irrigation.

SWEDISH PREPARATORY COMMITTEE FOR THE UNITED NATIONS WATER CONFERENCE. 1977. *Water in Sweden*. Stockholm: Ministry of Agriculture. Water recycling programs within Sweden.

TARPLEE, W. H., JR., et al., 1971. *Evaluation of the Effects of Channelization on Fish Populations in North Carolina's Coastal Plain Streams*. Raleigh, N.C.: North Carolina Wildlife Resources Commission. Good summary.

TEXAS WATER RESOURCES INSTITUTE AND THE TEXAS AGRICULTURAL EXPERIMENT STATION. 1984. "Storing Soil Moisture," *Water Currents*, Fall, pp. 3–6. Groundwater recharge and reuse as drinking water.

TOBIN, GRAHAM, AND BURRELL E. MONTZ, ed. 1983. *Water Resources Management*. Special issue of the *The Environmental Professional*. Fourteen articles that reflect the water research emphasis of geographers.

THOMAS, RICHARD E. 1985. "Reuse Due to Federal Wastewater Construction Grants." In *Future of Water Reuse: Proceedings of the Water Reuse Symposium*. Vol. 1. Denver, Colo.: AWWA Research Foundation. Discusses need for better university curricula in water reuse.

TROEH, F. R., et al. 1980. *Soil and Water Conservation for Productivity and Environmental Protection*. Englewood Cliffs, N.J.: Prentice-Hall. One of the better university textbooks on soil and water conservation.

U.S. GEOLOGICAL SURVEY. 1984. *National Water Summary 1983—Hydrologic Events and Issues*. Washington, D.C.: Government Printing Office. Important water document.

U.S. GOVERNMENT ACCOUNTING OFFICE. 1976. *Report to Congress: Better Federal Coordination Needed to Promote More Efficient Farm Irrigation, RED-76-116*, Washington, D.C.: U.S. Government Accounting Office. Provides good figures on water seepage in canals.

U.S. WATER RESOURCES COUNCIL. 1978. *The Nation's Water Resources: 1975-2000*. Washington, D.C.: Government Printing Office. Second National Water Assessment of 106 water resources subregions across the United States.

VIESSMAN, WARREN, JR., and CLAIRE WELTY. 1985. *Water Management: Technology and Institutions.* New York: Harper & Row. Engineering designs and objectives as they relate to human and environmental factors concerning water management.

WALTON, SUSAN. 1981. "Egypt After the Aswan Dam," *Environment,* May, pp. 30–39. Good summary.

WEIRETER, ROBERT. 1982. "Waste Not Wastewater: West: The Arcata Experiment," *American Forests,* June, pp. 38–53. Interesting discussion of the use of wetlands for wastewater treatment in Arcata, California.

WITTFOGEL, K. A. 1956. "The Hydraulic Civilizations." In William L. Thomas, ed., *Man's Role in Changing the Face of the Earth,* pp. 152–164. Chicago, Ill.: University of Chicago Press. Classic theory in water management.

World Environment Report. 1984. April 4, vol. 10, no. 7, p. 55. Contains a brief news item relating to the use of efficient low-flow toilets in West Germany.

WRIGHT, KENNETH, and WILLIAM C. TAGGART. 1976. "The Recycling of a River," *Civil Engineering,* November, pp. 42–46. Engineering consultants to the Denver Greenway Project discuss their conclusions.

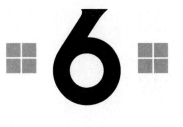

6

RANGELAND RESOURCES AND THEIR MANAGEMENT

While I know the standard claim is that Yosemite and the like afford the greatest natural shows, I am not so sure but that the Prairies and the Plains last longer, fill the aesthetic sense fuller, precede all the rest, and make North America's characteristic landscape.

Walt Whitman

Our country's rangelands are one of our most important renewable resources. They provide forage and roughage for livestock and wildlife, habitat for wildlife, and open space, recreational opportunities, and aesthetic benefits for humans. Rangelands stabilize soil and contribute to soil development and water retention. Furthermore, by reducing grain requirements, forage-based livestock production conserves energy and uses resources not readily usable by other means. Specifically, ruminants, like cattle and sheep, can digest and convert cellulose (one of the world's most abundant organic compounds) into foods people can use, such as meat, milk, cheese, and butter. Ruminants also supply other essential commodities, such as fertilizer, leather, wool, and even fuel.

Although the term **rangeland** to many Americans brings up images of cattle herds and horse-riding cowboys on the grasslands west of the Missis-

sippi River, the term actually includes all grasslands and shrublands (collectively called rangelands) as well as forest lands across the nation that support an understory of herbaceous or shrubby vegetation that provides forage for grazing and browsing animals. The U.S. Department of Agriculture (1981) provides a good definition of rangeland:

Rangeland is land on which the potential natural vegetation is predominantly grasses, grass-like plants, forbs, or shrubs; including land revegetated naturally or artificially that is managed like native vegetation. Rangeland includes natural grasslands, savannas, shrublands, most deserts, tundra, alpine communities, coastal marshes, and wet meadows, that are less than 10 percent stocked with forest trees of any size.

Despite fairly elaborate definitions, there is no real consensus among resource agency officials and academics as to what exactly constitutes range. In some studies, the pinyon juniper and chaparral plant communities of the western United States are classified as rangelands, whereas in other studies, they are classified under forest ecosystems. There is also major disagreement over the exact nature of the transition zone between forest and rangeland; some studies classify the transition zone as forest, others classify it as rangeland. The problem is that there is currently no agreed upon classification system.

In 1970, rangeland in the contiguous United States was inventoried under the Forest-Range Environmental Study (FRES) (Forest-Range Task Force 1972). The FRES report was an attempt by the U.S. Forest Service to conduct the first analytical ecosystems approach to rangeland classification on a nationwide basis. It was intended to supersede the only other rangeland survey of consequence, "The Western Range" (USDA Forest Service 1936), which was submitted to the Congress in 1936. The 1936 survey used a less sophisticated descriptive approach, emphasizing western range use, its condition, and future administrative strategies. This 1936 system is still with us today, since university professors and other researchers never really came to recognize the newer FRES report. Says Edward Slater, Office of Range, U.S. Forest Service, "The state of the art in terms of rangeland classification is that there is no state of the art. Both systems are currently acceptable." Until there is an agreed upon classification system, assessing rangeland data will continue to be difficult.

There is agreement, however, that America's growing number of people are putting increased demands on these rangeland resources. To meet these demands, our country's rangelands must be managed wisely. This chapter will begin by briefly looking at the extent and kinds of U.S. rangelands, their uses, and the causes of their depletion. The chapter will then concentrate on the management of rangelands for grazing, including some principles, policies, and techniques in rangeland conservation and management. We will then turn to efforts and techniques at preserving some of the remaining isolated patches of natural rangelands that still exist in the country. The chapter will conclude with a statement on the current status of our national rangelands, as well as a discussion of how you can personally get involved in helping conserve our rangeland heritage.

EXTENT, KINDS, AND USES OF RANGELANDS

Extent of Rangelands

Rangelands occur on every continent and on most large islands throughout the world. Shantz (1954) estimates that rangelands extend over 44 million km^2 (17 million mi^2) and constitute 24 percent of the world's vegetation. Included within his classification of rangelands are such dissimilar vegetation types as arctic herblands, savannas, steppes, and even dense bamboo jungles. True natural grasslands, according to Shantz, cover only about 9.25 million km^2 (3.57 million mi^2).

One-third, approximately 312 million ha (770 million acres), of this country's land area is classified as rangeland, mostly located in the western half of the nation (USDA 1984) (Figure 6-1). This includes natural grasslands like prairies and mountain meadows, shrublands like the treeless plains of Texas, and even coastal marshes and wet meadows. This U.S. Forest Service system of rangeland classification, however, does not include *improved pasture-*

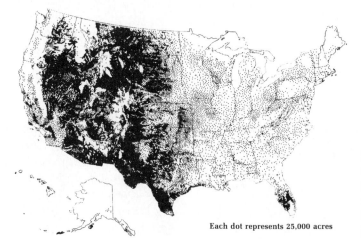

Each dot represents 25,000 acres

FIGURE 6-1 Rangelands in the United States. (From Maryla Webb and Judith Jacobsen, *U.S. Carrying Capacity—An Introduction* [Washington, D.C.: Carrying Capacity, 1982].)

land—grasslands dependent upon artificial seeding, fertilization, and irrigation.

Kinds and Uses of Rangelands

The 1970 Forest-Range Environmental Study (FRES) categorized all U.S. rangeland communities into seven different kinds of grassland ecosystems. What follows is a brief description of each kind.

The first grassland ecosystem is the *mountain grassland ecosystem,* and it is found primarily in the Western Mountain States adjacent to or surrounded by forested areas. At moderate elevations, these beautiful pastoral openings are surrounded by stands of Douglas fir, ponderosa pine, or lodgepole pine. Whether in the foothills at northerly latitudes or at high mountain sites, mountain grassland ecosystems are characterized throughout by bunchgrasses of the fescue and wheatgrass groups. In terms of land use, much of the lower elevations or foothills were converted to agricultural use soon after settlement, such as the Palouse Prairie Hills of north central Oregon. At moderate elevations there are livestock ranges, and the higher elevations serve as important summer ranges for big game, cattle, and sheep.

The *mountain meadow ecosystem* constitutes the second major kind of grassland. It consists of wet to intermittently wet sites in the forest zone of mountains in the western states. Typically, the topography is flat to gently sloping, basinlike, and adjacent to lakes and streams that keep the soil saturated for at least part of the growing season. The dominant vegetation is composed of grasses, sedges, and rushes, with some phreatophytic shrubs. With so many lakes and streams, the mountain meadow ecosystem provides excellent habitat for numerous species of wildlife, including fish, waterfowl, and beaver. At the higher elevations, these meadow ecosystems have not been threatened so much by cultivation as by roadbuilding and trails made by horses used for recreation.

The third kind of grassland is the *plains grassland ecosystem,* and it is located on the Great Plains—a broad belt of flat land that slopes gradually eastward from the eastern foothills of the Rocky Mountains to the Central States, where it gives way to the tall-grass prairie ecosystem. The plains grassland ecosystem (commonly known as the *short-grass steppe)* is dominated almost exclusively by blue grama *(Bouteloua gracilis)* and, through much of its range, by a companion species, buffalo grass *(Buchloe dactyloides).* Both are short in stature (under 1 m or 3.28 ft) and form a dense sod, giving thousands of square miles of rolling plains in North America a uniform smooth ap-

pearance. This kind of grassland covers an area larger than any other vegetation region in the United States, covering some 113 million ha (280 million acres). Although large areas of the plains grassland ecosystem have been converted to crop farming, the remainder is primarily used for rangeland.

The *prairie grassland ecosystem* (commonly known as the tall-grass prairie ecosystem) constitutes the fourth and perhaps the most luxuriant type of true grassland type in the U.S. rangeland country. The tall-grass prairie ecosystem lies on the flat to rolling hill land of the Central Lowland, between the deciduous forests of the East and the short-grass plains of the West. By far, the most important dominant grasses are two species of the genus *Andropogon*—little bluestem *(A. scorparius)* and big bluestem *(A. gerardi).* They constitute about 70 percent of the vegetation in this ecosystem and can reach heights of 2 m (6.56 ft). It is here that large herds of bison once grazed. Unfortunately for wildlife (as well as the rangeland industry), most of the tall-grass prairie is now gone, having succumbed to the plow. Its deep, dark, fertile soils, along with climatic conditions suited to growing corn and other valuable crops now form the fertile farmlands of America's corn belt. The remaining principal areas of concentration are in Nebraska, Kansas, Oklahoma, and the Dakotas.

The fifth kind of grassland, the *desert grassland ecosystem* (commonly known as the semidesert grassland or desert-plains grassland), occurs in scattered areas on tablelands of moderate to extreme relief in the Colorado Plateau region of Arizona, New Mexico, and Utah, as well as on the plains of southwestern Texas. This kind of grassland occurs mainly at elevations of less than 1300 m (4265 ft). This is the driest of the true grassland ecosystems, with most areas receiving between 25 and 50 cm (9.8 and 19.7 in.) of precipitation annually. These plateau lands are moderately to severely dissected by rugged canyons. The chief dominant grasses within the desert grassland ecosystem are several species of grama grass, especially black grama *(Bouteloua eriopoda),* curly mesquite *(Hilaria belangeri),* and three types of awn grasses *(Aristida).* Most of the desert grassland ecosystem is used as rangeland—providing one of the better year-round ranges in the country.

The sixth kind of grassland is the *wet grassland ecosystem.* This is perhaps the most diverse kind of grassland, since it includes the coastal wet prairies and marshes from the Mexican border to Long Island, New York (excluding the coastlines of Florida, Georgia, and the Carolinas), the Everglades, the palmetto prairie of southern Florida, the tule marshes in the California Trough, and the flood plains of the lakes of the Intermontaine Plateaus. The vegetation of this ecosystem is also diverse, with cordgrasses and saltgrass on the coastal prairies, wire-grass and saw-palmetto on the palmetto prairie, and tules, cattail, and soft flag on the tule marshes. As might be expected, there is no consistent pattern of land use in this ecosystem. In addition to livestock production, the land is used for hunting, fishing, trapping, and agriculture.

The seventh kind of grassland is the *annual grassland ecosystem.* This is the California steppe vegetation community, which occupies large areas of Central Valley of California and is found along the Pacific coast. These California annual or foothill grasslands have dominant plants such as wild oats (*Avena fatua*), soft chess (*Bromus mollis*), ripgut (*Bromus rigidus*), wild barley, and fescue. At higher elevations, perennial bunchgrasses may occur, such as needlegrass, creeping wildrye, and pine bluegrass. Much of the annual grassland ecosystem is now irrigated and forms the basis for one of the richest agricultural areas in the world, the Central Valley of California. At higher elevations in the annual grassland ecosystem, cattle grazing exists along with dryland farming.

RANGELAND DEPLETION

Despite the large extent and variety of our country's rangelands, this resource is diminished constantly through both natural and human causes.

Natural Causes of Depletion

Drought. Prolonged droughts can drastically modify vegetation. Of all the natural causes of rangeland depletion, ranchers fear droughts the most since they can do virtually nothing (beyond cloud-seeding) to control or modify this natural phenomenon. Cattle ranchers in Nevada, for example, constantly face water shortages and the possibility of a severe drought that can deteriorate the range plant community. In the northwestern section of the state, ranchers can anticipate that at least one year out of every 10 will be a drought year. Conditions get even worse as one moves farther south. For example, in Reno, Nevada, ranchers can anticipate between two and three drought years out of every 10, and in the southwestern section of the state, near Las Vegas, ranching is nearly impossible, with four to five years out of every 10 (on the average) experiencing a severe drought (Figure 6-2).

Droughts can severely deteriorate the range plant community. For example, Owen (1980) notes

that a 1934 drought in the Snake River plains of southern Idaho caused an 84 percent reduction in plant cover, as compared with the plant cover of 1932 in a study plot where livestock had been excluded. During the same drought year of 1934 in western Kansas, the drought killed 64.6 percent of plants on pastures that were only moderately grazed. More recently, from 1977 to 1981, a severe dry spell wilted crops and rangelands over parts of Montana, Wyoming, the Dakotas, and Minnesota. Only an occasional spear of grass poked through the dusty ranges, and ranchers and dairymen were forced to feed hay to stock that should have been munching on summer grass. In the hardest hit areas, such as eastern Montana, the drought also affected hay production, thus making hay scarce and expensive—$80 to $100 a ton. Not able to cope, some ranchers either sold off their stock or sent their cattle to farmers in states not stricken by the drought. No figures are yet available on the percentage of the range plant community affected by the 1977–1981 drought.

Competitors. A number of herbivorous animals, particularly grasshoppers, jack rabbits, prairie dogs, and kangaroo rats, compete with livestock for the range plant community. Within certain study areas on the Montana rangeland during the 1936–1937 drought, scientists recorded 25 grasshoppers per m^2, and these rangeland competitors demolished 67 percent of the total forage (Owen 1980). Drought conditions also provide favorable environmental conditions for population explosions of jack rabbits. According to Owen (1980, p. 252), ''. . . 75 antelope jack rabbits consume as much forage as 1 cow, and 15 eat enough to sustain 1 sheep.'' Owen also notes that the kangaroo rat of the southwestern United States is an important rangeland competitor. This rodent digs extensive burrow systems and stuffs these burrows with seeds and deposits gathered during nocturnal foraging. Given a kangaroo rat density of only 2 per acre, range scientists estimate these animals can bring about a decrement of 7.4 pounds per acre of forage.

Shrub Encroachment. Grasslands are periodically invaded by woody, low-value shrubs, such as sagebrush, juniper, creosote bush, burroweed, and mesquite. The mesquite (*Prosopis juliflora*) of the southwestern grasslands is considered by ranchers to be the worst pest of the many woody plant invaders. Mesquite receives this distinction because of its wide distribution, abundance, and aggressive encroachment on this country's rangelands. Ironically, grazing, particularly overgrazing, actually invites these invasions of other plants. Since grasslands ecologic-

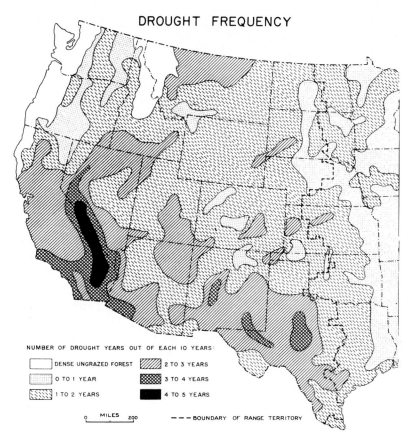

DROUGHT FREQUENCY

NUMBER OF DROUGHT YEARS OUT OF EACH 10 YEARS:

DENSE UNGRAZED FOREST		2 TO 3 YEARS
0 TO 1 YEAR		3 TO 4 YEARS
1 TO 2 YEARS		4 TO 5 YEARS

0 ⊢ MILES ⊢ 200   — — — BOUNDARY OF RANGE TERRITORY

FIGURE 6-2 Drought frequency. (Courtesy of U.S. Forest Service.)

ally occur between the wetter forests and the drier desert shrubland, continued grazing by animals that prefer grass (e.g., cattle) reduces grass, thereby allowing trees to invade from the forests and shrubs and succulents to invade from the desert. On the Texas prairie alone, over 20 million ha (50 million acres) of rangeland have been invaded by mesquite and juniper, thereby seriously lowering its livestock carrying capacity (Owen 1980).

Human Causes of Depletion

Cultivation. The encroachment of farmlands onto our nation's rangelands has already taken a heavy toll. Furthermore, this encroachment is likely to continue as our human population grows, and as we develop more sophisticated techniques for cultivating in dryland areas. Rangelands may be further restricted to those areas that are too dry, too wet, too cold, or too rocky for agriculture.

Overgrazing. In addition to direct land-use conversion that changes grazing land to crop production, humans have limited or deteriorated existing rangelands by using off-road vehicles, by using the

land for concentrated recreation, and by using herbicides. But of all human activities, the grazing of livestock has had the most profound effect.

Grazing not only reduces the amount of vegetative cover, but also affects future leaf and root growth by allowing other factors to come into play (Barnard 1964). Dung and urine are added to the soil; trampling causes soil compaction, which, in turn, affects rates of water infiltration and soil erosion, thereby altering seed and fruit dispersal. With this change in microenvironment, the interrelationships between grass species are affected, and the individual species is also affected. **Overgrazing** occurs when the grazing is so heavy and prolonged that it impairs future forage production. Characteristically, the native grass cover is replaced by invading plants of low nutrient value. Once virgin grassland, America's western rangelands are now predominantly covered with sagebrush and other weed species, and they are heavily eroded as a result of overgrazing. **Range condition** is a term used by rangeland management agencies to discuss the condition or quality of the range. The U.S. Forest Service defines range condition as ''an estimate of the degree to which the present vegetation and ground cover depart from that which is presumed to be the natural potential (or climax) for the site'' (USDA 1981, p. 158). In other words, the greater the departure from natural conditions in terms of ground cover, plant species composition, and production, the poorer the condition of the range.

The Bureau of Land Management (BLM) manages some 70 million ha (174 million acres) of rangeland in the arid West. In 1984, it classified 18 percent of its rangelands as being in either *poor condition* (lands that are stripped of much topsoil and vegetative cover) or *bad condition* (lands where the topsoil was gone and where vegetation was sparse, mostly composed of low-value plants) (Table 6-1). In both cases, overgrazing was the primary culprit. By comparison, the BLM classified 42 percent of its rangelands as being in *fair condition,* meaning that these lands were in better condition, yet the more valuable forage species had still been depleted and replaced by less palatable plants or by bare ground. Its remaining rangelands were either in *good condition* (31 percent) or in *excellent condition* (5 percent). The gradual improvement in range condition as indicated by the BLM in Table 6-1, however, may cloak the actual trend in the condition of our public rangelands. The BLM admits that the information contained in its various reports are not directly comparable because of changing methods of reporting the information (BLM 1985). For example, the Department of the Interior's report in 1975 was based on the range's ability to produce forage for livestock, whereas the 1984 condition class figures are based on a new method referred to as *ecological site inventories.* These inventories only cover approximately 40 million ha (99 million acres) of the total 70 million ha (174 million acres) of public rangelands. Professional ''judgment'' (guesswork?) was used to estimate the range condition of lands yet to be covered by the ecological site inventories. Although range management professionals in such agencies as the BLM claim that range condition has actually improved since the 1930s, changing classification systems and incomplete inventories raise questions about the actual figures used by these organizations.

When prolonged overgrazing is combined with severe drought, **desertification** may occur, which is the conversion or degradation of productive rangelands into pure desert. Although the exact process of desertification is not known, causal factors are cultivation of poor quality lands, overdrafting of the groundwater, poor drainage of irrigated lands, and land degradation from the use of off-road vehicles. The well-publicized Ethiopian famine of 1985 was primarily the result of desertification stemming from severe drought and overgrazing along the southern edge of the Sahara Desert in Africa. However, one need not look farther than North America to find examples of desertification (Figure 6-3). Harold Dregne, director of the International Center for Arid and Semi-Arid Land Studies at Texas Tech University, calculated that 2.8 million km² (1.1 million mi²) or 36.8 percent of the world's arid lands have undergone *severe* desertification and 27,193 km² (10,500 mi²) of North America have undergone *very severe* desertification (Dregne 1977). Furthermore, the North American area of 27,193 km² (10,500 mi²) of very severe des-

TABLE 6-1

Comparative percentages of public rangelands in excellent, good, fair, and poor condition (1936–1984)

	PERCENT BY CONDITION CLASS			
YEAR	EXCELLENT	GOOD	FAIR	POOR OR BAD
1936[a]	1.5	14.3	47.9	36.3
1966[b]	2.2	16.7	51.6	29.5
1975[c]	2.0	15.0	50.0	33.0
1984[d]	5.0	31.0	42.0	18.0

Source: Bureau of Land Management. 1985. *50 Years of Public Land: 1934–1984.* Washington, D.C.: U.S. Department of Agriculture, p. 20.

[a]Data adapted from *The Western Range,* Senate Document 199, 75th Congress, 2d Session.

[b]*The Forage Resource,* Pacific Consultants (1969).

[c]*Range Condition Report,* Department of the Interior (1975).

[d]Aggregation of all baseline resource records maintained at each of the Resource Areas within the BLM. Total acreage = 96%; the remaining 4% has not been rated for range condition.

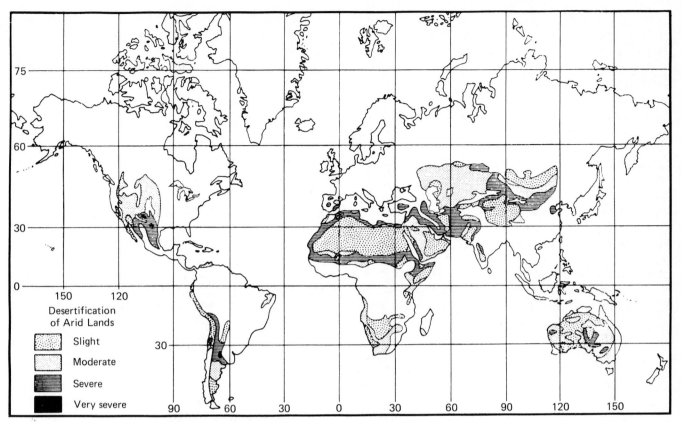

FIGURE 6-3 The degree of desertification in 1981. (From Harold E. Dregne, ''Combating Desertification: Evaluation of Progress,'' *Environmental Conservation*, vol. 11, no. 2 [1984], p. 115.)

ertification is approximately twice the African area of very severe desertification, which is 14,244 km² (5500 mi²) (Owen 1985).

There are three very severe areas of desertification in the United States: One is on the Navajo Indian Reservation, which is on the border of New Mexico and Arizona, and the other two areas surround El Paso, Texas. All three areas have been plagued by overgrazing. Dregne further estimates that about 91 million ha (225 million acres) within the United States, or approximately 10 percent of the nation's land area, have experienced severe or very severe desertification.

The case of the Navajo Indian Reservation provides a dramatic example of socially disruptive desertification in the United States. Sheridan (1981) notes several factors that have caused the Navajo land crisis. First, the Navajo's are experiencing a high population growth rate—about 3 percent per year, which is comparable to the rate in India or Mexico. In other words, over the last century the Navajo population has increased tenfold, whereas the land area of the

reservation has only increased threefold. With more mouths to feed, the Navajo are reluctant to cut back on their flocks. Second, the usual methods of livestock control, such as fencing, conflict with Navajo communal tradition. Although certain members of a clan may have a *customary use area* for grazing their flocks, other resources (timber, firewood, and water) are communal property, open to all who need them. Third, the current Navajo land tenure system further complicates proper land management. The land is not owned by individual Navajos, or even by the Navajo tribe, but rather by the federal government, which holds the land in trust for the tribe. On the other hand, individual Navajos exercise control over use rights to the land. Although federal efforts to control overgrazing began as far back as 1937, restrictions such as sheep permits based on each area's carrying capacity have been met with bitter opposition. Finally, overharvesting of shrubs, particularly four-wing saltbush, for cooking and for heat have contributed in a major way to desertification. The Navajo people are rapidly depleting the natural resource base (i.e., the vegetation) for their livestock. As one of the poorest groups in the nation, the Navajo overgraze the land because they have no alternative, thus pitting short-term interest against sustaining the land for future generations.

Pollution. Our rangelands are also facing serious threats from toxic chemicals and other forms of pollution. In Merced County, California, for example, the tainted water of Kesterson Wildlife Refuge is percolating into nearby grasslands. Milk samples from cattle at six dairies within the Grasslands Water District around Kesterson now have to be regularly tested by the State Department of Food and Agriculture. The refuge was closed in 1983 after the discovery of widespread deaths and deformities among birds nesting there. Scientists tentatively blame the deaths on selenium, a trace metal discharged into the marshy refuge from the San Luis agricultural drain on the west side of the San Joaquin Valley (Figure 6-4).

RANGELAND CONSERVATION AND MANAGEMENT

Range Management—More Than Just Science!

Although Americans did not invent range management, as a profession and a science, it is indeed American. Courses in range management began to be offered in western universities in the early 1900s. A. W. Samson, considered by many to be the father of range science, compiled in 1923 and 1928 the first principles of range management. However, the textbook that had the greatest impact on the evolution of the discipline was Stoddart and Smith's 1943 edition of *Range Management* (Vallentine and Sims 1980).

In their latest edition (1975), Stoddart and Smith (now with the help of Thadis W. Box) define range management as "the science and art of optimizing the returns from rangelands in those combinations most desired by and suitable to society through the

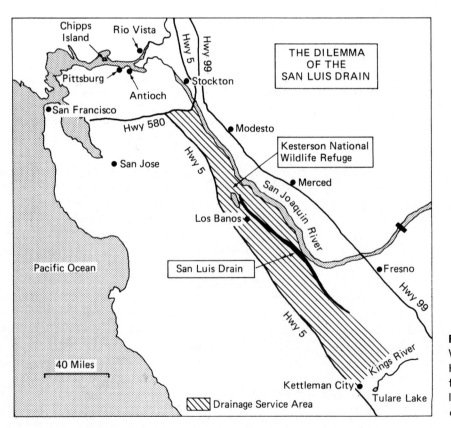

FIGURE 6-4 Kesterson National Wildlife Refuge. The dilemma: How does one drain agricultural fields without contaminating wildlife refuges? (From *San Jose Mercury News*, February 9, 1985.)

manipulation of range ecosystems.'' They point out that range management is more like the study of human ecology than the study of pure science, since it involves the physical sciences (the topographic, climatic, and hydrologic factors), the biological sciences (the plant and animal interactions), and, particularly, the social sciences (human institutions, technology, perceptions of grasslands, natural resource and ranch economics, multiple-use concepts, and land-use planning). Because of the integrated nature of range resources, range management is also closely tied to the management of soil, water, forests, and outdoor recreational resources.

Evolution of U.S. Range Policy

Beginning of the Problem. Some of our nation's rangelands have been grazed for over 460 years, dating back to 1519 when Ponce de Leon is believed to have introduced livestock into Florida. In his 1540 quest for the fabled seven golden cities of Cibola, the Spanish captain Coronado took with him ''1000 horses and 500 of our cows and more than 5000 rams and ewes'' on his march through what are now Kansas and Colorado (Barnes 1926). Escaped and abandoned animals from these original herds gradually stocked the range, adding to the already vast herds of large grazing animals (e.g., bison, elk, deer, and pronghorn antelope).

Grazing further intensified under the government's various land disposal schemes (Stoddart et al. 1975). For example, the Homestead Acts of 1862, 1909, 1912, and 1916 resulted in the cultivation and grazing of thousands of acres of land that was unsuited for these purposes. Furthermore, much adjacent public domain went unclaimed, for it was ''the land nobody wanted'' (Kremp 1981). It was the hot, dry, dusty, and rocky ''waste'' land that did not make homesteading worthwhile. Settlers did not want it since the land would be too hard to work and crop productivity would simply be too low. The government did not want it because it was mostly unforested, and its scenic qualities were not spectacular enough to have the land designated as a national park or forest. This unclaimed public domain was useful, however, as marginal grazing land. Beginning as early as 1850, cattle ranchers and sheep herders grazed their animals on this free, unregulated forage (Box et al. 1976). The Civil War, however, soon ruined markets and put the economy in disarray. Yet, left to their own devices, the tough, free-roaming Texas longhorn cattle not only survived, but multi-

plied. In order to find new markets for the cattle after the Civil War, the Texas cattle ranchers began rounding up the longhorn cattle and driving them north for shipment along the transcontinental railroad lines. Along the way they found a vast sea of grass that stretched from the Missouri River to the foothills of the Rockies, and their cattle arrived at their destination fatter than they were when they left Texas. Within a few short years, livestock ranches spread across the prairie all the way to the Canadian border. By 1880, the concept of an *open range* and *free grass* had become traditional throughout the West.

Despite the vast open range, this was also a period of bitter conflict between the cattle ranchers and the sheep herders. As the demand for wool and mutton increased, sheep grazing became highly profitable and sheep herding (especially from 1865 to 1901) became as spectacular a business as cattle ranching (Stoddart et al. 1975). Cattle ranchers resented having to graze their livestock on lands previously grazed by sheep, since sheep crop grass shorter than cattle. Cattle ranchers believed that sheep carried oil in their hooves that repelled cattle. The cattle ranchers further resented sheep herders because they were more mobile and could easily move to a new area once the forage became scarce. The cattle ranchers had to remain on the land because they needed a more permanent base of operation. Consequently, hostilities broke out between the cattle ranchers and sheep herders. Each side raided the other's herds and slaughtered livestock, and human lives were lost. Eventually, however, the cattle ranchers began to realize that the sheep industry was here to stay and was a natural part of the American West.

But one thing both cattle ranchers and sheep herders had in common: They overgrazed the range. Since neither group could afford to buy much land, they rushed to exploit the federally owned open range before others claimed the land. By the turn of the twentieth century, sheep had nibbled the grasses to the root and cattle had trampled the soil into dusty, barren landscapes (Box et al. 1976). It was the classic ''tragedy of the commons'' as clearly stated in 1968 by Garrett Hardin:

> Therein is the tragedy. Each man is locked into a system that compels him to increase his herd without limit—in a world that is limited. Ruin is the destination toward which all men rush, each pursuing his own best interest in a society that believes in the freedom of the commons.

This "If I don't use it somebody else will" philosophy coupled with the mid-1880s winter blizzards and dry summers all but ruined the western livestock industry. This set the stage for the need for conservation and range resource management.

The End of Free Grass. The introduction of barbed wire on the Great Plains in the 1880s first foreshadowed the closure of the open range (Dana and Fairfax 1980). Private stock herders began illegally to fence in sections of the public range. Although the action was unauthorized and constituted a trespass against the government, it did provide some indication about who was using certain portions of land. Furthermore, it provided stock herders an element of control over grazing patterns, thereby bringing some degree of stability over the western grazing lands. More importantly, the illegal fencing of hundreds of miles of public lands forced the government to establish federal policy on range use. The government first tried to forbid the enclosure of the public domain, authorizing fence destruction. Despite the efforts of President Cleveland and the Congress, the fences remained and eventually provided evidence of historic range use when the Taylor Grazing Act of 1934 later came into effect.

A second step in the gradual withdrawal of land from the public domain, and the consequent development of range conservation, came with changes in public attitudes towards forests and wilderness areas (Kremp 1981). With the destruction of forested lands in the East and Midwest by private timber exploiters, political support mounted for the reservation of lands specifically for their conservation and protection. The establishment of forest reserves (1891) and the National Forest System (1905) brought additional stability to those valuable grazing areas within the mountain regions. As early as 1906, for example, the U.S. Forest Service administered grazing rights, collected fees, and allocated livestock numbers to protect the forest's forage grasses, trees, and watersheds (Arrandale 1983). Although livestock grazing may be a minor use of our national forests now, in the early days of the U.S. Forest Service, the forester's main task was to reckon with range operators (Greeley 1951). As might be expected, the stock herders resented what they considered to be government interference in their rightful way of life. While range conditions gradually improved within the national forests, range conditions on the unregulated sections of the public domain continued to decline for over 30 years.

By the Dust Bowl years of the mid-1930s, the ranchers were ready to concede that a lawful limit on forage use was preferable to watching the land blow away. Consequently, the stock herders themselves supported passage of the Taylor Grazing Act of 1934 (Arrandale 1983). This third step towards controlling the open range was a major accomplishment for conservationists, for they had finally succeeded at getting the federal government involved in managing rangelands. Initially, the act provided for the administration of 32 million ha (80 million acres) in *grazing districts*—a concept similar to the Soil Conservation Service's soil districts (see Chapter 3 for further details). The Grazing Service, a new office within the Department of the Interior, was established to administer these districts in order to halt overgrazing on public lands, to institute projects designed to improve rangeland conditions, and to stabilize the chaotic livestock industry. From its inception, the Grazing Service was underfunded and relatively ineffective. Even though the stock herders supported its creation, they continued to oppose bitterly any federal attempts at lowering livestock numbers to within the carrying capacity of the land (Foss 1960).

In 1946, Congress consolidated the Grazing Service and the General Land Office into the Bureau of Land Management (BLM). Today, the BLM administers some 191 million ha (473 million acres) of public lands officially designated as National Resource Lands—190 million ha (470 million acres) of which are original public domain lands established in the course of national expansion. The balance are lands once privately owned but now under federal ownership as the result of various land laws and actions. The BLM manages approximately 70 million ha (174 million acres) of public rangelands, where more than 21,000 livestock operators graze about 9 million head of domestic livestock—cattle, sheep, goats, and horses. If judged by conditions prevailing at the time of the passage of the Taylor Grazing Act, the BLM's accomplishments (especially if one uses the BLM's range condition statistics) have been substantial; if judged by the potential use of the land, there remains much to be done.

Another step in grassland conservation and management took place in 1960, when the secretary of the Department of Agriculture designated 24 areas as *National Grasslands*. Administered by the U.S. Forest Service under the terms contained in the Taylor Grazing Act, these *demonstration areas* were established to illustrate how lands classified as unsuitable for cultivation could be converted to grasslands that would benefit both livestock and humans. Today, there are approximately 1.54 million ha (3.8 million acres) of these demonstration grasslands in the country. They are located mainly on the Great Plains, with some in Oregon and Idaho.

Although range experts generally agree that grasslands improved on most of the public rangelands after the Taylor Grazing Act, many BLM lands remain in poor shape (Arrandale 1983). For example, a 1974 study ordered by the Senate Appropriations Committee found that one-third of public lands were in *poor condition,* that is, lands producing far less forage than their biological capacity (Kremp 1981). Interior Secretary Thomas Kleppe even commented in a 1976 speech before the Society of Range Management that 87 percent of BLM rangelands were ''in something less than satisfactory condition'' (CEQ 1977).

This failure of the BLM to halt overgrazing on many of its lands brought about the landmark federal court decision referred to as the NRDC Grazing Case, also known as the *NRDC* v. *Morton* decision (Dana and Fairfax 1980). The Natural Resources Defense Council (NRDC), a national conservation organization, brought suit against the BLM for failing to prepare an Environmental Impact Statement (EIS) on the environmental effects of grazing and for continuing to grant grazing permits despite not having an EIS report. (The preparation of Environmental Impact Statements has been a federal requirement since the passage of the 1969 National Environmental Policy Act, or NEPA.) The U.S. Supreme Court ruled against Secretary of the Interior Morton, thus ordering the BLM to draft separate Environmental Impact Statements to assess the condition of the range and to consider alternative grazing policies. After further negotiation, the BLM and NRDC agreed to scale back the 212 site-specific grazing statements ordered by Judge Flannery to 144 separate Environmental Impact Statements, to be completed by 1988 (Arrandale 1983). The *NRDC* v. *Morton* decision was extremely significant for grassland conservation and management, since it authorized the BLM to limit grazing pressure aggressively, with or without the rancher's consent.

Just two years after the *NRDC* v. *Morton* decision, Congress passed the Federal Land Policy and Management Act (FLPMA) of 1976. This act, often referred to as the BLM Organic Act, further strengthened the agency's authority by stating that BLM's public lands be retained in public ownership, with BLM as the permanent resource management agency (Kremp 1981). Most stock herders had previously thought that the government would eventually sell the remaining public range to private interests (Arrandale 1983). What this new piece of legislation did was declare the federal government's intent to hold onto the wide open spaces in perpetuity, thus reversing the 200-year-old policy of disposal of all public lands. Furthermore, the act mandated that BLM manage its public lands under the principles of multiple-use and sustained yield, thereby declaring that rangeland was no longer to be managed just for livestock. The act further required that users of public lands pay a fair market value for such uses, that the BLM base its policy decisions on long-range management plans with citizen participation, and that the BLM review its lands to find roadless areas containing 2226 ha (5500 acres) or more for possible inclusion in the National Wilderness Preservation System. (See Chapter 10 for further details on the National Wilderness Preservation System.)

Current Range Policy. The Public Rangelands Improvement Act (PRIA) of 1978 is the most recent act dealing with the public rangelands (BLM 1985). This act (1) reemphasized the concepts expressed in the FLPMA, (2) established a grazing fee formula on a trial basis (1979–1985) that reflects annual changes in the costs of livestock production, and (3) established the Experimental Stewardship Program (ESP). This act was proposed and backed by James Watt, then director of the Mountain States Legal Foundation in Denver, Colorado, and the livestock industry.

The most controversial of the three sections of the act is the Experimental Stewardship Program. Its stated purpose was to provide incentives to, or rewards for, livestock operators whose stewardship resulted in improved conditions on their grazing allotments. Incentives were to be in the form of either grazing fee adjustments (i.e., operators would be allowed to pay up to 50 percent of their grazing fee in the form of range improvements) or *cooperative range management projects;* that is, special arrangements whereby individual ranchers, who in the eyes of BLM officials have had a good record of land stewardship because of their past record, would be free from the detailed supervision and regulation by the BLM.

Although environmental groups were persuaded by the livestock industry to support the act originally, they have recently concluded that the long-term cooperative range management projects are nothing more than a deceptive technique to transfer the control of public rangelands to private ranchers. In 1984, the Natural Resources Defense Council, with the Sierra Club, the Wilderness Society, Defenders of Wildlife, and the Animal Defense Council as co-plaintiffs, filed suit against the BLM, charging that the new policy violates the federal government's obligation to regulate private livestock grazing on the public lands, that it insulates livestock owners from BLM oversight, and that it hampers the public's legal right to participate in range management decisions.

In 1979, a political campaign known as the Sagebrush Rebellion heated up. Ranchers in the Nevada state legislature demanded state control over BLM lands. This was only the latest attempt since the 1930s to remove public lands (including national forests) from public ownership. Although the effort was unsuccessful, it had the backing of President Reagan, who once said, "I happen to be one who cheers and supports the Sagebrush Rebellion. Count me in as a Rebel." In his first term, President Reagan brought to office an administration sympathetic to ranchers. There was James Watt, as interior secretary; Garrey E. Carruthers (a man with close ties to the stock herders), as assistant secretary for land and water resources; and Robert L. Burford (a Colorado cattleman), as BLM director. Their goal was to revise BLM grazing policies essentially to put grazing policy back in the hands of the ranchers (Arrandale 1983). In the 1980s, ranchers continued to hold the sympathy of President Reagan and his administration. In 1982, grazing fee for private lands was $8.83 per *animal unit month (AUM)*, which is the amount of grass and other plants that one cow, one horse, or five sheep consume during one month. During that same year, ranchers had to pay only $1.82 per AUM for use of public rangelands, one-fifth the price of grazing on private lands (Arrandale 1983). Environmentalists claim that this is a direct government subsidy and the policy encourages overgrazing and consequent rangeland deterioration.

Furthermore, opponents maintain that the Sagebrush Rebellion, which is a "grass-roots" movement, may actually lead to "sagebrush"—not grass—in the long run! Cecil D. Andrus, secretary of the Department of the Interior under the Carter administration, stated that if the Sagebrush Rebellion rebels win and public lands are pried loose from federal jurisdiction, this country would quickly witness "the ultimate 'lockup' of the land" (Andrus 1980). He maintained that westerners and visitors from everywhere would face an increased number of fences and "KEEP OUT" signs, thereby restricting their access to what was once open range. In addition to a deteriorated range condition, he felt that scenic area and wildlife habitat, as well as air and watershed resources, would suffer. According to Andrus, only with continued federal management can we hope to maintain the land heritage of all Americans.

The debate will go on, but one thing is certain: The dominance of livestock grazing on public lands will increasingly be challenged by other special interest groups—especially those that represent wildlife, recreation, and mining interests (Kremp 1981). Consequently, public land agencies, such as the Bureau of Land Management and the U.S. Forest Service, will be under increased pressure to satisfy the interests of these various groups.

Techniques for Rangeland Conservation

Less controversial than rangeland policy are the numerous techniques that are available to maintain and actually improve forage production and the overall condition of the range. These techniques can be grouped into five major categories: (1) vegetation alteration, (2) soil alteration, (3) predator and competitor control, (4) stock manipulation, and (5) conservation ranch plans. We will now take a brief look at each one of these five categories.

Vegetation Alteration.   Rangelands can be improved by manipulating the vegetation to produce a higher proportion of palatable plants. Ideally, the process should reduce the proportion of open ground, provide a longer growing season, and eliminate unpalatable shrubs or injurious plants. Poisonous plants, such as larkspur found in the foothills and mountain grasslands of the Rocky Mountains, are a particular nuisance. According to Owen (1980), 4 percent of Western livestock are killed by poisonous plants each year. Other poisonous plants that affect grazing animals include fiddleneck, false-hellebore, knotweed, tarweed, wyethia, and white loco.

Undesirable brush and small plants can be controlled by mechanical methods, fire, chemicals, or biological methods. Each method has its advantages and disadvantages. *Mechanical* methods include plowing, disking, cutting, pushing, and chaining. Although the actual technique used varies according to the kind of ecosystem and the roughness of the topography, mechanical techniques are used primarily against such grassland invaders as mesquite, sagebrush, rabbitbrush, pinyon, chaparral, juniper, and oakbrush. Mechanical brush control is extremely expensive; it tears up the land; it must be done repeatedly; and the land affected must be reseeded with palatable grasses.

The use of *fire* is a more natural means of controlling unwanted brush, since it duplicates nature's way of vegetation alteration. In addition to removing rough herbaceous residue, prescribed burning also has other short-term advantages, such as improving the nutrient content of the new growth and increasing production. In the long term, however, prescribed burning is probably deleterious to rangeland. Owen (1980) has noted that unless the prescribed burn is hot enough to destroy mesquite completely, the mesquite will survive and grow more vigorously than before, thus putting the grasses at a disadvantage. Furthermore, burning can also lead to soil erosion due to loss of vegetation cover, soil compaction, and decreased water infiltration resulting from the reduction of mulch and weed invasion.

The use of *chemicals* and *biological* methods are more controversial techniques to control unwanted brush, since they may also bring long-lasting ecological side effects. Specifically, chemical brush control refers to the use of herbicides as the primary agent. Although herbicides can be applied by hand on the ground, aerial spraying is usually the choice of most ranchers since it is more economical. The chemical often used by ranchers is 2,4-D, since this chemical can kill broad-leaved plants while leaving grasses and other narrow-leaved plants unharmed. A more complex and, consequently, less used technique to control unwanted invaders is biological brush control. Here, ranchers, with the help of range scientists, use insects, fungi, viruses, and other biological measures to control brush species. As with any type of biological control, however, the desired results will not be as immediate as with the use of chemicals, and the long-term implications may also prove devastating to the grasslands.

Vegetation can also be altered to reduce insect populations and diseases that consume large amounts of vegetation and limit the seed supplies of many range plants. Although all treatment methods are applicable to this problem, the use of pesticides is the most common practice. Although in its infancy, a more ecological approach to control insects and diseases and at the same time to enhance range yields is the integrated management program (USDA 1981). (See Chapter 3 for further details.) Since insect populations are often attracted to various types of debris, the disposal of these waste products is one technique of rangeland conservation. Debris disposal, which could be in the form of burning, chaining, or simple removal, is also carried out to improve aesthetics, increase forage yield, and reduce fire hazard.

Timber thinning or *selective cutting* (see Chapter 7) is used to increase range grazing on commercial forest land. The U.S. Forest Service claims that the harvesting of mature tree stands will often result in temporary (5 to 10 years) production of grasses, forbs, and shrubs that are palatable to livestock (USDA 1981). Proper range management within forest grazing lands can also benefit timber production (e.g., grazing animals consume vegetation that com-

petes with trees). Uncontrolled grazing, on the other hand, can bring untold harm to the timber resource. It is imperative that timber thinning for range production be extremely well planned, coordinated, and controlled, or the overall productivity of the land will be impaired.

Range managers also used drainage and irrigation techniques to alter vegetation for the purpose of expanding or improving vegetation. *Drainage techniques* center around the draining or lowering of the water level on bogs, marshes, or other areas that sustain standing water. If lack of water is the problem, range managers will recommend that the rancher install ditches, sprinklers, and other forms of *irrigation techniques*. Of course, the rancher may find some of these suggestions economically unfeasible.

Finally, *range seeding* is an attractive, but controversial, method that can be used to hasten the rehabilitation of depleted ranges, to replace less palatable species, or to provide for emergency forage. Some ranchers, for example, will seed an area with chested wheatgrass in the early spring in order to give the native grasses an opportunity to develop more fully. The use of combinations of legumes and nonlegume grasses may even outyield pure seedlings, as well as prevent soil erosion (Kircher and Wallace 1982). Seeding methods include broadcasting (by hand or helicopter) or drilling—the use of mechanical drills to place plant seeds at a uniform depth in the soil. The artificial seeding of palatable grasses and legumes is controversial since it often involves the initial spraying of herbicides to remove unwanted vegetation, which can lead to the destruction of native plants and wildlife and cause some serious soil erosion problems. Furthermore, the seeding of nonnative species is frequently opposed. The Natural Resources Defense Council (NRDC) has often questioned, through litigation, BLM's reliance on the introduction of nonnative grasses as a management technique for the public range (Dana and Fairfax 1980).

Soil Alteration. Soil, though more difficult to alter than plants or animals, can also be treated to improve rangelands. *Mechanical treatment*—the physical disturbance of the soil through such practices as disking, chiseling, pitting, or contour furrowing—is used for a variety of reasons, such as controlling erosion, increasing water infiltration, improving the microclimate, preparing a seed bed, and increasing the nitrogen content of the soil by encouraging the spread of leguminous species.

Fertilization—the application of nutrients to soils for the purpose of improving forage production—has been practiced since the nineteenth century (Barnard

1964). Since many areas have been grazed (a nutrient extractive process) for decades without any plant nutrients being returned to the soil, these areas are likely to produce less feed than they originally produced. Consequently, they may lack essential nutrients, such as nitrogen, calcium, phosphorus, and potash. Other elements necessary for the nutrition of animals may also be missing in the soil, such as cobalt, copper, and molybdenum. On the positive side, fertilization (with reseeding) can double, and in some cases triple, the carrying capacity of the rangeland (Kircher and Wallace 1982). On the negative side, however, inorganic fertilizers are escalating in cost, and the practice—even with the use of light aircraft—is often not cost-effective. Fertilization is a technique best fitted to intensively managed, highly productive private lands (USDA 1981).

Predator and Competitor Control. Livestock are vulnerable to a number of predators, particularly coyotes, cougars, foxes, and predatory birds. In an effort to cut down on livestock deaths due to predators, western ranchers resort to such practices as shooting, trapping, and poisoning these so-called rangeland pests.

Perhaps the most controversial practice is the use of the poisonous Compound 1080 (sodium fluoroacetate). In 1972, President Nixon banned the use of the poison on federal grazing lands since it was found to have caused the deaths of many nontarget species, including prairie falcons, hawks, eagles, owls, bears, and even humans. Ten years later, in a response to ranchers' complaints of "unreasonable" losses of livestock to coyotes and other predators, President Reagan reversed the EPA ban on the use of Compound 1080. The new ruling, however, only permits the use of the potent chemical in toxic collars attached to the necks of lambs and goats and in single dose lethal baits under carefully controlled circumstances. Environmentalists are concerned that, once again, the compound might be used improperly. Furthermore, they argue, alternative predator control methods exist, such as the use of llamas and certain breeds of sheep dogs that are effective in warding off livestock predators (Miller 1988).

As coyotes and other rangeland predators are reduced, however, the populations of rodents, rabbits, and other rangeland *competitors* increase—animals that compete with livestock for forage. Owen (1980) notes that in one study of coyote feeding habits, 49.5 percent (by volume) of their diet was of grass-consuming rabbits and rodents, whereas only 14 percent of their diet was of livestock that they had actually killed. Owen, therefore, questions the practi-

cality of drastic reduction programs of natural predator populations, when, in the long run, this practice may lead to reduced rangeland production and greater economic losses than the few cattle or sheep lost initially to these predators. In other words, perhaps the "pests" are really beneficial after all.

Rangeland deterioration resulting from overgrazing is yet another cause of increased populations of competitors on a rangeland. As Owen (1980) has pointed out, rangeland pests (e.g., jack rabbits, prairie dogs, kangaroo rats, grasshoppers) are a *symptom* of range deterioration, not the cause. For some unexplained reason, their populations usually only peak after periods of serious overgrazing. And it is only during this period of population explosion that these competitors are really a problem on the range. If this is true, then limiting livestock grazing pressure, not the use of guns, traps, and poisons to eradicate competitors, is the answer to improve rangeland conservation.

If rangelands are to be protected, it is not just the stock herders with their cattle and sheep who must be controlled. There are roughly 63,000 wild horses and burros that run free across the western rangelands, and they, too, pose threats of overgrazing in environmentally sensitive ranges (Arrandale 1983). In fact, since 1971, these free-roaming horses and burros—symbols to some of the pioneer spirit of the West—have been under the protection of the federal government. The government stepped in to eliminate the often cruel practice of *mustangers*, who corralled the wild horses and burros and shipped them off to meat-packing plants. Now that wolves and other natural predators are mostly gone from the plains (partly a result of the government's indirect poisoning of nontarget species, as mentioned previously), horse and burro populations have exploded and the BLM and U.S. Forest Service are faced with controlling this threat to the rangeland. Between 1971 and 1981, these two agencies rounded up 32,500 horses and 5700 burros from the range (Arrandale 1983), and put them up for adoption by the American people. Whereas ranchers and state governments complain that the roundup is not occurring fast enough to stop herds of wild horses and burros from damaging the range, animal protection groups, such as the American Horse Protection Association (AHPA) and the Wild Horse Organized Assistance (WHOA), have challenged the legality of these BLM and U.S. Forest Service roundups.

Although the wild horses are not descendants of the fabled Spanish mustangs—animals that vanished long ago—but rather descendants of animals turned loose or escaped from ranchers during the

Great Depression, the thought of wild horses and other animals running free across the Western plains has a certain appeal that most Americans would like to preserve. Managing this heritage, however, will probably remain quite controversial for some time to come.

Stock Manipulation. In most cases, livestock need to be evenly distributed over a parcel of rangeland in order for the land to be properly grazed. Without *manipulation*, livestock have a tendency to congregate and overgraze certain sections of a pasture, for example, under clumps of shade trees or at watering points. Animal distribution can be improved by (1) selecting the appropriate type and breed of livestock, (2) using more fencing, (3) increasing the number and changing the distribution of watering points, (4) arranging for the proper placement of salt blocks and supplemental feeding areas, and (5) adjusting stocking rates and grazing systems. We will now take a brief look at each of these techniques designed to improve animal distribution, and consequently, to increase range productivity.

Selecting the proper livestock type and breed for a particular rangeland is just as important as having the proper type of forage plant (Owen 1980). For example, sheep normally do better on hilly terrain covered predominantly with shrubs, whereas cattle prefer level terrain covered mostly with grasses. Hereford cattle can withstand severe winter cold and can usually find enough food to survive, whereas the shorthorn breed cannot. On the other hand, Brahman cattle can withstand drought, heat, and pests, such as fleas and ticks.

Fencing and herding are expensive but necessary for proper herd distribution (Figure 6-5). This practice utilizes all types of range fences, including log-type fences used in heavy snow areas and barbed wire, steel post-type fences used in the plains. Electric fences are even used in some locales.

One disadvantage of fencing is that it can prove detrimental to the region's wildlife resources. In 1983, for example, a Wyoming rancher deliberately fenced off 96 km² (37 mi²) of critical winter habitat for over 2000 pronghorn antelope. Though his actions were legal under Bureau of Land Management regulations, the fence was merely his method of striking out against those who opposed coal leasing in Wyoming's Red Rim area. The Wyoming Wildlife Federation, contending that Red Rim provides the only escape for the pronghorns from harsh winter winds and deep snows, feared that the fence would result in thousands of dead antelope.

The strategic location of waterholes is a less ex-

FIGURE 6-5 Fencing—an important tool in managing livestock grazing on range. (Photo by author.)

pensive but effective method of getting livestock to parcels of a rangeland that are underused or completely unused (Figure 6-6). Water developments can be small (e.g., earth dams, pits, small spring developments, troughs, and wildlife "guzzlers") or large (wells, seeps, or ditches involving water storage and distribution systems).

Since most range animals crave salt, the placement of salt blocks away from streams, wet meadows, and waterholes is also a strategy used by ranchers to distribute livestock evenly over the land

FIGURE 6-6 The placement of water holes—a means of getting livestock to use undergrazed pastures. (Photo by author.)

FIGURE 6-7 The proper distribution of salt blocks can also serve to balance the use of rangeland. (Photo by author.)

(Figure 6-7). In most cases, salting areas, as well as supplemental feeding areas, should be 1 to 3 km (0.6 to 1.8 mi) from watering points (Herbel 1982). Keep in mind that salt is more than just a food supplement to most range animals. For example, if cattle undergo prolonged salt deprivation, they will eventually lose their appetites, weaken, and ultimately collapse (Owen 1980).

Ranchers can also manipulate their livestock by using a number of *grazing systems.* For example, **deferred grazing** excludes livestock from an area for a specified period of time in order to allow seeds enough time to send out new rhizomes and to allow old plants enough time to restore their vigor. **Deferred-rotation grazing** is a *systematic rotation* of deferred grazing, where a ranch is divided into three pastures, A, B, and C, and livestock are allowed to remain in each pasture for specific periods of time (Figure 6-8).

Perhaps the most controversial grazing system is **rest-rotation grazing,** which is a form of deferred-rotation grazing. In this system, at least one grazing unit (area of rangeland or pastureland) is rested from grazing for a full year. In 1960, the BLM began embracing the ideas presented in August L. Hormay's 1960 rest-rotation grazing research (Dana and Fairfax 1980). By the mid-1970s, it had become the major tool of range management efforts throughout the West. Connected to the rest-rotation strategy was the notion of the Allotment Management Plan (AMP), which requires a specific *stocking rate* (determining the number and kinds of animals allowed to graze a unit of land for a specified period of time) and expensive investments (by the government) for fencing, livestock watering tanks, and other facilities necessary for proper herd management. In 1974, the Bu-

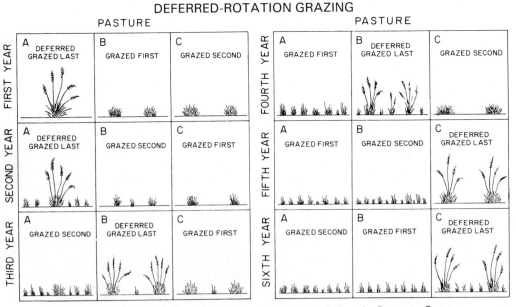

FIGURE 6-8 Deferred-rotation grazing. (From Ruben L. Parson, *Conserving American Resources,* 3d ed. [Englewood Cliffs, N.J.: Prentice-Hall, Inc., 1972], p. 320.)

reau was operating more than 1000 AMPs, covering over 10 million ha (25 million acres) of public land (Arrandale 1983). Although the technique may be of great benefit in some areas, it should not be viewed as a panacea for managing the entire public range. Kremp (1981) maintains that a blanket policy of rest-rotation grazing may not only prove economically unsound, but may actually deteriorate the range. He notes that a pasture within a rest-rotation scheme must be stocked two or three times as densely as under normal grazing schemes, thus raising questions as to the ultimate effect this will have on vegetation types, soil compaction, and range destruction. Furthermore, rest-rotation requires that the public range be crisscrossed with fences, thus increasing the mortality of antelope, deer, and other forms of wildlife. Kremp also questions why the BLM applies rotation schemes to pastures that are already in good condition, since ranges in good or excellent condition do not need rotation grazing, and in his opinion, deteriorate if the system is instituted.

Conservation Ranch Plans.   Rather than looking for a single panacea, a better approach is to develop a *conservation ranch plan*—a strategy that gives consideration to both range improvement and grazing schemes (Figure 6-9). With this technique, all practices that are beneficial and economic are integrated into one overall management plan that treats each site and situation differently. This is coordinated land management planning, since each range unit has different characteristics and must be managed accordingly.

Natural Grassland Preservation Efforts

These are the gardens of the Desert, these the unshorn fields, boundless and beautiful, for which the speech of England has no name—The Prairies. (William Cullen Bryant)

Aside from efforts to conserve and manage rangelands properly, efforts are also underway to preserve some of the nation's last remnants of natural grasslands for purposes other than grazing. Prairie preserves dot the Midwest, such as the Cayler Prairie in Iowa, the Ordway Memorial Prairie in South Dakota, and the James Woodworth Prairie Preserve, whose tiny 2.1 ha (5.3 acre) plot lies surrounded by suburban Chicago. Interest in preserving remnants of prairie is high, since the prairie contains more life than any other American habitat: 80 different mammals, 300 kinds of birds, and 15,000–18,000 species of insects (Pierce 1985). The prairie landscape provides enormous possibilities for scientific research, environmental education, and low-impact recreation.

A Tallgrass Prairie Preserve.   One area that environmental groups are working especially hard to preserve is an 80 km (50 mi) wide strip of land in eastern central Kansas and northeastern Oklahoma known as the Flint Hills. Flint Hills is one of the few remnants of tallgrass prairie where cattle have not replaced the native wildlife, where fences have not broken the prairie vistas, or where plowing and urban development have not decreased the prairie to a "postage stamp" in a sea of concrete. Environmentalists are striving to get a portion of the Flint Hills preserved as the newest unit of the National Park System—a Tallgrass Prairie.

Although interest in creating a prairie national preserve has existed for over 50 years, the National Park Service did not get serious about the idea until the 1950s, when it initiated its first study of alternative locations for the prairie park. Once the word got out that the National Park Service had found the Flint Hills site to be the most desirable for the purposes of preservation, cattle-grazing operators in the region, as well as other opponents to the preserve, began to thwart efforts by the National Park Service to pass the necessary legislation in Congress. The stock herders, some being fifth-generation family businesses, feared government restrictions on the land. Furthermore, they claimed that because of the soil's flintlike rock (unplowable limestone), the area was only good for grazing and governmental protection against agricultural encroachment was not necessary. Conservation groups, such as the National Parks and Conservation Association and the Nature Conservancy, however, continually reminded the stock herders that other forms of development—from highways to shopping centers to power plants—were nibbling away at the prairie. One specific example was the Kansas Power and Light Company's Jeffrey Energy Center in Pottawatomie County, which was expanding its power plants, coal storage areas, and reservoirs.

There are also other areas of contention. Ranchers within the Flint Hills area see themselves as better land stewards than the federal agencies (i.e., BLM and USFS) that are often in charge of range management on western public lands. Ranchers cite their practice of burning prairie grasses regularly to maintain productive grazing areas, observing sound soil and water conservation practices, and generally avoiding overgrazing. However, some conservation organizations, such as the Sierra Club, maintain that not all Flint Hills ranchers have this reverence for the

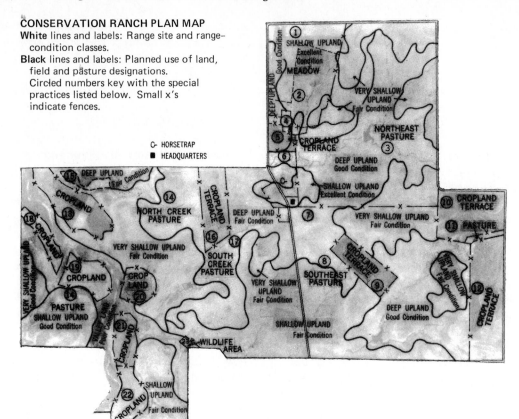

CONSERVATION RANCH PLAN MAP
White lines and labels: Range site and range-condition classes.
Black lines and labels: Planned use of land, field and pasture designations.
Circled numbers key with the special practices listed below. Small x's indicate fences.

C- HORSETRAP
■ HEADQUARTERS

CONSERVATION MEASURES

CULTIVATED FIELDS

General Practices

Weeds in tame pastures will be mowed high to avoid cutting grass needed for grazing.

Fire lanes will be maintained along public roads and other hazard areas.

One hundred to two hundred pounds of phosphate per acre will be applied each year to sweetclover fields.

Terraced fields will be cultivated on the contour.

Grain fields will not be grazed after March 15.

PASTURES

General Practices

The goal of range management will be to improve all ranges to good or excellent condition.

The goal on each range site will be to increase the key forage plants as follows:

Valley range site—
1. Big bluestem
2. Indiangrass
3. Switchgrass
4. Little bluestem

Shallow upland range site—
1. Little bluestem
2. Sideoats grama
3. Hairy grama

Deep upland range site—
1. Little bluestem
2. Indiangrass
3. Big bluestem
4. Sideoats grama

Very shallow upland range site—
1. Little bluestem
2. Sideoats grama

FIGURE 6-9 Conservation ranch plan. Planning for sustained-yield management on ranches. (Courtesy of USDA, Soil Conservation Service.)

land, and that, in fact, absentee landownership is on the rise, as well as overgrazing (King 1984).

Today, a tallgrass prairie sanctuary is a lot closer to reality than it was 50 years ago. For one thing, prairie preservationists have backed off on their original goal of seeking park designation, and now see *preserve* status as being politically more feasible. This designation will allow the Osage Indian tribe to maintain their mineral rights to the land, thus allowing

them to continue receiving valuable oil and gas revenues from the land—a right they have had since the beginning of the century. Cattle grazing will also be allowed under the preserve concept, at least until large enough herds of native ungulates exist. Theoretically, two ways of life—the Osage Indian culture and western cattle ranching—will be preserved, while the National Park Service manages the area to foster the return of the native prairie environment. Under this new scheme, the major obstacles have been resolved and it is now up to Congress to acquire the lands from willing sellers.

PROSPECTS FOR THE FUTURE

Presently, the nation's rangelands are in trouble. Over half of the rangeland in the contiguous 48 states is rated as being in *less than satisfactory condition;* that is, it produces less than 40 percent of its forage vegetation potential (USDA 1984). In general, the rangelands in worst condition are located in the Southwest—an area that has arid climate, prolonged grazing seasons, and a history of over 400 years of livestock grazing. The rangelands in the Plains States are in slightly better condition. The rangelands in best condition are the relatively isolated mountain meadows and mountain grasslands that are located at high elevations.

Intensification of Existing Problems

The demand for cropland, roads, and urban space is expected to continue the squeeze on our nation's rangelands in the decades ahead. By the year 2030, the country's rangelands may have decreased by as much as 23 million ha (57 million acres) (USDA 1984). Furthermore, the U.S. Department of Agriculture projects that the demand for range forage by domestic livestock will increase to 300 million animal unit months by the year 2030, a 40 percent increase over the 1976 level, not to mention the browsing and grazing requirements of wildlife, including wild horses and burros. The USDA estimates, for example, that 11 million animal unit months of forage are required to sustain the big game populations in the Western States. Unless there is a change in the supply of forage resources in relation to projected demands, the nation can look forward to a growing scarcity of forage resources, increased intensive grazing on remaining rangelands, rising prices of rangeland products, and rangeland deterioration.

Positive Signs and Success Stories

The demand for range grazing, which can lead to range deterioration, is derived from such factors as (1) the demand for livestock products (meat, hides, wool, tallow, and insulin), (2) the relative prices and costs of production of other feed sources (e.g., grain), and (3) a change in technology (e.g., feed substitutes). On all three fronts, as well as others, there are some positive signs and success stories that give reason for hope that some progress is being made in range conservation and grassland preservation.

1. *America's diet is changing.* The notorious "red-blooded American beef eater" is on the decline. Americans are eating less and less beef, and their collective decision to do so has sent shock waves over the Western plains. Per capita consumption of steak, roasts, hamburger, and other forms of beef has fallen dramatically, and ranchers and experts in agricultural economics see no sign of the decline abating. Americans still eat more beef than any other meat, but the gap is narrowing. Americans now eat more chicken, fish, and pork than previously. Industry experts believe there are two main reasons for the decline in beef consumption: (1) inflationary pressures, which keep beef prices proportionately higher than those of chicken and other meats, and (2) the consumer's increasing interest in eating a healthier diet (one with less fat) to minimize heart disease and other illnesses.

Since our customs, dietary habits, and attitudes towards beef and other foods are gradually changing, there may be a day in the relatively near future when our grasslands are used for more *protein efficient* or *rangeland efficient* animals. In other words, the differential efficiency of the animals themselves in converting grass into meat may dictate that we raise a certain type of animal to maximize protein production.

Already, on the vast, flat plains of Venezuela, one can witness one of the world's most unusual animal roundups—the herding of 100 pound, water-dwelling rodents called capybaras (Figure 6-10). The rodents share the range with herds of cattle and herders. Sunquist (1984), a biologist, has reported that capybaras are more efficient at converting grass into pounds of protein than either sheep or cattle. Because of their high fecundity (each female can produce 36 young in her lifetime), these species are considered a valuable resource for ranchers. According to Sunquist, "pound for pound, females produce five times more offspring, in terms of weight, than do other large grazers." With proper management, say other capybara experts, the meat-producing potential of capybaras may well exceed cattle in many areas of South America, and perhaps elsewhere. Since capybara meat is reported to be delicious, tasting something like a combination of beef and pork, some Americans might be willing to give it a try. But, are America's image-conscious stock herders ready to herd rodents?

On a similar note, perhaps America's livestock raising will gradually go indoors, at least on a partial basis, thus conserving grasslands for uses other than grazing. Noel Vietmeyer (1984), a staff member of the

FIGURE 6-10 A new kind of roundup for America? Venezuelan cowboys rounding up herds of capybaras. (Photo courtesy of Fiona C. Sunquist.)

National Academy of Sciences, notes that Peruvians presently raise guinea pigs in their bedrooms, and consume 70 million of them a year. Fed on table scraps and fresh alfalfa, this indoor livestock can produce meat more effectively in poor parts of the world than cattle, sheep, pigs, or goats. According to Vietmeyer, a farmer starting with one male and ten females can expect to have a herd of 3000 guinea pigs, also known as *cuy* (pronounced ''coo-ee''), within one year. Furthermore, he notes, some Peruvian government farms produce cuy like chickens. In one case, 1200 cuy, housed in 30 sheds, produced 100,000 animals annually.

Although it may take some drastic changes for Americans to begin raising guinea pigs in their bedrooms, the concept of indoor livestock raising has a certain appeal. During World War II, Americans planted Victory Gardens (food gardens within their backyards) to supplement the war effort. There may be a day when urbanites, like their rural counterparts, raise their own ''Victory Pens'' of animals in their garages or backyards. Already, one can find urbanites who raise chickens in their backyards, and certainly many American children have penned guinea pigs or pigeons for pets. What will it take to go from pets to protein supplements? One thing is for certain: Relieving the grazing pressure from America's traditional grasslands will help preserve this natural heritage.

2. *Experiments with alternative feeds.* U.S. ranchers are experimenting with various feed supplements that might further relieve pressure on our nation's grasslands. Generally speaking, stock herders will rely on grasslands as a base of food supply for their stock. But as the nutrient value of grasslands declines, stock herders will begin to introduce supplemental food. Also, when drought or government programs curtail grain production—driving up the price of corn and other traditional livestock feeds—shortages will occur in some areas, forcing ranchers to look for alternative sources of feed.

In 1983, for example, a severe drought hit the area near Kansas City, Missouri, devastating corn crops that were primarily used for livestock feed. The price of corn and other traditional feed supplements skyrocketed. Under these emergency conditions, ranchers began feeding their livestock a wide range of feeds, including stale bread and cookies, milk, distillery and brewery mashes, cheese, potatoes, oranges, wheat, beet pulp, whole cotton seeds, and alfalfa meal. Specialists from the U.S. Department of Agriculture then began to raise questions about the nutritional value of such alternative feeds. It was found, for example, that a pound of bread was equivalent in nutritional value to a pound of corn. Oddly enough, in 1983 farmers could purchase stale bread for less than half the price of corn, which was selling for $4 a bushel. In 1983, milk was even less expensive than corn. This is not to suggest that ranchers are going to turn from grasslands to milk and old chocolate chip cookies as a food source for their livestock. It does suggest, however, that scientists and ranchers are beginning to look at alternative feed sources that were hitherto not considered viable alternatives.

Researchers, for example, have begun testing leucaena, the so-called miracle plant, as fodder for cattle in many parts of the world. Leucaena grows in warm American latitudes, in Africa, and in the Pacific islands, and it has undergone intensive testing in Brazil, Central America, Hawaii, Indonesia, Mexico, the Philippines, and Taiwan. Leucaena has a reputation as a miracle plant because some varieties of leucaena grow 15.2 m (50 ft) tall in just six years, thus providing a rich source of firewood in regions where fuel is scarce. Its roots enrich the land with nitrogen. It resists drought and thrives in depleted tropical soils, checking erosion on steep slopes. Its seed pods contain edible beans. In Hawaii, where one species grows wild, cattle and goats thrive on its feathery leaves, which are said to be as nourishing as alfalfa.

However, this new form of fodder cannot be fed to cattle indiscriminately. When researchers fed the Hawaiian leucaena to Australian cattle, the animals lost hair and developed goiter and cancer of the esophagus. Scientists from the U.S. Department of Agriculture's Animal Disease Center in Peoria, Illinois, discovered that the first stomach of the Hawaiian livestock contains bacteria that digest and neutralize an otherwise toxic compound in leucaena. These necessary bacteria were found to be missing in the cattle of Australia, Texas, Iowa, and elsewhere. However, scientists may have come up with a solution to the problem. By transplanting bacteria from the digestive tracts of Hawaiian goats into the Australian cattle, the latter were able to digest the plant safely. Although more testing will certainly have to be done, leucaena appears to have considerable potential as fodder.

3. *Greater knowledge of ecological role of plants.* Plant scientists are discovering that certain common range pests, such as mesquite, actually make an important contribution to the ecosystem and should not be sprayed with herbicides or bulldozed. For example, Lawrence Gilbert, a University of Texas scientist, discovered that bacteria in the root nodules of mesquite convert atmospheric nitrogen into compounds useful in surrounding soil. Since nitrogen is critical for the growth of both grass and beef, Gilbert suggests that mesquite clumps be allowed to coexist with grass. By doing so, the rancher will save time and energy, and the environmental impacts from herbicide spray and soil compaction will be minimized.

4. *Alternative predator control methods.* Some ranchers are experimenting with alternative predator control methods. For example, in Oregon, sheep growers are trying an imported method of deterring coyotes: They are using guard dogs with some encouraging results. Guard dogs have long been in use in parts of Europe, but this technique for predator control has only recently been introduced to the United States. These specially bred and trained dogs live with sheep or goats almost as part of the flock and frighten away predators by barking. According to Yost (1985), guard dogs are being used in at least 35 states with some successful results. In one case, an Oregon sheep grower was suffering about 12.5 percent losses from predators until the first guard dog was put out. In the following three months, the sheep grower experienced not one single loss. When the dog was withdrawn from the sheep herd, the killing immediately began again. Other sheep growers experienced similar successes and are, consequently, finding that guard dogs are a valuable

tool in predator deterrence. For one thing, they are a lot cheaper and less controversial than the traditional control methods of poisoning (e.g., using Compound 1080), trapping, or shooting. Although using guard dogs may not be a panacea for predator problems, it is a tool that seems to be able to lessen the use of more potentially ecologically harmful practices.

5. *Grassland communities are being successfully reestablished on mined land.* The national drive towards energy independence, which began in the 1970s, has encouraged surface mining of coal, which has increased dramatically in many parts of the country. As surface mining has increased, grasslands have begun to disappear. To counter this, Congress mandated that mined areas undergo reclamation. Early revegetation efforts met with failure, helping to create an atmosphere of doubt regarding the ability of these lands to be repaired. However, reclamation technology has advanced to the point where the establishment of perennial grasses on mined lands has become highly probable. Ries and DePuit (1984), for example, have noted the successes that have been made in reestablishing grassland communities in the northern Great Plains. Although reestablished grasslands appear to be successfully providing forage for beef production in this region, questions remain regarding the long-term stability of these grasslands, their ability to sustain production, and whether or not toxic materials will somehow find their way into the vegetation.

6. *Increased multiple-use of grasslands.* Increasingly, grasslands are being recognized as valuable for uses other than livestock grazing. In 1979, a federal district court ruled in favor of the grazing rights of wildlife over livestock on the pasture in the Charles M. Russell National Wildlife Refuge in Montana. Specifically, the court upheld the right of the U.S. Fish and Wildlife Service to give priority to the food needs of pronghorn antelope, deer, and other species of wildlife, over the objections of local stock herders.

Scientific research is becoming another important use of grasslands. Grassland preservation organizations, such as Save the Tallgrass Prairie, Inc., point with pride to such areas as the *Konza Prairie Research Natural Area*, 3487 ha (8616 acres) of tallgrass prairie in the Kansas Flint Hills, about 20 minutes by automobile from Kansas State University. The Nature Conservancy (a national, private conservation organization) purchased the area in 1971 and 1977 as part of its efforts at preserving natural diversity, and later deeded the land to Kansas State University for long-term ecological research and education. Here, biologists examine the role of antelope, elk, and buffalo in the prairie ecosystem. Prescribed burning, as a management tool, is perhaps the most dramatic technique applied at the Konza. The Nature Conservancy's Samuel H. Ordway, Jr., Memorial Prairie—a 3075 ha (7600 acre) preserve in the prairie pothole and mixed grassland of north central South Dakota—also offers a model site for both grazing and burning.

In California, efforts are being made to preserve the rare natural areas known as *vernal pools*—unique self-contained ecosystems that occur within natural grassland communities in only a few areas in the world, specifically in central and southern California, southern Oregon, and in the Cape Province of South Africa (Zahn 1984) (Figure 6-11). Only here are the essential ingredients necessary for the formation of vernal pools: a mild Mediterranean climate; a thick, dense clay hardpan; and winter rainfall. Every spring in California, these depressions are transformed into a blaze of blossoming wild flowers. This is where in the late 1800s, naturalist John Muir described his walks in the Central Valley as "wading out in the grand level ocean of flowers." Conservation organizations, such as the Nature Conservancy and the Native Plant Society, have made significant strides in preserving the world's remaining vernal pools—one of Earth's most unusual phenomena—from encroaching farmland. These areas are being preserved for wildlife, such as the herds of tule elk that still roam amid the goldfield flowers of California, and wild flower enthusiasts will be able to, in the words of John Muir, "walk through a continuous bed of honey-bloom."

Grasslands are also beginning to be preserved as parks. In 1981, for example, Canada declared an area near Killdeer, Saskatchewan, as the site for the Grasslands National Park—the first park of its kind on the continent devoted exclusively to the prairie ecosystem. Although the specific boundaries have yet to be officially drawn, the park will consist of about 259 km^2 (100 mi^2), and may eventually cover a total of 932 km^2 (360 mi^2) (Lindahl 1982). Some grasslands have been converted to parks in Canada—even in sections such as southern Canada where the Canadian government owns little land and most of the land must therefore be drawn from private or provincial holdings. One would think that in the United States, where the federal government owns much more land and can therefore move more quickly on new park formation, there could be successful efforts at preserving some grassland remnants.

ACTION FOR RANGELANDS

Preventing the degradation and loss of our nation's rangeland resources, as environmental causes go, is hardly as glamorous as saving the whales or protecting the harp seals. Those most concerned about rangelands are a small band of well-informed range scientists, mostly westerners, and an even smaller group of midwestern prairie preservationists. Yet, we all have something at stake in conserving our rangelands and preserving remnants of our natural grassland heritage.

Personal Action Strategies

You can help conserve these rangeland resources by undertaking one or more of the following strategies for action:

1. Lower your consumption of beef products. Americans consume an average of 105 pounds of beef per person per year, and this puts a tremendous strain on our nation's rangeland resources, as well as on the energy and water resources that support the livestock industry. Furthermore, this American dietary habit causes ecological havoc around the world. Since 1950, the American demand for cheap, lean beef for hamburgers, hot dogs, and other fast-food items has caused Central American nations and other meat exporting nations to clear and burn huge tracts of their tropical forests—areas rich with endangered animals and exotic plant life—for the purpose of expanding their livestock industry to feed meat to Americans (Nations and Komer 1984). The world's ecological systems would be better off if Americans

FIGURE 6-11 Vernal pools with native California rangelands. (Photo by author.)

asked, "Where's the beef coming from and at what environmental price?"

2. *Encourage "grass-finished" meat production.* When you do eat meat, try to shift away from the *fedlot-finished* meat (a high energy-intensive system—one that will be harder to maintain as energy resources become more scarce) to *grass-finished* meat. The latter has three major benefits: (1) It is less energy intensive; (2) the meat has less fat, and, consequently, human health might be improved; and (3) ranchers, with an increase in demand for grass-fed beef, might be financially better off, which might allow them to invest in long-term range conservation practices. In other words, "vote with your pocketbook" by buying grass-fed meat products if you must eat meat.

3. *Call for the use of native grasses and flowers in urban landscaping.* Support conservation groups, such as the Grassland Heritage Foundation, that encourage the planting of native grasses and flowers in the urban landscape along roadsides, on the grounds of commercial buildings, and in city parks. Established prairie plantings in Kansas have helped prevent soil erosion and minimize costly maintenance. An example of this is the creative use of native grasses and flowers in the landscaping of Kansas City International Airport; here, visitors and residents alike now get a glimpse of the original Kansas landscape and city officials are pleased since these native grasses thrive without repeated mowings, watering, or the use of fertilizers, herbicides and insecticides.

4. *Support "flexible" grazing schemes.* A blanket grazing policy, such as the BLM's tendency to use rest-rotation as a standard policy on all its lands, is likely to do more harm than good. Support grazing systems and policies that are flexible and individually adapted to each particular geographic site. Inform others of the possible negative consequences of BLM policies that are not site specific.

5. *Call for a review of pesticide policies.* Brush and weed control, which is necessary for rangeland conservation, is often carried out as a single-shot practice and not as an ongoing part of a well-balanced and integrated management system. The use of pesticides as a brush control technique is often done in a careless fashion. Insist that the federal Environmental Protection Agency (EPA) annually review the pesticide policies of federal and state agencies in order to ensure the uniform interpretation and application of federal pesticide registration and permissible-use regulations. Furthermore, support those who are seeking control techniques that are more environmentally acceptable than chemical pesticides.

6. *Support rangeland research.* First of all, you can support grassland research centers, such as the Konza Research Prairie of Kansas State University. This unique, open-air laboratory is used as a yardstick to measure the differences between a balanced grass, soil, and water ecosystem and a resource-depleting cultivated system.

Second, you can support the work of rangeland research scientists who work at State Agricultural Experiment Stations, forestry schools, the U.S. Forest Service, the Bureau of Land Management, and the Soil Conservation Service. Range research has now turned from the earlier concentration on single-purpose range livestock grazing systems to an ecosystem approach that focuses on the interrelationships of multiresource productivity and use. This new ecosystem approach deals with forage production, livestock grazing, wildlife and fisheries habitat, watersheds, timber harvesting, and recreation. According to the U.S. Department of Agriculture (1981), research needs exist in the areas of *ecoysystem analysis* (understanding the structure of biological systems, their energy flows, nutrient cycles, water availability, and plant and animal interactions), *range resource inventory* (identifying and classifying range resources), *resource improvement* (finding better approaches to rehabilitating deteriorated rangelands), *coordination with other uses* (determining the impacts and tradeoffs among multiresource use interactions), and the *social and economic aspects of resource use* (determining the managerial alternatives for range grazing in relation to local, regional, and national socioeconomic needs).

Third, you can carry out some of your own research. You might begin by investigating the revolutionary and controversial ideas of Allan Savory, whom *Newsweek* has dubbed the "guru" of range management. Savory contends that western rangeland, though it is generally overgrazed, is still understocked (SCSA 1984). The problem, he contends, is the emphasis on light grazing. His solution to overgrazing and the spreading of desertification is heavy stocking and frequent movement of livestock according to the growth cycle of the plants. According to this scheme, which he calls *holistic resource management*, heavy grazing is more natural than light grazing, since (according to Savory) this herding effect mimics the impact on the land of the vast bison and pronghorn herds that evolved with range plant communities (Savory 1988). Savory notes that this herd effect has many attributes, including breaking up the surface capping, increasing soil porosity, and encouraging seedling establishment. Critics charge that his approach is nothing more than a system of short duration grazing that underrates the negative impact of heavy stocking rates. Savory's approach is getting conservation organizations at least to question the traditional means of restoring land, such as long-term range rest schemes.

7. *Join a range society or grassland preservation organization.* Range science and management took a major leap forward in 1948 with the creation of the first range society—the American Society of Range Management. The Society of Range Management (SRM) carries out many activities that will keep you informed and involved in grassland research and management. SRM sponsors annual meetings, hosts local chapter activities, publishes journals, such as the *Journal of Range Management,* and generally promotes the principles of range science.

Those more interested in native grassland preservation, rather than traditional range management, can join such groups as the Tallgrass Prairie Foundation, the Grassland Heritage Foundation, the Plains Resource Institute, or the Land Institute. All of the above, of course, are excellent sources of information, particularly if you are interested in the preservationist's perspective.

8. *Pursue an education and career in rangeland resources.* In 1916, Montana State University developed the first range management curricula in the United States. Today, range management curricula and degrees are still limited to only a handful of schools. Rangeland studies departments are located at Montana State University (Bozeman), Colorado A&M (Ft. Collins), Washington State University (Pullman), the University of Idaho (Boise), the University of California (Berkeley), Texas A&M (College Station), and the University of Minnesota (Minneapolis).

DISCUSSION TOPICS

1. Why is the Taylor Grazing Act of 1934 considered a milestone in range management?

2. What is a *grazing district* and how does it operate? Discuss the livestock operation and conservation strategies of the grazing district closest to your school.

3. What is the rancher's greatest environmental problem? What methods can be used to solve this problem?

4. List the pros and cons of using fire as a range management tool.

5. What is meant by the statement: Range pest populations represent the symptoms rather than causal factors of range deterioration? Provide examples.

6. What is the most serious livestock predator? What interesting fact arises when analyzing the relationships among sheep, rodents, rabbits, predators, and forage?

7. In terms of range management, what are the roles of the Bureau of Land Management (BLM), the U.S. Forest Service (USFS), and the Soil Conservation Service (SCS)? Use an example where their roles would be at odds with each other. How might this conflict be resolved?

8. Do federal crop allotment programs impact public rangelands? If so, how?

9. Suggest various ways that public land management objectives and private land operations be integrated to satisfy the various users and the management objectives.

10. Proper herd distribution is an important factor in good range management. List and explain a few approaches to stock manipulation.

11. Regarding range management, what types of field projects need to be undertaken in your local area?

12. Using land capability maps, AUM statistics, and other references from your local Soil Conservation District, pick a local ranch and design a Conservation Ranch Plan. Defend your criteria and methodology for the plan before the class.

READINGS

ANDRUS, CECIL. 1980. "The Attack on Federal Lands," *National Parks and Conservation Magazine,* April, pp. 9–10. Opposition to "Sagebrush Rebellion" by former Secretary of the Interior.

ARRANDALE, TOM. 1983. *The Battle for Natural Resources.* Washington, D.C.: Congressional Quarterly. Includes excellent chapter on the Bureau of Land Management and the livestock industry.

BARNARD, C., ed. 1964. *Grasses and Grasslands.* New York: Macmillan. Excellent background on the physical characteristics of grasses and grasslands as well as their susceptibility to human impact.

BARNES, WILL. 1926. *The Story of the Range.* Washington, D.C.: U.S. Department of Agriculture. Classic work on rangelands.

BOX, T. W., et al. 1976. *The Public Range and Its Management: Report to the President's Council on Environmental Quality.* Logan, Utah: Utah State University. Good general reference.

BUREAU OF LAND MANAGEMENT. 1985. *50 Years of Public Land: 1934–1984.* Washington, D.C.: U.S. Department of Agriculture. BLM brochure that summarizes 50 years of rangeland management from the BLM's perspective.

COUNCIL ON ENVIRONMENTAL QUALITY. 1977. *Environmental Quality—1976.* Washington, D.C.: Government Printing Office. One of several annual reports put out by the President's Council on Environmental Quality.

DANA, SAMUEL, and SALLY K. FAIRFAX. 1980. *Forest and Range Policy: Its Development in the United States.* 2d ed. New York: McGraw-Hill. A historical, chronological approach to forest and grassland policy in the United States from its beginnings to 1979.

DREGNE, HAROLD E. 1984. ''Combating Desertification: Evaluation of Progress,'' *Environmental Conservation,* vol. 11, no. 2, pp. 115–121.

DREGNE, HAROLD E. 1977. ''Desertification of the World's Arid Lands,'' *Economic Geography,* vol. 52, pp. 332–346. Significant study on desertification.

FOREST-RANGE TASK FORCE. 1972. *The Nation's Range Resources—A Forest-Range Environmental Study.* Forest Resource Report No. 19. Washington, D.C.: Forest Service, U.S. Department of Agriculture. The first national *ecological* appraisal of range resources in the United States.

FOSS, PHILLIP O. 1960. *Politics and Grass: The Administration of Grazing on the Public Domain.* Seattle, Wash.: University of Washington Press. History and development of U.S. grazing practices and policies.

GARRISON, GEORGE A., et al. 1977. *Vegetation and Environmental Features of Forest and Range Ecosystems.* Agricultural Handbook No. 475. Washington, D.C.: Forest Service, U.S. Department of Agriculture. One of the reports developed as part of the Forest-Range Environmental Study (FRES) of the Forest Service. Presents descriptive sketches of 34 soil-vegetation units, called ecosystems, covering the 48 contiguous states.

GREELEY, WILLIAM B. 1951. *Forests and Men.* New York: Doubleday. Good account of grasslands and grassland resource management within forested regions.

HARDIN, GARRETT. 1968. ''The Tragedy of the Commons,'' *Science,* vol. 162, pp. 1243–1248. A classic article dealing with the problems of managing public property.

HARRIS, DAVID R., ed. 1980. *Human Ecology in Savanna Environments.* New York: Academic Press. Examines the ways in which past and present human populations have adapted to and impacted tropical savanna environments.

HEARD, HAROLD F. 1975. *Rangeland Management.* New York: McGraw-Hill. Standard, intermediate-level college textbook for range science.

HERBEL, CARLTON H. 1982. ''Grazing Management on Rangelands,'' *Journal of Soil and Water Conservation,* March–April, vol. 37, no. 2, pp. 77–79. Management strategies for optimum production.

HODGSON, HARLOW J. 1976. ''Forage Crops,'' *Scientific American,* February, pp. 61–75. Geographically illustrates where different forage crops can be grown.

JASMER, GERALD E., and JERRY L. HOLECHEK. 1984. ''Determining Grazing Intensity on Rangeland,'' *Journal of Soil and Water Conservation,* vol. 39, no. 1, pp. 32–35. Maintains that no precise method exists for measuring grazing intensity that is simple, rapid, and accurate.

KAISER, FRED H., et al. 1972. *Forest-Range Environmental Production Analytical System: FREPAS.* Agricultural Handbook No. 430. Washington, D.C.: Forest Service, U.S. Department of Agriculture. Describes the analytical and computer capability of the FREPAS computer program used by the Forest Service for the Forest-Range Environmental Study (FRES).

KING, MADONNA LUERS. 1984. ''Preserving the Tallgrass Prairie,'' *Sierra,* May-June, vol. 69, no. 3, pp. 72–76. Interesting discussion from an environmentalist's point of view.

KIRCHER, HARRY B., and DONALD L. WALLACE. 1982. *Our Natural Resources.* Danville, Ill.: Interstate Printers and Publishers. Discusses rangeland resources from a traditional use perspective.

KREMP, SABINE. 1981. ''A Perspective on BLM Grazing Policy.'' In John Baden and Richard L. Stroup, eds., *Bureaucracy vs. Environment: The Environmental Costs of Bureaucratic Governance,* pp. 124–153. Ann Arbor, Mich.: University of Michigan Press. Excellent review of BLM grazing policy.

LIBECAP, GARY D., and RONALD N. JOHNSON. 1981. ''The Navajo and Too Many Sheep: Overgrazing on the Reservation.'' In John Baden and Richard L. Stroup, eds., *Bureaucracy vs. Environment: The Environmental Costs of Bureaucratic Governance,* pp. 87–107. Ann Arbor, Mich.: University of Michigan Press. Cultural ramifications of rangeland deterioration.

LINDAHL, MARY. 1982. ''At Last, A Prairie Park,'' *International Wildlife,* July–August, vol. 12, no. 4, pp. 42–47. Historical account of the preservation of Canada's Grassland National Park.

LITTLE, DENNIS, et al., eds. 1982. *Renewable Natural Resources: A Management Handbook for the 1980s.* Boulder, Colo.: Westview Press. A handbook for the concerned citizen as well as for resource managers and policymakers.

MILLER, G. TYLER. 1988. *Living in the Environment.* 5th ed. Belmont, Calif.: Wadsworth. Outstanding overall reference textbook for environmental studies.

NATIONS, JAMES D., and DANIEL I. KOMER. 1984. ''Chewing up the Jungle,'' *International Wildlife,* September–October, vol. 14, no. 5, pp. 14–16. Interesting discussion of how beef production is decimating Central America's forests.

OWEN, OLIVER. 1980. *Natural Resource Conservation: An Ecological Approach.* New York: Macmillan. Includes excellent rangeland chapter from a biologist's perspective, but the latest edition (1985) of this book does not have a separate chapter on rangelands.

PARSON, RUBEN L. 1972. *Conserving American Resources.* 3d ed. Englewood Cliffs, N.J.: Prentice-Hall. Classic university-level resource management textbook written in the geographical tradition.

PIERCE, ROBERT. 1985. ''Shaping a Tallgrass Sanctuary,'' *National Parks,* March–April, vol. 59, no. 3–4, pp. 28–29. Brief history of the efforts to create Tallgrass Prairie National Preserve.

RIES, R. E., and E. J. DEPUIT. 1984. ''Perennial Grasses for Mined Land,'' *Journal of Soil and Water Conservation,* vol. 39, no. 1, pp. 26–29. Discusses grassland communities that have been successfully established on mined land in the Northern Great Plains.

SAVORY, ALLAN. 1988. *Holistic Resource Management.* Covelo, Calif.: Island Press. A provocative and controversial look at conventional approaches to land management. An alternative comprehensive planning model is presented.

SHANTZ, H. L. 1954. ''The Place of Grasslands in the Earth's Cover of Vegetation,'' *Ecology,* vol. 35, pp. 143–151. Good source for determining the scientific classification of rangelands and their global distribution.

SHERIDAN, DAVID. 1981. ''Overgrazed and Undermanaged,'' *Environment,* vol. 23, no. 4, pp. 14–38. An interesting case study of desertification on the Navajo Indian Reservation.

SOIL CONSERVATION SOCIETY OF AMERICA. 1984. ''Rangeland Revolutionary,'' *Journal of Soil and Water Conservation,* July–August, vol. 39, no. 4, pp. 235–240. Interesting interview with Allan Savory and his ideas on ''Holistic Resource Management.''

SPRAGUE, HOWARD B., ed. 1974. *Grasslands of the United States: Their Economic and Ecologic Importance.* Ames, Iowa: Iowa State University Press. Good overview of the subject.

STODDART, LAURENCE, et al. 1975. *Range Management.* New York: McGraw-Hill. Classic textbook on the subject.

SUNQUIST, FIONA. 1984. ''Cowboys and Capybaras,'' *International Wildlife,* March–April, vol. 14, no. 2, pp. 4–9. Presents an alternative to traditional livestock raising.

U.S. BUREAU OF LAND MANAGEMENT. 1975. *Range Condition Report, Prepared for the Senate Committee on Appropriations.* Washington, D.C.: Government Printing Office. An important government survey of rangeland condition.

USDA, FOREST SERVICE. 1984. *America's Renewable Resources: A Supplement to the 1979 Assessment of the Forest and Range Land Situation in the United States.* Washington, D.C.: U.S. Department of Agriculture, Forest Service. Important update on an earlier Forest Service assessment of rangelands.

USDA, FOREST SERVICE. 1936. *The Western Range,* 74th Congress, 2d Session, Senate Document 199. The very first attempt by the U.S. government to classify its rangelands.

USDA, FOREST SERVICE. 1981. *An Assessment of the Forest and Range Land Situation in the United States.* Washington, D.C.: U.S. Department of Agriculture, Forest Service. An important Forest Service assessment of U.S. rangeland condition.

UNESCO/UNEP/FAO. 1979. *Tropical Grazing Land Ecosystems: A State-of-Knowledge Report.* Fontenoy, Paris: United Nations Educational Scientific and Cultural Organization. A large and comprehensive report on tropical grazing lands with a discussion of national development strategies and programs. Particular emphasis on improved management strategies at the village level in Third World countries.

VALLENTINE, JOHN F., and PHILLIP SIMS. 1980. *Range Science.* Detroit, Mich.: Gale Research. A guide to literature of range science.

VIETMEYER, NOEL. 1984. ''In Peru They Eat Guinea Pigs,'' *International Wildlife,* July–August, vol. 14, no. 4, pp. 16–17. Presents one alternative or supplement to traditional livestock production in the United States.

WAGNER, FREDERICK H. 1978. ''Livestock Grazing and the Livestock Industry.'' In H. P. Brokaw, ed., *Wildlife and America.* Washington, D.C.: Council on Environmental Quality. Estimates changes in the wildlife population with increasing livestock grazing.

WEBB, MARYLA, and JUDITH JACOBSEN. 1982. *U.S. Carrying Capacity–An Introduction.* Washington, D.C.: Carrying Capacity. Explicit account of the state of U.S. rangelands, their carrying capacity and ability to meet U.S. beef demands.

YOST, DICK. 1985. ''Oregon Goes for Guarding Dogs,'' *Defenders,* March–April, vol. 60, no. 2, pp. 10–15. Discusses Oregon sheep growers' successes with guard dogs as a predator control technique against coyotes.

ZAHN, GARY. 1984. ''Springing to Life,'' *National Wildlife,* vol. 22, no. 4, p. 407. Illustrates abundance of wildlife and wild flowers in California's remaining native grasslands.

7

FOREST RESOURCE MANAGEMENT

A tree: the grandest and most beautiful of all the productions of the earth.

William Gilpin,
Remarks on Forest Scenery, 1791

Most anthropologists believe that our early ancestors were tree-dwelling primates from a warm, moist geographic region. Although gradual weather changes eventually converted their tropical forest homes into open grassy savannas with scattered dry-land trees, it was from the forest that they originally satisfied their basic needs for food, shelter, and clothing. After more than three million years of biological and cultural evolution, human beings still rely on forest ecosystems for survival.

Today, forests occupy 33 percent of the total land area of the United States—300 million ha (740.2 million acres) in the 50 states (Clawson 1975). Only livestock-grazing on natural rangelands commands an equivalent area.

BENEFITS FROM THE FOREST

Value to Humans

Forests have provided a major source of food to humans throughout the centuries. The early forest dwellers on the North American continent gathered much of their food directly from the forests—roots, buds, nuts, berries, and larger fruits. Even today, residents of the forested areas of our country supplement their diet with game animals, such as deer, wild pigs, and birds. In many countries, forests are managed for the game crop in addition to the timber production. Forests have also served as grazing land for domesticated animals. For ages, horses, cattle, and sheep have foraged in the forests and have furnished humans with a reliable food supply.

The cultivation of forest soils has long produced abundant agricultural crops. In the eastern half of the United States, for example, early settlers cut down the forests to reveal a rich virgin soil. Although some of the cleared land was not suitable for agriculture, much of it, particularly along alluvial deposits, provided a reliable source of food.

Our early ancestors used trees both for shelter and for escape from their enemies. Gradually, they learned to use trees to build primitive shelters on the ground, covering the roof and walls with thatch made of leaves and grasses or with stretched and dried animal skins. They harvested the trees by **girdling** them; that is, by removing a band of bark from the trunk of a tree in order to kill it. Apparently they learned to clear the forests before they learned to put the open grasslands to any useful purpose. Despite all the alternatives to wood available today, almost all structures—houses, schools, offices, and factories—contain some material derived from the forest, whether it be in the form of timber or in the form of insulation or wood by-products.

Humans have long depended on the forest for leaves and raw materials for clothing. Hunter-gatherers used the fronds of palm trees. Modern urbanites wear rayon shirts made from wood pulp and coats made of forest-dwelling animal fur. Humans still derive much of their clothing from the forest and its wildlife.

In addition to food, shelter, and clothing, humans have derived numerous other benefits from forests. For thousands of years human beings have been using the forest as a source of energy, allowing them to cook foods that could not be eaten raw (e.g., manioc), and enabling them to extend their range of habitats. For over 500,000 years, wood has been *the* source of energy for human beings. In Third World countries, forest wood is still used primarily (80 percent) for fuel (Eckholm 1979).

The United States relied almost exclusively on firewood for energy until coal, around 1820, and petroleum, in 1859, began to dominate energy production. Following the OPEC oil embargo in 1973, firewood consumption in the United States has made a comeback as a source of heating fuel.

In our national forests, according to the National Wildlife Federation, the harvesting of firewood has increased *sevenfold* since 1973. In 1980, the U.S. Forest Service gave away 1.6 billion board feet of timber—the fuel equivalent of 7 million barrels of oil. In the same year, they also issued 480,500 permits to gather wood, and they estimate that an additional 219,000 people gathered wood from areas where permits are not required. Furthermore, extensive *timber-rustling* goes on without permission. In 1980, a single area of Oregon suffered timber thefts approaching $9 million in value. In the years ahead, wood may also provide a source of liquid fuels and a wide variety of petrochemical substitutes.

Forests also provide us with such commercially valuable products as mushrooms, gums, and drugs. For centuries, people have been turning to the "forest pharmacy" for medicine to relieve headaches, infections, and even malaria. Modern-day biologists are delving into the genetic secrets of the world's tropical rainforests before those vital resources are destroyed. Recently, the forest setting has been put to a more controversial use—marijuana growing. Some people have illegally preempted extensive areas of forest land, particularly in California, for marijuana cultivation. Some of those sites are protected by armed guards and hidden traps.

Forests also provide the most effective natural resource for the conservation of soil and water. The protective forest cover checks the flow of surface water and then slowly releases it in a clear, steady flow. It also replenishes the reserves of groundwater. In a healthy deciduous forest, for example, the forest litter and deep soil may have enough storage capacity for 36.8 cm (14.5 in.) of rain.

Many underdeveloped and even economically advanced societies continue to rely on wood and wood derivatives. Underdeveloped societies often cultivate their fields with wooden plows, transport their wares in wooden carts, and use wood to make furniture, fences, and household implements. Modern society, on the other hand, relies on forest products to make newsprint, linoleum, cellophane, plastics, and other common "necessities" of everyday living. In today's age of synthetic materials, it is easy to forget our continual dependence on the forest.

Beyond all these practical benefits, forests satisfy the human need for recreation, access to wilderness areas, and spiritual and mental health (Figure 7-1). They provide urbanites with opportunities for hiking, fishing, bird watching, camping, picnicking, and numerous recreational pursuits. Without trees, our environment would be desolate.

Ecological Services

In addition to the direct human benefits provided by trees and forests, forests perform irreplaceable ecological services. They assist in the global recycling of oxygen, nitrogen, carbon, and water. They reduce flood potential and recharge springs, and they pro-

FIGURE 7-1 Morning light illuminating forest floor. (Photo by Jurgen R. Meyer-Arendt.)

vide critical habitat for millions of plant and animal species. All these life-supporting services are powered by energy from the sun.

Effects on the Atmosphere. Forests have an influence on wind, air temperature, humidity, precipitation, evaporation, and various types of pollution. Although they generally have no effect on short-term weather conditions, they do have some effect on the long-term climatic conditions of a region. We can modify local climate to some degree by manipulating the density, sizes, and even kinds of trees in the area, the extent of the forest, its degree of slope, and its direction of exposure to the sun.

Probably the greatest effect of a forest on local climate comes from its ability to dissipate the velocity of wind and to direct the path of a wind upward and away from the forest floor. With winds only a few miles per hour within the forest (as opposed to winds 20 to 30 miles per hour outside the forest), rates of evaporation (from soil) and transpiration (from vegetation) are reduced, and drifting snows are curtailed in the forest.

The forest cover influences the temperature of the air by intercepting the sun's rays and providing shade. How great that influence is depends, of course, on the density of the forest. In general, forests moderate summer temperatures by 6 to 8 degrees and winter temperatures by 2 or 3 degrees (Sharpe et al. 1976).

Forests also modify humidity, precipitation, and evaporation. Because of transpiration from trees and other herbaceous material, the relative humidity in a forest is greater than over a bare field. A mature oak tree, for example, transpires approximately 189.3 L

(50 gal) of water per day during the hot summer months (Anderson and Holland 1982). By contributing substantially to local atmospheric moisture, forests may have an effect on the precipitation rate of an area—perhaps increasing rainfall above forest areas by as much as 2 or 3 percent as compared with non-forested areas (Sharpe et al. 1976). There is no question that the forest cover reduces the evaporation rate of moisture in the ground both within the forest and in some adjacent regions.

Forests provide a valuable service by reducing gas, particulate, and noise pollution. Trees help to purify the air by taking up small amounts of sulfur dioxide. Some scientists maintain that trees also absorb various water and soil pollutants through their roots. Furthermore, trees help abate noise pollution by providing a noise-absorbing buffer in urban areas.

Effects on Soil and Water. The forest canopy lowers the temperature of the soil both by providing shade and by insulating the soil with forest litter. Differences between the soil temperature of forest areas (e.g., 32°C in summer) and the soil of nearby open areas (21°C) may be as great as 11°C (Sharpe et al. 1976). The forest canopy also moderates soil temperature. Forest soil freezes and thaws more gradually than the soil in open areas.

The forest cover serves to preserve the composition of the soil. The branches, twigs, and leaves of the forest accumulate annually to form a litter that feeds hundreds of organisms, such as rodents, earthworms, and microorganisms. The decaying litter and burrowing animals keep the soil porous, fertile, and receptive to air circulation and water infiltration. Consequently, the forest acts as a reservoir for recharging groundwater, springs, and streams.

The forest is an effective agent in minimizing soil erosion and flood damage. The forest canopy reduces the velocity of falling raindrops; the forest humus acts as a sponge that keeps the rainwater from running off; and the roots of the trees reinforce the soil. As a result, the forest retards the loss of topsoil and plant nutrients and checks the movement of sediment into rivers and reservoirs.

Another ecological service performed by forests—flood prevention—is often overlooked. A good example of this occurred in a small chaparral-covered canyon in southern California (Sharpe et al. 1976). In 1974, fire destroyed the forest cover on approximately 2024 ha (5000 acres) of Pickens Canyon in Los Angeles County. Soon after, a torrential rainstorm brought a sudden flood that killed 34 people and destroyed 200 homes. Just a few miles away, San Dimas Canyon—a comparable watershed that had not been devastated by fire—experienced the same storm but suffered no flood damage. Observers have reported similar extremes in other areas.

Effects on Wildlife. The forest provides a habitat for wild animals, where they are protected from human intrusion. Each type of forest constitutes a different ecosystem, with its own community of plants and animals and supporting a variety of wildlife populations and densities.

FORESTS AND FORESTRY

Forests

Simply stated, a **forest** is a collection or a stand of trees in which most of the crowns touch. The canopy of a forest is generally closed. By contrast, a *woodland* is a stand of trees where the crowns only occasionally touch, forming a partially closed canopy. The more comprehensive term *forest ecosystem* denotes a complex, living community of trees, shrubs, vines, other plants, animals, soil and subsoil, water, and atmosphere. All these elements are mutually dependent and are in constant competition.

While some forests extend over vast wilderness areas, others are small tracts in urbanized areas. Many of them are *artificial ecosystems;* that is, they have been created by human beings. Although forests are generally regarded as *renewable resources*, the great age of many trees requires some modification of that view. **Old Growth** trees of Douglas fir, ponderosa pine, and western hemlock along the Pacific coast are from 500 to 1000 years old, and some California redwoods are more than 2000 years old. Such trees are clearly not renewable within the lifetime of anyone now alive.

Industrial foresters are keenly interested in an ecological phenomenon known as *forest competition*—the contest between different plant species to dominate a particular site. Whether or not a tree will thrive at a particular site depends on many environmental factors, including light, temperature, moisture, soil conditions, and the presence of the same or different species. To understand why certain species of trees occur in particular locations, foresters must know how all these factors interrelate.

Forest succession is another important aspect of forest ecology. Forests are constantly changing. They evolve in response not only to environmental factors but also to an internally controlled process known as *succession*. As different types of trees and accompanying vegetation invade a site, and others withdraw,

the nature of the forest community changes. Foresters recognize three stages of forest succession: pioneer, intermediate or subclimax, and climax. Since many valuable commercial trees die out during the intermediate stage, foresters strive to control the stages of succession in order to maximize the value of a particular site.

To help understand and manage forests, foresters have devised several systems of *forest classification*. One system is to classify forests by age, species, and species characteristics. For instance, foresters speak of **even-aged** forests in which relatively small age differences (usually only 10 to 20 years) exist between individual trees, and of **all-aged** forests in which trees exist of all ages. A **pure forest** is dominated by one tree species, whereas a **mixed forest** has a variety of species. Foresters refer to forest trees as either **tolerant** (those that can survive in shade) or **intolerant** (those that must have direct sunlight to survive). Commercial foresters use one classification system or another to argue for the harvesting of a particular stand of trees. For example, they claim that, because the Douglas firs of the Pacific Northwest are intolerant, they should be harvested in *sunlite blocks*, which is a less controversial way of saying that they should be clear-cut. (See the Harvesting Techniques section of this chapter for further details on clear-cutting.)

Forestry

Forestry is the science and art of managing forests so that they continually yield the maximum quantity and quality of forest products while sustaining their vital ecological services. Therefore, forestry embraces a wide range of activities: harvesting trees; protecting watersheds, wildlife habitats, and wilderness and recreational sites; maintaining stream erosion control projects; and safeguarding the aesthetic qualities of forests.

Forestry science consists of several specialized pursuits. The comprehensive term **forest resource management** usually includes *mensuration*, appraising, measuring, and projecting tree growth; *regulation*, deciding when and what trees are to be cut; and *valuation*, determining the value of specific trees and forest properties. In this chapter we will discuss several other aspects of the science: *silviculture*, the planting of trees; *protection*, techniques for combating disease, insects, and fire; and, finally, *policy*, the laws and regulations that determine the behavior code of those who engage in the science of forestry. Not surprisingly, it is policy that elicits the greatest public controversy and scientific debate.

FOREST REGIONS OF THE UNITED STATES

When the first European settlers landed in 1620, forests covered approximately half of the land area of present-day America. More than three centuries later, those original 800–900 million acres have shrunk to about 740.2 million acres. Only about one-third of the 2.3 billion acres of land in this country is now forested.

Types and Location of Forests

The major forests of the United States can be classified into a fairly small number of zones. At the broadest level of categorization, we can divide the contiguous 48 states into two units: western forest types and eastern forest types. The western forest extends from the Pacific Coast across the Rocky Mountains. Here evergreen *coniferous* trees, mostly softwoods, predominate. The eastern forest stretches from the Great Plains to the Atlantic. Here *deciduous* hardwoods and softwoods predominate.

According to a more detailed breakdown, the forest regions of the United States fall into six major zones: Northern Forest, Central Hardwood Forest, Southern Forest, Tropical Forest, Rocky Mountain Forest, and Pacific Forest (Figure 7-2). Within these zones, 10 species are of particular commercial value: Douglas fir, coast redwood, western hemlock, Sitka spruce, ponderosa pine, balsam fir, eastern white pine, sugar maple, white oak, and loblolly pine (Figure 7-3). Softwoods, which are ideal for pulp and construction, account for 74 percent of the United States timber harvest. The remaining 26 percent of the timber harvested consists of hardwoods, such as hickory, oak, and maple. The timber industry is now dominated by the lush Pacific Forest, but foresters predict that the South, with its rapid-growing pine forests, will ultimately take the lead.

The Northern Forest. The Northern Forest dominates the northeastern United States. It is centered around the Great Lakes, with southern extensions into the Appalachian highlands. This area is rich in conifers, such as balsam fir, eastern white pine, red, black, and white spruce, red or Norway pine, jack pine, white cedar, tamarack, and eastern hemlock. It is also rich in broad-leaved trees, such as sugar maple, aspen, beech, northern red oak, white oak, and basswood.

Two of the top ten commercial trees are abundant in this region: balsam fir (*Abies balsamea*) and

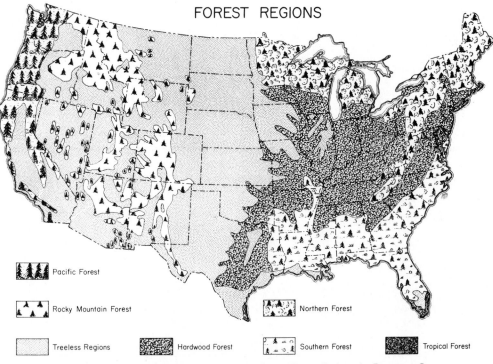

FOREST REGIONS

Pacific Forest

Rocky Mountain Forest

Treeless Regions

Hardwood Forest

Northern Forest

Southern Forest

Tropical Forest

FIGURE 7-2 Major U.S. forest regions. (From Ruben L. Parson, *Conserving American Resources,* 3d ed. [Englewood Cliffs, N.J.: Prentice-Hall, Inc., 1972], p. 335. Courtesy of U.S. Forest Service.)

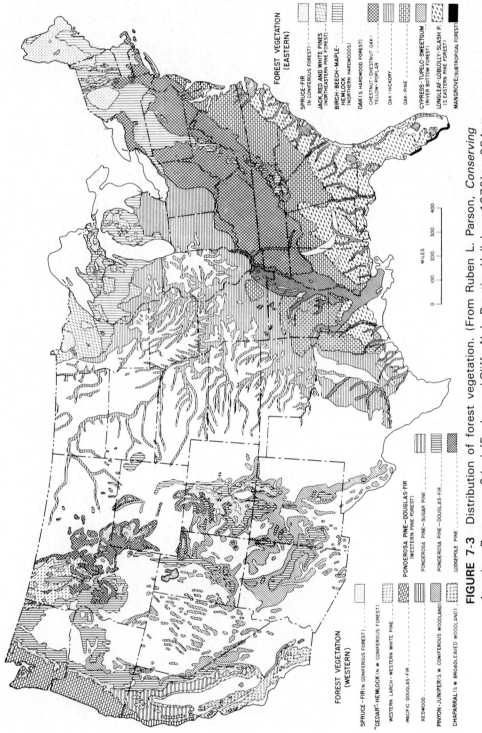

FIGURE 7-3 Distribution of forest vegetation. (From Ruben L. Parson, *Conserving American Resources*, 3d ed. [Englewood Cliffs, N.J.: Prentice-Hall, Inc., 1972], p. 334. Courtesy of U.S. Forest Service.)

FOREST VEGETATION (EASTERN)

- SPRUCE-FIR (N CONIFEROUS FOREST)
- JACK, RED AND WHITE PINES (NORTHEASTERN PINE FOREST)
- BIRCH-BEECH-MAPLE-HEMLOCK (NORTHERN HARDWOODS)
- OAK (S HARDWOOD FOREST)
- CHESTNUT-CHESTNUT OAK-YELLOW-POPLAR
- OAK-HICKORY
- OAK-PINE
- CYPRESS-TUPELO-SWEETGUM (RIVER BOTTOM FOREST)
- LONGLEAF-LOBLOLLY-SLASH P. (S EASTERN PINE FOREST)
- MANGROVE (SUBTROPICAL FOREST)

FOREST VEGETATION (WESTERN)

- SPRUCE-FIR (N CONIFEROUS FOREST)
- "CEDAR"-HEMLOCK (N W CONIFEROUS FOREST)
- WESTERN LARCH-WESTERN WHITE PINE
- PACIFIC DOUGLAS-FIR
- REDWOOD
- PINYON-JUNIPER (S W CONIFEROUS WOODLAND)
- CHAPARRAL (S W BROADLEAVED WOODLAND)
- PONDEROSA PINE-DOUGLAS-FIR (WESTERN PINE FOREST)
- PONDEROSA PINE-SUGAR PINE
- PONDEROSA PINE-DOUGLAS-FIR
- LODGEPOLE PINE

MILES
0   100   200   300   400

sugar maple (*Acer saccharum*). The balsam fir is also known as Canadian balsam and eastern fir. Millions of Americans know it as the familiar Christmas tree, with its pleasing symmetrical shape. The wood of the balsam provides pulp, its resin is used by pharmacists, and its needles are stuffed into aromatic pillows for the delight of tourists.

The sugar maple is found throughout the Midwest and the Great Lakes states, New England, and as far south as Louisiana. Sugar and syrup made from its sap are important crops in the New England states. One tree produces approximately three pounds of sugar a year. Since the wood of the sugar maple has an interesting grain and is easily polished, it is commonly used for furniture, cabinets, and musical instruments.

The Central Hardwood Forest. The Central Hardwood Forest extends from the Rio Grande to the shores of Cape Cod and to the southern portions of Wisconsin, Minnesota, and Michigan. Although some conifers are found there, including eastern white pine, Virginia pine, and shortleaf pine, broad-leaved hardwood trees predominate, including white oak, beech, red maple, northern red oak, hickory, elm, tulip or yellow popular, and white ash.

Two trees are of commercial significance in this region: white oak (*Quercus alba*) and white pine (*Pinus strobus*). Of the various members of the oak family in American forests, the white oak is the most familiar to residents of the eastern part of the country. The white oak can reach 2.4 m (8 ft) in diameter and can live for 600 years. Exceedingly hard when seasoned, oak wood is valued for flooring, furniture, and cabinetry, and for industrial applications ranging from bridges to whiskey barrels.

White pine is the tree that Pilgrims saw when they landed. Although it has been called the monarch of the eastern forest, it can be found in the Appalachian Mountains as far south as Georgia, and can be spotted as far west as eastern Minnesota. White pine was first used commercially to manufacture ship masts. White pine harvesting became a source of friction between the colonies and Great Britain just before the Revolutionary War when the British tried to preempt the supply for its own ships. Today the soft workable wood is widely used in furniture, paneling, and crates.

The Southern Forest. The loblolly, longleaf, shortleaf, and slash pines are predominant in the Southern Forest. This region is located in the southeastern United States, extending from eastern Maryland to eastern Texas, taking in portions of Missouri,

Arkansas, and Oklahoma. The abundant rainfall and long growing seasons of the region produce large volumes of timber in short periods of time.

The loblolly pine (*Pinus taeda*), for example, grows straight, tall, and strong. But, more important in terms of commercial output, it grows rapidly. In managed forests, loblolly is ready for harvesting after *only 12 years* of growth. Since it takes 153 acres of loblolly pine to produce one edition of the *Sunday New York Times*, it is easy to see why foresters have a strong interest in these trees. In the South, loblolly is planted by the millions, providing wood for plywood, lumber, and most important, pulp for paper production. The tree gets its popular name from *loblollies*—the local term for the moist lowlands that the species prefers.

The Tropical Forest. For most Americans, it is difficult to imagine that this country has its own tropical rainforests (forests usually associated with Third World countries located along the equator), yet rainforests do exist at the southernmost tips of Florida and Texas, and in Hawaii. Here, a wide variety of broad-leaved evergreen trees have adapted to the region's hot, humid climate. The leading species are mangrove, mahogany, and bay tree. Although these trees are not used as commercial timber, the forest absorbs runoff, reduces soil erosion, provides a varied wildlife habitat, and furnishes aesthetic pleasure.

The Rocky Mountain Forest. Also known as the Western Forest, the Rocky Mountain Forest extends over vast mountains and high plateaus from Mexico to Canada and from the Great Plains to the eastern parts of Oregon and Washington. Ponderosa pine grows on the lower, drier slopes of the Rocky Mountains; lodgepole pine grows on the cooler, wetter heights; and Engelmann spruce, Douglas fir, and true fir form a continuous forest at the highest elevations. In the northern Rocky Mountains, western larch and western white pine are locally important. The relatively low rainfall and short growing season of the Western Forest limit commercial activities in this zone.

The ponderosa pine (*Pinus ponderosa*) is the most important western timber pine and is second only to the Douglas fir in total stand in the United States. Being indigenous to the West, the ponderosa is found in all 11 western states and in Texas, Nebraska, North Dakota, and South Dakota.

The Pacific Forest. The Pacific Forest, sometimes called the West Coast Forest, contains some of the nation's largest trees. Of all the forest regions of the country, it has the most commercially valuable timber per acre, the principal species being Douglas fir, redwood, western hemlock, and Sitka spruce.

Sitka spruce (*Picea sitchensis*) grows in coast-hugging stands from California to Kodiak, Alaska. The soft, light, but strong wood, valued for pulp, was used for the frames of early airplaines, including Howard Hughes's *Flying Boat*, nicknamed the "Spruce Goose." Western hemlock (*Tsuga heterophylla*) has a fine texture and straight grain. Among western trees, this evergreen is second only to Douglas fir in volume harvested.

Douglas firs (*Pseudotsuga menziesii*) are huge trees, towering 60.1 m (200 ft) or more, with trunks 4.6 m (15 ft) in diameter, and with bark 0.3 m (1 ft) thick. Their strong, knot-free lumber makes them the most commercially valuable of all trees for lumber. Builders use lumber and plywood made from these trees for commercial buildings, schools, churches, and homes.

Redwood (*Sequoia sempervirens*) is another valuable tree of the Western Forest. It is one of the tallest, longest-living, and fastest-growing trees in the United States. One specimen towers 111.9 m (367 ft) over the forest. But its girth of 13.4 m (44 ft) cannot rival that of the shorter, bulkier *sequoias*, which have circumferences of more than 24.4 m (80 ft). In some stands, Sempervirens redwoods have an exceptionally fast growth rate of 0.91 m (3 ft) in diameter within 50 years, and they have lived as long as 2000 years.

Forest Ownership

America's forest: How large is it? Where is it? Who owns it? How productive is it? With projections indicating a doubling of timber demand by the year 2020, these are important questions. Approximately one-third (740.2 million acres) of the United States is covered with forests that are either commercial or noncommercial (Figure 7-4).

Commercial versus Noncommercial Forest Lands. There are approximately 487.7 million acres of *commercial* forest lands in the United States. These are forest lands that are either producing or are capable of producing crops of industrial wood and that have not been withdrawn from commercial harvesting. To qualify as commercial forest lands areas must be able to produce in excess of 20 cubic feet of industrial wood in natural stands per acre per year. Even inaccessible and difficult-to-work-in areas are included in this classification, except for small areas that are unlikely to produce wood under current

technology. Commercial forest lands also provide recreation, wildlife habitat, watershed protection, and animal forage.

All lumber, paper, and other forest products come from these 487.7 million acres of commercial land. The remaining 252.5 million acres consist of *noncommercial forests*. Some of these forest lands lie on inaccessible mountains or are situated where soil quality and drainage are poor. Certain areas that would qualify as commercial forests have been reserved for nontimber uses, such as parks, wilderness areas, and game refuges.

Of the total noncommercial forests, 228.3 million acres are classified as being incapable of producing enough trees per acre to make them profitable to harvest. The remaining 24.2 million acres of unavailable land would be capable of commercial production if certain statues or administrative designations were changed. For example, many potentially productive timberlands are currently classified as wilderness areas on which timber production is restricted. Timber companies must defer harvesting these areas until the public changes its mind on how to best use them.

Location and Ownership of Commercial Forest Lands. Approximately three-fourths of the total U.S. commercial forest lands are located in the eastern half of the country, nearly equally divided between North and South (Figures 7-2 and 7-3). The remaining one-fourth is located in the West, in Washington, Oregon, California, Idaho, Colorado, and Montana. The ownership of U.S. commercial forest lands breaks down as follows:

58 percent is owned by private citizens

14 percent is owned by lumber companies

28 percent is owned by government

Seventy-two percent is owned privately—either by citizens or lumber companies. Citizens own the most—58 percent (283.2 million acres). Only a small percentage—14 percent (68 million acres)—is owned by lumber companies. Most of their holdings are in the South (53 percent), the rest of their holdings are in the North (26 percent) and on the Pacific Coast (21 percent).

The public owns 28 percent, or 136.5 million acres. Twenty percent of this is owned by the federal government, mostly in the form of National Forests (89 million acres), Bureau of Land Management lands (5.8 million acres), and miscellaneous federal lands

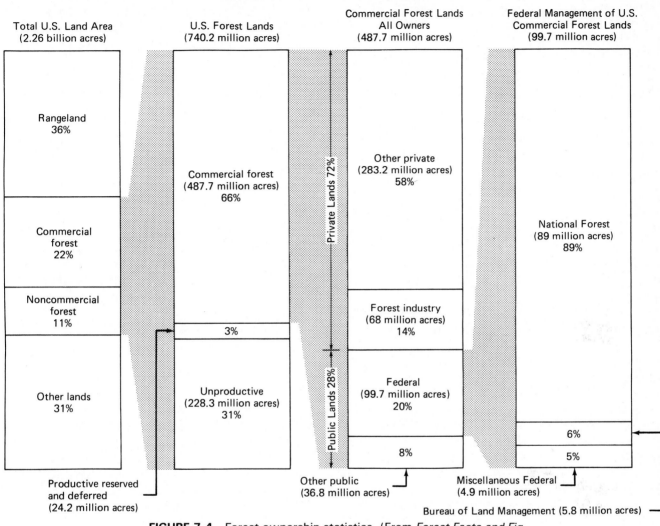

United States Forest Land Ownership Breakdown

FIGURE 7-4   Forest ownership statistics. (From *Forest Facts and Figures* [Washington, D.C.: American Forest Council, 1979], p. 1.)

(4.9 million acres). The remaining publicly owned commercial forest lands (8 percent, or 36.8 million acres) are in state, county, municipal, and Indian holdings.

Production Inventories. Geography and history both determined who would end up with the greatest share of hardwoods and softwoods. Hardwoods are found predominately in the East, where early settlers staked their claims prior to increased federal interference. Consequently, most of the hardwoods fell into the hands of private owners. As a result, many wood-processing plants in the East must rely on private owners for their timber, and in the West they must rely on National Forests and other public lands.

HISTORY OF AMERICAN FOREST MANAGEMENT

Forest Exploitation

Precolonial to 1620. Human beings have been living on the North American soil for 17,000 years. For most of that time, the forests were the exclusive domain of the Native Americans. Hunters and gatherers undoubtedly influenced forest succession by setting fires accidentally or in order to drive their prey past hunters armed with bow and arrow. With the advent of agriculture, American Indians in the East used fire to clear the land and to prepare it for the planting of crops. Many fires, of course, also occurred naturally. Cultural geographers and anthropologists are still trying to discover the ways in which these early inhabitants modified the primeval forest.

From 1620 to 1776. North America's second wave of settlers came upon over a hundred different conifers and broad-leaved trees in the eastern part of the country alone. The Europe from which they had fled had fewer than a dozen commercial tree species. The settlers viewed the forests as a mixed blessing. The forests provided building material, fuel, and game, but they also occupied valuable land needed for agriculture and pasture. Moreover, the forests harbored unfriendly Indians, confirming their fears that the forest was a dwelling place for hostile forces.

The settlers cleared the land for crops and began to harvest the white pine and oak of the forests for trade. By 1631, colonists in New Hampshire were exporting white pine to England, where the soft, clean, fragrant, fairly strong wood found a ready market. White pine was to dominate that market for 250 years. The English were also eager for oak to use in shipbuilding. According to a 1691 charter, all trees that were more than 60 cm (24 in.) in diameter at a height of 30 cm (1 ft) from the ground were to be set aside for the Royal Navy; the strongest and straightest were reserved for manufacture into ship masts (Sharpe et al. 1976). Despite the demands of the Crown, however, the colonists continued to harvest the forests for their own purposes.

The early colonists showed little concern for conservation. A few laws specified punishment for timber thieves and for anyone who set fire to a forest that could produce merchantable goods. But from 1620 to 1776 the forests east of the Allegheny-Appalachian Range were relentlessly harvested to clear new areas for settlement. Taming the wilderness meant cutting down the trees.

National Exploitation: 1776 to 1876. After the Revolution, the young nation hastened to develop its own navy to protect its growing commerce. The United States Navy was officially established in 1798. Immediately, the demand for ship timber increased. Between 1798 and 1833, several laws were enacted to reserve oak forests on the Gulf Coast of Florida for the navy, indicating the belief that the nation's sea power depended on the availability of forest resources.

The population of the nation quadrupled from 1820 to 1870, creating a vigorous home market for forest products. A steam sawmill was in use as early as 1830 at a plant near Pontiac, Michigan, and wood-burning locomotives traveling on wooden rails gave the country its first glimpse of rapid transportation.

The first logging locomotive came on the scene in 1852. The lumber industry, with its close link to the industrial revolution, enabled the young nation to break away from Europe industrially as well as politically.

As population increased, so did the desire for expansion. Between 1841 and 1871 new laws were passed to accelerate the harvesting of forests and the building of a transportation system to foster settlement. Two laws were of particular importance: the Preemption Act of 1841 and the Homestead Act of 1862. The *Preemption Act* made it possible for families to obtain at modest cost 64.7 ha (160 acres) for colonization, so long as they promised to improve the land and erect a dwelling. The *Homestead Act* was broader but similar in purpose. Both laws fostered settlement and encouraged wasteful exploitation of the forests.

Other laws further promoted westward expansion. Under various land grant acts, the first of which was passed in 1850, railroad builders received the right of way they needed to construct their railroad lines. But they also received, at no expense, alternating square mile *sections* (each being 6 mi^2) on each side of the railroad, and the right to purchase the remaining sections at $2.50 per acre. The railroaders, in turn, could sell these sections to settlers at a minimum charge. New towns and cities sprang up along the routes. The demand for building material skyrocketed, and by 1870 some 27,000 lumber-producing plants were busy producing forest products.

Exploitation of the forests followed a regional pattern. Although commercial logging had existed in New England since colonial times, it was not until loggers turned their attention to the pine forests of the upper Midwest that destruction truly set in. They followed wasteful cutting practices, left great quantities of slash (debris), and allowed forest fires to rage.

As the accessible forests vanished, the white pine loggers, with their exploitive philosophy, shifted from Maine to New York to Pennsylvania and eventually, in 1870, reached the forests of Minnesota and Wisconsin. In their haste, they wasted enormous amounts of their harvest, leaving great areas of slash. Eventually, the slash caught fire and destroyed millions of acres of forest, claiming thousands of human lives and destroying an untold number of wildlife species.

Within a few more years, the robber baron economy had reached the coniferous forests of the Southeast. Here, between 1900 and 1910, the lumber companies turned their attention to the longleaf, loblolly, and slash pines that sprang up as secondary growth on abandoned tobacco and cotton farmlands. The southern pines resisted destruction, however, because they are fast-growing, quickly regenerate themselves after a cutting, and actually benefit from limited burning.

Finally, the destructive forces reached the Pacific Northwest, particularly the states of Washington and Oregon, as well as northern California. About the same time the pine industry was growing up in the South, the Douglas fir industry was developing in the West. By 1905, Washington had become the leading wood-producing state, as it still is.

By this time, informed people were beginning to protest the way in which our forests were being exploited, and their concern gave rise to conservation proposals and public pressure for federal action.

Forest Conservation

Professional Forestry. The history of professional forestry falls into three distinct periods: origin and early development (1876–1897), growth (1897–1945), and science and technology (1945–present).

Although the years from 1876 to 1897 were marked by wasteful practices and unbridled exploitation, they also produced a campaign of public education and support that led to the creation of a forestry policy for federal lands. Five early dates are of particular significance.

1876 *Congress appoints special forestry agent.* Exactly a hundred years after the Declaration of Independence, the U.S. federal government appointed its first forestry agent—Dr. Franklin B. Hough, a physician, statistician, and naturalist from Lowville, New York. His appointment marked the beginning of federal attention to forestry. Dr. Hough's assignment was to gather data on the existing supply and the future demand for timber, to report on successful forest management techniques, and to seek a means to preserve and renew forests. His agency became the Division of Forestry within the Department of Agriculture, which, in turn, became the U.S. Forest Service.

1891 *Forest reserves are established.* The Creative Act of Congress, approved March 3, 1891, gave the president power to withdraw forest lands in the public domain from homesteading and to bring them under the management of the federal government. On March 31, 1891, President Benjamin Harrison set aside the Yellowstone Timberland Reserve, which surrounded Yellowstone National Park, as the first of the federal forest reserves (now known as national forests). This action marked the beginning of the National Forest System and provided the first evidence of a nationwide conservation movement. Over the

next 14 years, Presidents Harrison, Cleveland, McKinley, and Theodore Roosevelt proclaimed 60 forest reserves totaling 2.3 million ha (56 million acres). These reserves were administered by the General Land Office of the Department of the Interior, rather than by the Division of Forestry in the Department of Agriculture.

1897 *The Forest Service Organic Act is passed.* How were the newly created forest reserves to be managed? Were they to be preserved by keeping them untouched by humans? Or were they to be used under some carefully supervised production plan? The Forest Service Organic Act declared that the reserves were to be used to supply timber. That same philosophy governs the policy of the U.S. Forest Service today.

Between 1897 and 1945, the U.S. Forest Service came into being, the National Forest System was developed and expanded, and forestry became a recognized governmental profession. Accompanying these developments was a movement to conserve all natural resources and the widespread use of the word *conservation*.

1898 *Gifford Pinchot is named Forestry Head.* A year after the Forest Service Organic Act was passed, Gifford Pinchot was named head of the Division of Forestry in the Department of Agriculture. Since forest reserves were still under the jurisdiction of the Department of the Interior when he was appointed, all he could do was try to inform the public about the state of the nation's forests. When Theodore Roosevelt, a long-time admirer of Pinchot, was inaugurated, he appointed Pinchot, in 1901, as head of the newly named Bureau of Forestry and gave him limited responsibility for managing the nation's forest reserves.

1905 *The U.S. Forest Service is established.* Despite efforts to curb it, forest exploitation continued apace. Clearly further legislation was needed. The Transfer Act of February 1, 1905, transferred the management of the Forest Reserves from the Department of the Interior to the newly created U.S. Forest Service (the outgrowth of Pinchot's Bureau of Forestry) in the Department of Agriculture. Pinchot, the first Chief Forester, could now extend his authority to the public forest reserves. In 1907, the term *forest reserves* was replaced by *national forests*, because *reserves* implied that the forests had been withdrawn from use.

Supported by Roosevelt's keen interest, the U.S. Forest Service and its Chief Forester created new national forests and launched forestry as an authentic profession. Moreover, Roosevelt and Pinchot together sparked a new spirit of concern for the future of natural resources in the United States—a spirit that came to be known as the conservation movement. Supporters urged that wasteful practices be eliminated through the scientific management of resources. Pinchot was one of the principal architects of the influential conservation movement.

As the years passed, a series of landmark acts were passed. The Weeks Act of 1911 enabled the federal government to purchase lands to be managed as National Forests at the headwaters of navigable streams. The Clarke-McNary Act of 1914 extended that policy by enabling the federal government to purchase lands necessary for timber production and for the protection of navigation within the watersheds of navigable streams. Furthermore, the act expanded federal-state cooperation in the protection of state and private forests against fire. The Knutson-Vandenberg Act of 1930 provided federal funds for the purpose of reforestation in the national forests.

Since 1945, the role of science and technology in forest management has grown steadily. Following World War II, a determined effort was made to foster the concept that science and nature should work together in forest management. These years have also brought intervention in the management of the nation's forest lands. Some of the more significant legislative acts passed since 1945 follow.

1960 *The Multiple-Use Sustained Yield Act.* This act supplemented the Organic Act of 1897 by giving legislative status to what had long been the operating policy of the Forest Service—the management not only of timber, but of watershed, wilderness, wildlife, grazing, and recreation resources on forest lands. (We will return to this act later in this chapter.)

1973 *The Endangered Species Act.* This revision of an earlier act established protected status to threatened plant and animal species. (See Chapter 9 for further details.)

1976 *The National Forest Management Act.* This complex piece of legislation requires that all individuals involved in forest operations plan out their harvesting strategies in advance of timber harvesting for the purpose of minimizing environmental degradation of the site.

This increased role of the federal government, together with the legislation it has spawned, has complicated the life of career foresters by imposing a variety of burdens and restrictions on them. Still, the nation's forests have clearly benefited from the public policy of recent years.

Forest Administration. The forested areas of the United States are administered by five federal bureaus: (1) the Soil Conservation Service, which is concerned with woodlots and forests on privately owned farms; (2) the Tennessee Valley Authority, which oversees timberland management in the Tennessee Valley watershed; (3) the U.S. Fish and Wildlife Service, which encourages the proper management of fish and wildlife habitats; (4) the Bureau of Land Management, which handles certain timber and grazing lands in the western states; and (5) the U.S. Forest Service, which manages the national forests.

The National Forest System consists of 155 national forests (Figure 7-5) and 19 national grasslands, covering some 77 million ha (190 million acres) of publicly owned land. Most of this land is west of the Mississippi River. Overall, the National Forest System accounts for only 17 percent of all forest lands in the United States. Administratively, the Forest Service is made up of regions. Within the regions, the *national forests* are the administrative units, and within the national forests are *ranger districts*. These forests are managed under the Multiple-Use Sustained Yield Act of 1960 and the Forest Reserves Management Acts of 1974 and 1976.

Sustained yield means that the growth of trees must balance the wood lost by cutting, fire, disease, and pests. If that balance is maintained, the national forests will survive into perpetuity. Ideally, the principle of sustained yield should also be applied to forest products other than timber, including the promotion of abundant wildlife, healthy fisheries, livestock forage, and water supplies. Unfortunately, however, the yield of those products is often diminished in the effort to sustain the yield of timber. By 1965 *timber growth* had exceeded *timber cut*, which at first would seem encouraging in terms of forest conservation. Unfortunately, the figures refer only to the quantity cut; they say nothing about the quality of the wood being harvested or about the condition of the remaining forest—its soil, its watershed, its wildlife, and so on (Owen 1985).

The principle of **multiple use** requires that the management of the national forests take into account recreational, forage, watershed, and wildlife uses in addition to timber production. One of the guiding principles of the U.S. Forest Service is "the greatest good for the greatest number in the long run." Budgetary constraints often prevent the Forest Service from implementing that principle, however.

LOCATION OF NATIONAL FORESTS AND NATIONAL GRASSLANDS

FIGURE 7-5 National forests and grasslands. (From Ruben L. Parson, *Conserving American Resources,* 3d ed. [Englewood Cliffs, N.J.: Prentice-Hall, Inc., 1972], p. 355. Courtesy of U.S. Forest Service.)

The Forest Service faces a difficult task in trying to reconcile the conflicting interests of different groups. Timber companies want to convert the forests into office buildings, houses, and newspapers. Hikers and wilderness campers want to preserve the forests in more or less pristine condition. Hunters want to bag as much game as they please, but protectors of wildlife urge that animals be captured only on film. Resort owners want to attract paying guests, but local residents complain that outsiders cause forest fires and contaminate water supplies. The interests of all these groups are basically incompatible. The logger, the hunter, the bird-watcher, and the camper simply cannot all coexist on the same site. Still, U.S. foresters must try to work out acceptable solutions to balance these conflicting demands.

Foresters must act in accordance with the principle of multiple use and keep many objectives in mind. For example, as *watershed managers*, they must strive for maximum water yields, minimum soil erosion, and effective flood control. To increase water storage, they sometimes open up areas in the forest, since snow on the ground evaporates at a slower rate than snow caught in tree tops. This technique is particularly effective in the mountainous evergreen forests of the West, where most of the region's precipitation falls as snow. It also serves to reduce transpiration and increase stream flow. In their role

as watershed managers, foresters also try to prevent fires, overgrazing, and improper cutting methods in their effort to curtail erosion, sedimentation, and flooding.

In their role as *wilderness managers*, foresters often find themselves embroiled in heated controversy. A program known as Roadless Area Review and Evaluation (RARE), for example, has triggered a lively debate over which public lands should be given over to commercial use and which should be maintained as wilderness. Although the RARE process began in 1967 with RARE I, its initial conclusions were so unsatisfactory and controversial that the task of classifying roadless areas was begun again in mid-1977 (RARE II) and continues today. Foresters, under the RARE process, are called on to make recommendations on several sensitive issues: Which roadless areas should be added to the National Wilderness Preservation System? Which public lands should be released for multiple use? Which public lands should undergo further study before a decision is made on how they should be managed?

Commercial interests suspect that RARE is simply a strategy for getting most of the National Forest System designated as wilderness areas. Environmental organizations suspect that the RARE process will lead to the giveaway of potential wilderness areas. Whatever they recommend, foresters find themselves at odds with both the commercial interests and the wilderness advocates.

Foresters must also serve as *range managers.* Of the total acreage of our national forests and national grasslands, over half is devoted to cattle and sheep grazing, most of which is in the West. Foresters must ensure that the owners of those animals observe proper grazing seasons, repair erosion damage, re-seed grazed areas, keep salting facilities away from waterholes, use fences to confine their stock, and eliminate noxious plants.

Foresters are also *wildlife managers,* since one of the objectives of the U.S. Forest Service is to improve the habitats of wildlife and the diversity of species in forest and range ecosystems. As they try to increase or curtail the population of certain species, they must consider the type of forest they are dealing with, the mix of plant species, the stages in the succession of the forest, and the rotation of cuttings.

Certain trees provide excellent nesting sites or places of refuge for various species of birds. So-called snags are tree cavities favored by such hole-nesting species as woodpeckers, nuthatches, and owls. They also serve as perches and nesting sites for hawks and eagles. Snags occur most commonly in diseased or dead trees, however, and create fire and safety hazards. So the forester must decide whether to let them stand or to cut them out.

Several public and private forests have set aside extensive tracts for the exclusive purpose of encouraging wildlife. In some commercial forest, *buffer strips* of trees have been created along streams and highways to preserve wildlife habitats. Such strips also serve to check erosion and improve water quality.

Foresters try to limit clear-cuts (areas where all the trees are removed) to less than 20 ha (50 acres). Small, irregularly shaped open areas divided by zones of undisturbed forest add to the *edge* habitat frequented by such game animals as pheasant, rabbit, and deer. Fire lanes and logging trails also contribute to the edge habitat.

Controlled, or prescribed, burning is another management tool that foresters use to encourage wildlife. In the southern pine forests, for example, prescribed burning is used periodically to check the accumulation of litter (fuel), to minimize the competition between hardwoods and softwoods, and to control brown spot disease. After an area has been burned, seed-bearing plants spring up that provide food for a variety of birds. In central Michigan, prescribed burning is used to preserve open stands of jack pines that serve as nesting sites for the Kirtland's warbler, an endangered species. The burning keeps the height of the trees in the range of 1.5 m to 6.1 m (5 ft to 20 ft), which satisfies the nesting requirements of these birds. Prescribed burning to remove forest litter or underbrush is also becoming more commonly used in the arid forests of the Southwest.

FOREST RESOURCE MANAGEMENT

Without sound, scientific management the survival of our forests would be in jeopardy. Deforestation would disrupt watersheds, impair soil fertility, lead to the silting and flooding of stream valleys, and accelerate stream eutrophication. It would also alter local microclimates, impair wildlife habitats, destroy aesthetic values, wipe out recreational areas, and impede scientific research (Figure 7-6). The purpose of **forest resource management** is to maximize the use of the nation's forests while minimizing the potential for ecological disaster. Forest resource management consists of three major activities: harvesting, reforestation, and forest protection.

Harvesting

Whereas agriculture is the tillage of soil for the purpose of harvesting food crops, **silviculture** is the cultivation of forests for timber crops. Among the silvicultural techniques commonly used in the harvesting of forest products are *selective cutting, clear-cutting,* and *shelterwood cutting* (Figure 7-7). Less common techniques are *seed-tree cutting, naturalistic silviculture,* and *short-rotation silviculture.* Although each technique has its ardent proponents, the characteristics of each site should determine which technique is most appropriate for the task at hand.

Selective Cutting. **Selective cutting,** or *thinning,* is the careful removal of trees of specific species, size, or condition (Figure 7-8). Proponents of this technique point out that nature has always practiced selective cutting by culling out weak, diseased, or aged trees, thereby admitting light into the shaded forest.

This harvesting technique is appropriate in forests that contain trees of various ages or that contain several species of unequal commercial value, such as in mixed deciduous stands of hickory, oak, and walnut. Thinning is an excellent way to accelerate the rate of tree growth in the remaining forest, since it increases the availability of sunlight and soil nutrients.

Selective cutting also improves the quality of the trees. Since the seedlings are nurtured in the partial shade of a protective forest canopy, they grow up-

(a)

(b)

FIGURE 7-6 Negative effects of deforestation. (a) Severe soil erosion in clear-cut area. (b) Sediment-clogged stream near a clear-cut area. (From Bernard J. Nebel, *Environmental Science: The Way the World Works* [Englewood Cliffs, N.J.: Prentice-Hall, Inc., 1981], p. 196.)

ward instead of outward. As a result, the wood fiber is relatively straight, fine, and strong. Selective cuttings every five to 10 years are usually adequate to keep the quality of the growing stock at a high level.

Another advantage of selective cutting is that it guarantees a variety of species, ages, and stages of growth. Such variety protects the forest ecoystem against epidemics of insects and disease and reduces the need for herbicides, pesticides, and elaborate nursery programs for the propagation of new stock. Because selective cutting does not impair the natural appearance of forests, it is the method favored by hunters, anglers, nature observers, and hikers.

Selective cutting has certain drawbacks, however. The method can only be used with tolerant species, that is, tree species that can grow in the shade,

such as hemlock, beech, and maple. Moreover, great care must be taken to avoid damage to the residual trees as the designated trees are being harvested. Such precautions are expensive, because logging costs increase when small cuttings are made at frequent intervals. Finally, loggers often remove only the highest-quality trees (a practice known as *high grading*), leaving the poorer quality trees to reseed the area. As a result, the overall quality of the forest declines.

Conservationists favor selective cutting because it duplicates natural processes. Actually, however, when trees are culled out by such natural agencies as insects, disease, or fire, their remains rot on the ground and restore organic matter to the soil. Moreover, nature has no need for logging roads to remove

(a)

(b)

(c)

(d)

(e)

FIGURE 7-7 Major systems of silviculture. (a) Clear-cutting with natural regeneration; (b) clear-cutting with planting; (c) shelterwood cutting; (d) selective cutting; (e) coppice system (e.g., short rotation method). (Illustration by Tom Prentiss from Stephen H. Spurr, ''Silviculture,'' *Scientific American,* February 1979. Copyright © 1979 by SCIENTIFIC AMERICAN, Inc. All rights reserved.)

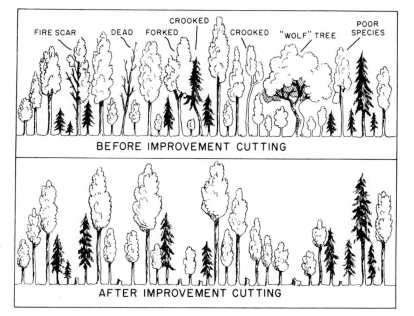

FIGURE 7-8 Sanitation cutting—one type of selective harvesting. (From Ruben L. Parson, *Conserving American Resources*, 3d ed. [Englewood Cliffs, N.J.: Prentice-Hall, Inc., 1972], p. 372. Courtesy of U.S. Forest Service.)

the felled trees. Selective cutting requires a maze of tote roads and skidder trails to provide access to the scattered trees chosen for harvesting. The heavy equipment driven over those roads compacts the soil and impedes the growth of the trees that remain.

Clear-cutting. In the harvesting technique known as **clear-cutting,** all the trees are removed from a given area (Figure 7-9). Today, 60 percent of all tree harvesting is done by this method. After the trees have been removed, the clearcut is reseeded, fertilized, and sprayed with pesticides and with herbicides to control animal and vegetative competition. In many respects, clear-cutting resembles the agricultural production of crops.

This tendency to regard trees as *crops* has made clear-cutting the most controversial approach to tree harvesting. Proponents of clear-cutting, for example, argue that it is the most appropriate technique for forests in which the trees consist of commercially useful species and are of relatively even age. Since all the trees can be cut from a single block or strip, there is

FIGURE 7-9 Clear-cut areas that will take decades to heal. (From Frederick R. Troeh, J. A. Hobbs, and Roy L. Donahue, *Soil and Water Conservation: For Productivity and Environmental Protection* [Englewood Cliffs, N.J.: Prentice Hall, Inc., 1980], p. 444. Courtesy of U.S. Forest Service.)

no need to hunt and pick. They also argue that clear-cutting is the most efficient technique in terms of time and energy expended. Since harvesting is done at one time and one place, the machinery can be moved about without damaging residual trees. The tree farmer simply clears space in which he can create a new forest of his liking. Few logging roads are needed, and time and money are saved.

Advocates of clear-cutting also point out that most commercial species do best in full sunlight in stands of even age. They claim that it is the only way to regenerate desirable species in certain regions, including walnut, yellow poplar, oak, and especially Douglas fir. Moreover, because clear-cut forests grow back quickly, they can also be harvested more frequently. And finally, the timber industry argues that clear-cutting makes it easy to remove infected trees from a section of forest. The section is simply cut out, and healthy trees replace the infected ones.

Opponents, on the other hand, see major flaws in the clear-cutting method of harvesting trees. They argue that clear-cutting creates an artificial forest of even-aged trees that are highly susceptible to disease, insects, and fire. In southeastern United States, for example, where natural forests with diverse species have been replaced with a monoculture of pine trees, clear-cut areas must be artifically seeded or planted. And to overcome competition from other species, herbicides have to be sprayed over clear-cut areas, subjecting animals and humans to unknown hazards. Many forest managers also point out that clear-cutting interferes with the runoff pattern of a region, thereby disturbing seasonal irrigation patterns on farms and rangelands below the harvested area.

Increased water runoff also means an increased loss of soil and soil nutrients. The removal of trees from a large area destroys the natural forest cover and exposes the soil to erosion and loss of nutrients. When researchers at Hubbard Brook, New Hampshire, clear-cut an experimental forest plot under scientifically controlled conditions, they found that the loss of nitrite in runoff increased 45-fold; the loss of potassium, 21-fold; the loss of calcium, 10-fold (Nebel 1981). Such a severe loss of nutrients is bound to have an effect on future tree growth. Timber companies have already begun to apply artificial fertilizers to clear-cut areas.

Soil compaction is also a problem in clear-cut areas. The sheer weight of the bulldozers and logging trucks used in clear-cutting changes the character of the soil and affects future tree growth. To circumvent this problem, timber companies have experimented with helicopters and helium balloons to lift the har-

vested trees from the forest. Logging by helicopter costs 20 times more than logging by tractor, however.

Wildlife habitats are also destroyed by large-scale clear-cuts. Few animals can survive on a barren piece of earth that has little food and shelter. It must be pointed out, however, that occasional, relatively small clear-cuts create additional *edge* and actually benefit certain wildlife species.

Finally, opponents of clear-cutting argue that this harvesting technique brings an aesthetic loss by leaving ugly, unnatural gashes in a forest. Along the highways of Washington and Oregon, for example, the motorist is often confronted with a dramatic contrast between lush green forests and clear-cut areas of stark desolation. The view from the air is even more startling. By blending clear-cut areas into the natural topography of the landscape, timber companies can at least reduce the visual impact of their activities. For example, it is now common to leave a buffer strip along highways for aesthetic purposes and to provide animal habitat.

Shelterwood Cutting.   In **shelterwood cutting,** trees are removed from only a portion of an area at any one time. That portion does not exceed 0.04 km², or 10 acres. Over a 10 to 15 year period the entire area will have been harvested. Shelterwood cutting combines some of the features of clear-cutting and selective cutting and is used to harvest either even-aged trees or uneven-aged trees.

In the first cut, called *preparatory cutting,* only the mature poorly formed or otherwise defective trees are removed. This thinning operation opens the forest floor to light penetration. The best trees are left standing to cast seed and to provide shelter for the seedlings. Once a good seed crop has been distributed, a second, heavier cut, known as *seed cutting,* is made of most of the remaining trees. Some mature trees are left to provide shelter for the young seedlings. In this cutting, between 30 and 60 percent of the stand is harvested. Finally, after the young seedlings are well established, a third and final cut, known as *removal cutting,* removes all the mature trees that remain (Stoddard 1978).

Like the proponents of selective cutting and clear-cutting, advocates of shelterwood cutting claim that the method parallels natural processes. They point out that ground fires have always swept through the forests, removing everything but the hardy mature trees. Those survivors drop seed to the ground and shelter the seedlings from the ravages of wind and rain.

Shelterwood cutting is appropriate for the harvesting of such tolerant species as redwood, sugar pine, and white pine that require shade during their early years (Stoddard 1978). It is used mainly in harvesting Norway (red) pine, white pine, and ponderosa pine in the southern pine forests.

The shelterwood technique had several advantages: Since it subjects the forests to only gradual change, seedlings, soil, and wildlife have time to adapt to the altered conditions. Since the seedlings develop from the choicest seed trees, they produce a high-quality forest. Moreover, the ample light admitted during the second and third stages enables the trees to grow rapidly. Finally, brush and undesirable hardwoods can be controlled without the application of herbicides.

Yet shelterwood cutting has certain disadvantages as well. Like clear-cutting, it generally produces an even-aged forest consisting of a single specie of tree. Consequently, the forest lacks the natural stability that comes with diversity. Like selective cutting, shelterwood cutting requires an extensive network of logging roads. Moreover, the seedlings are often damaged during the second and third cuts. Finally, since the timing of the cuts may not coincide with the most favorable market and price conditions, profits may be adversely affected.

Minor Harvesting Techniques. The *seed-tree method,* a variation of clear-cutting, eliminates all the trees within a stand except the best seed trees. Those trees are left close enough together to provide adequate pollination and seeding for a new crop. This method is seldom used, however, because it has several serious drawbacks: The trees that are left standing may be brought down by wind or ice and may fail to produce ample seed to reestablish the forest. Moreover, the seed trees are so few in number that it is difficult to harvest them after the new growth has become established. The seed-tree method has been used successfully with the southern longleaf pine, but it has failed with the northern pines because of the excessive invasion of brush into the growing area.

Naturalistic silviculture relies on natural forest diversity (a mixed stand of uneven age) and on natural succession (Spurr 1979). It has long been practiced in Europe, but it has only recently been seriously considered in this country. From time to time, partial cuts are made to ensure the highest economic return consistent with the maintenance of the forest. Because of its diversity, the forest suffers little damage from disease and insects, and advocates claim that the technique is relatively inexpensive and risk free. Although an even-aged forest of the same species will

usually bring in more dollars, a naturalistically managed forest can be profitable with the right combination of species and appropriate terrain.

Finally, *short-rotation silviculture* is a technique for producing large amounts of wood-fiber on so-called biomass plantations. Here, trees with maximum photosynthetic efficiency are intensively cultivated and frequently harvested. This technique somewhat resembles the *coppice system* that was widely used in the United States during the nineteenth century. In that system, stands of hardwood were harvested for fuel on a short-rotation cycle and were regenerated by means of sprouts taken from the stems.

Short-rotation silviculture is best suited to such fast-growing species as sycamore, cottonwood, and red alder. The trees are mechanically harvested on a rotational basis every two to four years when they are 3.0 to 6.1 m (10 to 20 ft) high and 2.5 to 5.1 cm (1 to 2 in.) in diameter (Spurr 1979). The sprouts are intensively cultivated and fertilized to produce the next crop. The harvest is converted into chips for fuel or into chemical feedstock. The system requires heavy investments in irrigation, fertilization, cultivation, and harvesting. Although experiments continue, no plantations of commercial size have yet used this system.

Decisions on what to grow and what harvesting technique to use must be based on the climate and soil conditions that exist at a particular site and on the regulations that govern the use of the site. Short-rotation silviculture could not be used in the national forests, for example, since it would violate the multiple-use concept.

Reforestation

Reforestation, the process of replanting denuded areas is a major component of forest resource management. It is accomplished by either natural or artificial methods.

Most forest owners depend primarily on *natural reforestation* to reestablish the forest after harvesting (Anderson and Holland 1982). They leave a few sturdy trees and simply rely on the wind and wildlife to disperse the seeds. In many areas, this system is effective and economical. However, nature often fails to seed in a new crop. Human intervention is then needed to help nature reforest a stand.

Artificial reforestation consists of using various tools—hand spreaders, tractors, and airplanes or helicopters—to supplement natural reseeding. In deciding which species to plant, foresters must first identify the climate and soil characteristics of the area to be reforested. Although they know which species do well in particular climatic zones (Figure 7-10), they choose those species that are indigenous to the area and gather seeds from nearby stands. For example, although slashpine is planted throughout the South (zones No. 11 and No. 18), it does best in its native habitat—the Gulf Coast, Florida, and Georgia.

Methods of Artificial Reforestation. The five most common methods of artificial reforestation are (1) planting wild seedlings, (2) direct seeding, (3) planting cuttings, (4) planting nursery-grown seedlings, and (5) planting containerized seedlings.

Digging up and transplanting *wild seedlings* is not widely practiced, since it requires a great deal of time and labor in the field and often proves uneconomical.

Direct seeding is a more widely used approach. In 1978, this technique was used on over 32,726 ha (80,865 acres) of U.S. land (Anderson and Holland 1982). This method of reforestation uses seeds that are chemically coated to discourage birds and rodents from eating them. The seeds may be scattered by using an old-fashioned cyclone seeder, by using conventional tractors with special attachments, or by using aircraft.

The *cuttings* used in reforestation are usually 20.0 to 30.4 cm (8 to 12 in.) long (Anderson and Holland 1982). They are cut from trees during the winter and are then planted in small holes dug with a metal spade. Only certain trees, such as willow and cottonwood, can be propagated from cuttings, however. For example, this method is used to regenerate cottonwood stands that are, in turn, used for pulp.

Planting nursery-grown seedlings is the most dependable method of artificial reforestation. According to Anderson and Holland (1982), this method has several advantages. The planter can choose a species with genetic characteristics that suit a specific purpose—for example, pine seedlings that will produce abundant gum. The seedlings develop quickly into

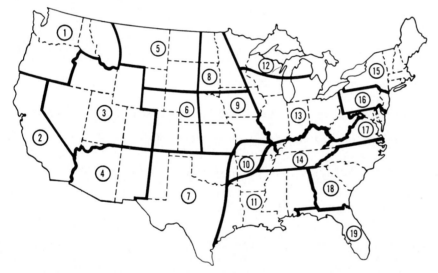

1. Douglas fir, western white pine, ponderosa pine.
2. Redwood, ponderosa pine, Douglas fir, white fir, Sitka spruce, Monterey pine, Monterey cypress, sequoia.
3. Ponderosa pine, Douglas fir, blue spruce, white fir.
4. Ponderosa pine, blue spruce, Arizona cypress, Rocky Mountain red cedar, Austrian pine, Chinese arborvitae.
5. Jack pine, white spruce, eastern red cedar, ponderosa pine.
6. Jack pine, ponderosa pine, eastern red cedar, western white spruce.
7. Eastern red cedar, ponderosa pine, Arizona cypress, Chinese arborvitae, one-seed juniper.
8. Ponderosa pine, white spruce, jack pine, European larch, northern white cedar.
9. Norway spruce, white spruce, blue spruce, eastern white pine, western white spruce, European larch, northern white cedar, eastern red cedar.
10. Shortleaf pine, eastern red cedar.
11. Loblolly pine, shortleaf pine, slash pine, longleaf pine, eastern red cedar, southern cypress.
12. Eastern white pine, red pine, jack pine, white spruce, balsam fir.
13. Eastern white pine, jack pine, Norway spruce, white spruce, blue spruce, northern white cedar, European larch, Douglas fir.
14. Shortleaf pine, eastern white pine.
15. White spruce, Norway spruce, eastern white pine, red pine, jack pine, European larch, northern white cedar.
16. Eastern white pine, red pine, pitch pine, northern white cedar, Norway spruce, European larch, white spruce.
17. Shortleaf pine, loblolly pine, eastern white pine, southern cypress, Norway spruce.
18. Loblolly pine, shortleaf pine, longleaf pine, slash pine, eastern white pine, Norway spruce, eastern red cedar, southern cypress.
19. Slash pine, longleaf pine, loblolly pine, southern red cedar, southern cypress.

FIGURE 7-10 Recommended species for forest planting, by climate zones. (From Charles H. Stoddard, *Essentials of Forestry Practice*, 3d ed., p. 86. Copyright © 1978 by John Wiley & Sons, Inc.)

established trees, and undesirable volunteer trees can be easily identified and eliminated. Even while young, the seedlings contribute to erosion control. The planter can control the spacing of the trees, and the seedlings produce even-aged plantations, which are easier to manage.

The method has disadvantages as well. The cost of the nursery stock may not be recovered until the trees are large enough to be thinned and sold, which may take 10 to 20 years. Replacing damaged stock is costly. And the initial investment may prompt the planter to incur further investment to protect against fire and other destructive agents.

The *cultivation of seedlings in containers* has become a profitable business, especially in the Pacific Northwest. Here seedlings of spruce and hemlock (and to a lesser extent pines and firs) are grown in great quantities in the controlled environment of the greenhouse. Between 1970 and 1977, the production of these *incubator babies* in the United States increased from fewer than a million to more than 65 million. The advantages of this approach are the following:

1. *Speed*—seedlings grown in a greenhouse are ready for planting in only five to seven months, which is three or four times sooner than seedlings raised in outdoor nurseries.
2. *Specialization*—seedlings can be conditioned for planting in inferior sites.
3. *Stability*—since such hard-to-grow species as hemlock respond well to the controlled atmosphere of the greenhouse, they consequently remain healthier when transplanted than seedlings grown in a nursery.
4. *Scheduling*—containerized seedlings can be planted earlier in the fall and later in the spring than nursery seedlings.
5. *Handling*—containerized seedlings can be tightly packed when transplanted, which makes them less vulnerable to damage. On rugged topography, seedlings must be planted by hand, but on relatively flat land mechanical tree planters speed the process. With a mechanical tree planter, seedlings can be planted at the rate of about 1000 per hour, at a lower cost than hand planting (Stoddard 1978).

Planting containerized seedlings has certain drawbacks, however. Greenhouse cultivation makes the seedlings somewhat susceptible to nutritional imbalances, disease, and other problems associated with monoculture production. Preparing the planting site for seedlings requires additional time and finan-

cial outlay. In some localities containerized seedlings cost twice as much as regular nursery-grown stock. For a time at least, containerized seedlings will probably supplement rather than replace the usual nursery-seedling approach.

Tree Fertilization. When the cost of reforestation is high, timber companies often fertilize reforested areas from the air to protect their investment. Although such fertilization is beneficial to the plants, there is some doubt as to whether or not the benefits outweigh the costs and the possibly detrimental environmental effects.

In the Pacific Northwest, forest industries have fertilized thousands of acres of forest land, particularly forests of Douglas fir, and are conducting research on tree fertilization. In the South, adding nitrogen to older forests and phosphorus to poorly drained stands along the Gulf coast and the Atlantic coastal plain has produced good results. Forest fertilization is just one more example of the general trend in this country toward monoculture tree farms—the production of trees as crops.

Monoculture is the cultivation of a single species—a field of oats, or a tree stand of Douglas fir—all of the same age and size. Despite the popularity of monoculture tree farms, they have been criticized by many professional foresters and ecologists for being highly vulnerable ecosystems susceptible to insects, diseases, and fire. Furthermore, they argue that these monoculture tree farms produce inferior trees as compared with the slower-growing trees of the natural forest. Critics also say that monoculture tree farms waste energy through excessive use of high technology, pollute the environment with their overuse of insecticides and herbicides, and are not responsive to other U.S. forest demands, such as the need for erosion and flood control, for abundant wildlife habitat, for scenic beauty, and for recreational opportunities.

Forest Protection

Another function of forest resource management is the suppression of environmental factors that are injurious to forests. Diseases, insects, and fire eradicate about one-quarter of the annual growth of U.S. commercially usable timber. To a lesser extent, animals, avalanches, and unusual weather conditions (storms, hurricanes, and floods) take their toll.

Diseases. Diseases and insects together account for more forest destruction in the United States and throughout the world than any other factor. Most diseases are caused by parasitic fungi, but other causes, such as tree viruses, contribute their share. In the United States, diseases account for 45 percent of timber losses per year. Examples of forest diseases are Dutch elm disease, chestnut blight, and, most recently, what is known as *air pollution disease.*

Dutch elm disease has eliminated more than two-thirds of America's elm trees. Researchers believe that it was carried to North America during the 1930s in a cargo of elm logs from Europe. The disease is transmitted either by bark beetles migrating from diseased trees to healthy trees or by the roots of diseased trees fusing with the roots of nearby healthy trees. Death is swift—few trees live more than two years after the start of the infection. Even today, the disease continues its slow spread throughout North America, currently threatening the more than 1 million elms in California.

Chestnut blight, a parasitic fungus that was accidentally introduced from the Orient around 1900, quickly spread through the eastern forests (Figure 7-11). By 1914, the chestnut was practically eliminated as a commercial species. The American chestnut was a large, attractive tree and was important for such industries as leather-tanning and construction. Today, most of the eastern American chestnuts have been destroyed.

Air pollution disease, a more recent phenomenon in America's forests, is currently the object of active research. Evidence suggests that it is threatening the well-being of forests around several metropolitan areas. For example, in a recent study of air pollution disease in the Central Valley of California, researcher Wayne Williams (1980) reported these findings:

1. Air pollution had severely damaged the yellow pine forests downwind from the Central Valley.
2. The dominant tree species, ponderosa and Jeffrey pines, were hypersensitive to oxidant air pollution.
3. Stands within the national forests studied had declined.
4. The disease was associated with the beginning of the smog season and grew worse when ozone levels exceeded federal and state standards.
5. The worst oxidant-damaged forests of southern California had growth losses as high as 83 percent.

There is no one best method for controlling forest diseases; instead, proper treatment depends on the nature of the disease. In the case of Dutch elm

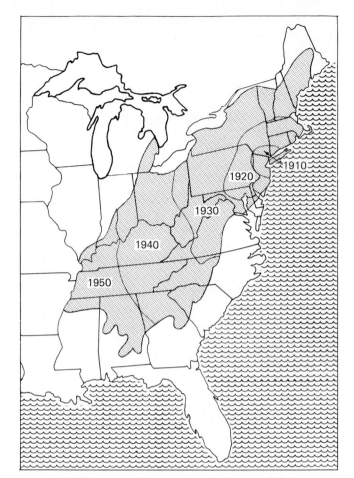

FIGURE 7-11   The spread of chestnut blight. (From Mike Toner, ''Is This the Chestnut's Last Stand?'' *National Wildlife*, vol. 43, no. 6 [October–November 1985], p. 26.)

disease, scientists are experimenting with sex attractants and parasites in an attempt to control the population of the bark beetle. They are also searching for ways to slow the disease by using fungicides. A newly developed fungicide, Lignasan-BLP, injected into healthy elms has produced encouraging, though inconclusive, results. Geneticists are also at work on the problem.

Sound forestry management offers the best hope for controlling forest diseases. Such management includes the removal of susceptible, infected, and dead trees, the protection of young trees from injury, and the maintenance of diversity within the forest. Disease control also requires the careful monitoring of imported timber that might be carrying parasites, and the reduction of air pollution, especially ozone, fluorine, and sulfur dioxide.

Insects.   Twenty percent of U.S. timber losses each year can be attributed to insect pests. Among the most destructive insect pests are the spruce budworm and the gypsy moth.

The spruce budworm, the "crocodile" of caterpillars, is native to North America. About every 40 years it defoliates the spruce and balsam forests of Maine and Canada. The budworm population is usually too small to cause major forest damage, but after successive years of warm and dry weather, the population can explode and millions of acres can be stripped barren.

The gypsy moth also causes large-scale forest defoliation. This pest came from Europe in 1869, when a naturalist brought specimens to Massachusetts hoping to breed disease-resistant silkworms by crossing the two. The cage in which the moths were held blew over, and the moths escaped into the forests. They have been eating their way across the country ever since. By 1979, 2 million acres in the eastern United States had been defoliated by gypsy moth larvae.

Again, sound forestry management offers the best control method for insect pests. Other measures may be employed, but some of them are very expensive and many impair the ecological health of the forest. DDT and related insecticides, for example, accumulate in food chains, kill large numbers of animals (including the natural predators of the pests), and, in the long run, become ineffective as a pest control. It is more desirable to introduce predators that are pest-specific, sex attractants that kill them, and sterilized male insects that curtail the population growth of the pest.

Preliminary evidence suggests that when trees come under attack by insects, the trees may actually relay messages with one another through pheromones (airborne chemicals). In response to the warning issued by neighboring trees, some trees change the chemical composition of their leaves to repel insects and disease. For example, oaks and sugar maples may raise the levels of toxins or downgrade the nutritional content in their leaves. If these findings are confirmed, they will have far-reaching implications for future pest-control programs.

Fire. Though they get more publicity than forest diseases and insects, fires account for only 17 percent of U.S. timber losses each year. Eighty-five percent of fires are started by humans, some by accident, others for malicious reasons. The rest are set off by lightning.

Compared to common *surface fires* that burn relatively coolly and slowly along the forest floor, *crown fires* travel swiftly through the forest canopy and can be extremely hazardous to humans and wildlife.

Crown fires have a long-lasting impact on the forest ecosystem. Less disastrous than crown fires, but nonetheless destructive, are *soil fires* that not only burn on the soil surface but also through the soil, consuming its humus and peat content. This type of fire can destroy heat-sensitive tree roots, upset the organic content of the soil and its water-absorption capacity, and eliminate billions of soil bacteria and fungi, which play a crucial role in forest ecology.

Roughly 30 percent of forest fires are set by children playing with fire or adults seeking revenge. In 1980, for example, arsonists seeking revenge against the government started many of the fires that blackened 40,470 ha (100,000 acres) of Appalachian forest land in Kentucky, Tennessee, West Virginia, and Georgia. Among their reasons for starting the fires were late welfare checks, government purchases of forest land, government management of timber and game, and even the hope of getting a job. The Forest Service used to hire local citizens to fight fires but abandoned the practice after discovering that some of them were setting fires just to obtain employment.

Some fires that are deliberately set have beneficial results, however. In the practice known as *prescribed burning* or *controlled burning*, foresters purposely set surface fires according to a carefully devised plan. The Forest Service once regarded all fires as bad, but it now realizes that some fires bring ecological benefits, such as the reduction of the crown fire hazard through the elimination of excessive surface fuel, the manipulation of forest succession to maintain valuable stands of trees, and the creation of open space and additional edge to improve wildlife habitat.

Whether or not controlled burning will benefit an area, however, depends on the nature of the site and on ecological conditions. Such burns are costly, since they can be applied only to small portions of the forest and sometimes get out of control, causing a serious liability problem.

Urban Forestry

Most people associate forests with remote wilderness areas, and yet a 28-million-ha (70-million-acre) forest, greater in size than all the forests managed by the U.S. Forest Service, exists in bits and pieces inside the nation's cities. This urban forest contains between 228 and 500 million trees worth $15 billion (Heinrichs 1981). Although 80 percent of the U.S. population lives within this forest, many urbanites "can't see the forest for the trees," and this vast forest is dying of neglect.

To check that decline, a new specialization

within forestry known as **urban forestry** has recently emerged. It is an outgrowth of the concern of civic groups, urban planners, and real estate developers for the quality of life in densely populated areas. Urban forestry embraces several activities, including landscape design, noise abatement control, tree planting, and tree maintenance.

Forested areas within cities contribute to the aesthetic quality of the urban environment. Such cities as Washington, D.C., Boston, New York, San Antonio, Seattle, Portland (Oregon), and San Francisco are especially rich in this natural resource.

Urban forests also help to moderate temperatures and humidity, abate wind velocity, and assimilate air pollutants. They attract a variety of birds, small mammals, and other forms of wildlife. Moreover, they serve to absorb noise, protect municipal watersheds, screen visual blight, and shield shopping centers, schools, and high-density neighborhoods. They bring a "breath of fresh air" to city dwellers. Merchants have even discovered that a well-landscaped environment *improves* business. Many a fading commercial district has been restored through urban reforestation.

Trees have a hard time surviving in the urban environment, however. They are particularly vulnerable to many of the diseases and pests that affect trees in more natural settings. For example, before the onslaught of Dutch elm disease there were 77 million elms in the towns and cities of the United States. Now there are only 34 million. Minneapolis spends most of its urban forestry funds battling the disease, and even the elms on the White House grounds are dying.

The cities of southern Florida are fighting an even more deadly blight called *lethal yellowing*—a disease now threatening the region's famous coconut palms. Out of an original 3 million palms, only 700,000 remain, and the number is dropping rapidly. In Dade County alone, lethal yellowing has killed 90 percent of the coconut palms. No means of controlling the disease, which is caused by organisms similar to both bacteria and viruses, has yet been found.

Urban trees suffer even greater attrition from mistreatment by human beings. They are often improperly planted and are either overwatered or underwatered. They are badly pruned by well-meaning citizens and careless utility companies. Their limbs are lopped off at random, making the trees vulnerable to disease and insect infestation. They are poisoned by dog urine, pesticides, and road salt. They are scarred by lawnmowers, cars, and bicycles, suffocated by air pollutants, cut and flogged by vandals, and buried by building contractors. Tree vandalism is

so widespread in some districts that city arborists plant two or three times as many trees as are actually needed, knowing that at least half of them will be hacked to death by vandals.

Urban reforestation is the primary management technique used to combat these natural and unnatural abuses. Trees are categorized according to their shape, growth rate, and urban tolerance, and according to their suitability to various *hardiness zones,* which specify average annual minimum temperatures (Elias and Irwin 1976). Most commonly, however, trees are selected for urban planting on the basis of their likelihood of survival and their ease of handling. Such criteria do not always produce genetically diverse plantings.

The primary management problems in urban forestry are a lack of public understanding, citizen apathy, and a lack of funds. Many people think that trees along city streets can take care of themselves. Actually, urban forests are artificial ecosystems that must be regularly maintained. The failure of many cities to pass ordinances defining who owns the trees and who is responsible for their care and maintenance leads to public apathy. Such apathy also stems from attitudes dating back to 1784, when insurance companies refused to insure a home with street trees. Recent *solar ordinances,* designed to protect the solar access rights of homeowners choosing to use solar collectors on their rooftops, often lead to the destruction of urban trees. The day may come when parts of the urban forest are cut down just to ensure that sunlight will fall on solar energy collectors.

Public apathy, in turn, leads to inadequate budgets. Some urban foresters consider themselves merely "morticians," because all they can afford to do is remove dead and dying trees. According to recent surveys, urban forestry receives approximately 0.05 percent of city budgets (Heinrichs 1981). And, as public funds grow scarcer, the prospects for adequate budgets for urban forestry grow even dimmer.

FUTURE PROSPECTS FOR THE NATION'S FOREST RESOURCES

The overall forest resources of the United States have remained relatively stable over the last decade. Except in the West, more timber was grown than was cut. Actually, this good conservation resulted, in part, from economic conditions that depressed the demand for timber. In 1982, for example, interest rates were so high that many people were priced out of the housing market. Home construction declined, and the lumber industry slumped. In the West, 138 of the 750 sawmills closed down, and 30,000 workers were discharged. Even university students suffered. The University of Oregon and the University of Washington, which are both supported in part by the lumber industry, experienced severe budget cuts, faculty layoffs, and the cancellation of many courses. In sum, the nation's forests have fared relatively well over the last several years, though for incidental reasons.

Pressures on the Nation's Forests

Three pressures are affecting the nation's forests: economic problems, energy shortages, and the worldwide timber famine. America's economic problems have prompted action to increase the timber harvest in order to stimulate the economy. In 1979, President Carter ordered a feasibility study on increasing the timber harvest on national forest lands. The Reagan administration actually called for increased harvests. In 1983, it proposed that 12.3 billion board feet be cut and sold—a 10 percent increase over the 1982 harvest. Believing that a major demand for housing was imminent, Assistant Secretary of Agriculture John Crowell, Jr., urged that production be stepped up. The timber industry applauded his message. Environmentalists, however, worried that such a policy would result in the destruction of what remained of the great stands of Old Growth Douglas fir in the Western Cascades, that wildlife would be affected, that new logging roads would aggravate erosion, and that land would be eliminated from possible inclusion under the national Wilderness Preservation Act. To lower the national debt, the Department of Agriculture even recommended selling some of its forest lands to private interests.

As energy shortages mount, pressure to harvest the energy of the forests is likely to increase. The nation's woodlands are now being thought of as energy production centers. *Energy plantations* are springing up across the country—fields of fast-growing cottonwood, alder, and even some tropical species. Many homeowners are installing woodburning stoves. There is some question, however, about whether enough firewood will be available a decade from now to fuel all those stoves. And the consensus seems to be that wood burning does increase air pollution.

Finally, the looming worldwide timber famine is about to have an effect on the use of the nation's forests. In 1979, for example, the National Wildlife Federation estimated that 20 million ha (50 million acres) of forests were harvested worldwide, mostly for fuel, but also for clearing new agricultural land. If the ex-

pected global firewood shortage does occur by the year 2000, the increased demands from the have-not nations may lead to a significant rise in the export of U.S. timber.

Positive Signs and Success Stories

There are many reasons for optimism about our forest resources, however. Since World War II, there have been major advances in forest policy, managment techniques, research, tree utilization, and in fostering improved attitudes toward forest resource management. A few are discussed subsequently.

1. *Legislation and new policy decisions.* The most significant advances in forest resource management have been in legislation and public policy rather than in management techniques. The Multiple-Use Sustained Yield Act (1960) was followed by the Wilderness Act (1964), the National Environmental Policy Act (1969), amendments to the Water Pollution Control Act (1972), the Endangered Species Act (1973), the Forest and Rangeland Renewable Resources Planning Act (1974), the National Forest Management Act (1976), and the Federal Land Management Policy Act (1976).

All these acts have had an impact on the ways in which public forest lands, and in some cases private forest lands, are managed. Most of them were passed in response to heightened public awareness of the natural environment and the need to manage forest lands in an environmentally sound manner. As a result, recreation management, habitat management, soil and water protection, and wilderness preservation have, at least in theory, gained equal emphasis with timber management on public lands. The multiple-use management program conducted by the U.S. Forest Service in Siuslaw National Forest, Oregon, has been eminently successful. Here some of the most valuable timber in the country is being harvested on geologically unstable terrain without jeopardizing the multimillion-dollar fishery.

The states are also beginning to regulate their forest resources. The California Forest Practices Act of 1973 is the most far-reaching forest statue yet enacted in the United States. It empowers the state government to protect forest resources by regulating the use of both private and public holdings. It provides for environmental protection by calling for fire protection, slash disposal, soil conservation, and watercourse protection. All plans to harvest timber must accommodate the recommendations of a professional, registered forester. Harvesting plans must include plans for regeneration, and the operator must obtain a permit before starting to log. Penalties for violations include denial and revocation of permits, injunctions, fines, and imprisonment.

2. Improved management techniques. Several innovative approaches to management techniques have appeared in recent years.

- *Improved harvesting and yarding systems.* The use of light *skyline systems* (cables stretched tautly between two points and used as a track to suspend and transport logs, so they do not drag along the ground) has reduced the impact of timber harvesting on the forest environment and has made possible the intensive management of previously inaccessible areas (Figure 7-12). In the near future, *helistats*—a combination of helicopter and aerostat (airbag)—will be used to lift and transport logs from areas where road access might be injurious to the forest. Hand-held computers may some day enable foresters to carry out on-the-spot analysis of tree growth and determine the value and the optimum harvest time for individual tree stands.

- *Coordination of silviculture and wildlife.* The scheduled use of silviculture to enhance the diversity of forest growth has led to considerable improvements in wildlife habitats.

- *National forest landscape management.* As a result of growing concern over the visual environment, the landscape's appearance now receives equal consideration with other forest resources. Working with landscape architects and silviculturalists, the Forest Service has issued guidelines to meet visual objectives.

- *Renewed attention to sound traditional methods.* In some areas, horse-logging is making a comeback, since it saves fuel and, under certain conditions, is ecologically sound. The use of goats to control fuelbreak vegetation (a *fuelbreak* is a lane of cleared vegetation to prevent fires from spreading), a common practice in Europe, is beginning to appear in the United States, particularly in the chaparral-covered forests of the West.

3. Major research advances. Several breakthroughs have been made recently in forest research (Spurr 1979):

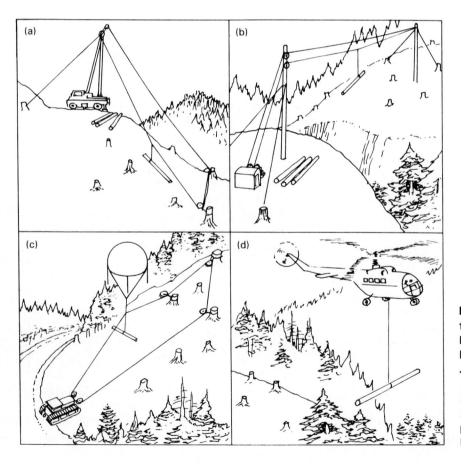

FIGURE 7-12 Log transport systems. (a) High-lead cable; (b) skyline cable; (c) balloon cable; (d) helicopter. (From Frederick R. Troeh, J. A. Hobbs and Roy L. Donahue, *Soil and Water Conservation: For Productivity and Environmental Protection,* © 1980, p. 447. Reprinted by permission of Prentice-Hall, Inc., Englewood Cliffs, N.J.)

- *Forest genetics.* Geneticists have made significant progress in the past few years in improving the growth, resistance, and quality characteristics of trees for specific locations. For example, they have improved the control of white pine blister rust through genetic selection.
- *Remote sensing.* Aerial photography and various types of remote sensing (e.g., electronic scanning devices in orbital satellites or spacecraft) are being used to inventory the nation's forests and other natural resources.
- *Atmospheric physics.* Researchers are studying the effect of weather on the movement of forest fires and are investigating ways to modify weather and control lightning.
- *Programming models.* Some useful linear programming models have recently been developed for scheduling harvesting and for other forest resource management operations.

4. More efficient utilization of resources. Timber companies are devising ways of reducing waste by using the entire tree. Even the stumps of harvested trees are being used as a source of cellulose for the manufacture of paper products and plastics. Computers are being used to reduce the waste from milling operations. The Oregon Sun Studs Company, for example, measures each log's precise configuration. A computer then uses that information to plot the first cut, increasing yield by as much as 25 percent.

5. New attitudes toward urban forestry. Many colleges and universities are offering new courses in architectural design, urban landscaping, and public relations for urban foresters. This new breed of professionals has already produced some innovative approaches. Lansing, Michigan, for example, plants 88 different tree species, based on cost, ease of transport, and potential for survival. This well-financed program is known as the Master Street Tree Conversion Planting Plan. Charlotte, North Carolina, has an easement program that enables the city to plant trees on a 4.6 m (15 ft) strip on the property of homeowners and to care for the trees for the first two years. After the two-year period, the homeowner receives full ownership and responsibility for the trees (Heinrichs 1981). Many cities employ arborists to identify historically significant, unusual, large, or rare tree species so that they can be legally protected.

6. New approaches to world forestry. Awareness of the natural resources crisis is bringing about a new approach to forest resources among the poorer countries of the world. Public officials in those countries spend most of their time protecting and managing government forest reserves. Consequently, residents often feel that the government is denying them access to products they desperately need. Many foresters in those countries are now trying to meet the needs of the people, while still honoring their own professional obligations.

In what is known as the *community forestry approach*, foresters act more as community organizers than as police. They engage in a variety of nontraditional activities: They plant grasses and trees to stabilize hillsides and shifting sands; they encourage private and municipal woodlots to produce fodder, utility poles, and fuel; they try to integrate the cultivation of trees into other cropping activities, a practice referred to as *agroforestry*; and they encourage villagers to raise forest trees along roads and irrigation canals. Community forestry is emerging as a powerful force in the struggle of the world's poor to meet their basic needs. Its success will relieve future demands on the forest resources of the United States.

ACTION FOR FORESTS

The demand for U.S. timber is expected to double by the year 2020. Preserving our forests to meet that demand, and to serve other uses as well, will not be an easy task. There are several ways in which you can help.

1. Support ecologically sound forestry policies.

- *Call for increased production on privately owned, nonindustrial forest lands.* Several major conservation groups, including the National Wildlife Federation, have pointed out that 283 million acres (4,000,000 privately owned woodlots) make up 59 percent of the nation's timber base. Much of that timberland is improperly managed. Improved management would step up the production of wood products and would also improve water quality, enhance wildlife habitats, and create new recreational opportunities. By providing more information, greater technical assistance, and more attractive tax incentives, the federal government could encourage landowners to increase their timber production.
- *Call for strict adherence to multiple-use standards in the national forests.* The public has many opportunities to comment on the management of our national forests. For example, concerned citizens can make their views

known on major policy decisions under the Forest and Range and Renewable Natural Resources Planning Act of 1974. Citizens can have an influence on environmental impact statements, timber management plans, the U.S. Forest Service, and congressional actions on management.

- *Support desirable methods for the control of fires, forest diseases, and insect pests.* Improved management and integrated pest controls are more desirable methods of control than the use of herbicides and pesticides.

- *Urge the elimination of wasteful practices.* The demand for timber can be reduced by cutting waste at the harvest site, during manufacturing, and in packaging. Waste can also be reduced by limiting our use of disposable paper products. Each year, we consume 273 kg (600 lb) of paper per person—much of it wasted. Check to see whether or not your college or university uses recycled paper, and whether or not your family recycles newspapers and magazines.

- *Support forest research.* How do even-aged and uneven-aged forests compare in productivity? How do pure and mixed stands compare in vulnerability to diseases, insects, and other destructive agents? Further research is needed on these questions and many others.

2. *Participate in forest decisions.* Foresters cannot protect all the nation's trees by themselves. Oakland, California, recently planted 2000 trees in one section of the city. Two years later, because of vandalism, only 10 trees were left (Heinrichs 1981). Local citizens must support the long-term planning efforts of urban foresters. Subscribe to the free monthly newsletters from government departments of forestry, or visit their local offices to get information. Join organizations concerned with forestry, and attend meetings of your state board of forestry.

3. *Develop community action projects.* In 1971, a 16-year-old boy named Andy Lipkis set out to replace the smog-sick pines of San Bernadino Forest in southern California. At first, his friends laughed at him. He had no money, no equipment, and no experience. But Andy Lipkis assembled a group of volunteers and planted 20,000 smog-tolerant seedlings. By

1982, he had founded Tree People, a national volunteer conservation group, which potted, planted, or gave away over 100,000 smog-tolerant and drought-tolerant pine seedlings.

4. *Join a CCC-type organization.* Several states have recently created CCC-type organizations, modeled after the Civilian Conservation Corps of the Great Depression years, in which young people become actively involved in forest conservation projects. These organizations have proved so successful that the National Association of Civilian Conservation Corps Alumni has launched a movement to create CCC II, a permanent corps to put people to work on forest management programs.

5. *Become a tree farmer.* With land taxes on the rise, landowners are searching for ways to put idle or unproductive forest lands to use. One way to ease the tax burden is to have woodland certified as a Tree Farm in the American Tree Farm System. To qualify, the woodland must be privately owned, must be managed for the growth and harvest of forest crops, and must be adequately protected from diseases, insects, overgrazing, and fire.

6. *Choose a career in forestry.* To become a certified forester you must have a degree from a professional forestry school accredited by the Society of American Foresters. According to Sharpe (1976), you may concentrate in one of five areas of forestry: (1) *biology,* including forest ecology, forest genetics, and dendrology; (2) *resource management,* including data processing, land surveying, and remote sensing; (3) *ecosystem management,* including fire science, forest entomology, and silviculture; (4) *social science,* including forest law, forest policy, and public relations; and (5) *resource administration,* including organizational administration and land-use planning. Recently, forestry schools have been adding courses in *environmental quality*—studies that bridge the natural and social sciences.

At the moment, forestry schools are producing more graduates than can be hired by public agencies and private companies. Still, there are opportunities in less traditional areas of forestry, such as managing and protecting the holdings of groups of small timberland owners, marketing forest products, doing forestry research, and providing environmental consulting.

DISCUSSION TOPICS

1. List and discuss the human benefits that are derived from forests.

2. Discuss the ecological services provided by forests.

3. What is the difference between a forest and a woodland? Can forests be classified as a *renewable* resource?

4. Discuss forest competition, forest succession, and for-

est classification as they relate to forest management. How does forest classification enter into the Douglas fir controversy?

5. Why is forestry regarded as an art as well as a science?

6. List and discuss the six major forest types and their geographic locations. What are the distinguishing characteristics of each region?

7. Who owns the nation's trees? What role have geography and history played in determining the ownership of U.S. timber resources?

8. What roles have Franklin Hough, Gifford Pinchot, and Theodore Roosevelt played in the history of U.S. forest conservation?

9. Compare and contrast the concepts of sustained yield and multiple use. When were these concepts established as U.S. forest policy? Discuss the problems inherent in the multiple-use concept.

10. Discuss the three major timber harvesting techniques and the pros and cons of each. Which one is most used in your region?

11. How do seed-tree cutting, naturalistic silviculture, and short-rotation silviculture differ? Why has naturalistic silviculture not been favored as a harvesting technique in the United States?

12. Discuss the advantages and drawbacks of the five major means of reforestation. What are the arguments for and against monoculture tree farming?

13. What are the four major diseases that affect forests? What methods do foresters use to control these and other diseases?

14. What are the major insects that plague trees? What management techniques are used to control them?

15. What are the characteristics of the three major fire classes?

16. Do fires serve any useful purpose? If so, what? Why do foresters use controlled (or prescribed) burning?

17. What trees can you identify in your own neighborhood? Do they appear to be in good health? Who is responsible for caring for them? Does your town or city have an urban forester on its staff?

18. How can the U.S. meet future timber demand? List the pros and cons of the several alternative strategies for meeting timber demand.

19. How do individuals contribute to the destruction of national forests, urban forests, and world tropical forests?

20. As energy prices go up, many Americans will switch to wood stoves for heating and cooking. What are the pros and cons of this practice? How does it relate to the global firewood crisis?

21. Argue for and against the selling of portions of the National Forest System to private industry as a means of helping to pay off the national debt.

22. What reasons do we have to be optimistic about the future of our forests?

23. How can you personally become involved in preserving our forest heritage? Which method are you likely to try?

READINGS

AMERICAN FOREST INSTITUTE. 1979. *Forest Facts and Figures.* Washington, D.C.: American Forest Institute. Highly informative fact sheet.

ANDERSON, DAVID A., and I. I. HOLLAND. 1982. *Forests and Forestry.* 3d ed. Danville, Ill.: Interstate Printers & Publishers. Emphasis on growing timber as a crop in the South.

BARRENT, JOHN W., ed. 1980. *Regional Silviculture of the United States.* 2d ed. New York: Wiley. Excellent text for regional approach to U.S. silviculture.

CLAWSON, MARION. 1975. *Forests for Whom and for What.* Baltimore, Md.: Johns Hopkins University Press. Good discussion of forest uses and policy.

DANA, SAMUEL TRASK, and SALLY K. FAIRFAX. 1980. *Forests and Range Policy: Its Development in the United States.* 2d ed. New York: McGraw-Hill. A standard textbook on the basic laws and principles of forest and range management.

DAVIS, KENNETH P. 1966. *Forest Management: Regulation and Valuation.* 2d ed. New York: McGraw-Hill. A highly technical book written for the professional forester interested in increasing timber yield.

DOUGLAS, J. SHOLTO, and ROBERT A. DE J. HART. 1976. *Forest Farming.* London: Watkins. Forest farming as a solution to the problems of world hunger and conservation.

ECKHOLM, ERIK. 1975. *The Other Energy Crisis: Firewood.* Washington, D.C.: Worldwatch Society. Good discussion of the use of the world's forests for firewood.

ECKHOLM, ERIK. 1979. *Planning for the Future: Forestry for Human Needs.* Washington, D.C.: Worldwatch Institute. Excellent suggestions for preserving and renewing the world's forests.

ELIAS, THOMAS, and HOWARD S. IRWIN. 1976. "Urban Trees," *Scientific American,* November, pp. 111–118. Excellent overview of urban forestry.

FOWELLS, H. A. 1965. *Silvics of Forest Trees of the United States.* Handbook No. 271. Washington, D.C.: U.S. Department of Agriculture. Informative work on silvics—the study of the requirements and processes of tree growth and the environment under which it takes place.

FROME, MICHAEL. 1974. *The Forest Service.* New York: Praeger. Good general history of the Forest Service.

FROME, MICHAEL. 1962. *Whose Woods These Are: The Study of the National Forests.* New York: Doubleday. Profiles of many of the nation's national forests.

HEINRICHS, JAY. 1981. "Tragedy of the City Forest," *American Forests,* April, vol. 87, no. 4, pp. 30–33. Excellent call for citizen participation in urban forestry projects.

HOUGH, FRANKLIN B. 1878–1882. *Report on Forestry: Prepared Under the Direction of the Commissioner of Agriculture in Pursuance of an Act of Congress Approved August 18, 1876.* 3 vols. Washington, D.C.: Government Printing Office. Classic work on the condition of American forests in the latter half of the nineteenth century.

HYDE, WILLIAM F. 1980. *Timber Supply, Land Allocation, and Economic Efficiency.* Baltimore, Md.: Johns Hopkins University Press. Argues that more efficient timber management will increase the extent of wilderness areas as well as timber yields.

LEOPOLD, STARKER A. 1978. "Wildlife and Forest Practice." In Howard Brokaw, ed., *Wildlife and America.* Washington, D.C.: Council on Environmental Quality. Effects of forest practices on the maintenance of wildlife habitat.

LITTLE, ELBERT L. 1978. *Important Forest Trees of the United States.* Forest Service Agricultural Handbook No. 519. Washington, D.C.: U.S. Department of Agriculture. Good summary of commercially important trees in U.S. forests.

MARSH, GEORGE PERKINS. 1864. *Man and Nature; Or, Physical Geography as Modified by Human Action.* New York: Scribner. Reprinted 1964. Cambridge, Mass.: Harvard University Press. Classic work on deforestation in both the United States and the Mediterranean region; relevant to current problems of environmental quality.

MCGUIRE, JOHN. 1982. "The National Forests: An Experiment in Land Management," *Journal of Forest History,* April, vol. 26, no. 2, pp. 84–91. Analysis of the problems facing the U.S. National Forest System.

NADEL, IRA BRUCE, and CARNELIA HAHN OBERLANDER. 1977. *Trees in the City.* New York: Pergamon Press. Summary of tree suitability to various urban situations.

NATIONAL ACADEMY OF SCIENCES. 1980. *Conservation of Tropical Moist Forests.* Washington, D.C.: National Academy of Sciences. Authoritive discussion of the loss of the world's tropical moist forests and what can be done about it.

NEBEL, BERNARD J. 1981. *Environmental Science: The Way the World Works.* Englewood Cliffs, N.J.: Prentice-Hall. Good introductory text.

OWEN, OLIVER S. 1985. *Natural Resource Conservation.* 4th ed. New York: Macmillan. Contains excellent chapter on forestry written by a biologist.

PARSON, RUBEN L. 1972. *Conserving American Resources.* 3d ed. Englewood Cliffs, N.J.: Prentice-Hall. Classic resource management textbook written in the geographic tradition.

ROBINSON, GLEN O. 1975. *The Forest Service: A Study in Public Land Management.* Washington, D.C.: Resources for the Future. A thorough study of the problems and controversies surrounding the resources managed by the U.S Forest Service.

ROBINSON, GORDON. 1988. *The Forest and the Trees: A Guide to Excellent Forestry.* Covelo, Calif.: Island Press. This book, written by the chief forestry spokesman for the Sierra Club since 1966, is essential reading for environmental activists, forestry professionals, and concerned citizens.

ROSTLUND, ERHARD. 1956. "The Outlook for the World's Forests and Their Chief Products." In Stephen Haden-Guest, John K. Wright, and Eileen Teclaff, eds., *A World Geography of Forest Resources,* American Geographical Society Special Publication No. 33, pp. 663–671. New York: Ronald Press. Well-informed summary of the facts and ideas that foresters must incorporate into their long-range planning.

SHARPE, GRANT W., et al. 1976. *Introduction to Forestry.* 4th ed. New York: McGraw-Hill. Still the best overall introductory textbook on forestry.

SIERRA CLUB et al. 1981. *A Conservationist's Guide to National Forest Planning.* San Francisco: Sierra Club. A guide prepared by several environmental organizations to help conservationists apply the National Forest Management Act regulations to planning.

SOCIETY OF AMERICAN FORESTERS. 1980. *Forest Policy Guidebook.* 2d ed. Washington, D.C.: Society of American Foresters. Good summary of the policies of the Society of American Foresters.

SPURR, STEPHEN. 1979. "Silviculture," *Scientific American,* February, vol. 240, no. 2, pp. 76–91. Outstanding discussion of various harvesting techniques.

STODDARD, CHARLES H. 1978. *Essentials of Forestry Practice.* 3d ed. New York: Wiley. An information-packed textbook.

TONER, MIKE. 1985. "Is This the Chestnut's Last Stand?" *National Wildlife,* vol. 43, no. 6, October–November, pp. 25–27. Discusses citizen action to save chestnut trees.

TROEH, FREDERICK, et al. 1980. *Soil and Water Conservation.* Englewood Cliffs, N.J.: Prentice-Hall. Contains good chapter on forest and grassland resource management.

USDA, FOREST SERVICE. 1982. *An Analysis of the Timber Situation in the United States, 1952–2030.* Forest Resource Report No. 23. Washington, D.C.: U.S. Department of Agriculture. Useful government statistics and analysis of U.S. timber situation.

USDA, FOREST SERVICE. 1981. *A Citizen's Guide to the Forest and Rangeland Renewable Resources Planning Act.* Washington, D.C.: U.S. Department of Agriculture. How citizens can get involved in planning the national forests.

USDA, FOREST SERVICE. 1973. *Silvicultural Systems for the Major Forests Types of the Unit.* Agricultural Handbook 445. Washington, D.C.: U.S. Department of Agriculture. Analysis of the suitability of the common silvicultural systems for each major forest type.

WILLIAMS, WAYNE T. 1980. "Air Pollution Disease in the California Forests. A Base Line for Smog Disease on Ponderosa and Jeffrey Pines in the Sequoia and Los Padres National Forests, California," *Environmental Science and Technology,* February, vol. 14, no. 2, pp. 179–182. Interesting case study of air pollution disease.

WILLIAMSON, RICHARD L. 1973. *Results of Shelterwood Harvesting of Douglas-Fir in the Cascades of Western Oregon.* Washington, D.C.: U.S. Department of Agriculture. States the position that shelterwood harvesting may be biologically and economically preferable to clear-cutting.

WINTERS, ROBERT K. 1974. *The Forest and Man.* New York: Vantage. Well-documented and readable account of the worldwide influence of humans on forests.

8

WILDLIFE RESOURCES

*That wildlife is merely something to shoot at is the
grossest of fallacies. It often represents that
difference between rich country and mere land.*
Aldo Leopold

WHAT IS WILDLIFE?

The term **wildlife** embraces all native life forms (except humans) that are not domesticated, including plants as well as animals. Wildlife connotes *wildness;* that is, *freedom,* not captivity or human manipulation, *independence,* not helplessness, and *renewability* through natural reproduction. When thinking of *wildlife resources,* however, most individuals have a more restrictive definition of wildlife—one that places an emphasis on animals, particularly land animals, such as birds, deer, and elk, rather than on fish in fresh water or fish and marine mammals in the ocean. Despite the fact that the latter animal categories have the same characteristics of wildness, they will be treated separately in Chapters 11 and 12.

The emphasis of this chapter will be on animals rather than plants, although wildlife managers are beginning to slowly take an interest in the perpetuation and preservation of certain wild plant species (e.g., wild flowers and rare cactuses) and their related ecosystems (Koopowitz and Kaye 1983). This increasing interest in wild plant species protection further supports the notion that the definition of wildlife is continuing to expand from the original narrow concept that included certain *animals* (particularly *game species* used for hunting and fishing) to the broader concept of the *animal kingdom* that includes the plant ecosystems upon which the animals are dependent (Brokaw 1978).

THE VALUE OF WILD SPECIES

Americans have attached eight major types of values to wild species and these, in turn, can be categorized

199

as either *aesthetic* and *intellectual* or *economic* and *practical* (Table 8-1). As will be illustrated throughout this chapter, as well as in the following chapter on wildlife resource management, the more tangible economic and practical values are often in direct competition with the more elusive long-term values that come under the category of aesthetic and intellectual values.

Economic and Practical Values

The earliest economic and practical value associated with wild species was the procuring of animals for subsistence or for the market place. In fact, one of the first federal conservation restrictions placed on wild species in America (the Lacey Act of 1900) was for the sake of preserving a *food source* (Bean 1978). The Lacey Act made it a federal offense to transport across state lines game taken or possessed in violation of state laws. As wildlife dwindled as a food supply, the *recreational* use of wildlife replaced the food source value as the most significant value associated with wild species; hunting and fishing simply became more for sport and entertainment than for subsistence or for market exchange.

As the country grew in size and complexity, other value systems associated with wild species began to dominate the national scene, such as the use of wildlife for *scientific* pursuits (Myers 1983). Conservationists and environmentalists argue that all plant and animal species must be preserved for they might contain hidden answers to scientific questions that have plagued humankind for centuries. So-called useless species, they point out, have already made major contributions to science, medicine, and thus human survival: An unimpressive mold on bread has provided penicillin, a leading antibiotic; wild grasses have been domesticated and become the worldwide staple crops of maize, wheat, rye, and oats; wild animals that were once thought of as merely pests were later domesticated to serve humankind as draft animals or as a food source. Today, biologists are particularly interested in preserving wild seeds, for it is with the wild genes that they have increased the production of wheat, maize, barley, potatoes, millet, and virtually all the major crops through selective crossbreeding. Industrialized nations like the United States rely on the wild genes found in Third World countries. Some have even gone so far as to say that seeds will replace oil as the political weapon of the future.

The conservation argument for preserving "useless" species continues today, and is illustrated by the Tellico Dam controversy. The U.S. Supreme Court ruled in June 1978 that the Tennessee Valley Authority (TVA) had to stop work on the Tellico Dam to save the snail darter (a three-inch-long inedible species of perch), which was protected under the Endangered Species Act. Until 1976, the snail darter was found only in the Little Tennessee River. Environmentalists sought to halt the Tellico Dam because the $145 million project would turn that river into a lake, thus destroying the snail darter's last known spawning ground. This little fish became a test of strength between environmentalists and the forces of growth and development. Developers, consequently, moved Congress to exempt the Tellico Dam from the act 15 months later.

Concerned that the dam would be completed, biologists in 1976 transplanted 710 of the fish to the Hiwassee River, a tributary that enters the Little Tennessee 16 km (10 mi) downstream from the dam. The dam's floodgates were subsequently closed, and until recently, those original 710 and their offspring were the only known survivors. In November 1980, however, the snail darter was found living on the Chickamauga, another tributary to the Little Tennessee, 113 km (70 mi) downstream. Biologists are still arguing whether or not the darter could have migrated on its own or whether somebody took a bucket of snail darters and dumped them in the Chickamauga. Although it is simply too soon to say, it appears that the snail darter has survived, at least temporarily, this destruction of its original habitat.

Scientists also value wild species for a variety of reasons beyond preserving a genetic pool. Seismologists, for example, are becoming more and more interested in the apparent ability of wild species, such as cockroaches, to foresee earthquakes. Although it is still a hypothesis, much of their interest stems from the success that the Chinese and others have had in predicting earthquakes from animal behavior. If cockroaches can indeed predict earthquakes, the idea is to use them by lining entire fault zones with stations containing earthquake-sensing cockroaches.

TABLE 8-1

The value of wild species

AESTHETIC AND INTELLECTUAL (ELUSIVE)	VERSUS	ECONOMIC AND PRACTICAL (TANGIBLE)
Historical		Food source
Artistic		Recreational
Educational		Scientific
Spiritual		
Biotic respect		

Aesthetic and Intellectual Values

Aesthetic and *intellectual* values associated with wild species are usually long term and have no immediate practicality or economic return. When a local citizens' group fights for the preservation of the American bald eagle, for example, it is doing so not for the preservation of a genetic pool for future generations, but rather for the preservation of a symbol of our nation—a wild species that has *historic* significance. When wildlife photographers spend hours, weeks, and months trying to obtain the right angle and exposure on a photograph of Canada geese in harmonious flight, these wild species represent an *artistic* value to the photographer. When teachers take their school children on field trips to observe and to learn from nature, wild species serve as an *educational* value that the instructors could not do without. When a lone hiker stands on a mountain top to watch hawks soar with the wind currents, the magnificence of these avian creatures provides a *spiritual* value that cannot be obtained by walking the concrete habitats of humankind.

Finally, let us not forget the least economic, the least practical value of all—simply respecting life forms other than our own. In arguing for the conservation of primates (Figure 8-1), for example, Teleki and Baldwin (1975, p. 79) nicely state a case for *biotic respect:*

We have stressed the need to protect primate populations in terms of their resource and revenue values. When stripped of all economic and academic justifications, however, the heart of the conservation issue is simply a matter of respect for another life form—one which not only serves as vital substitute for human beings in biomedical experiments, but also uniquely stimulates human emotion and curiosity, and stands alone as our nearest relative in the animal kingdom. Apes really need to be protected, not so they can become surrogates to mankind, but so they can be apes.

This aesthetic and intellectual value versus economic and practical value division is not always so cut and dry. Conservationists, for example, argue that aesthetic and intellectual values *are*, indeed, practical, citing that it is highly utilitarian to maintain biotic diversity for teaching purposes (educational values) and aesthetic experiences (artistic values). Likewise, hunters have argued that their activities are as much for aesthetic and intellectual values (e.g., spiritual values associated with the wilderness experience) as for economic and practical values (e.g., game animals obtained for food or as part of recreation). Despite its obvious oversimplification, it still can be stated that economic and practical values (which are often, but not always, *short term*) are frequently in direct conflict with the set of aesthetic and intellectual values that are generally more *long range* in character.

FIGURE 8-1 Biotic respect. Life-forms other than our own deserve our respect and protection. Diane Fossey, anthropologist and world expert on gorillas, spent most of her adult life studying gorillas in the wilds of Rwanda, Africa. She was one of the first to document the gorilla as a gentle creature. In 1985, she was found slain in her cabin on a game reserve in the East African nation of Rwanda. Many believe to this day that she was slain by poachers—the same individuals who regularly kill the endangered gorillas in order to cut off their heads and hands for sale as curios. (Photo courtesy of Peter Veit/DRK Photo.)

WILDLIFE AND ECOSYSTEMS

Habitat Requirements of Wildlife

Healthy and abundant wildlife requires the preservation, maintenance, or creation of suitable wildlife habitats. An organism's **habitat** refers to the sum total of environmental factors that a given species needs to survive and reproduce in a given area. The habitat of a wild animal has five major components: (1) **cover** (shelter); (2) food (nutrition and nourishment); (3) water; (4) **home range** (area habitually traveled); and (5) **territory** (area habitually defended).

Cover. Cover refers to vegetation or other material that provides protection to a wild animal. Cover can be any variety of things—a tuft of grass, a thorny bush, a tangle of vines, a leafy tree, a clump of trees, a log, a cliff, a cave, or a cavity in a live or dead tree. In urban habitats, cover could be any one of the above or even such things as a sewer, a culvert, or a house eave.

Protection is the key value of cover for wildlife. Cover protects wildlife from weather and predators. Trees that protect deer from winter winds and drifting snow and tree canopies that protect birds from the hot afternoon sun are examples of cover against weather. *Concealment* from predators is an additional value of cover. Grasses conceal (hide) rabbits and mice from overhead predators, such as hawks, or from landbound animals such as domesticated dogs and cats. A breeding site safe from predators is particularly important for wild animals that have a low reproduction rate. If a particular bird only hatches one egg per year, it is essential that its nest or burrow be safe from predators if it is to survive as a species.

Food. Proper nutrition, of course, is vital to the welfare of any organism, for it directly affects reproduction, growth, and eventual survival. Biologists classify animals according to their food habitats and diet preferences. Based on food habits, the three major categories of animals are (1) **herbivores** (plant eaters), (2) **carnivores** (meat eaters), and (3) **omnivores** (plant and animal eaters). Whereas a deer (a herbivore) might be content browsing on some low leafy vegetation, a lion (a carnivore) makes a diet strictly of meat, and a bear, raccoon, or human (omnivore) prefers a diet of meat and plants.

There are two major classifications of animals based on diet preferences: (1) **euryphagous** (from *Euros*, wide); and (2) **stenophagous** (Owen 1985). If an animal, such as a pheasant or opposum, prefers a varied diet, the animal is categorized as eurypha-

gous. Animals in this category are far more likely to survive in critical periods of weather because of the variety of foods upon which they can subsist. Animals having a very specialized diet, such as the Everglade kite, which feeds almost exclusively on the snail *Pomacea caliginosa*, or the spruce grouse, which feeds on only spruce and jackpine needles during the winter, or the caribou, which feeds almost exclusively on lichens, would be classified as stenophagous and, consequently, highly vulnerable in terms of shortages of the particular food type the species needs.

The practice of artificially feeding game during severe winter months when food supplies are lean can actually be detrimental. Emergency feeding is expensive, often ineffective, and may prove to be a disservice to wild animals, if not bringing direct harm. When sportsmen or landowners place bales of hay or piles of grain in a particular spot, this process often causes increased social strife within the natural pecking order, an increased chance of predation by exposure of the animals in concentrated groups out in the open, and an increased possibility of spreading disease by concentration of the animals and the consequent contamination of their food and water.

Furthermore, artificial feeding also causes certain species to become dependent on humans for their food supply. For example, feeding at a designated location will attract deer to the area, and they might become dependent on the handout and discontinue their search for food provided by nature. When people feed bears in Yosemite National Park, they unknowingly train the bears to associate food with people, and, instead of seeking food in the wild, the bears choose to visit garbage cans and, in several cases, have walked through screen doors and into cabins within the park.

Water. Like food, water is vital to the life of all organisms. It is essential for digestion, metabolism, cooling, lubrication, and other life processes. Most wild animals have three sources of water: (1) *free water* (water that can be found in lakes, streams, snow, or dew on vegetation), (2) *food water* (water contained in the food consumed), and (3) *metabolic water* (water produced during the metabolic breakdown of proteins, carbohydrates, and fats). Most animals can survive only a few days without water, whereas they can survive much longer without food.

Home Range. Wild animals also require a home range, which refers to an area occupied over long periods by one group of animals or an individual animal. It encompasses all of the places that they regularly visit, such as areas in which they feed, breed, relax, escape from the weather, and conceal themselves from predators. Animals that occupy a deteriorated habitat often maintain larger home ranges than those in a good habitat. The resource management implications of this fact become apparent when considering how often humans disrupt or degrade wildlife habitats. Hence, wild species that may be invading an area which is traditionally not their domain may be doing so as a result of human pressure on their preferred or accustomed habitat.

Territory. Not only do wild animals have home ranges (areas regularly visited), some also have territories, which are areas regularly defended. More often than not, the area is defended by a member of one species against other members of the same species. For example, a more-or-less geographically definable area is aggressively defended by a lion against other intruding lions. Whereas home ranges may overlap, territories definitely do not overlap.

The importance of suitable wildlife habitats that provide adequate cover, food, water, home range, and territory cannot be emphasized enough. Each species has specific habitat needs that must not be overlooked in the rush to alter an area. Failure to understand these needs often leads to irreversible habitat damage.

Population Dynamics

A population is the number of living organisms that inhabit a given area, for example, the number of tule elk that graze in the Owens Valley of California, or the number of wolves that exist in northern Minnesota. Defining the population of an area, however, is not easy since populations are always in flux—they are dynamic. **Population dynamics** are the factors that produce population changes, and they have several elements that must be considered: the number of organisms or individuals, the density of individuals per unit area, the productivity of the animals, and their age and sex structure. Reproduction rate, movement, and mortality are the three controlling factors in a given population.

Population levels are affected by various population controls within species. Some animals (not all) maintain fairly constant population levels by forms of social behavior that limit reproduction to avoid overexploitation of food resources (Wynne-Edwards 1964). Wildlife biologists once assumed that animals will produce young as fast as they can and that the main factors keeping population levels at fixed limits were predators, diseases, parasites, accidents, or starvation. This assumption does not stand up, however,

since there are animal species that maintain relatively fixed populations, yet have virtually no predators and are not readily subject to disease and other limiting factors; the eagle and lion are notable examples of animals that maintain fixed populations.

What this implies is that certain wild animals restrict their population levels and density by various behavior modes related to the availability of food resources. The territorial system most certainly is a mechanism by which bird species stake out breeding sites, thus putting a limit on crowding and thereby adjusting the density of the population to food resources. Wynne-Edwards has also suggested that *massed aerial maneuvers* of some birds, such as starlings, is a means by which the flock can determine the proper relationship of population density to food supply. He maintains that starlings fly over a given area, determine the availability of the food supply, then adjusted their flock automatically by increasing or decreasing their activities and range in order to improve the balance between number of individuals and availability of food supply (Figure 8-2). According to Wynne-Edwards, the *epideictic displays*, or ceremonial demonstrations, of some species, for example, the black grouse males, are a further means of animal population control. In the case of the black grouse male, the display appears to provide a measure of population density and serves to exclude some less lucky males from the group, by chasing them away.

FIGURE 8-2 Massed maneuvers. Starling maneuvers are an example of communal activity that appears to have the purpose of providing the flock with an indication of population density. If the density is too high or too low in relation to the food supply, the flock automatically increases the activities that will improve the balance. (Photo courtesy of Joe Munroe/Photo Researchers.)

Carrying Capacity. Requirements such as cover, food, water, and other essentials for life are components of yet another concept known as **carrying capacity.** It can be defined as the maximum number of animals that a habitat can *carry* or support indefinitely under a given set of environmental conditions. This concept applies to domesticated as well as to wild animals. Many factors influence the carrying capacity of habitat, such as the progression of the seasons, human land-use practices, plant succession, climate, and the types and numbers of other animals (including humans) in the habitat. Imagine a fenced hillside with a small herd of cattle grazing on its natural grasses. If the cattle overgraze the area, the habitat will be unable to *carry* or support the herd on a long-term basis, thus the cattle will exceed the carrying capacity of the habitat. If the cattle, however, can remain there indefinitely and not outstrip the hillside's natural food supply, then the herd can be said to be living within the carrying capacity of its habitat.

Biotic Potential (BP). Two major factors have an influence on the number of animals that can subsist within a given habitat: biotic potential and environmental resistance (Owen 1985). **Biotic potential** is the theoretical maximum rate at which a population can reproduce with unlimited resources and ideal environmental conditions. The average number of *potential* offspring of a particular species can also be considered its biotic potential. In wild birds, for example, biotic potential is affected by the breeding age of the individual, the *clutch size* (the number of eggs regularly produced at once), and the number of offspring annually. Animal population control methods, such as population density, sex ratios, and mating habits, also have an influence on biotic potential.

Environmental Resistance (ER). **Environmental resistance** involves the factors that tend to limit or regulate the maximum potential size of a population. It refers to all the forces (both physical and biotic) that cause death or a lowering of the reproductive rate, such as severe physical conditions (drought and floods), natural calamities (hurricanes, tornadoes, and earthquakes), human impacts (forest fires), environmental contamination (poisoned food or water supplies), or habitat destruction (draining natural potholes, swamps, or marshlands). **Predation** is the situation in which an organism of one species, the **predator** (e.g., a carnivore), captures and feeds on an organism of another species, the prey (e.g., a herbivore). Predation and predators are certainly biotic components of environmental resistance, for they directly pare down the number of potential animals within a given habitat.

Various forms of parasites and *diseases,* of course, are other biotic forms of environmental resistance that often plague animal populations. Some wildlife biologists broadly define disease to include not only common infections, but also such things as injuries, birth defects, changes due to malnutrition, and certain tumors. Although it is common to find parasites in many healthy animals, excessive numbers can cause disease, as seen in the brain worm disease of deer and the meningeal worm disease of moose.

One of the predominant forms of wild waterfowl disease is **botulism,** resulting from anaerobic bacteria that thrive on dead organisms. *Clostridium botulinum,* the bacterium which acts as the causative agent, produces a powerful poison that kills waterfowl, particularly in the western parts of North America.

In the wild, when ER (environmental resistance) is low and BP (biotic potential) is high, the particular species in question is likely to experience a **population explosion**—any rapid increase in the number of organisms in a given area in which the **population density** (the number of individuals per unit area) would increase, placing a greater pressure on the available food supply. As the food supply becomes utilized and destroyed, this once rapidly multiplying species might undergo a **population crash** (a *dieback* resulting from the large population exceeding the ability of the environment to support it, i.e., a decline in the population that results from the population exceeding its carrying capacity).

Wildlife populations can also be classified as either irruptive, cyclic, or stable (Owen 1985). A wildlife population that *irregularly* experiences a population explosion, increase in density, and resulting population crash would be classified as an **irruptive population**—one that is highly erratic and unpredictable. A **cyclic population** is one that *regularly* has its ups and downs—regular intervals of rapid population and population density increases, followed by crashes, and then by further increases. Finally, a **stable population** is one that remains at a rather *constant* level, once having reached the carrying capacity of the habitat.

Management Implications. In wildlife conservation, increasing the numbers of threatened or endangered species is obviously important; likewise, controlling the numbers of certain animals (e.g., the number of wild burros in a canyon) at a conservative level is also an important task of the wildlife biologist and conservationist. There are various ways in which humans can manipulate animal population dynamics to attain their particular objectives, such as adjusting animal density, food quantity, and the harvest season. Specific examples will be provided in the following chapter on wildlife resource management.

EXTERMINATION OF WILDLIFE

All animals will eventually become extinct, including the human animal. Biological extinction is a natural evolutionary process. Since life began on Earth (3.2–3.5 billion years ago), only 2 million of the estimated 500 million species of plants and animals that ever existed are here today. Hence, *99.5 percent of all species have become extinct* (Ziswiler 1967). If biological extinction is the rule rather than the exception, you might ask why environmental scientists are concerned about the extinction of animals. The answer is that humans have vastly *accelerated* these natural evolutionary processes to the point of bringing ecological disruption to Earth (Eckholm 1978, Ehrlich and Ehrlich 1981, Fisher et al. 1969, Scheffer 1974).

Causes of Animal Extermination

There are several major factors that cause animal extermination. In decreasing order of importance, they are as follows: (1) restricted and modified habitat, (2) commercial market hunting, (3) introduction of exotics, (4) sport hunting, (5) pest and predator control, (6) hunting for food, (7) wildlife trade, and (8) pollution. Other factors, such as low biotic potential, genetic assimilation, nonadaptive behavior, and specialized diet add to the reasons why animals may become extinct. A combination of the above factors, not just a single factor, usually drives an animal species to extinction.

Restricted and Modified Habitat. Without question, habitat modification, restriction, or elimination has had the greatest effect on the status of wildlife in the United States. The effect has been brought about primarily by agricultural expansion, forest harvesting, prairie conversion, inland waterway modification, seashore manipulation, and general urbanization and its accompanying technological developments.

Agriculture has had one of the most profound effects upon American wildlife (George 1966). Human population growth, resettlement, and land development for agriculture has brought on changes in plant and animal communities, diminished wildlife cover, accelerated eutrophication of lakes and wetlands, and caused an overall loss of habitat diversity (**odd areas,** woodlots, marshlands, etc.) (Table 8–2). These developments, of course, have reduced animal species. With over 20 percent of the continental United States now in cropland, and another 25 percent in pasture, North America's plant and animal communities have experienced drastic habitat disruption as a result of the spread of agriculture (Burger 1978). Although habitat alteration has certainly benefited some species, the overall effect of the spread of agriculture has been the reduction of wildlife diversity.

The *harvesting of timber* from our forest lands has disrupted much indispensable habitat for wildlife (Bandy and Tabler 1974). The current trend in forest management still gives greater priority to maximum wood yield over optimum wildlife habitat. With the increased demand for forest products, the timber industry uses practices that are often harmful to some wildlife populations—practices such as clear-cutting, even-age planting, the intensive use of herbicides to kill shrubs that compete with young conifer seedlings, the use of poisoned grains to kill rodents that eat tree seedlings, and the use of highly controversial aerial sprays for the control of insecticides and fungicides.

The conversion of America's public grasslands (as well as modern ranching practices in other areas) is often detrimental to wildlife and wildlife habitats (Buttery and Shields 1975). In the Hawaiian Islands, for example, natural brushlands are converted to artificial grasslands for meat production. Bulldozers scrape the hillsides clean of natural grasses and brush; introduced grasses, such as pangola grass, are disk-harrowed into the soil; synthetic fertilizers are applied by aerial spraying; barbed wire fences are constructed around the perimeter of the field; herbicides are regularly applied to so-called weed plants that compete with the human-desired monocultural species; and predator animals are shot, poisoned, or scared away from the herd animals. All of these practices, and more, directly or indirectly alter or totally destroy wildlife habitats.

We can look to South Dakota for a case in point. The ring-necked pheasant, a nonnative bird imported from China in 1881, has adapted well to our nation's prairie lands. But a drought in the 1970s forced this issue: Should domesticated animals prevail over wild species when an area is faced with severe environmental constraints, such as a drought, a flood, or other natural calamity? An estimated 30 percent of the ring-necked pheasant population nests along roadsides in parts of South Dakota (Figure 8-3). Fear-

TABLE 8-2

Agriculture and wildlife

HISTORICAL PERIOD OR TREND	AGRICULTURAL PRACTICE	DESCRIPTION	IMPLICATION FOR WILDLIFE
First Americans (Indians)	Small scale	Planted crops on alluvial soils or in forest openings created by girdling or burning trees	Only local effect on wildlife; likely favorable, since small clearings increase habitat diversity
Early Americans (Europeans) (1838)	Introduction of steel moldboard plow	Allowed the breaking of grass-bound sod; cropland traditionally wrested from forests; grasslands—world's richest soil	Tall grasslands began to vanish under the plow; prairie wildlife reacted to rapid human settlement; wilderness prairie animals—gray wolf, bison, elk, and pronghorn—began to decline
Post–Civil War (1900)	Rapid mechanization of agriculture	Numerous inventions, such as McCormick reaper; establishment of land-use patterns	Wilderness animals continued to vanish; introduced exotic species began to prosper (e.g., boll weevil); increased bird depredation of crops; cropland patterns and fire prevention end prairie fires, thus changing habitat openings
Dust Bowl years (1930s)	Moderate scale; increasingly mechanized	Drought and intensive use of soils brought on massive soil erosion problems—soil depletion, fertility loss, silting of waterways	Change in plant and animal communities
Post–World War II (1945-) "Big Farming"	Large scale; highly mechanized	Tractor replaced horse, freeing millions of acres from pasture and fodder production	Loss of habitat diversity
	Development of hybrid grain	Farm machinery grew larger, more efficient, more specialized; farm size increased; shift to monoculture—single crop farming	Wildlife cover diminishes as continuous row cropping replaces trees and fences of smaller farmsteads
1950s	Emphasis on synthetic fertilizers	Synthetic nitrogenous fertilizers replace animal manure and "green manure" of plowed down hay	Rapid eutrophication of lakes and wetlands, with consequent ill effects on aquatic wildlife
	Population shift from farm to city	Abandoned farmsteads torn down; Americans lose touch with land	Accelerated destruction of wildlife shelter (gardens, lilac bushes, shade trees); first-hand understanding of principles of ecology is lost
1960s	Agribusiness replaces family farm; increased use of synthetic fertilizers *and* pesticides	Corporate farming—concept of "factory farm"; concern for world grain markets	Mechanical harvesters (e.g., corn pickers) increase waste grain, leading to shift in certain waterfowl wintering grounds; rice monocultures bring on similar shift in flight patterns
1970s–present	Land reclamation projects (draining and filling); "land forming" (leveling and filling surface irregularities with heavy equipment)	Vast drainage of marshlands for farmlands; irrigation projects; stream channelization (clearing of riparian habitat) in efforts to "conserve" irrigation water	Increased loss of wetlands and consequent waterfowl habitat; irrigation projects bring shift in crop varieties and threat to groundwater supplies; accelerated loss of hedgerows, odd areas, potholes, and woodlots; reduced species diversity

Source: Compiled from Burger, George V. 1978. "Agriculture and Wildlife." In Howard P. Brokaw, ed., *Wildlife and America.* Washington, D.C.: Government Printing Office, pp. 89–107.

ing the failure of their hay crops for livestock feed, ranchers were able to pressure the governor to lift a state ban on roadside mowing, thus resulting in habitat destruction during the prime breeding season of the ring-necked pheasant. Furthermore, the ranchers requested nearby wildlife refuges be opened up as hay reserves during periods when their own grasslands were overgrazed. Although wildlife refuges

FIGURE 8-3 Ring-necked pheasant. (upper) The ring-necked pheasant, once a flourishing game bird in South Dakota, faces some serious trouble there as its habitat continues to be destroyed. (Photo courtesy of Hugh M. Halliday/ Photo Researchers.) (lower) An estimated 30 percent of the pheasant population nest along roadsides in parts of South Dakota. (Photo courtesy of Leonard Lee Rue III/Photo Researchers.)

were intentionally designed to protect and preserve habitat, not to produce feed for livestock, many of South Dakota's ranchers saw the refuges as a place to salvage their own herds. The question that plagues environmentalists, however, is whether or not the opening up of these wildlife refuges to cattle grazing is merely a means of *rewarding the rancher who allows his rangelands to become overgrazed.*

Urbanization, and its accompanying technology,

has taken a heavy toll on wildlife habitats (Stearns 1972). Urbanization means people, and people mean industrial parks, shopping centers, housing developments, and sanitary landfills—all of which need space.

The filling of San Francisco Bay is a classic example of wildlife habitat loss. Since the 1850s, the bay has been filled to provide space for various urban-related uses: harbor facilities, salt evaporation ponds, sanitary landfills, airports, industrial parks, and housing developments. In addition, the bay was indirectly filled by the heavy loads of silt sent down by the hydraulic mining for gold in the Sierra Nevada Mountains between 1850 and 1884. Since 1850, the total bay system (water areas and marshlands) has shrunk in size by approximately *30 percent* (Figure 8-4). If it were not for the creative ideas and determination of local conservation leaders, the filling of San Francisco Bay would not have been halted.

Direct Hunting by Humans. For over 99 percent of human history, humans have been hunter-gatherers and have had a direct effect upon wildlife (Smith 1976). Thirty-nine percent of today's endangered species have become endangered as a result of hunting: commercial hunting (21 percent), sport hunting (12 percent), and hunting for food and clothing (6 percent) (Miller 1982). Furthermore, all three forms of hunting remain controversial (Clarke 1979, Klein 1977).

The development of synthetic products has helped decrease the number of animals hunted for hides, furs, feathers, tusks, and other animal products, but certain species remain threatened as a result of such *commercial* pursuits. For example, the International Union for the Conservation of Nature and Natural Resources (IUCN) reports that ivory poachers are now using new techniques to kill elephants, such as machine gunning, poisoning them with fruits filled with battery acid, and the poisoning of waterholes. Poisoning waterholes, of course, also becomes a threat to the nontarget species that share the same habitat, including humans.

In Canada's eastern coastal waters, the harp seal is annually slaughtered for its fur. Opposed to this form of wildlife "management," protesters from Greenpeace, the Fund for Animals, and other conservation groups have painted seals with a harmless organic dye on their white coats to render their pelts commercially valueless. In 1980, the total allowable number of harp seal pups to be killed by Canadian and Norwegian seal hunters was legislatively set at 180,000. But as Nicholas Rosa has pointed out, these quota systems are often exceeded (Rosa 1976).

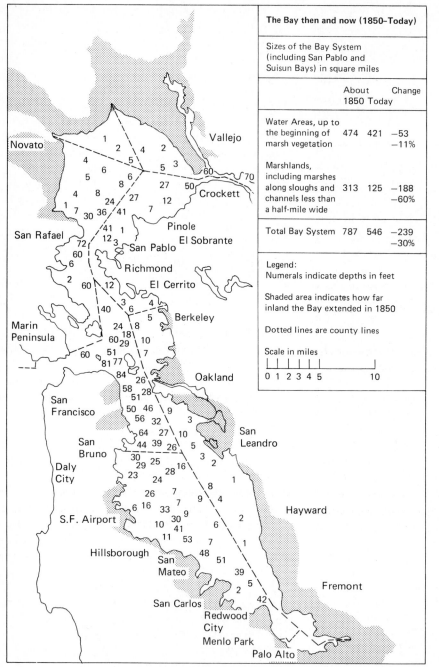

The Bay then and now (1850–Today)		
Sizes of the Bay System (including San Pablo and Suisun Bays) in square miles		
	About 1850	Change Today
Water Areas, up to the beginning of marsh vegetation	474 421	−53 −11%
Marshlands, including marshes along sloughs and channels less than a half-mile wide	313 125	−188 −60%
Total Bay System	787 546	−239 −30%

Legend:
Numerals indicate depths in feet

Shaded area indicates how far inland the Bay extended in 1850

Dotted lines are county lines

Scale in miles
0 1 2 3 4 5   10

FIGURE 8-4 The shrinking bay. Various urban-related landfill projects have caused San Francisco Bay to shrink approximately 30 percent since 1850. (Reprinted with permission of the San Francisco Examiner. © 1989 The San Francisco Examiner.)

Whereas one could possibly argue the legitimacy of the procurement of ivory and furs as the commercial by-products of animal hunting, hundreds of thousands of animals are commercially slaughtered in order to fulfill such questionable desires as manufacturing a fly swatter from the tail of a dead gnu, a wastepaper basket from the foot of an elephant, or a home decoration from a mummified baby alligator (Wagner 1971). This use of animal products is certainly an unnecessary strain on the animal kingdom, not to mention that it is morally bankrupt!

Sport hunting has been and continues to be a major threat to wildlife, particularly large game animals such as the elephant, tiger, rhinoceros, and leopard. Most of India's famous and beautiful Bengal tigers, once flourishing but now facing extinction, have been eliminated by licensed or privileged sport hunters, in addition to poachers and cattle herders who have poisoned them. Romanticized by Ernest Hemingway and Robert Ruark, big game hunting in Africa drew rich sport hunters from around the world, including President Teddy Roosevelt—a leading conservationist—for the experience of shooting East Africa's big game (Figure 8-5). Fortunately for the animals, however, Kenya and other African governments are starting to restrict or totally ban big game hunting in order to save their nation's dwindling stocks of wildlife. Cameras with zoom lenses are beginning to replace the rifle, and many who tread in Hemingway's footsteps prefer to capture their trophies on film rather than carrying the skins and stuffed heads back home to hang on their hunting den wall.

The now extinct passenger pigeon *(Ectopistes migratorius)* was once one of the most numerous birds on the North American continent. Several factors caused its extinction: disease, resulting from crowding; low biotic potential (only one egg per nesting); several storms; restricted habitat, resulting from land clearing; and *sport hunting* (Schorger 1973). In the 1860s, killing passenger pigeons was considered an attractive sport, and shotguns, fires, traps, artillery, and even dynamite were used to mount massive attacks on the species. In 1907, a lone hunter shot the last *wild* pigeon of its kind, and in 1914, the last *captive* pigeon died in the Cincinnati Zoo, thus ending the species existence for perpetuity.

Hunting for food was a major cause of extermination in early America (Reiger 1978). Although such hunting has declined sharply in recent years, America's wildlife history is marred with examples of excessive hunting for food.

The near extinction of the American bison *(Bison bison)* was the result of many factors, the original major impact being the westward movement of the railroads in the late 1860s and the professional hunters employed to provide the construction crews with bison as their basic food supply. Later, millions of bison were shot by hide hunters, and, finally, the deliberate

U.S. government policy to subdue the Plains Indians by taking away their primary food supply, the bison, was in reality an early form of biological warfare. These three factors diminished the numbers and range of the bison on the North American continent. Today, the few remaining bison herds on ranges in the western United States are protected by laws.

Introduced Species. Exotic species introductions account for approximately 16 percent of the exterminations and extinctions of wildlife species. When a species is introduced to a new environment, either accidentally or deliberately, the consequences are often unpredictable and undesirable (Ehrenfeld 1970). The biological effects of exotic species introductions cannot be forecast. Hence, introducing species is a game of "ecological roulette" in which many mistakes have been made and gains have been slight.

Purposeful introductions (the intentional introduction of exotic organisms) have been many in America. A few introduced species have become important game animals. The ring-necked pheasant *(Phasianus colchicus)* from Asia is a success story in most areas, since it not only took hold in this country, but did so with minimal disruption of the local habitat niches. Likewise, the introduction of the brown trout *(Salmo trutta)* from England and Germany blended into America's ecosystems without harmful consequences.

Most purposeful introductions, however, have proven disastrous. Exotic birds have often been introduced by immigrants who missed seeing and hearing the species that they had known in their homeland. For example, the house sparrow *(Passer domesticus)* was introduced from England, resulting in damage to grain crops, fruit crops, trees, and houses. Eventually it displaced such native species as swallows, wrens,

FIGURE 8-5 Last of the white hunters. As African game laws become stricter, "legal hunters" are trading in their rifles for cameras with long lenses. "Illegal hunters" (poachers), however, are on the rise. (Photo courtesy of George Rodger/Magnum Photos.)

and martins (Laycock 1966). The starling *(Sturnus vulgaris)* is reported to have been introduced by one individual who wanted to introduce to America all of the bird species mentioned in Shakespeare's writings. Starlings are now well established in most of the continental United States, and they have caused untold millions of dollars of crop and fruit damage, as well as having caused jet aircraft to crash.

Some birds have been intentionally introduced to act as a **biological control** for insect pests. The cattle egret *(Bubulcus ibis)* was introduced to Hawaii from Florida in 1959 to control insect pests but in the long run it may prove to be detrimental to native ground-nesting birds, such as the eastern meadowlark *(Sturnella magna).* The egret apparently has taken to feeding on newly hatched meadowlarks.

Alien mammals have been repeatedly introduced into the continental United States since 1900. The nutria *(Myocastor coypus)* is a cat-sized rodent that was intentionally imported from Argentina for the get-rich-quick schemes of some Americans. Originally reported to be a superior fur animal, nutria were shipped to the states, only to be later turned loose by the breeders when they found the pelts would not get a good price. Nutria became well established and began causing severe damage to agriculture, levees, and marsh ecology. (On the positive side, however, nutria have become an important ingredient of some local economies, such as in the bayou lands of Louisiana.)

Accidental introductions are the nonintentional introductions of exotic organisms, including any introductions conducted without a specifically defined purpose or long-range goal. Whereas many parts of the United States have received accidental introductions, Hawaii and Florida have been the recipients of the greatest numbers of exotic organisms. The giant African snail *(Achatina fulica)* accidentally made its way to the Hawaiian Islands. There, it destroyed crops and vegetation, and the shells of the dead snails even changed the pH of the soils, thus acting as an additional detriment to crops (King 1968). The most famous accidental introduction of all is the walking catfish *(Ciarias batrachus)* (Courtenay 1970). This native fish of southeast Asia is thought to have escaped a fish farm in the community of Parkland, west of Deerfield Beach, Florida, and "walked" into nearby canals. From there, the fish spread north and has the potential of becoming a dominant species, perhaps to the *exclusion* of some native species (Figure 8-6).

When it comes to exotic species introductions, several facts become apparent:

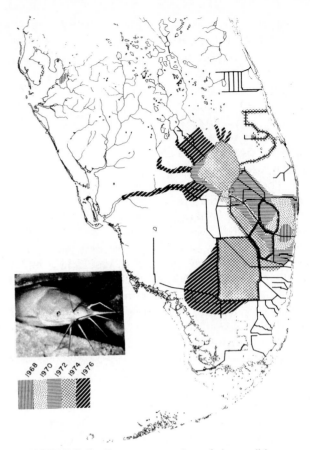

FIGURE 8-6   Range expansion of the walking catfish in Florida shown in biennial increments. (From W. R. Courtenay, Jr., "The Introduction of Exotic Organisms." In Howard P. Brokaw, ed., *Wildlife and America* [Washington, D.C.: Government Printing Office, 1978], p. 244. Source: Francis McKittrick Watkins.)

1. Releases have not always resulted in the establishment of the exotic species, but more often than not, if it does become established, it is likely to be detrimental to the new ecosystem.

2. So-called scientifically thought out intentional releases are often just as detrimental as accidental releases; again, it is virtually impossible to predict how exotic organisms will behave in a new environment.

3. Introduced exotic organisms take years to reach their potential; what may have first appeared as a beneficial introduction at the time of establishment may become a destructive one later.

4. It is extremely difficult to predict the potential harm or benefit of the introduction of

foreign parasites and disease organisms that ride along with the imported or introduced floral and fauna.

5. If eradication of the exotic species becomes necessary, it could be costly both financially and ecologically.

Pest and Predator Control. When humans domesticated plants and animals some 10,000 to 15,000 years ago, they unintentionally invited competition with other undomesticated species. **Pests** are free-living organisms that, at times, exert detrimental effects on other wildlife, vegetation, agricultural crops, and livestock. Many also threaten public health and safety. A *predator* is any organism that captures and eats other animals or plants. The line between these two definitions, however, is often unclear. For example, is the boll weevil a pest or predator? Some would argue that it is as much a predator as a coyote. As humans slowly became more sophisticated at growing plants and raising livestock, they also had to learn how to protect these domesticated species from the ravages of animal damage.

In the United States, pest and predator control can be traced back to 1630 in the Massachusetts Bay colony, where eagles, bears, mountain lions, wolves, and coyotes had *bounties* placed on their heads (Allen 1962). Early U.S. settlement was a period when Americans hated and feared their competitive co-predators and a governmental policy of extermination of predators began. Sometimes the governmental response to animal damage was the total extermination of the target species, such as the now extinct Carolina parakeet, which fed on fruit crops. In other cases, governmental response led to the near extinction of a target species, such as the mountain lion and wolf, which preyed on livestock.

Government-sponsored pest and predator control programs have also brought about the indiscriminate poisoning of nontarget species, many of which were the national predators of the pest that the government was trying to curtail. The near elimination of the black-footed ferret—the natural predator of the prairie dog—is a case in point (McNulty 1971). In southwestern Wyoming, the government, at the insistence of ranchers, undertook the systematic poisoning of prairie dog towns to preserve grass for livestock. Unfortunately, the poison campaigns also affected the natural predators of the prairie dog—hawks, eagles, falcons, coyotes, and particularly the black-footed ferret. These poisoning efforts were so severe that both the white-tailed prairie dog and the

black-footed ferret are now on the list of endangered species and are protected by law.

Animals that once were considered pests are, in many cases, turning out to be a necessary element within the ecological web of life. Wildlife biologists, for example, are now finding that the prairie dog takes the pressure off other animals that may otherwise serve as prey for the predators; that is, if there are fewer prairie dogs to eat, the coyotes prey more heavily on cattle and sheep. Attacks on livestock, hence, are lessened when there is natural prey in the area.

In a few cases, governmental attempts at animal damage control have been total failures, such as its unsuccessful attempt to control the coyote *(Canis latrans)* population in the southwestern United States (Leydet 1977; Pringle 1975, 1977). While government carries on a ceaseless warfare against the coyote, the animals have actually *increased* since earlier days, and much of this increase in coyotes is ironically a direct result of human modification of the landscape—overgrazing by livestock results in a greater abundance of rabbits and hares on farms and on ranch lands, which, in turn, creates an increased food supply and suitable habitat for coyotes.

Furthermore, coyotes show an uncanny ability to foil human hunters—springing traps before removing the bait, avoiding poisoned food, and digging several dens to minimize the danger caused by the human discovery of any single one. They travel either singly or in packs. They can eat almost anything—insects, rats, rabbits, large deer, household garbage, fruits, and berries. Coyotes also are able to sustain a very high mortality rate. After the removal of many coyotes, their reproduction rates seem to go into "overdrive"—an apparently built-in reproduction control that adjusts the size of their litters to their density in any given area. This ability to outsmart humans has allowed the coyote to proliferate, and it is now found in every state except Hawaii.

Coyotes are not the only form of wild dog that has proven to be a predator problem to humans. In Australia, the dingo still remains a dirty word among the country's sheep herders. The dingo, a species of wild dog that is usually yellow and about the size of a German shepherd, preys heavily on rabbits, wallabies, and other grass-eating animals, including sheep. Although Australia's war against the dingo has sharply reduced sheep losses—and the population of wild dogs—their immediate victory may be short lived. Recent government studies indicate that if the dingo becomes extinct, the herbivores will proliferate and compete more vigorously with Australia's sheep for pasturage. The result would be a far more serious threat to the sheep than is now caused by the dingoes. From an ecologist's point of view, the dingo may turn out to be one of the sheep rancher's better friends.

Although avian predators, such as the golden eagle, and certain owls and hawks have caused livestock ranchers and fishermen concern enough to occasionally demand an eradication program, *avian pests* have more recently caught the public's attention (Figure 8-7). For example, millions of blackbirds descended in 1975 on various farming and residential areas of Kentucky and Tennessee (Fichter 1980). Residents complained of crop damage, health problems (the birds infected humans with histoplasmosis—a lung-damaging fungus), and general inconvenience (bird droppings forced people to walk under umbrellas from their front door to their automobile in the driveway). In 1976, another blackbird invasion reopened a bitter controversy between the effected populace and out-of-town conservationists: Whether or not the roosting invaders should be sprayed with Tergitol, a detergent that washes away the protective oil coat on the birds' feathers and thus causes them to freeze to death. In 1975, after a Tergitol spray killed 500,000 birds in Kentucky, environmentalists from Washington and New York raised such an outcry that the Environmental Protection Agency banned the use of the detergent against the birds. But, will the ban hold in the wake of future blackbird invasions? And, what alternative blackbird control methods are available to wildlife resource managers? These questions and more will be pursued in the following chapter.

For now, it is simply important to note here that many forms of wildlife are considered to be in direct competition with human endeavors, either as predators or as pests. Furthermore, government officials have reacted to public outcries by undertaking eradication campaigns, many of which have had a deleterious impact on wildlife.

Pets, Zoos, and Scientific Research. International trade in live animals for pet stores, zoos, aquariums, and biomedical research laboratories accounts for approximately 5 percent of the extermination and extinction of wildlife species. Many of the imported animals are on the endangered species list and, therefore, are smuggled illegally into the country. Whether entry into the United States is legal or illegal, hundreds of thousands of animals die in the process of capture, shipment, or storage after purchase. Wild animals have specific requirements in regard to temperature, humidity, dietary needs, and spatial needs, and many of these requirements are either unknown or ignored, thus resulting in high animal fatalities.

The neighborhood pet store is often thought of as a wholesome operation, where a family can spend hours gazing at a variety of potential pets, from domesticated puppies and kittens to exotic wild mammals, birds, reptiles, amphibians, and fish. What is often ignored, however, is that such pet-loving nations as the United States, the United Kingdom, and Germany have had deleterious effects on wildlife communities in Third World countries as a result of their obsession to keep an animal captive in a cage or an aquarium in their home (Ehrenfeld 1970, Tuan 1984).

Zoos and aquariums, although important for species preservation, have also had a negative impact on world wildlife resources. For some zoo keepers, acquiring a green tree python, a Johnson's crocodile, or a Fiji iguana is worth the gamble of possibly being arrested for buying smuggled animals that are protected by international treaty. Some of the nation's largest and most prestigious zoos have been caught either purposely or unwittingly buying smuggled animals that are extremely rare and endangered. Clearly, as long as collectors and exhibitors are willing to pay the price for rare animals, smugglers will be willing to take the risk to ship them.

Even the medical profession has had an effect on wild species. Although zoos and aquariums do not breed all the species they get from the wild, in overall numbers they are net *producers* of wild mammals. Biomedical researchers, on the other hand, are net *consumers*. During 1972–1973, biomedical research facilities consumed an estimated 130,000 captured and imported wild primates but only produced 4682 primates by captive breeding (National Academy of Sciences 1975). The demand for apes and monkeys by centers of medical and pharmaceutical research is so heavy that this has encouraged the smuggling of wildlife. Some leading U.S. pharmaceutical companies, for example, negotiate directly with animal dealers, often not asking where the animals were obtained. Medical research is obviously important for human betterment and welfare, but it should not mean the total elimination of such primates as chimpanzees and orangutans.

Pollution and Other Sources. Various forms of air and water pollution have caused approximately 3 percent of the exterminations and extinctions of wildlife species (Table 8-3). Many of the major environ-

Red-winged blackbird

There may be more red-wings than any other U.S. bird — at least it was the most often sighted species in a recent survey. The male's red wing patch is unmistakable, though the drab female looks more like a large sparrow.

House sparrow

The house sparrow, an English import, is number two on the most sighted species list. It looks as ordinary as it is common, but you can tell the male by its black bib and white cheeks.

Starling

The starling has been so successful since it was brought here from Europe that it's now probably our least loved bird. In winter, it's drab and spotty, but in summer, it acquires a metallic sheen. Its numbers now seem to be declining.

Mourning dove

This habitué of telephone lines is hunted for sport in many states — the annual kill is around 50 million, yet the population remains stable.

Western meadowlark

This abundant westerner is a frequenter of fields and fencerows. The southern part of its range overlaps with that of a near twin, the eastern meadowlark.

Common grackle

As the starling population dwindles, the grackle bids fair to replace that much maligned species as the number one pest bird, particularly in the East.

Horned lark

The seventh most sighted bird in recent surveys, the horned lark likes open spaces, and takes as readily to coastal flats as it does to plains.

Robin

Some people think the robin is the most common bird, but that's probably because it's so urbanized and because the male, with its orange breast, is so visible. Actually, there are probably three times as many red-winged blackbirds.

Common crow

Sometimes a pest, the crow prefers to live in fairly well-structured colonies. The great horned owl is an archenemy, and a group of crows will attack one on sight.

Barn swallows

Aptly named, barn swallows can be found on almost any farm, where they build distinctive mud nests, usually in or on buildings. It is the only swallow with a forked tail.

FIGURE 8-7 Five of the top ten are "pests." Of the 10 bird species you are most likely to see every day, five of them—the starling, house sparrow, grackle, crow, and red-winged blackbird—can become terrible nuisances. (Adapted from Roger Tory Peterson, *A Field Guide to the Birds* [Boston: Houghton Mifflin Co., 1980].)

TABLE 8-3
Pollution effects on fish and wildlife

TYPE OF POLLUTION	HUMAN NEED	SOURCE OF POLLUTANT	SPECIFIC CASES
Pesticides and PCBs (polychlorinated biphenyls)	Disposal of unwanted products	Landfill site—pesticides wrapped in paper bags accidentally unearthed by construction activities	Hundreds of fish killed in Austin, Texas
	Pest eradication (sand fly)	Pesticide application to salt marsh	A million fish killed in Florida
	Disease eradication (Dutch elm disease)	DDT application to elm trees	151 birds killed in New Hampshire
	Cleansing solution	Rinse water used to clean a pesticide truck rig enters stream	A river in Mississippi was closed to fishing for one year and 100,000 fish died
	Disposal of industrial wastes	Kepone discharged from a pesticide manufacturing plant	Chesapeake Bay fishing industry idled in Virginia
	Food products	Pesticide application to agricultural fields	Eggshell thinning inhibited reproduction in California brown pelican
			Premature births in California sea lions
Sewage and industrial waste	Disposal of industrial waste	2600 gallons of cyanide solution dumped down storm drain	40,000 fish killed in Illinois
	Disposal of sewage water	Sewage plant failure and resulting overflow: consumption of dissolved oxygen from water as organic matter breaks down	Thousands of fish died in waters off San Jose, California
	Disposal of sewage sludge	Offshore dumping	Delaware and Maryland clams contaminated with heavy metals, thus closing shellfishing areas
	Fallibility (room for accidents)	Runoff from a chemical plant fire	6000 to 10,000 fish killed in Jacksonville, Florida
Petroleum in ocean waters	Energy—satisfied by a rapid increase in the quantities of crude and refined petroleum that are transported by sea	Tanker collision	*Torrey Canyon* tanker spill on the south coast of England—30,000 marine birds died
		Oil platform failure	Santa Barbara oil platform spill resulted in 3700 dead birds
		(Other sources: discharge of ballast waters by tankers; accidental discharge from ships)	
Thermal pollution	Energy—satisfied by steam- or nuclear-powered electric generating plants	Discharge of cooling waters	Numerous fish killed in the northeastern Great Lakes region
Environmental radioactivity	Energy—satisfied by nuclear power technology	Inevitable leaks and spills of highly contaminated waste products; release to the atmosphere of radioactive gases such as tritium, krypton-85, and two isotopes of xenon	Species such as the California condor (*Glymnogyps californianus*) or the whooping crane (*Grus americana*), which have reached low population numbers, can ill afford any radiation-induced mortality or deleterious mutations
Airborne toxics	Aluminum for industrial or domestic use	Fluoride emissions from smelting plant	Habitat destruction—ponderosa pine in and around Glacier National Park in Montana have been injured
	Transportation	Photochemical oxidants (smog) from automobiles	14,000 square miles of vegetation in Southern California have been harmed
Acidic precipitation	Energy—satisfied by burning fossil fuels	Power plants and smelters	Spotted salamanders (*Ambystoma maculatum*) are no longer able to

TABLE 8-3 (Continued)

TYPE OF POLLUTION	HUMAN NEED	SOURCE OF POLLUTANT	SPECIFIC CASES
	with a high sulfur content		breed in melt ponds near Cornell University in Ithaca, New York, because winter snows are too acid
			Low pH in freshwater lakes was found to eliminate the salmon and trout population in southern Norway
			Long-term effects on wildlife: reduction in forest growth, erosion of cuticles of leaves, leaching of nutrient salts from soils
Erosion	Energy, irrigation, and flood control	Runoff in the form of silt and mud	Wildlife population in and along Nile River affected with construction of Aswan High Dam in Egypt. The dam stopped the natural flow of nutrients downstream, thus collapsing fish populations that formerly existed off the mouth of the river and where food organisms were dependent on the nutrients carried out during floods
People	Recreation in open space	Crowding in parks, on lakes, and generally in the "great outdoors"	Visitors illegally feed black bears in Yellowstone National Park, thus upsetting natural feeding habits, cycles, and human-animal relationships

Source: Compiled from Arnold, Dean E. 1979. "Environmental Pollution: Effects on Fish and Wildlife Management." In Richard D. Teague and Eugene Decker, eds., *Wildlife Conservation: Principles and Practices.* Washington, D.C.: The Wildlife Society, pp. 79–85; Riseborough, Robert W. 1978. "Pesticides and Other Toxicants." In Howard P. Brokaw, ed., *Wildlife and America.* Washington, D.C.: Government Printing Office, pp. 218–236; and National Wildlife Federation. 1980. "Toxics and Wildlife," *National Wildlife,* p. 32-D.

mental toxicants affecting, or potentially affecting, wildlife result directly from the rapid increase in energy, forest production, and agriculture. For example, acidic precipitation, environmental radioactivity, petroleum pollution, and thermal pollution result from our efforts at energy production; herbicides and pesticides are increasingly used in silviculture; and America's monocultural practices in agriculture encourage and frequently require increased uses of herbicides and pesticides. Such practices either bring direct wildlife mortality or sublethal effects, such as reduced vigor, modified behavior, retarded growth, and impaired reproductive function. *Any long-term solution to solving pollution-wildlife problems will ultimately require developing ecologically responsible methods of harnessing energy, producing timber, and growing crops* (World Resources Institute and the International Institute for Environment and Development 1986).

ENDANGERED SPECIES' CHARACTERISTICS

Natural-Related Characteristics

Some animal species have *natural* peculiarities that make them more susceptible to extinction. Animals that have a low reproductive rate *(low biotic potential)* are very vulnerable to storms and diseases (Owen 1985). The female California condor, for example, lays only a single egg every other year. Since there are only about 20 females left in the world, the loss of a single egg is critical to the survival of this species. Understandably, there was a public outcry in 1980 when a condor chick died of heart failure and shock while being handled by an inexperienced field worker as part of a captive-breeding program for the preservation of the species. The female blue whale (*Balaenoptera musculus*) cannot bear more than one calf every two years, and most females bear no more than two offspring by age 10. In addition to its low biotic potential, the blue whale also has another problem—its large size. Whales, like elephants and bisons, are *large and visible,* thus making them easy targets for hunters.

Stenophagous animals, ones that maintain a very *specialized diet,* are also prone to becoming extinct, since their food source can be easily eliminated by natural or human action (Owen 1985). The destruction of eucalyptus trees, whether by blight, drought, forest fires, or human removal, would result in extensive koala mortality since these animals eat only the leaves and buds of this particular tree. Not only does the blue whale have a low reproductive rate *and* its large size and visibility going against it, it *also* has a very specialized diet—shrimplike krill found in polar upwelling zones.

Nonadaptive behavior is a further characteristic of species susceptible to extermination or extinction. Once again, the blue whale can be used as an example; its nonadaptive behavioral characteristic is its tendency to congregate in Antarctic feeding grounds, thus making it easy for whale hunters to spot and kill it. A Hawaiian bird, the wedge-tailed shearwater, experiences high mortality as a result of its attraction to illuminated lampposts along island roadways. A more dangerous game is that which is played by the redheaded woodpecker, which likes to race automobiles, flying directly in front of the grill and often succumbing to the roar of the automobile (Ehrenfeld 1970, Owen 1985).

The red wolf may be one of the next mammals to become extinct as a result of **genetic assimilation—**interbreeding with another species. As the coyote *(Canis latrans)* increases its territory, it is crossing with the nearly extinct red wolf *(Canis niger)* to form coyote-red wolf hybrids. If this hybridization continues, it is possible that the purebred red wolf will fade in numbers, thus eliminating the species *Canis niger* (Lovejoy 1976, Owen 1985).

Human-Related Characteristics

Certain animals are also very susceptible to extermination or extinction due to *human-related factors* (Miller and Botkin 1974, Terborgh 1974). The peregrine falcon is highly susceptible to pollution and pesticides; the elephant ranks high as a game animal; the blue whale has a high economic value for its oil; and the Carolina parakeet was exterminated for causing damage to crops. Predator animals, such as the lion and the wolf, that feed on livestock or game animals are also highly susceptible to human wrath and revenge.

CONCLUSION

Less than 10 percent of all mammals (Ehrenfeld 1970) and plants (Smithsonian Institution 1975) are clearly threatened with biological extermination. Yet, there is obviously good reason why conservationists are concerned about the plight of endangered species. Among the species that are likely to disappear next, because of natural causes, human-related causes, or other causes, are those listed by Thomas Lovejoy in Table 8-4. If the red wolf and other animals are to remain viable species on Earth, human action in the form of *wildlife resource management* may be necessary to prevent further deterioration of animal numbers and habitats. We turn to this subject in the following chapter.

TABLE 8-4

Species that are likely to disappear next

BIRDS	MAMMALS	REPTILES AND AMPHIBIANS
Kakapo (New Zealand owl parrot)	Red wolf	Round Island boa (two species) (Indian Ocean)
Puerto Rican parrot	Golden lion marmoset (Brazil)	Gavial (India)
Chatham Island robin (New Zealand)	Pigmy hog (Assam)	Orinoco crocodile (Panama)
Blewitt's owl (India)	Mesopotamia fallow deer	Israeli painted frog (Panama)
	Hispid hare (Assam)	Golden frog (Panama)
	Yellow-tailed woolly monkey (Peru)	
	Pileated gibbon (Malaysia)	

Source: Lovejoy, Thomas, 1976. ''We Must Decide Which Species Will Go Forever,'' *Smithsonian,* July, vol. 7, no. 4, pp. 52–59.

DISCUSSION TOPICS

1. Define the term *wildlife*. What indicators in your community support the idea that the definition of wildlife has broadened in recent years?

2. Ask a few of your friends about the values they associate with wildlife. What values most often occur? Why?

3. Explain, with numerous examples, why there is no such thing as a useless species. Along these lines, why is it that even traditional biologists are getting involved in conservation politics when it comes to saving tropical rain forest ecosystems?

4. Why was the Tellico Dam–snail darter controversy so significant?

5. Discuss the case for *biotic respect*. How does this concept relate to the present-day controversy between animal-rights groups and medical researchers? Furthermore, what about the coyote that devastates domesticated sheep? In your opinion, does it deserve biotic respect?

6. Discuss the pros and cons to sport hunting. In this particular case, how do aesthetic and intellectual values come into conflict with economic and practical values?

7. Define habitat. List and explain its five major components. What is the difference between protection and concealment?

8. What do omnivores and animals classified as stenophagous have in common? Relate your discussion to the probability of extinction.

9. List several reasons why the artificial feeding of wildlife can actually be detrimental.

10. List and discuss three sources of water for wildlife.

11. What is the difference between home range and territory? Can you provide some local examples of where urban developers ignored the home range or territory of certain species?

12. Define and illustrate the relationship between biotic potential, environmental resistance, and carrying capacity.

13. Discuss the three classifications of wildlife populations. How might this information be useful to environmentalists, wildlife resource managers, and urban planners?

14. Since 99.5 percent of all wildlife species have become extinct, why should anyone be concerned about preserving the remaining wildlife species? Should an urban dweller be less concerned about the preservation of wildlife species than a rural dweller? Why?

15. Using examples from your own community, discuss the eight major factors that cause animal extinction. In your area, what factor seems to have the greatest impact on wildlife deterioration or extinction?

16. Discuss the natural peculiarities that some animals have that make them more susceptible to extinction.

17. Some animals are also susceptible to extermination due to human-related factors. Explain and provide examples of these factors.

READINGS

ALLEN, DURWARD L. 1962. *Our Wildlife Legacy*. New York: Funk & Wagnalls. Good historical account of pest and predator problems in the United States.

ARNOLD, DEAN E. 1979. "Environmental Pollution: Effects on Fish and Wildlife Management." In Richard D. Teague and Eugene Decker, eds., *Wildlife Conservation: Principles and Practices*, pp. 79–85. Washington, D.C.: The Wildlife Society. Good summary.

BANDY, P. J., and R. D. TABLER. 1974. "Forest and Wildlife Management: Conflict and Coordination." In H. C. Black, ed., *Wildlife and Forest Management in the Pacific Northwest*. Corvallis, Oreg.: School of Forestry, Oregon State University. Excellent description of wildlife disruption associated with timber harvesting.

BEAN, MICHAEL J. 1978. "Federal Wildlife Law." In Howard P. Brokaw, ed., *Wildlife and America*, pp. 279–289. Washington, D.C.: Government Printing Office. Good historical analysis.

BROKAW, HOWARD P. 1978. *Wildlife and America*. Washington, D.C.: Government Printing Office. Important book.

BURGER, GEORGE V. 1978. "Agriculture and Wildlife." In Howard P. Brokaw, ed., *Wildlife and America*, pp. 89–107. Washington, D.C.: Government Printing Office. Good summary.

BUTTERY, ROBERT F., and PAUL W. SHIELDS. 1975. "Range Management Practices and Bird Habitat Values." In *Proc. Symp. Mgt. Forest and Range Habitats for Nongame Birds*. Forest Service General Technical Report WO-1, pp. 183–189. Washington, D.C.: U.S. Department of Agriculture. Informative discussion.

CAIN, STANLEY A. 1972. *Predator Control—1971: Report to the Council on Environmental Quality and the Department of the Interior by the Advisory Committee on Predator Control*. Washington, D.C.: Government Printing Office. Important government report.

CAIN, STANLEY A. 1978. "Predator and Pest Control." In Howard P. Brokaw, ed., *Wildlife and America*, pp. 379–395. Washington, D.C.: Government Printing Office. Excellent discussion.

CLARKE, C. H. D. 1979. "Hunting and Fishing Values and

Concepts.'' In R. D. Teague and Eugene Decker, eds., *Wildlife Conservation Principles and Practices*, pp. 7–10. Washington, D.C.: The Wildlife Society. Brief overview.

COURTENAY, W. R., JR. 1970. ''Florida's Walking Catfish,'' *Ward's Natural Science Bulletin*, vol. 10. no. 69, pp. 1, 6. Brief discussion of a classic example of ''accidental introduction.''

COURTENAY, W. R., JR. 1978. ''The Introduction of Exotic Organisms.'' In Howard P. Brokaw, ed., *Wildlife and America*, pp. 237–252. Washington, D.C.: Government Printing Office. Excellent summary.

DASMANN, RAYMOND F. 1984. *Environmental Conservation*. 5th ed. New York: Wiley. Classic introductory college textbook on environmental management.

DASMANN, RAYMOND F. 1981. *Wildlife Biology*. 2d ed. New York: Wiley. A well-known book in its field.

DUNLAP, THOMAS R. 1988. *Saving America's Wildlife*. Princeton, N.J.: Princeton University Press. Historical account of how animal ecology and management developed as a scientific discipline.

ECKHOLM, ERIK. 1978. *Disappearing Species: The Social Challenge*. Washington, D.C.: Worldwatch Institute. Detailed account of wildlife extinction.

EHRENFELD, D. W. 1970. *Biological Conservation*. New York: Holt, Rinehart & Winston. Important book.

EHRLICH, PAUL, and ANNE EHRLICH. 1981. *Extinction*. New York: Random House. Excellent discussion of the causes of wildlife extinction.

FICHTER, GEORGE S. 1980. ''Too Many Blackbirds?'' *National Wildlife*, April–May, pp. 33–36. Interesting discussion of birds that are considered by many to be pests.

FISHER, J., et al. 1969. *Wildlife in Danger*. New York: Viking Press. Historical account of animal extinction.

GEORGE, JOHN L. 1966. ''Farmers and Birds.'' In Alfred Stefferud, ed., *Birds in Our Lives*, pp. 396–403. Washington, D.C.: U.S. Bureau of Sports Fisheries and Wildlife. Good discussion of birds and American agriculture.

KING, W. 1968. ''As a Consequence Many Will Die,'' *Florida Naturalist*, vol. 41, no. 3, pp. 99–103, 120. Interesting account of the giant African snail and its accidental introduction to the Hawaiian Islands.

KLEIN, DAVID R. 1977. ''The Ethics of Hunting.'' In John Hendee et al., eds., *Principles of Wildlife Management*. Washington, D.C.: Government Printing Office. Good summary.

KOOPOWITZ, HAROLD, and HILARY KAYE. 1983. *Plant Extinctions: A Global Crisis*. Washington, D.C.: Stone Wall Press. Documentation of this most misunderstood threat to our planet with keys to plant conservation.

LAYCOCK, G. 1966. *The Alien Animals*. Garden City, N.Y.: Natural History Press. Excellent overview of the problems of introduced species.

LEYDET, FRANCOIS. 1977. *The Coyote: Defiant Songdog of the West*. San Francisco: Chronicle Books. Readable account of problems associated with coyotes and predator control.

LOVEJOY, THOMAS. 1976. ''We Must Decide Which Species Will Go Forever,'' *Smithsonian*, July, vol. 7, no. 4, pp. 52–59. Includes interesting discussion of genetic assimilation.

MCNULTY, FAITH. 1971. *Must They Die? The Strange Case of the Prairie Dog and the Black-Footed Ferret*. New York: Doubleday. Detailed study.

MILLER, G. TYLER, JR. 1982. *Living in the Environment*. 3d ed. Belmont, Calif.: Wadsworth. Outstanding introductory college textbook on environmental management. Also see later editions.

MILLER, R. S., and D. B. BOTKIN. 1974. ''Endangered Species: Models and Predictions,'' *American Scientist*, vol. 62, no. 2, pp. 172–181. Good discussion of wildlife extermination or extinction due to human-related factors.

MYERS, NORMAN. 1983. *A Wealth of Wild Species*. Boulder, Colo.: Westview Press. Comprehensive discussion of the direct economic benefit that humanity derives from wild species.

NATIONAL ACADEMY OF SCIENCES. 1975. *Nonhuman Primates: Usage and Availability for Biomedical Programs*. Washington, D.C.: National Academy of Sciences. Good discussion of the effects of biomedical research on wildlife extinction.

NATIONAL WILDLIFE FEDERATION. 1980. ''Toxics and Wildlife,'' *National Wildlife*, November, p. 32-D. Readable account.

OWEN, OLIVER S. 1985. *National Resource Conservation: An Ecological Approach*. 4th ed. New York: Macmillan. Contains two outstanding chapters on wildlife extinction and management.

PRINGLE, LAURENCE. 1977. *The Controversial Coyote: Predation, Politics, and Ecology*. New York: Harcourt Brace Jovanovich. Detailed study.

PRINGLE, LAURENCE. 1975. ''Each Antagonist in Coyote Debate is Partially Right,'' *Smithsonian*, vol. 5, no. 2, pp. 74–81. Interesting discussion of the coyote controversy.

REIGER, GEORGE. 1978. ''Hunting and Trapping in the New World.'' In Howard P. Brokaw, ed., *Wildlife and America*, pp. 42–52. Washington, D.C.: Government Printing Office. Excellent discussion.

RIPLEY, S. DILLON, and THOMAS E. LOVEJOY. 1978. ''Threatened and Endangered Species.'' In Howard P. Brokaw, ed., *Wildlife and America*, pp. 365–378. Washington, D.C.: Government Printing Office. Good summary.

RISEBROUGH, ROBERT W. 1978. ''Pesticides and Other Toxicants.'' In Howard P. Brokaw, ed., *Wildlife and America*, pp. 218–236. Washington, D.C.: Government Printing Office, Excellent overview of pollution effects on fish and wildlife.

ROSA, NICHOLAS. 1976. ''Managing the Seals: To What End?'' *Oceans*, September–October, vol. 9, no. 5, pp. 57–59. Useful discussion of the harp seal controversy.

SCHEFFER, VICTOR B. 1974. *A Voice for Wildlife*. New York: Scribner. Good discussion of wildlife extinction due to human activities.

SCHORGER, A. W. 1973. *The Passenger Pigeon*. Norman, Okla.: Oklahoma University Press. Historical account of the extinction of the passenger pigeon.

SMITH, ROBERT LEO, ed. 1976. *The Ecology of Man: An Ecosys-*

tem Approach. New York: Harper & Row. Holistic discussion of wildlife and cultural evolution.

SMITHSONIAN INSTITUTION. 1975. *Report on Endangered and Threatened Plant Species of the U.S.* Washington, D.C.: Government Printing Office. Important document.

STEARNS, F. 1972. "The City as Habitat for Wildlife and Man." In T. Detwyler and M. Marcus, eds., *Urbanization and Environment.* Belmont, Calif.: Duxbury Press. Excellent chapter about wildlife within cities.

TELEKI, GEZA, and LORI BALDWIN. 1975. "Breeding Programs Aim to Keep This a Planet of the Apes," *Smithsonian,* January, vol. 5, no. 10, pp. 76–81. Interesting discussion of captive breeding programs.

TERBORGH, JOHN. 1974. "Preservation of Natural Diversity: The Problem of Extinction Prone Species," *BioScience,* vol. 24, pp. 715–722. Good discussion of wildlife extinction related to human factors.

TUAN, YI-FU. 1984. *Dominance and Affection: The Making of Pets.* New Haven, Conn.: Yale University Press. A provocative book about the psychological impulse to "make pets."

WAGNER, RICHARD H. 1971. *Environment and Man.* New York: Norton. Excellent introductory college textbook on environmental quality planning.

WORLD RESOURCES INSTITUTE AND THE INTERNATIONAL INSTITUTE FOR ENVIRONMENT AND DEVELOPMENT. 1986. *World Resources 1986: An Assessment of the Resource Base that Supports the Global Economy.* New York: Basic Books. Comprehensive survey of global resources.

WYNNE-EDWARDS, V. C. 1964. "Population Control in Animals," *Scientific American Reprint,* August, pp. 1–8. Fascinating discussion of natural population controls within wildlife species.

ZISWILER, V. 1967. *Extinct and Vanishing Animals.* New York: Springer-Verlag. Global and evolutionary picture of wildlife extinction.

9

WILDLIFE RESOURCE MANAGEMENT

Introduction

Wildlife Problems
  and Management Strategies

Prospects for the Future

Action for Wildlife

The long fight to save wild beauty represents democracy at its best. It requires citizens to practice the hardest of virtues—self-restraint.

Edwin Way Teale

INTRODUCTION

Wildlife resource management may be defined as the manipulation of habitats, wildlife populations, and people for the dual purpose of serving the best interest of (1) the animals themselves and (2) the economic, social, and cultural goals of people (Giles 1969). The science of wildlife management is based on the fundamental principles of ecology, which are based on the interactions within natural communities of living organisms, plant and animal successions, and wildlife population dynamics.

Putting this *science* of wildlife management into practice is the work and *art* of many specialists, including social scientists and humanists. But primarily, it is the duty of the *wildlife resource manager*—a professionally trained individual who may gather data through research, apply scientifically sound solutions to wildlife species or habitat problems, conduct on-the-ground management programs, enforce

regulations, and administer programs and properties. Their task, essentially, is to maintain viable wildlife populations, help prevent excessive damage by wildlife that causes economic hardship, and satisfy the public desire for abundant and diversified wildlife. This is not an easy task, since society is riddled with conflicting interest groups—hunters, bird-watchers, farmers, backpackers, and public safety officers. Dense flocks of red-winged blackbirds, for example, may thrill the nature photographer but disturb the rice farmer whose fields the birds use as feeding habitat. The wildlife manager must, therefore, strive to *balance* these conflicting interests.

In a broader sense, wildlife management entails the search for and application of ways to minimize the causes of wildlife extinction. Historically, American biologists, conservationists, environmentalists, and legislators have sought methods to solve or curtail the problems for wildlife that result from restricted and modified habitat; from direct hunting by humans; from introduced species; from controlling pests and predators; from the activities of pets; from the work of zoos and scientific researchers; and from pollution.

Several trends can be discerned by looking at America's history of wildlife conservation (Table 9-1). First, there is a trend from managing *game* species to protecting *nongame* endangered species. Second, there is a movement from an interest in *single-species* protection to an interest in total *biome* preservation. Third, there is a greater concern with pollution's devastating effects. Fourth, there is an increasing role on the part of the federal government in wildlife protection and enforcement. Finally, there is an ever broadening definition of wildlife. Over the years, several wildlife resource management techniques have been devised, such as protective laws, habitat acquisition, and habitat development. We now turn to look at these strategies in more detail.

WILDLIFE PROBLEMS AND MANAGEMENT STRATEGIES

Coping with Restricted and Modified Habitat

Habitat Acquisition and Preservation. If the encroachment of urbanization and agriculture upon wildlife habitat is the major cause of wildlife extinction in America, then slowing the rate of habitat elimination is of prime importance in wildlife preservation. Efforts towards preserving habitat can be divided between the public and private sectors. Management in *public lands*, in turn, can be further divided into federal efforts and state efforts, as well as the efforts of regions, counties, cities, and smaller communities. The United States contains some 315 million ha (778 million acres) of public lands, and if it were not for these public lands many species of American wildlife would not have survived—the whooping crane (Aransas National Wildlife Refuge in Texas); the bald eagle (Chippewa National Forest in Minnesota); and the grizzly bear (Yellowstone National Park in Wyoming and Glacier Park in Montana). *Private lands*, however, account for the majority of the land in the United States, hence, the proper management of these privately owned lands is critical to wildlife habitat. Unfortunately, wildlife habitat on private lands is much more vulnerable, since private lands often change ownership when economic incentives enter into the picture; that is; preserving wildlife often takes a back seat to building subdivisions, planting rice, or cutting timber.

Approximately 95 percent of all *public lands* in the United States are federally owned. Four principal agencies administer these lands: the National Park Service, the U.S. Forest Service, the Bureau of Land Management, and the U.S. Fish and Wildlife Service. The Department of Defense, the Water and Power Resources Service (Bureau of Reclamation), the Bureau of Indian Affairs, the Atomic Energy Commission (Nuclear Regulatory Commission and the Energy Research and Development Administration), and the Tennessee Valley Authority are also involved in some form of wildlife management, but to a much lesser extent.

Our *national parks* not only conserve unique natural or historic sites, they also protect wildlife and wildlife habitats. Also administered by the Park Service are our country's *national monuments*—areas of lesser scenic uniqueness, but nonetheless important as wildlife habitats. Some Park Service policies that relate directly to wildlife include enforcing hunting and fishing restrictions; encouraging native species; restricting the artificial feeding of wildlife; keeping people on trails and at designated campsites and away from critical nesting or breeding areas; and, more recently, encouraging less use of the private automobile and other polluting devices within park territories. But, more important than any specific policy, the national park or the national monument is a major protective device to *lock up* land that might otherwise be encroached upon by developers, agriculturalists, or other private interests. Despite this obvious benefit, however, a few wildlife specialists maintain that, with the exception of Alaska's parklands, national parks make rather poor wildlife habitats in the United States.

The growth in acreage of our *national forests* can further increase the protection of lands from human encroachment, if *properly managed* (Clawson 1974, 1975; Siderits 1975). In theory, the U.S. Forest Service is *supposed* to practice a policy of *multiple use*, which means conservation of the national forest for water, recreational uses, wilderness, grazing, and wildlife, as well as for timber. However, with outside pressure to increase timber yields from our national forests, the Forest Service sometimes adopts practices that are detrimental to wildlife populations—practices such as monoculture planting; clear-cutting; pesticide spraying; and mining, which contributes to the toxic pollution of streams and lakes, disrupts drainage systems, removes vegetation, and encourages soil erosion and destruction. Despite some detrimental practices, however, keeping lands in a national forest status is probably more protective to wildlife than opening the land to private ownership and exploitation.

TABLE 9-1

Historical highlights in American fish and wildlife conservation

DATE	LEGISLATION OR EVENT	KEY POINTS	HELPED RELIEVE WILDLIFE EXTERMINATION PROBLEM(S)[a]					
			(1)	(2)	(3)	(4)	(5)	(6)
1900	Lacey Act	Federal government's first significant step into wildlife law enforcement; made it a federal offense to transport across state lines game taken or possessed in violation of state laws; required a federal permit to import *any* exotic wildlife. Act further strengthened by amendments in 1935		X	X	X	X	
1900–1909	Theodore Roosevelt's administration	148 million acres added to national forests; first 28 national wildlife refuges established	X					
1911	Formation of American Game Protection Association	Predecessor of the American Game Association, which was succeeded in 1936 by the annual North American Wildlife Conferences		X	X			
	Fur Seal Treaty	Treaty between Russia, Japan, Canada; saved the Alaska fur seals from extinction		X				
	Bayne Law	New York state law to prohibit the sale of all game birds, domestic or foreign, which belonged in the same family as species protected in New York state		X	X			
1916–1918	Migratory Bird Treaty and Migratory Bird Treaty Act	Treaty with Canada; protected songbirds; prohibited traffic in all wild migratory birds; established management of migratory game birds; set stage for similar treaties with Mexico, Japan, and USSR		X	X		X	
1925–1948	Period of Aldo Leopold, "Father of American Wildlife Management"	Conducted game surveys; established game policy; convinced SAAMI (Sporting Arms and Ammunition Institute) to establish first doctoral fellowships in the wildlife field; first professor of wildlife management in the United States; published *Game Management* text in 1933; wrote classic *Sand County Almanac* in 1948	X	X	X	X	X	
1929	Migratory Bird Conservation Act (Norbeck-Anderson Act)	Authorized a national system of waterfowl refuges and a Migratory Bird Commission to implement it; funds lacking for acquisition due to onset of Great Depression years	X					
1934–1935	Period of Jay N. "Ding" Darling as chief of the Bureau of Biological Survey	Secured emergency funds for establishing waterfowl refuge system; established Cooperative Wildlife Research Unit program in universities to assure professionally trained wildlife managers; initiated first nationwide effort to census wintering waterfowl; instigated the First North American Wildlife Conference continued today under sponsorship of the Wildlife Management Institute; organized and became first president of National Wildlife Federation; reorganized and revitalized the Bureau of Biological Survey into an effective agency (Fish and Wildlife Ser-	X	X	X	X	X	X

TABLE 9-1 (Continued)

DATE	LEGISLATION OR EVENT	KEY POINTS	HELPED RELIEVE WILDLIFE EXTERMINATION PROBLEM(S)[a]					
			(1)	(2)	(3)	(4)	(5)	(6)
		vice); instigated the American Wildlife Institute (later Wildlife Management Institute), which provided financial support to many wildlife conservation activities; influential in establishing the Duck Stamp Act, which provided money for acquiring waterfowl habitat from the sale of mandatory duck stamps to hunters; helped get through Congress the Fish and Wildlife Coordination Act, which required that federal, state, and other agencies cooperate in increasing wildlife populations and access the effects of pollution on wildlife						
1937	Pittman-Robertson Act (Federal Aid to Wildlife Restoration Act)	Provided a new source of funds for wildlife research and development from a tax on firearms and ammunition, resulting in nationwide upgrading of employment and professionalism in wildlife field	X	X	X	X	X	
1961	Wetlands Loan Act (and Wetlands Inspection Act of 1962)	Established loans from future duck stamp funds for acquiring and protecting small wetlands (potholes), which are too small to be administered as National Wildlife Refuges	X					
1964	Wilderness Act	Brought much wilderness lands (and its wildlife habitats) under federal jurisdiction and protection	X	X	X	X	X	X
1966	Endangered Species Conservation Act	Predecessor to 1973 Endangered Species Act which gave federal government far greater authority, responsibility, and scope; see 1973 Act	X	X	X	X	X	X
1968	Scenic and Wild Rivers Act	Preserved free-flowing streams (and riparian habitats) from further physical encroachment or development	X	X	X	X	X	X
1969	National Environmental Policy Act (NEPA)	Not directly concerned with wildlife management, but has related purposes: to promote efforts which will prevent or eliminate damage to the environment and biosphere; to create conditions under which humans and nature can exist in productive harmony; implies that proposed federal actions will be examined and understood *before* actions are taken; EIRs (Environmental Impact Statements) must be written	X	X	X	X	X	X
1972	Marine Mammal Protection Act	Intent was to conserve animals such as whales, polar bears, walruses, sea otters, and seals; established a moratorium on hunting or importing the marine mammals; encouraged the active participation of the public in implementation process; first broad federal legislation to preempt state authority for the management of resident wildlife	X	X			X	X
	Marine Protection Research and Sanctuaries Act	Required that the Environmental Protection Agency issue permits before material could be dumped into coastal or ocean waters by any U.S. citizen; gave Com-	X					X

(*continued*)

TABLE 9-1 (Continued)

DATE	LEGISLATION OR EVENT	KEY POINTS	HELPED RELIEVE WILDLIFE EXTERMINATION PROBLEM(S)[a]					
			(1)	(2)	(3)	(4)	(5)	(6)
	(Ocean Dumping Act)	merce Department authority to create sanctuaries "for the purpose of preserving or restoring . . . areas for their conservation, recreational, ecological, or aesthetic values"						
1973	Endangered Species Act	Mandated close cooperation with states; authorized federal financial aid to states for endangered species programs; extended endangered species protection to plants as well as animals; required protection of *threatened* species as well as *endangered* species (including hunting and killing, as well as selling, exporting, or importing of their hides, pelts, or feathers); prohibited any private, state, or federal project that would jeopardize endangered species or destroy or modify critical habitats; encouraged public participation in the implementation of act; further reduced the rights of states in wildlife matters	X	X	X	X	X	X
1974	Sikes Act	Reinforced the authority of states to manage resident wildlife on certain federal lands (Bureau of Land Management; Forest Service; National Aeronautics and Space Administration; Energy Research and Development Administration)	X	X	X	X	X	X
1976	Fisheries Conservation and Management Act	Gave authority to eight regional fisheries management councils to formulate plans and programs for the regulation of fishing in their respective jurisdictions, subject to the approval of the Secretary of Commerce (federal government has last say, thus again preempting states' rights). Councils may set seasons, catch limits, gear limits, size limits; define fishing areas; and restrain amount of fishing effort	X	X				

Source: Compiled from Swanson, Gustav A. 1979. "Historical Highlights in American Wildlife Conservation." In Richard D. Teague and Eugene Decker, eds., *Wildlife Conservation: Principles and Practices.* Washington, D.C.: The Wildlife Society, pp. 3–6; and Dingell, John D., and Potter, Frank M., Jr. 1978. "Federal Initiatives in Wildlife Management." In Howard P. Brokaw, ed., *Wildlife and America.* Washington, D.C.: Government Printing Office, pp. 302–309.

[a](1) Restricted or modified habitat; (2) Direct hunting by humans; (3) Introduced species; (4) Pest and predator control; (5) Pets, zoos, and scientific research; (6) Pollution and other sources.

BLM lands refer to those public lands administered by the Bureau of Land Management (BLM). The BLM administers more public land than all the other federal land agencies combined. Although these public lands help protect wildlife habitat from encroachment, historically grazing and mining have had a higher priority than wildlife protection and management in BLM policy. However, with the passage of the 1976 BLM Organic Act, this public agency must now administer a multiple-use policy wherein wildlife and other resources on BLM lands must receive greater attention. Nearly half of the fees received for grazing on the public lands are now earmarked for correcting the problems of overgrazing—the most serious threat to wildlife on BLM lands.

Our *national wildlife refuges* are perhaps the public lands most intensively managed with wildlife in mind. The *National Wildlife Refuge System*—a collection of lands and waters selected for their value to America's wildlife populations, particularly migratory birds and rare mammals—involves over 400 refuges totaling 14 million ha (34 million acres), and the system is still growing (Figure 9-1). Three federal acts laid the groundwork for the system: (1) the 1929 Migratory

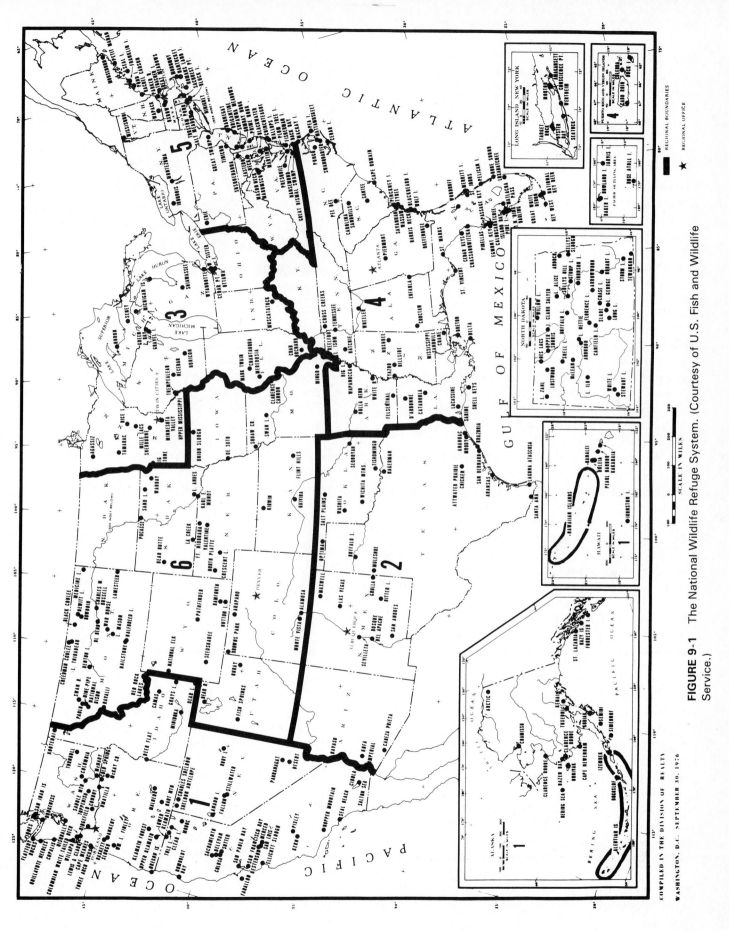

FIGURE 9-1 The National Wildlife Refuge System. (Courtesy of U.S. Fish and Wildlife Service.)

Bird Conservation Act, which provided authority for the purchase of lands needed for migratory bird refuges; (2) the 1956 Fish and Wildlife Act, which authorized the acquisition of refuge lands for the conservation and protection of all kinds of wildlife; and (3) the 1966 Endangered Species Preservation Act, which provided for refuges to protect vanishing wildlife and gave official recognition to the national wildlife refuges as a system. Although many more acres of wetlands (marshes, swamps, lakes, and streams) must be added to the national chain of refuges if water-loving species are to survive as a basic resource, the United States can take pride in knowing that it has the largest system of wildlife habitats *in the world*.

These wildlife refuges have brought an extended life to certain rare and endangered species: the whooping crane (Aransas Refuge in Texas); the trumpeter swan (Red Rock Lakes Refuge in Montana); the key deer (Key Deer Refuge in Florida); the desert bighorn sheep (Cabeza Prieta and Kofa Game Refuges in Arizona and the Desert Wildlife Range in Nevada); the albatross and other oceanic birds, the Laysan duck, the Laysan and Nihoa finches, the Nihoa millerbird, and the Hawaiian monk seal (Hawaiian Islands Refuge).

Americans often think of wildlife refuges as simply places where some government agency is trying to protect the land for wildlife or where the lonely private hunter waits patiently in a duck blind to shoot a favorite species of game bird. Wildlife refuges, however, provide many more services to the public—*recreational facilities* (hiking, sightseeing, bird-watching, biking, and sometimes boating and swimming); *farmland* (the farmer plants specified crops for migratory birds on refuge lands in return for a share of the harvest); *grazing land* (forage is provided for ranchers in times of local shortage); *timber land* (management is for optimum wildlife benefits rather than for maximum timber production); and even *energy resources* (oil and gas production, which, however, is becoming more controversial as oil, gas, and other mineral operations become more complex and challenging). These services to the public, in turn, translate into dollars for local economies, which share in the revenues from grazing, haying, and the selling of timber, and oil, gas, and other mineral products.

Perhaps the greatest service of all to the public is the National Wildlife Refuge System's role in preserving areas to be used for *environmental education*—places where the nation's citizens can observe natural ecosystems, the interplay of wildlife species, and the ways that humans can live in harmony with other creatures on this planet (Figure 9-2). Funding for the maintenance of existing areas and for the purchase of

FIGURE 9-2 San Francisco Bay National Wildlife Refuge. (Photo by author.)

new wildlife refuges must be increased so that environmental interpretation programs, scientific research, and wildlife preservation can continue into perpetuity.

Several federal agencies, such as the U.S. Forest Service, the Bureau of Land Management, and the U.S. Fish and Wildlife Service, also manage what are known as *natural areas*—areas of land or water that have essentially retained (or recovered) their primitive conditions, for example, undisturbed natural estuaries, alpine meadows, prairies, and streams. Natural areas, in turn, may also include what are referred to as *natural heritage areas* or *natural history areas*. These areas may include areas that are *not* natural but deserve special management because of some significant natural feature, whether it be archaeological, geological, or biotic (e.g., an endangered species of plant or animal) (Thom 1979).

The federal government is most noted for its management of *wilderness* natural areas—usually large areas (several thousand or more acres) where natural forces predominate or can be restored. The Wilderness Act of 1964 greatly increased the protection of certain natural areas, as did the Land and Water Conservation Fund Act of 1965, the Fish and Wildlife Conservation Act of 1968, the National Environmental Policy Act of 1969, the Endangered Species Conservation Acts of 1969 and 1973, and the Resource Planning Act of 1974. The Wilderness Act of 1964 allowed Congress to classify roadless tracts of 2024 ha (5000 acres) or more in the national forests, national parks, BLM lands, and fish and wildlife refuges as wilderness areas, thus making them part of the *National Wilderness Preservation System*. (See Chapter 10 for further details.) In preserving wilderness, of course, one also preserves the wildlife species that are associated with or dependent upon the land, water, and nutrients within the habitat.

Hendee and Schoenfeld (1979) identify three major types of wilderness wildlife: (1) wilderness-dependent wildlife, (2) wilderness-associated wildlife, and (3) common wildlife found in wilderness. *Wilderness-dependent wildlife* requires wild, extensive, and undisturbed habitats for survival (e.g., the grizzly bear and the mountain caribou in Idaho's Panhandle National Forest). *Wilderness-associated wildlife* includes species that are indeed associated with wilderness habitats or are merely *perceived* by humans to be associated with a given habitat (e.g., the ptarmigan in the high alpine country of western wilderness areas). *Common wildlife found in wilderness* are those species that are found in wilderness areas but also live in many neighboring, more modified landscapes. These species are neither dependent upon wilderness nor associated with human perception with wilderness. Although these three categories are not always clear-cut (e.g., grizzly bears range over nonwilderness areas of Montana as well; eagles occasionally occur on heavily grazed western ranges), categorizing wilderness wildlife can be an important management aid (Table 9-2).

State governments, like the federal government, own and administer their own natural areas, forests, and parks, which are significant wildlife habitats. State natural areas (sometimes called natural areas, scientific areas, nature preserves, or wildlife management areas) are usually administered by a state conservation department. New York, for example, has numerous tracts of state-owned lands designated as wildlife management areas. Since there are wildlife management areas in 36 of New York's 62 counties, one does not have to travel far to enjoy these wildlife lands (Dickinson 1980). Fortunately, most of the states have initiated similar natural area programs to preserve wildlife habitats that are either too small or are not considered significant enough for the federal government to protect.

Despite the many accomplishments of wildlife conservation on public lands, three major problems are increasing on these federal and state lands: (1) *competition for resources*, (2) *underfunding*, and (3) *polarization*. Economic pressures upon the public lands are mounting; more timber, mineral, and grazing lands are in demand. At the same time, financial support for land acquisition, maintenance, and wildlife work on these public lands is shrinking. Furthermore, there is a growing polarization between the *consuming users* (hunters and fishermen) and the *nonconsuming users* (bird-watchers, hikers, and photographers). Conservationists (including hunters), however, must remain united if wildlife is to have any chance to be protected. As habitat acquisition of public lands and maintenance on public lands become more difficult, the private sector will play a greater role in wildlife preservation.

Many *private lands* are owned and administered for the public good by such nonprofit private organizations as the Nature Conservancy, the Trust for Public Land, the Izaak Walton League, and many others. Private organizations that acquire and currently manage natural areas have several important conservation roles (Table 9-3). Their primary role is to "get government rolling," since new government programs in any field are seldom initiated from within government. Government programs are fostered because of needs perceived and articulated by one or more groups of organized citizenry. In other words, government *rarely creates* new programs; it *merely reacts* to the citizen outcry. This fact should give assurances to the student and the average citizen who falsely believe that you cannot change government. You can change government policy!

There are numerous techniques that private citizens and organizations can use to help ward off wildlife habitat loss (Table 9-4). They range from the least protective (merely informing a developer of the existence of natural areas and wildlife habitats through the use of an environmental impact statement) to outright purchase of the land that is to be protected (e.g., fee simple acquisition).

The private organization that has the best track record at land acquisition and consequent protection of ecosystem diversity is the Nature Conservancy. It is a national, nonprofit, membership-sponsored conservation organization. Over 1.5 million acres (660 preserves in 49 states, the Virgin Islands, Canada, and the Caribbean) have been preserved through the efforts of the Conservancy and its members since the organization was formed in 1950. To safeguard natural areas and wildlife, the Conservancy (1) identifies the most important areas, through its natural area identification program; (2) acquires land, either through gift, purchase, or by assisting government, (3) provides long-term stewardship for hundreds of Conservancy-owned preserves (the Conservancy retains ownership of a majority of its projects, and other areas are conveyed to public or private conservation groups or educational institutions for ownership and management); and (4) strives to increase public awareness and education of the need to safeguard natural areas.

Habitat Improvement. Once a wildlife habitat has been acquired and protected from urban en-

TABLE 9-2

Wilderness wildlife management

STEPS	OBJECTIVES	GUIDELINES
1. Inventory all *wilderness-dependent species* in the designated wilderness area	To seek natural distributions, numbers, and interactions of indigenous species of wildlife	Consider wildlife as but one component of the composite wilderness resource
2. Inventory characteristics of the natural habitat on which they depend	To the greatest extent possible, allow natural processes to control wilderness ecosystems and their wildlife	Recognize the necessity for wilderness management because nature alone is powerless to prevent the impact of ever-present human influences
3. Assign a *high* wilderness management priority to monitoring and preserving these natural conditions	To keep wildlife wild, their behavior altered as little as possible by human influence	Plan only for the actions necessary to meet wilderness wildlife objectives, in management plans prepared for each individual wilderness area
4. Inventory *wilderness-associated species* and their habitats. Assign *moderate* wilderness management priority	To permit viewing, hunting, and fishing where such activities are biologically sound, legal, and conducted in the spirit of the wilderness experience	Follow a principle of nondegradation in area management; that is, strive to prevent further degradation of the naturalness present in individual areas, but seek restoration of naturalness in areas where it is below a minimum standard
5. Inventory *common species*. Assign *lowest* wilderness management priority	Whenever appropriate, to favor the preservation of rare, threatened, and endangered species dependent on wilderness conditions	Allow natural processes to shape wilderness habitat, encouraging fire and avoiding predator and plant disease controls
	Within the constraints of all transcending legislation applicable to wildlife in a particular wilderness, to seek the least possible degradation of the qualities that make for wilderness—naturalness, solitude, and absence of permanent visible evidence of human activity	Where natural processes must be supplemented or simulated, employ the minimum tool necessary to do the job
		Insulate wilderness areas with compatible management practices on adjacent lands
		Manage for indigenous wild plant and animal species
		Regulate user impact in keeping with carrying capacity principles, but not in such a way as to degrade wilderness experiences
		Promote a wilderness ethic among users so that more people can enjoy wilderness while minimizing their impact
		Cultivate hunting and fishing practices that protect the wilderness environment and foster experiences that depend on wilderness conditions
		Step up wilderness wildlife research, using methods that do not degrade the wilderness environment or the experiences of other users
		Accept the practical realities that dictate varying approaches by different agencies on individual areas, but work toward a consistent, if broad, framework for managing wildlife in all wilderness areas

Source: Compiled from Hendee John C., and Schoefeld, Clarence A. 1979. "Wildlife Management for Wilderness." In Richard D. Teague and Eugene Decker, eds., *Wildlife Conservation: Principles and Practices.* Washington, D.C.: The Wildlife Society, pp. 197–203.

TABLE 9-3

Role of private organizations in wildlife protection

| ROLE | EXAMPLES | |
	INSTIGATING PRIVATE ORGANIZATION	ACCOMPLISHMENT
They initiate new government agencies, reform old ones, and start new programs	American Ornithologists' Union	Instrumental in creating the Bureau of Biological Survey, which eventually became the U.S. Fish and Wildlife Service
	American Ornithologists' Union with the Audubon Society	Its leaders persuaded Theodore Roosevelt to create a chain of Federal Bird Reservations, which was later to become a part of the National Wildlife Refuge System
	Izaak Walton League	Conceived the Outdoor Recreation Resources Review Commission that eventually led to the creation of the Land and Water Conservation Fund Act of 1965, which has financed new federal and state wildlife refuges as well as parks and recreation areas
	The Wilderness Society	Conceived the idea of the Wilderness Act, which established the National Wilderness Preservation System
They secure passage of basic laws	National Audubon Society	Drove through legislative bodies laws outlawing feather trade
	New York based conservation organizations	Provided the impetus for Lacey Act of 1900
They sue	Environmental Defense Fund	Instrumental in getting DDT and some other *hard pesticides* (the synthetic organic chemicals that persist in the environment and poison wildlife) banned in the United States; helped stop the Cross-Florida Barge Canal
	Natural Resource Defense Council	Forced U.S. Soil Conservation Service to comply with National Environmental Policy Act to modify or abandon many plans for channelized streams
They conduct educational programs	National Audubon Society	Publications, lectures, workshops, lawsuits, legislative campaigns
	National Wildlife Federation	Periodicals, conservation courses for children and ''conservation summits'' for adults
They raise money and buy land for wildlife	The Nature Conservancy	Since its formation in 1950, it has purchased more than a million acres, most of which have wound up as additions to the National Wildlife Refuge System, the National Parks, or the National Forests
	Izaak Walton League	Acquired key rangelands for the National Elk Range in Wyoming
They conduct or sponsor research	New York Zoological Society	Sponsored field studies in Alaska as early as 1900
	National Wildlife Federation	Since 1957 has contributed $367,000 in research grants to scholars
They apply the power of knowledge	American Ornithologists' Union or the American Society of Mammalogists	Distinguished scholars from these organizations are listened to with respect
They fight local battles to save wildlife	Izaak Walton League, Maryland Chapter	Forced the Army Corps of Engineers and the Washington Suburban Sanitary Commission to replace a flood control structure that for 20 years had blocked anadromous shad and herring from spawning areas on the northwest branch of the Anacostia River
	National Aububon Society, Tacoma Chapter	Stopped proposed highway from going through important marshland

Source: Compiled from Stahr, Elvis J., and Callison, Charles H. 1978. ''The Role of Private Organizations.'' In Howard P. Brokaw, ed., *Wildlife and America.* Washington, D.C.: Government Printing Office, pp. 498–511.

TABLE 9-4

Methods used to give protective status to nature areas and wildlife habitats

TECHNIQUE[a]	DESCRIPTION	BENEFITS	DISADVANTAGES
1. Environmental impact statement analyses	Informs developers of the existence of natural areas so they can be avoided	Helps starve off immanent threats of destruction; developer learns of problem through numerous mechanisms: permit application procedures, public project reviews, public interest lawsuits, public hearings; public planning agencies; private planning corporations; as well as NEPA, EIRs	Lowest level of protection; depends on *voluntary* avoidance of natural areas; short-term profit motive may prevail
2. Notification and management assistance	Informs an owner that he or she has a natural area	Many a natural area has been destroyed because the owner was unaware of its significance; individuals tend to conserve scarce (valuable) resources	Possibility of backfire; landowner may destroy scarce resource (e.g., the oldest tree in the state) to diffuse public interest
3. Registration	Places that natural area on an official *registry* by nonbinding agreement between the owner and the resource agency	Registration formalizes the owner's intent to maintain an area in its natural state; gives an area some protection by public recognition of its significance	Intentional destruction, although rare, can still occur
4. Designation	Normally involves public land and is accomplished by administrative action of the managing agency	Designated areas are recognized and included in management plans, property inventories, and other official documents	Often considered by public land managers to be an extra burden on their time, thus rarely use this protective device
5. Dedication	A legally binding commitment between a public or private owner and the state to permanently set aside a natural area	Gives a very high level of protection even if the area is in private ownership; often cannot be undone without the mutual agreement of several different signatures	Requires complicated state legislation, often in the form of a state natural area systems act
6. Less than fee acquisition	Establishment of a protective agreement such as a conservation development *easement* without actual acquisition by the managing agency	Depending on the arrangement, protection may be permanent as in a dedication; circumvents the problem of trying to financially manage the resource	Public ownership of a natural area (or portions thereof) does not guarantee protection. Such rights might eventually be put to some public use other than conservation
7. Fee simple acquisition	Acquires *full title ownership* of a tract for the purpose of designation or dedication as a natural area	Highest level of protection	There are limits to managing resources—the burden of *financially* maintaining the lands over the long run

Source: Compiled from Jenkins, Robert. 1978. "Habitat Preservation by Private Organizations." In Howard P. Brokaw, ed., *Wildlife and America*. Washington, D.C.: Government Printing Office, pp. 424–426; and Thom, Richard H. 1979. "Natural Areas and Natural Heritage Areas." In Richard D. Teague and Eugene Decker, eds., *Wildlife Conservation: Principles and Practices*. Washington, D.C.: The Wildlife Society, pp. 194–195.
[a]Listed in the approximate order of the level of protection achieved. The higher the number, the greater the level of protection.

croachment or other forms of habitat destruction, it may still need to be manipulated to provide a better habitat for wildlife (Yoakum 1979, Yoakum et al. 1979). The purpose of habitat improvement is twofold: First, it is to provide quality habitat where it has deteriorated or where a specific habitat component (e.g., cover, water, or food) is insufficient; and, second, it is to maintain habitat quality. In most cases, habitat manipulation refers to those methods and

techniques specifically designed by wildlife managers to increase cover, water, and food for wildlife populations. Habitat manipulation is applicable in urban areas as well as in the rural scene, but let us first look at what possibilities exist for habitat manipulation on the farm and on nonfarm rural sites.

Good soil and water conservation practices on the farm *simultaneously* improve wildlife habitat (Table 9-5). In addition, however, *cover* can be improved by

TABLE 9-5

Managing lands to meet wildlife requirements

CROPLAND	PASTURELAND	RANGELAND	WOODLAND
Practices helpful to wildlife:			
Cropping systems that include grass-legume meadows	Grazing within the carrying capacity of the pasture	Proper grazing and salting	Protection from unwanted fire and harmful grazing
Liming and fertilizing	Liming and fertilizing	Watering places for livestock	Selective cutting in small woodlands
Stripcropping	Reseeding, renovating, or overseeding with legumes	Reseeding	Leaving den trees when cutting hardwood timber
Cover crops	Building ponds for livestock water	Construction on walkways in marshy range	Piling brush near the edge of the woods
Stubble-mulch tillage		Partial brush removal	"Release" cutting to increase production of acorns, nuts, and other tree seeds useful for wildlife food
Delaying mowing of headlands, roadsides, and watercourses until after the nesting season			Cutting trees out of woodland borders to increase the growth of shrubs for food and cover
Leaving unharvested one-eighth to one-fourth acre of grain next to good cover			Clear-cutting when harvesting aspen and western conifers
			Seeding clovers and grasses along roads and trails and in woodland openings
Practices harmful to wildlife:			
Clean fall plowing	Uncontrolled burning	Overgrazing	Uncontrolled burning and grazing
Mowing of watercourses and headlands before ground nesting birds have hatched	Overgrazing	Complete brush removal	Cutting of all den trees
Burning of ditchbanks, fence rows, and crop residues	Complete clean mowing early in the season		

Source: Compiled from U.S. Department of Agriculture. 1969. *Making Land Produce Useful Wildlife, Farmers' Bulletin No. 2035.* Washington, D.C.: U.S. Department of Agriculture.

(1) odd areas, (2) woodlots, (3) living fences, (4) wildlife borders, (5) windbreaks, and (6) streambank protection. **Odd areas** are parcels of "waste" land that are already good for wildlife and need to be protected or areas that can be changed into good wildlife habitat. On the farm, odd areas are often the problem areas such as rock exposures, gullies, eroding streambanks, sinkholes, and sand blowouts, but they could also be abandoned roads, railroad rights-of-way, gravel pits, or pieces of good land that are cut off from the rest of a cultivated field by a stream, drainage ditch, or gully (Figure 9-3). Such odd areas, when possible, should be fenced off to prevent cattle from grazing and trampling herbaceous ground cover that might serve as a suitable food source for particular forms of wildlife.

Many farms have "miniforests" or **woodlots** adjacent to them. Proper woodlot management will not only magnify its forestry value, but it will also enhance its value as wildlife habitat. Management of woodlots might entail selective cutting for sustained yield (which admits enough sunlight for undergrowth to prosper and shelter animals) and protection against uncontrolled burning and grazing. The planting of **living fences** can also greatly enhance the number and quality of wildlife on a farm. Although the invention of barbed wire in 1874 made the farmers' fences neat, these wire fences offered wildlife no cover. Living fences composed of native or exotic shrubs (e.g., osage orange and multiflora rose) are not only more aesthetically pleasing to the eye but also provide food, cover, and travel lanes for cottontails, pheasants, quail, and other forms of wildlife, and they help prevent soil erosion as well.

Wildlife borders are primarily used to control soil erosion, but they simultaneously provide cover and sometimes even food for wildlife. There are two types of wildlife borders: (1) those made of grasses

FIGURE 9-3 Wildlife on the farm. Farm practices that conserve soil and water resources also conserve wildlife. On a well-managed farm, problem areas such as rock exposures, gullies, and eroding streambanks become, through conservation, habitats for wildlife and assets to the human tenants. (From Ruben L. Parson, *Conserving American Resources,* 3d ed., © 1972, p. 433. Reprinted by permission of Prentice-Hall, Inc., Englewood Cliffs, N.J.)

and legumes, and (2) those made of shrubs or shrubs and conifers. Wildlife borders also make use of an area that might otherwise be considered waste (e.g., areas in which satisfactory grain crops are hard to grow or turnrows along the edges of cropland fields). The advantage of creating wildlife borders is that they benefit the farmer in a multitude of ways: soil erosion control, production of more insect-eating songbirds; greater numbers of pollinating insects, and greater numbers of game and nongame birds and mammals.

Windbreaks that have been planted along crop fields to help control wind erosion also serve as additional cover for wildlife. This particular type of cover is valuable for it increases the *edge* quality of the habi-tat—the **ecotone** or *marginal edge* where one kind of animal and plant community environment meets another kind.

Streambank protection is another method by which farmers directly control soil erosion (bank cutting, property loss, and silt loading in streams) and also indirectly provide wildlife cover, food, and water. With the aid of soil and water engineers, the causes of streambank erosion (e.g., overgrazing or fallen trees that deflect water from its normal direction of flow) and wildlife habitat loss can be minimized (Figure 9-4).

Various techniques can also be used on the farm to improve water availability for wildlife populations.

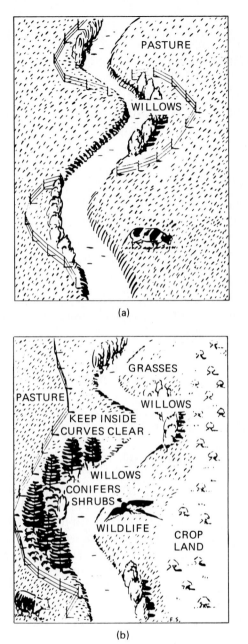

(a)

(b)

FIGURE 9-4 Streambank correction methods for wildlife. (a) Deep streams with high banks can be enhanced for wildlife in this fashion. (b) Shallow streams with low banks can be enhanced for wildlife with this method. (From *Making Land Produce Useful Wildlife, Farmers' Bulletin No. 2035* [Washington, D.C.: U.S. Department of Agriculture, 1969].)

Water development methods include creating or manipulating existing natural waterholes, springs, and seeps; building reservoirs and small ponds; and diverting drainage ditches. Many farmlands have natural depressions where runoff waters accumulate. These natural waterholes need to be preserved for

wildlife, and, sometimes, these areas can also be improved by deepening the catchment or trench that leads to the basin. In some cases, underlying geological strata will allow the development of springs and seeps where none previously existed. Reservoirs and small ponds can sometimes be created by building a earthen dam across a drainage ditch (Figure 9-5). Not only can the pond provide water for deer and wild turkeys, but also it can provide resting, feeding, and breeding places for ducks and other waterfowl. Ponds also help the farmer in preventing floods and the consequent soil erosion. Furthermore, ponds store water for livestock, irrigation, orchard spraying, and fire protection for farm buildings. Ponds can also be a source of fish production. Water catchment systems (also known as *gallinaceous guzzlers* or just *guzzlers*) are often simple devices that capture precipitation in the drier farmland regions, as well as elsewhere (Figure 9-6).

Finally, the proper manipulation of drainage ditches can also benefit wildlife populations. Since drainage ditches filled with trees and shrubs may be good for wildlife but cannot provide the necessary drainage of adjacent fields, the first aim in good ditchbank management is to establish and keep grass on the banks.

In addition to cover improvement and water development, *food production* can also be enhanced for wildlife populations on farmlands (Yoakum 1979). This can be done by four primary means: (1) fruit production, (2) browse planting improvement, (3) herbaceous plantings, and (4) aquatic plant development.

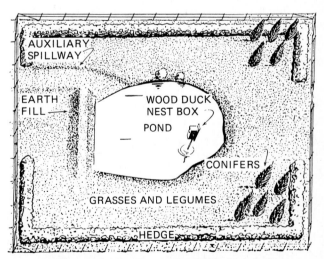

FIGURE 9-5 Ponds and wildlife on farms. (From *Making Land Produce Useful Wildlife, Farmers' Bulletin No. 2035* [Washington, D.C.: U.S. Department of Agriculture, 1969].)

FIGURE 9-6 Water development for wildlife. In the arid West, resource managers often construct water catchment devices known locally as "guzzlers." The concrete apron directs rainwater to an underground storage tank. A float valve maintains a constant level of water in a trough for wildlife, such as these chukar partridge. (From James D. Yoakum, "Habitat Improvement." In Richard D. Teague and Eugene Decker, eds., *Wildlife Conservation: Principles and Practices* [Washington, D.C.: The Wildlife Society, 1979], p. 136.)

Fruit production refers to the propagation (the direct planting of desirable seeds or transplants), release (the removal of competitive plants), and protection (the guarding of the fruit species until they reach fruit-producing age or protection of the fruit itself from consumption by undesirable organisms) of fruit-producing species for wildlife. Examples of tree and shrub species that would be used for fruit production are cherry, ash, beech, gum, oak, and hickory. In many cases, fruit production is combined with developing shelterbelts, windbreaks, living fences, and gully or waterway plantings.

Improving browse (the shoots and twigs of shrubs and trees used by wildlife for food) can also improve food production. This may entail simply the *topping* or cutting back of old growth, which allows the more desirable succulent young twigs and stems to be maintained at browse level. Or it may involve more extreme forms of plant manipulation such as chaining or cabling, spraying, burning, and seeding. The latter are browse manipulation techniques often used for improving forage for livestock, but they can, when carefully practiced, benefit wildlife.

Purposeful *herbaceous plantings* (usually in conjunction with other land management activities such as soil stabilization after wildfire burns, timber stand improvement, or the restoration of roadside cover) can benefit food production for wildlife. Wildlife benefits the most when a mixture of seedlings are used—forbs and browse, as well as grass plantings.

The fourth and last major technique for increasing food production for wildlife on farmlands is *aquatic plant development*. Farmlands adjacent to natural marshlands can improve the food and cover of these areas for wildlife by simply fencing out grazing animals. The habitat manager can also use a variety of other techniques to intersperse open water and marshland: (1) *controlling water level* by the use of dikes, embankments, spillways, level ditching, and plugs; (2) *creating openings* by using controlled burning and the use of explosives to improve the channels and openings that wildlife require for movement between nest site and feeding areas; and (3) *pothole blasting* by using explosives to make deep holes in marshlands with a fairly high water table, thus improving nesting sites for particular kinds of marshland species.

Many of the above techniques of habitat manipulation on farmlands, of course, can also be used in nonfarm rural areas. Three additional types of habitat manipulation are mainly found in nonfarm rural areas: (1) manipulating ecological succession, (2) constructing artificial islands, and (3) developing artificial nests and nest sites. *Manipulating ecological succession* is a difficult and somewhat controversial technique to improve wildlife cover (Dasmann 1981). Since plant and animal communities change as the physical environment (available sunlight, moisture, wind velocity, and soil fertility) changes, wildlife managers have attempted to control ecological succession by using such techniques as controlled burning, controlled flooding, herbicide spraying, plowing, and logging. If *climax associated species* (e.g., caribou, bighorn sheep, and grizzly bear) were desired, then the creation of state and national refuges would be the management technique, since these animals need a relatively undisturbed climax community (possibly a wilderness) in which to survive. *Mid-successional species* (e.g., ruffed grouse, moose, and white-tailed deer) are temporary phenomena, as is the vegetative community upon which they feed. To keep these temporary species around permanently requires habitat disturbance by humans on a regular basis. Quail and rabbit are classified according to Dasmann as *low-successional species,* and this type of animal is greatly dependent on major disturbances of the ecological succession by humans, such as an abandoned cornfield or cotton field or a road cut that is invaded by windborne or animal-borne seeds. It is probably safe to say that as humans use up and degrade more and more landscapes, it will be to the benefit of low-successional species, but at the expense of climax-associated species.

Constructing artificial islands is one means of improving nesting and resting sites where conditions for certain wildlife species are not quite optimal. During dry periods, bulldozers or draglines can form ridges and islands within marshlands or ponds, and these human-made islands can boost waterbird populations. A 1977 Bureau of Reclamation project created 62 artificial nesting islands for Canada geese in Canyon Ferry Lake near Townsend, Montana, and since then there has been a threefold increase in the numbers of Canada geese in this area (Owen 1980).

Dredge islands have been made for years by the U.S. Army Corps of Engineers (Davids 1978). In most cases, however, the primary motivation to build dredge islands was to find a means of disposing of the sand, mud, and shells removed during the dredging of rivers, bays, and pleasure boat harbors. Disposal of this waste has been a constant headache for engineers, especially since environmental impact statements have been required. No longer allowed to indiscriminately dump the dredged material, the Corps of Engineers has had to find ecologically sound ways of converting this waste into a resource, and one fairly acceptable method has been the creation of artificial islands designed as new wildlife habitats. Some state fish and game departments, however, have brought about construction delays by asking pertinent questions: How is the island going to be built and maintained? Who is going to fund it? Who is going to operate and manage the new reserve? Are they ecologically safe for wildlife? Constructing a mud island may sound at first like a simple habitat improvement idea, but, as always, ecological, economic, and political questions complicate the issue.

Creating artificial nests and nest sites by using cyl-

inders, boxes, or platforms can sometimes substitute for natural nest sites in otherwise suitable habitat (Figure 9-7). For example, nest boxes have been useful for songbirds and ducks. Squirrels, geese, and birds of prey have benefited from elevated nesting platforms in areas of fluctuating water levels. Although these human-made wood, metal, and chicken wire fabrications are far less aesthetically pleasing to humans than natural nests and have to be regularly maintained and protected against extreme weather conditions and vandalism, they appear to serve the reproduction function as well as natural nests. Such structures are even *more* effective in some cases as protection against human machines (tractors, automobiles, and mowers), predators, and nest site competitors.

Whereas good soil and water management practices on the farm are also good for wildlife populations, the same is not true of profitable timber operations. Maximum production of timber in forests often drastically alters the structure and species composition of plant communities, which, in turn, has significant effects on wildlife. Large-scale wildlife goals, therefore, must be accomplished through timber management because timber management affects many acres, is well financed, dramatically affects wildlife habitat, and has great impact on wildlife. In comparison, traditional wildlife habitat management affects fewer acres, has less financial backing, has less influence on wildlife habitat, and has less impact on wildlife.

Forests *can* be managed for wildlife habitats as well as for timber products; in fact, on public lands this is mandated by several federal laws. Congress has continuously reiterated the concept of multiple use, which in its broadest sense implies the maintenance of a reasonable representation of native animals on all major soil and vegetation types, not just on the infertile sites that are too poor in quality to grow good timber. To meet this congressional mandate, there are several techniques that the timber manager can use to preserve forest and wildlife diversity, with moderate, but not excessive, sacrifice in board foot production and economic yield. In the majority of cases, these techniques involve (1) leaving snags and potential snags in the forest; (2) leaving dead and down woody material on the forest floor; (3) protecting cliffs, talus, and caves; (4) making minimal impact in riparian zones; (5) using prescribed fire (controlled burns) to alter the successional stage; (6) leaving strips or corners of mature trees uncut; (7) keeping clear-cut blocks small; (8) maintaining small uneven-aged stands, although even-aged stands are simpler to manage mechanically; and (9) resisting the

(a)

(b)

FIGURE 9-7 Artificial nests and nest sites. (a) Where natural tree cavities are lacking, resource managers can construct artificial nesting structures such as these for wood ducks. (b) In areas with excessive fluctuating water levels, nesting structures can be elevated. (From James D. Yoakum, ''Habitat Improvement.'' In Richard D. Teague and Eugene Decker, eds., *Wildlife Conservation: Principles and Practices* [Washington, D.C.: The Wildlife Society, 1979], pp. 137–138.)

excessive use of herbicides and pesticides (Thomas 1979).

Leaving snags and potential snags in the forest is critical for many species of plants (fugus, moss, lichen), invertebrates (moth, beetle, ant), birds (pileated woodpecker, flicker, nuthatch), and mammals (bat, flying squirrel, marten). A snag is essentially a standing dead or partially dead tree from which the leaves and most of the limbs have fallen. Snags are used in a variety of ways by snag-dependent wildlife: cavity nesting (woodpeckers, squirrels, song birds); exterior nesting (brown creepers, birds of prey); roosting (birds of prey, turkey, bandtail pigeon); perching and singing (songbirds); communication (woodpeckers); hunting perches (birds of prey, flycatchers); food storage (small mammals); and protection from weather (many species).

Traditionally, foresters practice what is called *sanitation cutting*—the cleaning out of dead and crooked trees (snags) in order to leave only the straight, healthy, and uniform specimens (see Chapter 7). This was often done under the guise of increased timber production, fire prevention, and safety. Today, however, foresters are beginning to take a second look at the importance of snags within the forest. Increased emphasis on recent federal laws on management of publicly owned forest lands for wildlife and numerous scientific reports that con-

clude that birds may play a significant role in the regulation of insect populations (Beebe 1974) have spurred the U.S. Forest Service to reexamine their past management policy.

However, as timber harvest is intensified, there will likely be a desire and a tendency to eliminate the Old Growth stands that produce the large snags most used by snag-dependent wildlife. To help circumvent this problem, foresters have attempted to *produce* snags by three methods: (1) retaining snags in managed stands and foregoing the cutting of certain commercially valuable trees to meet wildlife habitat goals; (2) delaying harvest until the dominant trees are considerably larger (long rotations of either stands or selected trees); and (3) killing suitable trees intentionally if they are appropriately located and the correct size and species for wildlife use (Thomas 1979). The latter technique is the most controversial for it has not been proven that snag-dependent wildlife will take to these human-created habitats.

Foresters can also help maintain wildlife populations by *leaving dead and down wood materials* (logs, stumps, root wads, bark, and piles of limbs) on the forest floor. Not only are these components of the forest important for mineral cycling, nitrogen fixation, and fire, they are also important as hiding cover, feeding sites, food sources, and as perching, dusting, and nesting areas (Figure 9-8). The male blue grouse,

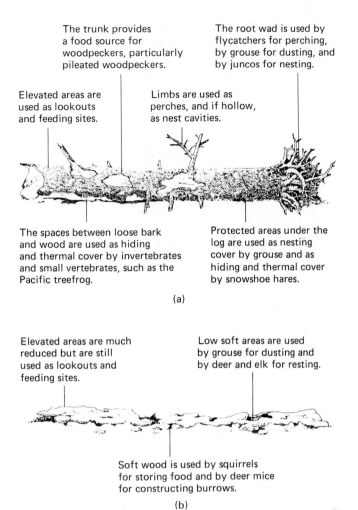

The trunk provides a food source for woodpeckers, particularly pileated woodpeckers.

The root wad is used by flycatchers for perching, by grouse for dusting, and by juncos for nesting.

Elevated areas are used as lookouts and feeding sites.

Limbs are used as perches, and if hollow, as nest cavities.

The spaces between loose bark and wood are used as hiding and thermal cover by invertebrates and small vertebrates, such as the Pacific treefrog.

Protected areas under the log are used as nesting cover by grouse and as hiding and thermal cover by snowshoe hares.

(a)

Elevated areas are much reduced but are still used as lookouts and feeding sites.

Low soft areas are used by grouse for dusting and by deer and elk for resting.

Soft wood is used by squirrels for storing food and by deer mice for constructing burrows.

(b)

FIGURE 9-8 Protecting dead and down woody materials for wildlife. (a) A recently fallen tree showing those structural features important for wildlife. (b) A decayed log—still a benefit to wildlife. The male blue grouse, for example, uses a decayed log for his courtship display. (From Jack Ward Thomas, ed., *Wildlife Habitats in Managed Forests—The Blue Mountains of Oregon and Washington*, Agricultural Handbook No. 553 [Washington, D.C.: U.S. Department of Agriculture Forest Service, 1979], p. 79.)

for example, even requires a log to stage his courtship display. As the nation's energy shortage becomes more acute, the male blue grouse and other dead and down wood-dependent wildlife will likely be competing with humans who seek an ever increasing amount of forest litter for use in their home fireplaces and wood-burning stoves.

Protecting cliffs, talus, and caves is another means by which the forester can benefit wildlife populations (Thomas 1979). Cliffs are used for feeding and reproduction by amphibians (woodhouse toad, Pacific treefrog), reptiles (western fence lizard, western rattlesnake), birds (Canada goose, golden eagle, peregrine falcon), and mammals (black bear, bobcat, bighorned sheep). The peregrine falcon is particularly interesting because, although it is now considered a cliff-nester, records indicate that it once nested in the cavities of snags. Apparently, as the great trees on which they depended were harvested, many peregrine falcon took up residence in cliffs as secondary habitats. The felling of the big trees, their original habitat, was certainly at least a partial cause for their

status as an endangered species in the United States (Scott et al. 1977).

There are numerous types of caves, and wildlife uses them in many ways. Birds (barn owl, screech owl) and mammals (coyote, gray fox, wolverine) use caves for feeding and reproduction. Furthermore, they provide shelter from extreme weather conditions, protection from predators, and isolation from the outside world. Protecting talus (the mass of rock debris that collects at the bottom of a cliff) is also an important wildlife habitat consideration for the forester. Various amphibians (long-toed salamander, woodhouse toad), reptiles (side-blotched lizard, gopher snake), birds (turkey vulture, red-tailed hawk, prairie falcon, mountain bluebird), and mammals (mountain goat, lynx, least chipmunk, striped skunk) use this rubble for feeding and reproduction purposes. Talus areas, as well as cliffs and caves, are unique habitats that are often rare and fragile. Foresters must identify, evaluate, and possibly protect these areas from the activities of timber harvesting.

Unfortunately, most of the above management

procedures that enhance wildlife habitats also cut into the profits of the timber operator. Therefore, tradeoffs must be identified, and, of course, this is standard operating procedure under the multiple-use management concept. As long as the loss in wood available for harvest is equated with the loss of dollars and jobs, the wildlife manager within public forest lands will have an uphill battle to preserve the vestiges of wildlife within the forest. Even greater will be the difficulty of preserving wildlife habitats and populations within the 73 percent of the commercial forest lands that are in private hands. These forests are not under congressional mandate and, hence, there is little incentive for private businesses to forego maximum profit for the purpose of preserving some wildlife species within the forest biota.

Wildlife habitat can also be improved in developed or *urban areas*, and this is particularly important since more and more land is being developed by the spreading urban centers (Laurie 1979, Leedy et al. 1978). Stearns (1972) categorizes three types of city wildlife: (1) *those that get along with humans* and are somewhat dependent upon them for food, cover, and nesting sites (birds such as pigeons, starlings, English sparrows, nighthawks, chimney swifts; mammals such as Norway rats, house mice, cats, dogs); (2) *those that tolerate humans* for their advantage (birds such as blue jays, robins, woodpeckers; mammals such as gray squirrel, cottontail rabbits, chipmunks, skunks, bats); and (3) *those that shun humans* (migratory birds; mammals such as the white-tailed deer, coyotes, black bear). Maintaining a balance of these wildlife types in the city is the difficult task of the urban wildlife manager.

There are several ways in which cities can improve developed habitat for wildlife (Table 9-6). All cities, for example, have *neglected areas*—areas that are not particularly used, such as abandoned parking lots, little-used alleys, and school grounds that are no longer in use. With minimal investment, these neglected areas can prove useful to wildlife. In some cases, *planned neglect* of these so-called neglected areas is exactly what they need (Stearns 1972). Much valuable wildlife habitat is wasted because Americans are generally overly tidy and want to mow or trim vegetation more than is actually necessary for fire prevention, safety precaution, or aesthetics. The utility right-of-way is the classic example of an area that *needs* to be neglected. Rather than regularly mowing, trimming, or using herbicides on the grasses and shrubs underneath and near a utility right-of-way, the corridor of open space should be purposely neglected to improve urban wildlife habitat.

Just as the borders of agricultural fields can be managed for *edge* habitat, so too can *streets and highways* within the city (Leedy 1975). A *multiflora* rose living fence along a highway edge will do more for wildlife populations than a neatly mowed grassy strip. If a strong metal center divider is deemed necessary for safety reasons, it can be easily hidden underneath living fences so that both safety and wildlife habitat can be enhanced. And most important, the use of herbicides for weed control along roads, streets, and highways must be curtailed. This would save the taxpayers money, add one less pollutant to the soil, water, and air, and improve human as well as wildlife habitat. Selecting *street trees* that attract songbirds and other desirable species is another means of improving developed areas for wildlife (Santamour et al. 1976). Careful management of *city parks* can also enhance wildlife populations (Odum 1971). Good park management for wildlife would encompass such techniques as protecting certain shrubbery, understory, snags, and dead and down woody materials. Furthermore, the site on which a park is originally located is of the utmost importance to wildlife.

Many *institutional grounds*, such as traditional university campuses, are very parklike and can be managed similarly for wildlife (Odum and Davis 1969). In both cases, the designer and manager of these kinds of grounds must balance the desires of the football-throwing human animal who wants large expanses of neatly mowed grass with occasional tall trees against the needs of the cover-seeking wild animal that prefers dense and scrubby shrubs and medium-height trees.

Cemeteries, church yards, and greenbelts also have great expanses of space that could be more properly managed for wildlife. Just as the multiple-use management plan applies to public forest lands, an adapted version of this concept can be applied to these areas (Finkler 1975). For example, Forest Lawn Cemetery in Buffalo, New York, serves as a bird sanctuary as well as a human burial site. The streams, rivers, and lakes in our cities also need to be protected for wildlife, as well as for water quality, aesthetics, and other reasons (Tourbier and Westmacott 1976). Preserving or repairing *riparian habitat* within existing or newly developed areas is of utmost importance for wildlife. *Insect pests* and other forms of pests abound within our cities, and the methods used in dealing with these nuisances often have a profound affect on wildlife populations (Olkowski et al. 1976).

Much has been written about habitat improvement within the backyards of *privately owned residences*

TABLE 9-6

Methods for improving wildlife habitat in developed areas

ELEMENTS OF THE CITY	ASSOCIATED WILDLIFE MANAGEMENT PRINCIPLES	EXAMPLES OF GOOD MANAGEMENT FOR WILDLIFE
Neglected areas	Maximize use of little-used areas (parking lots, streets, alleyways, school grounds) as open space for recreation and wildlife Revise outdated city ordinances against weeds that are beneficial to wildlife	A barren rooftop that has been converted to a rooftop garden An alley junkyard that has been converted into center block paths linking neighborhood to neighborhood A vacant lot that has been developed into vest-pocket parks Areas that have been purposely left scrubby: stream and riverbanks; railroad and utility rights-of-way; dumps; open storm sewers; industrial wastelands
Streets and highways	Manage highway rights-of-way as edge habitat valuable for wildlife Avoid the crossing of wetlands and the channelization of streams Avoid the crossing of migration routes of reptiles and amphibians Minimize mowing of grassy center dividers and edges of highways Selectively use (or better yet, do not use) herbicides for weed control	A multiflora rose living fence along roadway A highway center divider that is made up of shrubs rather than a lone metal barricade Borrow pits and earth fills (resulting from highway construction) that have been converted to wetland for waterfowl, furbearers, etc. Tunnels or culverts underneath roadways to protect migration routes of wildlife
Street trees	Select tree species according to: 1. value for wildlife 2. tolerance of city conditions 3. noise reduction Avoid use of single species (monoculture)	Trees that attract songbirds, yet are resistant to salt from street deicing and air pollution Mixture of tree species that are resistant to an epidemic of Dutch elm disease
City parks	Retain some natural brushy or shrubby cover in areas away from paths Protect some snags (dead standing trees) and dead and down woody materials (logs, stumps)	 Shrubbery and understory vegetation that was preserved for songbird populations (mockingbirds, brown thrushes, etc.) Hollow trees that have been preserved for wildlife food sources and den trees
Institutional grounds	Strive for a diversity of plant species and forms that provide ground cover and foliage at *intermediate* as well as at tall tree levels	University campuses and government buildings and grounds that have medium-height trees and dense cover for wildlife nesting and escape cover (rather than tall trees scattered in large expanses of lawn)
Cemeteries, greenbelts, churchyards	Select vegetation that requires less mowing	Cemeteries that have been managed as partial bird sanctuaries (Forest Lawn Cemetery in Buffalo, New York)
Streams, rivers, lakes	Preserve high-quality streams and other water bodies Improve those stream bodies and water bodies that need improving Create additional impoundments or wetland Eliminate or minimize water pollution	Riparian habitats that have been preserved against stream channelization Rivers that have been cleaned up (Willamette River, Oregon) Concrete areas that have been replaced with ponds or pools for waterlilies and tropical fish
Insect pests	Use biological control measures in lieu of pesticides that are harmful to wildlife Use of mixture of native species of plants that are less subject to disastrous die-offs	The attempt to stop the Mediterranean fruit fly (medfly) by releasing thousands of sterilized male medflies (Santa Clara County, California)
Privately owned residences	Convert lawns and concrete areas in backyard to native meadows and natural open spaces Plant wildlife-attracting trees and shrubs	Living fences of honeysuckle or holly Properly placed bird baths, feeders, and bird boxes Windbreaks of junipers, spruces, or pines A group of fragmented private backyards converted into neighborhood recreational areas open to all

Source: Data from Leedy, Daniel L., Maestro, Robert M., and Franklin, Thomas M. 1978. *Planning for Wildlife in Cities and Suburbs.* Washington, D.C.: Fish and Wildlife Service; Stearns, Forest, and Montag, Tom. 1974. *The Urban Ecosystem: A Holistic Approach,* Community Development Series, vol. 14; and Laurie, Ian C., ed. 1979. *Nature in Cities: The Natural Environment in the Design and Development of Urban Green Space.* New York: Wiley.

(National Wildlife Federation 1974). Unless a person has bought a new unlandscaped home, the process of converting existing yards into wildlife-attracting habitats is slow and expensive. Yet, when putting in a new lawn, question its size and very existence; when replacing a dead tree or bush, consider putting in one that is beneficial to wildlife. Regarding private homes, however, what really needs to be done is to get the country's developers and landscape architects to "think wildlife" when designing new towns, communities, building structures, and the surrounding grounds, thereby incorporating wildlife habitat concepts into the original planning of a new urban complex, rather than trying to correct or re-adapt the site at a later date (Figure 9-9).

Because of the very serious traffic hazards created by birds, wild burros, and other wildlife species, *airports* are one of the few components of the city that must *keep out* wild animals (Solman 1974). Methods exist to make existing airports less attractive to wildlife, such as eliminating nearby open dumps, thinning pine plantations near runways, and draining surrounding marshlands. Future airports, ideally, should be located in areas that attract minimal wildlife to begin with, such as sandy land with good drainage.

Techniques for Managing Direct Hunting by Humans

Wildlife Law Enforcement. **Game laws** (restrictions and regulations on hunting, trapping, and fishing) have been in existence since the colonial period in America (Morse 1979). Originally, game laws were enforced by local peace officers, but later by special officers known as *wardens* or *protectors* (Bavin 1978). Today, most wildlife law enforcers are known as either game wardens or conservation officers and possess college degrees in wildlife resource management.

Various wildlife management techniques come under the heading of protective game laws:

1. *Bag limits* are restrictions on the species and number of individuals taken while hunting or fishing.
2. *Closed seasons* are restrictions on the season or the time of day for hunting and fishing.
3. *Firearm restrictions* determine the type of firearm, trap, or fishing equipment used, for example, laws against the use of machine guns and lead shot for hunting waterfowl.

(a)

(b)

FIGURE 9-9 Habitat preservation within newly planned communities. (a) In Santa Cruz, California, developers of the Neary Lagoon Project protected trees and topography, thereby reducing soil erosion, preserving habitat for wildlife, and maintaining the aesthetics of the area. The additional effort also increased property values. (b) Water bodies naturally attract various forms of wildlife. (Photos by author.)

4. *Accessory restrictions* determine the use of dogs and other equipment. Today, wildlife law enforcers are being pressured by conservation groups to question the ethical (if not legal) use of modern technological accessories that make the "hunt" appear meaningless, such as four-wheel-drive vehicles, walky-talkies, and mobile flood lights.

5. *Market prohibitions* are laws against hunting for the market place.

Threatened and endangered species legislation is a second and more recent category of wildlife law enforcement (Bean 1977, Ramsay 1976). While early wildlife management techniques focused on game laws, it soon became evident that effective conservation of wildlife also required protection of habitat. Since outright habitat acquisition was more often than not financially prohibitive, lawmakers were faced with the challenge of finding some means to protect lands from the worst effects of highway and dam construction, draining, filling, clear-cutting, and generalized industrialization. Legislation such as the Fish and Wildlife Coordination Act (1934), the Endangered Species Conservation Act (1966), the National Environmental Policy Act (1969), and the Endangered Species Act (1973) tightened controls over the major causes of wildlife extinction, including direct hunting (Table 9-1).

As protective legislation broadened, so did the problems of wildlife law enforcement (Bavin 1978, Ramsay 1976). Conservation officers, originally only concerned with regulating hunters and fishermen, must now deal with the handlers (importers and exporters, shipping companies, carriers, and brokers) and the recipients (pet dealers, zoos, propagators, taxidermists, and retailers) of wildlife and wildlife products.

Shooting Preserves and Animal Propagation. The negative effects of direct hunting by humans can be partially controlled by encouraging hunters to use **shooting preserves**—areas privately owned or leased for the purpose of releasing pen-reared game birds, usually upon payment of a fee by the hunter. This concept has also been referred to as *fee hunting, pay-as-you-go hunting,* and *put-and-take shooting* (Kozicky and Madson 1979).

Shooting preserves throughout the United States are increasing due to several factors: shrinking public hunting grounds; stricter laws on existing public hunting grounds; increased antihunter sentiment; and improvements in propagation methods, which

permit game birds to be produced at lower costs, thereby ensuring encounters with game on shooting preserves near metropolitan areas (Kouba 1976). Some would contend, however, that shooting preserves are the worst of all possible hunting options and represent little sportsmanship. Regardless, the number of shooting preserves will probably continue to multiply and provide hunting opportunities, particularly for urban hunters, while *conserving other areas for other purposes.*

Site Management. Influencing the spatial distribution of hunters to wildlife is another wildlife management tool (Thomas et al. 1976). The idea is to understand the behavior of hunters in relation to the characteristics of the hunting area. Such area characteristics include its proximity to roads and trails, its camp sites, and its parking lots. Some early findings indicate that *changing trail layout,* more than any other kind of land management, increases or decreases hunter-game contact. By removing or adding some trail signs and making others more or less conspicuous, contacts between hunters and wildlife can be increased for a greater game harvest or reduced if *preservation* is the goal. Hunting is *conservation* if it is done properly.

Wildlife law enforcement, shooting preserves, and site management are the three major means used to control the adverse effects of direct hunting by humans. *Although nearly impossible to apply to shooting preserves,* the concept of *balanced biotas* should be the management objective. This management philosophy calls for the maintenance of natural environments in hunting areas, maintaining an abundant and varied animal life—an environment that is indeed *wild* and true to life. According to Dasmann (1984, p. 372):

> Wildlife to be worth preserving should be wild, and to be wild it should be rich and varied, with predators as well as prey. If wildlife management is to concentrate on the sheer production of meat, eliminating all that conflicts with or feeds on the cherished herbivores, it becomes then only another form of animal husbandry, a useful and profitable pursuit, but lacking those qualities associated with the word "wild."

Dealing with Introduced Species

Stricter Laws and Regulations. Due to numerous past experiences involving the adverse effects of fish introductions, such as the environmental disruption caused by the introduction of the carp, most states already have regulations governing the importation, possession, and introduction of nonnative fishes. And most states already prohibit the introduction of any species of fish not native to that state.

Courtenay (1978) has called for new and stricter laws and regulations regarding exotic organisms. First, at the state level, he has suggested that *all* (not just most) states have regulations on the introduction of nonnative fishes. Second, all states should have restrictions regarding organisms other than fishes. To date, only few states actually regulate the introduction of birds, and this was primarily a reaction to the environmental disruptions brought about by the introduction of the English sparrow in 1865 and the European starling in 1880. Third, since an introduction of an organism in one state has the potential of spreading to adjoining states, it is of the utmost importance that states cooperate with adjoining states in the drafting of regulations regarding introductions. Fourth, stricter enforcement of existing and new regulations will be required. For example, even in some states that do have the necessary laws or regulations, there continues to be an increase in the number of exotic species. Finally, legislators must be convinced of the seriousness of exotic introductions, for it is the legislator who often allocates (or does not allocate) funds for enforcement of the laws.

Much can also be done at the federal level. For example, new and stricter federal laws governing the introduction of nonnative aquatic organisms into interstate drainages could be enacted. Federally sponsored and operated laboratories to examine fish disease and parasite problems could also be accelerated. Federal regulations on interstate commerce in exotic species could be reexamined, since states alone are incapable of keeping such unwanted traffic from crossing their borders. Finally, federal recognition and funding to slow down the spread of introduced exotic species could be increased.

Intensified Research. Most introductions have been failures, either because a desired introduction did not take hold or because it did become a part of the ecosystem but later had adverse affects. To prevent future failures, detailed research must be required prior to any introduction. All aspects of the ecology of the proposed introductions must be thoroughly studied. Information should be collected on the organism's predators, diseases, climate preferences, and cover, food, and water needs.

As a general rule, this country would probably be better off if it had a policy that prohibits further introductions of exotic organisms. However, since such a policy is unlikely, perhaps a more realistic policy would be to allow (1) *no introductions except if faced with no realistic alternative,* and (2) *no introductions except after a detailed and careful evaluation* (Courtenay 1978).

Managing Pests and Predators

Public Awareness Programs. Many accusations against predators are either untrue or overly exaggerated, and, therefore, hard evidence must be found regarding the predator in question. For example, the crow was often accused by duck hunters of eating eggs and ducklings. It was later found that crows primarily eat crop-destroying insects. The barn owl, long persecuted by farmers for raiding chicken yards, was later discovered to eat mostly the pestiferous starlings and English sparrows. In both cases, further investigative research proved the accused ''criminal'' animal to be beneficial to humankind (Owen 1980). Even if a wild animal is found to be the culprit in a pest problem, public awareness programs can help enlighten citizens to the problem and increase their willingness to try alternative paths for controlling the pest. In Pasadena and South Pasadena, California, for example, such programs were instrumental in creating ordinances that prohibit residents from feeding coyotes and other mammalian predators in urban areas. This nonfeeding policy was adopted in preference to lethal trapping programs.

Soft Path Solutions. There are numerous pest and predator problems and a variety of techniques to deal with them. But to minimize ecosystem disruption, the resource manager should try to pursue the *softest path* possible given the particular circumstances (Table 9-7). Rather than poisoning adult coyotes with Compound 1080 via tainted sheep collars (the *hard path* approach), sheep ranchers might try the softer path of using *adversive agents,* such as using Tabasco sauce on samples of mutton to condition coyotes against killing their domestic stock (Miller 1982). Other nonlethal means of preventing livestock losses would be the use of scare devices, fences, or guard dogs.

Rather than shooting often destructive wild horses and burros (the *hard path*), the Bureau of Land Management developed the Adopt-a-Horse Program (the *soft path*) (Stocker 1980). At one time wild horses and burros were shot by ranchers or caught and sold for dog food. Now wild horses and burros taken from public lands in the West are offered with certain restrictions to private citizens. About 20,000 have been adopted into almost every state since the program be-

TABLE 9-7

Major types of control technology

TYPE	TECHNIQUE OR DEVICE	EXAMPLES	CHARACTERISTIC
Lethal control	Gassing Shooting Poisoning	Gassing woodchucks; Poisoning orchard field rodents; bounty hunting	Most direct method; *hardest path* (greatest chance of causing ecosystem disruption)
Preventive control	Fencing Frightening devices Chemical repellents Trapping-transfer of offending animals	Deer-proof fences; bird roost repellents; carbide exploders to repel blackbirds; trapping transfer of tule elk from Owens Valley to Hamilton Range, California	
Physiological control	Modifying the offending animals' ability to survive, resist other control measures, or reproduce	Use of sprayed detergents on blackbirds to induce exposure symptoms and chemo-sterilant application in pigeon control	
Environment control	Making the damage areas *less* attractive to the offending species or by improving habitat for them on alternate areas	Vegetation removal in airport vicinity to prevent starling concentration hazardous to aircraft; waterfowl refuges to offer attractive resting and feeding areas as an alternate to croplands	Least direct method; *softest path* (least likely to cause ecosystem disruption)

Source: Data from Cummings, Maynard W. 1979. "Wildlife Damage Problems." In Richard D. Teague and Eugene Decker, eds., *Wildlife Conservation: Principles and Practices.* Washington, D.C.: The Wildlife Society, pp. 167–171.

gan in 1973. While the roundup and adoption program is aimed at the wild horses and burros, it also preserves another historic "species"—the American cowboy. Except for the helicopters and the two-way radios used, the roundups have not changed too much in 100 years. To date, some would consider this program quite successful. Others, however, still insist that the burros are nonnative pests and are not worth the time, cost, and human energy expended for their preservation.

Stricter Regulations. At the same time that softer paths of pest and predator control techniques are being pursued, stricter regulations on the use of pesticides, herbicides, and predator poisons should be enacted. A real beginning was made with the 1972 presidential executive order that stopped the poisoning of all predators on federal lands or by government employees anywhere. In the same year, the Environmental Protection Agency also reduced in number the types of poisons that are allowed to be used against predators (Miller 1982). In 1980, Interior Secretary Cecil D. Andrus disallowed the use of Compound 1080, the poison used to kill coyotes. The livestock industry, however, fought back. In 1982, President Ronald Reagan rescinded Andrus's ban, authorizing the use of Compound 1080 in sheep collars. Since Compound 1080 also kills nontarget scavengers (both birds and mammals) that feed on the coyote carcasses, this poison and other ecologically devastating poisons should be taken off the market.

Besides supporting public awareness programs that question the accusations against predators, seeking the softest path of control possible, and calling for stricter regulations on pest and predator poisons, several underlying principles can be adhered to when dealing with pest and predator control problems:

1. Support only those animal control programs that are justified biologically and sociologically, as well as economically. More often than not, the easiest, fastest, and cheapest solution was the one previously used.

2. Recommend that only the minimum necessary control be applied. Controlling pests and predators is merely a problem of getting their population levels down to tolerable levels. It is *not* necessary to eradicate every wild burro, for example, to solve the wild burro problem, any more than it is necessary to kill every snail in your backyard to get rid of your snail problem.

3. Urge that control programs be regulated

closely by state or federal laws. We have all read accounts about the indiscriminate use of traps, snares, poisons, dogs, gas, and even germ warfare. Many of the methods are cruel and at times destructive to the environment (LaBastille 1976).

4. Encourage continuing research into the field of alternative animal control techniques, especially the soft path approaches. Not only must resource managers have better techniques of controlling and preventing animal damage, but also they need more accurate methods to assess the damage caused by wildlife and more sophisticated means to measure the effectiveness of damage control programs once they are in operation.

Controlling Pets, Zoos, and Scientific Research

Biome Preservation Programs.   As wild populations of animals kept as pets, kept in zoos, and used in scientific research dwindle, environmentalists search for ways to conserve these animals. One such attempt is UNESCO's Man and the Biosphere Program (MAB). This is a massive effort aimed at identifying and delineating the world's different kinds of biological areas, ranging from Alaska's tundra to Africa's deserts. The program focuses on the major extensive ecological homogeneous areas, known as *biomes*, such as the desert-sagebrush areas of Arizona, Mexico, and California; the Douglas fir, cedar, and hemlock forests of the Northwest; the swamps and marshlands of the South; the tropical rain forests of the tropics and the tiagas; and the coniferous forests of North America and Asia. The Man and the Biosphere Program is a collective international effort sponsored by the United Nations Educational Scientific and Cultural Organization (UNESCO), the National Science Foundation, and the U.S.–USSR Environmental Agreement, a compact calling for cooperative environmental research by the two countries. Its aim is to protect these different biological regions, to see that the world does not lose plant and animal life (and the genes contained in them), and to conduct ecological research. There are already in the United States more than a dozen experimental ecological preserves under intensive scientific scrutiny, and they are considered part of the Man and the Biosphere Program.

Stricter Enforcement of Foreign Game Laws.   In many countries, such as Kenya, game laws were rarely enforced until decreases in some species became suddenly apparent. The United States, through its international commissions, must continue to encourage strict foreign game laws. As one can imagine, however, this is not always practical nor possible.

Economic Alternatives for Foreign Villagers.   Many foreign nationals have always made their living by selling wildlife, and, therefore, strict game laws are a great economic burden for them. Ecuadorian wildlife managers have outlined a proposal that might get around this problem. They have made large areas of the Amazon Basin into national parks, and they intend to train local Indians to become salaried park guards—guardians of the animals, rather than human predators of the animals. In addition to the problem of financing this proposal, there is always the question of whether or not the Indians will easily accept the idea. There is also the greater question of whether or not this wildlife preservation effort will be worth the disruption of the cultural heritage of the Indians that this livelihood has provided. *Manipulating cultures to preserve wildlife is tricky business and must be handled cautiously. Many a society has been destroyed by governments imposing demands that are culturally not acceptable.*

Stricter Enforcement of Existing U.S. Regulations.   The United States has had regulations against wildlife trade since the dawn of conservation law, but of the laws enforcement was rare. The Lacey Act of 1935 prohibited importation into this country of any wildlife acquired illegally in another country. The Endangered Species Act of 1969 banned the importation of any animals on the endangered species list. But not until 1973 did many nations become serious about controlling the illegal sale and smuggling of wildlife and wildlife products.

In 1973, 80 nations met to draft the Convention on International Trade in Endangered Species of Wildlife Fauna and Flora (CITES) (King 1978). In a sense, "passports" are now required for animals—dead or alive—that pass from one country to another, putting the burden of enforcement on the importing countries. The program went into effect in 1975, and now over 60 nations have signed and ratified the treaty.

Another new enforcement technique, supported mainly by the World Wildlife Fund, is an organization called TRAFFIC (Trade Records Analysis of Fauna and Flora in Commerce). This organization monitors the movement of animal products around the world. The information is supplied upon request to government, CITES officials, and conservationists. With offices operating in London, Washington, D.C., Nairobi, and with others opening in Frankfurt and

Tokyo, TRAFFIC provides the first reliable source of data about the numbers of animals and amount of animal products being moved around the world. TRAFFIC thus acts as an *arm of documentation* for law enforcement agencies.

New U.S. Legislation.   As long as there is a *demand* and it is *legal* to sell certain wildlife products, the stricter enforcement of laws regulating imports merely drives the trade "underground." For example, in U.S. pet stores, collectors of exotic birds will pay more than $10,000 for a hyacinth macaw. At leading national department stores, the fashion industry pushes trendy western-style boots trimmed with lizard skin. Although these items are being sold *legally* in this country, their transit through world commerce may have been *illegal*.

Essentially, wildlife trade provides things for people who do not need them. No one really needs a leopard coat! Legislation should be enacted that forbids pet stores, furriers, and other retailers of wildlife and wildlife products from selling species that are classified by world organizations as either threatened or endangered. U.S. laws should allow imports only from those nations that can prove they are practicing strict conservation measures regarding endangered species.

Wildlife Farming.   Claiming that the demand for wildlife products will never dwindle, many animal dealers, tanners, and bureaucrats have suggested that wildlife be farmed like domesticated pigs, cattle, or chickens. The notion calls for either *controlled harvests* on large natural preserves where the desirable animals are protected (e.g., the South African game reserves) or ranching operations where animals of one kind (monocultures) are artificially reared. In fact, two crocodile ranching operations, both owned by Papuans and managed by Australians, are already under way at Lae and Port Moresby. Because these ranching operations may reconcile economic need and a wildlife preservation need, an exception to the CITES ban on saltwater crocodiles has been granted to Papua New Guinea. The logic goes that if crocodiles can be ranched, why not leopards, tigers, or cheetahs? Although wildlife farming is not a new idea and has widely been done for years, there is, nevertheless, a growing interest in this method of increasing animal numbers.

Conservationists, on the other hand, question the validity of the wildlife farming concept for two reasons: (1) *identification*—since it is impossible to tell whether or not a saltwater crocodile skin or other animal product was raised or poached, identifying illegal animal products will be very difficult; and (2) *demand*—farming an endangered species may merely create a market for it and further encourage the poaching of those animals that are still running wild. Obviously, the role of wildlife farming as a preventive or corrective technique in wildlife resource management has yet to be determined. Another question, of course, is whether or not wildlife farming is merely a new form of animal husbandry and thus more properly belongs in the realm of similar pursuits—cattle ranching, sheep herding, and so on. How "wild" is a crocodile *farm*?

Frozen Zoos.   Alarmed about the rapid disappearance of exotic animals, the nation's zookeepers are now looking toward what are commonly known as *frozen zoos*—genetic banks of sperm and fertile eggs that can be shipped to breeding centers in five or six major locations. Notice that, as with the wildlife farming technique, we are dealing here with a concept that is essentially a captive breeding program to ensure species survival. Again, it raises the question whether or not this technique is wildlife management or animal husbandry. Regardless, in 1980, 650 representatives of 200 American and Canadian zoos and aquariums met at the conference of the American Association of Zoological Parks and Aquariums and endorsed the concept of the frozen zoo. Although animals have long been exchanged among zoos for breeding purposes, this new program would extend this service to large centers where all types of animals would be sent by zoos for "honeymoons" or *artificial insemination*.

Increased Education.   Since wildlife trade laws are only as good as the officials who inspect the shipments, it is paramount that all *customs officers* attend seminars taught by animal experts and visit zoos and museums to see and to learn to identify exotic species. *Tourists* can also be educated to check regulations before buying wildlife or wildlife products abroad. And most important, the *general public* can be educated so that their major conservation tool—the money they spend—can be used to change the practices of wildlife trading businesses. In most developed countries, for example, public pressure has succeeded in forcing the fur garments made from spotted cats out of shop display windows and even off the streets. Major fashion showrooms in some countries have now agreed to stop creating coats made from endangered species. Since the fashion industry has often set the stage for the demise of many animals, it needs to be looking for alternative and more ecological modes of expression, such as the design of coats from dyed Persian lamb hides.

Keeping Pollution within Allowable Levels

Environmental Impact Analysis. Since pollution is such a multifaceted problem and must be attacked along several different fronts, prior environmental analysis of a given site can help foresee and possibly prevent potential ecological disruption. A *baseline ecological survey* should be required before any major new development occurs within an area, particularly if the area has drainage basins that are highly susceptible to pollution. Questions need to be *increasingly* asked about the possible negative effects of logging, mining, and pesticide application on wildlife populations and their habitats. The cost of the survey should be borne by the developer and the results should be made public. *Environmental impact reports* that attempt to predict the long-range environmental effects of new proposals should be written and analyzed prior to project development. New agricultural areas, for example, often require the damming of rivers, the building of pumping stations, and the construction of complex irrigation systems. Major new developments that conflict with long-term resource conservation might have to be foregone.

Land-Use Controls. To protect inland waters from contamination, for example, hazardous dump sites should be *zoned* away from critical wildlife habitats. San Jose, California, for example, discovered that a hazardous waste transfer station was located directly next to the San Francisco Bay National Wildlife Refuge and that a spill of hazardous materials could enter nearby tributaries and severely affect the site. Limits should also be placed on the amount of physical alteration allowed on inland waters. Limits should be placed on the channelization, filling, and draining of wetlands. Such controls would help protect riparian habitat that is vital to wildlife. Land-use controls could also be used to adjust agricultural practices so that land use is according to *land capability*, along the lines already devised (but not always adhered to) by the U.S. Soil Conservation Service. Such controls might also entice some commercial farmers to switch to more organic systems of food production (using recycled crop wastes, livestock manure, and municipal sludge), thereby minimizing the use of synthetic fertilizers, herbicides, and pesticides, which are harmful to wildlife. The organic farming benefits to wildlife, of course, are enormous (Danko and Wilson 1976).

Ecological Monitoring. If a new project is allowed in an area, its operation needs to be carefully monitored so that any environmentally negative consequences of the project can be identified immediately and possible corrective measures put into effect. For example, if clear-cutting is to be allowed, the creeks, streams, and river channels within the drainage basin need to be watched carefully for increased levels of sedimentation that can suffocate fish and alter riparian habitat. Ideally, such monitoring should be done by agencies *independent* of the project.

Legislation. Legislation that attempts to restrict the release of chemical compounds into the environment should be supported. As mentioned earlier, stricter controls of pesticides, herbicides, and predator poisons are desperately needed. Hazardous waste cleanup legislation, such as the ''Superfund,'' must be continually supported. The intent of this type of legislation is to have a source of readily available federal funds for the purpose of immediate corrective action after a hazardous waste accident. Much wildlife (and human) exposure can be reduced if the cleanup after a toxic waste spill is quickly done. Too often in the past, action has not been taken until after the guilty party has been legally identified.

Applied Research. Research needs to shift from identifying the effects and causes of pollution damage (talking about the problem) to studying ways of ending pollution. Ecological methods of harnessing energy, such as using renewable nonpolluting sources of energy, like solar energy, need to be studied.

PROSPECTS FOR THE FUTURE

The downward trend of wildlife resources in the United States appears to be stabilizing as a result of years of hard work in wildlife management, habitat protection, and pollution abatement. Specifically, those concerned with wildlife, ''wildlifers,'' have been successful or have made significant strides in eight areas of endeavor: (1) more land has been placed under public control; (2) restoration of certain species has been achieved; (3) an environmental approach to wildlife management has been encouraged; (4) the public attitude toward predators has been changed; (5) the banning of certain harmful chemicals has been achieved; (6) there has been an increase in river and stream protection; (7) new timber harvest rules have been initiated; and (8) international organizations, conventions, and sanctuaries have been started. All of these and more serve as *positive signs* that wildlife deterioration can be slowed down and even reversed if *citizens have the will to do it*.

Positive Signs and Success Stories

1. *Increased amounts of land placed under public control.* One of the many measures of success in wildlife conservation over the last few decades can be seen in the increased amount of land placed under public control. Each year, the number of wildlife sanctuaries, public hunting grounds, public fishing lakes, and wilderness areas has steadily increased. The world's largest system of wildlife habitats is in the United States. The most impressive is the National Wildlife Refuge System, which is administered by the U.S. Fish and Wildlife Service. Over 400 protected areas, covering approximately 14 million ha (34 million acres), make up this system that protects wildlife and provides breeding grounds for wildlife, particularly for migrating birds and endangered species. Some 315 million ha (778 million acres) of public lands can be found in the United States, much of which can provide habitat for a diversity of wildlife, if properly managed by the states and by the federal government (Swanson 1979).

2. *Increased restoration of certain species.* A second encouraging sign is the number of species that are making a comeback after nearly becoming extinct. Once annihilated to near extinction by hide hunters in most of its range, this country's largest reptile—the American alligator—is no longer thought to be threatened with extinction. Strict enforcement of federal and state laws protecting the reptile has brought about its comeback. In fact, in some areas of Louisiana and Florida, alligators are so numerous that they have become public nuisances, crawling on golf courses, resting on roads, and, in one instance, killing a teen-aged bather.

Another animal that has been taken off the endangered species list is the gray wolf of Minnesota. Under the endangered species classification it was illegal to kill the gray wolf, and this protective device enabled the number of gray wolves to rise to an estimated 1200 in Minnesota alone. As its numbers rose, however, so did the complaints from local ranchers that their livestock was being preyed upon by wolf packs. One of the reasons that the gray wolf was reclassified from an **endangered species** (one threatened by extinction in at least a significant portion of its range) to a **threatened species** (one likely to become endangered in the foreseeable future) was

so that the U.S. Fish and Wildlife Service could occasionally "harvest" a wolf that had repeatedly bothered a rancher.

While much of the world is losing its few remaining large wild mammals, the United States has been very successful in reversing the trend within its own boundaries. Pronghorns, elk, mule deer, white-tailed deer, and even the majestic moose are on the rise. Wildlife managers can also point with pride at the apparent comeback of numerous other species, such as the Alaskan fur seal, the Hawaiian goose (or nene), the whooping crane, the wild turkey, the key deer of southern Florida, the trumpeter swan, the bald eagle, the peregrine falcon, and the osprey.

3. *Environmental approach to wildlife management.* Since 1970, the "New Conservation Movement," more commonly called the "Environmental Movement," is a third encouraging sign, for it differs from the traditional conservation movement in that it goes far beyond the traditional concern of hunters and anglers for the preservation of game species and habitats (Table 9-8). The New Conservation Movement is broader in scope and attempts to initiate positive proposals based on the demands of the overall public; the principle of ecosystem diversity; the measure of progress as sustainability; the spirit of cooperation between private, state, and federal authorities; the support received from general public funds; the interests of nonconsumptive recreational users—campers, bird-watchers, and backpackers, as well as the consumptive recreational users—hunters, trappers, and anglers; the clientele of diverse interest groups and associations (e.g., the Wilderness Society and Ducks Unlimited); and the ecological and environmental research that helps maintain genetic diversity of both flora and fauna. Although this is the direction that wildlife management seems to be headed, *and rightfully so*, there is no guarantee that any of these objectives, such as sustaining ecological diversity, will be achieved (Caulfield 1979, Scheffer 1976).

However, there are several innovative programs that serve as indicators that wildlife managers are moving in this broader direction. Most impressive of all are the rising number of federal, state, and private *nongame programs*—programs aimed at maintaining or restoring ecosystem diversity (Graul et al. 1976). Several recent acts of the federal government have been beneficial to nongame as well as game species (e.g., the Water Quality Act, the Endangered Species Act, and the Washington Convention on Endangered Species). Furthermore, in 1980, the Senate and

TABLE 9-8

Changing approaches to wildlife management

CATEGORY	PAST APPROACH	EMERGING APPROACH (NEEDED, BUT NOT YET FULLY ACHIEVED)
Strategy	Negative, defensive strategy (private, state, or federal fish and wildlife interests *reacted* defensively to the proposals of others)	Positive, offensive strategy (concerned agencies *initiating* positive proposals)
Political support	Based upon (1) the demands of fishermen and hunters; (2) the desires of manufacturers of hunting and fishing equipment and supplies	Based upon the demands of the general public, not just hunters and fishermen
Primary concern	To maintain a sustained yield of preferred fish and wildlife—"shootable game"	To maintain ecosystem diversity and natural communities; to maintain "balanced biotas"
Primary belief	Economic development is the chief measure of human progress	Ecological health and sustainability is the chief measure of human progress
Authority	State authority provided basic legal authority for fish and game management, except in respect to migratory waterfowl, endangered species, and anadromous and commercial fisheries where federal authority reigned supreme; constant controversy between state and federal agencies over the authority to manage wildlife	Clear understanding of federal and state responsibilities, so that the U.S. Fish and Wildlife Service can undertake national leadership in its allocated sphere without fear of state repudiation and to allow states to feel secure in their own realms
Financial support	Almost solely from state license fees paid by fishermen and hunters, and from federal taxes on guns, ammunition, and fishing tackle	Broadened financial backing to collect fees from general public, and possible federal taxes on cameras, film, binoculars, camping gear, and other outdoors equipment; appropriation of general state funds to support its broadened responsibilities so as to escape from its present financial trap of limited, legislatively dedicated revenues
Traditional land uses (e.g., farming, grazing)	Often in competition with those of fish and wildlife, and resource agencies often resolved the competition in favor of fishermen and hunters	Competition resolved equally—taking into consideration the interests of the "antikiller" (the camera- and binocular-carrying hiker); multiple-use management plans for farmers and ranchers that will provide new rural income from all renewable resources including wildlife and related recreation
Clientele ties	Resource agencies fostered strong ties with narrow-visioned clientele groups, such as Trout Unlimited, Ducks Unlimited, Sport Fishing Institute	Clientele broadened to include all who are interested in the survival of natural living things, such as Sierra Club, the Wilderness Society, the Nature Conservancy, the Trust for Public Land
Research	Research aimed at improving sustained yield of desired species for hunters and fishermen	Broad-based ecological research and survey with closer operational relationships with environmental protection, forestry, park, recreation, state comprehensive planning, and other concerned agencies

Source: Adapted from information in Caulfield, Henry P., Jr. 1979. "Political Considerations." In Richard D. Teague and Eugene Decker, eds., *Wildlife Conservation: Principles and Practices.* Washington, D.C.: The Wildlife Society, pp. 45–48.

House passed versions of a nongame bill that authorized funds for state fish and wildlife agencies to plan and implement nongame conservation activities. Since urban wildlife is usually of the nongame variety and hunting is seldom allowed in urban areas, this nongame legislation will serve to encourage wildlife that can be enjoyed in a nonconsumptive way.

Some states have developed nongame wildlife programs, particularly for endangered species and raptorial species. Washington State, for example, has an excellent program for protecting its coastal zone areas, particularly areas where there are nesting sea birds or marine mammal populations. California has established over 18 ecological reserves for endangered species like the Morro Bay kangaroo rat. Michigan's Living Resources Program has been important for the Kirtland warbler and other species. Some states even have nongame wildlife state income tax "checkoffs," whereby taxpayers designate a portion of their refunds for nongame conservation. Missouri, California, Oregon, Minnesota, and New York are among the states with active "wildlife checkoff" programs.

Private agencies are getting into the act of preserving nongame species. Utility companies, for example, are becoming concerned about the fish, wildlife, and plant species that utilize the land and water areas around their power facilities. In many cases, they have studied and protected these resources. In California, the Pacific Gas and Electric Company has protected, among others, the endangered salt marsh harvest mouse and raptors utilizing transmission towers and lines. Particularly impressive is the work of the Florida Power and Light Company to benefit such endangered species such as the manatees, the sea turtles, and the American crocodile. But what is the motive for such wildlife protection? Is it out of direct concern for wild animals? Is it for public relations or to abate the opposition of environmentalists? One could argue, perhaps, that it does not really matter what the motive is as long as the result is satisfactory.

Universities are also moving in the direction of nongame species research. Dr. Tom Cade of Cornell University is involved in a program to reestablish peregrine falcon populations in Eastern cities. Peregrines hatched in the laboratory have been placed in Baltimore, Maryland, and in Washington, D.C., as well as on off shore islands on the East coast. Peregrines are attracted to cities because of the clifflike elevated buildings. Recently, several captive-bred falcons released early in the program mated and fledged young.

4. Changing public attitudes toward wildlife. Aldo Leopold would probably be pleased to see that America is apparently moving, although very slowly, in the direction of *quality* enjoyment of wildlife (Brown et al. 1979, Wagar 1979). In 1949, Leopold identified five components of wildlife enjoyment. Briefly stated, they are as follows:

- *Thinking trophy*—the lowest level—the pursuit of game animals for hides and trophies.
- *Thinking nature*—the feeling of oneness with nature.
- *Thinking healthy*—the enjoyment of the simple pleasures, such as breathing fresh air and viewing a change of scenery.
- *Thinking ecologically*—perceiving nature with an understanding of the principles of ecology.

- *Thinking husbandry*—the highest level—caring and being responsible for resources, their preservation, and their management.

Stephen Kellert of the Yale School of Forestry and Environmental Studies undertook one of the most comprehensive wildlife attitude surveys ever conducted, and it showed Americans favoring the protection of wildlife for nonconsumptive purposes (Kellert 1979, 1980). Some of the interesting findings of this study are as follows: Out of 3107 people interviewed in the nationwide survey, more people were willing to pay higher prices for commodities in order to protect wildlife habit. Seventy-six percent voted in favor of wildlife, whereas 20 percent voted for the selective cutting of timber; 60 percent voted in favor of wildlife, whereas 34 percent voted for reduced grazing on public land. In the area of wildlife program funding, the public seems to be willing to broaden the traditional sources of wildlife funding by placing an excise tax on birdseed, feeders, birdhouses, and birdbaths, with the proceeds going to programs that emphasize nongame species. A surprising result of the survey was that although more than two-thirds of those questioned were in favor of a sales tax on furs and off-road vehicles (and even a majority of the trappers and off-road vehicle enthusiasts surveyed approved of such taxes), the voters were less enthusiastic about program funding through taxes on backpacking and camping equipment; bird-watching equipment and supplies; and wildlife books, art, and magazines.

The Kellert study also showed that Americans, while approving of hunting for meat and wildlife population control, disapproved of hunting purely for recreation and for sport. Americans particularly disapproved of the hunter who seeks trophies to hang on the wall. Although hunting for management purposes was acceptable, public attitudes towards common predators has apparently changed. Animals such as the gray wolf and mountain lion, which were once considered villains to be exterminated, are now more widely regarded as desirable and necessary parts of natural ecosystems.

All these findings seem to indicate that Americans favored protecting wildlife at the expense of jobs, housing, and development projects. As we all know, however, what we say and what we do are not always the same, and therefore caution must be exercised when reading these indicators. Nevertheless, the trend seems to be in the direction of a broadened concept of wildlife resources, and the U.S. Fish and Wildlife Service plans to use these reports to define broad policy guidelines and directions and to provide for public education programs in the future. *People's opinions and behaviors are just as important,* if not more so, than management techniques in influencing the success or failure of a conservation program.

5. *Banning of certain harmful chemicals.* A fifth positive sign indicating that wildlife deterioration can be lessened is seen in the banning of certain herbicides and pesticides. In 1972, for example, the Environmental Protection Agency banned the use of DDT for most purposes in the United States. DDT, DDD, and DDE residues have now dropped in many bird species (Johnson 1974), and many threatened or endangered species are now on the comeback, including prairie falcons (Enderson and Wrege 1973), ospreys (Puleston 1976), and brown pelicans (Anderson et al. 1975, Wurster 1976).

Strict antipollution law enforcement appears to be responsible for the dramatic reproductive improvement of these species, but other factors may also have had an effect, as was the case with the California brown pelican. Biologists generally agreed that the reproductive failure of the brown pelican in the late 1960s and early 1970s was due to collapse of thin-shelled eggs during incubation. DDT and DDE apparently interfered with the brown pelicans' calcium metabolism, making the shells of their eggs so thin that the eggs tended to break before the offspring hatched. But biologists also pointed out that there is a relationship between breeding success and the availability of food during the breeding season. Specifically, the diet of the brown pelican during the breeding season consists almost exclusively of anchovies. The high concentration of anchovies in 1979 in the Santa Barbara Channel north of Santa Cruz and Anacapa Islands was almost certainly an important factor in the pelican's breeding success. Furthermore, closures of nesting areas and adjacent waters to the public permitted the birds to breed with relatively little disturbance.

6. *River and stream protection.* Another good sign is that our federal and state legislators are beginning to see the value of river and riparian habitat protection. In 1968, the National Scenic and Wild Rivers Act preserved a number of free-flowing streams and riparian habitats from further physical encroachment and development. Several states followed suit by developing their own riparian protection plans with the notion of preserving certain segments of rivers from encroachment until they could qualify for federal protection (see Chapter 10 for further details). State departments of fish and game are even beginning to get involved in managing and protecting rivers and ri-

parian habitats—something heretofore not considered part of the traditional role of these departments, which have historically regulated just hunting and fishing.

7. *New timber harvest rules.* A seventh positive sign, which should prove encouraging to "wildlifers," is the new set of rules and regulations that many timber industries must now follow prior to harvesting a particular area. Broadened public support for wildlife protection has brought about changes in forestry philosophy.

Logging operation planners and workers on private lands in several states are now required to consider the welfare of fish and wildlife and to take special precautions to protect habitat (Reynolds 1980). Prior to harvesting a stand, loggers must follow specific *timber harvesting plans* prepared in advance by registered professional foresters. These plans receive multidisciplinary and public review to assure that all significant environmental factors are considered. The timber harvest plans are scrutinized by members of a review board representing agencies such as the state department of forestry (often the agency that accepts or rejects the timber harvest plan), the state departments of fish and game, and the state regional water quality control board.

A specific example of the new approach to timber harvesting is seen in the extraordinary mitigation measures that were taken in California to protect osprey nests (White 1979). When it was revealed that timber harvesting could not continue on Elk River Timber Company lands in lower Elk River drainage in Humboldt County without a loss in nest productivity, the Elk River Timber Company agreed to provide additional nest trees and construct artificial nest platforms. The success of these platforms has yet to be determined, but nevertheless, the cooperation exhibited by this particular timber company is encouraging and can serve as a model for other logging industries.

8. *International organizations, conventions, and sanctuaries.* A final positive indicator of wildlife habitat improvement can be seen in the growing number of international organizations, conventions, and sanctuaries that have been formed to protect wildlife resources on a worldwide scale. Despite opposing economic and political pressures, international wildlife protection and management has made headway throughout the world. Worldwide efforts have been led by such organizations as the International Union for the Conservation of Nature and Natural Resources (IUCN), the World Wildlife Fund (WWF), and the International Council for Bird Preservation (ICBP). Just as there is an ecology of nature, nations have begun to realize that there must also be an *ecology of law*—agreements among nations to ensure that conservation is a success. Neither air or water pollution nor animals respect political borders! Some interesting preservation techniques and innovative ideas have come out of such international conventions as the Convention of International Trade in Endangered Species (CITES), the International Convention on Migratory Species, the World Heritage Convention, and the European Convention. Countries are talking to each other and becoming increasingly concerned about the protection and the preservation of wildlife species and habitats.

The number of international sanctuaries is also increasing. The Indian Ocean Sanctuary, which was proclaimed by the International Whaling Commission, and the whale sanctuaries of Mexico and Argentina are particularly innovative approaches. The Kluane–St. Elias–Wrangell Mountains World Heritage Site is a unique proclamation of an international sanctuary by the United States and Canada under the World Heritage Convention. And, as mentioned earlier in this chapter, UNESCO'S Man and the Biosphere Program (MAB) and its system of biosphere reserves are innovative.

Anticipated Problems

Wildlife deterioration seems to be slowing down and stabilizing in the United States, but the question is for how long. Can the many successes of wildlife managers, conservationists, and environmentalists hold out against the burgeoning problems that face the nation and the world? Wild animals and wild places are feeling the effects of the nation's energy and economic woes: wildlife habitats continue to be threatened; rangeland continues to deteriorate in the West; intensive farming and urban and suburban sprawl continue to gobble up uncounted acres of habitat; and pollution continues to haunt too many rivers and lakes.

Brokaw (1978) identifies two underlying problems for wildlife management: (1) *the lack of education*—people still do not understand that we are inextricably dependent upon wildlife; and (2) *the problem of the commons*—short-run special interests will have a tendency to be dominant over the long-term social need of ecosystem health. The first problem will require additional research and education—not an easy task considering the large size of the population to be educated and the reluctance of educational institutions to adopt new programs; the second problem will require economic incentives and government regulation—an even more difficult task considering the presence of powerful special interest groups (including the environmentalists) and an unwieldly bureaucracy.

ACTION FOR WILDLIFE

If you are interested in wildlife protection, there are several ways that you personally can become involved on different levels: (1) become aware of your personal habits; (2) support existing and new wildlife management principles and policies; (3) help fund wildlife conservation programs; (4) become active in private organizations; (5) take part in wildlife training and research; and (6) participate in wildlife education, conservation programs, and careers. One can support wildlife by becoming involved in only one way or in all six ways, depending upon your time constraints, finances, and level of commitment.

1. *Become aware of your personal habits.* Much can be done by simply altering any personal habits that are detrimental to wildlife resources (National Audubon Society 1976). For example, the National Audubon Society recommends the following actions:

- Use your *consumer power* to alter business practices.
- Use pesticides only when and where you are sure you really have a problem.
- Use herbicides sparingly, or preferably not at all.
- Use your *voting power* to help establish, protect, and fund wildlife refuges, wilderness areas, parks, wild and scenic rivers, and ecological reserves.
- Question the so-called authorities and experts. Do not assume they are always ''in the know.''

2. *Support existing and new wildlife management principles and policies.* You can be a great help by supporting the specific policies of the Wildlife Society:

Hunting

- Endorse the principle that hunting, when properly regulated, is a biologically sound means of managing wildlife populations.
- Encourage the expansion of programs for hunters designed to increase their knowledge of wildlife ecology and hunting ethics.

- Encourage the development of high-quality shooting preserves, consistent with need and demand, as part of a balanced program of public and private wildlife management.

Trapping

- Recognize that trapping has been and currently is a successful technique for capturing animals for specific purposes.
- Encourage the development of improved traps, better and more humane trapping techniques, and efficient alternative methods of taking animals.

Animal Damage Control

- Support the use of only the most efficient, safe, economical, and humane methods to control depredating animals, and advocate effective and humane lethal control only when other methods are unsatisfactory.
- Urge that all control programs directed at wildlife populations and species be regulated closely by state or federal laws.

Alterations of Stream, Riparian, and Wetland Habitats

- Encourage legislation that promotes the maintenance and wise management of stream, riparian, and wetland habitats and their biota.
- Encourage governments to exercise jurisdiction over water rights to set minimum flow rates for streams and minimum levels for lakes and reservoirs that are necessary to maintain ecologically viable aquatic systems.

Threatened and Endangered Species

- Encourage the enactment of legislation and the enforcement of existing laws designed to safeguard their wild populations.
- Foster research on their biology to provide a valid basis for their restoration and management.
- Promote public support for the restoration, conservation, and management of threatened and endangered species.

On a broader scale, you can support the federal government's efforts at preparing a comprehensive national policy for the management of fish and wildlife resources. According to Kimball (1980), such a policy must have four ingredients: (1) *an ecosystem approach*—the policy must encompass all forms of wildlife—game and nongame, endangered species, as well as those in abundance, and migratory as well as nonmigratory species; (2) *a cooperative spirit*—the policy must encourage cooperation among all governmental agencies and concerned private groups to foster and nurture public awareness of the values and benefits stemming from proper conservation of fish and wildlife; (3) *species diversity*—the policy must encourage coordination among these same agencies to produce optimum varieties and numbers of fish and wildlife; and (4) *mutual authority and recognition*—the policy should recognize *both* the responsibility of state wildlife agencies to manage fish and resident wildlife on federal lands (except where contrary federal laws exist) and the authority of the federal government to manage wildlife habitats and regulate the public use of its lands.

3. *Help fund wildlife conservation programs.* State wildlife programs receive funding from a variety of sources—license revenues (from hunting and fishing licenses); federal aid funds (from the Pittman-Robertson Act); general funds (appropriations and state taxes earmarked for wildlife); and other revenues—returns from lands and investments, commercial licenses, and so forth. All of these funding sources and more are necessary for successful wildlife conservation.

At a very personal level, however, you can help by joining one of several professional wildlife organizations, such as the National Audubon Society, the National Wildlife Federation, the Nature Conservancy, or Ducks Unlimited. By being a member, you will be supporting the work of wildlife research scientists, educators, communications specialists, and conservation law enforcement officers.

Since the goals of federal wildlife law have broadened substantially to include preservation of wildlife other than game animals and game fish, you can also support efforts to broaden the revenue base for wildlife conservation. Michael Bean (1978) has suggested several ways to do this, such as encouraging nonhunters to purchase duck stamps and broadening the tax base under the Pittman-Robertson and Dingell-Johnson Acts.

Taxable products and services that might be appealing both to hunters and nonhunters are such items as nature publications; stamps, posters, and art prints; wildlife walks and camps; programs for the physically handicapped and shut-ins; camera-hunting classes; and instructions for attracting wildlife. Through effective promotion by personal selling, attractive advertisements, and wildlife editorials or columns, wildlife agencies in conjunction with your moral and financial support can help broaden wildlife revenues (Schick et al. 1976).

4. *Become active in private wildlife organizations.* You can go beyond being just a subscribing member of a private wildlife organization and actually volunteer your services. Many organizations, such as the National Audubon Society, the League of American Sportsmen, and the American Wildlife Institute, are dependent upon concerned citizens who are willing to devote a few hours per week to various essential tasks. Refuges within the National Wildlife Refuge System are continually in need of volunteers to staff offices, lead nature walks, and repair facilities.

5. *Support wildlife training and research.* You can also help wildlife resources by supporting the further development of new courses, programs, departments, and institutes that have a wildlife focus within our nation's colleges, universities, and private research institutions. Special attention must be given to broaden traditional wildlife management programs so as to incorporate the concepts and procedures and working tools developed by the social sciences, particularly human ecology, anthropology, sociology, economics, political science, history, geography, and social psychology (Teague 1979).

Wildlife training and research programs that ne-glect studying the social, political, economic, legal, and cultural implications of wildlife resource management and ecology are pure folly since *the solution to most wildlife management problems depends on the habits, behaviors, and views of humans.* Since biology departments within our colleges and universities handle most wildlife training, they could easily broaden and strengthen their wildlife programs by incorporating existing courses from other departments into the wildlife training. Such courses as environmental law, environmental economics, and human ecology can be taught as part of wildlife training programs. Your support of multidisciplinary and interdisciplinary education will help traditional wildlife management programs move in the right direction.

6. *Participate in wildlife education, conservation programs, and careers.* Perhaps the ultimate commitment to wildlife is to select a lifetime career in the field. This could mean being a traditional wildlife biologist on a public refuge, working as a wildlife specialist for a timber company, being a free-lance wildlife writer or photographer for various wildlife magazines and journals. Whether in wildlife management, wildlife research, wildlife public relations, wildlife education, or wildlife law enforcement, opportunities exist for those individuals who seek serious preparation and are prepared for fierce competition for employment.

DISCUSSION TOPICS

1. Define *wildlife resource management.* Why is it necessary for wildlife resource managers to be more than just pure biologists? Provide some examples.

2. What is the difference between a game and nongame species? Why should wildlife managers strive for balanced biotas?

3. What are the three types of wilderness wildlife? Provide examples.

4. List and discuss various ways that wildlife resource managers can tackle the problem of loss of wildlife habitat. Discuss how wildlife habitat has been lost in areas adjacent to your neighborhood.

5. Pick the closest farm to your house. Make a diagram that illustrates how that farmer can improve the land for wildlife enhancement. Meet with the farmer and discuss your diagram. Record the farmer's reaction to various aspects of your plan. Report your findings back to class.

6. Check with your city's planning department. Find out what attention, if any, it gives to streambank protection for wildlife.

7. Actually construct a guzzler for wildlife. Test out the device in a neighboring field that has abundant wildlife. If you are a photographer, record your results on film.

8. What is the difference between climax-, mid-, and low-successional species? Using specific animals as examples, illustrate how this information is of value to the wildlife resource manager.

9. Discuss the pros and cons of the construction of dredge islands as a technique in wildlife resource management. Are dredge islands being constructed in your local area? Do the benefits outweigh any drawbacks?

10. Why is sanitation cutting detrimental to wildlife? Provide examples with specific animals.

11. Discuss the concept of planned neglect. What areas adjacent to your neighborhood deserve to be managed accordingly? Who would be against this type of management strategy? Why? Is there any room for compromise? If so, how?

12. Construct a large-scale map of your county's major

highway systems. Using a clear plastic overlay, map out the various types of vegetation within the median strips as well as along the borders of the highway route. Make another overlay sheet that illustrates an improved wildlife habitat scheme—one that is safe for both wildlife and for automobile passengers.

13. Study an institution's grounds within your local area, whether it be a campus, a churchyard, or a cemetery. How might it be improved for wildlife? Discuss your proposal with those in charge.

14. Interview three developers within your local area. Find out how much, if any, attention they devote to wildlife when they draft their various development schemes. What are they willing and not willing to do to protect wildlife?

15. Visit a wildlife refuge within your local area. Find out what kind of wildlife law enforcement techniques are used at the refuge. Are they well accepted by the public? Are they religiously enforced by the refuge manag-

ers? Are any of the existing laws due for modification? If so, how?

16. Why is the shooting preserve the antithesis of balanced biotas? Why should we still have shooting preserves?

17. Discuss the pros and cons of owning domestic animals as pets. Be sure to discuss this question as it relates to the concerns of the wildlife resource manager.

18. Visit your local pet store and record where various animals come from. Do you suspect the proprietor of conducting illegal trade in animals? Why?

19. Discuss the advantages and disadvantages of wildlife farming.

20. Visit your local zoo. Find out to what degree it uses the frozen zoo technique in wildlife preservation.

21. List and discuss various ways that you personally can get involved in wildlife preservation. Which activities are you already doing, are likely to do in the near future, and are not likely to do in your lifetime?

READINGS

ANDERSON, D. W., et al. 1975. "Brown Pelicans: Improved Reproduction Off the Southern California Coast," *Science*, vol. 190, pp. 806–808. Detailed explanation of the comeback of the brown pelican.

BAILEY, JAMES. 1984. *Principles of Wildlife Management*. New York: Wiley. Emphasis on the applications of ecology to the management of wildlife populations and habitats.

BAVIN, CLARK R. 1978. "Wildlife Law Enforcement." In Howard P. Brokaw, ed., *Wildlife and America*, pp. 350–363. Washington, D.C.: Government Printing Office. Excellent history of U.S. wildlife law enforcement.

BEAN, MICHAEL J. 1977. "The Endangered Species Act Under Fire," *National Parks & Conservation Magazine*, June, vol. 51, no. 6, pp. 16–20. Readable account of U.S. threatened and endangered species legislation.

BEAN, MICHAEL J. 1978. "Federal Wildlife Law." In Howard P. Brokaw, ed., *Wildlife and America*. Washington, D.C.: Government Printing Office. Detailed overview of threatened and endangered species legislation.

BEEBE, SPENCER B. 1974. *Relationships Between Insectivorous Hole-Nesting Birds and Forest Management*. New Haven, Conn.: Yale University School for Environmental Studies. (Multilithed.) Brief discussion of the role of birds in insect control within forests.

BROKAW, HOWARD P. ed. 1978. *Wildlife and America*. Washington, D.C.: Government Printing Office. Comprehensive study.

BROWN, THOM L., CHAD P. DAWSON, and ROBERT L. MILLER. 1979. "Interests and Attitudes of Metropolitan New York Residents and Wildlife." In *Transactions of the 44th North American Wildlife and Natural Resources Conference*. Washington, D.C.: Wildlife Management Institute. Interesting case study of public attitudes toward wildlife.

CALDWELL, LYNTON K., et al. 1976. *Citizens and the Environment: Case Studies in Popular Action*. Bloomington, Ind.: Indiana University Press. Includes good discussion of successes in international wildlife protection and management.

CAULFIELD, HENRY P., JR. 1979. "Political Considerations." In R. Teague and E. Decker, eds., *Wildlife Conservation: Principles and Practices*, pp. 45–48. Washington, D.C.: The Wildlife Society. Good summary of the political aspects of wildlife conservation.

CLAWSON, MARION. 1971. *The Bureau of Land Management*. New York: Praeger. Includes informative discussion of wildlife management on BLM lands.

CLAWSON, MARION, ed. 1974. *Forest Policy for the Future: Conflict Compromise Consensus*. Washington, D.C.: Resources for the Future. Good summary.

CLAWSON, MARION. 1975. *Forests for Whom and for What?* Baltimore, Md.: Johns Hopkins University Press. Includes discussion of forest policy related to wildlife management.

COURTENAY, WALTER R., JR. 1978. "The Introduction of Exotic Organisms." In Howard P. Brokaw, ed., *Wildlife and America*, pp. 237–252. Washington, D.C.: Government Printing Office. Outstanding overview of this factor in wildlife extinction.

CUMMINGS, MAYNARD W. 1979. "Wildlife Damage Problems." In R. Teague and E. Decker, eds., *Wildlife Conservation: Principles and Practices*, pp. 167–171. Washington, D.C.: The Wildlife Society. Excellent discussion of wildlife damage problems and alternative methods of control.

DANKO, ROBERT, and PETER WILSON. 1976. "Make Way for Organic Agriculture," *Conservation News*, vol. 41, no. 9, pp. 6–7. Brief discussion of the benefits of nonconventional agriculture for wildlife.

DASMANN, RAYMOND F. 1976. *Environmental Conservation.* 4th ed. New York: Wiley. Outstanding general conservation textbook. Also consult the more recent (1984) edition.

DASMANN, RAYMOND F. 1981. *Wildlife Biology.* 2d ed. New York: Wiley. Includes classification of wildlife types as they relate to ecological succession.

DAVIDS, RICHARD C. 1978. "Managing America's Man-Made Islands," *Exxon-USA,* 4th quarter report, pp. 16–21. The creation of artificial islands for habitat development.

DICKINSON, NATHANIEL R. 1980. "State Land/Wildlife Management Area: For Everybody," *The Conservationist,* vol. 34, no. 4, pp. 10–14. Interesting discussion of New York's wildlife management areas.

DINGELL, JOHN D., and FRANK M. POTTER, JR. 1978. "Federal Initiatives in Wildlife Management." In Howard P. Brokaw, ed., *Wildlife and America,* pp. 302–309. Washington, D.C.: Government Printing Office. Excellent summary.

DUNLAP, THOMAS R. 1988. *Saving America's Wildlife.* Princeton, N.J.: Princeton University Press. Historical analysis of wildlife resource management in America.

ENDERSON, J. H., and P. H. WREGE. 1973. "DDE Residues and Eggshell Thickness in Prairie Falcons," *Journal of Wildlife Management,* vol. 37, pp. 476–478. Illustrates the positive effects of banning certain harmful chemicals.

FINKLER, EARL. 1975. *The Multiple Use of Cemeteries.* Planning Advisory Series Report No. 285. Chicago: American Society of Planning Officials. Buffalo, New York's Forest Lawn Cemetery—a bird sanctuary.

GILES, R. H. ed. 1969. *Wildlife Management Techniques.* Washington, D.C.: The Wildlife Society. Important book.

GRAUL, WALTER, RICHARD DENNEY, and JOHN TORRES. 1976. "A Species-Ecosystem Approach for Nongame Programs," *Wildlife Society Bulletin,* Summer, vol. 4, no. 2, pp. 78–79. Good description.

HENDEE, JOHN C., and CLARENCE A. SCHOENFELD. 1979. "Wildlife Management for Wilderness." In Richard D. Teague and E. Decker, eds., *Wildlife Conservation: Principles and Practices,* pp. 197–203. Washington, D.C.: The Wildlife Society. Classifies types of "wilderness wildlife" and appropriate management schemes.

JENKINS, ROBERT. 1978. "Habitat Preservation by Private Organizations." In Howard P. Brokaw, ed., *Wildlife and America,* pp. 424–426. Washington, D.C.: Government Printing Office. Methods used to give protective status to prime wildlife habitats.

JOHNSON, DAVID W. 1974. "Decline of DDT Residues in Migratory Songbirds," *Science,* vol. 186, pp. 841–842. Excellent overview.

KELLERT, STEPHEN R. 1980. *Activities of the American Public Relating to Animals.* Washington, D.C.: U.S. Fish and Wildlife Service. Important study often referred to by the U.S. Fish and Wildlife Service.

KELLERT, STEPHEN R. 1979. *Public Attitudes Toward Critical Wildlife and Natural Habitat Issues.* Washington, D.C.: U.S. Fish and Wildlife Service. Important study on public attitudes toward wildlife resources.

KIMBALL, THOMAS. 1980. "On Establishing a National Fish and Wildlife Policy," *National Wildlife,* May, p. 24-B. Maintains that four ingredients are necessary for establishing a valid wildlife policy.

KING, F. WAYNE. 1978. "The Wildlife Trade." In Howard P. Brokaw, ed., *Wildlife and America,* pp. 253–271. Washington, D.C.: Government Printing Office. Excellent overview.

KOUBA, LEONARD J. 1976. "The Evolution of Shooting Preserves in the United States." *The Professional Geographer,* May, vol. 28, no. 2, pp. 142–146. Provides interesting historical background to the concept of the shooting preserve.

KOZICKY, EDWARD L., and JOHN B. MADSON. 1979. "The Shooting Preserve Concept." In Richard D. Teague and E. Decker, eds., *Wildlife Conservation: Principles and Practices,* pp. 156–160. Washington, D.C.: The Wildlife Society. Good discussion of the advantages and disadvantages of shooting preserves.

LABASTILLE, ANNE. 1976. "A Delicate Balance," *National Wildlife,* June–July, vol. 14, no. 4, pp. 29–32. Vivid description of brutal animal control programs.

LAURIE, IAN C., ed. 1979. *Nature in Cities: The Natural Environment in the Design and Development of Urban Green Space.* New York: Wiley. Excellent book on how to bring back wildlife to urban areas.

LEEDY, DANIEL L. 1975. *Highway Wildlife Relationships, Vol. 1: A State-of-the-Art Report.* Springfield, Va.: National Technical Information Service. A how-to book on how to improve highways for vehicle travel and wildlife.

LEEDY, DANIEL L., ROBERT M. MAESTRO, and THOMAS M. FRANKLIN. 1978. *Planning for Wildlife in Cities and Suburbs.* Washington, D.C.: Fish and Wildlife Service. Excellent how-to book on improving wildlife habitat within cities.

LEEDY, DANIEL L., and LOWELL W. ADAMS. 1984. *A Guide to Urban Wildlife Management.* Columbia, Md.: National Institute for Urban Wildlife. Excellent overview.

LEEPSON, MARC. 1977. "Protecting Endangered Wildlife," *Editorial Research Reports,* September 16, pp. 683–700. Provides international perspective on wildlife protective efforts.

LEOPOLD, ALDO. 1949. *A Sand County Almanac and Sketches Here and There.* New York: Oxford University Press. A classic work on environmental ethics written by the father of wildlife resource management.

MILLER, G. TYLER, JR. 1982. *Living in the Environment.* Belmont, Calif.: Wadsworth. Outstanding introductory textbook on environmental studies. Check more recent editions.

MOEN, A. N. 1983. *Agriculture and Wildlife Management.* Lansing, N.Y.: CornerBrook Press. Good summary.

MORSE, WILLIAM B. 1979. "Law Enforcement—A Management Tool." In Richard D. Teague and Eugene Decker, eds., *Wildlife Conservation: Principles and Practices.* Washington, D.C.: The Wildlife Society. Provides historical perspective on game laws in the United States.

NATIONAL AUDUBON SOCIETY. 1976. *The Environment and What You Can Do.* National Audubon Society. Brochure.

Provides numerous ideas on how individuals can modify their personal habits to protect wildlife.

NATIONAL WILDLIFE FEDERATION. 1974. *Gardening with Wildlife—A Complete Guide to Attracting and Enjoying the Fascinating Creatures in Your Backyard*. Washington, D.C.: National Wildlife Federation. Good summary with excellent illustrations.

ODUM, EUGENE P. 1971. "Ecological Principles and the Urban Forest." In *Proceedings, Symposium on Role of Trees in the South's Urban Environment*, pp. 78–81. Athens, Ga.: Center for Continuing Education, University of Georgia. Illustrates how city parks can be managed to enhance wildlife populations.

ODUM, EUGENE P., and SHARON DAVIS. 1969. "More Birds in the Bushes from Shrubs in the Plans," *Landscape Architecture*, October, p. 36. Describes how to manage institutional grounds, such as college campuses, for wildlife habitat improvement.

OLKOWSKI, W., et al. 1976. "Ecosystem Management: A Framework for Urban Pest Control," *BioScience*, vol. 26, pp. 384–389. Excellent description of the relationship between wildlife and urban insect control.

OWEN, OLIVER S. 1980. *Natural Resource Conservation: An Ecological Approach*. New York: Macmillan. Includes excellent chapter on wildlife resource management. Also consult the more recent edition.

PULESTON, DENNIS. 1976. "Ospreys and the DDT Ban," *EDF Letter*, March, p. 2. Interesting comments related to the return of the osprey.

RAMSAY, WILLIAM. 1976. "Priorities in Species Preservation," *Environmental Affairs*, Fall, vol. 5, no. 4, pp. 595–616. The need to set priorities in threatened and endangered species legislation.

REGENSTEIN, LEWIS. 1975. *The Politics of Extinction*. New York: Macmillan. Detailed account of the international politics involved in wildlife preservation.

REYNOLDS, FORREST. 1980. "Improve Logging Practices to Protect Wildlife," *Outdoor California*, March–April, pp. 16–18. Methods by which foresters can help protect wildlife.

SANTAMOUR, F. S., JR., H. D. GERFOLD, and SILAS LITTLE, eds. 1976. *Better Trees for Metropolitan Landscapes, Technical Report NE-22*. Upper Darby, Pa.: U.S. Forest Service. The proper selection of street trees for wildlife enhancement.

SCHEFFER, VICTOR B. 1976. "The Future of Wildlife Management," *Wildlife Society Bulletin*, Summer, vol. 4, no. 2, pp. 51–54. An interesting look into the future of wildlife resource management.

SCOTT, VIRGIL E., KEITH E. EVANS, DAVID R. PATTON, and CHARLES P. STONE. 1977. *Cavity-Nesting Birds of North American Forests*, Agricultural Handbook No. 511, November, Washington, D.C.: U.S. Forest Service. Important study, which describes in detail the necessity of protecting cliffs, talus, and caves on forest lands.

SCHICK, MORE, DEGRAAF, and SAMUEL. 1976. "Marketing Wildlife Management," *Wildlife Society Bulletin*, Summer, vol. 4, no. 2, p. 64. Innovative advertising strategies to broaden wildlife revenues.

SIDERITS, KARL. 1975. "Forest Diversity: An Approach to Forest Wildlife Management," *Forestry Chronicle*, vol. 51, no. 3, pp. 99–103. A discussion of the multiple use concept as it applies to wildlife resources.

SOLMAN, VICTOR E. F. 1974. "Aircraft and Wildlife." In *Wildlife in an Urbanizing Environment*, pp. 137–141. Amherst, Mass.: University of Massachusetts Cooperative Extension Service. Good description of how to make airports less attractive to wildlife.

STAHR, ELVIS J., and CHARLES H. CALLISON. 1978. "The Role of Private Organizations." In Howard P. Brokaw, ed., *Wildlife and America*, pp. 498–511. Washington, D.C.: Government Printing Office. The important role that private organizations play in wildlife protection.

STEARNS, F. 1972. "The City as Habitat for Wildlife and Man." In T. Detwyler and M. Marcus, eds., *Urbanization and Environment*. Belmont, Calif.: Duxbury Press. Excellent chapter on how to preserve or improve wildlife habitat within urban areas.

STEARNS, FOREST, and TOM MONTAG. 1974. *The Urban Ecosystem: A Holistic Approach*. Community Development Series, vol. 14. Prepared by the Institute of Ecology for the National Science Foundation's Research Applied to National Needs (RANN) program (Washington, D.C.). Methods for improving wildlife habitat in developed areas.

STOCKER, JOSEPH. 1980. "Battle of the Burro," *National Wildlife*, August–September, vol. 18, no. 5, pp. 14–16. Informative discussion of the problems of managing burros—an animal considered by many to be a pest.

SWANSON, GUSTAV A. 1979. "Historical Highlights in American Wildlife Conservation." In Richard D. Teague and Eugene Decker, eds., *Wildlife Conservation: Principles and Practices*, pp. 3–6. Washington, D.C.: The Wildlife Society. Excellent summary.

TEAGUE, RICHARD D. 1979. "The Role of Social Sciences in Wildlife Management." In Richard D. Teague and Eugene Decker, eds., *Wildlife Conservation: Principles and Practices*, pp. 55–60. Washington, D.C.: The Wildlife Society. Calls for the inclusion of more social science training for wildlife managers.

THOM, RICHARD H. 1979. "Natural Areas and Natural Heritage Areas." In Richard D. Teague and Eugene Decker, eds., *Wildlife Conservation: Principles and Practices*, pp. 194–195. Washington, D.C.: The Wildlife Society. Illustrates how federal agencies classify wild lands.

THOMAS, JACK WARD, ed. 1979. *Wildlife Habitats in Managed Forests—The Blue Mountains of Oregon and Washington*. Agricultural Handbook No. 553. Washington, D.C.: U.S. Department of Agriculture, Forest Service. Important government study.

THOMAS, JACK WARD, JOHN D. GILL, JAMES C. PACK, WILLIAM M. HEALY, and H. REED SANDERSON. 1976. "Influence of Forest-Land Characteristics on Spatial Distribution of Hunters," *Journal of Wildlife Management*, July, vol. 40, no.

3, pp. 500–506. Describes site management as a technique to protect wildlife.

TOURBIER, JOACHIM, and RICHARD WESTMACOTT. 1976. *Lakes and Ponds, Technical Bulletin 72*. Washington, D.C.: Urban Land Institute. Illustrates how lakes and ponds are vital for urban wildlife.

U.S. DEPARTMENT OF AGRICULTURE. 1969. *Making Land Produce Useful Wildlife, Farmers' Bulletin No. 2035*. Washington, D.C.: U.S. Department of Agriculture. A how-to manual for improving wildlife habitat on the farm.

WAGAR, J. V. K. 1979. "Quality in Wildlife Management." In Richard D. Teague and Eugene Decker, eds., *Wildlife Conservation: Principles and Practices*, pp. 11–15. Washington, D.C.: The Wildlife Society. Excellent explanation of the reasons for demanding quality wildlife.

WHITE, JACK. 1979. "Urgan Renewal for Osprey," *Outdoor California*, January–February, pp. 25, 32. Brief discussion of the mitigation measures required in California to protect the osprey.

WURSTER, CHARLES F. 1976. "Postscript on Pelicans," *EDF Letter*, March, p. 2. Brief note on the comeback of the brown pelican.

YOAKUM, JAMES D. 1979. "Habitat Improvement." In Richard D. Teague and Eugene Decker, eds., *Wildlife Conservation: Principles and Practices*, pp. 132–139. Washington, D.C.: The Wildlife Society. Excellent discussion of how to manipulate lands to improve wildlife habitat.

YOAKUM, J., W. P. DASMANN, R. SANDERSON, C. M. NIXON, and H. S. CRAWFORD. 1979. "Habitat Management Techniques." In S. Schemintz, ed., *Wildlife Management Techniques*. Washington, D.C.: The Wildlife Society. Detailed account within a very important and often referred to textbook.

10

WILDERNESS AND OPEN-SPACE PRESERVATION AND MANAGEMENT

Types of Preservation
Principles and Techniques of
    Open-Space Management
Prospects for the Future
Action for Open-Space Preservation

We need the tonic of wildness—to wade sometimes in marshes where the bittern and the meadow-hen lurk, and hear the booming of the snipe; to smell the whispering sedge where only some wilder and more solitary fowl builds her nest, and the mink crawls with its belly close to the ground.
Henry David Thoreau, *Walden*

Most Americans are aware that environmental movements have something to do with protecting pristine areas of the countryside. They often use terms such as **parks**, **open space**, and **wilderness** interchangeably. Actually, each term has a specific, well-defined meaning that will be elaborated on as the chapter develops. Geographer Nicholas Helburn (1977) suggests that human beings have a profound need for natural things whether it be the virgin wilderness or the flower bed in a well-tended garden. Between these two extremes on the *wildness continuum* are the National Wildlife Areas, the National Wild and Scenic Rivers, the National Trails, the National Parks, forests, deserts, wetlands, farmlands, state and regional parks and campgrounds, downtown parks, penthouse gardens, and suburban lawns. Others have also studied the wilderness concept, from the classic wilderness authors, such as Leopold (1949) and Muir (1954), to the contemporary authors, such

as Tuan (1971), Klein (1976), and Price (1981). The purpose of this chapter is to explore Helburn's wildness continuum, to differentiate between the major types of open space, to discuss their peculiar problems, and to suggest some general management strategies. Let us begin at the far end on the wildness continuum—those areas that are closest to virgin wilderness.

TYPES OF PRESERVATION

Federal Systems

The National Wilderness Preservation System. The American Heritage Dictionary of the English Language defines **wilderness** as ''any unsettled, uncultivated region left in its natural condition.'' The Wilderness Society, a nationally recognized organization, defines wilderness as "an area where the earth and its community of life are untrammeled by man, where man himself is a visitor who does not remain." After a century of tumultuous debate—dating back as far as painter George Catlin's 1882 proposal to preserve a huge wildland area in the Great Plains—the federal government passed the Wilderness Act of 1964, which provided for the protection of specific wilderness areas through the National Wilderness Preservation System. This act expanded upon the above definitions:

> An area of wilderness is further defined to mean in this Act an area of undeveloped federal land retaining its primeval character and influence without permanent improvements or human habitation, which is protected and managed so as to preserve its natural conditions and which (1) generally appears to have been affected primarily by the forces of nature with the imprint of man's work substantially unnoticeable; (2) has outstanding opportunities for solitude or a primitive and unconfined type of recreation; (3) has at least five thousand acres of land, or is sufficient size to make practical its preservation and use in an unimpaired condition; and (4) may also contain ecological, geological, or other features of scientific, educational, scenic or historical value.

In federally designated wilderness areas many activities are forbidden: the construction of roads, dams, buildings, and other permanent structures; timbering; and the operation of motorized vehicles and equipment. Grazing is permitted only in areas that had been designated as grazing areas before the Wilderness Act of 1964; mining was permitted only through 1983. The act does, however, permit a wide range of relatively *low impact* recreational activities in wilderness areas: hiking, camping, mountain climbing, canoeing, rafting, cross-country skiing, and in some cases hunting and horseback riding. But even these activities are strictly controlled.

Instead of creating a new federal agency to administer these lands, the Wilderness Act left their management to the agencies that were already managing them. The act required each agency (the U.S. Forest Service, the National Park Service, the U.S. Fish and Wildlife Service, and the Bureau of Land Management) to protect the wilderness qualities of the land in its jurisdiction. By establishing *wilderness zones* within existing national forests, parks, and wildlife refuges, Congress simply confirmed the role of these agencies in protecting wilderness areas.

The Wilderness Act also authorizes the managing agencies to fight fires, to suppress insect infestations, to take emergency measures to safeguard the health and safety of wilderness users, and to take other necessary actions. But the most zealous defenders of the wilderness protest that even the fire roads, lookout towers, patrol cabins, and the motorized vehicles used by the agencies in their routine management of the land impair the wilderness experience.

When it was set up in 1964, the National Wilderness Preservation System consisted of 3.7 million ha (9.1 million acres) of national forest land—all of it already under the management of one agency or another. The Wilderness Act authorized Congress to add to that land (Figure 10-1), and since 1964 Congress has indeed brought additional acres into the system. It has added other wilderness tracts under the Endangered American Wilderness Act of 1978 and the Alaska Lands Act of 1980. Despite these impressive gains, wilderness areas account for only 3.4 percent of all the land in the United States and only 11.7 percent of all government-owned lands (Table 10-1).

Even so, a battle is raging over energy production rights and mineral leasing in the wilderness areas. Industrialists claim that vast supplies of energy and minerals are locked up in the wilderness sites and that those supplies should be exploited, such as the minerals of the Overthrust Belt along the eastern edge of the Rocky Mountains. Environmentalists reply that Congress scrutinized the sites before designating them as wilderness areas and excluded most of the known energy reserves from their boundaries. According to some estimates, only 2 percent of our total oil and gas reserves lie within designated wilderness areas. Furthermore, in 1982, the Congressional Office of Technology Assessment showed that billions of tons of coal reserves already leased to private enterprises were going unused, mainly because of the lack of demand. So, environmentalists ask, why should the government rush to issue more leases? Why not wait until there is a need to exploit these energy reserves?

Environmentalists present what they insist are legitimate needs for preserving the wilderness rather than opening it up to further exploitation. Nash (1978) has identified several major arguments used by ecologists and environmentalists in defense of wilderness: First, scientists need the wilderness as a means of measuring the *impact of civilization* on the natural environment. Just as medical scientists need healthy people, ecologists need healthy, balanced areas where natural mechanisms can be observed

National Wilderness Preservation System
September 1983

FIGURE 10-1 The National Wilderness Preservation System. (Reprinted from *National Wilderness Preservation System*, Sierra Club, 1983).

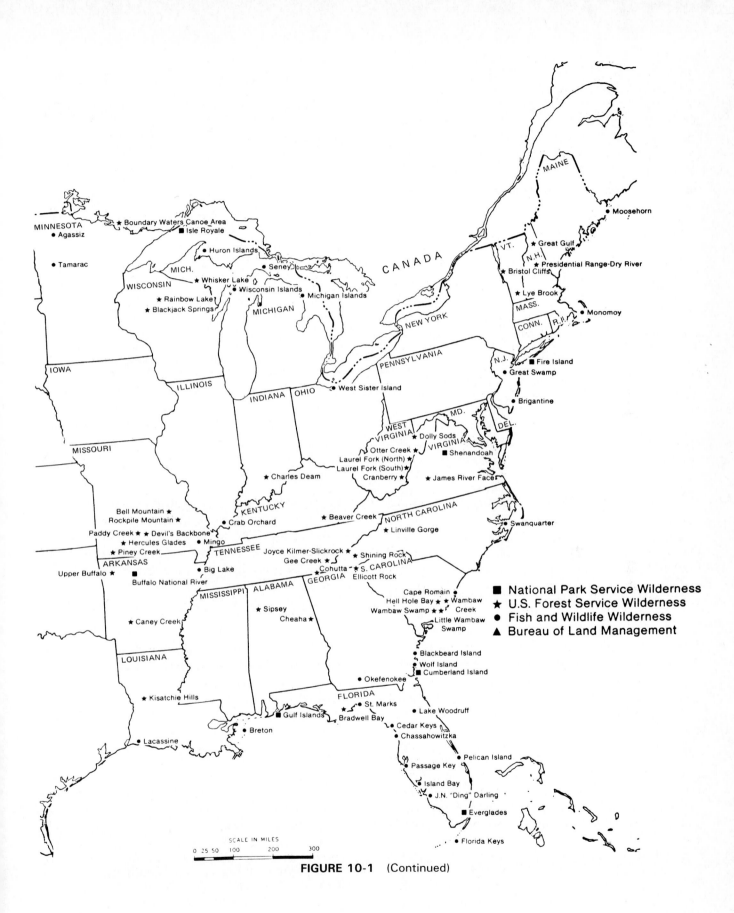

FIGURE 10-1 (Continued)

TABLE 10-1

National wilderness preservation system (NWPS)

AGENCY	NUMBER OF NWPS UNITS	AGENCY'S NWPS ACREAGE	TOTAL AGENCY ACREAGE	PERCENTAGE OF AGENCY LAND IN NWPS	PERCENTAGE OF TOTAL NWPS ACREAGE	AGENCY'S NWPS ACREAGE AS PERCENTAGE OF: TOTAL ACREAGE OF THESE 4 AGENCIES	U.S. LAND AREA
U.S. Forest Service (USFS)	165	25,252,800	190,719,100	13.24 %	31.65%	3.7	1.1
National Park Service (NPS)	36	35,334,500	79,018,000	44.71 %	44.28 %	5.2	1.5
Fish & Wildlife Service (FWS)	65	19,208,300	88,827,900	21.62 %	24.06%	2.8	0.8
Bureau of Land Management (BLM)	3	12,000	315,991,900	0.004%	0.01%	0.002	0.0005
TOTAL	269	79,807,600	674,556,900		100.00%	11.7%	3.4%

Source: Sierra Club. 1983. *The National Wilderness Preservation System.* Brochure.

Largest Unit: Wrangell–St. Elias, Alaska, 8,700,000 acres.

Smallest Unit: Pelican Island, Florida, 6 acres.

functioning under normal conditions. Second, society as a whole needs to preserve refuges of *biological diversity* in order to safeguard for the future what remains of natural gene pools. Third, the availability of natural landscapes helps sustain *mental health*. Every weekend, thousands of Americans flee the confines of the city to walk through the forest or to stroll along a quiet beach. Some opportunity for direct contact with nature seems to be a psychological necessity for human beings. And not everyone is fortunate enough to live in a house with a view of the natural world. Fourth, some people report that they experience a feeling of *oneness, of harmony,* in natural surroundings. Ralph Waldo Emerson, Henry David Thoreau, and John Muir, for example, testified to the religious experience they underwent in the fields and forests remote from human habitations. Fifth, Nash maintains that the presence of the wilderness helps foster *social diversity* and *human dignity*. In place of the regulations, cultural institutions, and uniformity imposed by civilization, the wilderness offers experimentation, freedom, and self-realization. To novelist Wallace Stegner, it represents "the geography of hope." Sixth, Nash maintains, as did historian Frederick Jackson Turner in 1893, that the wilderness is a major influence in the shaping of the *American character.* It was during the pioneering days, according to Turner, that independence and individualism were born, that a democratic society arose, and that the concept of equal opportunity emerged. To these observers, the preservation of the wilderness is essential to the preservation of American culture. Sev-

enth, Nash points out that some of the most creative minds have found *inspiration* in the natural landscape: Thoreau, Emerson, and numerous others in literature (Brooks 1980); John James Audubon, Albert Bierstadt, and Thomas Cole in painting (Novak 1980); Aaron Copeland and John Denver in music; and Ansel Adams and Eliot Porter in photography. The unspoiled countryside seems to provide that which is essential for artistic endeavor—what geographers and others refer to as a *sense of place*. Finally, says Nash, efforts to preserve the wilderness remind citizens that they themselves are ultimately responsible for the environment. We tend to forget that we are dependent on the earth's natural resources for our very *survival*. We assume that water comes from the kitchen faucet rather than from rivers and underground reservoirs; that meat comes from plastic-wrapped packages in the supermarket rather than from living animals; and that gasoline comes from filling stations rather than from oil found deep beneath the surface of the earth. To walk the wild country sharpens our awareness of *where things come from* and reminds us of how dependent we are on natural resources.

The National Wilderness Preservation System provides a counterbalance to the pressures being exerted on the environment by the federal government's rush to sell public lands, states' rights movements, urban demands for additional water, and oil and mineral exploration. The system is certain to be a major factor in the preservation of the future. Additional insights into the National Wilderness Preservation System can be obtained from Fox (1981), Allin (1982), and

Nash (1982). For the Wilderness Society's agenda for the National Wilderness Preservation System, consult their 1984 publication entitled *Toward the Twenty-First Century.*

The National Wild and Scenic Rivers System

Past these towering monuments, past these mounded billows of orange sandstone, past these oak-set glens, past these fern-decked alcoves, past these mural curves, we glide, hour after hour . . . (Major John Wesley Powell, 1869)

Powell's account is of a day adrift on the Colorado River in Utah's Glen Canyon—once one of the grandest landscapes on the continent. Today, its fern-decked alcoves are flooded, its oak-set glens are submerged. In the opinion of David Sumner (1981), author and landscape photographer, it stands as a symbol of what happens to a river when its flow is dammed. Environmentalists mourn the loss of Hetch Hetchy, of Glen Canyon, and of Flaming Gorge on the Green River. On Helburn's wildness continuum, *free-flowing rivers are probably the linear equivalent of the wilderness area.* Yet, of the 5.6 million km (3.5 million mi) of rivers, streams, creeks, and brooks in this nation, only 0.3 percent enjoy any protection (Figure 10-2).

In 1968, the National Wild and Scenic Rivers System (Figure 10-3) was created to protect American rivers that possessed exceptional recreational and scenic values. This system was to parallel in concept the National Wilderness Preservation System. Its main purpose was to prevent the construction of

FIGURE 10-2 The Tuolomne River in California, one of the latest rivers to be included in the National Wild and Scenic Rivers System. (Photo by author.)

dams and other structures on what remained of the nation's free-flowing rivers. It initially included segments of eight rivers flowing a total of 1292 km (803 mi) in seven states.

The system protects only segments of rivers, because few rivers in the United States remain truly wild from their headwaters to their mouths. Most riverine areas are heavily settled and suffer the abuse arising from dense concentrations of population. Moreover, since rivers traverse vast expanses of territory (much of it inhabited), it is politically difficult to protect entire rivers. The act that established the Wild and Scenic Rivers System identified three categories of river environment.

1. *Wild rivers*—the most free-flowing (that is, undisturbed by humans) rivers or sections of rivers, which are generally inaccessible by road, have no impoundments (e.g., water reservoirs), and have no buildings along their banks.
2. *Scenic rivers*—relatively free-flowing rivers or section of rivers with a few recreational facilities, which are accessible by road.
3. *Recreational rivers*—rivers or sections of rivers that are still aesthetically pleasing despite small developments along their banks (including farms and towns) and that are easily accessible by roads, railroads, and small airfields.

Few of the rivers designated under the act fall entirely into one classification. For example, Missouri's Eleven Point River is classified as *scenic* throughout its length. In contrast, segments of Oregon's Rogue River (Figures 10-4 and 10-5) and California's Feather River fall into all three classifications. The framers of the act were wise in recognizing that a given river might fit all three environmental categories. Had they insisted on preserving only the wildest rivers, they would have excluded sections of rivers with great scenic and recreational value.

Environmentalists argue, however, that the National Wild and Scenic Rivers System includes only fragments of the nation's great rivers. Why, they ask, are such glorious rivers as the Colorado in the Grand Canyon and the renowned Stanislaus River in California not included? And why, they ask, has so little progress been made toward designating additional rivers to the system? By 1981, only 61 rivers had been brought into the national system (26 of them as a result of the 1980 Alaska National Interest Lands Conservation Act). This is far short of the short-term congressional goal of 100 protected rivers and the

Note: Hawaii is not included on this map because it has no designated National Wild and Scenic Rivers or rivers under study for inclusion in the system.

FIGURE 10-3 The National Wild and Scenic Rivers System. (Courtesy of the National Park Service and U.S. Forest Service.)

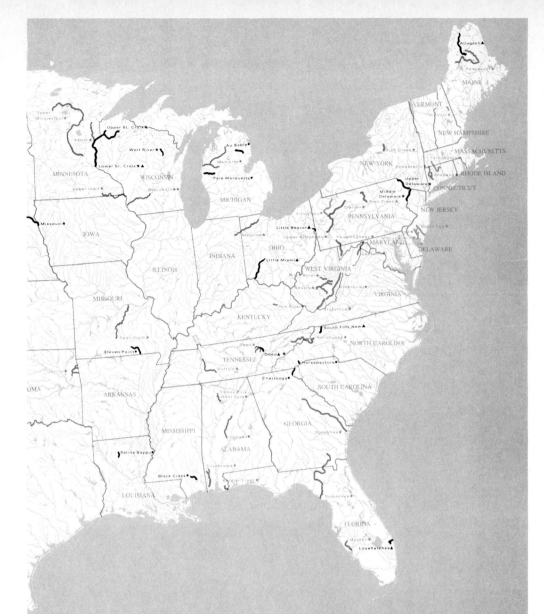

National Wild and Scenic Rivers System

As Authorized by Public Law 90-542, as Amended.   **August 1988**

Legend   Management or Study Responsibility
■ **Existing Components**   ★ **Department of the Interior**
■ **Study Completed**   ● **Department of Agriculture**
■ **Study in Progress**   ▲ **State/Local**

The National Wild and Scenic Rivers System is comprised of selected rivers of the Nation which, with their immediate environments, possess outstandingly remarkable scenic, recreational, natural, cultural and other similar values. River areas included in the system shall be preserved in free-flowing condition, and shall be protected for the benefit and enjoyment of present and future generations.

For further information contact:
United States Department of the Interior   United States Department of Agriculture
National Park Service   Forest Service
P.O. Box 37127   P.O. Box 96090
Washington, DC 20013-7127   Washington, DC 20090-6090

FIGURE 10-3   (Continued)

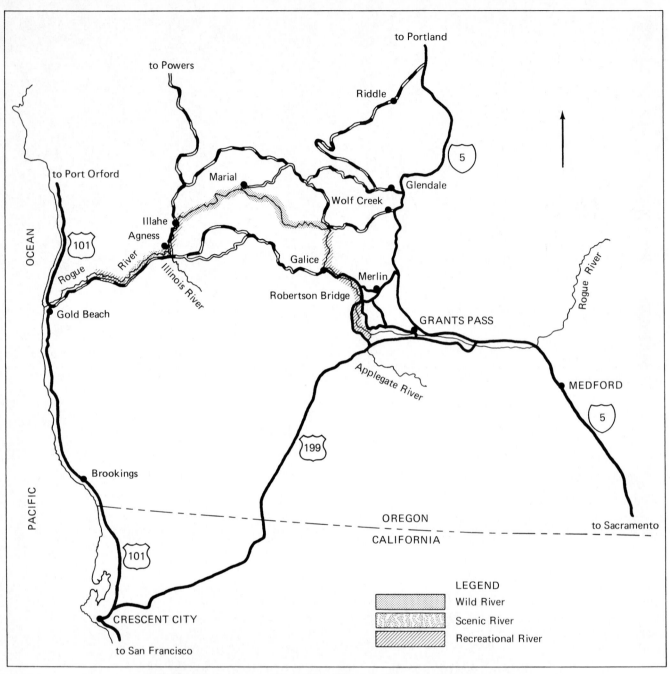

FIGURE 10-4 Rogue River Classification. (Courtesy of U.S. Forest Service.)

conservationists' long-term goal of 550 to 600 protected rivers by 1990. To date, the system has brought under protection only about 11,265 km (7000 mi) of the country's rivers and streams, which total 5.6 million km (3.5 million mi). During this same period, over 14,484 km (9000 mi) of rivers have undergone channelization, which may involve clearing, widening, and deepening the original channel or lining it with concrete (Sumner 1981).

Sumner (1981) concludes that there are several reasons for the disappointing progress in river preservation: (1) the criteria used for classifying rivers are confusing; (2) the preliminary studies that have to be undertaken before a river is designated for protection often drag on for 10 years or more, with a great deal of work being duplicated by various agencies; (3) for a river to be designated for protection, Congress must vote its approval twice; (4) many of the people

(a)

(b)

(c)

FIGURE 10-5   Scenes of the Rogue: (a) wild; (b) scenic; (c) recreational. (Photos by author.)

who live along the rivers that are being considered for protection regard the system as a ''federal land grab,'' and they feel that the federal government is meddling in their private affairs; and (5) the managers of the system tend to concentrate on the preservation of wild rivers and to slight the need to preserve scenic and recreational rivers.

Regardless of the problems, the building of a national river preservation system is a worthy goal. For further details on the National Wild and Scenic Rivers System check the 1980 report of the Heritage Conservation and Recreation Service, as well as their subsequent reports. Rennicke (1985) has also written on this subject.

The National Trails System.   Another ambitious federal undertaking was launched in 1968 when Congress approved the National Trails System Act to ex-

pand the network of hiking and horseback trails across the country. The act identified two types of trails: National Scenic Trails and National Recreation Trails. On *scenic trails* only hiking and related uses are permitted; motorized equipment is banned. The purpose of the act is to safeguard the scenic, natural, and historic qualities of the designated areas. Wherever possible, the trails are laid out so that they bypass highways, power transmission lines, and other human developments. The Appalachian Trail (Figure 10-6) and the Pacific Crest Trail, the first trails to be brought into the system, follow the major north-south mountain ranges of the nation.

In 1980, President Carter approved the North Country National Scenic Trail, which runs 5224 km (3246 mi) along the northern border of the country, from the southern tip of Lake Champlain in New York to the Red River of the North in North Dakota.

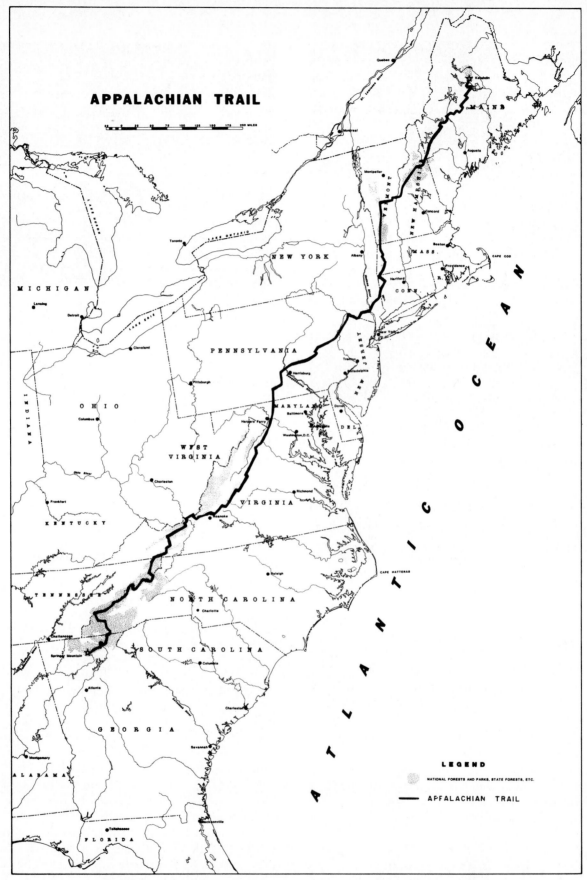

FIGURE 10-6 Map of the Appalachian Trail. (Courtesy of the National Park Service.)

This trail cuts across a variety of landscape types. In working out its route, planners took into account the scenery and terrain along the way, points of geological and historical interest, opportunities to incorporate existing trails (of which they used 547 km, or 340 mi), and land ownership. Almost half of the trail runs through land owned by federal or state governments. It traverses national forests, state forests, a national lakeshore, a national grassland, state wildlife areas, and historic sites. Only 5 percent of the trail passes through developed or urbanized areas, while 61 percent of the trail is through forested areas and the rest runs through agricultural and open areas such as the Badlands in North Dakota. Approximately 50 million people live within 161 km (100 mi) of the trail, and half the U.S. population can reach it within a half-day's drive. Although the trail is a legal reality, officials estimate it will be at least 20 years before it is fully completed and open to the public from one end to the other.

Recreation trails, the second type of national trail, are located near cities, where they are available to large urban populations. Snowmobiles, trail bikes, and other forms of motorized vehicles are permitted on these trails. The emphasis is on recreation rather than scenic beauty.

As under the National Wilderness Preservation System and the National Wild and Scenic Rivers System, existing federal agencies (U.S. Forest Service, the National Park Service, the Bureau of Land Management, the U.S. Fish and Wildlife Service) continue to manage sections of these recreational trails within their jurisdictions. The National Trails System Act makes it possible to add more trails to the system after appropriate study and with congressional approval.

The National Park System. Since the establishment of Yellowstone National Park in 1872—the world's first national park—the United States has led the way in preserving natural areas through its National Park System. Over a hundred nations have followed suit by setting up their own systems of national parks. In 1916, the U.S. Congress established the National Park Service under the Department of the Interior. The National Park Service immediately assumed the management of areas that had already been designated as national parks, including Yellowstone National Park (1872), Yosemite National Park (1890), and Grand Canyon National Monument (1908).

The National Park Service has several goals: to preserve the spectacular scenery and natural areas on public lands, to preserve wildlife that is capable of withstanding limited human contact, and to provide buffer zones to protect fragile wilderness ecosystems. Fishing, camping, and the use of street vehicles are permitted in most national parks, but mining, hunting, timber harvesting, and off-road vehicles are forbidden.

The Park Service, as it is generally called, now manages 30.8 million ha (76 million acres), consisting of 37 national parks and 285 national monuments (the larger units being in Alaska and in the western United States) (Figure 10-7). It also manages numerous national lakeshores and seashores, recreation areas, various national preserves, natural areas, national military parks, and national memorial parks. We will take a closer look at the major components of the National Park System.

National parks are large areas of unusual scenic and recreational importance (Runte 1979). For the most part, economic development is restricted to services that are provided for visitors to the parks. (The types and numbers of such services, however, are quite controversial.) National parks can be created only by an act of Congress.

One of the most recent parks to be brought into the National Park system was the Channel Islands National Park, created in 1980. This group of five islands lies off the Pacific coast between Los Angeles and Santa Barbara, California. Of all the national parks so far established, this park seems most likely to retain its pristine character. Since island ecosystems are more fragile than mainland systems, the Park Service is more concerned with protecting the ecology of the Channel Islands than with fostering recreational use by the public.

These islands support an uncommon variety of wildlife. On the rocks of San Miguel Island, for example, as many as 15,000 sea lions and California seals can be seen basking in the sun during their mating season. Anacapa Island provides the only stable rookery for the brown pelican on the Pacific coast. Eleven other types of sea birds inhabit the islands, and hundreds of dolphins and gray whales pass through Santa Barbara Channel between the Channel Islands and Baja California on their seasonal migrations.

National monuments are generally smaller than national parks and are somewhat less impressive in scenic value. The 1906 Antiquities Act made it possible for national monuments to be created through presidential proclamation, rather than through an act of Congress. As a result, the president can act *quickly* to protect areas from commercial exploitation. Presi-

FIGURE 10-7 National Park System. (From Freeman Tilden, *The National Parks* [New York: Knopf, 1982], pp. 2–3.)

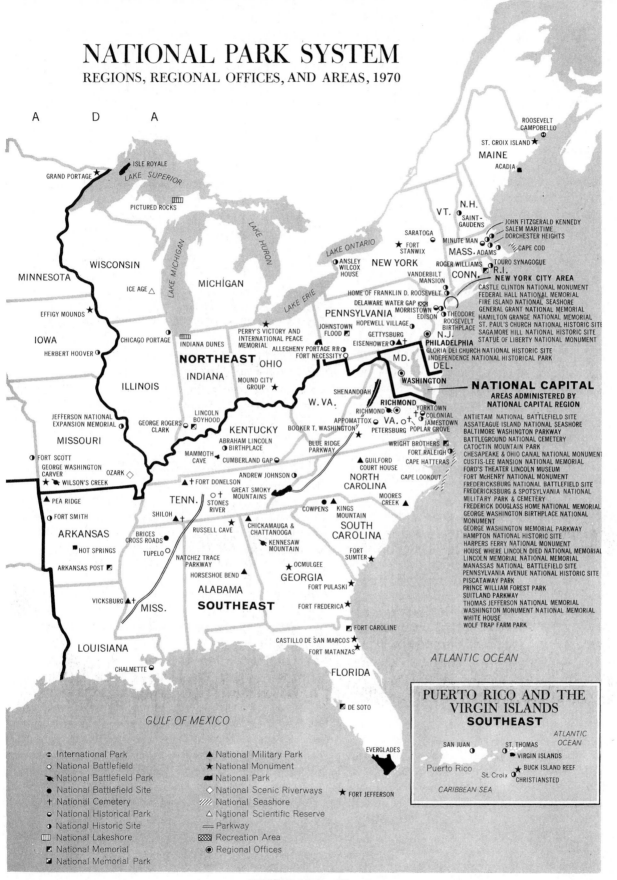

NATIONAL PARK SYSTEM
REGIONS, REGIONAL OFFICES, AND AREAS, 1970

A   D   A

ISLE ROYALE
GRAND PORTAGE ★
LAKE SUPERIOR
PICTURED ROCKS

MINNESOTA
WISCONSIN
MICHIGAN
ICE AGE △
LAKE MICHIGAN
LAKE HURON

EFFIGY MOUNDS ★
IOWA
CHICAGO PORTAGE ○
HERBERT HOOVER ○

INDIANA DUNES
PERRY'S VICTORY AND INTERNATIONAL PEACE MEMORIAL
LAKE ERIE

NORTHEAST
OHIO
INDIANA
ALLEGHENY PORTAGE RR ○
FORT NECESSITY ○
MOUND CITY GROUP ★
ILLINOIS

JEFFERSON NATIONAL EXPANSION MEMORIAL ○
GEORGE ROGERS CLARK ○
LINCOLN BOYHOOD
KENTUCKY
MISSOURI
ABRAHAM LINCOLN BIRTHPLACE ○
MAMMOTH CAVE
CUMBERLAND GAP ○
W. VA.
SHENANDOAH
BLUE RIDGE PARKWAY
BOOKER T. WASHINGTON ○

FORT SCOTT ○
GEORGE WASHINGTON CARVER ○
OZARK ◇
★ WILSON'S CREEK

PEA RIDGE ▲
FORT SMITH ○
ARKANSAS
ANDREW JOHNSON ○
FORT DONELSON ▲
GREAT SMOKY MOUNTAINS
STONES RIVER ○ †
TENN.
SHILOH ▲ †
RUSSELL CAVE ○
BRICES CROSS ROADS ○
CHICKAMAUGA & CHATTANOOGA ▲
HOT SPRINGS ■
TUPELO ○
KENNESAW MOUNTAIN ★

ARKANSAS POST ⊠
NATCHEZ TRACE PARKWAY
HORSESHOE BEND ▲
OCMULGEE ★
VICKSBURG ▲ †
ALABAMA
MISS.
SOUTHEAST
FORT FREDERICA ★
GEORGIA
FORT PULASKI ★

LOUISIANA
CHALMETTE ○
FORT CAROLINE
CASTILLO DE SAN MARCOS ★
FORT MATANZAS ★

GULF OF MEXICO
FLORIDA
DE SOTO ⊠
EVERGLADES

★ FORT JEFFERSON

ROOSEVELT CAMPOBELLO ✪
ST. CROIX ISLAND ★
MAINE
ACADIA ■

VT.   N.H.
SAINT-GAUDENS ○
SARATOGA
FORT STANWIX ★
MINUTE MAN ○
JOHN FITZGERALD KENNEDY ○
SALEM MARITIME ○
DORCHESTER HEIGHTS ○
MASS. ADAMS ○
CAPE COD
NEW YORK
ANSLEY WILCOX HOUSE ○
ROGER WILLIAMS ○
TOURO SYNAGOGUE ○
VANDERBILT MANSION ○
CONN.   R.I.

NEW YORK CITY AREA
CASTLE CLINTON NATIONAL MONUMENT
FEDERAL HALL NATIONAL MEMORIAL
FIRE ISLAND NATIONAL SEASHORE
GENERAL GRANT NATIONAL MEMORIAL
HAMILTON GRANGE NATIONAL MEMORIAL
ST. PAUL'S CHURCH NATIONAL HISTORIC SITE
SAGAMORE HILL NATIONAL HISTORIC SITE
STATUE OF LIBERTY NATIONAL MONUMENT

HOME OF FRANKLIN D. ROOSEVELT ○
DELAWARE WATER GAP ⧓
PENNSYLVANIA
MORRISTOWN ○
EDISON ○
THEODORE ROOSEVELT BIRTHPLACE ○
JOHNSTOWN FLOOD ○
HOPEWELL VILLAGE ○
GETTYSBURG ▲ †
EISENHOWER ○
N.J.
PHILADELPHIA ○
GLORIA DEI CHURCH NATIONAL HISTORIC SITE
INDEPENDENCE NATIONAL HISTORICAL PARK
MD.
DEL.
WASHINGTON ●

NATIONAL CAPITAL
AREAS ADMINISTERED BY NATIONAL CAPITAL REGION

RICHMOND
APPOMATTOX ○
PETERSBURG ▲
VA. ○ †
YORKTOWN
COLONIAL
JAMESTOWN
POPLAR GROVE †
WRIGHT BROTHERS ★
FORT RALEIGH ○
CAPE HATTERAS
NORTH CAROLINA
CAPE LOOKOUT

GUILFORD COURT HOUSE ▲
MOORES CREEK ▲
COWPENS ○
KINGS MOUNTAIN ▲
SOUTH CAROLINA
FORT SUMTER ★

ANTIETAM NATIONAL BATTLEFIELD SITE
ASSATEAGUE ISLAND NATIONAL SEASHORE
BALTIMORE WASHINGTON PARKWAY
BATTLEGROUND NATIONAL CEMETERY
CATOCTIN MOUNTAIN PARK
CHESAPEAKE & OHIO CANAL NATIONAL MONUMENT
CUSTIS-LEE MANSION NATIONAL MEMORIAL
FORD'S THEATER LINCOLN MUSEUM
FORT McHENRY NATIONAL MONUMENT
FREDERICKSBURG NATIONAL BATTLEFIELD SITE
FREDERICKSBURG & SPOTSYLVANIA NATIONAL MILITARY PARK & CEMETERY
FREDERICK DOUGLASS HOME NATIONAL MEMORIAL
GEORGE WASHINGTON BIRTHPLACE NATIONAL MONUMENT
GEORGE WASHINGTON MEMORIAL PARKWAY
HAMPTON NATIONAL HISTORIC SITE
HARPERS FERRY NATIONAL MONUMENT
HOUSE WHERE LINCOLN DIED NATIONAL MEMORIAL
LINCOLN MEMORIAL NATIONAL MEMORIAL
MANASSAS NATIONAL BATTLEFIELD SITE
PENNSYLVANIA AVENUE NATIONAL HISTORIC SITE
PISCATAWAY PARK
PRINCE WILLIAM FOREST PARK
SUITLAND PARKWAY
THOMAS JEFFERSON NATIONAL MEMORIAL
WASHINGTON MONUMENT NATIONAL MEMORIAL
WHITE HOUSE
WOLF TRAP FARM PARK

ATLANTIC OCEAN

PUERTO RICO AND THE VIRGIN ISLANDS
SOUTHEAST

SAN JUAN
PUERTO RICO
ST. THOMAS
VIRGIN ISLANDS
BUCK ISLAND REEF
St. Croix
CHRISTIANSTED
CARIBBEAN SEA
ATLANTIC OCEAN

Legend:
- ⊕ International Park
- ○ National Battlefield
- ★ National Battlefield Park
- ● National Battlefield Site
- † National Cemetery
- ○ National Historical Park
- ○ National Historic Site
- ⫿⫿⫿ National Lakeshore
- ⊠ National Memorial
- ⊠ National Memorial Park
- ▲ National Military Park
- ★ National Monument
- ■ National Park
- ◇ National Scenic Riverways
- ⧄ National Seashore
- △ National Scientific Reserve
- ══ Parkway
- ⊞ Recreation Area
- ◉ Regional Offices

FIGURE 10-7 (Continued)

271

dent Carter used this power in 1978, when he established a large number of national monuments in the state of Alaska.

National recreation areas are park units set aside primarily for recreational purposes. Lumbering, grazing, and mining are permitted in some of these areas, as long as these activities do not interfere with the primary purposes.

One type of national recreation area is the *national urban park*. The first such park was the Gateway National Recreation Area, which was created in 1972. Located partly in New York and partly in New Jersey, the park consists of 10,927 ha (27,000 acres) around the Hudson River estuary. It includes splendid sand-pit beaches and a vast wetland, Jamaica Bay on Long Island, which is the only wildlife refuge adjoining a subway line. Golden Gate National Recreation Area (also established in 1972) provides recreational facilities for the San Francisco Bay metropolitan community. This Golden Gate greenbelt, together with adjacent parklands, consists of some 48,564 ha (120,000 acres). Almost all these parklands are contiguous, and this vast park is unique among the recreational resources of the nation's cities. Both parks reflect the new urban emphasis of the National Park Service. Speaking in support of urban national parks, former Interior Secretary Walter J. Hickel once said, "We have got to bring the natural world back to the people, rather than have them live in an environment where everything is paved over with concrete and loaded with frustration and violence" (Foresta 1984, p. 185). As a result of that statement, national urban parks are sometimes referred to as "Parks to the People." There are now eight federal greenbelt parks adjacent to large cities, and plans are afoot to create more of them.

National seashores and national lakeshores are created as a response to the American love for shorelines, coasts, lakes, and the sea. Like the national recreation areas, these areas are usually located near large urban centers, such as New York or Chicago. The National Park Service currently administers 10 national seashores and four national lakeshores (all on the Great Lakes).

What about the ecological health of these various components of the National Park System? In 1983, former Interior Secretary James Watt said, "The national parks are in better shape than they have been in years." But according to a 1980 report issued by the National Park Service, entitled "State of the Parks," conditions are far from ideal (Figure 10-8). After surveying 310 of the 323 National Park Service areas, the National Park Service reported the following:

- Activities *outside* the park boundaries are threatening 132 of these areas. Fifty-six are threatened by exploration for gas, oil, geothermal energy, and hardrock minerals.
- Logging activities directly *outside* park boundaries are causing damage in 25 areas.
- Water-quality problems generated by activities *outside* park boundaries are emerging in almost every park area. Furthermore, acid rain is destroying 20 areas and is suspected of damaging 62 others.
- Air pollution caused by smoke or contaminants from *outside* the parks threatens 94 areas. A total of 140 areas are suffering from air-quality problems of one sort or another.

Our seashore parks, such as Cape Hatteras, are being threatened by off-road vehicles that damage fragile ecosystems. Padre Island, the Gulf Islands, and Fort Jefferson are experiencing visual pollution and threats of oil spills from offshore oil drilling. Natural processes, such as the distribution of beach sand, are being disturbed by coastal development. At Cape Lookout National Seashore in North Carolina, for example, the beach erosion is so severe that the park's historic lighthouse is being undermined.

In Yellowstone National Park the proposed geothermal development of nearby Island Park may permanently disrupt the activity of Old Faithful and over 100 other geysers and springs that depend on a delicate balance of temperature and flow rate within the subterranean system. The survival of Yellowstone's grizzly bears is also in jeopardy as logging, mining, and oil and gas development in adjacent national forests impinge on their natural habitat. Energy development is also causing serious problems in other national parks. For example, the Four Corners power plant and other power plants are affecting parks in the Southwest. Coal production is adversely affecting Bruce Canyon National Park in Utah. And, to add to existing problems, potentially harmful nuclear-waste facilities are being planned for locations adjacent to parks, such as the one proposed for a location near Utah's Canyonlands National Park. The hydroelectric plant at Glen Canyon Dam has altered the flow of water through the Grand Canyon. As a result, rafting through the Canyon has been affected. Furthermore, smog drifting inland from Los Angeles, fumes from copper-smelting plants in Arizona, and exhaust from nearby power plants have so polluted the air of the Grand Canyon that on 100 days a year visitors cannot see clearly from one rim to the other. Acid rain resulting from energy production is affecting such notable

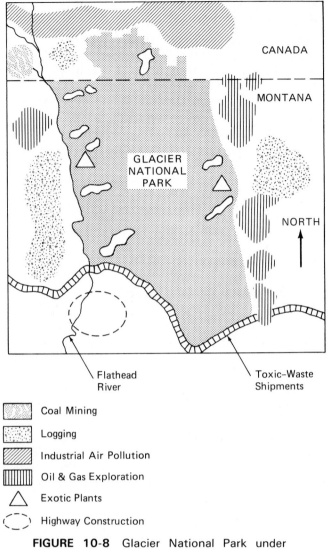

Flathead
River

Toxic-Waste
Shipments

▨ Coal Mining

▨ Logging

▨ Industrial Air Pollution

▨ Oil & Gas Exploration

△ Exotic Plants

(⌒) Highway Construction

FIGURE 10-8 Glacier National Park under siege by oil and gas exploitation, timber harvesting, highway construction, industrial air polllution, and toxic-waste shipments. (Map by Bob Conrad for *Life* Magazine, July 1983.)

parks as Shenandoah, Acadia, and Voyageurs, damaging vegetation and killing fish in their lakes and streams (see Chapter 11 for further details). Although acid rain is most serious in the Midwest and in the East, it is recognized as a nationwide problem.

To the occasional visitor, the National Park System seems to be in reasonably good shape except for some air pollution and occasional overcrowding. But those who live year-round in the parks—the superintendents and their staffs—are in a better position to observe the changes that are taking place, and these are the people who compiled the gloomy National Park Service report. The National Park Service's "State of the Parks" report succeeded in calling con-

gressional attention to some serious park management problems. Considering Interior Secretary Donald P. Hodel's 1988 request for increased wildland to be opened for coal mining—approximately 1.6 million ha (4 million acres)—the 1980 National Park Service report appears *not* to have exaggerated the plight of the parks. For additional insight into the problems, policies, and programs of the National Park Service, see Foresta (1984), Tilden (1982), and the Conservation Foundation (1985).

State Systems

Several state systems parallel federal efforts to preserve the natural environment. Most of these systems are located near large cities and thus serve the recreational needs of urban populations. Although they generally tend to be less extensive than national reserves, they contribute significantly to the nation's conservation efforts.

Wilderness Preservation Systems. A number of state legislatures have created wilderness areas. To define wilderness, they have used many of the words and phrases that we find in federal legislation, such as "areas where the earth and its community of life are untrammeled by man and where man himself is a visitor who does not remain," and "areas affected primarily by the forces of nature," and "areas consisting of at least 5000 acres of land." And, as in the federal system, these state wilderness areas are generally set up in parks. In California, for example, Santa Rosa Mountains State Wilderness (a portion of Anza Borrego Desert State Park in San Diego County) and Mount San Jacinto State Wilderness in Mount San Jacinto State Park in Riverside County are part of the California State Wilderness System.

River Preservation Systems. In 1981, 26 states had river preservation systems. With the notable exceptions of the Oregon, California, and Minnesota systems, however, most of these state systems are relatively ineffectual. Some of them prohibit dams but do nothing to protect shorelines. Others actually cause harm. For example, when a state classifies a river as "wild or scenic," it succeeds mainly in attracting public attention to the river and promotes overuse by visitors. If the state fails to regulate public attendance, it creates increased pressures without imposing adequate controls. Moreover, the state systems are commonly understaffed and underfunded.

State Parks. State parks consist of relatively spacious areas of scenic distinction, often accompanied by historical, archaeological, ecological, and geological features. Although state parks are generally smaller than federal parks, there are exceptions. New York's Adirondack State Park, for example, contains 1.5 million ha (3.7 million acres) of privately owned land and 930,810 ha (2.3 million acres) of state-owned land. Its combination of public and private holdings makes this vast facility unique among state parks. By simply drawing a boundary around the areas they wanted protected, the designers brought everything into the park that happened to be there, from vacation homes to small towns. The Adirondack Park Agency oversees both public and private land within the park. Roderick Nash (1978) claims that a system of this sort is well-suited to areas where the desire to conserve nature arises years after settlement has taken place.

Coastal Zone Management. The federal Coastal Zone Management Act of 1972 encouraged states to inventory and protect the scenic and recreational resources of their coastlines. The act recognized the high value Americans place on their seashores and coastlines as parts of the wildness continuum.

California, with its vast coastline, has led the way in coastal regulation. In 1972, it established a Coastal Zone Conservation Commission, which, in turn, created six regional commissions consisting of local government officials and private citizens. These regional commissions have since been combined into one statewide commission, which is authorized to control development from the mean high-water mark to a line 914 m (3000 ft) inland. Its purpose is to preserve, restore, and enhance coastal resources in situations where local efforts to resolve land-use conflicts or to bring about needed projects have been less successful.

Despite the many opportunities to conserve scenic and recreational resources, many of the state coastal management systems, like the California system, are beset by political problems. Indeed, some critics (particularly landowners, entrepreneurs, and realtors) predict the death of the state coastline commissions in response to cuts in federal and state budgets and pressure from local governments. In 1983, for example, environmentalists attacked the governor of California for using the state's budgetary crisis as an excuse for dismantling the coastal commission through severe budget cuts.

County and City Efforts

The origin of the local park dates back to 1634, when Boston established its Common as an acceptable site for grazing cows (Nash 1978). Since then, the local park has emerged as an important recreational source. County and city parks are rarely meant to protect natural scenery. Rather, they provide urbanites with a little breathing space and an opportunity to be closer to nature. *County parks* do help to conserve vegetation and wildlife, but they are used mainly as picnic areas, baseball diamonds, and playing fields. *City parks* range in size from Central Park in New York City and Golden Gate Park in San Francisco to tiny *vest-pocket* parks.

Undeveloped parks are natural areas owned by city park departments that have not yet been developed for recreational use (including the installation of picnic tables, latrines, trail signs, and parking lots). These areas generally have limited public access or none at all, and they are relatively free of human activity. On the wildness continuum, they rank higher than developed parks. Undeveloped parks provide an urban habitat for thousands of song birds, small herds of deer, and such animals as skunks, raccoons, and squirrels (Figure 10-9). Even though city dwellers may not be able to enter these areas, they can enjoy the song birds that visit their backyards, and joggers, bicyclists, and photographers can delight in a natural landscape within city limits. These undeveloped areas are usually scheduled for development as soon as funds are available. The current crisis in public funding, however, has led to a temporary postponement of much development. Environmentalists applaud that delay and hope that park officials will come to realize that *open land within the city need not be developed in order to be enjoyed.*

PRINCIPLES AND TECHNIQUES OF OPEN-SPACE MANAGEMENT

> Nature is painting for us, day after day pictures of infinite beauty if only we have the eyes to see them. (John Ruskin)

Open-space management is *more of an art* than a science, since there are seldom clear-cut answers to worrisome problems. Yet judgments must be made. In the following section we will look at some of the principles and techniques available to the open-space manager. Although they are most applicable in true wilderness areas, many of them are appropriate to the management of county and city parks as well.

Certain basic principles serve open-space managers as a conceptual framework within which to make their management decisions. The following principles, adapted from the authoritative works of

(a)

(b)

(c)

FIGURE 10-9 Guadalupe Oak Grove Undeveloped Park, San Jose, California. (a) Mule deer (*Obdocoileus hemionus*) walking on rolling, grassy upland; (b) pair of American kestrel (*Falco sparverius*) perched atop a dead California oak tree; (c) cow grazing on grassy hillside. The city's Parks and Recreation Department leases the land to ranchers for the purpose of increasing department revenue and for fire prevention. By grazing cattle and horses within the undeveloped parkland, the grass is kept short, thereby helping to prevent grassland fires within the heart of the city. (Photos by author.)

John Hendee (1977, 1978) is suggestive rather than all inclusive.

Open-Space Management Must Take into Consideration the Management of Adjacent Lands. Open-space areas are not isolated entities; they are affected by activities in adjacent areas. This was the major point made in the National Park Service's "State of the Parks" report. For example, logging roads and timber harvesting on adjacent land has a notable effect on any wilderness area. And, conversely, the management of a wilderness area may have a significant effect on the management of adjacent areas. For example, controlled burning within a national park may cause smoke pollution and fire losses in areas outside the park.

To minimize this problem, open-space managers have suggested that a *buffer zone* be created—a belt of land around the boundary of the open space.

Clearly, some means must be devised to protect open spaces from the deleterious effects of activities conducted in adjacent areas.

Protecting a Natural Area Means Protecting Its Ecosystem. Open-space managers must develop a single plan for dealing with the interrelationships among all the component parts of the area. For example, in wilderness management, one must consider the effect of fishing on shoreline vegetation and soil erosion as well as on fish populations.

Open-Space Managers Should Respect Human Values as Well as the Integrity of Flora and Fauna. Wilderness areas were not set aside only for the sake of their flora and fauna. They were also set aside for the benefits to humans that can be derived from their use. Concentration on the benefits that humans can derive from open space is *anthropocentric* (human-centered) management. Concentration on the ecological integrity of the area is *biocentric* (plant and animal-centered) management. When possible, open-space managers should strive for a balance between these two extremes of management. A management philosophy that insists on preserving the absolute purity of the wilderness may trigger a public backlash that will threaten future funding.

Open-Space Management Requires the Management of People. Although the term *wilderness* suggests an area free of controls, an area in which visitors can do as they like, the very survival of the wilderness requires that human activities be carefully supervised and controlled. Recreational pursuits impose a highly unnatural influence on wilderness areas, and open-space managers must influence, modify, and, if necessary, *control* human activities in order to minimize their impact on the wilderness environment.

Open-Space Managers Must Have Clearly Defined Objectives. Open-space managers must be guided by formal plans that include precise statements of their goals and objectives. Without such prescriptions, management tends to be unorganized and sometimes counterproductive. For example, a series of minor decisions on the number and location of trails, on the number and type of trail signs, and on

the various restrictions on what visitors can and cannot do will impair the value of the wilderness unless these decisions are coordinated by an overall plan.

Open-Space Managers Must Be Sensitive to the Carrying Capacity of an Area. The *carrying capacity* of an area is the amount of use that area can tolerate without suffering an unacceptable impact. For example, an excessive number of visitors to a wilderness area impairs the environment and destroys the very solitude that the visitors are seeking (Figure 10-10). Carrying capacity is a relative term, however; it specifies no exact number but rather a range of activity suggested by the use to which an area is put. Moreover, carrying capacity varies from time to time. For example, during a drought, when the biological communities are experiencing physical stress, the carrying capacity of an area declines and human use should be curtailed.

Management Should Strive to Reduce Impacts Selectively. Since various uses produce different impacts, open-space managers should restrict use on the basis of specific impacts rather than adopting all-inclusive restrictions. One approach is to rank users according to the impact they are likely to have on the area. For example, large groups of horseback riders will have a greater impact than small groups; large

(a)

(b)

FIGURE 10-10 Horsepacking and questions of carrying capacity in Emigrant Wilderness Area in Yosemite National Park, California. (a) A seemingly remote pristine valley fits the wilderness concept. (b) Approaching the same valley is a "horsepack train" carrying 35 individuals. Just how many horsepack trains can one valley experience per season before the "wilderness" is lost? (Photos by author.)

parties of overnight campers will have a greater impact than small parties; and so on. The manager should impose the most stringent restrictions on those users who will have the greatest impact.

Management decisions should be *site-specific* as well as impact-specific. Within a given wilderness area, for example, restrictions may be needed in only a few locations, perhaps along heavily used trails bordering lakes and streams. Moreover, only *seasonal* restrictions may be needed, as in early spring when vegetation is easily damaged or on summer weekends when human use is greatest.

Open-Space Managers Should Impose Only Those Regulations That Are Necessary to Achieve Objectives. Excessive management impairs the very values and feelings that make the wilderness experience so desirable—feelings of freedom, spontaneity, and a sense of escape. Only those regulations should be imposed that are necessary to achieve the objectives that the manager establishes. The ideal approach is a form of *traffic management*, in which users are informed about the current condition of the area and are invited to use alternative trails and campsites. If the situation is critical, of course, it may be necessary to forbid camping at damaged sites. Ordinarily, however, the wilderness experience is likely to be more enjoyable when the manager says, ''Try the alternative campsite down the way—I think you'll like it,'' rather than, ''You'll be fined if you use this campsite.''

Open-Space Managers Should Observe the Concept of Nondegradation. Managers should strive to maintain or improve the environmental conditions at each site in order to forestall deterioration. Certain sites within a wilderness area are bound to be more natural and less despoiled than others. Those sites should be maintained at their high level of environmental quality and should not be permitted to degenerate to the level of lower-quality sites. For example, the relatively undisturbed areas of the intermountain West should not be permitted to decline in environmental quality just because the wilderness areas of southern California have suffered from greater degradation. Nor should what are regarded as acceptable levels of impact in the eastern United States be taken as acceptable levels for the western United States.

Hendee also maintains that the nondegradation concept permits upgrading an area or restoring its quality. Whether or not humans should try to improve on the natural state of an area is a controversial matter, however. Environmentalists who applaud efforts to restore natural conditions and natural processes may oppose efforts to wipe out campsites, to plant trees and shrubs, and to fertilize and water the vegetation.

Open-Space Managers Should Strive for a Degree of ''Wildness.'' Whatever the activities that take place in a given area, Hendee concludes, open-space managers should strive to preserve in these areas the greatest degree of wildness possible. It is easier, of course, to provide a context of wildness in remote wilderness areas than in downtown vest-pocket parks. Yet the managers of certain county and city parks are working with landscape architects to capture a *sense of wildness* even in those vestiges of open spaces. Since sense of wildness is a perceived phenomenon (Nash 1982), geographers and others are exploring the role of environmental perception in wildland recreation management (Stankey 1971, Saarinen 1974).

For additional information on wildland principles, policies, and strategies, consult Brockmann and Merriam (1979), Shechter and Lucas (1978), Washburne and Cole (1983), Hammitt and Cole (1987), and Wellman (1987).

PROSPECTS FOR THE FUTURE

The National Wildlife Federation reports that the open spaces of the United States continue to shrink. The ''wide open spaces'' that attracted immigrants to America for more than 300 years are vanishing, and our perception of the land is changing.

The Decline of Open Space in America

Open space in America is declining for three major reasons: the continuing increase in population, the migration of people from the cities to the countryside, and the cutback in public funds.

Citing 1980 census figures, the National Wildlife Federation reports that there are 64 people for every square mile in the United States—50 percent more than just 30 years ago. Despite a slowdown in the birth rate, the U.S. population grew from 203 million in 1970 to 226 million in 1980. Projections indicate that this rate of growth, coupled with immigration, will continue for the next 80 years before it levels off. This trend can only intensify the crowding, pollution, and aesthetic degradation of the open space that still survives—as exemplified by actual and perceived threats to our national parks (Table 10-2).

Where are all these people going? The population is shifting to the suburbs, to the small towns,

TABLE 10-2

Threats to the national park system

Bar chart: Total Number of Threats Reported (y-axis) by Threat Category (x-axis). Legend: open bars = Adequately Documented by Research; shaded bars = Known or Suspected Threats which Require Research to Adequately Document.

Threat Category	Known or Suspected (shaded)	Adequately Documented (open)	Total
Air Pollution	637	55	692
Water Quality/Quantity	396	70	466
Aesthetic Degradation	629	456	1085
Physical Removal of Resources	491	147	638
Exotic Encroachment	421	181	602
Visitor Physical Impacts	404	101	505
Park Operations	257	100	357

Source: National Park Service. 1980. *State of the Parks—1980. A Report to the Congress.* Washington, D.C.: U.S. Department of the Interior.

and to rural lifestyles, according to U.S. Census demographers. This shift will strain existing public utilities, transportation systems, and recreational areas, and the demand for new housing will eliminate much of the remaining open space.

Whenever the nation's economy shows signs of strain, federal officials threaten to raise money by selling "surplus" public lands. Former Interior Secretary James Watt, for example, once said, "What better way to raise some of the revenues that we so badly need than by selling some of the land and buildings that we don't need." (National Wildlife Federation 1983, p. 37). Of the 299 million ha (740 million acres) owned and managed by federal agencies, vast tracts consist of grassland, forest, wilderness, wildlife refuge, and parkland. Much of that open space will be lost forever if the federal government succeeds in its efforts to sell it.

Budgetary constraints also impede the acquisition of new open space. When money is available, other priorities claim what little capital resources are available. An example of this occurred in 1982 when Congress earmarked $98 million for new park acquisitions, but the money was spent by Interior Secretary James Watt on park maintenance that still did not prevent the deterioration of the parks.

Positive Signs and Success Stories

On a more pleasant note, some progress is being made in protecting land and rivers, in restoring parks, in providing recreation on private lands, and in creating a nationwide outdoor code of ethics. Certain changes in federal policy are also having a beneficial, though indirect, effect on our open spaces. In 1979, Congress passed an Omnibus Parks bill designed to preserve a significant portion of our national heritage and to expand recreational opportunities for Americans. This bill designated 809,400 ha (2 million acres) as wilderness, added 12 new areas to the National Park System, created 5 new national trails, and protected 8 river sections from development. In 1983, President Reagan signed the Coastal Barrier Resources Act, which was designed to protect 975 km (606 mi) of barrier islands and fragile beach along the Gulf and Atlantic coasts by curtailing federal aid for highway and other developments. This act was a major turning-point in national policy. Previously, the federal government had spent millions of dollars a year to control nature on these islands and beaches through such efforts as sand stabilization projects and road development.

Other policy changes are occurring among the state governors. In 1983, for example, Florida Governor Bob Graham unveiled a program to restore the Everglades by restricting development and by restoring the "River of Grass" at the southern end of the peninsula. The governor said, "Whatever the price, the price of inaction is higher still. . . . The price is the extinction of the Florida panther, the pollution of our drinking water, the death of a national park, the loss of countless fish and wildfowl. . . ." Environmentalists applauded Graham's efforts to reverse the destructive trends that threaten the Everglades.

Progress is also being made in the opening up of private lands to recreation. Currently, many private properties are closed to the public because the owners fear that they will be subjected to lawsuits growing out of injuries sustained on their property. The National Wildlife Federation and other groups have devised a model act that clarifies liability and provides for the punishment of trespassers. If adopted by the states, the act would enable landowners to open their lands with less fear of litigation.

In 1980, the National Conference on Outdoor Ethics met to devise a code of ethics. That code urges visitors to open spaces not to litter, disturb agricultural fields, break fences, or fish or hunt without permission. Environmentalists hope that this conference and other similar conferences will help generate nationwide promotion of an outdoor code of ethics.

Finally, there have been some encouraging reversals in federal policy. In 1981, for example, decades of intense highway construction came to an end. With the interstate highway system nearly completed, the Reagan administration imposed large budget cuts on future highway construction. Twenty-five years of building federally funded highways had urbanized America, destroying millions of acres of wildlife habitat, farmland, and open space.

Despite these encouraging signs, however, the recent record on the preservation of America's open space has been generally unfavorable, and conservationists need the help of every citizen in reversing this trend.

ACTION FOR OPEN-SPACE PRESERVATION

The idea of wilderness needs no defense. It only needs more defenders. (Edward Abbey)

Nearly all the efforts to conserve wilderness and the other open spaces (including the creation of national parks) result from the determination of *a few concerned individuals*. Citizens must take the initiative; the government merely responds to pressure from the citizens. There are several ways in which you can help preserve America's natural beauty (Gillette 1972).

1. *Preserve or upgrade your own neighborhood.*

- *Fight the war against litter and graffiti.* Litter and graffiti are costly and ugly forms of pollution. One study indicates that it costs taxpayers more to pick up and dispose of an empty bottle than the customer paid for the full bottle at the store! Avoid littering, and pick up the litter of others. There will always be people who litter, and city budgets make it impossible to send out clean-up crews to every neighborhood. Someone has to clean up the mess, and you can take the lead. You can turn the chore into a positive experience by inviting family members and sympathetic neighbors to make it a weekend social event. In January 1989, the successes of some New York anti-litter community organizations even made national news.

- *Urge restrictions on billboards and overhead utility lines.* Billboards and overhead utility lines mar the landscape and turn roads and highways into ugly thoroughfares (Lewis et al. 1973). Support legislation to restrict billboards and above-ground utility wires in open space areas.

- *Encourage zoning for open space.* Encourage your local government to adopt zoning that will guarantee some degree of wilderness within easy reach. A pleasant community attracts customers and employees to local stores and enhances real estate investments.

In other words, increased wilderness *can* mean increased profits.

- *Recycle a vacant lot.* If you are tired of looking at the trash-filled vacant lot across the street or that boarded-up, burned-out building down the block, work to convert it into a vest-pocket park. There are numerous urban land programs, such as the Trust for Public Land, whose purpose is to help citizens do just that. The Trust for Public Land has aided more than 15 neighborhood land trusts in Oakland, California, New York City, and Newark, New Jersey (Bolton 1979).

2. ***Support the efforts of city, county, and state agencies to preserve open space.*** At the city and county level, support proposals for the maintenance of parks and the protection of open space—particularly wetlands, woods, shorelines, and streams (White 1968). Free or low-cost camping and recreation facilities near major urban areas will make it unnecessary for city dwellers to visit national parks and thus lessen the strain on those already overused resources. City officials often ignore the possibility of incorporating nearby rivers, streams, and creeks into greenbelts and open-space areas. Docent programs, which mobilize volunteer efforts in state and local parks, can be encouraged.

3. ***Help protect national parks.*** The National Park Service publishes numerous citizen's action guidebooks that are available from its headquarters in Washington, D.C. (e.g., National Parks and Conservation Association 1979). The National Park Service welcomes comments on publications such as its "Statement for Management" (SM) and its "Development Concept Plan" (DCP). Become familiar with the various management techniques that help ease the strain on our park system. For example, support regulations calling for advance campground reservations and for restrictions on the number of climbers and hikers by means of quotas and permits. Support higher fees for people who want to bring cars or motor homes into a park, and encourage the phasing out and relocation of hotels and concession stands within parks. Encourage the prohibition or limitation of cars and other motorized vehicles in the more heavily used national parks. Yosemite National Park, for example, has already instituted such measures.

4. ***Monitor mining activities in wilderness areas.*** You can help protect natural areas from unnecessary or improper mining in several ways:

- *Learn about the leasing process.* Inquire about the leasing status of the parks you are familiar with and ask about the future plans of the responsible agencies (usually the U.S. Forest Service or the Bureau of Land Management). Those agencies are under no obligation to issue leases to mining operations, and their management plans should include specifics on their leasing policy.
- *Monitor development plans.* Once a mineral resource lease has been issued to a mining operation, it is difficult to halt road construction, drilling, and seismic blasting. But you can urge that the timing of such activities be adjusted to avoid those seasons of the year in which the region's wildlife is particularly vulnerable. After the mining activities have ceased, insist that all roads be obliterated and the disrupted land restored to its natural state.
- *Publicize unacceptable activities.* The controversial behavior of figures such as former Interior Secretary James Watt and lesser officials is always newsworthy. Inform your local newspaper and broadcasters of any threats to natural areas that you learn about.
- *Consult conservation organizations.* Some of the major conservation organizations, such as the Sierra Club, maintain *leasing* committees to coordinate the activities of conservationists interested in protecting public lands. Those committees will give you information on how you can help.

5. ***Join land protection organizations.*** Consider joining such wilderness conservation organizations as the Wilderness Society and the National Parks and Conservation Association. Support land-purchasing organizations, such as the Nature Conservancy. Originally established in 1917 to preserve rare and endangered ecosystems for scientific purposes, the Nature Conservancy has expanded its preservation efforts to include scenic and recreational resources as well.

6. ***Offer an easement on your property.*** If you or your family happen to own property with some natural character that you want to preserve, you might consider offering a conservation easement to a land trust, park board, or a private conservation organization such as the Nature Conservancy. Such easements *freeze* the land, preventing further development in perpetuity, and provide the landowner with a reduction in property taxes.

7. *When the time comes, donate a piece of your property.* A great many of the protected wilderness areas in the United States are the result of private philanthropy. Whether for altruistic reasons or for their heirs' financial benefit, landowners can bequeath open land to a private conservation group or government agency for public use. Unlike arrangements under conservation easements, the outright donation of land leads to the transfer of title and ownership. If you have no land of your own to bequeath (few of us do), ask whether or not your family or a family business owns any wildland.

8. *Choose a career in open-space management.* Open-space managers work in remote wilderness areas, suburban neighborhoods, and inner-city enclaves. Their jobs are many and varied. They can work as facilities maintenance personnel; park rangers; outdoor recreation planners; landscape architects; foresters; soil, range, and wildlife conservationists; and park managers, supervisors, and administrators. The essential requirements for such a career are an understanding of the natural environment, skill in physical planning, and training in maintenance and operation. An understanding of human behavior is also an advantage, since open-space management is primarily the management of people.

Does such a career appeal to you? If so, see if you can find part-time, summer, of after-school employment in one of these areas. Many college and university departments have internship programs in which you can gain experience and make professional contacts. Competition for jobs in open-space management is growing more intense, and the better prepared you are, the better your chances for employment.

DISCUSSION TOPICS

1. Discuss the concept of the wildness continuum. How does a wilderness differ from a national park in terms of purpose and permissible uses?

2. List and discuss at least five reasons why we should preserve wilderness areas. Which reasons coincide most closely with your personal values?

3. Why is it difficult to preserve the entire length of a river? Distinguish between the three major river classifications included in the National Wild and Scenic Rivers Act.

4. Discuss the two major trail classifications in the National Trails System.

5. Distinguish between national parks, national monuments, national recreation areas, and national seashores in terms of purpose and permissible uses. Which do you or your family visit most often? Why? What impact has human use had on the areas you are familiar with? Have you observed any effort to reduce that impact?

6. What are the major programs facing the national parks? How might they be remedied?

7. How do the efforts of the states to protect wilderness areas resemble federal efforts? How do they differ?

8. What is an undeveloped park? Why do environmentalists advocate that more land be preserved in this condition? What management problems might such parks create?

9. List and briefly explain the 10 major principles governing wilderness and open-space management. Compare the levels of difficulty that would be incurred in incorporating each principle into the management of wilderness areas, national parks, and city parks.

10. What management techniques are available for maintaining the proper carrying capacity of our national parks? Discuss the pros and cons of each technique.

11. Discuss several ways in which you might foster "wilderness" in your own neighborhood. Which would be most likely to be effective? Why?

12. List and discuss several ways in which you can personally help preserve the open-space tradition of the United States.

READINGS

ALLIN, CRAIG W. 1982. *The Politics of Wilderness Preservation.* Westport, Conn.: Greenwood Press. An examination of how policymakers have dealt with wilderness issues since American independence.

BOLTON, CHARLES. 1979. *Citizen's Action Manual: A Guide to Recycling Vacant Property in Your Neighborhood.* Washington, D.C.: Government Printing Office. A how-to manual prepared by the Trust for Public Land.

BROCKMANN, FRANK C., and LAWRENCE C. MERRIAM, JR. 1979. *Recreational Use of Wild Lands.* 3d ed. New York: McGraw-Hill. Detailed overview of recreational resource management.

BROOKS, PAUL. 1980. *Speaking for Nature: How Literary Naturalists from Henry Thoreau to Rachel Carson Have Shaped America.* Boston: Houghton Mifflin. Fascinating account of how these literary figures have shaped wilderness values.

CONSERVATION FOUNDATION. 1985. *National Parks for a New Generation.* Washington, D.C.: The Conservation Foundation. Excellent analysis of the programs, policies, and problems of the National Park System.

DETWYLER, THOMAS R., and M. G. MARCUS, eds. 1972. *Urbanization and Environment: The Physical Geography of the City.* Belmont, Calif.: Duxbury Press. Excellent study.

FORESTA, RONALD A. 1984. *America's National Parks and Their Keepers.* Washington, D.C.: Resource for the Future. Excellent study of the U.S. Park Service as a bureaucracy and of the system.

FOSTER, CHARLES. 1987. *The Appalachian National Scenic Trail.* Harpers Ferry, W.Va.: Appalachian Trail Conference. Detailed study.

FOX, STEPHEN. 1981. *John Muir and His Legacy: The American Conservation Movement.* Boston: Little, Brown. The role of John Muir and his wilderness concept in the history of the American conservation movement.

GILLETTE, ELIZABETH, ed. 1972. *Action for Wilderness.* San Francisco: Sierra Club Books. Practical manual for activists or would-be activists in a wilderness preservation campaign.

GROVE, NOEL. 1988. "The Trail: Ribbon of Yesterday," *The Nature Conservancy,* March–April, vol. 38, no. 2, pp. 12–17. Discusses the role the Nature Conservancy played in safeguarding sections of the Appalachian Trail.

HAMMITT, WILLIAM E., and DAVID N. COLE. 1987. *Wildland Recreation: Ecology and Management.* New York: Wiley. Very good university textbook on the subject.

HART, JOHN. 1979. "Parks for the People: The National Debate," *Sierra,* September–October, pp. 45–49. Informative discussion about urban parks.

HELBURN, NICHOLAS. 1977. "The Wildness Continuum," *The Professional Geographer,* vol. 29, no. 4, pp. 333–337. Interesting discussion of the concept of wilderness.

HENDEE, JOHN, et al., eds. 1977. *Principles of Wilderness Management.* Washington, D.C.: Government Printing Office. Useful collection of articles.

HENDEE, JOHN, et al., eds. 1978. *Wilderness Management.* Washington, D.C.: U.S. Department of Agriculture. The manager's "bible" on wilderness management.

HERITAGE CONSERVATION AND RECREATION SERVICE. 1980. *Nationwide Rivers Inventory: Phase I.* Washington, D.C.: U.S. Department of the Interior. The federal government's attempt to provide a uniform data base for designating rivers to be protected under the National Wild and Scenic Rivers Act.

KLEIN, DAVID R. 1976. "Wildness Part I. Evolution of the Concept," *Landscape,* vol. 20, no. 3, pp. 36–41. Interesting historical analysis of the wilderness concept.

LEOPOLD, ALDO. 1949. *A Sand County Almanac and Sketches Here and There.* Fair Lawn, N.J.: Oxford University Press. Classic book on the cultural values of the wilderness.

LEWIS, PIERCE F., et al. 1973. *Visual Blight in America.* Washington, D.C.: Association of American Geographers, Commission on College Geography, Resource Paper No. 23. Introduction to the problem of landscape deterioration.

MUIR, JOHN. 1954. *The Wilderness World of John Muir.* With an introduction and interpretive comments by Edwin Way Teale. Boston: Houghton Mifflin. Cultural values of the wilderness as described by one of America's leading wilderness advocates.

NASH, RODERICK. 1978. *Nature in World Development: Patterns in the Preservation of Scenic and Outdoor Recreation Resources.* New York: The Rockefeller Foundation. Brief, but excellent, outline of American approaches to wilderness and open-space preservation.

NASH, RODERICK. 1982. *Wilderness and the American Mind.* 3d ed. New Haven, Conn.: Yale University Press. A classic book on American attitudes toward wilderness.

NATIONAL PARKS AND CONSERVATION ASSOCIATION. 1979. *Citizen's Action Guide to the National Park System.* Washington, D.C.: National Parks and Conservation Association. A discussion of how citizens can get involved in parks, from resolving current problems to establishing new parks.

NATIONAL PARK SERVICE. 1980. *State of the Parks—1980. A Report to the Congress.* Washington, D.C.: U.S. Department of the Interior. Recent analysis of the status of U.S. Park Service lands.

NATIONAL WILDLIFE FEDERATION. 1983. *National Wildlife,* February–March, p. 37. Brief news item regarding the current status of wilderness in America.

NOVAK, BARBARA. 1980. *Nature and Culture: American Landscape Painting.* Fair Lawn, N.J.: Oxford University Press. Wilderness as portrayed by American landscape painters.

PALMER, TIM. 1984. "A Time for Rivers," *Wilderness,* Fall, vol. 48, no. 166, pp. 12–19. Good analyses of the successes and failures of the National Wild and Scenic Rivers System.

PRICE, LARRY W. 1981. *Mountains and Man: A Study of Process and Environment.* Berkeley, Calif.: University of California Press. Comprehensive analysis of mountain environments and human history.

RENNICKE, JEFF. 1985. "America's Wild and Scenic Rivers," *Sierra,* March–April, vol. 70, no. 2, pp. 54–58. Brief but informative overview.

RUNTE, ALFRED. 1979. *National Parks: The American Experience.* Lincoln, Neb.: University of Nebraska Press. Comprehensive history of the national park idea.

SAARINEN, THOMAS F. 1974. "Environmental Perception." In Ian R. Manners and Marvin W. Mikesell, eds., *Perspectives on Environment.* Washington, D.C.: Association of American Geographers, Commission on College Geography,

Publication No. 13, pp. 252–289. Environmental perception as it relates to outdoor recreation and environmental amenities.

SHECHTER, MORDECHAI, and ROBERT C. LUCAS. 1978. *Simulation of Recreational Use for Park and Wilderness Management.* Baltimore, Md.: Resources for the Future. Applying computers to wildland management.

SHEPARD, P. 1967. *Man in the Landscape.* New York: Knopf. Classic wilderness book.

SHOMAN, JOSEPH J. 1971. *Open Land for Urban America: Acquisition, Safekeeping, and Use.* Baltimore, Md.: Johns Hopkins University Press. Basic techniques in open-space preservation and maintenance.

STANKEY, GEORGE H. 1971. *The Perception of Wilderness Recreation Carrying Capacity: A Geographic Study in Natural Resources Management.* Ph.D. dissertation, Michigan State University, Department of Geography. Ann Arbor, Mich.: University Microfilms, no. 71–23, 246. Illustrates one approach for determining the relevancy of the diverse perceptions and attitudes of different types of wilderness users.

STRANAHAN, SUSAN. 1984. "Green But Not Growing," *National Wildlife,* October–November, vol. 22, no. 6, pp. 33–35. Discusses the mounting problems of U.S. urban parks.

SUMNER, DAVID. 1982. "Oil and Gas Leasing in Wilderness—What the Conflict is all About," *Sierra,* vol. 67, no. 3, pp. 28–34. Interesting discussion.

SUMNER, DAVID. 1981. "Rivers Running Free: Building the Wild and Scenic System," *Sierra,* September–October, vol. 66, no. 5, pp. 42–50. Informative discussion of the problems inherent in building a national river protection program.

TILDEN, FREEMAN. 1982. *The National Parks.* New York: Knopf. A well-illustrated study.

TUAN, YI-FU. 1971. *Man and Nature.* Washington, D.C.: Association of American Geographers, Commission on College Geography, Resource Paper No. 10. Valuable source for conceptual orientation.

WARD, E. NEVILLE, and BETH KILLHAM. 1988. *Heritage Conservation—The Natural Environment.* Waterloo, Ont.: University of Waterloo Press.

WASHBURNE, RANDEL F., and DAVID N. COLE. 1983. *Problems and Practices in Wilderness Management: A Survey of Managers.* Ogden, Utah: U.S. Department of Agriculture. Excellent discussion of use characteristics, management problems, and management techniques within the National Wilderness Preservation System.

WELLMAN, J. DOUGLAS. 1987. *Wildland Recreation Policy.* New York: Wiley. Outstanding historical information on the individuals, laws, and agencies associated with wilderness preservation and management in the United States.

WHITE, WILLIAM H. 1968. *The Last Landscape.* New York: Doubleday. Open-space preservation in the urban context.

WILDERNESS SOCIETY, THE. 1984. "Towards the Twenty-First Century," *Wilderness,* Summer, vol. 48, no. 165, pp. 34–39. Excellent discussion of their agenda for the National Wilderness Preservation System.

■11■

FRESHWATER FISHERIES MANAGEMENT

Types of Freshwater Habitats

Threats to Freshwater Fisheries

Freshwater Fisheries Management

Prospects for the Future

Action for Freshwater Fisheries

The Quality of Fishing Reflects the Quality of Living
                    Motto of the Sport Fishing Institute

Americans are demanding more fish and a higher quality fishing experience. According to the National Oceanic and Atmospheric Administration, per capita consumption of fish and shellfish in 1987 was a record 7 kg (15.4 lb). This increased demand for fish is partly due to the health-conscious 1980s, with doctors and other health specialists stressing that fish is lower in fat and higher in protein than beef, poultry, and other food products. Since some of America's fisheries are located in freshwater habitats (e.g., lakes, streams, reservoirs, and ponds), fisheries managers, resource economists, and others are interested in sustaining these freshwater resources, as well as this country's marine or saltwater fisheries. This chapter will concentrate on freshwater fisheries. Freshwater habitats, the characteristics of inland fisheries, related management techniques, and policy strategies will be discussed. The chapter will conclude with a look at new trends in freshwater fisheries management, and it will provide some ideas on how you can personally get involved in protecting this nation's freshwater fisheries.

TYPES OF FRESHWATER HABITATS

There are two major types of freshwater habitats: lotic and lentic. **Lotic** environments include fast-moving freshwater bodies, such as streams and rivers. Lakes, reservoirs, ponds, and bogs are inland water bodies that have water that moves very slowly, and consequently, are termed **lentic** environments (Figure 11-1). An inconsistency in terminology exists, however, when categorizing types of lentic and lotic habitats, as will be shown subsequently.

Natural Freshwater Habitats

For the purpose of this chapter, lakes and streams will be classified as *natural habitats* and reservoirs and

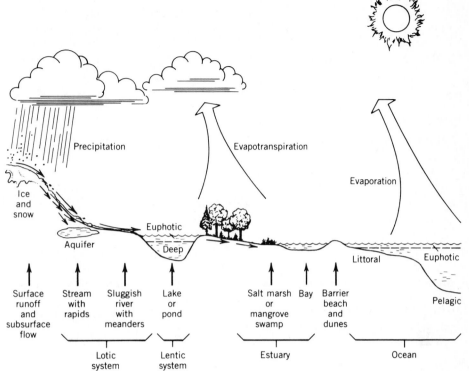

FIGURE 11-1 The lotic and lentic systems as part of the hydrologic cycle. (From Richard T. T. Forman and Michael Godron, *Landscape Ecology*, p. 45. Copyright © 1986 by John Wiley & Sons, Inc.)

ponds as *artificial habitats* or human-made impoundments. Although reservoirs and ponds can be created by nature, they are generally thought of as water bodies constructed by humans (e.g., a reservoir behind a dam has been constructed by water engineers; a sedimentation pond has been built by a farmer).

Lakes.   In America, natural lakes occur primarily in the northern states and are generally a result of glacial action. Depending on conditions (e.g., the actual glacial process, the type of soil, and the temperature range), these natural lakes may be either deep and *oligotrophic* (nutrient poor) or shallow and *eutrophic* (nutrient rich). Cold-water or cool-water fish communities predominate in this northern lakes region. In the southeastern United States (e.g., in Florida and Louisiana), one finds predominantly natural lakes resulting from limestone solution and tectonic movements. Here, the lakes are mostly shallow and eutrophic. Obviously, warm-water fish communities are favored in this type of habitat. In high altitude areas of the United States, another major category of lake exists—the alpine lake. This type of habitat is formed by either glacial or volcanic processes and favors cold-water species of fish.

The natural lake ecosystem has three major zones: littoral, limnetic, and profundal. The **littoral zone** is the shoreline of a lake, which some authori-

ties extend out as far as 200 m (656 ft) in depth; between 60 m (197 ft) to 200 m depth is usually denoted as *sublittoral*. This relatively shallow region of the lake has emergent plants (e.g., bulrushes and cattails), floating plants (e.g., duckweed and water lilies), and submergents (e.g., pondweed and pickerel weed). Fisheries within this region can include yellow perch, northern pike, sunfish, mussels, and clams. Beyond the littoral zone is the **limnetic zone**. This is the open-water surface layer of a lake, where sunlight can penetrate, but it is too deep to support rooted aquatic plants. Plankton and fish are the principal plants and animals of this zone. The **profundal zone** extends from the bottom of the limnetic zone downward to the lake bottom. This area has insufficient sunlight for photosynthesis. This is the area of settling and of decomposition of organic matter (e.g., twigs and leaves, fish skeletons, and animal excreta) that forms the **benthic** or bottom zone that is eventually recirculated as minerals within the lake. For a comprehensive overview of the role of lakes in the landscape see Burgis and Morris (1987).

Streams.   Fish also live in freshwater streams. A stream can be defined as a body of flowing water, where it is merely a rill on a farmer's field or a large river like the Mississippi or Missouri. Ecologists, hydrologists, and water resource managers generally discuss stream characteristics in terms of (1) stream-land interaction; (2) water flow; (3) structure and function of stream corridors; (4) stream orders; and (5) biological zonation. Let us very briefly look at some of these characteristics.

Streams must be thought of in terms of *stream-land interaction,* or the stream's relationship to an entire terrestrial watershed. Although it is convenient in this chapter to separately discuss lakes, streams, reservoirs, and ponds, the above are all integral parts of the whole stream ecosystem. Much of the biota and productivity of the stream is a direct result of inputs or influences from the surrounding environment. For example, a stream often receives important organic material and energy from falling leaves and twigs from overhanging trees, shrubs, and other forms of vegetation.

Water flow and degree of aeration also affect stream fisheries. Since the velocity of stream currents is determined by the gradient of the land, **stream gradient** has an effect on where certain fish, such as black bass (smallmouth and largemouth bass) are located. Compared to deep lakes, streams are more sensitive to pollution from oxygen-demanding wastes. In fact, the oxygen reduction that can result from human sewage can destroy entire fisheries.

Streams also have corridors of riparian vegetation that are different from the surrounding environment (Figure 11-2). In addition to its better known role as a soil erosion and water level control (i.e., the prevention of downstream flooding), the stream corridors also serve as a *natural highway* for the movement of terrestrial animals (and plants) across the landscape (Forman and Godron 1986). Furthermore, these riparian corridors have an effect on water temperature, and thus, stream fisheries.

Streams are classified according to **stream order,** or their position in a drainage network (Figure 11-3). *First-order streams* are generally the smallest unbranched members of the stream network that flow year round; *second-order streams* are the result of the coalescence of two first-order streams; and so on. As stream orders increase, so does the degree of environmental change (e.g., flow rate, water contamination, oxygen depletion, etc.). Consequently, some fish species inhabit only the clear waters (with lush riparian corridors) of the first-order (feeder) streams. Other fish species prefer the higher order muddy streams that result from runoff in rural agricultural areas. Still other fish communities can survive the urban scene—areas that characteristically have rivers which are sluggish, with little shade, and are heavily contaminated with urban wastes.

Streams also have *biological zones* resulting primarily from differences in stream gradient and water temperature (Table 11-1). As the zone changes, so does the presence of certain fish species. Huet (1959) illustrates how these zones apply to a subwatershed of the Susquehanna River in North America.

Artificial Freshwater Habitats

Human-built reservoirs and ponds also add substantially to the number of lentic resources. A brief look at the characteristics of these resources will help set the stage for a discussion of freshwater fisheries management.

Reservoirs.   A **reservoir** is an area where water is collected, stored, and regulated. Often, it is the result of building a dam at a suitable point across a valley. In most cases, reservoirs are built with the intention of being multipurpose—providing a number of services, including irrigation, flood control, navigation, hydroelectric power generation, and recreation. The contribution of reservoirs to the total number of lentic habitats in America is on the increase. In 1900, America only had 100 reservoirs, yet by 1980, it had about 1500—approximately 4 million ha (9.9 million acres) of reservoirs (Noble 1980). Much of this reser-

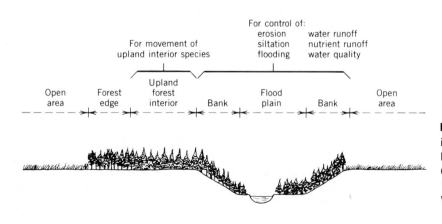

FIGURE 11-2 A stream corridor: its structure and function. (From Richard T. T. Forman and Michael Godron, *Landscape Ecology,* p. 147. Copyright © 1986 by John Wiley & Sons, Inc.)

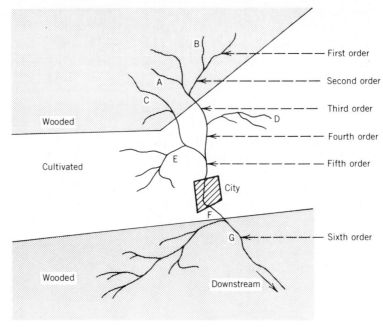

FIGURE 11-3 Classification of a stream according to stream orders. Fish can move from point B to point A, but not to Point D or E because of agricultural runoff. Similarly, fish in points D and E cannot move to points F and G because of urban runoff. (From Richard T. T. Forman and Michael Godron, *Landscape Ecology*, p. 150. Copyright © 1986 by John Wiley & Sons, Inc.)

voir building has taken place in Tennessee, the Dakotas, Texas, and California. On certain rivers in the Southwest, such as the Colorado River, America's demand for irrigation and potable water has spawned hundreds of reservoirs that regulate almost the entire river system (Stanford and Ward 1986).

Fisheries within reservoirs favor exotic fish at the expense of native species; native fish simply cannot survive the uncompromising environment of the artificial reservoir. When fisheries, mostly sport fisheries, are established with introduced species in reservoirs (e.g., the striped bass in Lake Mead), they often go through a boom and bust cycle due to a variety of environmental reasons.

Ponds. To a lesser extent, ponds also contribute to the lentic resource. A **pond** can be defined as a quiet body of water, smaller than a reservoir, that is generally of artificial construction. Most ponds are less than 2 ha (4.9 acres) in size. In addition to traditional *farm ponds* that are used for the collection of irrigation runoff and associated sedimentation, there has been a recent proliferation of private and public ponds near suburban housing developments for the

TABLE 11-1

Biological zonation of streams

NAME	PREDOMINANT LOCATION	TEMPERATURE	AVERAGE CURRENT	GRADIENT	BOTTOM	WATER POOLS	VEGETATION	SEDIMENTATION	OXYGENATION
Trout zone	Small headwaters	Cool	Rapid	Steep	Sand, gravel, cobbles, boulders	No pools or backwaters	Few—no rooted plants	None	Very good
Grayling zone (sucker, roach)	(A) Riffles (B) Deeper runs	Warm	Rapid–moderate	Moderate	Gravel, cobbles	Short pools	Weed beds absent	None	Good Good
Barbel zone (minnow, sucker)	Upper stretches of larger rivers	Warm	Moderate	Moderate	Gravel, sand	Extensive backwater in eddies	Weed beds present	Few	Fair–good
Bream zone	Lower stretches of larger rivers	Warmer	Slow	Low	Silt, sand	Long, deep pools	Weed beds present	Fine silts, organic matter	Poor

Source: Information compiled from Cooper, Edwin L. 1980. "Fisheries Management in Streams." In Robert T. Lackey and Larry A. Nielsen, eds., *Fisheries Management*, pp. 297–322. Boston: Blackwell Scientific; personal interview with Jerry Smith, Professor of Geology, San Jose State University.

expressed purpose of recreation, with an emphasis on fishing (Noble 1980). Because of their small size and location near urban centers, management of these fisheries presents a different set of problems.

THREATS TO FRESHWATER FISHERIES

Despite the high *biotic potential* (reproductive capacity) of freshwater fish, approximately 70 percent of each fish population dies every year (Owen 1985). The primary forms of environmental resistance working against fish are habitat loss, water contamination, drought, competition, predation, and fishing pressure. A brief look at these forms of environmental resistance will help one understand why our lakes, streams, reservoirs, and ponds are not always teaming with fish.

Habitat Loss

Just as with the other forms of wild animal species, loss of habitat plays a major role in the success or failure of a freshwater fish population. In terms of the freshwater fisheries, habitat loss is a result of two major causes: (1) logging and road construction, and (2) dams and water diversion projects.

Logging and Road Construction.   Management plans for forests often overlook the impact of logging and road construction on streams and freshwater fisheries. For example, in a 1985 report to the regional forester for Montana and Idaho, the National Wildlife Federation found that the U.S. Forest Service overvalued timber and grazing on forest land at the sacrifice of fisheries important to the region's recreation industry. The report cited how road construction was detrimental to the area's fisheries because it eliminated shoreline habitat, caused sedimentation which smothered fish eggs, obstructed the movement of fry, and ruined food sources.

The National Wildlife Federation report also found that the U.S. Forest Service's management plans for all 13 western forests had the same flaw—an undervaluing of the importance of fisheries to a region. Furthermore, it criticized the USFS for not sufficiently analyzing the impact of forest activities on fish outside the forests—information they are legally responsible for providing.

Dams and Water Diversion Projects.   Urbanization has a tremendous effect upon our nation's lotic and lentic resources and its associated freshwater fisheries. In an effort to build and maintain our cities, we channelize streams to help control flood runoff, we build diversion channels to carry drinking and irrigation water from wet to dry regions, and we dredge and fill the coastal portions of rivers and estuaries. (See Chapters 4 and 5 for further details on the hydrological impact of humans.)

The Colorado squawfish and the Atlantic salmon are two examples of fish species that are losing habitat as a result of dams and diversion projects. The Colorado River used to cascade wild and free for approximately 2414 km (1500 mi), from the Continental Divide to the Gulf of California. It was a time when the Colorado squawfish (referred to as the "white salmon" by early European settlers) migrated several hundred miles to reach spawning grounds, which is believed to be the longest migration of any freshwater fish in North America. Today, however, gigantic dams and water diversion projects have transformed its habitat. According to many biologists, when you prevent squawfish from moving around, its numbers apparently decline. Between 1981 and 1985, 33 new water-diversion projects had been initiated or approved in the upper basin of the Colorado River, and dozens of other projects are on the drawing boards for consideration in the near future. Consequently, fisheries biologists are not optimistic about the long-term future of this already endangered species.

On the other side of the continent, the Atlantic salmon is also facing a similar fate as a result of habitat loss, as well as other factors, such as water pollution and an overzealous commercial fishing industry. The Atlantic salmon swims in the Merrimack River, just north of Boston, Massachusetts. When the Merrimack was a free-flowing river, thousands of Atlantic salmon swam from the Massachusetts coast to the river's cool headwaters in the mountains of New Hampshire to spawn. Today, the Atlantic salmon in the Merrimack is no longer bountiful. Seven existing dams in the Merrimack watershed have seriously disrupted the Atlantic salmon's migratory path. In 1987, biologists from the U.S. Fish and Wildlife Service maintained that Atlantic salmon restoration was possible if the existing dams were equipped with modern fish-passage facilities (e.g., fish ladders, fish elevators, etc.). However, they also maintained that restoration would only be possible if no new dams were built. Unfortunately, new ones are being discussed, such as the controversial hydroelectric dam proposed for Sewalls Falls in Concord, New Hampshire. For a detailed study of the impact of smaller construction projects (e.g., dikes and revetments) on fisheries, see Sandheinrich and Atchison (1986).

Water Contamination

Environmental changes caused by agricultural and industrial waste effluents can be detrimental to freshwater fisheries (Hellawell 1986). Since the causes of water pollution were discussed in Chapter 4, what follows is merely a brief look at some of the negative consequences of water contamination on freshwater fisheries.

Silts and Sediments. Soil erosion impacts freshwater fisheries in three major ways—physically, chemically, and biologically (Table 11-2). For example, sedimentation literally smothers hundreds of thousands of salmon fish eggs annually; oysters and clams react to highly turbid waters by physically closing up and not feeding, thereby growing less and providing less food in the food chain; and invertebrates, such as mussels, will not settle on soft, sediment-clogged stream beds. The impact of off-site erosion on freshwater fisheries is extremely serious, and, according to LaRoe (1986), the problem can only be approached by revolutionizing our current agricultural practices. (See the section on Habitat Protection in this chapter and Chapter 3 for further details on minimizing off-site soil erosion).

Oxygen-Demanding Wastes. The release of excessive organic nutrients in urban stormwater and sanitary sewage results in a loss of dissolved oxygen in related water bodies. If the release occurs abruptly, it can result in direct fishkills. If the level of dissolved oxygen decreases gradually, the area can experience a shift in fish species. For example, as dissolved oxygen levels decrease, there can be a shift from a predominance of trout, whitefish, and chub to a predominance of perch, bass, and pike. Eventually, oxygen levels fall further and carp and sunfish become dominant (Wheeler 1979). For a detailed look at cultural eutrophication and the causes of the depletion of dissolved oxygen, see Henderson and Markland (1987).

Toxic Chemicals. A number of scientists are now concerned that DDT, PCB, dioxin, and other post–World War II chemicals are causing cancerous growths on fish (Figure 11-4). According to Morell (1984), bullheads in the Buffalo River, which drains into Lake Erie, had high rates of liver cancer; 12 percent of the bottom-dwelling English sole found in the waters of Puget Sound, near Seattle, Washington, had malignant liver tumors; and the list goes on. Not surprisingly, the contaminated waterways of America's industrialized areas had the highest reports of fish with cancers (Figure 11-5).

People who eat chemically contaminated fish may also be at a higher risk of getting cancer. According to a 1988 study by two University of Michigan graduate students, the current FDA Action Levels—levels at which Great Lakes states should warn people against eating certain fish—are too high to protect against cancer. Reducing the levels of toxic chemicals in our waterways is particularly difficult, since chemicals that are now banned in the United States (e.g., DDT, aldrin, and dieldrin) are still used

TABLE 11-2

Impact of silts and sediments on freshwater fish

I PHYSICAL EFFECTS	II CHEMICAL EFFECTS	III BIOLOGICAL EFFECTS
Increased water turbidity:	**Increased organic materials:**	**High turbidity:**
Reduced light penetration	Increased biochemical oxygen demand	Reduced sight for feeding
Reduced photosynthesis	Decreased dissolved oxygen levels	Change in type of fish present
Reduced production of phytoplankton and benthic aquatic plants	Possible fishkills	Possible delay in spawning
	Increased nutrient loads:	Change in fish behavior patterns
Deposition of sediments:	Increased eutrophication of waterbodies	Clogged gills
Smothering of fish eggs	Increased algal blooms	Weakened organisms more susceptible to disease
Quantitative reduction in food	Changes in types of plants and fish	Physically smothered organisms and outright death
Qualitative reduction in food	Lowered dissolved oxygen	
Change in channel configuration:	Possible fishkills	**Changes in streambed:**
Elimination of depressions in streambed	**Increased associated chemicals:**	Some plants cannot root
Streambed becomes shallower and broader	Insecticides and herbicides enter food chain	Some larvae will not settle
Erosion along streambanks	Bioaccumulation	
Loss of riparian habitat	Endangered animal and human health	
Increased water temperatures		

Source: Information compiled from LaRoe, Edward T. 1986. "Instream Impacts of Soil Erosion on Fish and Wildlife." In Thomas E. Waddell, ed., *The Off-Site Costs of Soil Erosion.* Washington, D.C.: The Conservation Foundation.

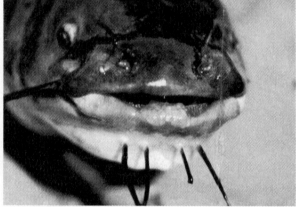

FIGURE 11-4 (upper) A tumor-ridden catfish from Florida; (lower) lip tumor on a bullhead catfish from Ohio's Black River. (Courtesy of photographer Chip Clark and the Smithsonian Institution.)

in Central America and South America, and those chemicals return to the United States by winds and precipitation.

Even if we discount the problem of toxic chemicals entering our waterways indirectly, we still have a problem in this country with banned chemicals. In Alabama, the town of Triana continues to suffer from the 1947–1970 disposal of DDT-laden wastewater into a drainage ditch that flowed into Indian Creek. For over 23 years, the U.S. Army's Redstone Arsenal disposed of 5.7 million L (1.5 million gal) per day of DDT into a drainage ditch (Stranahan 1984). Today, Indian Creek—a stream the town's people had previously depended on for protein (fish) and their drinking water supply—is off limits.

Acid Rain. In July 1987, 2000 high-priced BMW automobiles were pockmarked and scarred by a storm of acid rain in Jacksonville, Florida. In some cases, the rain dissolved the paint down to the metal. More important, however, our nation's lakes and streams and their associated fisheries are suffering. In 1988, the National Wildlife Federation noted that the biological health of approximately 16,000 lakes and streams in the United States was severely impaired. The Adirondacks Lakes Survey Corporation, which is made up of utility companies and state researchers, studied over 1500 lakes in New York's Adirondack State Park to discover the effects of acid rain. The scientists found that 25 percent of the lakes were *dead*—meaning no fish could be found. Another 20 percent of the lakes were so acidic that they had to be classified as *endangered*. Three quarters of the dead lakes had waters as acidic as tomato juice. Lakes in the Adirondacks are particularly susceptible to acid rain because they are located in the first mountains encountered by the acid-laden clouds that drift east from the Midwest, and because many of the lakes are quite small (40 percent are less than 4 ha, or 10 acres)—the smaller the water volume, the less water there is to dilute the acid rain.

The effect of acid rain on our nation's fisheries is obviously very serious. Acidic water bodies can cause fish to suffocate by eroding gill membranes. Yellow perch and lake trout begin to die at pH 4.5; smallmouth bass at pH 5.5; and so on. Acid rain can also indirectly kill fish. Acidic precipitation can leach aluminum from surrounding soils. Once the aluminum enters a stream, fish die of asphyxiation as a result of their gills being clogged. For additional information on acidification of freshwaters, see Cresser and Edwards (1987).

Drought

In 1988, much of the United States was undergoing a drought and the news media continually reminded us of the plight of the American farmer. Little was said, however, about the plight of our nation's fish. In Nevada's Truckee River reservoirs, for example, the water levels were so low that spawning grounds for the endangered Lahontan cutthroat trout and the cui-ui were nonexistent. In the Dakotas, high water temperatures eliminated or sharply reduced the production of bass, walleye, and northern pike at federal hatcheries. Declining flows also affected federal fish hatcheries in South Carolina and Georgia that are dependent upon water from area streams. To many U.S. Fish and Wildlife Service fisheries biologists, the 1988 drought was a missed year for natural reproduction of several fish species.

1. Puget Sound—Liver cell cancer in English sole and starry flounder.

2. Yaquina Bay, Oregon—Blood cell neoplasms in blue mussels.

3. Santa Ana, California—Benign mouth tumors in white croaker (none reported since improvements made in nearby sewage system).

4. Gulf of California—Pigment cell tumors in croaker.

5. Torch Lake, Michigan—Liver cancer in sauger and walleye.

6. Lake Michigan, Lake Huron, Lake Ontario and Lake Erie—Goiters in coho salmon, Gonad tumors in carp, skin tumors on sucker and catfish.

7. Fox River and Des Plaines River, Illinois—Liver cell cancer in brown bullhead catfish, and various types of neoplasms in 15 other fish species.

8. Black River, Ohio—Liver cell, bile duct and mouth cancers in bullhead catfish.

9. Tuskegee, Alabama—Benign mouth tumors in black bullhead catfish (rate declining since procedures improved in local sewage plant).

10. Niagara River, Buffalo River and Lake Erie—Various neoplasms in goldfish, white sucker, walleye, redhorse sucker and drum. Liver cancer in brown bullhead catfish.

11. Deep Creek and Pleasant Valley lakes, Maryland—Liver cancer and bile duct cancer in white sucker.

12. New England coast from Maine to Rhode Island—Blood cell neoplasms in clams and oysters.

13. Sakonnet River, Rhode Island—Tooth tumors in cunners.

14. Hudson River Estuary, New York—Liver and pancreatic cancers in tomcod.

15. Chesapeake Bay—Bile duct tumors in white perch, and blood cell neoplasms in oysters and clams.

16. Central Florida—Cancer of mouth and benign skin tumors in brown bullhead catfish.

17. Florida Keys—Nerve and pigment cell tumors in damselfish and slippery dick, snapper and schoolmaster.

FIGURE 11-5 Areas in the United States where diseased fish have been repeatedly found. (Courtesy of artist Susan Sanford and MedSciArt Co.)

Competitors and Predators

Fish must also compete with other animals (including other fish) for food as well as deal with intense predatory pressure. For example, fish eat fish (e.g., muskellunge eat minnows); predatory birds such as osprey, kingfishers, herons, and egrets eat fish; reptiles such as garter snakes and snapping turtles eat fish; and mammals such as bears, otters, and minks eat fish. And, of course, humans catch and consume fish. In general, predation has the greatest impact either when fish populations are high or when fish populations are low (e.g., when the populations are diseased, parasitized, or starving) (Owen 1985).

Some of the most aggressive competitors are now being introduced into freshwater bodies through the discharge of ballast water from ocean-going vessels. In 1987, for example, the northern European river ruffe (*Gymnocephalus cernuum*) was discovered in Lake Superior's Duluth Harbor (SFI Bulletin August 1988). This perchlike fish, which is native to Northern Europe, entered the Great Lakes through ballast discharge. The Great Lakes Fishery Commission (GLFC) maintains that ruffe can rapidly dominate native fish populations, citing how white-fish production in ruffe-infested Russian lakes has been reduced by 50 percent. Other exotic species introduced in the Great Lakes by ballast water are the "water fish" (*Bythotrephes cederstroemi*), the European flounder, the Chinese mitten crab, the Asian clam, as well as a variety of marine algae, worms, clams, and mussels. Many of these introduced animals turn out to be highly adaptable and undesirable.

Overfishing by Humans

One merely has to go to America's favorite fishing holes on the first day of fishing season to realize that humans are one of the greatest predators of fish. According to the periodic *National Surveys of Fishing,*

Hunting, and Wildlife Associated with Recreation, conducted at five-year intervals by the U.S. Fish and Wildlife Service, fishing remains the prime outdoor recreational activity for the American family. For example, from 1980 to 1985 (the latest survey period), the growth rate in fishing participation (1.8 percent per year) exceeded the growth rate of the U.S. population (1.3 percent per year). In terms of fishing pressure, the survey found that anglers fished at least 900 million days in the 13 million ha (33 million acres) of fresh water located within the contiguous 48 states exclusive of the Great Lakes. After making certain assumptions, it ultimately concluded that every square foot of water received a fishhook at least 1.5 times during 1985. The figures are indeed sobering.

FRESHWATER FISHERIES MANAGEMENT

Managing freshwater fisheries as ecosystems is no easy task since humans have historically used streams for exploration, colonization, political boundaries, hydropower, industrial development, recreation, navigation, mass transport, agricultural irrigation, a source of urban water supply, and waste disposal. In terms of these competing uses, fisheries have played, and most likely will continue to play, a secondary role in water resource usage. Most fisheries biologists maintain that it would be utopian to think one could ever succeed at managing streams and lakes for a diverse natural biota. But if that is true, then what is freshwater fisheries management?

Freshwater fisheries management can be defined as the manipulation of freshwater habitats and fish populations to maintain and possibly increase fish harvests for commercial and recreational uses. Although the ideal is to develop balanced biotas, the market value of a species and what the fisherman wants to catch often dictate how freshwater bodies are managed. Fisheries managers also have their own idea of what the ideal fish should be (Table 11-3) and manage accordingly.

In order to maintain, improve, or increase fish populations, fisheries managers use a variety of techniques at their disposal. Let us briefly look at the following major methods: habitat improvement, habitat construction, biotic manipulation, regulation, and habitat protection.

Habitat Improvement

Fishery habitats can be altered to increase the competitive advantage for desirable species, and, more important, to increase the total carrying capacity for

TABLE 11-3

The ideal fish

1. Attractive (good public image) and tasty
2. Easy to eat (few nuisance bones)
3. In demand by sport fishermen
4. In demand by industry for commercial products
5. Well adapted to its habitat
6. Able to hold its own against predators
7. Be a fast-growing herbivore
8. Not violate cultural taboos
9. Not transport human diseases, parasites, or toxins
10. Should be indigenous to the area

Source: Information compiled from Cooper, Edwin L. 1980. "Fisheries Management in Streams." In Robert T. Lackey and Larry A. Nielsen, eds., *Fisheries Management*, pp. 297–322. Boston: Blackwell Scientific.

maximum biomass (of fishes) production. Techniques include altering the land (e.g., constructing bank stabilization and artificial spawning structures), the vegetation (e.g., using cover manipulation and weed control), and the water (e.g., regulating water level and degree of aeration). As Owen (1985) has noted, one positive habitat manipulation often leads to other positive effects.

Altering the Land. For years, fisheries managers in the dairy state of Wisconsin have had to deal with the problem of streams being deteriorated by ditching and cattle grazing. To correct the problem, they have tried such habitat improvement techniques as covering cattle-crossing areas with crushed stone or gravel, stabilizing streambank erosion by fencing out cattle, and building rock deflectors to direct stream currents. Fisheries managers also alter land for the purpose of improving cover for fish. Techniques range from shoring up existing overhangs, to designing artificial reefs from old automobile tires, to submerging and anchoring discarded Christmas trees.

Where suitable natural spawning sites are poor, such as a stream or lake bottom heavily laden with mud, fisheries managers have created artificial spawning sites with sand and gravel, and, in some cases, even with nylon mats. Other techniques include placing rip-rap in appropriate places, digging artificial spawning channels, and providing barrels or similar containers for fish to spawn in. In a study of the brook trout population in Lawrence Creek, Wisconsin, such habitat alterations proved to be quite successful (Cooper 1980).

Altering the Water. Fisheries managers alter water in four major ways by controlling level, turbidity, aeration, and fertility. By manipulating water level, fisheries managers can change vegetation, control spawning, and affect predation. For example, to eliminate shallow-water spawners like the common carp, reservoir water levels can be lowered so the eggs of this undesirable species can be exposed or isolated (Noble 1980). If prey species are overabundant, lowering water levels can force them from the aquatic vegetation that serves as their cover, thus making them more susceptible to predators. Conversely, northern pike need marshy areas for spawning, and raising reservoir levels may provide additional favorable sites for this highly desirable species (Lager 1956).

Most recreational fishes suffer direct adverse effects from excessive turbidity. Turbidity can be reduced by (1) directly adding green or dry organic matter to a turbid pond; the organic matter, upon decomposition, causes the dry particles in the water to precipitate; (2) establishing plant growths on reservoir bottoms during drawdown of the water level; and (3) applying chemicals such as alum or gypsum to the water. For long-term results, however, the chemical technique also requires fertilization. (See the fertilization section of this chapter for further details.)

Enhancing the oxygen levels of water is a technique often used by fishery managers. Typically, cold-water fishes require oxygen levels above 5 mg/L, and warm-water fishes require above 3 mg/L (Noble 1980). In the winter, however, snow can blanket a frozen lake, thereby reducing photosynthetic production of oxygen. The result is oxygen depletion and *winterkill*. To eliminate the problem, fishery managers can increase oxygen production by several techniques, such as removing the snow cover with snow plows, opening up sections of the lake with dynamite, or strategically placing artificial motorized aeration devices. These same aeration devices can be used to control oxygen depletion in lakes during the summer.

Finally, fishery managers can alter the fertility of the water. Sometimes freshwater bodies are naturally infertile—lacking the necessary phosophates, nitrates, and carbonates. Generally, this is due to the characteristics of the surrounding watershed. To correct the problem in small bodies of water, fishery managers can increase phytoplankton production and fish populations by directly adding organic fertilizers (e.g., manure and hay) or, more commonly today, by adding inorganic agricultural fertilizers. Increasing water fertility by such techniques has only met with limited success and has often resulted in *disaster* (e.g., overfertilization which leads to excessive phytoplankton blooms, leading to oxygen depletion and consequent fishkill).

Altering the Vegetation. Freshwater habitats can also be improved by altering associated aquatic vegetation. Although fish populations require aquatic vegetation as cover for young fish, as a surface on which food organisms can grow or attach, and as a source of oxygen, excessive vegetation can actually be destructive to a fishery. For example, too much cover can result in an upset in predator-prey relationships. When a fish population can easily escape its predators, overpopulation and stunting of fish size can result. Furthermore, overly thick vegetation deprives phytoplankton of needed nutrients, and the eventual decomposition of that same vegetation can result in a decrease in the level of dissolved oxygen. To the human senses, large accumulations of decomposing aquatic vegetation can also be aesthetically undesirable. The top three water weeds in the United States are water hyacinth, water chestnut, and the lotus.

There are three methods to manipulate aquatic vegetation: mechanical, chemical, and biological. Mechanical control methods include such techniques as water level manipulation (exposing submerged vegetation will dry it out; drowning vegetation will limit sunlight) and the use of various cutting machines mounted on raftlike boats (Figure 11-6). The nice thing about harvesting weeds with a cutting machine is that the harvested aquatic plants can be later churned up into compost to be used as a soil additive (Henderson and Markland 1987).

Chemical control methods include the spraying or dusting of water bodies with algicides, herbicides, or pesticides. Repeated doses, however, have proven to have several disastrous effects for freshwater ecosystems. For example, the Fairmont Lakes in Minnesota had been dosed with copper sulphate (an algicide) for more than 58 years. Although this practice temporarily rid the lake of excessive algal growths, several deleterious effects later occurred, such as fishkills resulting from lowered dissolved oxygen levels and copper toxicity (Henderson and Markland 1987). This is a good example of where the use of chemicals—often considered the cheaper and easier way to go—can later prove in the long run to be bad economically as well harmful to the ecosystem.

In recent years, fisheries managers are becoming increasingly interested in exploring various biological methods for controlling excessive aquatic vegetation. According to Henderson and Markland (1987), the ideal fish for aquatic weed control must (1) control a variety of weeds without interfering with

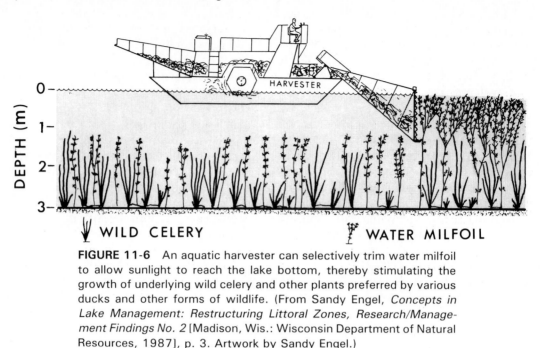

FIGURE 11-6 An aquatic harvester can selectively trim water milfoil to allow sunlight to reach the lake bottom, thereby stimulating the growth of underlying wild celery and other plants preferred by various ducks and other forms of wildlife. (From Sandy Engel, *Concepts in Lake Management: Restructuring Littoral Zones, Research/Management Findings No. 2* [Madison, Wis.: Wisconsin Department of Natural Resources, 1987], p. 3. Artwork by Sandy Engel.)

other fish species, (2) be hardy, easy, and economical to use, and (3) supplement the fishery size. In the United States, the species that come closest to meeting these requirements are the grass carp and common carp. Fisheries managers have also used other organisms for weed and algae control, such as crayfish and *Tilapia*—a cichlid introduced from Africa. Snakes, turtles, beetles, snails, and some mammals have been used for weed control. Of these organisms mentioned above, the use of *Tilapia* seems to be the most promising.

Finally, Engel (1987, p. 1) notes that "thinking like a landscape architect" has led to some recent creative approaches to managing aquatic vegetation. In this approach, entire lakes and bays are viewed as "aquascapes—underwater real estate needing better design." The first step is to prepare a *lake-use map*, thereby indicating preferred areas for swimming, boating, angling, and nature study, in association with the various types of aquatic vegetation present. Second, the lake is zoned into areas of similar use (e.g., sailing, swimming, and fishing). Finally, a management strategy is tailored to each type of zone: intensive plant management in the swimming and boating zones, channelization in the angling zones, the planting of cattails and bulrushes in waterfowl shoreline zones, and the leaving alone of little used zones. According to Engel, this approach has several benefits: (1) It recognizes weedbeds as potential assets; (2) it enhances lake recreation without sacrificing biotic diversity; and (3) it provides an approach

that is more balanced and creative than treating the entire lake in the same way.

Habitat Construction

In addition to improving upon existing habitats, fisheries managers can also construct new habitats in the form of reservoirs, artificial lakes, and farm ponds. According to Owen (1985), the United States already has at least 1000 reservoirs of over 202 ha (500 acres), and by the year 2000, it will have approximately 3 million farm ponds that contribute 68 million kg (150 million lb) of fish annually to the American diet.

There are certain design criteria that must be considered when constructing ponds and small reservoirs. For example, they must be constructed in a way to allow for drawdown and draining, so that fisheries managers can manipulate the water level. Drop structures (a concrete device to help prevent the upstream migration of fish), vertical standpipes (principal spillways to allow the release of moderate inflows) and emergency spillways (wide overflow areas for heavy water flow) are considered essential components of most ponds and small reservoirs (Noble 1980). Additional components include amenities for the angler and the general recreationist, such as fishing piers, boat launch sites, and safety rails.

Managing these artificial impoundments requires many of the same skills and techniques involved in manipulating natural habitats. For example, fish within ponds can get diseases from parasitic protozoa, tapeworms, roundworms, fungi, algae, leeches, bacteria, and viruses. To help control fish diseases, pond managers use a variety of management techniques, ranging from water manipulation, to the use of disinfectants and antibiotics, to the genetic improvement of the fish stock.

Biotic Manipulation

In addition to manipulating habitats (including habitat improvement and habitat construction), fisheries managers can also manipulate the actual fish population. This can be accomplished by three major methods: (1) predator control; (2) competitor control; and (3) artificial propagation, which includes stocking, aquaculture, and the breeding of pollution-resistant fish or so-called superior fish. A brief look at these management techniques would now be beneficial.

Controlling Predators. Since predators help keep fish populations from outstripping the carrying capacity of a water body, one can easily see how thinning (reducing) the predator population would be likely to increase the population of a desirable fish species. For example, Alexander (1977) reports that in the more severe climates of North America, merganser ducks and other fish predators annually take more trout than do anglers. Although the fisheries manager might please the angler by reducing the number of merganser ducks, and thus possibly increase the number of trout, he or she might, by doing so, also incur the wrath of hikers, bird enthusiasts, and animal protectionists. Like so many resource management problems, fisheries managers too must face questions involving tradeoffs and compromise.

The classic example of the effect of a predator on a fish population is the story of the lamprey. In the 1940s and 1950s, the Great Lakes were plagued by the sea lamprey—the blood-sucking so-called vampires of the deep. Descended from an early class of primitive jawless fish, the eellike sea lamprey uses a sucking disklike mouth to attach itself to a fish and rasp a hole in the fish's scales. Once attached, the lamprey drains blood and other body fluids from its prey, often killing the host fish. In 1987, officials of the Great Lakes Fishery Commission estimated that a single sea lamprey can kill 18 kg (40 lb) of fish in the year and a half it is an active parasite. Even those fish that survive attacks by the sea lamprey are left with ugly, round scars, which make them less marketable.

In the 1950s, fisheries managers built dams, constructed electrical barriers on streams, and used chemical compounds such as 3-trifluoromethyl–4-nitrophenol to control the lamprey invasion. Officials of the commission declared the management strategy a success, citing, for example, that the number of spawning sea lampreys in northern Lake Huron alone had declined from 100,000 a year in 1970 to about 10,000 a year in 1980. By 1987, however, fisheries managers discovered that the lampreys were once against threatening Great Lakes fish. The lampreys, being highly adaptable to different environments, were apparently avoiding the small, easily treated streams and were now breeding in the broad, deep channels of the St. Marys River (between Lake Superior and Lake Huron) and St. Clair River (between Lake Huron and Lake St. Clair). Since these rivers are too large to be chemically treated, scientists are now looking for other management techniques, such as biological controls. In the rivers of Michigan's Upper Peninsula, fisheries managers are experimenting with a new method wherein male lampreys are chemically sterilized and released. The idea is to reduce the percentage of successful breedings. If the technique proves successful, a broader study will be later conducted in the St. Marys River in the early 1990s.

Despite numerous examples of the failure of chemicals to control predators for any length of time, fisheries managers continue to use this approach. In 1987, for example, officials of the California Department of Fish and Game used the chemical rotenone to kill all the fish in Kaweah Lake and its 241 km (150 mi) of tributaries spreading across Kings and Tulare counties. Local anglers, recreation business operators, water users, and environmentalists were outraged because rotenone, like so many chemicals, is a nonselective toxin—it kills all fish indiscriminately. The Department of Fish and Game, along with commercial fishermen, however, argued that this fish-kill plan was the most efficient method of keeping the predatory white bass out of the Sacramento–San Joaquin Valley Delta—thus protecting the highly profitable salmon and striped bass populations that are harvested for market. Like the sea lamprey story, the quick *chemical fix* technique may later prove not only ineffective at controlling predator populations, but it may also prove to be disastrous to the long-term health of the freshwater ecosystem.

Controlling Competitors. Removing competitors or undesirable fish is another type of biotic manipulation known as *rough* or *trash fish control.* Nongame species that are often considered useless or trash fish by the fisheries manager are gizzard shad, carp, suckers, and bowfins. The removing of rough fish with toxicants (e.g., rotenone) and restocking with trout or other game species is a well accepted practice in the ponds and lakes of North America. Other removal methods include encouraging the commercial harvesting of the unwanted species, seining, using spawning controls, and manipulating water levels.

Although such practices may "thin" overabundant, stunted fish, and thus prove beneficial in the short run, there are several drawbacks that come with the practice. First, the results are only *temporary* and thus *ineffective* in the long run. Rough fish easily reestablish themselves as part of the fish community. Second, the practice of using nonselective toxins often endangers rare native species, thus reducing biotic diversity and the overall health of the freshwater ecosystem. Third, fish toxicants can be misapplied (e.g., too much may be applied at the wrong time, such as during the colder months when the detoxification process occurs relatively slowly) and thus prove disastrous. Finally, fish toxicants may escape the control area by overflowing, thus negatively impacting downstream areas.

Ballast water introductions of exotic species can be fairly simply and cheaply controlled. Ocean-going vessels can be required to exchange their ballast water at sea before entering freshwater lakes. Routine spot sampling of ballast water and inspection of ship's logs at entry points (e.g., at the St. Lawrence Seaway) would help ensure that ship captains were making the required mid-ocean exchange of ballast water. Vessels found with ballast water containing undesirable organisms or without the proper log entries would not be permitted entry into inland waterways.

Artificial Propagation.   In addition to thinning undesirable species, fisheries managers manipulate fish populations by using various methods of artificial propagation. The techniques of aquaculture, stocking, and the engineering of superior fish come under this category.

Aquaculture, also known as fish culture or fish farming, can be defined as the raising of fish in captivity—in tanks (Figure 11-7) or in raceways—for direct consumption or for release into streams, lakes, reservoirs, or ponds. Aquaculture includes the culture of such species as catfish, salmon, trout, and crawfish for human food; striped bass, largemouth bass, and bluegill for sportfishing; and golden shiner and fathead minnow for fish bait. The U.S. Fish Hatchery system has over 93 national hatcheries and support facilities (Anderson 1987).

The Hudson River Striped Bass Hatchery, which is operated by EA Science and Technology of Middletown, New York, is an example of a successful

FIGURE 11-7   Fish-rearing tanks in a hatchery. (Photo by Lowell Georgia/Science Source/Photo Researchers.)

hatchery. Located 64 km (40 mi) north of New York City on the eastern shore of the Hudson River estuary, this hatchery produced and released in 1987 more than 330,000 fingerling striped bass for direct-release into the Hudson River, and more than 1,400,000 fingerlings during the previous five years. But how many fingerlings survived once they were released? According to an annual Hudson River Shoreline Fisheries Survey conducted by the New York State Department of Environmental Conservation (NYSDEC), fish tags indicated that more than one- quarter of the striped bass found were from the Hudson River Striped Bass Hatchery, thus making this hatchery the largest single contributor to an extensive striped bass restoration project being coordinated by the U.S. Fish and Wildlife Service (SFI Bulletin, June 1988).

But the use of hatcheries as a fisheries management technique has its drawbacks. First, hatcheries are capital intensive—they require expensive facilities, expensive maintenance programs, and an expensive payroll for personnel. For example, Anderson (1987) notes that trout (fish about 20–25 centimeters, or 8–10 inches in length) which are reared in a hatchery and then transplanted cost approximatley 81 cents a pound. Second, hatcheries can be plagued by viruses and other diseases. In hatcheries within the Great Lakes Region, such as the U.S. Fish and Wildlife Service's Iron River Hatchery and

Michigan's Marquette Hatchery, epizootic epitheliotropic virus disease (EEVD) is now causing havoc with local efforts at lake trout restoration. In 1988, the virus was so severe that all fish at the Iron River Hatchery had to be destroyed, as well as a good portion of the fish at the Marquette Hatchery, resulting in a total loss of about 2.5 million fish for 1988.

Despite these drawbacks, the practice of aquaculture is on the rise in the United States. Some researchers, such as Lee (1987), see U.S. fisheries in transition, from an *open-access fisheries*, where fish are harvested from the wild, to a *closed-access fisheries*, where fish are raised in captivity (aquaculture) so that certain fish stocks can be the private property of individuals, states, and corporations. Lee cites how some anthropologists, such as Courtland Smith of Oregon State University, see this change as a natural evolution, similar to the evolution of humans from hunters and gatherers to agriculturalists (i.e., from individuals hunting wild animals to individuals harvesting their own domesticated livestock). To defend his case, he notes how the catfish industry in the United States has made such a transition. According to Lee, 90 percent of the catfish marketed in the United States today is produced through aquaculture, whereas historically, catfish were caught by commercial fishermen harvesting wild stocks. The salmon fishing industry and some other fishing industries are also making a similar transition, says Lee.

There is no question that the potential for aquaculture is good and that its importance in providing food will increase as the world's population grows. To lower capital investment costs, researchers are investigating the traditional practices of aquaculture in Third World countries that emphasize *polyculture*—the growing of fish and agricultural crops simultaneously. In the Philippines, for example, carp or *Tilapia* are grown together in rice fields (Figure 11-8). According to Avault (1980), fish production within these fields can reach 200 kg/ha (441 lb/acre) despite the fact that the fish are never fed by hand. Furthermore, rice production may also increase, since the fish fertilize the soil with their waste products, eat harmful insects, and till the soil through their normal body movements.

Fish reared in captivity can then be either sold directly to market or used to stock streams, lakes, reservoirs, or ponds. There are two major goals of **stocking** programs: (1) to maintain existing populations; and (2) to increase the size and numbers of fish available for recreational anglers. Fisheries managers may attempt to meet those goals by using an **introduction**—a fish species not present in the habitat at the time of the stocking program. An *endemic* species (i.e., a native species which is indigenous to the habitat) may be introduced, or the fisheries manager may choose to add an *exotic* species (i.e., a nonnative) to the habitat. Fisheries managers have been so successful at introducing exotic species that fisheries biologists, environmentalists, and even some fisheries managers are beginning to question the validity of such stocking programs.

Although there have been beneficial introductions, such as the European brown trout, stocking programs can do more harm than good if not carefully studied and planned in advanced. Even with advanced studies, predicting the outcome of an introduction is almost impossible (Noble 1980). Examples of mistakes made by fisheries managers are numerous, such as the introduction of the white amur

(a)

(b)

FIGURE 11-8 Aquaculture mixed with agriculture. (Photos courtesy of Dr. James Avault, Jr., Louisiana State University.)

(grass carp) from Malaysia for weed control, and the introduction of the European carp as a food source. Introductions may lead to harmful results, such as the decline or elimination of native species by competition, predation, or hybridization (i.e., genetic swapping) (Moyle 1976).

Stocking can also lead to a vicious cycle known as *fishing pressure-stocking* (Cooper 1980). For example, if anglers know that a section of a stream is being stocked with trout, it often leads to increased fishing pressure on that section of the stream, which in turn leads to demands for increased levels of stocking. To decrease fishing pressure, fisheries managers could take a *no-stocking policy*, but that would not be popular with most anglers. Thus, the fisheries manager is caught in a "no-win" situation.

The latest form of artificial propagation is the development of pesticide or acid-resistant strains of fish through selective breeding experiments. For example, scientists at Cornell University are artificially breeding new strains of trout that are tolerant of the low pH levels often found in the 214 different lakes of the Adirondacks region of New York State. In studies conducted in the 1970s, scientists found that over half of the lakes had pH levels of less than 5.0, compared to the 5.6 pH level of unpolluted rainwater. (Recall, the lower the pH level, the more acidic is the water.) Of those same acidified lakes, over 82 percent were barren of fish (Crane 1984).

Most fisheries managers and biologists admit, however, that manufacturing pollutant-resistant fish is only a stopgap measure or band-aid technique until the worldwide society finds a means to drastically reduce the causes of acid rain. Those in favor of developing such "superior fish" argue that it is better to do at least something to help keep trout available for the recreational anglers than to wait for the acid rain problem to be solved. Environmentalists and a number of researchers, however, worry that developing pollution-resistant fish may give the public and legislators the wrong impression—that acid rain is no longer a national and worldwide problem. Says Fred Johnson, a Pennsylvania Fish Commission official, "creating an acid-resistant trout is like straightening the deck chairs on the *Titanic*" (Crane 1984).

Fishing Regulations

A more traditional means by which fisheries managers have cared for their resource is the practice of placing restrictions on anglers. There are five major types of such restrictions—all with their advantages and drawbacks (Table 11-4). Fisheries managers may close a specific area to fishing *(closed-area)*, or forbid fishing during a particular season when fish are more vulnerable *(closed-season)*, or restrict the number *(creel-limit)* or the size of fish taken *(size-limit)*. They may also restrict the types of fishing techniques used (e.g., the use of dynamite or poison) or support state or national legislation protecting particular endangered species. To establish restrictions in a responsible manner, however, fisheries managers must first have studied the ecosystem in question as well as know the total clientele they are serving. When it comes to using restrictions, says Cooper (1980), fisheries managers must be *adaptable* and take into consideration the full spectrum of users of the resource and not just consider the meat-hungry angler.

Occasionally, scientists, environmentalists, and anglers unite in order to call for stricter regulations on a fish species. In 1988, for example, the winter run of chinook salmon in the Sacramento River in northern California was so low that the California Sportfishing Protection Alliance, the Defenders of Wildlife, the Sierra Club, and the American Fisheries Society (a 7000 member scientific association) filed suit against the National Marine Fisheries Service (NMFS) for not giving the salmon threatened status under the Endangered Species Act.

The NMFS refused to give salmon threatened status, since such an action would have a huge impact on river users, such as federal agencies that had pending hydroelectric projects. Instead, it requested that the Bureau of Reclamation maintain water flow during critical months, and that the California Department of Fish and Game continue their habitat restoration projects (Price 1988).

Habitat Protection

Fisheries managers are slowly beginning to realize that *many of the above management techniques would not be required if fishery habitats were protected in the first place.* Consequently, fisheries managers are starting to make the transition from the quick-fix solution used in their lake, stream, reservoir, or pond to the longer-term solution of finding ways to prevent problems from occurring in the first place.

Stream improvement programs, for example, are now beginning to focus on the entire human-land relationship within a watershed. Attempts are being made to find financial incentives to get farmers to practice good soil and water resource management, to get industries to cut down on the pollutants that produce acid rain, and to get water developers to consider fisheries when constructing small or large dams. To reduce the impacts of off-farm soil erosion and runoff, for example, fisheries managers now real-

TABLE 11-4

Major types of fishing regulations

TYPE	DESCRIPTION/PURPOSE	ADVANTAGES	DISADVANTAGES
I Closed-season or closed-area restrictions	Restricts fishing during periods of the year when fish are more vulnerable (e.g., breeding periods)	Scatters fishing pressure in time and space; protects eggs and future young fish	Impractical for large geographic areas; most anglers consider it too much interference with their fishing opportunity; may not really protect the resource
II Size limits	Restricts harvesting fish under a certain size	Helps assure the presence of a certain species (e.g., predator species that help control rough fish); greater opportunity for an angler to land a large specimen; creates "psychological goals" for fisherman to strive for	Not always effective in sustaining total numbers of a species; mortality of released fish possible
III Creel-limits	Restricts number of fish taken	Divides the resource among fishermen; creates "psychological goals" for fishermen to strive for; minimizes the chance of overharvest	Does not really protect the resource
IV Fishing technique restrictions	Outlaws fishing with highly destructive devices (e.g., dynamite; poison; seines; barbed, multiple-point hooks)	Helps prevent the destruction of the habitat as well as the fish population; improves "sporting" aspect	People who already fish this way would often not have any reservations about continuing the practice under restrictive laws
V Legislation	National laws that can protect endangered species (e.g., Endangered Species Act)	Can bring national attention (and protection) to a species	Complexity and multiplicity of restrictions; difficulty of telling fish species apart; legislation can be reversed as politics change

Source: Information compiled from Cooper, Edwin L. 1980. "Fisheries Management in Streams." In Robert T. Lackey and Larry A. Nielsen, eds., *Fisheries Management*, pp. 297–322. Boston: Blackwell Scientific; Noble, Richard L. 1980. "Management of Lakes, Reservoirs, and Ponds." In Robert T. Lackey and Larry Nielsen, eds. *Fisheries Management*, pp. 265–295. Boston: Blackwell Scientific: and Owen, Oliver, 1985. *Natural Resource Conservation: An Ecological Approach.* 4th ed. New York: Macmillan.

ize they must get involved in reversing the causes of agricultural soil erosion in the last 50 years—the trends toward monoculture, larger fields, bigger and heavier equipment, compacted soils, higher pesticide use, and farming closer to streams. Without addressing these problems, anything the fisheries manager does on site will only be a temporary solution—a mere reaction to a problem rather than a solution.

PROSPECTS FOR THE FUTURE

Fisheries management of inland waters in the United States has been practiced for over 100 years, and it is likely that management will intensify in the near future. Recreational and commercial fishing is increasing, fishermen are becoming more and more organized in official groups, and other users of aquatic resources are demanding that our nation's lakes, reservoirs, streams, and ponds be managed in a way

that is also suitable to their interests. Over the past century, only a few fisheries management techniques have been developed, such as fish culture, stocking, predator control, and the other techniques previously discussed in this chapter. It is obvious that new techniques (and especially attitudes towards management) need to be developed to meet the challenge of the future.

Positive Signs and Success Stories

Despite all the problems that fisheries managers must face, they (and you) should have reason for hope. What follows below is a brief discussion of some of the many positive signs and success stories that can be found across the nation.

1. *Some beneficial agricultural trends.* America is waking up to the fact that agricultural practices that intensify soil erosion and contaminate our water supplies cannot continue. We are moving toward a more *sustainable* or *low-input* agriculture—one that encourages minimal or more efficient use of pesticides and fertilizers, conservation tillage, contour plowing and terracing, and the protection of riparian vegetation and associated waterways (see Chapter 3 for further details).

2. *Greater appreciation of urban streams and lakes.* A movement is underway in America to preserve or restore its urban streams and lakes. When the new towns of Columbia, Maryland, and Woodlands, Texas, were developed, the ecological diversity of the stream valleys were purposely retained (Spirn 1984). In 1984, neighbors in Oakland, California, stood in front of a flood control district bulldozer that was stripping a section of Glen Echo Creek. A video of the incident convinced the Oakland City Council to order the creek redesigned and revegetated. Because of these efforts, the creek is now part of a wildlife refuge rather than a concrete channel. Similar neighborhood groups that promote watershed restorations are forming all over the nation.

3. *The comeback of certain fish species in select regions of the country.* Salmon, for example, are making a comeback into many Pacific Coast rivers, such as the mighty Columbia River in Washington and Oregon's Rogue River. Salmon declined within the Pacific Northwest due to many common abuses: excessive sedimentation of streams resulting from poor logging and agricultural practices, dams that blocked migration or mauled fish in their hydroelectric turbines, and overfishing. The reversal was brought about by a number of factors, such as (1) better dam management, which included helping smolts move down stream (Figure 11-9) and having a better understanding of how water discharges from dams affect salmon runs; (2) an increased number of hatcheries and increased hatchery production; (3) new regulations (e.g., the Northwest Power Act of 1980 gave salmon migration equal priority with the need for hydroelectric power from the Columbia River; and (4) improved ocean conditions, including the return of cool, nutrient-rich water to the Northwest following the end of the tropical El Niño current in 1984.

4. *Successes at protecting wild species and wild environments.* Alarmed that certain wild strains of

FIGURE 11-9 Ferrying salmon (wild and hatchery-reared smolts) to a navigation channel below the lower granite dam on the Snake River. (Courtesy of photographer Doug Wilson.)

trout were disappearing because of antiquated fishing regulations, hatchery stocking, and poor land management, a number of anglers and state biologists in the West recently developed new management programs for protecting the remaining wild trout populations. They discovered that wild trout (trout not raised in a hatchery) respond best to protected trout habitat. By 1986, eight states had wild trout programs, wherein certain rivers were designated as nonstocking waters. Restrictions on tackle and strict limits on the fish taken (including catch and release regulations) were also imposed. This increased protection of native trout habitats and wild trout species is particularly encouraging. To fisheries biologists and environmentalists, it means the protection of diverse habitats and genetic diversity (genetic "money in the bank"); to anglers, it means a more aesthetically pleasing recreational experience (i.e., catching a wild trout as opposed to a "factory" fish).

5. *Increasing respect for nongame species.* Not only are fisheries managers and anglers changing their attitudes about the need for protecting wild game species, they are simultaneously beginning to recognize the value of protecting nongame species— species they used to call "trash fish." For example, so-called trash fish are now beginning to be seen for their food value and usefulness in medical research (e.g., the garfish is used for neurological studies; the *Tilapia*, for cataract research; and the catfish, for insulin research). The next step, of course, will be to appreciate such nongame species for their *role within the ecosystem*, as opposed to any anthropocentric or human need which these creatures can fulfill.

6. *Growing trend toward skill rather than kill.* Anglers are changing their ethics in other ways as well, such as the recent trend toward what is commonly called tag and release, catch and release, or reduced-kill fishing. According to the Sport Fishing Institute, this bodes well for recreational fishing, since releasing caught fish (1) recycles fish for other anglers, (2) heightens ecological awareness among anglers, and (3) fosters a better relationship between anglers and fisheries biologists (e.g., the tagging of fish by anglers provides biologists with needed raw data on fish history, feeding habitats, fish migration, and so forth). Conferences on angling ethics are now being held, such as the 1987 conference sponsored by the Izaak Walton League of America. In addition to the tag and release system being encouraged, solutions are sought to correct poor ethical practices, such as the violation of fishing regulations, the abuse of nongame fish species, the overcrowding of certain streams and lakes, the improper handling of the catch, and the wasting of important portions of the catch.

7. *Increasing voluntary efforts.* Across the country, conservationists, anglers, and local citizens are uniting for the purpose of becoming *stream doctors* or stream protectors. They are volunteering their time and energy to help state wildlife agencies plant riparian vegetation, move boulders, clean up litter, and conduct fisheries studies. As Johnson (1985) has noted, the American public is beginning to put their heart and soul into stream protection.

8. *Discovery that all lake bottoms are not biological deserts.* Finally, it should be encouraging to know that scientists are finding more life at the bottom of large water bodies than they previously believed was there. In 1986, for example, researchers from Michigan State University descended 396 m (1300 ft) to the bottom of Lake Superior and found the area to be teaming with life, with such species as sculpin (a minnow-sized fish), burbot (a member of the cod family), and hydra (a tiny jellyfish-like organism).

ACTION FOR FRESHWATER FISHERIES

There are a number of things that you personally can do to get involved in protecting this country's freshwater habitats and fisheries. They range from writing your legislators to choosing a career in freshwater fisheries management.

1. *Urge your legislators to fully staff and fund U.S. Forest Service fisheries programs.* Nearly one third of all steelhead and salmon caught by America's fishermen were spawned in National Forests, yet the U.S. Forest Service rarely receives adequate funding for fisheries enhancement programs—many of which are already planned but await funding. Under the Reagan administration, for example, timbering and road building generally received 90 percent of optimal funding compared with 25 percent of optimal funding for fisheries programs. And if "money talks," one could argue that adequately funded fisheries programs would pay for themselves. For example, the National Wildlife Federation notes that the proposed $6 million Harding River Fishway in southeastern Alaska would likely produce $2 million worth of salmon each year.

2. *Support your state's fish restoration projects.* The Wallop-Breaux Trust Fund—a trust fund established in 1984 in order to more than quadruple the amount of money going back to the states

for sport fish restoration projects—is constantly threatened. This fund is generated by a special excise tax levied on fishing equipment (e.g., fishing rods, artificial lures, and tackle boxes), motorboat fuel, and import duties on some types of boats. In 1987, President Reagan wanted to divert $25 million from this trust fund to other purposes. Conservationists argued that this was an illegal raid on the fund, that the states needed this money, and that such shell game tactics would only open the door for other diversions of funds raised through user fees. You can help by lending your support to those individuals and conservation organizations that believe in maintaining the original intention of the Wallop-Breaux Trust Fund—to restore fish habitat and fisheries.

3. *Take a stand on acid rain.* Unless the problem of acid rain is resolved, fisheries managers are going to increasingly concentrate on producing artificially bred "superior fish" to withstand a more acidic environment. Fisheries managers admit this is not what is really needed. Let the members of Congress know that you consider the acid rain problem a real threat to the planet and cite some of the following recommendations by the Soil Conservation Service of America (SCSA): (1) the United States and Canada should accelerate their efforts at international agreements on acid rain; (2) clean-air legislation in the United States and Canada should be strengthened, not weakened; (3) monitoring networks should be expanded; (4) economic incentives (e.g., tax write-offs, low-interest loans and grants) should be provided to encourage reductions in air pollution emissions; and (5) conservation programs that reduce the use of fossil fuels should be emphasized.

4. *Become a fisheries volunteer.* If acid rain is your major concern, for example, you can join the National Audubon Society's volunteer Citizens' Acid Rain Monitoring Network. In 1988, the society had over 80 volunteers nationwide using acid rain testing kits. Each month, the National Audubon Society distributes the data collected to local and national news media and to members of Congress, thus heightening public awareness of the acid rain problem in this country. For other types of fisheries-related volunteer organizations, check with your state's fish and game office or with the fisheries specialist in biology, natural resources, or environmental studies on your campus. There is no doubt that fisheries professors can use some help monitoring nearby lakes and streams with the *dichotomous key* (Marshall et al. 1987) and other techniques for analyzing the health of a freshwater ecosystem.

5. *Choose a career in fisheries management.* If you are the type of person who enjoys sloshing around in cold water wearing knee-high rubber boots, or setting gill nets, or measuring and weighing fish, you just might like to consider pursuing a career in freshwater fisheries management. Although the jobs are few, and the pay is relatively low, the opportunity to be outdoors is a definite benefit. Furthermore, you will have the knowledge that you are helping to protect a great American heritage—our wonderful streams and lakes, their associated riparian habitats and fisheries, and the right of future generations to observe, to photograph, and to wet a line in a favorite fishing hole (Figure 11-10).

FIGURE 11-10 A healthy freshwater ecosystem—a heritage worth preserving for wildlife (elk, moose, buffalo, bear) as well as for humans. (Courtesy of photographer R. Valentine Atkinson.)

DISCUSSION TOPICS

1. Visit your local fish market. Identify which species come from freshwater streams, lakes, or aquacultural operations. Find out where those species are coming from. What fisheries management problems exist at those specific locations?

2. Map out the natural and artificial freshwater habitats within the nearest watershed to your house. Key the map according to the recreational and commercial fisheries, the specific species harvested, and the major fisheries problems. Discuss your findings in class.

3. Are the lakes in your region oligotrophic or eutrophic? If eutrophic, identify the sources of the nutrients.

4. What is the difference between the littoral, limnetic, profundal, and benthic zones of a lake? How do these zones affect fisheries?

5. Map out the major streams and creeks within your county. Key on the map those sections of these rivers that need restoration. Also key the map according to what agencies and governmental bodies have jurisdiction over these river sections. Discuss the political programs facing fisheries managers at those sites.

6. Discuss the major threats to freshwater fisheries in your local watershed or county. What management techniques have proved successful? What techniques have failed?

7. Map out the location of fish hatcheries in your state. How many are there? Why are they located where they are? What species are these hatcheries most interested in propagating? What management problems occur at these hatcheries?

8. Is aquaculture being practiced in your city, county, or state? If not, why not? If so, where, and what is being propagated? What management problems are being encountered?

9. How did the drought of 1988 affect fisheries in your area? What management strategies were used to help fisheries during this critical period?

10. Discuss your state's fishing regulations. Which ones seem to be working? Failing? Why?

11. What species have been introduced in your local area? Where? Have there been unforeseen problems?

12. What is the attitude of your state's freshwater fisheries managers toward the use of toxicants? Where did they use them last? Have there been follow-up studies at the sites where toxicants were once used? If so, what were the major findings of these studies?

READINGS

ALEXANDER, GAYLORD R. 1977. "Food of Vertebrate Predators on Trout Waters in North Central Lower Michigan," *Pap. Michigan Acad. Sci. Arts Ltrs.* Michigan Academician, N.S., vol. 10, no. 2, pp. 181–195. Good discussion of the impact of duck populations on trout.

ANDERSON, STANLEY H., et al. 1987. *Environmental Science.* Columbus, Ohio: Merrill. Useful introductory textbook.

AVAULT, JAMES A. 1980. "Aquaculture." In Robert T. Lackey and Larry A. Nielsen, eds., *Fisheries Management*, pp. 380–411. Boston: Blackwell Scientific. Excellent overview.

BOYLE, ROBERT H., and R. ALEXANDER BOYLE. 1983. "Acid Rain," *The Amicus Journal*, Winter, pp. 22–37. Brief review of the problem.

BURGIS, MARY, and PAT MORRIS. 1987. *The Natural History of Lakes.* Cambridge: Cambridge University Press. Excellent overview of natural and human-made lakes in the landscape.

COOPER, EDWIN L. 1980. "Fisheries Management in Streams." In Robert T. Lackey and Larry A. Nielsen, eds., *Fisheries Management*, pp. 297–322. Boston: Blackwell Scientific. Excellent summary.

CRANE, JILL. 1984. "Aswim in Acid Waters," *National Wildlife*, October–November, vol. 22, no. 6, pp. 22–23. Interesting discussion of how scientists in New York are breeding "superior fish" that can survive in polluted lakes.

CRESSER, MALCOLM, and ANTHONY EDWARDS. 1987. *Acidification of Freshwaters.* Cambridge: Cambridge University Press. Discusses the interacting physical, chemical, and biological processes that regulate the acidity of freshwaters.

DAVIES, B. R., and K. F. WALKER, eds. 1986. *The Ecology of River Systems.* Boston: Dr. W. Junk. State-of-the-art information on the ecology of running waters, with emphasis on large drainage basins.

ENGEL, SANDY. 1987. *Concepts in Lake Management.* Madison: Wis.: Department of Natural Resources. Interesting discussion of restructuring littoral zones.

FORMAN, RICHARD T. T., and MICHAEL GODRON. 1986. *Landscape Ecology.* New York: Wiley. Analysis of the structure, function, and dynamics of altered landscapes.

GANGSTAD, EDWARD. 1986. *Freshwater Vegetation Management.* Fresno, Calif.: Thomas. Detailed discussion of aquatic vegetation and various methods of control.

GOUDIE, ANDREW. 1986. *The Human Impact on the Environment.* 2d ed. Cambridge, Mass.: MIT Press. Basic textbook for introductory courses in environmental studies that stresses landscape changes, environmental hazards, and land degradation.

HELLAWELL, J. M. 1986. *Biological Indicators of Freshwater Pollution and Environmental Management.* London: Elsevier Applied Science. Comprehensive overview.

HENDERSON, S. B., and H. R. MARKLAND. 1987. *Decaying Lakes: The Origins and Control of Cultural Eutrophication.* New York: Wiley. Detailed analysis.

HORNBLOWER, MARGOT. 1983. "How Dangerous is Acid Rain," *National Wildlife*, June–July, vol. 21, no. 3, pp. 4–11. Brief summary of the problem.

HUET, MARCEL. 1959. "Profiles and Biology of Western European Streams as Related to Fish Management," *Trans. Amer. Fish. Soc.*, vol. 88, pp. 155–163. Good illustration of the concept of *biological zones*.

JOHNSON, PHILLIP. 1985. "Smoothing the Way for Salmon," *National Wildlife*, June–July, vol. 23, no. 4, pp. 30–35. Interesting account of how volunteers who are helping protect salmon are making a difference in the Pacific Northwest.

LABASTILLE, ANNE. 1981. "Acid Rain: How Great a Menace?" *National Geographic*, November, vol. 160, no. 5, pp. 652–680. Very readable summary of the problem.

LACKEY, ROBERT T., and LARRY A. NIELSEN, eds. 1980. *Fisheries Management.* Boston: Blackwell Scientific. Comprehensive analysis.

LAGER, KARL. 1956. *Freshwater Fishery Biology.* Dubuque, Iowa: Brown. Good basic textbook.

LAROE, EDWARD T. 1986. "Instream Impacts of Soil Erosion on Fish and Wildlife." In Thomas E. Waddell, ed., *The Off-Site Costs of Soil Erosion.* Washington, D.C.: The Conservation Foundation. Excellent analysis of the problem.

LEE, DANNY C. 1987. "A New Era in Fisheries," *Resources*, Winter, no. 86, pp. 17–19. Interesting article on catfish aquaculture and salmon ranching.

MARSHALL, T. R., et al. 1987. *Using the Lake Trout as an Indicator of Ecosystem Health.* Technical Report No. 49. Ann Arbor, Mich.: Great Lakes Fishery Commission. Application of the dichotomous key—a computer program for ecosystem monitoring.

MILLER, G. TYLER. 1988. *Living in the Environment.* 5th ed. Belmont, Calif.: Wadsworth. Outstanding introductory textbook for environmental studies.

MORELL, VIRGINIA. 1984. "Fishing for Trouble," *International Wildlife*, July–August, vol. 14, no. 4, pp. 40–42. Discusses the cancer epidemic in freshwater fish.

MOYLE, P. B. 1976. "Fish Introductions in California: History and Impact on Native Fishes," *Biological Conservation*, vol. 9, pp. 101–118. Good discussion of hybridization and other problems resulting from fish introductions.

NOBLE, RICHARD L. 1980. "Management of Lakes, Reservoirs, and Ponds." In Robert T. Lackey and Larry A. Nielsen, eds., *Fisheries Management*, pp. 265–295. Boston: Blackwell Scientific. Excellent overview.

OWEN, OLIVER. 1985. *Natural Resource Conservation: An Ecological Approach.* 4th ed. New York: Macmillan. Contains an excellent introductory chapter on freshwater fisheries management from a biological point of view.

PALMER, TIM. 1986. *Endangered Rivers and the Conservation Movement.* Berkeley, Calif.: University of California Press. Very readable book that surveys America's endangered rivers.

PRICE, ANDERS A. 1988. "Ruination of the Winter Run," *Sierra*, May–June, vol. 73, no. 3, pp. 80–81. Discusses attempts to protect the chinook salmon in the Sacramento River through regulation.

SANDHEINRICH, MARK B., and GARY J. ATCHISON. 1986. *Environmental Effects of Dikes and Revetments on Large Riverine Systems.* Vicksburg, Miss.: U.S. Army Engineers Waterways Experiment Station. A government report that reviews several projects conducted under the auspices of the Environmental and Water Quality Operational Studies Program, which was managed by the U.S. Army Engineers Waterways Experiment Station.

SFI. 1988. *SFI Bulletin*, January–February, no. 391. Washington, D.C.: Sport Fishing Institute.

SFI. 1988. *SFI Bulletin*, June, no. 395. Washington, D.C.: Sport Fishing Institute. Contains newsbrief regarding the Hudson River Striped Bass Hatchery.

SFI. 1988. *SFI Bulletin*, August, no. 397. Washington, D.C.: Sport Fishing Institute. Contains newsbrief regarding the problem of exotic biota in ship ballast water.

SPIRN, ANNE W. 1984. *The Granite Garden.* New York: Basic Books. A comprehensive look at urban nature and human design.

STANFORD, J. A., and J. V. WARD. 1986. "Reservoirs of the Colorado River." In B. R. Davies and K. F. Walker, eds., *The Ecology of River Systems.* Boston: Dr. W. Junk. An excellent chapter on the subject.

STRANAHAN, SUSAN. 1984. "The Town that Ate Poison," *National Wildlife*, June–July, vol. 22, no. 4, pp. 16–19. Discusses stream contamination in Triana, Alabama.

WHEELER, ALWYNE. 1979. "Fish in an Urban Environment." In Ian C. Laurie, ed., *Nature in Cities.* New York: Wiley. Excellent overview.

▪12▪

MARINE RESOURCE MANAGEMENT

How inappropriate to call this planet Earth, when clearly it is ocean.

Arthur C. Clarke

The oceans of our planet contain vast, diverse resources. For centuries, nations have struggled with one another to win their "fair share" of that rich natural abundance. Politicians and the owners of commercial fisheries make long-range forecasts of the availability of ocean resources. Conservationists, environmentalists, and government agencies worry about the long-range effects of pollution and the ultimate destruction or depletion of those resources.

Human beings derive a rich range of benefits from the oceans. Fish, shellfish, and other marine life furnish an abundant source of protein. The oceans help to replenish the oxygen supply of the earth's atmosphere and, to a limited but increasing extent, provide a source of water that is treated for domestic and industrial use. Through their role in the hydrologic cycle, the oceans furnish an almost limitless supply

of water for human consumption. The oceans also provide a source of fertilizers for agricultural and pastoral lands. In Oregon, for example, the wastes from crab and shrimp processing plants are used in the production of nitrogen and phosphorus fertilizers for cattle ranchers and dairy farmers. For thousands of years, the oceans have allowed ships to transport commercial products to international ports. In the last decade especially, large tankers have carried an increasing volume of goods, a trend that is likely to continue. Finally, the oceans and their shorelines provide humans with opportunities for a wide range of recreational and aesthetic experiences.

Despite all these benefits, human beings have subjected the oceans to overexploitation and contamination. We are exploiting the biotic resources of the oceans at an unprecedented rate, with many fisheries harvested at rates that exceed the limits deemed acceptable by marine biologists. Offshore waters have also become dumping grounds. Contaminants ranging from sewage to toxic industrial wastes to radioactive materials are being ''buried'' at sea, often in complete ignorance of how such contaminants will affect the marine ecosystem.

In this chapter, we will concentrate on the *marine biotic resources* that border the United States. (We will discuss the mineral potential of the oceans in Chapter 13.) We will explore the types of marine environments, the marine food chains, the major techniques for managing fisheries, and the ways in which you can help conserve marine resources. We turn now to a discussion of that unique ecosystem, to its physical and biotic components, and to the conservation and management of the biotic resources of the oceans.

TYPES OF MARINE ENVIRONMENTS

A rewarding approach to understanding the various types of marine environments is first to examine the topography of the oceans and then to explore the ecological zones of the oceans.

Topography

Among the many distinctive topographic features of the oceans, two are of particular importance in the management of marine resources: the continental shelf and the continental slope (Figure 12-1). The **continental shelf** is the part of the ocean floor adjacent to a continent or an island. It slopes gently at first (usually an angle of 1 degree or less) and then more steeply; finally, where the slope increases markedly (at an angle of 2 to 5 degrees), the continental shelf gives way to the **continental slope**. The continental shelf has an average width of about 65 km (40 mi), although in some areas it extends to over 1000 km (621 mi) (Ross 1980). Taken together, the shelves underlie an extremely large portion of the ocean and are equivalent in total area to that of some continents. The maximum depth of the shelves is approximately 200 m (656 ft).

In relatively shallow waters above the continental shelves, photosynthesis produces an abundance of vegetation. Moreover, the rivers of the adjacent land contribute a rich supply of nutrients. As a result, the continental shelves are the world's most productive fishing grounds. Not surprisingly, many legal controversies have arisen among maritime nations

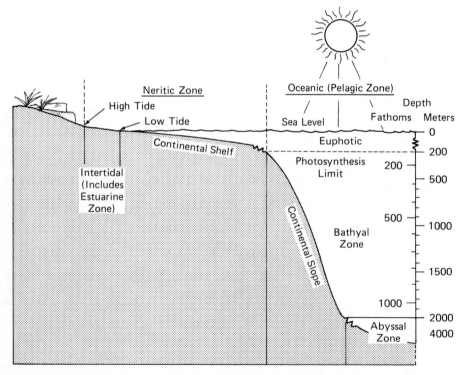

FIGURE 12-1 Zones of the marine ecosystem.

over exactly where the continental shelf ends and the continental slope begins. Since fishing in the open sea is less rewarding than fishing over the continental shelf, fishermen are naturally jealous of their fishing rights in these waters.

Ecological Zones

The major *ecological zones* of the ocean environment are the *neritic* (green water) zone and the *oceanic* (blue water) zone.

The Neritic Zone. The **neritic zone** is the relatively shallow zone that extends from the high tide mark of the coastline to the edge of the continental shelf. This area is strewn with abundant organic material derived from the remains of shellfish, sea urchins, and coral. Although this zone represents only 10 percent of the total ocean area, it is the habitat of 90 percent of all sea organisms. Sunlight penetrates its shallow waters, enabling photosynthesis to take place in the minute aquatic plants called phytoplankton. The phytoplankton, in turn, support microscopic aquatic animals (zooplankton) and bottom-feeding invertebrates, which eventually support larger fish suitable for human consumption.

Nearest the coastline in the neritic zone is the **intertidal zone**. This section of the shoreline (including *estuaries*) is periodically covered with seawater at high tide and is exposed at low tide. The organisms that live in this region must be able to tolerate exposure to air as well as immersion in saline waters. A wide variety of animal and plant communities inhabit this intertidal zone, from limpets, barnacles, and periwinkles (in the upper zone) to invertebrate animals and algae (in the middle zone), to sea palms, abalones, and eel grasses (in the lower zone).

Within the intertidal zone along some coastlines is an even more productive zone, the *estuarine zone*. **Estuaries** are narrow, fragile stretches along the coastline where fresh water from a river mixes with salt water from the sea. Estuaries are one of the most productive ecosystems known. For further details on the estuarine environment, consult Wilson (1988). Estuaries have several unique ecological characteristics:

1. *Wide Salinity Ranges.* Estuarine waters are *brackish*—that is, they are a mixture of fresh water from a river and salt water from the ocean. Their salinity may vary daily with the tides. Salinity also varies seasonally, depending on the amount of precipitation, snowmelt, and runoff.

2. *Tidal Fluctuation and High Turbulence.* The water level of an estuary regularly rises and falls with the tides. This movement creates high turbulence that limits light penetration and, consequently, restricts the phytoplankton population, but the movement also flushes the estuary.

3. *High Concentrations of Dissolved Oxygen.* The high turbulence of water in the shallow estuaries produces high concentrations of dissolved oxygen.

4. *Intermediate Water Density.* Estuarine water density generally occurs between the two extremes of fresh water (1.00 sp gr) and salt water (1.03 sp gr), although it is tidal action that determines the actual density.

5. *Fluctuating Water Temperature.* Since the shallow estuarine basins are exposed to extreme tidal action, the water temperature fluctuates from day to day and from season to season.

6. *High Concentration of Nutrients.* Estuaries trap and thereby concentrate nutrients as they are carried from the land by rivers and from the ocean by the tides.

7. *Nursery for Fisheries.* The estuarine environment provides a production area for an estimated 65 percent of the saltwater fish, clams, oysters, crabs, shrimp, and lobsters that are harvested by U.S. fishermen. Some marine species spend part of their life cycle in the estuarine environment in search of food, while others spend their highly vulnerable larval period in this ecological nursery. Consequently, marine life is directly dependent on the conditions that prevail in the estuarine regions.

The impact of human activities on the neritic zone has been severe (Morrissey 1988). Because of its accessibility, the intertidal zone was the first area to be exploited. Then, as the technology of boat-building and fishing advanced, harvesting moved farther and farther out into the neritic zone.

To the casual observer, estuaries often appear as desolate, insect-infested regions that might as well be used for dumping waste products or for the development of housing, business, or industry. Such a view has disastrous consequences. Beyond their essential role in the support of marine organisms, estuaries contribute substantially to the nation's economy. Serious damage to the estuarine ecosystem would destroy a significant supply of protein and would jeopardize the nation's commercial fishing industry. Moreover, estuarine zones provide a natural mechanism for pollution and flood control. They absorb and thereby dispose of great quantities of pollutants from coastal waters, and they protect the coastline from destructive waves generated by violent storms. Finally, the estuarine environment furnishes shelter and food for a wide variety of birdlife: coastal birds (pelicans, cormorants, and birds of the sandpiper family), long-legged marsh waders (bitterns, egrets, herons, and ibises), predator birds (marsh hawks, ospreys, and bald eagles), and migratory birds (ducks and geese). Environmentally and aesthetically, the estuarine environment is a rich natural resource worthy of preservation.

The Oceanic Zone. The second major marine environment is the **oceanic zone**. This vast blue water region beyond the continental shelf constitutes about 90 percent of the total area covered by the oceans (Meadows and Campbell 1988). Its net primary productivity is very low, however, so low, in fact, that it is sometimes called a *biological desert.* Vertically, the oceanic zone consists of three regions: (1) the euphotic zone, (2) the bathyal zone, and (3) the abyssal zone (Figure 12-1).

Commercial fishermen are most interested in the upper reaches of the **euphotic zone**. Light penetrates this area, enabling photosynthesis to take place. The euphotic zone extends downward approximately 200 m (656 ft). This is the greatest depth to which sunlight can penetrate the ocean and is known as the *photosynthesis limit*. Abnormally high concentrations of organic or inorganic substances may on occasion prevent light from penetrating to that level, however. Below the euphotic zone is the **bathyal zone,** a dark, intermediate layer of water that extends to the bottom of the continental slope, approximately 2000 m (6562 ft). Here organisms must depend for sustenance on the *fallout* of dead plant and animal materials from the euphotic zone or else make regular visits into the euphotic zone. Many species, including whales, migrate between the two zones. Because of the lack of light, the enormous water pressures, the low temperatures, and the limited supply of nutrients, productivity in the bathyal zone is low. This zone is of little importance to commercial fishermen. Below 2000 m (6562 ft) is the **abyssal zone,** which is even less important commercially. The few creatures that live in this inhospitable realm feed on one another and on whatever nutrients drift down from above.

CHARACTERISTICS OF THE MARINE ENVIRONMENT

Most of the fish consumed by humans are high in the marine food chain, at the fourth tropic level. These species at the high tropic levels are relatively scarce and hence are expensive to catch—much fuel, time, and human labor are required to capture these species. For example, swordfish, which is the product of a long food chain, is scarce. By contrast, anchovies (having a short food chain) are available in larger quantities and, consequently, are less expensive to harvest. This is not to say, however, that all large marine organisms have long food chains. Baleen whales, for example, feed relatively low on the food chain, consuming tiny shrimplike crustaceans called *krill (Euphausia superba)* (Reid 1988).

Gathering fish and shellfish from the oceans is a very costly undertaking. Generally speaking, the more scarce the fish, the more costly the venture, and hence the greater the cost to the consumer. Costs further increase when normal oceanic patterns are disrupted, as discussed below.

Feeding Migrations and Economics

Fish migrate from areas that are deficient in nutrients to areas of nutritional abundance. When these normal patterns are disrupted, they can cause havoc to marine organisms, and, ultimately, to the fishing industry. An interesting example of disrupted feeding migration is associated with a warm-water current known as **El Niño**. This current arrives off the western coast of South America approximately every seven years around Christmas time *(El Niño* is a Spanish term for the Christ Child). In 1982, El Niño was exceptionally strong and it traveled up the western coast of North America. It altered the weather patterns, raised ocean temperatures, and disrupted the normal supply of nutrients. Ultimately, this "warm water out of place" had a significant effect on local fisheries.

Scientists are not certain what causes El Niño, but most of them believe that it occurs when the trade winds, which usually blow along the equator from east to west, slacken or reverse and bring warm water from the western Pacific against the coast of Peru. There it breaks into currents that flow north and south. As a result, the normal horizontal feeding patterns of fish are disrupted, and the fish migrate away from their usual feeding grounds (Figure 12-2). In September of 1983, for example, barracuda, marlin, ocean sunfish, sailfish, great sea turtles, and several

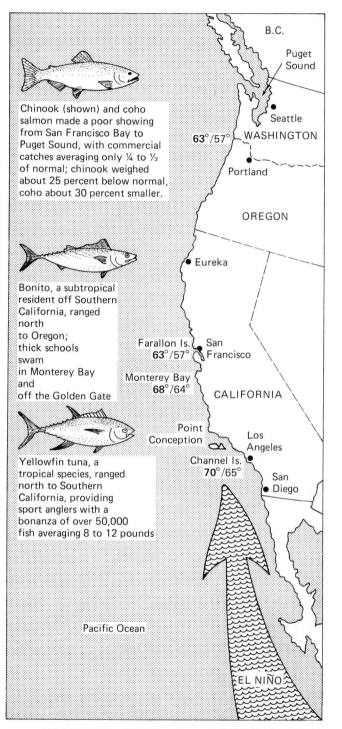

Chinook (shown) and coho salmon made a poor showing from San Francisco Bay to Puget Sound, with commercial catches averaging only ¼ to ⅓ of normal; chinook weighed about 25 percent below normal, coho about 30 percent smaller.

Bonito, a subtropical resident off Southern California, ranged north to Oregon; thick schools swam in Monterey Bay and off the Golden Gate

Yellowfin tuna, a tropical species, ranged north to Southern California, providing sport anglers with a bonanza of over 50,000 fish averaging 8 to 12 pounds

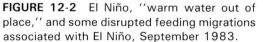

FIGURE 12-2 El Niño, "warm water out of place," and some disrupted feeding migrations associated with El Niño, September 1983.

species of sharks appeared off the coast of Washington, where the water temperature was about 18°C (65°F) instead of its normal 13°C to 15°C (55°F to 59°F). This movement of warm water to the north brought dramatic ecological changes. Certain tropical and subtropical fish migrated northward along warm-water corridors, providing commercial fishermen (and sport anglers) with species they had rarely seen in those waters.

The warm water of El Niño also inhibited the normal **upwelling** of cooler, nutrient-rich water from the ocean depths, thereby disrupting the normal food chain. Scientists discovered that the kelp forest canopy was reduced and that there was a scarcity of forage (herring, juvenile rockfish, anchovy). As a result, many fish, including salmon, went hungry. In fact, the 1983 harvest of salmon off California, Oregon, and Washington was the worst in 50 years. Catches were far below normal, and the fish weighed 25 to 30 percent below average. Many salmon fishermen turned to the more plentiful albacore. Farther north, however, Alaska's salmon fisheries harvested a record number of sockeye (red) salmon.

Destructive Agents

Although most marine organisms have a high *biotic potential*—that is, they have a high capacity for rapid population growth—they must, nevertheless, withstand an enormous barrage of destructive agents.

Natural Factors. Predators (birds, sharks, and otters), parasites (flukes, tapeworms, and crustaceans), red-tide organisms (excessive numbers of marine protozoans and their accumulated wastes), and adverse winds all serve to deplete fish populations.

From time to time, various unexplained causes also deplete fish populations. For example, in 1964, 1974, and 1980, massive invasions and subsequent dieoffs of anchovies occurred in the yacht harbor at Santa Cruz, California. Each time, about 400 tons of the tiny fish swam into the harbor, settled in, and milled around the commercial fishing boats and recreation yachts until they exhausted all the dissolved oxygen in the water. Then they died, leaving their rotting carcasses in the harbor.

In 1983, marine scientists became aware that coral reefs were dead or dying over vast expanses of the Pacific Ocean and in certain areas of the Atlantic. The immense coral reefs and the algae they attract provide shelter and feeding grounds for lobsters, fish, and thousands of smaller creatures, and they protect coastal areas from waves and storms. According to one explanation, a combination of factors, centering on El Niño, has warmed the tropical waters to temperatures that corals find intolerable.

Human-Related Factors.   In addition to all these natural destructive agents, marine organisms must cope with human threats, including overharvesting, the destruction of habitats, and contamination.

Overharvesting is one of the major causes of the depletion of many fish. The sea is a public domain over which no single nation has sovereignty. So it is not surprising that its resources are often ruthlessly exploited (Keen 1988). Numerous crustaceans and fish have been overharvested, especially shrimp, anchovies, and sardines. Off the North Atlantic coast, cod, ocean perch, and haddock have long shown signs of overexploitation. If these species and others are to be protected, future harvests will have to be regulated in accordance with sound ecological principles.

Marine mammals suffer even more severely from human exploitation. Fish have a high biotic potential, but most marine mammals rely on the survival of the one or two offspring that are produced annually. For example, the whaling industry has had a long history of bringing about a severe decline in whale numbers. For years they had been in hot pursuit of the world's largest animal, the blue whale *(Balaenoptera musculus)* until the International Whaling Commission in 1964 took steps to prevent further harvesting.

Other sea mammals continue to be the victims of overharvesting. In 1978, for example, it came to light that the fishermen of Iki Island off Japan had been carrying out for years the regular execution of thousands upon thousands of dolphins, which they viewed as competitors for their catches of yellowtail, squid, cuttlefish, and hamachi (Figure 12-3) (Jones 1980). Until the Marine Mammal Protection Act was passed in 1972, U.S. tuna fishermen accidentally killed more than 200,000 dolphins annually in their tuna nets. Though the toll has been reduced, the accidental killing of dolphins continues (Godges 1988).

Fur seals have also been overharvested. The Guadalupe fur seal was nearly destroyed in the nineteenth century, and the Pribilof or northern fur seal had come close to extinction early in the twentieth century. By 1910, the population of northern fur seals had declined from about a million to 17,000. Fortunately, a change in management regarding this species has increased that number to about 1.5 million, which allows a sustained harvest of 80,000 annually. The harvesting of the snowy white harp seal has also sparked heated controversy in recent years. In 1980, a Canadian federal fisheries department estimated the seal population at 1.4 million and set the annual harvesting quota at 180,000 pelts. Sealers claim that the financially strapped fishermen of eastern Canada rely on the seal harvest for their very survival until the start of the new fishing season, but environmentalists protest that the harp seal is a victim of wanton cruelty and its slaughter a horrifying attack on the sacredness of the environment.

The manatee, the marine mammal which gave rise to the mermaid legend, is another species endangered by humans (Norris 1978). Near extinction by 1979, only 1000–1200 manatees now survive in Florida's waterways. Government biologists fear that these one-ton, slow moving and slow to reproduce mammals will at last be exterminated by accidental encounters with barges, speed boats, and water skiers. Almost every living manatee now has cuts and

FIGURE 12-3 Japanese fishermen slaughter dolphins to protect their fishery. (Courtesy of photographer Howard Hall.)

deformities from boat propellers (Figure 12-4). Fishing hooks and nets, dams, and chemical pollution have also taken their toll.

Another human-related threat to marine fisheries is the *elimination of the habitat* of many species. This threat is especially acute in the coastal wetlands—the shallow-water marshes and tideflats of lagoons, estuaries, and sloughs. Long considered to be little more than swamp, many coastal wetlands have been filled for highways, airports, and waste-disposal sites, or they have been drained to control mosquito infestations. The wetlands have five purposes, serving as nutrient-rich nurseries for fisheries, as wildlife habitats, as buffers that protect the shoreline from the impact of tides and waves, as natural agents to accommodate floodwaters, and as pollutant filters. Although the public is growing increasingly aware of the importance of wetlands, these fragile areas are still vulnerable to developers eager to meet the demand for shore facilities.

California, for example, with its warm weather and coast-oriented population, has permitted the destruction of much of its wetland habitat. The state's marine shoreline extends for 3862 km (2400 mi), from the steep, rocky headlands of the north to the semi-arid coastal plains and terraces of the south. Its 110 coastal wetlands include tidal-flushed river mouths, saline lagoons, and nutrient-rich embayments. According to the Institute of Marine Resources in La Jolla, California, the total coastal and estuarine area of the state has been reduced from 154,190 ha (381,000 acres) at the turn of the century to the present total of 50,588 ha (125,000 acres)—a reduction of 67 percent. As in other maritime states, California's precious wetlands have been converted into housing tracts, factory sites, and marinas (Figure 12-5).

Contamination is yet another human-related cause of the deterioration of marine fisheries. The most severe pollution has been in the neritic zone—especially the estuaries. But the oceanic zone has also become a dumping ground for human wastes. The pollution of the ocean waters is not always deliberate, of course. The accidental spilling of toxic materials in shipping lanes is a regular occurrence. Fly ash from coal-fueled power plants has been found in sediment 356 m (1167 ft) deep in the mid-Atlantic. Vast though the oceans are, they are vulnerable to the effects of solid-waste dumping, oil spillage, pesticide and toxic chemical contamination, radioactive waste disposal, and thermal heating.

For decades, barges and ships have been dumping solid waste at designated sites off the Pacific, Gulf, and Atlantic coasts. In some cases, the accumulation of waste materials has become so great that its spatial distribution can be mapped. The New York Bight, for example, is one of the most heavily used dumping areas in the world. Every year, 8.6 billion kg (9.5 million tons) of waste are dumped into this area, covering 104 km^2 (40 mi^2) of the ocean bottom (Miller 1988). The effect on the marine ecosystem has been severe: lower oxygen concentrations and the reduction or elimination of populations of small marine plankton (protozoans, crustaceans, and algae) and crabs. Although still practiced, dumping on this scale is coming under stricter federal regulation.

An estimated 6 billion kg (7 million tons) of oil

FIGURE 12-4 The manatee. (Courtesy of U.S. Fish and Wildlife Service.)

FIGURE 12-5 Anaheim Bay in Orange County, California, once a large and productive marsh area, has been transformed by human activities. (Courtesy of the Institute of Marine Resources, La Jolla, California.)

are entering the oceans every year. Ten percent comes from the natural oozing of crude oil from deposits below the sea bottom. The rest comes from a variety of other sources, such as oil-contaminated river runoff, offshore oil rig leaks, the disposal of ballast water from ships, and marine transportation accidents. Oil pollution of the marine environment has many adverse effects, including food chain contamination, reduced photosynthetic rates, and the direct death of marine organisms.

The pesticides that find their way into the marine environment come from the croplands and forests of the coastal areas, from deliberate dumping into the ocean by pesticide manufacturers, or from shipping mishaps at sea. For example, in 1984, during a storm in the North Sea, a Danish freighter dropped 20 tons of a fatal herbicide known as Dinoseb. Oceanographers believe the drums are located in less than 61 m (200 ft) on the Dogger Bank, a large sandbank in the middle of the North Sea that serves as a breeding ground for cod, mackerel, and herring. If those drums are not recovered before they split open, heavy fish mortality can be expected. Moreover, ocean currents may carry the pesticide to other fishing grounds, causing widespread damage to marine food chains.

Perhaps more ominous than pesticides are such toxic chemicals as copper, mercury, lead, arsenic, and cyanide that have entered the marine environment mostly by deliberate dumping. An international treaty to control the dumping of poisonous chemicals

went into effect in 1972, but not all nations signed it, and even those that did may have occasionally violated it (Owen 1985).

Nuclear reactors discharge low-level radioactive wastes that find their way into the oceans. The world's ever-expanding fleet of nuclear-powered submarines also discharges radioactive wastes into the oceans. Until two decades ago, the United States even dumped radioactive waste at sea in steel drums, and may be on the verge of resuming that practice. The U.S. Navy, eager to dispose of the radioactive old reactors of outdated nuclear submarines, wants to sink the vessels in deep water. The U.S. Department of Energy (DOE) hopes to use the oceans as a dumping ground for thousands of tons of contaminated soil from abandoned atomic weapons facilities. And the nuclear power industry, already under attack for disposing of low-level wastes onshore, hopes to return to the disposal of waste materials in the ocean.

Only low levels of radioactive contaminants need be present to affect marine organisms. Marine biologists report that 0.2 microcuries of radioactivity will seriously disrupt fish egg development (Owen 1985). Despite such warnings, Great Britain and other nations of Western Europe continue to dump radioactive wastes at sea.

Finally, marine organisms in certain areas are exposed to *thermal pollution*. Several nuclear power plants are located in coastal areas where they use seawater as a coolant. The temperature of the water may be as much as 15 to 20 degrees higher when the water is returned to the ocean. Recent studies suggest that thermal pollution may significantly reduce the normal growth rate of certain species, such as sand crabs, which form an important link in the oceanic food chain.

MAJOR MARINE FISHERIES OF THE UNITED STATES

Like terrestrial resources, marine fisheries and their associated fishing differ greatly from one region to another: Maine has its lobsters and pots or box traps; Chesapeake Bay has its oysters and dredges; the Gulf of Mexico has its shrimp and trawls; California has its tuna and purse-seines; and Alaska has its salmon nets and traps (Parson 1972). (See pages 318–322 for a discussion of the major types of fishing devices.) The marine fisheries of the United States can be grouped into three major regions: the Atlantic, the Gulf, and the Pacific (Bennett 1983).

The Atlantic Region

The Atlantic region encompasses the eastern coast of the United States, from Maine to the southern tip of Florida and all Atlantic waters under the control of U.S. law (Figure 12-6). Some people also include Atlantic waters outside U.S. control that are regularly visited by U.S. fishermen. The Atlantic region embraces four subdivisions: New England and the

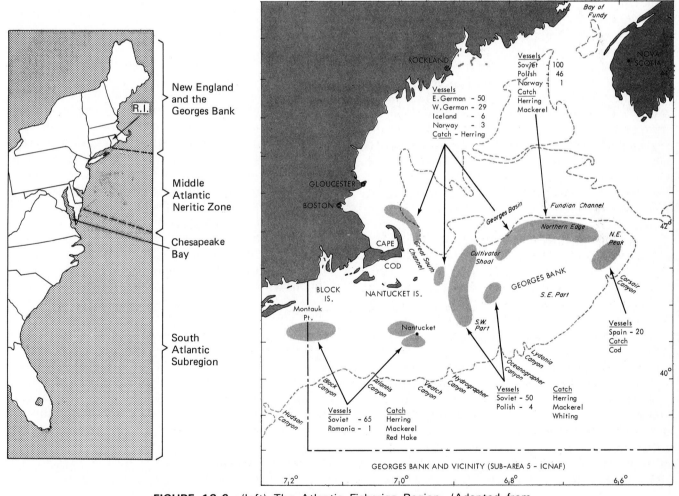

FIGURE 12-6 (left) The Atlantic Fisheries Region. (Adapted from Charles F. Bennett, *Conservation and Management of Natural Resources in the United States,* p. 235. Copyright © 1983 by John Wiley & Sons, Inc.) (right) Blowup of Georges Bank and vicinity. (Courtesy of *Commerical Fisheries Review.*)

Georges Bank, the Middle Atlantic Neritic Zone, Chesapeake Bay, and the South Atlantic Subregion.

New England and the Georges Bank. This was the first fishing ground of the American colonists. Then, as now, activity is centered on the Georges Bank—a 51,796 km² (20,000 mi²) area off Massachusetts. Located within the neritic zone, as are most New England fisheries, the Georges Bank is the world's richest fishing ground, providing 17 percent of the total U.S. annual catch. The upwelling currents, combined with the contour of the sea floor, concentrate nutrients in this area and support a great variety of sea life. Scallops, clams, worms, and snails feed on the abundant plankton and, in turn, supply ample food for haddock, pollock, cod, and flounder.

The peculiar combination of bottom contour and upwelling, however, also makes the Georges Bank especially vulnerable to oil pollution. The ocean currents around the Georges Bank form a closed circle, called a *gyre*. When a spill occurs, the gyre keeps the oil trapped in the area and prevents it from being dispersed to greater ocean depths. An oil spill persists long enough there to kill fish and eggs and destroys the local fisheries for as long as four to five years. A three-way struggle has emerged over the proper management of the Georges Bank: oil interests want the privilege to explore for oil; commercial fishermen want to protect their livelihood; environmentalists would like to turn the area into a marine sanctuary. This controversy will probably go on for many years to come.

The Middle Atlantic Neritic Zone. The stretch of coastal waters from southern New England to Chesapeake Bay is rich in crustaceans and fish. Scallops, menhaden, and flounder dominate the commercially valuable species. Overfishing by both U.S. fishermen and foreign fishermen has impaired this fishery, as has widespread pollution.

Chesapeake Bay. South of the Middle Atlantic Neritic Zone is Chesapeake Bay—a highly productive area with an abundance of oysters, clams, crabs, and fish. Chesapeake Bay is in trouble, however. In 1983, after a $27 million study, the Environmental Protection Agency reported that Chesapeake Bay is "clearly an ecosystem in decline." Since 1970, harvests of their famous blue crab have fallen off, and the oyster harvests have declined by a third from the 1960 level. The main problem is pollution, together with a long history of overfishing. Phosphorus and nitrogen runoff from agricultural fields and municipal sewage treatment plants is accelerating eutrophication—the growth of algae that consume dissolved oxygen, thereby suffocating marine animals. Industrial chemicals also flow into the bay. The three bay states—Virginia, Maryland, and Pennsylvania—must somehow raise at least $1 billion to protect the estuary from further deterioration.

The South Atlantic Subregion. The South Atlantic subregion extends from Cape Hatteras to southern Florida. Oysters, shrimp, and blue crabs dominate the commercial fisheries in the northern half, while mackerel, spiny lobster, mullet, and shrimp dominate in the southern half. With no major shipping lanes, and distant from large metropolitan areas, the South Atlantic subregion has been temporarily spared the degree of pollution encountered by the more northern regions.

The Gulf Region

The second major marine fishery is the Gulf of Mexico, which extends from Florida to the coastal borders of Texas and Mexico (Figure 12-7). Among the several factors that account for the abundant harvests of this region are these: The Mississippi River and many smaller rivers release their nutrient-rich waters into the Gulf, miles of shallow sunlit waters stretch along the coast, and the extensive estuarine systems act as efficient nurseries for marine organisms. These three factors provide a neritic zone that extends for many miles out into the Gulf, producing ideal ecological conditions for a variety of marine life.

Commercial shrimp fishing has been a major component of the region's economy for over a century. This multimillion-dollar industry depends on the well-being of the estuarine systems along the Gulf Coast. For example, pink shrimp spend part of their life cycle in the mangrove swamps of the Everglades before moving as adults into open marine waters. Consequently, the management of this fishery depends on the survival of the Everglades habitat. Grouper, mullet, and red snapper are also important in the fisheries of the Gulf region. Oysters and menhaden are important in the eastern section of this region (Alverson 1978).

The Pacific Region

The third major fishery is located on the Pacific Coast (Figure 12-8). Five subregions make up the Pacific region: the Alaska subregion, the Washington and Oregon area, the Northern California area, the Central California area, and the Southern California area.

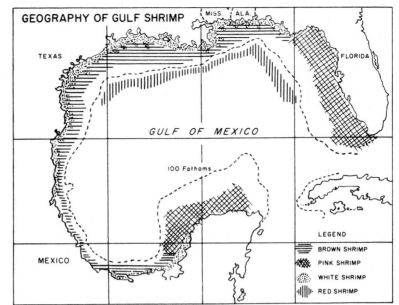

FIGURE 12-7 Geography of gulf shrimp. (From Ruben L. Parson, *Conserving American Resources* [Englewood Cliffs, N.J.: Prentice-Hall, Inc., 1972], p. 472.)

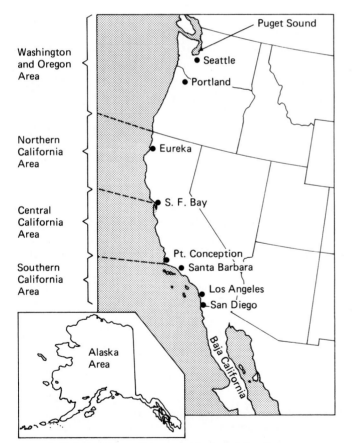

FIGURE 12-8 The Pacific Fisheries Region. (Adapted from Charles F. Bennett, *Conservation and Management of Natural Resources in the United States*, p. 234. Copyright © 1983 by John Wiley & Sons, Inc.)

The Alaska Subregion. In this northernmost section, salmon and king crab are the major fisheries, along with Dungeness crab, halibut, and scallop.

Despite a long history of overfishing, the salmon harvest is still number one in terms of tonnage of marine fish. The annual catch, however, is 50 percent less than what it was in the 1930s. There are several reasons for this decline: ignorance of the habitat requirements of the fish, inadequate fishing regulations, overfishing, poor management of the canneries, and degradation of the fishing grounds, particularly near the shore. When salmon spawn, they migrate up freshwater streams along the coast. Over the years, however, those streams have been severely degraded by soil erosion from mining operations, dam building, logging, and by pollution from sawmills and paper pulp mills. Some salmon populations migrate beyond the U.S. fisheries 200-mile limit, thereby embroiling other nations in the management of this fishery.

Other fisheries in the Alaska subregion, such as the Alaska king crab fishery, are also in trouble. Once considered an inexhaustible resource, the king crab, which is found almost exclusively in seas along the southern Aleutian coastlines, may be facing an irreversible decline. Experts disagree on what is causing the declining king crab stocks, citing such causes as parasitic disease, the increased activity of marine predators, warmer oceanic currents, and overharvesting. Curiously, in the seven years from 1974 through 1980, more king crab was taken from the Bering Sea than had been taken in that area in the 20 years from 1953 through 1973. After 1981, however, king crab stocks collapsed. In a 1983 trawl survey, all the adult females captured were found to be barren, with no eggs in their brood pouches. The survey also reported that the crab population was the lowest ever recorded. Alarmed, the Alaska Department of Fish and Game ordered the total shutdown of the king crab fishery. With its gradual closing (the Kodiak Bay and Bristol Bay fisheries were the first to shut down), production in the 1983–1984 season was expected to total about 11 million kg (25 million lb), as compared with nearly 91 million kg (200 million lb) at its peak season in 1980–1981.

The Washington and Oregon Area.

The numerous fisheries along the coasts of Washington and Oregon include harvesting such species as albacore, Pacific hake, Dungeness crab, ocean perch, salmon, oysters, and clams.

The clam fishery in this area is beset by the relatively minor, though persistent problem of *recreational digging,* which seems to be contributing to the disappearance of clams from the Pacific coast. From 1954 to 1974, clam production dropped from over 50,000 cases a year to approximately 15,000 cases. In 1965 alone, 50,000 recreational diggers harvested 800,000 razor clams, which was equivalent to half of the total commercial catch in the Pacific region. Although laws now exist to limit recreational diggers, enforcement has been poor.

The Northern California Area.

Extending from the Oregon border across San Francisco Bay, the Northern California area supports a broad range of commercial fisheries, including salmon, sole, Dungeness crab, and herring.

Every January, the herring harvest in San Francisco Bay provides a fascinating sight for onlookers. During this spawning season, schools of herring swim in to lay their eggs on rocks and seaweed in the shallows of the bay, and an armada of fishermen swarm frantically about the bay to set their nets. The Pacific herring *(Clupea harengus pallasi)* is harvested not so much for its meat as for the yellowish roe found in the female herring. The Japanese regard the roe as a delicacy, and most of the catch is shipped to Japan. In the 1984 season, that total herring catch was approximately 7250 tons, worth approximately $9 million. Although the roe constitutes only 10 to 15 percent of this total weight, the rest of the fish is not wasted; it is processed into fish oil, pet food, and fish meal.

The Central California Area.

The fisheries in this area, between San Francisco Bay and Point Conception, consist mainly of catches of shrimp, abalone, and ocean perch, along with lesser amounts of salmon, albacore, and Dungeness crab off the San Francisco coast. Salmon fishing here is on the decline. Fishermen are being subjected to higher equipment costs, shorter fishing seasons, and stricter limits on the number of salmon they can take.

The Southern California Area.

This southernmost area of the Pacific region extends from Point Conception to the Mexican border. Here the commercial harvests include bluefin and yellowtail tuna, shrimp and lobster, swordfish and barracuda. White sea bass, mackerel, and anchovy are also important commercial species.

This area is the scene of heated disputes between fishermen, environmentalists, and the general public. One source of friction is the accidental killing of porpoises during the harvesting of tuna. At the heart of the controversy is the purse-seine method of harvesting tuna—now the most common method used by commercial tuna fishermen. (See pages 318–322 for a further discussion of the purse-seine technique.) The net used is about a mile long and 183 to 213 m (600 to 700 ft) deep, and it has a 10.8 cm (4.25 in.) mesh. It is set in a large circle around a school of tuna. When the circle has been closed, it is hauled in by the cable, and the tuna are trapped when the bottom of the net closes. For some reason, yellowfin tuna are often located below groups of porpoises, and many of these animals get swept up in the purse-seine net with the tuna. Prior to 1976, when the federal government established limits on the number of allowable porpoise kills, hundreds of thousands of these air-breathing mammals died each year with the tuna harvest. To meet the government limits on porpoise kills (the limit in 1982 was 20,500) the fishermen had to reduce the mesh size of their nets. The tuna fishermen then threw up their hands in despair, complaining that environmentalists, state and federal regulations, competition from foreign fleets, and the general state of the economy were driving them out of business.

MARINE RESOURCES AND THEIR CONSERVATION

There are various management techniques for conserving and improving the nation's fisheries. We will now briefly look at some of the more significant ones.

Regulations

To sustain optimal fishing harvests, managers of marine resources regulate the pressure on existing stocks. They regulate the *areas* in which fishing can be carried on, the *seasons* in which fishing is permitted, the *methods* of harvesting, and the *size* of fish that can be taken, as well as the *total catch*. Unfortunately, these regulations are often set without the complete knowledge of a species' preferred environment, the factors that promote its growth and breeding, and how it interacts and competes with other marine organisms. Marine scientists do know, however, that for every fishery there is a point of *maximum sustainable yield* (MSY) (Figure 12-9). If harvesting is done beyond that point, the value of the harvesting effort decreases. Profit is generally maximum at levels below the MSY, as shown by part E1 of Figure 12-9. Beyond the MSY, overharvesting eventually becomes unprofitable, as shown by the points beyond E3 in Figure 12-9. Marine resource managers impose regulations to prevent the fishery from reaching those unprofitable levels.

The fishery policy of the United States has taken years to evolve, beginning back in 1871 with the establishment of the Fish Commission (Alverson 1978). The federal role in fishery management has gradually expanded over the years, until now it extends to such activities as gear research, exploratory fishing, and assistance programs to fishermen, such as supplying market information, grants, and low-interest loans. Today, the National Marine Fisheries Service (NMFS) is the primary federal agency responsible for fisheries management in this country. It operates a number of

large laboratories and stations, explores the high seas with its research vessels, and monitors domestic and foreign fishing fleets to see that they abide by current U.S. fishing regulations. In a sense, the NMFS is to marine fisheries what the Soil Conservation Service is to soil management and what the United States Forest Service is to forest management.

One of the more important recent policies that the NMFS must enforce is the Marine Mammal Protection Act (MMPA). In 1972, Congress enacted the Marine Mammal Protection Act, which, with certain exceptions, imposed a moratorium on the taking of marine animals. One of those exceptions, the accidental taking of porpoises in tuna fishing, has been the subject of numerous court actions (Eberhardt 1977). In 1976, the MMPA directed the National Marine Fisheries Service to set a yearly limit on the number of porpoises that fishermen can kill in their pursuit of tuna. The tuna fishermen protested that the limit destroyed their ability to compete with foreign fleets, and many of them went out of business. Environmentalists have countered that there are ways of catching tuna without killing porpoises (see pages 318–322), but the tuna industry finds it easier and cheaper to continue old methods than to adopt new ones. The MMPA has decleared that the annual porpoise kill eventually "must be reduced to insignificant levels approaching zero." It has not, however, specified precisely what those levels are.

Another significant regulatory act is the Fisheries Conservation and Management Act (FCMA) of 1976. Perhaps the most comprehensive fishery law in U.S. history, this act established a fishery conservation and management zone (FCZ) off the U.S. coasts that extends from the seaward end of the **territorial sea** to 200 nautical miles from shore. All U.S. states maintain individual fishing jurisdiction off their coasts out a distance of 3 nautical miles, with the exception of the Gulf Coast of Florida and Texas, which have 9 nautical mile territorial seas (Ross 1980). Congress passed the FCMA to check the rapid depletion of the marine biomass, including such valuable species as haddock, cod, and flounder. Between 1968 and 1975, the marine biomass in U.S. waters declined by 65 percent, largely as the result of overfishing by domestic and foreign ships. Under this extended jurisdiction, the United States has assumed complete management of most fish. Certain migratory tunas, however, are exempt from this ruling.

Specifically, the FCMA established eight Regional Fishery Management Councils to prepare plans for fishery management within their respective regions. Each council is to include among its mem-

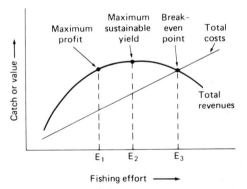

FIGURE 12-9 Fishing value as compared to fishing effort (number of boats, days at sea, and so forth). (From G. H. Knight, *International Law of Fisheries*, Louisiana State University Teaching Aid, Issue No. 2, Center for Wetlands Resources.)

bers commercial fishing industry workers, sport anglers, environmentalists, university professors, consumers, and state representatives. The councils must also create scientific advisory panels, oversee public hearings, review fishing policies of foreign fleets, and periodically report to the Secretary of Commerce. Their recommendations, on the approval of the Secretary of Commerce, govern the "where, what, and how much" of U.S. commercial fishing and the foreign fishing allowed in American waters.

It is too early to evaluate the effectiveness of this act, although results so far have been encouraging (Hill 1980) (Figure 12-10). In the first year the law was in effect, the haddock catch increased 110 percent and the cod catch increased 42 percent. From 1976 to 1979, U.S. exports of food fish more than doubled, from 111 million kg (244 million lb) to greater than 251 million kg (553 million lb). The value of those products almost tripled, to more than $1 billion in 1979. Despite the resentment of fishermen when they are told that they cannot fish certain species at specified times, most of these same fishermen would agree that the FCMA has been a boon to their industry. For additional information on regulations as a management tool, see Hildreth and Johnson (1983), Hollick (1981), Johnston (1981), and Keen (1988).

Improved Fishing Gear and Techniques

The use of better fishing gear and techniques in recent years has increased food production and has helped conserve our marine resources. There are three basic types of fishing gear: *purse-seine, trawl,* and *dredge* (Figure 12-11). With long purse-seines, fishermen can capture an entire school of fish with one setting of their nets. Trawls are bag-like nets that are dragged through the water behind boats called trawlers. They enable fishermen to follow and overtake their quarry. Dredges, on the other hand, are several-feet-wide devices that actually scrape animals, such as oysters and clams, off the seafloor. In addition to these basic types, many other devices are used, such as gill nets, traps, and weirs. Electronic gear techniques are also becoming popular in the U.S. fisheries (Figure 12–12), and marine scientists are experimenting with certain chemicals to attract fish. They are even considering the possibility of training one species of fish to help locate other species, as suggested by the association of porpoises with tuna.

Marine scientists are also working on new devices and strategies to conserve marine resources. To help reduce the loss of porpoises in tuna fishing, for example, they developed the *Medina Panel* (also called the Medina Strip)—a sort of "super apron" that is attached to the purse-seine (NMFS 1979) (Figure 12-13). This device is used in combination with a maneuver known as *backdown*, in which the boat is eased back to let one end of the net sink. As it does, most of the porpoises are able to escape. Unfortunately, this technique can be used only when weather conditions are favorable. Despite stricter fishing regulations and

SOME RESULTS OF "200-MILE" LAW

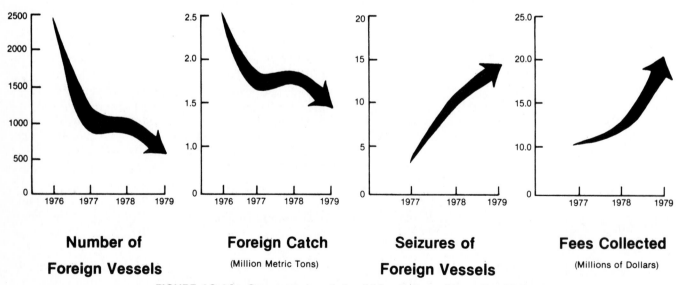

Number of Foreign Vessels

Foreign Catch (Million Metric Tons)

Seizures of Foreign Vessels

Fees Collected (Millions of Dollars)

FIGURE 12-10   Some results of the 200-mile law. (From Gerald D. Hill, "Fishermen Enter 4th Year of Conservation," *NOAA Magazine,* May–June 1980, p. 16.)

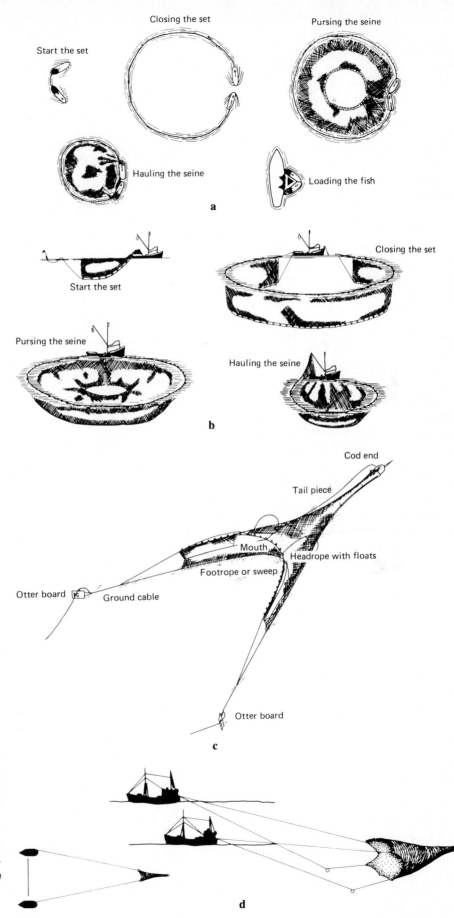

Start the set · **Closing the set** · **Pursing the seine** · **Hauling the seine** · **Loading the fish**

a

Closing the set · **Start the set** · **Pursing the seine** · **Hauling the seine**

b

Cod end
Tail piece
Mouth
Headrope with floats
Footrope or sweep
Otter board
Ground cable
Otter board

c

FIGURE 12-11 Some methods of catching fish. (a) Two boats and mothership method of purse seine; (b) one-boat purse-seine operation; (c) otter trawl gear; (d) pair trawl; (e) dredging operation; (f) lobster pat trawl; (g) longline gear; (h) gill nets. (From David A. Ross, *Opportunities and Uses of the Ocean* [New York: Springer-Verlag, 1980], pp. 164–166.)

d

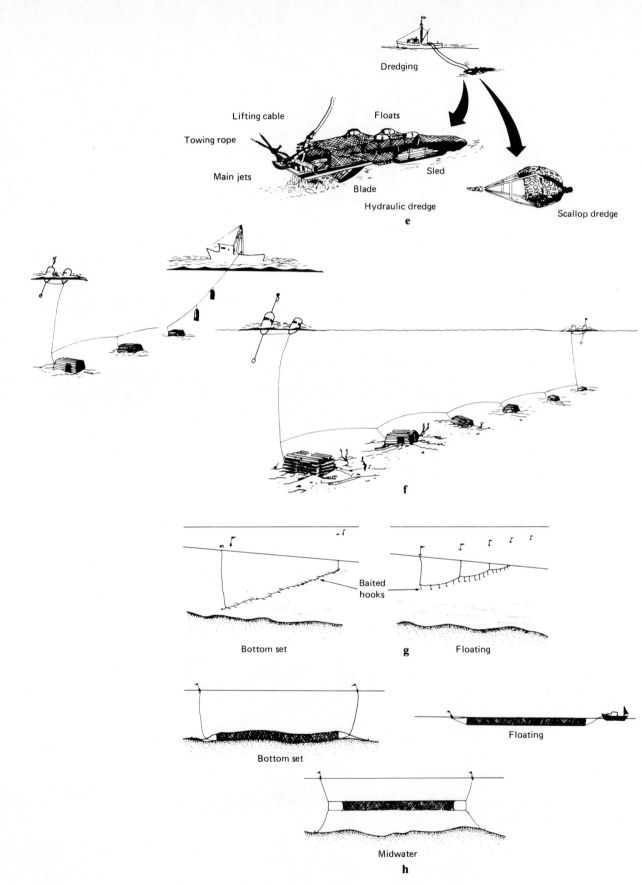

Dredging

Lifting cable
Floats
Towing rope
Main jets
Sled
Blade
Hydraulic dredge
Scallop dredge

e

f

Baited hooks

Bottom set
g Floating

Bottom set
Floating

Midwater

h

FIGURE 12-11 (Continued)

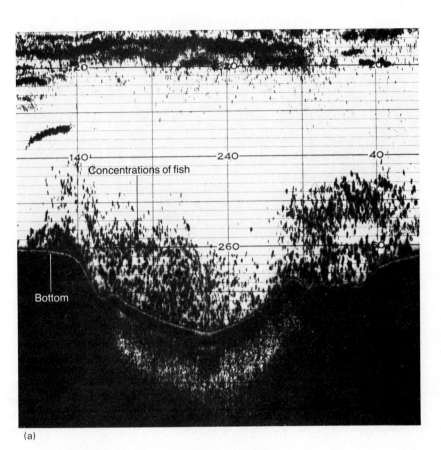

(a)

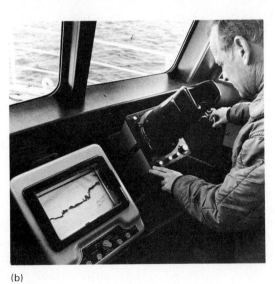

FIGURE 12-12 Echo-sounding record used to locate concentrations of fish. (Courtesy of Raytheon Marine Company.)

(b)

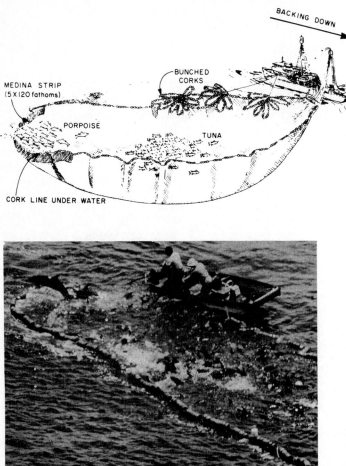

FIGURE 12-13 (upper) Tuna boat equipped with Medina Strip (also called Medina Panel). (lower) Fishermen helping porpoise escape from the net during "backdown." (Courtesy of the National Marine Fisheries Service [NMFS].)

improved fishing techniques, dolphins are still facing major problems (Godges 1988).

Protection Against Natural Predators

By protecting certain marine organisms from their natural predators, humans can increase their own share of available resources. For example, the oyster, one of America's favorite mollusks, has over a dozen predators. One of its worst predators is the starfish, and fishermen have used suction dredges and even chemicals to eliminate this fearsome predator (Parson 1972). By disrupting natural balances, however, such techniques may lead to a biotic chain reaction that will upset the local ecosystem.

Habitat Protection

Taking steps to protect the natural habitat is a conservation technique that is all too often overlooked. For one thing, we can protect fish habitats by practicing good soil and water conservation techniques. (See

Chapters 3 and 5 for examples.) Commercial fishermen can harvest their catches without devastating the ocean bottom. Sound coastal zone management and pollution abatement also serve to protect fish habitats.

Protecting the estuaries along our coasts is of particular importance (Morrissey 1988, Wilson 1988). The task is not easy, however, since most of the coastline is owned and managed by private citizens. Although the United States does not have a national land-use policy, the Coastal Zone Management Act passed in 1972 provides federal aid to coastal states with the hope that they will voluntarily develop programs to protect their coastlines. Moreover, it entrusts the management of coastal zones to the states and pledges the federal government to abide by their decisions. Unfortunately, several of the state coastal commissions and their federally approved management plans have been weakened by the actions of their state legislatures and by the appointment of pro-development commission members. For further information on coastal zone management, see the literature of the Office of Coastal Zone Management (1979) and the Center for Natural Areas (1980).

Protection of the marine habitat depends, of course, on stringent control of pollution—most recently *plastics* and *marine debris* pollution. According to recent reports (e.g., SFI 1987), plastics and other marine debris coming from boats, ships, and oil platforms may be just a serious, if not more serious, than some better known marine pollutants, such as oil. Ultimately, the solution to marine debris and other forms of pollution lies in a socially and economically acceptable combination of various approaches, in conjunction with serious international regulation (*Business Week* 1987, Keckes 1983, Malins 1980, and Williams 1979).

Fish Farming

We can also conserve our natural stocks of marine resources by supplementing them with fish grown in artificial or controlled environments. This can be done by either aquaculture or mariculture.

Aquaculture. **Aquaculture** (land-based fish farming) is normally carried on in canals, lakes, ponds, or rice paddies. Just as farmers must fertilize their crops, aquaculturalists must fertilize their ponds with natural fertilizers (fish wastes or animal wastes) or artificial fertilizers to stimulate the growth of phytoplankton. The phytoplankton, after being consumed by zooplankton, are then consumed by the fish. Aquaculture is commonly practiced in many parts of the world, and it supplies about 10 percent of the global marine harvest.

But in the United States aquaculture is still in its infancy—production in 1975 was only 65,000 metric tons, about 3 percent of the total U.S. fish and shellfish commercial harvest. This limited amount, however, still constituted (in 1975) about a quarter of our salmon production, about two-fifths of our oyster production, and about half of our catfish and crawfish production. To help counter the deterioration of wild fish stocks, the Sport Fishing Institute (1988) and other aquatic conservation organizations support the further development of this industry.

Mariculture. Since bays and estuaries trap a good part of the nutrients flowing down from the land, they can be used to produce large yields of desirable marine species in sections of bays, in suspended cages, or in metal tanks. This practice of farming the sea is called **mariculture**. Scientists from the National Marine Fisheries Service, for example, are experimenting with suspended oyster culture, whereby the oysters are grown on structures suspended into the proper water habitat. Limited quantities of shrimp and oysters are now being produced by mariculture in the United States. Unfortunately, however, the increasing contamination of our coastal estuaries will probably prevent the widespread use of mariculture.

PROSPECTS FOR THE FUTURE

The future volume of the U.S. fish harvest is not likely to rise substantially above the 1980 figure. Most marine scientists agree that U.S. fisheries in the Atlantic and the Pacific are, for all practice purposes, fished to capacity, if not overfished. Whereas aquaculture holds some hope for the future, pollution of sea water, particularly in estuarine zones, will prevent mariculture from making any significant contribution to U.S. supplies.

Continuing Problems

There is reason to believe that the U.S. fish harvest may even decline by the year 2000, mainly because of overfishing and pollution. According to Alverson (1978), certain common features help explain the pathology of many U.S. fisheries. Most of them developed during a period of minimal regulations on fishing; they simply responded to economic demands. Furthermore, they arose in a rather limited geographic territory and then spread over the entire range of the species they hunted. Over the last 50 to 100 years, their catches slowly increased and then rapidly declined due to overfishing or pollution. And finally, they have been directly affected by technological innovations (electronic fish-finding equipment) and increasingly sophisticated boats (superseiners) that enhanced fish harvests. Given the unlikelihood that the U.S. fish catch will increase in the future, U.S. consumers will turn more and more to the world supply. Unfortunately, world fisheries are even more seriously threatened by overfishing and pollution.

Positive Signs and Success Stories

Despite overfishing and the effects of pollution, there are some encouraging signs for the marine fisheries, which we will now discuss.

1. *Resiliency of the oceans.* Despite the fear that pollutants would transform the oceans of the world into cesspools, most of them have managed to assimilate many types of contamination and maintain their

stability. That is the conclusion of a four-year survey released in 1982 by the Regional Seas Program of the United Nations Environmental Program. Several international bodies and nearly 100 scientists from 36 countries contributed to this survey. In the 1970s, concentrations of such toxic substances as DDT, polychlorinated biphenyls (known as PCBs), other chlorinated hydrocarbons, and harmful metals were readily detectable in samples of ocean water. In 1982, by contrast, most PCBs were barely measurable. The samples on which these reports were based were taken from large ocean areas several hundred miles from shore. Conditions in coastal areas, which receive the greatest amount of pollution, are less encouraging. According to the survey, whereas animal and plant communities in the open ocean can recover from an oil spill within a matter of weeks or months, recovery in tidal areas may take decades, particularly where the oil has penetrated the bottom sediments.

Although the survey reports that the world's 328 million cubic miles of ocean are not in immediately jeopardy, it expresses some major concerns. In the Northern Hemisphere, where nations are trying to clean up both the air and the water, the picture is fairly encouraging. In the Southern Hemisphere, however, underdeveloped countries are now using the poisonous chemicals once used by many industrial nations, and there the oceans are deteriorating. Moreover, the survey cautions against the trend toward increasing contamination from heavy metals, carbon dioxide, radioactive materials, sewage microorganisms, and newly developed chemicals. It urges the careful monitoring of this trend, the introduction of strong regulations on existing pollutants, and the halting of any new contaminants into the oceans.

2. *Progress in controlling ocean dumping.* The oceans are capable of breaking down or absorbing certain wastes. They are less capable of resisting other contaminants, however, including radioactive wastes, persistent and nondegradable synthetic organic compounds, metals that are toxic to marine organisms, and toxic chemicals that are biologically magnified. The dumping of such toxic materials must be either banned or limited until we gain a better understanding of their ecological ramifications.

Some progress has been made. By 1975, for example, 54 countries had agreed to halt the dumping of several types of contaminants, including chemical and biological warfare munitions, high-level radioactive wastes, and certain pesticides and kinds of oil. They further agreed that permits should be required for the dumping of other toxic materials, such as lead, cyanides, and arsenic. Although the agreement does not apply to all forms of ocean dumping, it is a significant international step towards regulating this form of marine contamination.

In 1975, Congress also passed the Ocean Dumping Act, which bans the dumping of all wastes (except dredged materials) by U.S. ships without a permit from the U.S. Environmental Protection Agency (EPA). Since 1981, the EPA has banned the dumping of city sewage sludge and all other wastes that it deems harmful to the marine environment (Miller 1988).

3. *Advances in international sea law.* International efforts are being made to adopt an environmentally sound Law of the Sea Convention. In 1974, the United Nations Conference on the Law of the Sea was convened as a forum to negotiate a treaty that would regulate virtually every aspect of human use of the oceans. By 1983, that treaty, known as UNCLOS III, had been approved in principle by 124 governments, including France, Japan, and Canada. To date, the United States has not approved it, protesting that it does not guarantee U.S. companies access to deep seabed minerals.

Sixty nations must ratify that treaty before it goes into force (Ross and Knauss 1982). Once ratified, the Law of the Sea Treaty will provide an important international framework for the protection and conservation of the marine environment and its resources. Earlier attempts have been made to regulate ocean pollution, but only on a piecemeal basis. The new treaty deals with pollution in a *comprehensive* manner. It builds on various International Maritime Organization treaties, the United Nations Environment Program's transactions, and standards set by the 1972 Stockholm Declaration on the Human Environment. For many nations, ratification of the treaty will mean that for the first time they will be legally bound to protect marine resources.

4. *Programs to encourage sensitivity to the environment.* The fishing industry itself has launched several new programs to promote environmental sensitivity. For example, an innovative program known as the Whale Hotline has relieved the plight of whales in the waters off Newfoundland (Horwood 1984). Formerly, when a whale or some other large mammal got caught in their nets, fishermen simply shot the animal. Now they call the Whale Hotline and a team of specialists will rush to the scene, any time of the day or night, to release the animal without destroying it. As of mid-1984, over 150 whales (mostly humpbacks, fins, and minkes) have been rescued under this new program.

5. *Cetacean sanctuaries.* Several **cetacean sanctuaries** have recently been established to protect whales, dolphins, and other cetaceans (fishlike aquatic mammals). These are areas in which no cetacean may be killed, harassed, harmed, or taken captive. Human activities are forbidden that might interfere with such biological functions as feeding, breeding, or migrating. Under proper control, scientific research and public attendance are permitted. By 1979, four cetacean sanctuaries had been created: the gray whale sanctuary in Guerrero Negro, Mexico; a right whale sanctuary in the Gulf of St. Jose, Chubut Province, Argentina; a humpback whale sanctuary at Maui, Hawaii; and a finless porpoise sanctuary in the Hiroshima Sea, Japan. The International Union for the Conservation of Nature and Natural Resources (IUCN) and other organizations have proposed that additional sanctuaries be established.

6. *Possible halt to whaling in high seas.* It may not be too long before whaling is halted altogether on the high seas. Each season, the International Whaling Commission (IWC) lowers the total number of whales that can be killed in the coming season. In the 1983 season, according to the National Wildlife Federation, only 8000 whales could be harvested, as opposed to 10,000 in the previous year.

7. *Some successful fisheries management plans.* The Fisheries Conservation and Management Act of 1976, which established eight Regional Fishery Management Councils, has spawned several creative fishery management plans. The northern anchovy fishery plan developed in 1978 by the Pacific Fishery Management Council, for example, has been described by many marine resource managers as an innovative model of long-range planning. All such plans, however, must come under constant critical review to evaluate their effectiveness. In the opinion of J. L. McHugh, professor of marine resources at the State University of New York, the United States must develop management plans that will truly maintain fishery resources at optimum levels—something, he claims, that has never been done. Evidence of this can be seen in the poor management of striped bass, salmon, clams, oysters, river herring, and a few other species. Although our efforts to date have not been very promising, management plans for the northern anchovy fisheries management, as mentioned previously, may be steps in the right direction.

8. *Living resources—a new concept in fisheries management.* A new concept has entered into marine fisheries recently, although it has been recognized for years. That is the concept of managing ma-

rine biotic resources as a whole, rather than fishery by fishery as if each were totally independent of one another. In other words, *ecosystem-oriented management regimes* would be established, focusing not just on harvest limits for the specific species (e.g., krill) but on the effect commercial harvesting would have on all dependent organisms within the food chain (e.g., whales). Here, the emphasis would be on the *prevention of depletion* rather than attempts at after-the-fact protection, as is currently the case with whales and many fisheries resources.

9. *The comeback of some fishes and marine mammals.* According to the National Wildlife Federation, certain fishes and marine mammals are making a comeback as a result of changes in harvesting practices. Off the Labrador coast, for example, fishermen are catching large numbers of cod again—primarily due to a 322 km (200 mi) fisheries zone established in 1977 to restrict foreign trawlers from exploiting their banks. Although this simple management technique may not work for all fished-out waters around the world, it seems to be working in Labrador for cod.

Alaska has been the scene of some major marine mammal comebacks. For example, the northern fur seal, once exploited by the Japanese, the Russians, and the Americans, has now made a comeback as a result of a 1911 treaty, which allows harvesting within a sustainable yield. The Pacific walrus has also made a comeback in Alaska, brought about primarily by two factors: (1) discontinuance of commercial overfishing by the USSR in the 1950s, and (2) strict state regulation of walrus hunting by subsistence cultures.

ACTION FOR MARINE RESOURCES

It is conceivable that the survival of humanity may depend in large measure on our success in preserving a marine environment that will assure maximum yields of fish for human consumption. You can help achieve that goal by engaging in the activities discussed subsequently.

1. *Support ecologically sound marine policies.* Your support of the following polices can help preserve our marine environment:

- *On the marine environment in general.* Encourage legislators to pay attention to the management of marine biotic resources and to set harvesting quotas that are ecologically sound. Support national and international research programs on toxic pollutants.

- *On coastlines and estuaries.* It is on the transition zones between land and water that humans are inflicting the greatest ecological stresses. To help achieve an acceptable balance between the economic and ecological uses of coastal areas, urge that all major wetlands be carefully inventoried, with an indication of the potential demographic, industrial, and recreational encroachments. Encourage government officials to set up and support management programs that stress minimizing environmental degradation. Support prohibitions on irrelevant coastal uses (e.g., the use of the sand dunes for auto racing), and urge that cultural, historic, and aesthetic sites be protected. Foster public appreciation of estuaries as highly productive ecological systems, and guard your right as a citizen as to how these wetlands are to be used.

2. *Advocate the creation of ecological reserves.* Sometimes the only way to rescue a critical habit from destruction is by outright purchase—the buying of a piece of property and holding it as an ecological reserve. Areas most urgently in need of rescue are those that are ecologically unique, that contain threatened or endangered flora and fauna, and that provide a habitat for aquatic and terrestrial wildlife. Two programs set up for that purpose are the *National Marine Sanctuaries Program (NMSP)* and the *National Estuarine Sanctuary Program (NESP)*. The NMSP has created the Point Reyes–Farallon Islands National Marine Sanctuary, which embraces 2590 km² (1000 mi²) off San Francisco, and the Key Largo Coral Reef Marine Sanctuary, which includes 259 km² (100 mi²) of coral communities off the southeastern

coast of Florida. By 1989, the NESP had taken steps to protect 18 critical estuarine habitats (Figure 12-14).

3. *Support the use of underutilized species and wasted parts of fish.* One way to strengthen fisheries is to increase their harvest of underutilized species (Ross 1980). Remember, what is a "trash fish" to one person is a delicacy to another. Squid and shark may not be the favorite food of Americans, but they are well liked by people in other parts of the world. Several Pacific fish are underutilized: Pacific cod, lingcod, sablefish (or black cod), and bonito (tuna). Moreover, we can learn to use the entire fish, as foresters use every part of the trees they harvest. When fish are taken for their liver or to be filleted, for example, the carcass, including the viscera, bones, and all other parts, should not be discarded. With improved technology, these parts can be turned into fish protein concentrate (FPC) and other valuable products.

4. *Eat lower on the food chain.* You can select marine organisms at your local supermarket that are lower on the food chain and that are more abundant than the predators at the top of the food chain. Krill, for example, has a flavor similar to that of shrimp. It has a high protein content and is extremely abundant—its total mass is estimated at over 10 trillion pounds. (If krill is harvested on a wide scale, however, marine resource managers must be careful not to destroy this major food source for certain species of whales.) Several varieties of seaweed are also highly nutritious. In certain Asiatic countries, seaweed constitutes as much as 25 percent of the human diet (Ross 1980).

5. *Join a private marine conservation group.* Consider joining an oceanic society or conservation

FIGURE 12-14 Estuarine sanctuaries. (Courtesy of the National Oceanic and Atmospheric Association [NOAA].)

group. The Oceanic Society, the Cousteau Society, and the National Coalition for Marine Conservation support marine conservation. Greenpeace, Sea Shepherd International, and the American Cetacean Society focus primarily, but not exclusively, on preserving marine mammals.

6. *Pursue a marine-oriented education and career.* In the early 1960s, rising public interest in the oceans led Congress to create commissions on marine issues and to develop a national ocean policy. In

1966, it established the National Sea Grant College Program to help universities to foster scientific, technological, social, political, and economic expertise in the use of oceanic resources. Sea Grant colleges and universities exist across the nation. The conservation and management of marine resources call for a knowledge of economics, politics, law, geography, and environmental studies as much as a knowledge of biology. Students who are considering a career in the management of marine resources have a wide range of courses and programs from which to choose.

DISCUSSION TOPICS

1. What are the major features of the ocean? How does each relate to biological productivity?

2. Explain the phenomenon known as upwelling. Why is it so important to fisheries?

3. List five major human benefits derived from the world's oceans. Can you name some additional benefits?

4. There are various ways of categorizing the ocean environment. Name two major ways and explain each in detail.

5. Why is the continental shelf generally richer in marine biotic resources than the continental slope? Which suffers greater degradation as a result of human activities?

6. List and describe seven characteristics of the estuarine environment. In what ways are human activities affecting estuaries?

7. The open sea has been referred to as a "biological desert." Explain.

8. Explain the relationship between marine food chains, the types of fish that Americans like to eat, and overfishing by American fishermen. If you elected to eat lower on the marine food chain, what types of fish would you choose at your local supermarket?

9. What is krill? How does it relate to whales and to the possibility of whale extinction?

10. Explain the relationship between marine food chains, feeding migrations, and the phenomenon known as El Niño.

11. List and explain four major natural factors that deplete

fish populations. Can you think of any other natural causes that might affect fish populations?

12. In addition to natural destructive agents, marine populations must cope with pressures from humans. Discuss three major categories of human pressure on marine fisheries.

13. Debate the following statement: The ocean is vast and can dilute various pollutants, therefore, we need not worry about dumping our wastes in the ocean.

14. Should offshore oil wells be banned? Under what circumstances?

15. Discuss the pros and cons of various ways of controlling oil pollution.

16. America's fisheries can be grouped according to three major geographic areas. Discuss each—their geographical extent, their major fisheries, and their marine resource management problems.

17. Discuss the advantages and the disadvantages of the various methods by which marine resource managers can conserve and improve our nation's fisheries.

18. What is the difference between aquaculture and mariculture? Which do you think has the greater potential? Why?

19. Despite all the problems facing the world's oceans, there are some reasons for optimism. List and discuss at least nine indications that all is not lost as far as preserving our marine resources.

20. How can you personally get involved in conserving the world's oceans and their biotic resources?

READINGS

ALVERSON, D. L. 1978. "Commercial Fishing." In Howard P. Brokaw, ed., *Wildlife and America*, pp. 67–85. Washington, D.C.: Government Printing Office. Overview of the changing economic status of the U.S. commercial fishing industry.

BENNETT, CHARLES F. 1983. *Conservation and Management of Natural Resources in the United States.* New York: Wiley. The marine section contains useful geographic boundaries for U.S. fisheries.

BUSINESS WEEK. 1987. "Troubled Waters," *Business Week.*

October 12, pp. 88–104. Businesspersons discuss the serious predicament of the world's oceans and argue how something must be done immediately to improve the situation.

CENTER FOR NATURAL AREAS. 1980. *An Annotated Bibliography of Coastal Zone Management Work Products.* Washington, D.C.: Office of Coastal Zone Management, U.S. Department of Commerce. Excellent compilation of state, territory, and federal work projects produced through funding authorized by the Coastal Zone Management Act of 1972.

EBERHARDT, L. L. 1977. "Optimal Management Policies for Marine Mammals," *Wildlife Society Bulletin,* vol. 5, no. 4, pp. 162–169. Discusses the problems of interpreting the Marine Mammal Protection Act of 1972.

GODGES, JOHN. 1988. "Dolphins Hit Rough Seas Again," *Sierra,* May–June, vol. 73, no. 3, pp. 25–27. Discusses how regulatory stalls and a growing foreign tuna fleet are undermining previous successes at protecting dolphins.

GREENBAUM, DANIEL. 1983. "Promoting Environmental Sensitivity Within the Fishing Industry," *The Environmentalist,* vol. 3, pp. 199–208. Describes Resources for Cape Ann, a local program based in Gloucester, Massachusetts, designed to encourage environmental sensitivity within the fishing and shellfishing industry.

HILDRETH, RICHARD G., and RALPH W. JOHNSON. 1983. *Ocean and Coastal Law.* Englewood Cliffs, N.J.: Prentice-Hall. Cases, status, and regulations governing resource ownership, management, and use in the three coastal geographic zones.

HILL, GERALD D. 1980. "Fishermen Enter 4th Year of Conservation," *NOAA Magazine,* May–June, pp. 14–17. Discusses the results of the Fishery Conservation and Management Act of 1976.

HOLLICK, ANN L. 1981. *U.S. Foreign Policy and the Law of the Sea.* Princeton, N.J.: Princeton University Press. Examines the political and legal aspects of the U.S. ocean policy of the last 40 years, with special attention to the UN Conference on Law of the Sea.

HORWOOD, HAROLD. 1984. "Setting Free the Whales," *International Wildlife,* vol. 14, no. 1, pp. 5–11. Describes the Whale Hotline—an innovative alternative to killing whales, dolphins, and other marine mammals that are accidentally caught in fishermen's nets.

JOHNSTON, DOUGLAS M., ed. 1981. *The Environmental Law of the Sea.* Gland, Switzerland: International Union for the Conservation of Nature and Natural Resources (IUCN). A useful guide to the state of marine conservation law and policy. Puts the environmentally relevant aspects of the UN Conference on Law of the Sea into global and historical perspective.

JONES, HARDY. 1980. "Why the Dolphins Died," *International Wildlife,* September–October, vol. 10, no. 5, pp. 4–10. Includes dramatic photographs of dolphin kills by the Japanese to protect their fishery.

KECKES, STEPHAN. 1983. "Protecting the Marine Environment," *Ambio,* vol. 12, no. 2, pp. 112–114. Discusses causes and effects, management options, and socioeconomic consequences of marine pollution. Concludes with priorities for the 1980s.

KEEN, ELMER A. 1988. *Ownership and Productivity of Marine Fishery Resources: An Essay on the Resolution of Conflict for the Use of the Ocean Pastures.* Blackburg, Va.: McDonald & Woodward. Geographer Keen argues that the common ownership of marine fishery resources has contributed to the decline of fishing stocks. He calls for a change to a full ownership system.

LACKEY, ROBERT T., and LARRY A. NIELSEN, eds. 1980. *Fisheries Management.* New York: Wiley. Stimulating and informative text for students of fisheries management.

MALINS, DONALD D. 1980. "Pollution of the Marine Environment," *Environmental Sciences and Technology,* vol. 14, no. 1, pp. 32–37. Raises important questions regarding types of pollutants entering the marine environment.

MARX, WESLEY. 1981. *The Oceans: Our Last Resource.* San Francisco: Sierra Club Books. A highly readable book that provides a sensible and hopeful prospect for our coexistence with the oceans.

MEADOWS, P. S., and J. I. CAMPBELL. 1988. *An Introduction to Marine Science.* 2d ed. New York: Wiley. Excellent introduction to the study of the sea.

MILLER, G. TYLER. 1988. *Living in the Environment.* 5th ed. Belmont, Calif.: Wadsworth. Contains an excellent section on ocean pollution.

MORRISSEY, SIOBHAN. 1988. "Estuaries: Concern over Troubled Waters," *Oceans,* June, vol. 21, no. 3, pp. 23–27, 61. Outstanding summary of the problems facing our nation's estuaries.

NATIONAL MARINE FISHERIES SERVICE. 1979. *Report of the National Marine Fisheries Service for the Calendar Year 1978.* July. Washington, D.C.: U.S. Department of Commerce. See subsequent reports as well.

NORRIS, KENNETH. 1978. "Marine Mammals and Man." In Howard P. Brokaw, ed., *Wildlife and America,* pp. 320–388. Washington, D.C.: Government Printing Office. Good historical overview of human use and abuse of marine mammals.

OBENG, L. E. 1983. "The Control of Pathogens from Human Waste and Their Aquatic Vectors," *Ambio,* vol. 12, no. 2, pp. 106–108. Discussion of virus and bacteria pathogens in human waste and the disposal problems they present for communities.

OFFICE OF COASTAL ZONE MANAGEMENT. 1979. *The First Five Years of Coastal Zone Management: An Initial Assessment.* Washington, D.C.: Office of Coastal Zone Management, National Oceanic and Atmospheric Administration. A look at the success and failures of the first five years of the Coastal Zone Management Act of 1972.

OWEN, OLIVER S. 1985. *Natural Resource Conservation: An Ecological Approach.* 4th ed. New York: Macmillan. Contains an excellent chapter on marine resources from a biological perspective.

PARSON, RUBEN. 1972. *Conserving American Resources*. Englewood Cliffs, N.J.: Prentice-Hall. Classic introductory textbook in natural resource management.

PEQUEGNAT, W. E. 1983. ''Aquatic Baseline Studies for Environmental Impact Assessment,'' *Water International*, vol. 8, no. 4, pp. 180–190. Good discussion of the relative ecological importance of the various zones of the marine environment.

RADWAY, ALLEN K. 1980. *Conservation and Management of Whales*. Seattle, Wash.: University of Washington Press. Comprehensive study.

REID, WALTER V. 1988. ''Managing the Southern Ocean Krill Fishery,'' *Resources*, Spring, no. 91, pp. 11–13. Excellent discussion of the krill fishery.

ROSS, DAVID A. 1980. *Opportunities and Uses of the Ocean*. New York: Springer-Verlag. Explores the present and future utilization of the world's oceans.

ROSS, DAVID A., and JOHN A. KNAUSS. 1982. ''How the Law of the Sea Treaty Will Affect U.S. Marine Science,'' *Science*, September, vol. 217, pp. 1003–1008. Discusses how the treaty will affect the way U.S. marine scientists operate in the ocean.

SFI. 1987. ''The Growing Problem of Marine Debris,'' *SFI Bulletin*, March, no. 382, pp. 6–7. Brief, but excellent, source on marine debris—its sources, and suggestions on reducing the problem.

SFI. 1988. ''The Role of Aquaculture in Marine Fisheries Management,'' *SFI Bulletin*, June, pp. 1–2. Brief summary of the Sport Fishing Institute's position on aquaculture.

VALIELA, IVAN. 1984. *Marine Ecological Processes*. New York: Springer-Verlag. Outstanding textbook on the processes that control marine ecosystems, communities, and populations.

WILLIAMS, JEROME. 1979. *Introduction to Marine Pollution Control*. New York: Wiley. A holistic approach to coping with marine pollution, including discussions of the physical, chemical, biological, legal, and sociological considerations regarding marine pollution control throughout the world.

WILSON, JAMES G. 1988. *The Biology of Estuarine Management*. London: Croom Helm. Comprehensive study.

NONFUEL MINERAL RESOURCES

Nothing surely is so disgraceful to society, and to individuals, as unmeaning wastefulness.
Count Rumford Essay X (1804)

INTRODUCTION

Industrialized nations are highly dependent on the use of mineral resources. Television sets, high fidelity systems, automobiles, computers, cameras, and most things associated with a high standard of living are dependent upon mineral resources. One merely has to look around the university campus to find examples. The buildings are constructed from such materials as stone, brick (clay), sand, gravel, steel, cement, glass, and asphalt and hidden within the walls, ceilings, and floors of those same campus buildings are electrical and plumbing fixtures consisting of copper, brass, lead, asbestos, iron, and steel. Gypsum (used in plaster and wallboard), fiberglass, or rock wool may also be used as insulating material. The interior of those same buildings may be painted with mineral pigments (e.g., zinc, iron, and titanium) and have plastic chairs made from minerals (e.g., petroleum products), movie screens made from steel and sand, and light bulbs, porcelain fixtures, and other items made from mineral products.

Minerals are derived from the earth in a solid form (e.g., stone), in fragments (e.g., sand), as a liquid (e.g., oil), or as a gas (e.g., natural gas). The U.S. Bureau of Mines and the U.S. Geological Survey

(1981) officially define a mineral resource as "a concentration of naturally occurring solid, liquid, or gas material in such form and amount that economic extraction of a commodity from the concentration is currently or potentially feasible."

Minerals are generally classified either as nonrenewable metallic and nonmetallic minerals (e.g., sand, stone, lead, copper, mercury, and zinc) or as nonrenewable mineral fuels (e.g., oil, natural gas, coal, and uranium). This chapter will discuss the nonfuel minerals that are valued for electrical conductivity, strength, corrosion resistance, and other factors necessary for manufacturing products within industrial societies. The following chapter will focus on the fossil fuels (coal, oil, and natural gas) and other mineral fuels necessary to run America's homes, businesses, industries, and transportation systems.

There are over 100 nonfuel minerals traded in the world market today (Chiras 1985). Many of these minerals are used to manufacture products for the typical American home (Table 13-1). Note that in a list of nonfuel minerals within the home, it is still necessary to mention the mineral *fuels* that are used in a nonfuel way, such as petroleum products within synthetic fibers. The U.S. Bureau of Mines (1975) estimates that each person in the United States consumes approximately 10,011 kg (22,070 lb) of new mineral material (excluding energy resources) each year.

To understand America's mineral predicament better, we will first look at the sources and availability of mineral resources. This will be followed by a brief introduction to the extraction process, including surface, subsurface, and seabed mining. From there, we will turn to the environmental impact of mineral development, followed by a look at methods to regulate the industry. Then, the status of nonfuel minerals will be discussed, including U.S. supplies and the global outlook. A substantial section of the chapter will be devoted to strategies for stretching existing mineral supplies, since this is the section that discusses how we can help solve our mineral problems. Finally, the chapter summarizes prospects for the future and concludes with ways in which you can personally get involved in mineral conservation and management.

MINERALS: SOURCES AND AVAILABILITY

Sources

The Earth's Crust. Most of our minerals come from the earth's crust. Although the earth's crust ranges from 4.8 to 80.5 km (3 to 50 mi) thick, it is at

TABLE 13-1

Major mineral products in the typical American home

Building materials	Sand, gravel, stone, brick (clay), cement, steel, aluminum, asphalt, glass
Plumbing and wiring materials	Iron and steel, copper, brass, lead, cement, asbestos, glass, tile, plastic
Insulating materials	Rock, wool, fiberglass, gypsum (plaster and wallboard)
Paint and wallpaper	Mineral pigments (such as iron, zinc, and titanium) and fillers (such as talc and asbestos)
Plastic floor tiles, other plastics	Mineral fillers and pigments, petroleum products
Appliances	Iron, copper, and many rare metals
Furniture	Synthetic fibers made from minerals (principally coal and petroleum products); steel springs; wood finished with rotten-stone polish and mineral varnish
Clothing	Natural fibers grown with mineral fertilizers; synthetic fibers made from minerals (principally coal and petroleum products)
Food	Grown with mineral fertilizers; processed and packaged by machines made of metals
Drugs and cosmetics	Mineral chemicals
Other items	Windows, screens, light bulbs, porcelain fixtures, china, utensils, jewelry: all made from mineral products

Source: Keller, Edward A. 1985. *Environmental Geology.* 4th ed. Columbus, Ohio: Merrill.

present only economically and technically feasible to mine the uppermost layer. Cameron (1986) notes that the world's deepest oil wells only go down 9144 m (30,000 ft) and the world's deepest mines only go down 3658 m (12,000 ft).

Using the average composition of the earth crust (Table 13-2), Cameron also makes some interest-

TABLE 13-2

Composition of the earth's crust (in parts per million)

Oxygen	464,000	Cerium	67	Uranium	2.7
Silicon	282,000	Copper	55	Bromine	2.5
Aluminum	82,000	Yttrium	33	Tin	2
Iron	56,000	Neodymium	28	Arsenic	1.8
Calcium	41,000	Lanthanum	25	Germanium	1.5
Sodium	24,000	Cobalt	25	Molybdenum	1.5
Magnesium	23,000	Scandium	22	Tungsten	1.5
Potassium	21,000	Lithium	20	Holmium	1.5
Titanium	5,700	Nitrogen	20	Europium	1.2
Phosphorus	1,050	Niobium	20	Terbium	1.1
Manganese	950	Gallium	15	Lutecium	0.8
Fluorine	625	Lead	12.5	Thulium	0.25
Barium	425	Boron	10	Iodine	0.5
Strontium	375	Thorium	9.6	Thallium	0.45
Sulfur	260	Samarium	7.3	Cadmium	0.2
Carbon	200	Gadolinium	7.3	Antimony	0.2
Zirconium	165	Praseodymium	6.5	Bismuth	0.17
Vanadium	135	Dysprosium	5.2	Indium	0.1
Chlorine	130	Ytterbium	3	Mercury	0.08
Chromium	100	Hafnium	3	Silver	0.07
Rubidium	90	Cesium	3	Selenium	0.05
Nickel	75	Beryllium	2.8		
Zinc	70	Erbium	2.8		

Source: Cameron, Eugene N. 1986. *At the Crossroads: The Mineral Problems of the United States.* New York: Wiley.

ing observations regarding the relative abundance of minerals. For example, the first 9 elements (oxygen through titanium) make up 99 percent of the earth's crust, with the next 10 elements (phosphorus through chlorine) making up only 0.5 percent of the crust. All the remaining elements add up to only 0.2 percent of the crust. Relative abundance, however, must be weighed against the difficulty of extraction. Generally speaking, the more difficult to extract a mineral, the more costly the process—both in terms of dollars and energy.

Mineral Deposits: How They Are Formed. Raw mineral materials are found in a **mineral deposit**. A mineral deposit can be defined as any solid form (rock) that contains an element or compound useful to society.

Mineral deposits are shaped by four major processes: (1) cooling and crystallization, (2) weathering, (3) solution, and (4) deposition. During the *cooling and crystallization* of molten material (magma), such mineral commodities as iron, titanium, chromium, and phosphate are formed. The *weathering* of existing rocks creates another class of mineral deposits, such as calcium phosphate (an excellent source of phosphate for fertilizers) and bauxite (the aluminum-rich

material from which the metal can be extracted). Other mineral deposits (e.g., gold, silver, copper, lead, molybdenum) are a result of *solutions* that have deposited minerals in a branching fracture, such as the gold vein found in granite rock. *Deposition* is the final major process by which minerals are formed. In this case, minerals are mechanically accumulated in sheetlike deposits. For example, sandstone is the result of a river gradually dropping its mineral particles in sections of reduced water velocity.

Availability

Ore and Grade. Not all mineral deposits from the earth's crust are extractable at the present time. Consequently, geologists and mineral resource managers make distinctions, using such terms as *ore, grade, reserves,* and *resources.*

An **ore** is a mineral deposit that can be extracted under current (1) economic, (2) technological, (3) political, and (4) social conditions. In order for the extraction process to be *economically* feasible, the mineral material must be of the proper **grade** or tenor, that is, the mineral matter must contain enough of the element wanted. A *high-grade ore* is one that has high concentrations of the desired element (e.g., a copper ore that is 3 percent copper); a low-grade ore would have a relatively low concentration of the desired element (e.g., a copper ore that is only 0.3 percent copper). The size, shape, composition, and location of the mineral deposit in the earth's crust also affects the cost of the mining and processing operation. Furthermore, these factors (particularly the location of the mineral deposit) affect whether or not a project is *technologically* feasible.

Location also plays an important role in determining whether or not it is *politically* feasible to mine a mineral deposit. Antarctica provides a case in point. Geologists have recently found a wealth of various mineral deposits in Antarctica. To date, neither the United States nor the Soviet Union has territorial claims to that region, nor portions thereof. When world supplies of various minerals dwindle and it becomes economically feasible to mine that region, a rash of political obstacles will first have to be surmounted. Furthermore, if mining a mineral deposit in Antarctica's fragile ecosystem would create unacceptable environmental damage, the mineral deposit would not qualify as an ore.

Finally, a mineral deposit cannot be classified as an ore unless its extraction would be *socially* acceptable. Half Dome in Yosemite National Park contains certain mineral resources. However, Americans today would not stand for the defacement of such a national treasure. Consequently, there are strict rules and regulations regarding mining in national parks (see Chapter 10). Although it is hard to fathom that Half Dome in Yosemite National Park could someday be classified as an ore, there are those that have proposed it. However, one thing is certain, and that is change. Society changes its mind; technological improvements are made; political obstacles vanish (or appear); and mining operations, once considered uneconomical, all of a sudden become economically feasible.

Resources and Reserves. Once a mineral deposit is classified as an ore, the calculated tonnage of the desired mineral matter in the deposit becomes a **reserve,** in the same sence that one's financial reserve is one's liquid assets (i.e., money in the bank). (See Figure 13-1 for an illustration of the difference between resources and reserves.) By adding up the reserves of phosphorus in the United States, for example, geologists can estimate the nation's total phosphorus reserves. Unfortunately, this still does not answer the question as to how much phosphorus will be available from U.S. deposits in the future.

Although at first appearing simple, the concept of *reserve* is highly complex when applied to actual mining circumstances. Much of the complexity is a result of inadequate knowledge about the reserve (Figure 13-1). To help refine the concept, geologists have identified three basic categories of reserves: (1) *proven reserves*—those thoroughly explored and measured, (2) *probable reserves*—those partially explored and indicated, and (3) *possible reserves*—those reserves inferred by calculating and projecting from the above two types. Human judgment and error increase substantially as one passes from estimates of proven reserves, to estimates of probable reserves, to estimates of possible reserves.

THE EXTRACTION PROCESS

There are basically three methods of extracting mineral reserves: (1) surface mining, (2) subsurface (un-

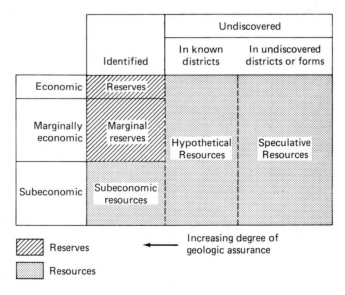

FIGURE 13-1 Classification of mineral resources used by the U.S. Geological Survey and the U.S. Bureau of Mines. (From Edward A. Keller, *Environmental Geology*, 5th ed. [Columbus, Ohio: Merrill, 1988], p. 357.)

derground) mining, and (3) seabed mining. Each method has its peculiar advantages and disadvantages.

Surface Mining

Surface mining is the extraction technique used to mine 90 percent of the nation's rock and mineral resources (Moran et al. 1986). It entails the removal of the *overburden* or overlying materials (e.g., topsoil, subsoil, and other strata) to expose the desirable mineral seam. Once the overburden is removed, large power shovels can scoop giant loads of mineral deposits in very short periods of time. Surface mining, itself, can be subdivided into its basic types: (1) open pit mining, (2) strip mining, and (3) dredging. The nature of the mineral deposit, as well as its shape, attitude, and depth, often determines the mining technique used.

Open Pit Mining. Approximately 80 percent of the annual production of minerals in the United States comes from **open pit mining** (Cameron 1986). This technique is used primarily for the extraction of iron (e.g., in the Lake Superior district), phosphate (e.g., in Florida), copper, or gravel. The larger open pits for granite or limestone are known as *rock quarries*. Compared to subsurface mining, open pit mining is cheaper (a few dollars per ton as compared with $20 or more per ton), provides for high recovery (80 percent of the ore may be recovered as compared with 40 percent for underground mines) and safer (underground mining cave-ins are notorious). There is no question, however, that open pit mining causes more environmental abuse than subsurface mining. This will be discussed in greater detail under the heading of "Environmental Impact" within this chapter.

Strip Mining. Strip mining is a surface mining technique that is environmentally more devastating than open pit mining, since it uses huge power shovels such as the Big Muskie (Figure 13-2). There are two principle types of strip mining: (1) area and (2) contour. **Area surface mining** is a mining technique that is employed on flat to gently rolling topography. The technique involves stripping away the overburden to expose the mineral deposit, and putting the overburden in an adjacent trench previously created by the extraction of the desired mineral element (Figure 13-3). The process leaves behind a rugged landscape of parallel ridges resembling a washboard (Figure 13-4). Area surface mining is used for extracting phosphate rock (in Florida, Idaho, and

FIGURE 13-2 A giant shovel used for strip mining coal. Note the size of the shovel in relation to the cars at its base. (From Bernard J. Nebel, *Environmental Science: The Way the World Works* [Englewood Cliffs, N.J.: Prentice-Hall, Inc., 1981], p. 564. Department of Energy photo by Schneider.)

North Carolina), gypsum (in many parts of the country), and coal (in Illinois and western Kentucky). On mountain landscapes, **contour surface mining** is the technique most often used. This method entails cutting a shelf, bench, or terrace into the side of a hill or mountain. Overburden is then dumped down the hillside on the previously built terrace. This technique is used primarily for the extraction of coal seams in the Appalachian Mountains. Of the two types of strip mining, contour is noted for being the most environmentally destructive.

Dredging. Where waves and currents have deposited sands and sands rich with valuable heavy metals (e.g., the iron-titanium oxide mineral ilmenite), **dredging** is the surface mining technique used for extracting minerals from streambeds and seabeds (Figure 13-5). With this method, chain buckets and draglines or suction devices are used to extract unconsolidated materials, such as sand and gravel, including gravels that are gold or tin-bearing. Unfortu-

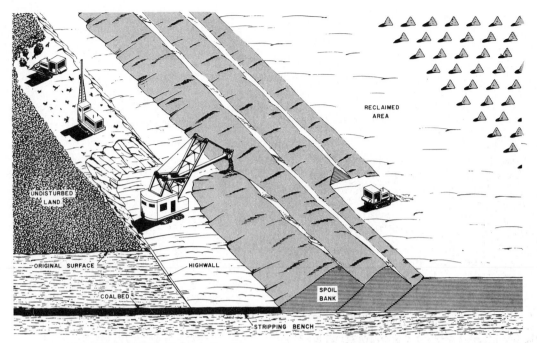

FIGURE 13-3 Schematic diagram of area strip mining of coal. (From U.S. Department of the Interior.)

FIGURE 13-4 Area strip mining of coal near Nucla, Colorado. (From Ruben L. Parson, *Conserving American Resources,* 3d ed. [Englewood Cliffs, N.J.: Prentice-Hall, Inc., 1972], p. 267.)

FIGURE 13-5 A 1400-ton floating dredge mines sand from the Mississippi River. The huge machine inhales sand from the channel, like a vacuum cleaner, then transports the sand through a pipe to a desired location. (Photo by AP/World Wide Photos.)

nately, the dredging process can disturb aquatic ecosystems by stirring up silt, which can lead to fish-kills.

Subsurface Mining

When the overburden is too deep to be removed economically, **subsurface mining** is the technique often used. There are basically two types: (1) the room-and-pillar method and (2) the solution method. In the *room-and-pillar method*, underground cavities or "rooms" are excavated, the resulting rooms being large enough to allow the movement of miners, equipment, and the removal of ore (Figure 13-6). Much of the mineral deposit is left behind to act as supporting posts or *pillars* to support the mine roofs. Tragically, miners are sometimes crushed under the weight of collapsing mine roofs in mining disasters. Whereas the room-and-pillar system is used for extracting nonsoluable minerals, *solution mining* is a technique for extracting salt, potash, and other underground soluble minerals. Specifically, hot water is pumped down an *injection well* to dissolve the mineral deposit. The mineral-rich solution is then pumped up an *extraction well* to the surface where the water is allowed to evaporate.

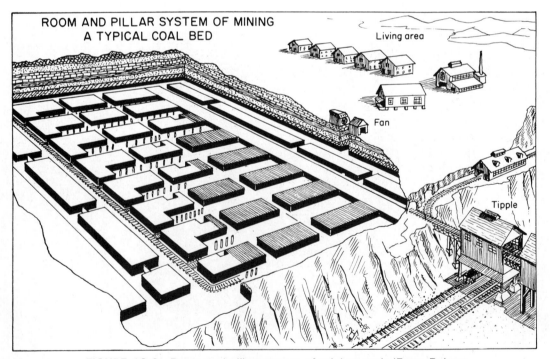

FIGURE 13-6 Room-and-pillar system of mining coal. (From Ruben L. Parson, *Conserving American Resources*, 3d ed. [Englewood Cliffs, N.J.: Prentice-Hall, Inc., 1972], p. 266.)

Seabed Mining

Although the great bulk of the nation's mineral resources comes from terrestrial mining, the last 35 years have seen a heightened interest in seabed mining. For example, in 1972, 80 percent of the nation's production of magnesium came from one company in Texas that used seawater as the raw material (Keller 1985). Although minerals can be obtained from seawater itself, most interest in seabed mining has to do with exploiting minerals on the continental shelf and deep-ocean floor.

Continental Shelf Minerals.   There is much interest in exploiting mineral deposits on the *continental shelf,* which is the submerged seaward extension of a continent. For example, phosphate deposits are mined on the continental shelf off North Carolina. However, terrestrial mining of phosphorite rock is preferred, since the seabed phosphate deposits are of a lower quality. Within the Hawaiian Archipelago, cobalt-rich manganese deposits have been found on the tops and flanks of its seamounts, or submarine mountains.

Deep-Ocean Floor Minerals.   In the last decade, there has been increasing interest in exploiting minerals on the ocean floor, particularly those minerals associated with (1) hydrothermal vents and (2) manganese nodules. *Hydrothermal vents* can be found at the Gorda Rise, a relatively unexplored seafloor ridge 161 km (100 mi) off the northern California and Oregon coasts. The Golda Rise stretches for over 322 km (200 mi) in a north-south direction. Geologists estimate that high-grade ore containing iron, copper, zinc, nickel, cobalt, silver, and a range of more exotic metals, such as molybdenum and vanadium, are present in these seabed ridges. Since the ridges are located over 4.8 km (3 mi) below the ocean surface, a new generation of *aquaminers* would have to be created—underwater robots that are controlled by computers in ships on the ocean surface. The prospect of mining this area is controversial, since according to some marine geologists, the United States is more likely to be mining the moon and the asteroid belt before mining is begun on the Gorda Rise.

An interesting aspect of the Gorda Rise is its formation. Marine geologists believe that the ridge is the juncture of two massive plates in the earth's crust, with the plates pulling apart at the rate of approximately 5 cm (2 in.) per year. As the plates separate, cold seawater infiltrates the rock fractures where it is superheated by molten volcanic rock. The hot seawater leaches minerals from the rock, rises because of convection, and then precipitates its mineral wealth on the ocean floor. Sulfide deposits (containing copper, zinc, iron, and trace elements of silver) settle near the vents, which are called *black smokers.* Other minerals take longer to cool and settle to the seabed, thereby providing a "rain of pure metal" for miles from the hypothermal vents.

In addition to the massive sulfide deposits associated with hypothermal vents, marine geologists have been fascinated for years with the prospect of mining *manganese oxide nodules,* which contain percentages of manganese (24 percent), iron (14 percent), copper (1 percent), nickel (1 percent), cobalt (0.25 percent), as well as several other vital minerals (Chiras 1985). Most nodules are the size of potatoes, though they may range in size from tiny grains to stones weighing hundreds of pounds (Figure 13-7). In most cases the nodules are discretely distributed, but in some locales they are welded together forming a continuous pavement. They are found at depths ranging from 3658 to 4572 m (12,000 to 15,000 ft). One of the most promising zones that has manganese nodules lies within the Clarion and Clipperton fracture zones southeast of Hawaii (Figure 13-8). Here, McKelvey and associates (1979) have estimated that the nodules contain more than 1.8 percent nickel, plus copper, not to mention the 30 to 40 percent manganese content—all of which are highly strategic metals. Mining of the nodules is technologically feasible, but the ore is currently not economically competitive with terrestrial sources.

FIGURE 13-7   Manganese nodules. (Photo by Florida State University, courtesy of the National Geophysical Data Center, Boulder, Colorado.)

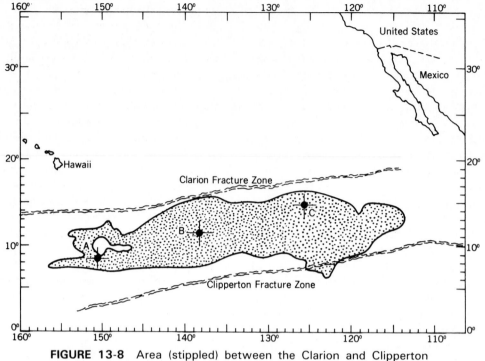

FIGURE 13-8 Area (stippled) between the Clarion and Clipperton Fracture Zones in which manganese nodules contain more than 1.8 percent nickel plus copper. (From Eugene N. Cameron, *At the Crossroads: The Mineral Problems of the United States,* p. 276. Copyright © 1986 by John Wiley & Sons, Inc.)

ENVIRONMENTAL IMPACT OF EXTRACTION AND PROCESSING

The environment bears a heavy price for the benefits that we enjoy from mineral consumption. The actual environmental impact depends upon such interrelated *physical* factors as topography, rock types, hydrologic conditions, and climate, and upon such *cultural* factors as the size of the operation, the mining techniques used, and the degree of environmental regulations imposed. Although there is some environmental impact in the mineral exploration stage (e.g., from exploratory drilling and gathering geological samples), the troublesome impact on land, water, air, and biological resources occurs at the latter stages of mineral extraction and mineral processing.

Impact of Extraction

Land Disruption and Abuse. Surface mining results in the most apparent environmental impact—that of land disruption and abuse. Approximately 0.25 percent of the total land area of the United States is disrupted by surface mines and quarries (Keller 1985). U.S. farmlands are gobbled up by surface min-

ing at a rate of approximately 80,940 ha (200,000 acres) per year (Miller 1986). In the Rocky Mountains, Owen (1985) reports that mining operations have degraded approximately 101,175 ha (250,000 acres) of wilderness beauty. Furthermore, the trend is for larger and larger surface mining operations, such as the Bingham Canyon copper mine in Utah. Keller (1985) notes that this is one of the world's largest mining operations, covering 8 km² (3 mi²) and extending 800 m (2624 ft) deep.

Soil Erosion and Sedimentation. Land scarring also produces other forms of environmental degradation, such as soil erosion. Soil erosion is intensified as a result of the elimination of soil-holding vegetation, the sculpturing of sheer cliffs susceptible to erosion, and the creation of mining waste piles that lie unprotected against rain and wind. According to Keller (1985), mining operations may increase sediment production by as much as 1000 times the natural rate. As streams fill with sediment, their ability to provide habitat for aquatic plants and animals is severely affected: Photosynthetic levels and concentrations of dissolved oxygen are reduced; stream temperatures are increased; fish-spawning sites are destroyed; and fish populations decline. (See Chapter 11 for further details.)

Water Pollution. Closely related to the problem of soil erosion and sedimentation is the concern over water pollution resulting from *acid mine drainage.* This phenomenon occurs when rainwater drains off abandoned mine wastes that are rich in sulfur compounds, thus producing sulfuric acid. This runoff then lowers the pH of streams, thereby acidifying and severely disrupting the aquatic ecosystem. In the United States, 60 percent of acid mine drainage comes from runoff originating on coal-mine wastes. In Appalachia alone, acid mine drainge runoff from coal-mine wastes accounts for the pollution of over 16,000 km (10,000 miles) of waterways (Moran et al. 1986). In addition to sulphuric acid, runoff can also carry dangerous levels of trace elements such as cobalt, copper, cadmium, lead, and molybdenum. When concentrated in water, soil, or plants, these trace elements, when consumed, can cause serious illness or even death.

Air Contamination. Finally, extracting minerals from the ground also adds to the problem of air pollution. When the vegetation is stripped from the land, winds sweep over the mine dumps adding large amounts of dust to the atmosphere. The most severe air contamination problems, however, result from the processing of minerals, which will be discussed in the following section.

Impact of Processing

Waste Accumulation. Since few mineral ores are more than 30 percent pure and some less than 1 percent, most mineral ores must go through a processing stage. One of the major environmental problems associated with mineral processing is what to do with the overburden and *tailings*—the waste product that remains after ore processing. These waste accumulations are usually found right at the mine site, since, ordinarily, large volumes of the ore-bearing rock must be processed and transportation of the ore to a processing plant would not be economically feasible. In the United States, it has been estimated that 7.4 metric tons of mine waste is generated per person each year. These stony, nutrient-poor waste piles make the landscape ugly, inhibit vegetation growth, and consequently are unattractive for wildlife. When the waste mounds are uranium tailings, such as at one time could be found in Colorado and other Western states, the mounds are downright dangerous. In the 1950s and 1960s, for example, radioactive tailings

were used by the construction industry in Grand Junction, Colorado. Over 5000 commercial buildings, schools, and homes were constructed with radioactive foundations (Owen 1985).

Air Pollution. In addition to radioactive waste piles and foundations that can increase the likelihood of lung cancer, the smelting of ores can release a variety of potentially lethal toxins. For example, arsenic and sulfur dioxide may be released when copper is processed, or cadmium may be released when zinc is smelted. Satellite photographs record the damaged vegetation resulting from toxic emissions, such as can be seen in Ducktown, Tennessee; Palmerton, Pennsylvania; and Sudbury and Wawa, Ontario (Cutter et al. 1985). In terms of human cancer death rates, arsenic smelter workers are three times as likely to come down with lung cancer, and cadmium smelter workers have twice the expected lung cancer rate (Miller 1986).

ENVIRONMENTAL REGULATION

The environmental decade of the 1970s heightened public concern about industries that damaged the environment. The mining industry was quickly identified as a major culprit that needed regulation. The type and degree of regulation imposed was often related to the type of ore sought after and the methods used to obtain it. Industries that extract nontoxic minerals such as sand, gravel, or crushed stone were less severely regulated than industries that mine and process ores that can produce toxic substances, such as those found in the sulfide ores. There are four major categories of environmental regulation that apply to the mining industries: (1) federal laws and international treaties, (2) leasing controls, (3) pollution and safety controls, and (4) land reclamation requirements.

Federal Laws and International Treaties

In 1970, the U.S. Congress passed the Resource Recovery Act. This act merely *encouraged* mining industries to carry out their activities in a less environmentally harmful manner. It did lay, however, the foundation for a stronger piece of federal legislation that was passed in 1977—the Surface Mining Control and Reclamation Act. In addition to regulating strip mining nationwide for the first time, this act established standards for leasing policy, for mining operations and safety, and for land reclamation. Aspects of the act related to leasing policy, mining operations and safety, and land reclamation will be discussed later. The first major regulation of deep seabed resources came in 1980 when Congress passed the Deep Seabed Hard Minerals Act. Under this act, the National Oceanic and Atmospheric Administration (NOAA) is authorized to not only license deep-sea mining operations but also to establish and promulgate rules related to environmental protection.

International efforts to regulate the mining industry are also underway. In 1982, 117 nations signed the United Nation's Law of the Sea Treaty. One of the main purposes of this law was to place deep-sea mining under international regulation. Unfortunately, 47 nations rejected the treaty, including the United States, England, West Germany, Belgium, Italy, and Japan. The Reagan administration rejected the treaty primarily because it believed that it would hinder American exploitation of ocean minerals. The Law of the Sea Treaty still faces an uphill battle. It was designed only to affect the ratifiers, and to date, only nine nations have ratified the treaty.

Dissatisfied with the progress and intent of the Law of the Sea Treaty, President Reagan in 1983 proclaimed an Exclusive Economic Zone (EEZ) extending 200 nautical miles offshore from U.S. coastal borders (Figure 13-9). As Cameron (1986) notes, President Reagan's EEZ policy is highly significant since it (1) opens 10,100,220 km^2 (3,900,000 mi^2) to exploration and development of mineral resources, an area equal to more than six times the present U.S. public domain; (2) guarantees *security of tenure* to U.S. mining organizations; and (3) places the management of mineral resources (including environmental regulation) in the hands of the National Oceanic and Atmospheric Administration and the Department of the Interior. Following the lead of the United States other countries quickly followed suit. Bernier (1984) reports that over 50 nations now have Exclusive Economic Zones. How strict enviriomental regulations will be enforced within these EEZs has yet to be seen.

Leasing Controls

Many federal and state laws use *leasing controls* to regulate mineral production. A case in point is the National Wilderness Act of 1964, which forbade new mineral leases in designated wilderness areas after 1983. Whereas the mining industry has long claimed that this has hindered mineral exploration, environmentalists have been quick to point out that only 25 percent of all public lands are off limits to mineral production, that Congress excluded major potential mineral production areas from the designated wilderness areas, and that Congress can open up wilderness areas for production in the case of a national emergency (Miller 1986).

When leases for mineral production are available, obtaining one is no easy task. A mining company must undergo an almost endless round of procedures, including the filing of the initial application for permits, taking part in public hearings, and preparing environmental impact statements. For example, the International Nickel Company began exploration in 1952. In 1975, the company determined that it had already spent $9 million dollars just on exploration, and that it would still have to get 31 permits from various federal and state agencies. In addition, public hearings and reports would have been required for each permit application. If all requirements had been met, it would have taken five years before mining could have begun. Consequently, they abandoned the project (Cameron 1986). Are all these procedures unnecessary *time costs* that discourage mineral exploration and production, as is contended by the mining industry, or are they merely *time requirements* that are necessary for good environmental management? One thing is certain: The controversy will continue for many decades.

Pollution and Safety Control

Mining industries are required by law to abide by various pollution and safety regulations. People in the mining industry often complain, however, that environmental regulations are not carefully designed or implemented. Barton (1980) cites the example of an environmental regulation that led to the closing of a lead-zinc mine in southwest Wisconsin. Effluent water from the mine contained, on average, about 2.5 parts per million (ppm) of zinc, approximately the same as the groundwater that drained into the mine. Although the Public Health Service recommended at the time a maximum of 5 ppm, the Environmental Protection Agency set 0.5 ppm zinc as the maximum allowable level coming from the mine. Instead of acceding to the requirement to lower the zinc content of its water effluent to what it considered an unreasonable level, the owners of the mine chose to close the plant. Likewise, between 1970 and 1980 eight zinc smelting plants were forced to close because environmental regulations could not be met. During this same period, zinc imports increased from 25 to 62 percent (Miller 1986).

In-depth studies by such organizations as the National Wildlife Federation (NWF) indicate that many of the pollution controls established by the 1977 Surface Mining Control and Reclamation Act are simply not being enforced. In 1985, for example, the

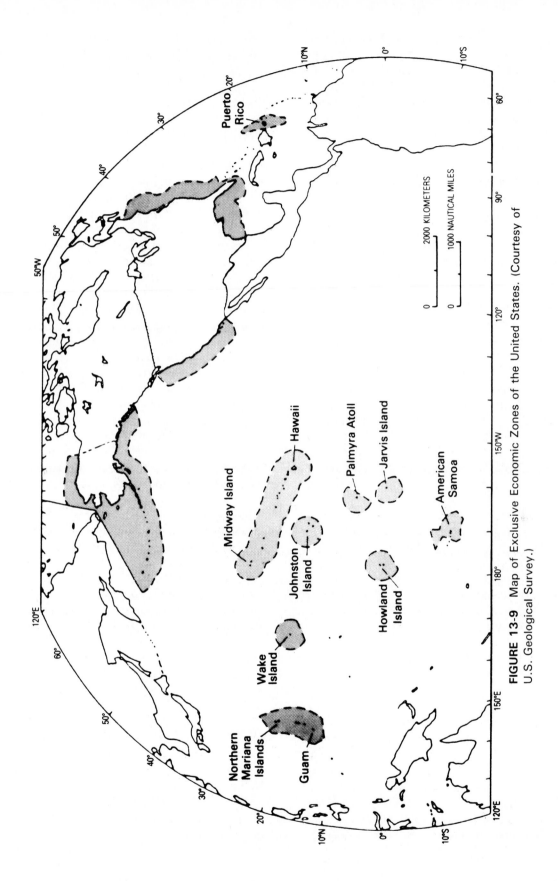

FIGURE 13-9 Map of Exclusive Economic Zones of the United States. (Courtesy of U.S. Geological Survey.)

NWF found that at least 6000 coal sites had been mined since 1977 without the legally required pollution controls. The federal Office of Surface Mining (OSM) did not bother to collect over $200 million in fines owed by law-breaking coal mining operators, and the rate of collection continued to drop. Between 1979 and 1983, 4000 coal operators were ordered to halt illegal mining, with over half ignoring the order. Such statistics have led the National Wildlife Federation and other conservation organizations to conclude that the federal Office of Surface Mining is riddled with poor management. Congressman Morris Udall, chairman of the House Interior and Insular Affairs Committee, has said the following about the OSM: "I cannot recall any time in my Congressional career when I have been faced with such overwhelming evidence of bureaucratic incompetence and dereliction of duty" (International Wildlife 1985, p. 26).

Land Reclamation Requirements

The 1977 Surface Mining and Reclamation Act provided the first real boost for the reclamation of surface-mined lands.

During the actual mining process, reclamation entails the use of various techniques such as terraces, sediment basins, and diversion dams to help control soil erosion and acid mine drainage. Once the mining operation is over, reclamation requires the grading of steep slopes, the replacing of topsoil, and the revegetation of the disturbed land with either annual or perennial vegetation, cultivated crops, or ponds and lakes. Commercial or natural fertilizers are sometimes applied if needed.

Unfortunately, not all lands that have experienced the detrimental effects of mineral extraction have been reclaimed. In a 1982 study by the Bureau of Land Management, W. Johnson and J. Paone recorded some rather startling statistics (Table 13-3). In the years between 1930 and 1980, 69 percent of the total area used by the mining industry was for surface mining, yet only 55 percent had been reclaimed. Furthermore, of the total land area utilized, only 47.4 percent had been reclaimed. The greatest percentage of reclaimed land was in the Midwest (Figure 13-10).

Why is so little land reclaimed? There are two major reasons: (1) lack of adequate environmental conditions, and (2) lack of specific legislation related to nonfuel mineral sites. Ninety percent of the nation's low-sulfur coal is produced in the arid and semiarid West, where environmental conditions are not adequate for current methods of land reclamation. Specifically, rainfall is often insufficient to reestablish vegetation; many scientists claim that 25.4 cm (10 in.) of annual rainfall is the minimum requirement for reclamation projects. Furthermore, the West has fewer plant species that are adaptable for such projects. In addition to inadequate environmental condi-

TABLE 13-3

Land used and reclaimed by the mining industry in the United States by area of activity (1930–1980)

AREA OF ACTIVITY[a]	UTILIZED, KM²	PERCENT OF TOTAL LAND UTILIZED	RECLAIMED, KM²	PERCENT RECLAIMED
Surface area mined (area of excavation only)	15,920	69%	8,735	55.0%
Area used for disposal of overburden waste from surface mining[b]	3,683	16%	1,910	52.0%
Surface area subsided or disturbed as a result of underground workings[c]	425	2%	24	5.6%
Surface area used for disposal of underground mine waste	770	3%	103	13.4%
Surface area used for disposal of mill or processing waste	2,242	10%	210	9.4%
Total[d]	23,067	100%	10,927	47.4%

Source: Keller, Edward A. 1985. *Environmental Geology.* 4th ed. Columbus, Ohio: Merrill.
[a]Excludes oil and gas operations.
[b]Includes surface coal operations for 1930–1971 only.
[c]Includes data for 1930–1971 only.
[d]Data may not add to totals shown because of independent rounding.

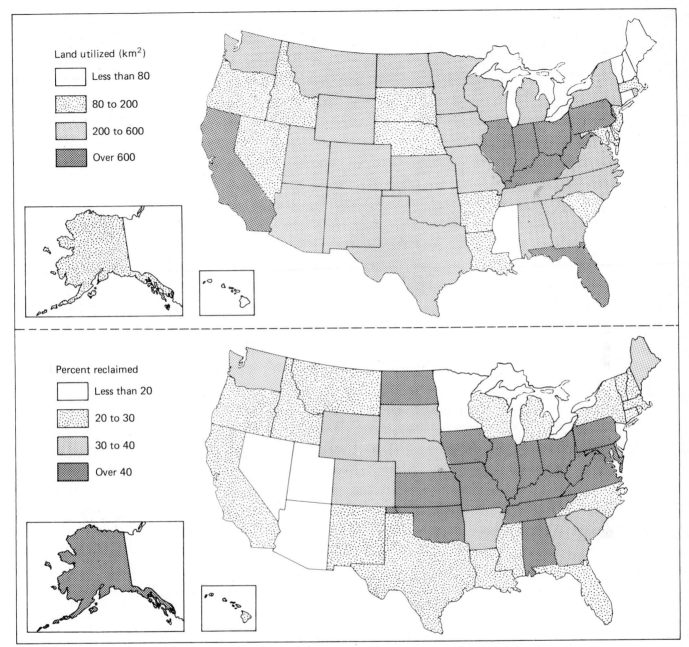

FIGURE 13-10 Geographic distribution of land mined and reclaimed from 1930 to 1980. (From Edward A. Keller, *Environmental Geology,* 5th ed. [Columbus, Ohio: Merrill, 1988], p. 378.)

tions for land reclamation, there simply are no federal laws that require reclamation of nonfuel mined lands, and if there are state laws, they are generally weak. Part of the explanation for this situation is that the public has put a higher priority on reclaiming areas that have been strip mined for coal.

To conclude this section, it is important to remember that mining operations occupy only a small percentage of the total land of the United States (Ta-

ble 13-4). In the western states, mining operations in each state do not exceed 0.2 percent of the area. Mining industries have used these figures to argue they are not "raping" the land, and, consequently, should not be singled out for stricter environmental regulations. Although it is true that mining operations do not occupy as much land as the National Wildlife Refuge System (35.9 million ha or 88.7 million acres) or the National Park Service (31.2 million ha or 77.0 mil-

TABLE 13-4

Land use in the United States in 1980

LAND USE	MILLIONS OF ACRES
Agriculture	
Cropland	413.0
Grassland pasture and range	985.7
Forest land grazed	179.4
Farmsteads, farm roads	10.9
Total, agriculture	1589.0
Wildlife refuge system	88.7
National park system	77.0
Urban and built-up areas	68.7
Forest Service wilderness	25.1
Highways (1978)	21.5
Mining	5.7
Airports (1978)	4.0
Railroads (1978)	3.0
Other	388.1
Total, all uses	2270.8

Source: Cameron, Eugene N. 1986. *At the Crossroads: The Mineral Problems of the United States.* New York: Wiley.

lion acres), one can hardly argue that wildlife refuges and parks disturb the land more than mining operations. Such industry arguments that are based on acreage mined do not justify the relaxation of pollution controls.

STATUS OF NONFUEL MINERALS

U.S. Reserves and Resources

General Status Report. We have examined the sources and availability of mineral ores as well as the difference between mineral resources and reserves. We have also described the major extraction techniques and their potential environmental impacts. And we have described efforts to regulate these operations. It is now time to assess the *mineral position* of the United States, that is, this country's ability to supply its mineral needs from its own resources.

First, there are those nonfuel minerals in which this country has *essentially no reserves* (Table 13-5). Examples of minerals in this category include such important minerals as manganese, cobalt, tantalum, aluminum, tin, and asbestos; and there are many more. These minerals exist in this country, but environmental, economic, or political reasons make it more desirable to import these materials. Note in Table 13-5 how the United States depends upon foreign sources that have the potential for political, economic, or military disruption.

Second, there are those nonfuel minerals for which the United States has a *reserve deficiency* (Table 13-5). In this case, U.S. reserves are significantly greater than in the above category, yet they are still deficient to meet this country's industrial needs. Examples in this category include mercury, silver, tungsten, zinc, and gold. For this category of minerals, the United States can rely on foreign sources that are politically, economically, and militarily more stable—nations such as Canada and Mexico.

Finally, the United States has certain mineral reserves and resources (both identified and undiscovered) that will be adequate well beyond the year 2000. Examples in this category include reserves of magnesium (a lightweight metal that can substitute for other metals), boron, titanium, and molybdenum, silicon, phosphorus, potash, and many, many more. (Boron, titaninum, and molybdenum are ferroalloys used with iron.) According to the U.S. Geological Survey, sand and gravel are the most important minerals besides oil located within 322 km (200 mi) of U.S. coasts. The USGS expects to find about 400 billion tons of these common constrution materials in the EEZ (Exclusive Economic Zone) proclaimed by President Reagan.

Strategic and Critical Minerals. The United States government is naturally concerned that someday some political organizations or mineral cartels may be formed that restrict the importing of minerals that are of strategic and critical importance for the U.S. military and industrial machine. According to the U.S. government, *strategic minerals* are those that are essential for military defense, but unfortunately must be imported from foreign sources. Such strategic minerals include chromium, manganese, cobalt, and platinum. As Cutter and associates (1985) have pointed out, it is an interesting twist of fate that much of the supply of strategic minerals to the United States currently comes from two nations that are often at odds with this country: the Soviet Union and the Republic of South Africa. To put it another way, over 50 percent of some 24 strategic minerals must be imported from other nations (Figure 13-11). This naturally has some military planners worried. *Critical minerals* are likewise important for national defense, but the U.S. has either some domestic supplies or the help of some friendly nations that can supply the needed materials in case of a national emergency. Nickel, copper, and vanadium fall under this classification. Over 30 minerals have been classified as either strategic or of critical importance to our nation. Uses for these minerals run the gamut from lead for car batteries, to copper for electrical wiring, to bauxite for construction, to silver for photography.

TABLE 13-5

Deficiency of U.S. reserves of selected nonfuel minerals. Foreign sources subject to potential interruption by political, economic, or military disruption are shown in lighter print.

	Commodity	Adequacy of U.S. Reserves for Cumulative U.S. Demand 1982–2000 (0 10 20 30 40 50 60 70 80 90 100%)	Major Foreign Source
Essentially No Reserves	Manganese		Gabon, Brazil
	Cobalt		Zaire
	Tantalum		Malaysia, Thailand, Canada
	Columbium		Brazil, Canada
	Platinum group		South Africa, USSR
	Chromium	~10%	USSR, South Africa
	Nickel	~10%	Canada, New Caledonia
	Aluminum	~10%	Jamaica, Australia
	Tin	~10%	Malaysia, Bolivia
	Antimony	~10%	South Africa, Bolivia
	Fluorine	~12%	Mexico, South Africa
	Asbestos	~20%	Canada, South Africa
	Vanadium	~20%	South Africa, Chile
Reserve Deficiency	Mercury	~30%	
	Silver	~40%	Canada, Mexico
	Tungsten	~45%	Canada, Bolivia
	Sulfur	~60%	Canada, Mexico
	Zinc	~68%	Canada, Mexico
	Gold	~72%	Canada, USSR
	Potash	~92%	Canada, Israel

Source: U.S. Geological Survey, 1984.

To help prevent shortages of strategic and critical minerals during wartime, the U.S. government has established a policy of *stockpiling*. The Strategic and Critical Materials Stockpiling Act of 1946 called for the purchase and storage of strategic and critical minerals. The policy called for the federal government to purchase enough materials to last three years in the event of war. In 1986, the United States was stockpiling 93 materials, 80 of which were nonfuel minerals (Miller 1986). For some materials, current procurement and stockpiling is at or over 100 percent of the required three-year supply; examples in this category would be manganese, diamonds, silver, tin, and tungsten. For various political and economic reasons, the United States has been less successful at procuring other minerals, such as copper, nickel, and vanadium (Van Rensburg 1986).

Tallies of U.S. mineral reserves and resources can help one understand this country's mineral posi-

tion, but as Cameron (1986) rightfully points out, such data represent only one element of the mineral position of the United States. To see the entire picture, one must also look at (1) the nation's capacity to smelt, refine, and process the mineral raw material, and (2) the nation's capacity for converting those products into finished goods. This would entail looking at the entire structure of the American mineral-based industry, which is beyond the scope of this chapter and book. Suffice it to say that determining a country's mineral position is extremely complex and any serious student of the problem can look forward to years of highly detailed analysis.

World Reserves and Resources

Determining the mineral position of the world is even a more difficult task (Leontief et al. 1983). Yet it must be done, since much of the U.S. nonfuel mineral sup-

*Traded as columbium.

FIGURE 13-11   The United States is dependent on 25 other nations for more than 50 percent of its supply of 24 strategic materials. (Reprinted with permission from *Chemical and Engineering News,* May 11, 1981, p. 21. Copyright 1981, American Chemical Society.)

ply comes from abroad. What follows is a brief discussion of the estimated global supply of nonfuel mineral resources and the problems that can occur when making estimations regarding depletion rates.

Status Report. In 1982, the U.S. Bureau of Mines estimated the world reserve base for important nonfuel mineral commodities. It unsurprisingly found that the global reserve base for some nonfuel minerals was *very large* (e.g., cement, lime, gypsum, and clay). In addition there were *large* supplies of other minerals (e.g., iron ore, phosphate rock, bauxite, potash). But there were *relatively small* supplies of others (e.g., tin, tungsten, mercury, cobalt) (Table 13-6). Keep in mind, however, that world estimates for some minerals are more accurate than for others. For example, are the figures provided by the underdeveloped countries (UDCs) as accurate as those provided by the generally more technologically sophisticated developed countries (DCs)? Are the figures on strategic minerals provided by Communist bloc countries as reliable as those provided by Western bloc nations? These and other questions complicate any at-

tempt to accurately estimate the world reserve base for nonfuel minerals.

Forecasting the future availability of world supplies of nonfuel minerals is even more complex. In Table 13-6, Cameron (1986) illustrates one forecasting method. If one takes the world reserve base as currently estimated for each commodity (Column A), and divides it by the figure for production (Column B), one gets what is called the Reserve Base/Production Index (RB/P) for each mineral. In this case, the RB/P index indicates how many year's supply (at the 1980 production rate) remains in the reserve base. Cameron rightfully concludes, however, that the RB/P index is limited in its usefulness. For example, it does not tell us at what rates a mineral can be produced in the future, nor does it tell us anything about the economic requirements needed for future production.

The issue with mineral resources is not so much one of actual extinction or exhaustion, but rather one of the cost of maintaining an adequate supply. One mines until the costs of mining exceed the value of the mineral. There are also social and cultural factors

TABLE 13-6

*World production, reserve base, and reserve base production index
for some important mineral commodities*

MINERAL	RESERVE BASE (THOUSANDS OF TONS)[a]	PRODUCTION 1980 (THOUSANDS OF TONS)[a]	RESERVE BASE PRODUCTION INDEX (RB/P)
Salt	∞	181,600	∞
Magnesium	∞	351	∞
Cement	Very large	978,000	Very large
Lime	Very large	131,623	Very large
Gypsum	Very large	78,290	Very large
Clays (common)[b]	Very large	449,000	Very large
Sodium carbonate	>43,200,000	8,459	>5,107
Sodium sulfate	5,100,000	2,169	2,351
Chromite	7,540,000	10,725	703
Potash	18,739,000	30,722	610
Vanadium	18,250	40	456
Manganese ore	12,000,000	29,000	414
Cobalt	9,200	33	279
Feldspar	>1,000,000	3,782	>264
Boron minerals	>300,000	1,175	>255
Phosphate rock	38,580,000	151,000	255
Bauxite	24,581,000	99,165	248
Ilmenite	905,000	3,979	227
Iron ore	231,056,000	1,090,432	212
Nickel	111,000	850	131
Fluorspar	645,000	5,000	129
Molybdenum	12,975	120	108
Antimony	5,175	74	70
Copper	562,000	8,421	67
Tungsten	3,813	60	63
Sulfur	2,976,000	56,900	52
Zinc	319,670	6,340	50
Talc and pyrophyllite	330,000	7,366	45
Mercury[c]	7,200	191	38
Lead	148,810	3,885	38
Barite	244,000	8,114	30
Asbestos	114,600	5,314	22
Tin	3,307	272	12

Source: Cameron, Eugene N. 1986. *At the Crossroads: The Mineral Problems of the United States.* New York: Wiley.

[a]Data from U.S. Bureau of Mines, *Mineral Commodity Summaries,* 1982 (production) and 1985 (reserve base).

[b]There are no data for world reserves of special types of clays.

[c]The standard unit for mercury is the flask, a flask being 76 lb. Numbers given are thousands of flasks.

that can put a nonfuel mineral in the category of *limited supply*, factors such as a nation's technological know-how, its degree of political stability, or its application of conservation and environmental protection measures.

Depletion Time and Depletion Curves. In addition to the RB/P index, mineral specialists use the concept of *depletion time* to help make forecasts. **Depletion time** is defined as the period required to consume 80 percent of the available (known or estimated) mineral supply. To illustrate depletion time, *depletion curves* are drawn that represent different sets of assumptions. In Figure 13-12, for example, depletion Curve A represents a *throwaway society*—one that mines, rapidly consumes products, and throws away resources. In this case, the hypothetical resource has a short lifespan. Curve B represents a *conserving society*—one that has moderate consumption and practices conservation techniques. With conservation has come an extended depletion time for the resource. Finally, Curve C represents a *conserving and recycling so-*

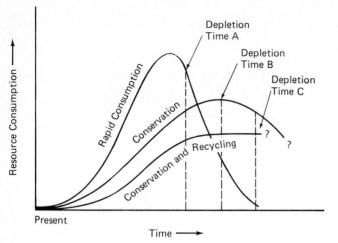

FIGURE 13-12 Depletion curves. (Adapted from Daniel B. Botkin and Edward A. Keller, *Environmental Studies: Earth as a Living Planet* [Columbus, Ohio: Merrill, 1987], p. 466.)

ciety—one that reduces consumption, reuses products, and recycles wastes. In this scenario, the resource's depletion time has been further extended.

The problem with depletion curves is that they are based on *assumptions*, not facts. If one assumes certain things will happen (e.g., that there will be new geological discoveries and technological breakthroughs), one might get an optimist scenario for the future. Or, if one assumes the development of certain negative factors (e.g., political instability; environmental contamination), one could get a pessimistic view of the future.

A good example is Goeller and Zucker's (1984) projected global population growth and demand for nonrenewable materials over the next century. They concluded that the world would not run short of any element before the year 2050. They clearly state, however, that their theory is based on several assumptions: (1) that society will continue to want a good supply of minerals at a reasonable cost, (2) that world population will not exceed 8.5 billion by the year 2100, (3) that science and technology will develop appropriate technological solutions, and (4) that world societies will develop along current lines (i.e., pastoralists will remain pastoralists, traditional agriculturalists will remain traditional agriculturalists, and so on). However, has science and technology always provided a technological fix to our problem? Do not traditional societies undergo cultural change? It should be clear from the above set of highly questionable assumptions that error could easily be introduced into their estimates. The bottom line: Always question the set of assumptions behind any depletion curve.

STRATEGIES FOR STRETCHING EXISTING MINERAL SUPPLIES

One thing that mineral forecasters do agree upon, however, is that demand for mineral resources will greatly increase in the future. Consequently, all nations must place a premium on stretching their existing mineral supplies as much as possible. There are five basic approaches to conserving mineral resources: (1) improving extraction techniques, (2) finding substitutions, (3) recycling materials, (4) practicing reuse and conservation, and (5) promoting exploration. The cost of many, if not most, of these techniques will raise the cost of mineral commodities and, consequently, consumer products, but the cost must be borne if future generations are to have an adequate supply of mineral resources and a healthy environment in which to live.

Improving Extraction Techniques

Over the last few decades there have been a number of new technologies developed that have allowed the extraction of low-grade mineral deposits—deposits that were once not economically feasible to mine. The low-grade deposits can then be stockpiled until demand or advanced technology warrants their use. Since 1900 the grade of copper ore has been reduced by a factor of ten—from 27.2 to 2.72 kg (60 to 6 lb) of copper per ton (Owen 1985). Moran and associates (1986) also note that when low-grade ores are recovered from old abandoned mines, there is a significant energy savings (a 20 percent savings in the case of copper extraction).

However, there are two basic limits to this strategy. First, many metals simply exist in the earth's crust in *concentrations too low* to make mining always economically feasible. For example, lead, nickel, and tin often occur in low concentrations. Second, the availability of cheap energy and water is a limiting factor. The mining industry has made great strides in its ability to extract low-grade ores, but it has been at the cost of an enormous consumption of energy and water—two of our nation's most precious natural resources. Consequently, other nonfuel mineral conserving strategies must also be employed.

Finding Substitutions

Substitution is a form of cultural adaptation wherein a society (1) uses more abundant minerals in place of less abundant ones, (2) uses a renewable resource as a substitute for a nonrenewable nonfuel mineral resource, or (3) develops a synthetic substitute for a natural material. We will now briefly look at these three types of substitution strategies.

Use of More Abundant Minerals. Examples of this first substitution strategy would be the use of aluminum and titanium in place of steel for airplanes and automobiles; the use of glass instead of tin-plated containers; glass fibers instead of copper wires in telephone cables; and magnesium instead of zinc in certain chemicals. Fortunately, many of our most abundant metals (e.g., iron, aluminum, titanium, and magnesium) can serve as substitutes for many scarcer metals. There is also a broad range of substitutes for some minerals. In certain applications, for example, chromium can be substituted with one of six different minerals—zinc, nickel, aluminum, molybdenum, titanium, or vanadium (Cameron 1986).

Use of Renewable Resources. The second substitution strategy is to replace a product designed from a nonrenewable mineral resource (e.g., aluminum or brick siding for home construction) with a product developed from a renewable forest (e.g., wood or plywood siding). Since it requires substantially less energy to produce wood than to extract mineral resources, much energy savings can be accomplished. Unfortunately, however, our nation's forests (including the wildlife in those forests) would then pay the price for switching to this renewable resource.

Use of Synthetic Materials. The final substitution strategy calls for the creation of synthetic materials to replace natural minerals. Plastics, for example, have now replaced many steel parts in houses and buildings. Furthermore, plastics are increasingly replacing other minerals (e.g., lead, zinc, and copper) in automobiles. In industry, synthetic diamonds and other abrasive materials are now beginning to replace natural diamonds. This third technique certainly fits the overall national trend of replacing natural products (e.g., natural fibers in clothes; natural rubber in tires) with synthetic products. If it is true that plastics and other synthetic products take substantially longer to *breakdown* (decompose) into the environment, then one must question the logic behind increasing our dependence on the synthetic substitution strategy.

Problems. Substitution as a conservation strategy, however, has additional limitations. First, critics contend that this strategy reinforces citizens' unrealistic faith in science and technology—a belief that a substitute can be found for any nonfuel mineral resource that is in short supply. Although this may prove someday to be true, there are currently certain materials that have no known substitute, such as the helium needed for low temperature refrigeration. Second, critics contend that substitutes are often of inferior quality. Nothing, for example, beats silver for photochemicals, gold for certain electrical components, or chromium in stainless steel. Finally, critics contend that synthetic products, such as plastics, are made up from minerals that are already in short supply, such as oil. As mentioned previously, discarded synthetic products also litter the landscape for longer periods of time. Substitution is definitely a useful conservation strategy, but it is clearly not a panacea for pending mineral shortages.

Recycling

A highly attractive means by which to stretch our existing supplies of mineral resources is recycling. **Recycling** can be defined as the recovery, reprocessing, and refabrication of metallic components from society's industrial discards. The United States alone generates more than 180 million metric tons of household and industrial solid waste each year (Botkin and Keller 1987). New Yorkers produce more solid waste per capita than any people in the world. New York City alone discards 24,000 tons of solid waste each year (Environmental Defense Fund 1985). Much of this is discarded "urban ore," since it contains materials that can be recycled or used to generate energy.

Advantages. There are numerous benefits to recycling, such as increasing the *residence time* of minerals (i.e., the time a mineral remains in use), while at the same time decreasing all of the following factors: the use of virgin resources, the amount of land disruption, the degree of air pollution, and the need for new landfill sites.

Enormous amounts of energy are also saved by recycling rather than processing virgin materials. For example, there is a 90 to 97 percent energy reduction when aluminum is manufactured from recycled aluminum (e.g., from an aluminum beverage can) as compared with when it is manufactured from bauxite (virgin aluminum ore) (Table 13-7). Citing a 1982 study of the U.S. steel industry, Moran and associates (1986) also note that there would be a 6 percent total energy savings in steel manufacture if steel were manufactured from scrap metal. That does not sound like much at first, but that energy savings amounts to 0.6 percent of the total U.S. energy use. Even more energy savings would be made if some materials were *reused* rather than refabricated. For example,

TABLE 13-7

Environmental benefits derived from substituting secondary materials for virgin resources

ENVIRONMENTAL BENEFIT	ALUMINUM	STEEL	PAPER	GLASS
		(percent)		
Reduction of energy use	90–97	47–74	23–74	4–32
Reduction of air pollution	95	85	74	20
Reduction of water pollution	97	76	35	—
Reduction of mining wastes	—	97	—	80
Reduction of water use	—	40	58	50

Source: Letcher, Robert Cowles, and Mary T. Sheil. 1986. "Source Separation and Citizen Recycling," in William D. Robinson, ed., The Solid Waste Handbook. New York: Wiley.

Miller (1986) notes that there are 80 billion throwaway beverage cans manufactured annually in the United States. If returnable bottles were used instead, enough energy would be saved to provide electricity for 13 million people annually. (See the "Reuse and Conservation" section for further details.)

One of the major successes in recycling can be seen in the recycling of the automobile. The discarded automobile is a prime example of an "urban ore" by virtue of its metal content of 89.5 percent (primarily steel, iron, aluminum, copper, lead, and zinc) and its nonmetal content of 10.5 percent (primarily rubber, glass, cardboard, and textiles). According to Davis (1972), nearly 90 percent of the millions of automobiles that are discarded in the United States annually are recycled. Since abandoned vehicles are a major problem in this country, imagine what the American landscape would look like if millions of abandoned vehicles were not dismantled by auto wreckers and their materials recycled!

An unusual example of recycling has begun in Palo Alto, California. Not too long ago it was discovered that the ash from the incineration of the city's sewage sludge contained large concentrations of copper (8000 ppm), silver (660 ppm), gold (30 ppm), and phosphorus (6.6 percent) (Gulbrandsen et al. 1978). Palo Alto is located in the heart of the "Silicon Valley," the nickname given to the Santa Clara Valley because of its large concentration of electronic and photographic industries. It is the waste from these industries that is the source of the gold, silver, and other urban ores to Palo Alto's sewage. The city currently has a contract with a private company to extract (recycle) these ores.

What is particularly attractive about recycling is its tremendous potential as a mineral conserving technique. Another example comes from the fertilizer industry. In the past, the fertilizer industry mined certain rocks for phosphate. It was later discovered that the mine tailings contained fluorine—a mineral required by chemical and metallurgical industries. The tailings, once considered a waste product, now contribute to more than half the domestic production of fluorine (Cameron 1986). History also indicates that the potential for recycling is great. As geographer Ruben Parson once noted (1972), nearly everything metallic was recycled during World War II to defeat Hitler's war machine, ranging from abandoned railroad tracks, to broken machinery, to tin cans. According to Miller (1986), currently only 10 percent of waste in the United States is recycled, whereas Japan and many European countries recycle 40 to 60 percent of their waste. Again, the potential for "waste as ore" or "trash as cash" is great.

Barriers. In the United States, recycling as a mineral conserving technique still has some obstacles to overcome. The first problem is one of *dispersion.* Discarded materials are distributed throughout the world and dumped in tens of thousands of locations. Consequently, the resource is often in *low concentration* and economically unfeasible to recover. Tungsten is an example of a material that is found in such low concentrations that it is simply cheaper to import the virgin mineral material from abroad. Only when the *low entropy ores* (concentrated ores) are depleted does it become economically feasible to recycle. Municipalities, however, are running out of solid waste disposal sites. As the problem intensifies, it will become more profitable to minimize waste through recycling, not to mention the associated environmental benefits of recycling.

A second obstacle to widespread recycling occurs during the manufacturing process. Some products are designed in a manner that it makes them uneconomical to recycle. Chiras (1985) used the example of the orange juice can, which is typically made of paper lined on the inside with foil and having top and bottom lids made of metal. Unfortunately, says Chiras, the lids are made up of two different alloys, thereby making them economically and technologically difficult to recycle effectively. By contrast, some products (e.g., aluminum cans and newsprint) are easy to recycle. Also at the manufacturing level there are obstacles to recycling, such as (1) using manufacturing processes that require virgin materials and (2) not considering the *real cost* of the product, which would affect the disposal costs of the product.

There are other obstacles to recycling, such as its sensitivity to economic fluctuations. In the early 1970s, for example, there was a metal recycling boom. Many small recycling centers developed and flourished. By 1975, however, an economic recession had set in and many of these same businesses declined—the recycling of zinc decreased by 27 percent, copper decreased by 30 percent, and stainless steel decreased by 43 percent (Moran et al. 1986). By 1976, however, the nation had experienced an economic recovery and so did the recycling industry.

In addition, there are the numerous institutional barriers to recycling. For example, the federal government provides millions of dollars worth of tax breaks and *depletion allowances* to mining industries to encourage the rapid extraction of virgin materials from the earth's crust. Since the recycling industry does not receive such subsidies, mining companies have an unfair economic advantage. Furthermore, the federal government hinders recycling industries by having them pay higher rates for trucking and rail cargo transportation of scrap materials. The mining industry pays lower rates for the transport of virgin mineral materials. In addition, many Americans are unwilling to recycle household goods such as glass bottles, aluminum cans, and newspapers. This negative attitude toward recycling only encourages the federal government to maintain cargo rates and other practices that discriminate against recycling. As Americans increasingly respect recycling as a mineral conserving technique, such federal discriminatory practices may disappear.

Despite the many obstacles to recycling as a mineral conserving technique, it remains *one of our most attractive strategies for the future*. It must be kept in mind, however, that even recycling is not a panacea to solve the continually rising demand and inevitable losses in mineral reserves. As Chiras (1985) has noted, 100 percent recycling of a given material is simply impossible; much is simply lost through inefficiencies in processing. Other mineral conserving techniques will also have to be practiced.

Reuse and Conservation

Closely associated with recycling is the concept of *reuse and conservation*. This is perhaps the most fundamental conservation technique since it is founded on the premise that Americans overconsume resources. With only 5 percent of the world's population, which inhabits only 6 percent of the global land area, the United States gobbles up 23 percent of the world's nonfuel mineral resources (Moran et al. 1986). It is no wonder that environmentalists call for conservation strategies that minimize the consumption of nonfuel mineral resources.

There are three basic approaches to reducing the consumption of nonfuel mineral resources: (1) increase product durability, (2) reuse products, and (3) practice general resource conservation. Manufacturers could build products that are more durable so that they will last longer. Refrigerators, stoves, washing machines, dryers, cars, and other products are often designed by manufacturers with *planned obsolescence* in mind, that is, they are intentionally designed to break down or wear out within short periods of time. For example, if automobiles were made twice as durable (and the technology is available to do this), the automobile industry's consumption of metals would be cut in half (Owen 1985). There is no question, however, that the selling price of the automobile would be substantially higher.

Much savings in mineral resources (both nonfuel and fuel) would be realized if people practiced *reuse*, that is, the use of a product for a second time without any refabrication of the material. The returnable bottle is the classic example. Despite the fact that it takes three times more energy to recycle (crush and remelt) a glass bottle as it does to reuse (clean and refill) it, 80 percent of this country's beverage containers are "disposable" (nonreturnable) bottles and cans (Miller 1986).

Finally, environmentalists praise *general resource conservation* as an ecologically sound strategy to stretch nonfuel minerals and other natural resources. There would be tremendous savings in nonfuel mineral resources if we simply eliminated some wasteful practices that are unnecessary for maintaining a high standard of living. For example, some American households have a radio and television set in every bedroom and a car for every person in the family. Is this level of energy and matter consumption necessary? Must the ideal American kitchen have every electrical device imaginable? Is it really necessary to have a vacation (second) home in the mountains or a beach house on the coast? When is enough, enough?

Exploration

Despite general resource conservation, recycling, and the other techniques to stretch our mineral supplies, further exploration and mineral discovery will be necessary to sustain this nation. As Cameron (1986, p. 187) has said, "Unless mineral deposits can be discovered, there will be nothing to conserve." Unfortunately, most of the easily recognizable and accessible deposits (e.g., the Mesabi Range iron deposits in Minnesota and the Comstock silver lode in Nevada) have already been discovered in this country. Consequently, future exploration will be more difficult and costly. Since much of Asia, Africa, and Latin America have yet to be explored for mineral deposits, there is promise that their territories will yield some interesting discoveries.

For the last 150 years, the primary mineral explorer in this country has been the U.S. Geological Survey. Various state geological organizations, special agencies (e.g., the Department of Energy and the Tennessee Valley Authority), mining industries, and university geologists and geophysicists have also participated in mineral exploration. Despite all this intensive investigation, 50 percent of this country has yet to be mapped in sufficient detail to provide enough adequate knowledge for mineral exploration. Since our information of the earth's crust is incomplete, there is a good chance that new mineral discoveries will be made as we learn more about our world. Some American scientists are already making plans to mine the moon. In 1985, a NASA advisory group recommended that the United States establish a permanent lunar base early in the next century. One of its purposes would be to mine the moon and the asteroids for materials that can help space travel. It was suggested, for example, that the lunar miners extract liquid oxygen and hydrogen from lunar soil to fuel spacecraft, use moon dust to make cement, and mine metals such as iron and nickel.

As one can easily imagine, there are several drawbacks to exploration as a mineral conservation strategy. Mineral exploration is a financially risky venture, even without embarking upon the grandiose schemes of lunar exploration. As Moran and associates (1986) have aptly demonstrated, only 100 out of every 10,000 potential sites where a deposit might exist will merit the high cost of exploratory mining. Of those 100 exploratory sites, only one is likely to end up as a productive mine.

Low concentrations of many minerals also dis-

courages exploration. For example, it is believed that seawater contains an inexhaustible supply of such minerals as zinc, sodium chloride, uranium, tin, molybdenum, nickel, copper, and cobalt. Yet to extract just 0.003 percent of the yearly U.S. consumption of zinc from seawater, one would have to process a volume of water equivalent to the combined annual flow of the Hudson and Delaware rivers (Miller 1986). Such low concentrations lead to high energy input and exorbitant costs in dollars.

Those who wish to expand mineral exploration are also up against environmentalists and members of the general public who fear additional land abuse, pollution, and loss of landscape aesthetics that would result from heightened mineral exploration. Although admitting that mineral exploration can create environmental havoc if not properly monitored, people in the mining industry feel that locking exploration out of 65 percent of U.S. public lands (e.g., the national parks, the wildlife refuges, and the national forests) is excessive and discriminates against the mining industry (Owen 1985).

PROSPECTS FOR THE FUTURE

Intensification of Existing Problems

Nonfuel mineral production in the United States faces numerous problems. Two problems, in particular, are likely to intensify: (1) the problem posed by increased demand for nonfuel mineral resources and (2) the problem posed by mineral exploration that is in conflict with efforts to protect the environment.

Increased Demand. The U.S. mineral position is already weak with regards to numerous metals and is likely to become weaker through the year 2005 as a result of increased demand. In one study of 18 of our most important nonfuel mineral resources, it was projected that demand for those resources would increase by 3 percent per year, thereby doubling within 23 years (Chiras 1985). On a global scale, says Chiras, the world will consume three to four times more nonfuel resources between 1980 and 2000 (in just 20 years) than were consumed previously in all of human history. Although projections of future rates of mineral demand will vary, there is little question that increased demand for nonfuel mineral resources is one of the major problems facing the United States and the world.

Increased Conflict. As the demand for nonfuel mineral resources increases, exploration and development of the earth's mineral resources will likely intensify, thereby heightening the conflict between the mining industry and those concerned principally with environmental protection. Already, the mining industry maintains that the U.S. conservation movement has (1) severely restricted mining access to lands in the public domain, (2) placed unnecessary administrative rules and regulations on lands that are legally open to exploration, and (3) added exorbitant costs to mining exploration and development for the purpose of environmental protection. The net result, claims the mining industry, is that the protection of wilderness areas, wild and scenic rivers, and wildlife refuges has a higher priority for the U.S. public than the exploration for metal and other nonfuel mineral resources. As Cameron (1986) has noted, the withdrawal of lands from exploratory mining in Alaska protected the last great "wilderness frontier" (as perceived by the environmentalist) but eliminated the miner's last great "mineral frontier" in America.

Positive Signs and Success Stories

Despite the gloom and doom that is usually associated with the future of mineral resources in this country, there are some signs that give reason for hope. In recent years, for example, there have been major improvements in the areas of recycling, environmental abuse reduction, federal defense of public lands, product design, and exploration.

1. *Recycling is coming of age.* With landfills overflowing, many cities are now rushing to develop large-scale, sophisticated systems for recycling materials. In 1987, for example, city officials in San Jose, California, voted to spend $1.8 million for a weekly curbside recycling program of household metals, glass, and newsprint in an effort to recycle 36 percent of the city's garbage by 1991 (Figure 13-13). While San Jose's curbside recycling program is based on voluntary participation, other cities and states have

FIGURE 13-13 (upper) Recycling truck in San Jose, California. (lower) City employee tosses newspapers in newspaper section at back of recycling truck. (Courtesy of City of San Jose, California.)

established mandatory systems. In 1987, New Jersey became the first state in the nation to have a mandatory recycling law. According to this recent law, the state's 567 communities will be expected to recycle 25 percent of their waste within the next two years. Other cities and states are looking to establish mandatory recycling programs. Recycling analysts estimate that the city of San Francisco could make $23 million a year by recycling 50 percent of its waste through a mandatory program. The city currently spends $20 million annually to truck its garbage 97 km (60 mi) away to another county.

Whereas the 1970s recycling scenario was played out by a few environmentally conscious individuals hoping to improve the quality of the nation's forests, air, and land resources, today's recycling scenario is played out by large cities hoping to avert a garbage crisis. Regardless of the motive, however, the amount of trash America generates almost promises to make recycling as common here as it is in Japan and Holland.

2. *Environmental abuse reduction.* Largely because of public pressure and environmental legislation, the mining industry has made some strides in cutting back on the environmental abuses for which it was noted in the 1960s and early 1970s. In a few cases, the bitter confrontations of the past have been replaced by peaceful collaboration between the mining industry, environmental groups, and state and federal regulatory agencies. For example, Wells (1985) discusses the unusually cooperative spirit that went into the planning of Chevron Resources' phosphate mining operation north of Vernal, Utah. Both mining officials and Utah's Division of Wildlife called for the reclamation of the mined land so that it could eventually become a state wildlife refuge. More constructive collaborations of this kind are needed if conflicts are to be avoided. Sometimes, however, the only way to resolve a conflict is to go to court.

3. *Federal support of public lands.* Recently, the federal courts seem to be ruling in favor of environmental protection. In 1986, a federal court upheld the U.S. Interior Department's refusal to grant leases for phosphate mining in the Osceola National Forest in Florida. The court agreed with the Interior Department and the National Wildlife Federation that the mining companies would not be able to restore the proposed mined area to its original purposes—conservation of timber and watersheds.

In 1987, just one year later, an even more significant federal court decision was passed regarding the beautiful Big Sur region in California. Acting under the 1872 Mining Act, a mining family had staked 32 mining claims in the Los Padres National Forest. The family intended to mine limestone from the scenic peaks that overlook the California coast. In 1981, the U.S. Forest Service had given the family permission to start mining the area. Two years later, however, the California Coastal Commission informed the family that it would have to cease work, since the property was inside the five-mile coastal strip designated for special environmental protection. The family filed suit, contending that the state had no right to impose its standards on federal lands. After a series of lower court battles, the U.S. Supreme Court reversed the decision of the U.S. 9th Circuit Court of Appeals in San Francisco (*California Coastal Commission* v. *Granite Rock Company*, 85-1200). It concluded that the state of California could impose its own stricter environmental regulations on the site.

This is probably the most important state-federal decision concerning federal lands that has been made in the last decade. The ruling clears the way for state officials to enforce strict regulations on federal land where they believe the federal government has been lax. This is a very significant development considering how much land is held by the federal government. The federal government owns 44 percent of the land in California and nearly one-third of the land nationwide. As one might suspect, local conservation agencies are delighted with this recent decision.

4. *Products are being made more durable and are miniaturized.* Industrialists are begining to make products that are smaller, last longer, and consequently utilize less mineral resources. Industry is already adapting automobiles, calculators, computers, refrigerators, ovens, and other "American necessities" to the pending mineral-scarce world. Although the size and weight of the automobiles of the late 1980s is slightly greater than the size and weight of those built in the 1970s, Americans are not likely to return to the gas guzzling, oversized automobiles of the 1950s and 1960s. It is also unlikely that Americans will return to the giant computers or bulky Burroughs adding machines of the 1950s, or return to other products that have now been miniaturized as a result of the invention of the microchip. As America's mineral resources become scarcer, this trend toward product durability and miniaturization will probably continue—a trend that conserves mineral resources.

5. *New exploration techniques are being discovered.* In recent years, there have been a number of new tools, concepts, and approaches to mineral exploration. Remote sensing (the use of orbiting satellites, infrared film, radar sensing devices, etc.) has greatly aided geologists in selecting exploration sites. New knowledge of the mechanics of plate tectonics (the movement of the earth's crustal plates) has forced geologists to question previous theories on the formation of mineral deposits.

In 1986, the U.S. Geological Survey reported that geologists are now even using trees to prospect for valuable metals. Scientists recently found that young spruce, fir, and pine trees absorb approximately 30 different elements, including a number of valuable metals, through their roots and transport them to their needles. By analyzing the leaves of these trees, scientists can get a reliable picture of the metals present in the ground below.

6. New mineral deposits have been found. Some of the previously mentioned techniques are beginning to pay off in actual mineral discoveries. In 1984, for example, U.S. scientists discovered undersea deposits of cobalt that were twice as rich as previous concentrations found in the Pacific Ocean. The deposits are located between the Hawaiian Islands and American Samoa, a region designated by President Reagan for mineral development by the United States. What is particularly significant about this discovery is that the United States previously had no domestic source for cobalt. Cobalt is classified as a strategic metal, since it is used for welding, alloys, magnetic materials, and for hardening armor plate.

ACTION FOR NONFUEL MINERAL RESOURCES

If this country is to meet its future nonfuel mineral resource demands, it is going to take personal commitment on the part of each and every American citizen. Here are several ways in which you can personally get involved:

1. Demand a continual evaluation of the mining industry and its regulators. Both the mining industry and its regulators must be constantly monitored for inefficiencies and policies that allow unnecessary environmental abuse. In 1985, for example, the National Wildlife Federation demanded a comprehensive evaluation by Secretary of the Interior Donald Hodel of the management and policies of the Office of Surface Mining. Keeping similar pressure on the mining industry and its regulators helps to encourage responsible mining.

2. Call for changes in institutional and industrial procedures. Tax breaks and depletion allowances that encourage primary production at the expense of recycling need to be modified or eliminated. Industries need to simplify, and, where possible, to standardize the specifications for certain materials, for example, standardizing the composition of the alloys in automobile parts. This would make recycling easier and less expensive, since it would eliminate the problems presented by a multiplicity of specifications. Call for governments and institutions at all levels to require the purchasing and use of recycled products. For example, recycled paper can be used for tax forms, reports, and laws; recovered rubber can be used in the paving of public roads; and re-refined oil can be used in government vehicles. It is important to get governments involved because of the high volume of their purchases. By creating a large market demand for recycled products, the price per unit will decrease, thus reducing costs for all. Imagine how much paper would be saved if all our elementary schools, high schools, colleges, and universities recycled paper!

Since superfluous packaging further complicates waste management and recycling, it is important that you put public pressure on the packaging industry to develop their products with waste reduction and energy efficiency in mind. You can help do this by not buying products that are overly packaged.

3. Support state bottle bills. In 1972, Oregon pioneered a state law requiring a deposit on beverage containers. Eventually, New York, Vermont, Maine, Michigan, Connecticut, Iowa, and Massachusetts followed suit. Within just two years of the implementation of a deposit law in New York, for example, $19 million was saved on solid waste disposal costs, $50 million was saved in clean-up expenditures, and $50 to $100 million was saved on energy; net employment also increased by 3800 jobs (Pollock 1987). If your state does not already have a deposit law, you can work towards the passage of a *bottle bill*. If it does, you could still work toward the creation of a national deposit law that would help states draw up uniform policies.

4. Support bills that limit or ban some plastics. Since plastics are not biodegradable, lawmakers in at least seven states have introduced bills to limit or ban some plastics products, such as plastic disposable diapers, plastic tampon applicators, and numerous plastic fast-food containers. Frustrated by the proliferation of new plastic products, West Germany and Denmark have already taken steps to ban certain plastic items. Other governments are placing taxes on these so-called one-way containers. Your support of this type of legislation is needed.

5. *Support stricter air and water pollution regulations.* As noted earlier, the recycling of mineral resource materials (e.g., scrap steel and scrap aluminum) reduces air and water pollution. Generally speaking, the stricter the environmental regulations on industry, the more economically feasible recycling becomes. Consequently, you can help recycling become economically feasible by calling for stricter pollution controls.

6. *Encourage higher landfill fees.* It is estimated that more than half of the landfill sites in the United States will be filled by the year 1990 (Pollock 1987). Part of the problem is that many of these sites still have fees that are artifically low. By encouraging higher landfill fees, solid waste collection agencies and private solid waste haulers will have greater incentive to incorporate salvage and recycling strategies into their normal pick-up service.

7. *Support associated research and development.* You can lend your support to the research and development associated with new techniques of mineral exploration and processing, and with the utilization or disposal of mineral waste. Much research, for example, needs to be done in the field of plastics recycling. In order for plastics to be recycled, manufacturers will have to be able to identify one plastic resin from another. Until such a plastic identification system is developed, manufacturers will not recycle the scrap (Letcher and Sheil 1986). The recycling of plastics is critical since the percentage of plastics in U.S. municipal landfills has nearly doubled in the last 10 years, constituting approximately 8 percent of the total volume (Pollock 1987).

8. *Reduce the energy and matter flow through your lives.* Finally, you can help the mineral resource picture by cutting back on your own demand for these resources. Buy used, reconditioned (recycled) products when possible. Avoid energy and mineral guzzling gadgets for the home. Choose returnable bottles over recyclable aluminum. *Whether a home, a car, or some other ''necessity,'' maintain a preference for small over large, used over new, efficient over inefficient, renewable over nonrenewable.* Of course, also question what you consider to be life's necessities. As Tolstoy and others have suggested, *changing the world first begins by changing one's personal behavior.*

In summary, the above recommendations will help America move toward a recycling society. According to Pollock (1987, p. 121), ''the countries that make the transition to a recycling society most quickly and smoothly will have the healthiest environments and the strongest economies.'' Only a few would disagree.

DISCUSSION TOPICS

1. Describe the four basic processes by which a mineral deposit is formed.

2. What is the difference between a mineral resource and a mineral reserve? How can mineral reserves expand? How can they shrink? In recent years, have mineral reserves in the United States increased or declined? How can this trend be explained? Is this trend likely to continue?

3. Describe the three types of surface mining. Since surface mines cover less than 0.5 percent of the total land surface of the United States, the mining industry maintains that federal and state officials overregulate their industry in comparison to others that use much larger sections of territory. Debate the industry's argument and the environmentalist's reply.

4. Why has there been increased recent interest in hydrothermal vents and manganese nodules? Discuss the technical, economic, political, and ethical problems associated with mining these resources.

5. What are the environmental impacts associated with surface mining, subsurface mining, and seabed mining? How might dredging for manganese nodules affect the economics of the fisheries in the Pacific Northwest?

6. Describe the multitude of problems associated with creating a Law of the Sea Treaty. How does the Law of the Sea Treaty relate to President Reagan's policy of Exclusive Economic Zones?

7. Describe the physical and cultural barriers to land reclamation. How might these barriers be overcome?

8. What is the status of nonfuel minerals in the United States? Why is it so difficult to predict? Do we have enough supplies of strategic and critical minerals? Debate the issues related to stategic minerals, importation policies, and national security.

9. Draw a diagram illustrating the concept of depletion time. Use three depletion curves, each representing a different set of assumptions.

10. Discuss the advantages and disadvantages of the following methods of stretching our current mineral reserves: (1) improved extraction techniques, (2) substitution, (3) recycling, (4) reuse and conservation, and (5) exploration.

11. List and discuss six positive signs associated with the future of mineral resources in this country. Would mineral industrialists see all of these as "positive signs"? What additional positive (or negative) indicators do you see?

12. List several ways in which individuals can help this country meet its future nonfuel mineral resource demands. Which items are you already doing? Which items are you likely to do under the right circumstances? Which items are you unlikely to ever do?

13. Using a topographic map of your region, identify the mining quarries marked by the U.S.G.S. Which sites are still in operation? Visit and photograph the sites. Identify the mining techniques used. Record the sites various environmental impacts. What local, state, or federal agencies regulate the site? Is the land scheduled for reclamation after the mining operation closes?

14. A number of mining quarries are located adjacent to or directly within urban areas. How might urban planners make better use of abandoned quarries or sand and gravel pits?

15. Debate the ethical questions related to mineral exploration, processing, and consumption. For example, the United States has less than 6 percent of the world population yet consumes approximately 20 percent of the world's nonfuel mineral resources. Is this immoral?

READINGS

BARTON, P. B. 1980. "Public Perspectives of Resources," *Economic Geology*, vol. 233, no. 12, pp. 25–29. Includes good discussion of the reasons for mine closures that are related to the cost of environmental regulations.

BERNIER, L. 1984. "Ocean Mining Activity Shifting to Exclusive Economic Zones," *Engineering and Mining Journal*, vol. 185, no. 7, pp. 57–60. Good historical account of recent trend toward the establishment of EEZs.

BOTKIN, DANIEL B., and EDWARD A. KELLER. 1987. *Environmental Studies: Earth as a Living Planet*. Columbus, Ohio: Merrill. General introductory textbook in environmental studies. Contains brief chapter on mineral resources.

CAMERON, EUGENE N. 1986. *At the Crossroads: The Mineral Problems of the United States*. New York: Wiley. Excellent book representing the mineral industrialist's point of view. A must for anyone serious about studying America's mineral problems.

CHIRAS, DANIEL D. 1985. *Environmental Science: A Framework for Decision Making*. Menlo Park, Calif.: Benjamin/Cummings. A good basic university textbook in environmental studies.

CUTTER, SUSAN L., et al. 1985. *Exploitation, Conservation, Preservation: A Geographic Perspective on Natural Resource Use*. Totowa, N.J.: Rowan and Allanheld. A spatial approach to resource management.

DAVIS, F. F. 1972. "Urban Ore," *California Geology*, May, pp. 99–112. Good description of the discarded automobile as *urban ore*—an urban waste product that becomes a valuable resource.

ENVIRONMENTAL DEFENSE FUND. 1985. *The Economic Advantages of Recycling Over Garbage Incineration in New York City*. New York: Environmental Defense Fund. Good case study.

GOELLER, H. E., and A. ZUCKER. 1984. "Infinite Resources: The Ultimate Strategy," *Science*, February, pp. 456–62. Technical analysis of America's mineral situation.

GULBRANDSEN, R. A., et al. 1978. *Gold, Silver, and Other Resources in the Ash of Incinerated Sewage Sludge at Palo Alto, California—A Preliminary Report*. Washington, D.C.: U.S. Geological Survey Circular 784. Excellent example of the concept of *urban ore*.

International Wildlife. 1985. Vol. 15, no. 6, November–December, p. 26.

JOHNSON, W., and J. PAONE. 1982. *Land Utilization and Reclamation in the Mining Industry, 1930–1980*. Washington, D.C.: U.S. Bureau of Mines, Information Circular 8862. Excellent statistical summary.

KELLER, EDWARD A. 1985. *Environmental Geology*, 4th ed. Columbus, Ohio: Merrill. Contains an excellent chapter that emphasizes the geological aspects of mineral resources. Also see later editions.

KRAUSKOPF, K. 1967. *Introduction to Geochemistry*. New York: McGraw-Hill. Includes excellent analysis of the composition of the earth's crust.

LEONTIEF, W., et al. 1983. *The Future of Nonfuel Minerals in the U.S. and World Economy*. Lexington, Mass.: Lexington Books. Nicely illustrates the complexities of mineral forecasting.

LETCHER, ROBERT COWLES, and MARY T. SHEIL. 1986. "Source Separation and Citizen Recycling." In William D. Robinson, ed., *The Solid Waste Handbook*, pp. 215–258. New York: Wiley. Good discussion of the problem of recycling plastics.

MCKELVEY, V. E., et al. 1979. "Manganese Nodule Resources in the Northeastern Equatorial Pacific." In J. J. Bischoff and D. Z. Piper, eds., *Marine Geology and Oceanography of the Pacific Manganese Nodule Province*, pp. 747–762. New York: Plenum. Good summary.

MILLER, G. TYLER. 1986. *Environmental Science: An Introduction*. Belmont, Calif.: Wadsworth. Basically Miller's *Living in the Environment* (1985) textbook, minus the chapters on economics, politics, and ethics.

MORAN, JOSEPH M., et al. 1986. *Introduction to Environmental Science*. 2d ed. New York: Freeman. Excellent introductory environmental science textbook, which stresses scientific principles and the natural functioning of the environment.

NEBEL, BERNARD J. 1981. *Environmental Science: The Way the World Works.* Englewood Cliffs, N.J.: Prentice-Hall. Standard introductory textbook.

OHLE, E. L. 1975. "Economic Geologists, SEG, and the Future," *Economic Geology,* vol. 70, pp. 612–622. Contains good graphics on total area occupied by mining operations in the United States.

OWEN, OLIVER S. 1985. *Natural Resource Conservation: An Ecological Approach.* 4th ed. New York: Macmillan. Contains good chapter on mineral resources, emphasizing relationships to biological systems.

PARSON, RUBEN L. 1972. *Conserving American Resources.* 3d ed. Englewood Cliffs, N.J.: Prentice-Hall. Classic resource management textbook written in the geographical tradition.

POLLOCK, CYNTHIA. 1987. "Realizing Recycling's Potential." In Lester R. Brown et al., eds. *State of the World 1987.* New York: Norton. Comprehensive article on the advantages, barriers, and potential of recycling.

U.S. BUREAU OF MINES. 1975. *Mining and Minerals Policy.* Washington, D.C.: Government Printing Office. Annual report of the secretary of the interior.

U.S. BUREAU OF MINES and U.S. GEOLOGICAL SURVEY. 1981. *Principles of a Resource: Reserve Base Classification for Minerals.* Washington, D.C.: U.S. Geological Survey. Important report.

VAN RENSBURG, W. 1986. *Strategic Minerals.* Englewood Cliffs, N.J.: Prentice-Hall. Comprehensive source.

WELLS, H. 1985. "Expansion at Vernal," *Chevron Focus,* January–February, pp. 1–5. Discusses cooperative effort at Chevron Resource's phosphate-mining operation in Vernal, Utah.

■ 14 ■

CONSERVATION AND RENEWABLES: THE SOFT ENERGY PATH

*There is a time for everything, and wisdom is to
know what is appropriate for our times, what to
take forward and what to leave behind.*
           Warren Johnson, Geographer (1985)

On January 2, 1989, the editors of *Time* magazine
broke a long-standing tradition—the tradition of de-
voting the new year's first edition to the "Man or
Woman of the Year." In the opinion of the magazine's editors, one subject was so pressing that it had
to be again brought to national and international attention, and that subject was the state of planet
Earth. Consequently, "Planet of the Year: Endangered Earth" was their cover story. The *Time* report
reminded us of how the world's scientists are now
becoming increasingly concerned about the possibly
negative consequences of the so-called *greenhouse effect,* such as warmer temperatures, rising seas, shoreline erosion, droughts, and the deteriorating ozone
layers in Earth's atmosphere and the accompanying
increase in cancer-causing doses of ultraviolet light
which that will cause. Even the conservative U.S. Environmental Protection Agency now forecasts major
greenhouse effects. The magazine went on to discuss
the serious problems of the deteriorating forests, the

loss of genetic diversity, the accumulating waste
products, and the need for radical changes in the way
that humans, particularly Americans, do things—including how we grow our food, construct our residential and commercial buildings, and design our
systems of transportation.

An underlying major cause of many of the problems has to do with the *types* of energy we have selected to use, with the *methods* that we utilize to capture that energy, and with our wasteful *use* of that
energy once we have obtained it. For a general review
of America's energy situation, and a discussion of the
pros and cons of various nonrenewable and renewable energy sources, several excellent introductory
textbooks in environmental studies cover the subject,
such as Owen (1985), Miller (1988), and Moran and
associates (1986). For greater historical depth on the
energy debate, consult Melosi (1987), Blackburn
(1987), and the World Commission on Environment
and Development (1987). The annual reports of the

U.S Energy Information Administration, such as their publication *Energy Facts 1987,* are a good source for keeping up on the ever-changing figures on U.S. energy production and use.

The purpose of this chapter, however, is not to condense or review previous studies. Rather, unlike the previous chapters in this book, this chapter takes the stand that an energy future dominated by fossil fuels and nuclear energy is a draconian bargain, that *it is time to stop the energy debate and accept the notion that energy conservation along with renewable energies are the only viable alternatives if we want a healthy, sustainable planet.* Although renewables will be briefly discussed at various points, the key focus of this chapter will be energy conservation.

DEFINITIONS AND BENEFITS

The simplest, cheapest, and greatest energy resource in the United States is **energy conservation.** By energy conservation, we mean (1) *reducing energy use* (e.g., turning off unneeded lights, turning down the furnace thermostat or air conditioner, and walking more and driving less) and (2) *increasing energy efficiency* (e.g., developing new machines and technologies that do the same amount of work, or more, for less energy expenditure, as can be seen in the design of light-weight automobiles with fuel-efficient engines).

The beauty of energy conservation is that it can lessen so many of the problems that the United States and the world are facing (Flavin and Durning 1988). For example, this soft path approach to energy resource management lessens acid rain, lessens the possibility of climatic change, and improves environmental aesthetics. Carbon emissions from a typical European car can be cut in half (approximately 450 kg or 992 lb annually) by raising the fuel efficiency to 50 miles per gallon of gasoline. Flavin and Durning also calculate that if worldwide energy efficiency were improved by 2 percent annually, the more catastrophic possibility of climatic change would be lessened, since the world's temperature would remain within 2°F of present levels. If energy demands were cut back, the need to construct new power plants and to erect open space-destroying utility towers would be reduced. Consequently, open space and other aesthetic aspects of the environment would be preserved.

In addition to the environmental benefits of energy conservation, Flavin and Durning argue that it would also improve national security, conserve energy without sacrificing economic growth, and even save money. National security would be improved since energy conservation lessens our dependence on oil from the Middle East. For example, they noted as U.S. automobiles became more fuel efficient (using 13.1 mpg in 1973 to using 17.9 mpg in 1985), U.S. gasoline consumption was reduced by 76 million liters (20 million gal) per year, thereby reducing oil imports by 1.3 million barrels per day.

Furthermore, cutting back on energy use does not mean sacrificing economic growth (Williams 1987). In fact, quite the contrary is true. According to a 1988 report by researchers at the University of California at Berkeley and at California Polytechnic State University, since the Organization of Petroleum Exporting Countries (OPEC) oil embargo in 1973, Americans not only conserved enough energy to save $45 million on their energy bills, but also they enjoyed a *35 percent rise* in gross national product. On a global scale, Flavin and Durning (1988) note that energy conservation now saves $250 billion annually, thus giving them reason to conclude that energy conservation is "one of the best buys in town." For insight into the potential of conserving even more energy while still increasing the U.S. gross national product, see Blackburn (1987).

Renewable energy (renewables) can be defined as those *nondepleting* or *continuous income* sources of energy, that pass through the environment as a *current* or *flow.* The sun (solar power), wind (wind power), rivers (hydropower), tides (tidal power), the natural growth of plant life (biomass), and the earth's internal heat (geothermal power) are all referred to as renewables (Foley 1987). By contrast **nonrenewable energy** is any *noncontinuous* forms of energy that remain in *static stores* until released by human technologies. Consequently, they have also been referred to as *capital sources* of energy, since they are limited (finite) and must be *drawn out of the bank* by humans. Examples include the fossil fuels (coal, oil, and natural gas) and nuclear fuel (Twidell and Weir 1986). Of these two energy classes, this chapter will only deal with the renewables.

Why emphasize the renewables? Compared with the nonrenewables, renewable energy sources are environmentally benign and cost-effective. They also help improve national security, work towards decentralization and regionalism, and improve environmental awareness among citizens. The literature is full of horror stories resulting from the use of fossil fuels. For example, fossil fuel pollutants are damaging trees (31 million ha or 77 million acres in central and northern Europe alone), causing premature human deaths (50,000 in the U.S. annually), and contributing to the greenhouse effect (as seen in the 30 percent increase in atmospheric carbon dioxide concentrations since 1860, and the 9 percent increase since 1960) (Shea 1988). Renewables are not environmentally perfect, but compared with the fossil fuels and nuclear fuel, they are the safe and clean way to go.

Furthermore, a commitment to renewable energy sources will help stabilize the U.S. economy (Matare 1989). According to the Worldwatch Institute (Washington, D.C.), most of the industrial world (including the United States) will be completely dependent on Middle Eastern oil by the year 2000. An intensified use of renewables will provide us the *flexibility* we will need in our ever-changing, highly unpredictable and volatile world. Closely related to the question of maintaining economic viability is the question of maintaining national security. Obviously, the less we are dependent on imported oil, the less vulnerable we will be to threats against our national security. An increased dependence on home-grown biofuel, for example, would help keep our planes, ships, and tanks fueled for national emergencies.

Renewables are also attractive because they arrive *dispersed* in the environment, thus allowing a move toward the *decentralization* of society. Individual houses, buildings, and industries can be generating more of their own power through active and passive solar designs, for example. Decentralization would also have the positive effect of helping to bring about a rebirth of *regionalism*, that is, a rebirth of the differences in living patterns and styles of buildings that were once found throughout the nation and the world. The extreme opposite of this would be centralization, which requires horrendous investments, large impersonal bureaucracies, and governmental controls to protect (in theory) the general public, as can be seen in the building and maintenance of nuclear power facilities. Because nuclear and fossil fuel facilities are large scale, complicated, and potentially dangerous, these forms of technology *isolate* individuals from the environment. By contrast, renewable sources have a tendency to *involve the individual* in the landscape. One can sense and visualize the flow of sun, wind, rivers, tides, waves, and the growth of plants. Consequently, say Twidell and Weir (1986), society will become more knowledgeable and conscious about its natural environment with renewable resources, just as the 1989 drought all of a sudden sensitized Americans to rainfall and the geography of drought. Let us now turn to the major sectors of our

society where energy conservation and renewables can be applied.

CONSERVATION AND RENEWABLES: PAST SUCCESSES AND POTENTIAL BY SECTOR

Residential and Commercial Structures

Americans have succeeded in radically reducing energy use per household and per unit floor area in commercial structures. From 1950 to 1973, for example, energy use was *increasing* (2 percent per year for households; 1 percent per year for commercial buildings). Since the oil embargo of 1973, however, energy has been *declining* in both sectors by about 1.5 percent per year (Rose 1986). Much of this savings resulted from (1) reducing heat loss and (2) improving the efficiency of internal uses.

Reducing Heat Loss. In addition to the well-known practice of weatherstripping and caulking around doors and windows, much energy (and money) can be saved by the proper use of insulation and window designs. Although tremendous savings have already been made, Flavin and Durning (1988) argue that we now have the technological ability to construct buildings that use one-third as much energy as is presently used. They cite, for example, how the average U.S. home consumes 160 kilojoules of heating energy per square meter of floor space per degree-day, whereas new Swedish houses consume just 65, some new Minnesota homes use just 51, and some individual units in Sweden use just 18 kilojoules.

The key to many of the previously cited energy savings has been the practice of superinsulating buildings. **Superinsulation** refers to doubling the normal insulation recommended for buildings and constructing an airtight liner into the walls. These houses are so well insulated that space heat is mostly obtained from sunlight radiating through windows and heat generated from people, stoves, and other appliances; very little heat is required from a traditional furnace. Indoor air pollution and the buildup of humidity is prevented by the use of ventilators with air-to-air heat exchangers (Blackburn 1987). *Constructing such super-efficient homes costs only 5 percent more, and those same additional costs can be regained in energy savings within just 5 years.* Although there are 20,000 superinsulated buildings in North America, with approximatey 5000 new ones being built each year, this type of construction represents less than 1 percent of total new housing construction (Flavin and Durning 1988). Obviously, increasing the percentage of superinsulated buildings is a conservation technique worth pursuing.

Since one-third of the heat loss from U.S. homes is from closed windows (Figure 14-1), researchers are also exploring various ways to improve the efficiency of windows (Raloff 1988). One technique is to raise the R value of windows from R-1 (the insulating value of a typical single pane of glass) to R-2 by using double-glazed windows. This can be further raised to R-4 by using double-paned windows with one pane coated with an infrared-radiation reflector, such as tin oxide, and by putting argon gas between the panes. By the mid-1990s, Flavin and Durning (1988) believe advanced technologies will allow windows to achieve the same insulating value as walls, which have an R value of 11. Miller (1988) predicts that window R values may even reach R-15, thus allowing a contractor to design a house with as many windows as possible without worrying about heat loss. Just as many of us now wear photochromatic prescription eyeglasses that darken when we go out in the sun, residential and commercial buildings of the future may even have light-sensitive glass that clears during winter months to let in more sunlight and darkens during summer months to keep interiors cool, thus reducing the use of furnaces and air conditioners.

Internal Energy Uses. Improvements in the efficiency of furnaces (space heat), air conditioners (space cooling), lights, and appliances have already conserved much energy, and there is much potential for additional savings. In 1980, for example, space heating accounted for approximately 60 percent of *final residential energy use*, which is primary energy use

minus losses brought about by the generation, transmission, and distribution of electricity (Williams 1987). Much energy loss results from the use of conventional gas furnaces, which send 25 percent of the heat they generate up the chimney. According to Flavin and Durning (1988), new, more efficient *condensing furnaces* are on the market—furnaces that cool and condense exhaust gases, thereby reabsorbing much of the heat rather than losing it. In addition to reducing fuel use for space heating by 28 percent, large ugly chimneys are replaced by small exhaust vents, and less air pollutants are produced (Hirst et al. 1986).

There are also air-conditioning units that are available today that are *twice* as efficient as those presently used in most commercial and residential structures. In 1984, for example, Lennox made an air-conditioning unit with an energy efficiency ratio of 15, as opposed to the ratio of 6 or 7, which is the average range for existing central units. Since most newly installed units have an energy efficiency ratio ranging from 7 through 9, much energy savings can be made by encouraging the installation of the more efficient units (Blackburn 1987).

Since approximately one-third of the electricity produced in American power plants is used to run household appliances, it is critical that we design highly efficient refrigerators, stoves, washers, dryers, water heaters, and other forms of appliances. Refrigerators are now available that are twice as efficient as the statistical existing average refrigerator (e.g., a Whirlpool, which requires 750 kilowatt-hours of electricity per year as compared with the statisical existing average of 1500 kilowatt-hours) (Flavin and Durning 1988). According to John H. Morrill, an energy specialist, ''If all the households in the U.S. had the most efficient refrigerators currently available, the

FIGURE 14-1 American windows leak as much energy as flows through the Alaskan pipeline. (Photo by author.)

electricity savings would eliminate the need for about 12 large nuclear power plants'' (Raloff 1988).

Other appliances can also be made to be more efficient. Blackburn (1987) notes that stoves can be better insulated, use electronic ignition rather than pilot lights, have better conduction from burners to pans. Clothes dryers can be retrofitted with heat recuperators. Similar ideas can be adapted to hot water heaters, washing machines, and so on. Unfortunately, says Blackburn, most American appliance manufacturers still oppose efficiency standards just like their counterparts in the automobile industry resist fuel efficiency standards. However, now that more efficient Japanese appliances are entering the U.S. market, Amerian appliance manufacturers will be forced to compete.

A revolution is also occurring in the way that we light our buildings. Since lighting consumes 20 to 25 percent of U.S. electricity—the equivalent of 100 power plants' worth—a rush is on to develop a better light bulb (Raloff 1988). Already, new more efficient light bulbs are available, such as an 18-watt fluorescent, which is equivalent in light output to a 75-watt incandescent bulb, but lasts 10 times longer. Flavin and Durning (1988) also note that packages of new efficient bulbs, more efficient controls and reflectors, and high-frequency ballasts can reduce energy requirements for illumination in commercial buildings by 75 percent. They cite, for example, how the University of Rhode Island recently cut their energy consumption for lighting by 78 percent, resulting in an annual savings of $200,000 on their electric bill.

We already have some commercial buildings that seem to have an ''intelligence'' of their own. These so-called *smart buildings* monitor indoor and outdoor temperatures, the location of people, and distribute cool or warm air to only where it is needed, thus saving substantial amounts of energy. Additional savings will be made when this systems approach to space heating and cooling is coupled with some of the newer lighting technologies on the horizon, such as *super-high-frequency ballasts* (cycling at 100 million hertz per second, not at 20,000 hertz, the typical cycling of high-frequency ballast, nor at 60 hertz, the average cycling of conventional fluorescent lighting) and *microelectronic sensors* that turn lights on and off as people enter and leave rooms. For additional information on possible energy savings in residential and commercial buildings, see Beaman (1987) and Hirst and Keating (1987).

A technological fix approach is not the only possible way of improving energy conservation within commercial and residential structures. For example, state and federal legislation can require that all build-ings sold pass an insulation and weatherproofing test, just as they now must pass termite inspection. Newly built houses could also be required to be a certain percentage more energy efficient than conventional houses of the same size (see the Davis, California, example later in this chapter). The legislative possibilities are almost endless for ensuring energy efficient buildings.

Industry

A second major sector of our economy that uses enormous amounts of energy is industry, which includes manufacturing (78 percent), mining (10 percent), agriculture (6 percent), and construction (6 percent) (Ross 1987). Industry has been the sector in our society that has led the way in bringing about better energy efficiency, mostly because increased efficiency means increased profits. Moreover, it has done this *without* decreasing production. From 1973 to 1986, for example, U.S. energy use by industry decreased by 17 percent, while industry enjoyed a 17 percent increase in production (Flavin and Durning 1988). Let us briefly look at how energy savings can continue to be made in manufacturing and agriculture.

Manufacturing. Eighty percent of the energy use in manufacturing goes into the production of six major categories of products. In order of energy use these products are chemicals, metals, petroleum refining, paper, cement, and glass products (Blackburn 1987). Since the production of *chemicals* is the largest industrial use of energy in the United States, approximately 22 percent of the energy consumed by industry, it is important that major strides be made in energy conservation in this area. Roughly one-third of this energy use is for raw materials (mostly oil and natural gas), while two-thirds is for energy fuels. Improved processing techniques that reduce waste and co-generation and other heat recovery devices can help reduce energy use. From 1972 to 1985, such techniques reduced the consumption of energy within the U.S. chemical industry by 34 percent (Flavin and Durning 1988). For additional energy conservation techniques related to the chemical industry, see Sheppard (1987).

In regards to the production of such *metals* as steel and aluminum, major energy savings can be made. In steel production, for example, Ross (1987) notes there are three categories of ways in which manufacturing efficiency can be improved:

1. *Management for conservation,* for example, having regular inspections to see that mo-

tors are turned off when not in use; scheduling maintenance programs; and using infrared scanners and other sophisticated inspection equipment.

2. *Radical process change,* for example, substituting basic oxygen and electric arc furnaces for the traditional open-hearth furnaces. These relatively new systems recycle scrap steel and cut energy costs in half. Another example would be the substitution of continuous casting—the formation of steel directly into a desired shape—for the more energy wasteful process of cooling and reheating ingots.

3. *Energy conservation retrofits,* for example, using the Paul Wurth bell-less top—a device that fits on top of an ironmaking furnace for the purpose of better controlling the distribution of materials. It has been reported to reduce coke rate and furnace maintenance requirements, while at the same time increasing overall production.

Of course, *if America made a long-term commitment to smaller and lighter automobiles and increased product durability, there would be less need for steel production in the first place.* As total steel use declines in America, the older, less energy efficient plants could be torn down—a process that has already begun. See Collins (1987) for additional insights into the U.S steel industry and energy use patterns.

Making aluminum is extremely energy intensive. Energy savings can be made, however, by substituting new methods of aluminum reduction for the traditionally used method, which is known as the Hall-Heroult smelting process—the most energy intensive stage of the production process. According to SERI (1981), these new processes can reduce energy consumption by more than one-third. Container legislation that encourages recycling (re-melting) aluminum cans for scrap would also help conserve energy, since re-melting scrap takes only 5 percent of the energy normally required in the Hall-Heroult smelting process (Rose 1986). In addition to conserving energy, recycling aluminum cans would help conserve landfill space and the aesthetic values of the environment. For insight into how the aluminum industry reacted to the energy shock of 1973, consult Peck (1988).

Energy savings can be made in the other areas of manufacturing as well. For example, Blackburn (1987) notes that energy use in *petroleum refining* can be reduced by using greater efficiency in the processing stage as well as by reducing the overall use of petroleum products throughout the economy. The current methods of producing *pulp and paper* also waste much energy, particularly in the pulp drying and repulping stages. In 1975, Dow Chemical listed numerous ways in which the paper industry could reduce its energy usage by 33 percent over a five-year period (Institute for Energy Studies 1979). One such method that has already been established at many paper plants is co-generation. For further details about the U.S. paper industry, see Lancey (1987). The *cement* industry is also making strides in energy conservation. The most notable energy savings in that industry are made by the use of a dry production process. Blackburn (1987) notes that the *flat process* in flat *glass* production has reduced energy use by 30 percent. He also mentions that if Americans reused glass containers (not re-melting them so they can be reformed into new glass products), the glass industry would reduce energy use by 67 to 83 percent.

Agriculture. America is known worldwide for its highly productive system of agriculture. But this short-term success story has been at the cost of increasing energy dependence and energy inefficiency. For every calorie of food produced, the American farmer uses 10 to 20 calories of fossil fuel (Clark 1975). In 1980, most of that energy (82.4 percent) went toward the *processing and distribution* of the food, which included (1) transporting the crop from the farm to the processor, (2) processing the crop (e.g., cleaning, preparing, packaging, and storing), and (3) transporting the crop to the supermarket (Figure 14-2). Only 17.6 percent of the energy used in U.S. agriculture went toward *production,* that is, producing crops with fertilizers and pesticides, using field machinery, using field transportation, using irrigation, drying crops, and so forth (Poincelot 1986). Since many of the energy saving techniques associated with the processing and distribution stage of the agricultural production system are discussed in other sections of this chapter, the following discussion will be limited to just those energy conserving techniques that can be applied to the production stage. In decreasing order of energy intensiveness, let us look at how energy savings can be made in the production categories of fertilizer and pesticide use, field machinery use, transportation, irrigation, and crop drying.

American farming is currently dependent upon synthetic fertilizers and pesticides—products that in themselves are energy dependent. For example, it takes fuel energy to mine, refine, transport, and apply fertilizers. In 1980, the production and application of synthetic fertilizers and pesticides accounted for approximately 40 percent of the energy require-

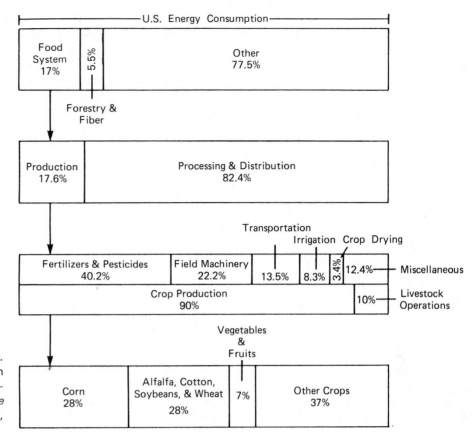

FIGURE 14-2 Flow chart of U.S. energy consumption, based on 1980 data. (From Raymond Poincelot, *Toward a More Sustainable Agriculture* [Westport, Conn.: AVI, 1986], p. 34.)

ment for crop production (Poincelot 1986). Reduction of synthetic fertilizer and pesticide usage is one way of conserving our energy resources.

Synthetic fertilizers can be replaced by other less energy-intensive sources of nitrogen, such as legumes, organic wastes, and even information. The use of leguminous forages after harvest, of course, is not a new idea. America's farmers use to be *leguminous farmers* long before they became *chemical farmers*. Legumes can be either *annual* (e.g., soybeans, *Glycine max*), *perennial* (e.g., alfalfa, *Medicago sativa*), or *biennial* (e.g., sweetclover, *Melilotus*). The favorite legume for forage purposes and energy reduction is alfalfa, since it leaves much nitrogen in the soil for succeeding crops. According to Heichel (1978), the use of proper rotation schemes that alternate alfalfa with food crops can reduce nitrogen needs up to 50 percent. With improvements through plant breeding, says Poincelot (1986), the value of alfalfa in conserving energy will be further increased.

But what about crop yields? Will they decline with the increased use of legume rotation schemes? No, not necessarily. According to Francis and King (1988), precise information about legumes and their nitrogen fixing abilities, the effects of various rotation

schemes, and proper timing can reduce energy requirements *without* changing yields.

Energy costs can also be reduced by the use of organic wastes, which include manures (range droppings), sewage sludge, crop residues, and compost. Since 90 percent of the annual manure production (175 million dry tons) is already applied to the land (Poincelot 1986), substituting manure for chemical fertilizers has its limitations. Furthermore, manures are difficult to handle, expensive to transport, and can cause environmental problems (e.g., surface runoff combined with manure can cause water contamination) if not properly applied. However, if our commercial farms gradually become more diversified, like our organic farms where animals and crop production are in close proximity, at least the transportation expense of moving manure would be eliminated, thus making the use of manure for nitrogen more attractive.

In a sense, information can also substitute for nitrogen. The careful scrutiny of soil tests can help farmers determine if they can maintain yields with reduced applications of chemical fertilizers. According to Francis and King (1988), farmers can use far less chemical fertilizers than normally recommended and still maintain normal yields. Furthermore, they note that farmers could further reduce their application rates of chemical fertilizers if they shot for yields based on an average of their past five years, as opposed to the common practice of shooting for the ever higher yields.

In terms of the crop production energy budget, pesticides comprise only 2 percent, as compared to 98 percent for fertilizers (Poincelot 1986). Consequently, cutting back or totally eliminating pesticide usage will not save a substantial amount of agricultural energy. Nevertheless, there is still some energy savings with lower pesticide use, not to mention the obvious benefit of helping to maintain environmental quality. Therefore, it is important that we at least mention some alternatives to pesticide use on the farm.

Prior to World War II and the introduction of chemical pesticides, farmers used a variety of pest control techniques that were quite effective—techniques collectively known a **cultural** or **bioenvironmental controls.** For example, *crop rotation,* allowed the farmer to alternate susceptible and nonsusceptible crops to reduce insect populations; *biological pest-control methods* used information about insect predator-prey relations; *sanitation schemes* removed organic debris that served as breeding places for insects; *field planning* allowed for the proper spacing of crops to minimize damage (a bruised plant can invite insect or disease investation); *plant timing* schemes used information about the best time to plant crops to avoid certain pests; *barriers* were created with hedgerows or alternative rows of different crops (strip cropping) so that insects would have a more difficult time spreading.

Farmers stopped using these practices when pesticides were introduced. Why? It seemed to be less work and to be less complicated to just open a bag of pesticides. Today's farmer, however, is gradually beginning to realize that taking this seemingly easier route may actually lead to *more work* and to *more complications* in the long run, especially now that they have to deal with long-term land problems (e.g., contaminated soil and water), health problems (e.g., the various cancers and other chronic diseases that they and their hired labor are experiencing), and marketing problems (e.g., the American public's demand for pesticide-free farm products). For additional information on the alternatives to pesticide use, see Francis and King (1988) and Poincelot (1986).

Since approximately 20 percent of agricultural energy goes toward the operation of farm machinery (Poincelot 1986), decreased utilization or more efficient utilization of farm machinery can make substantial energy savings. One related conservation technique is the *reduced or no-tillage system.* For example, the number of gallons of diesel fuel that are required per acre vary from 1.84 gal per acre for conventional tillage with moldboard plow), to 1.12 gal for reduced tillage with chisel plow, to 0.63 gal for reduced tillage with chisel plow, to 0 gal for no-tillage systems (Frye and Phillips 1981). Even though the no-tillage system requires the use of pesticides to control weeds, this system still remains the most energy efficient (Poincelot 1986). Additional ways to improve the operation of farm machinery include (1) *choosing the best fuel* (e.g., diesel fuel remains the least expensive and most energy efficient, though it also creates the most air pollutants), (2) *downrating tractor horsepower* (i.e., making sure the tractor bought or rented fits the scale of farm operation, and (3) scheduling *regular machine maintenance*—a practice that can result in a 25 percent increase in fuel efficiency (Bloome et al. 1981).

Additional energy savings on the farm can be made in the areas of transportation, irrigation, and crop drying. Since transportation uses approximately 14 percent of the total energy requirements for agricultural production, it ranks third behind the use of fertilizers and pesticides and the use of farm machinery (Figure 14-2). Methods to conserve energy in the transportation category include (1) making sure that existing vehicles are properly tuned and lubricated, (2) substituting numerous minimal cargo trips with one or two trips with full loads, (3) replacing worn-out vehicles with ones that are smaller, lighter, and more fuel efficient, and (4) eventually modifying vehicle engines to run on farm-produced renewable resources, such as ethanol, which is produced from the fermentation of corn or other grains. Only after these steps are taken can farm transportation become more self-sustaining (Poincelot 1986).

Irrigation uses about 8 percent of the energy required for crop production. There are various methods by which farmers can conserve irrigation energy. One method is *system alteration,* that is, replacing a high-energy intensive irrigation system with one that uses less energy. For example, surface irrigation systems function according to gravity flow, whereas sprinkler systems require pumps, most of which are electrical; trickle or drip irrigation systems require pumping, but they use minimal energy since they require low water pressure.

Irrigation energy savings can also be made in irrigation systems by *reducing the frequency of pumping.* Farmers often irrigate their crops during months when it is not necessary, simply because they do not know better. Education programs that discuss specific water requirements for crops can help farmers keep pumping frequency to a minimum, and thereby save water as well as energy. If pumps are used, *proper maintenance* of those pumps can also help conserve energy until *more efficient models* are purchased, or better yet, until those fossil fuel driven pumps are replaced with *ones driven by renewable energy.* Pumps can be driven by windmills (an old idea that is now having a resurgence) or the promising photovoltaic power system (Figure 14-3).

Irrigation energy costs can also be cut by pursuing various methods of *irrigation efficiency* (e.g., applying water only at night, thereby reducing evaporation, and eliminating leaks and seepage) and by *improving management* through the use of computers and moisture detection devices to determine optimal irrigation schedules. According to Poincelot (1986), improvements in equipment efficiency and management practices can result in an energy savings of 30 to 50 percent for water pumping. For additional information on the methods used to conserve irrigation energy, consult Arco (1982), Batly and associates (1975), Eisenhauer and Fischbach (1977), Jensen and Kruse (1981), Poincelot (1986), Ross (1978), Stetson and associates (1975), and White (1978).

Approximately 3 percent of the total energy consumed during crop production is expended for crop drying. Farmers dry crops so that they are more easily stored, less likely to overheat and to spoil, and less prone to insect investations. Drying also gives the farmer more flexibility. It permits earlier harvesting, the growing of later-maturing cultivars with greater yields, and, in some locations, double cropping (Poincelot 1986).

Since most crop-drying facilities are currently dependent on liquid propane or natural gas, this is an area where some energy savings can be made

(Frye and Phillips 1981). One technique is *field drying.* According to Elmore and Hanway (1984), if the appropriate hybrid is chosen (one with a shorter maturation period so that grain fill can complete before the frost), most of the drying (of maize, for example) can occur in the field before harvest. *Solar grain drying* is another possible alternative method that is proving attractive. This technique uses a flat-plate, air-type solar collector, which usually sits on the ground next to the grain bin. According to Heid and Trotter (1982), a well designed solar dryer has a cost-payback of three-and-one-half to five years, thus making it economically feasible. Additional energy conservation techniques associated with crop drying include *low-temperature drying* and *dryeration.* Dryeration is the practice of removing grain from the dryer while still hot, thus allowing the grain to complete the dehydration process under natural aeration. The idea is simple, similar to the notion of removing a steak from the barbeque prior to the time it has reached its desired level of cooking. Once off the fire, the steak continues to cook because of residual heat for the few minutes it takes to get to the dinner table. Similarly, the grain continues to lose moisture once it is outside the drying bin. For additional information on alternatives to conventional crop drying, consult Guceri (1983), Heid and Aldis (1981), and Jenkins (1989).

Transportation

About one-fourth of the energy used in the United States goes towards getting people and goods from one place to another. Forty-five percent of that energy is used by automobiles. The rest is used by freight trucks, buses, trains, airplanes, as well as by freighters, barges, and pipelines. Let us briefly look

FIGURE 14-3 Use of photovoltaic panels to pump water from aquifer on an organic farm in Santa Cruz, California. (Photo by author.)

at how energy can be conserved in a few of these different forms of transportation.

Automobiles and Trucks. Most Americans love going about in their private automobiles, and it is pure fantasy to think that they are going to give up this mode of transportation entirely, or even reduce their use substantially—at least in the near future. Consequently, it is paramount that our *automobile culture* develop (and buy) cars that are extremely energy efficient. Various engineering, design, and legislative techniques currently exist for improving fuel economy.

In 1973, automobile gas mileage in the United States reached its lowest average point—approximately 13 miles per gallon (mpg) (Blackburn 1987). In 1989, the average new American car gets twice the gas mileage. Even greater gains are possible by (1) developing more fuel efficient engines and transmission systems, (2) reducing drag coefficient, (3) reducing rolling friction, and (4) making cars smaller and lighter. Such techniques could raise automobile fuel efficiency to between 51 and 78 mpg by the year 2000. *The cost to the buying public would be an additional $120 to $330 per vehicle (in 1980 dollars), which is less than a high-quality car stereo* (Flavin and Durning 1988).

American automakers, and their buying public, must take fuel economy seriously. With the oil glut of the late 1980s, American carmakers lost interest in the research and development of fuel efficient automobiles. While the United States is falling further behind, the Japanese and Europeans are pushing forward and developing more fuel efficient technologies. Already, according to Flaving and Durning (1988), four-passenger autos with fuel efficiencies of nearly 100 mpg have reached the test tracts of these countries.

Such gains in fuel economy have come from a variety of sources. More *efficient engines* were designed that more fully use the combustion process. The standard gearbox was replaced with more *efficient transmission systems*, such as Subaru's continuously variable transmission (CVT), which is 20 percent more efficient than a three-speed automatic transmission. The *drag coefficient* (a measure of wind resistance) was reduced by new aerodynamic designs (e.g., by sloping the front hood and grill, rounding edges, and smoothing the underside of the vehicle). *Rolling friction* was reduced by using more efficient tires, such as radial tires, which improve gasoline mileage by approximately 5 percent. *Auto weight* was reduced by using plastic body panels and aluminum parts, as is done on the Honda CRX HF. Finally, additional fuel economy was gained by using *microelec-*

tronics to keep the engine, transmission, and steering mechanisms finely tuned.

Legislating automobile standards and consumer incentives is another means of increasing fuel economy. Congress has failed, however, to go beyond the 27.5 mpg fuel economy standard that it set in 1985. Worse yet, in October 1988, the Department of Transportation acceded to requests by General Motors Corporation and the Ford Motor Company to *lower* the fuel economy requirement for 1989 cars from 27.5 to 26.5 mpg. In other words, Congress legislated in the wrong direction, thereby making it easier for the return of the gas-guzzler. Just as in the 1960s, many domestic and foreign automakers are now promoting greater horsepower cars. According to Blackburn (1987), as well as many other energy specialists, automakers and the American auto-buying public have neither foresight nor hindsight. Perhaps, he says, we need an oil crisis with long gas lines every six years just to keep us moving in the right direction—toward greater fuel efficiency.

Americans should also be working towards an all new transportation technology, such as the development of electric or solar-powered cars. According to Matare (1989), there are growing indications that the safer, quieter, and less polluting electric car may soon be competing with the extremely polluting gasoline-powered automobile. For example, he cites a 1984 Argonne National Laboratory study that calculates that by the year 2000, the total annual cost of fueling and maintaining a 30 mpg car will be $1133, as compared with the average yearly cost of $320 for a compact electric vehicle with a range of 160 km (100 mi). Improvements in fuel efficiencies for gasoline-powered cars, however, may offset the cost advantage of electric vehicles.

Perhaps a better indication of the likelihood of electric automobiles taking over city streets (and possibly the highways) is to look at what is now technologically feasible. By 1988, German car makers had designed what many believe to be the first really viable electric car—one that is suitable for more than mere city streets. The Pohlmann EL can reach a top speed of 125 kph (78 mph) and has a range of 160 km (100 mi). This striking performance is a result of lightweight design and construction principles, new engine concepts, and the use of a nickel-iron battery.

Switzerland is also leading the way in the development and use of practical electric cars. In 1988, more than 50 street-legal *solarmobiles* (battery-powered cars charged by solar cells mounted atop the vehicle) were in use in Switzerland, with the possibility of greater numbers being used in the near future. The most popular car was SunCraft's Sulky Solar and

Rotaver's Solarmobile, both of which can cover 100 km (62 mi) at speeds from 40 to 60 mph. These light, silent, and nonpolluting cars sell for under $10,000 (in 1989 dollars).

There is no question that Amerians have grown accustomed to cars with top speeds of at least 160 kph (100 mph), with breathtaking acceleration, and with virtually unlimited range. *But if Americans are given the choice between driving electric vehicles or car pooling in gasoline-powered automobiles, or using mass transit, there is no question in this author's mind that Americans would choose their own personal, private, and sporty electric car.*

Gradually switching from gasoline-powered cars to electric cars will also entail a few other changes in American society. For example, increased use of electric cars will mean an increased need for electric power. In order not to rely on coal, oil, and nuclear power, solar energy power plants and other means of capturing renewable energy will need to be intensified (Matare 1989). Furthermore, one's private electric car will need to be used for short-range commuting, while using other means, such as bus, rail, and aircraft, for long-range travel. For additional information on the feasibility of electric vehicles in the near future, see Argonne National Laboratory (1984) and Wilson and associates (1989).

As far as trucks are concerned, they, like the auto, can also be made more energy efficient. Such techniques as new aerodynamic designs or retrofits (e.g., air deflectors), better maintenance, more efficient engines (e.g., turbocharged diesel engines), better transmissions, and improved tires (e.g., radial tires) can save energy. According to Blackburn (1987), prototypes of trucks exist that are 40 percent more energy efficient than existing models. Blackburn also notes that deregulation has helped reduce the number of empty runs. Developing policies that totally eliminate trucks that return empty after reaching their destination would further conserve fuel.

Ships and Planes. Energy savings can also be made in the way that we design our freighters, cruise ships, and aircraft. Already there are examples of what the anthropologist John Bodley calls the *paraprimitive solution*—solutions to problems that incorporate the best technologies of the present and the past. For example, Windstar Sail Cruises has built two of the most innovative ships in the history of cruising—the *Wind Star* and the *Wind Song* (Figure 14-4). These 134 m (440 ft) long, 62 m (204 ft) high cruise ships combine state-of-the-art computerized technology with an old technology that uses renewable energy—sails that capture wind. These fuel conserving cruise ships are the prototypes of what cruise ships may look like in the future. There are also examples of freighters that have *metal sails* to conserve energy.

Some new aircraft designs are also adapting paraprimitive solutions to conserve energy. For example, McDonnell Douglas is combining computer-aided designs and high-tech materials with an old idea—the *propeller*—in what aircraft engineers call an *unducted-fan engine*, or UDF. More simply, it is called the *propfan*. This new power plant consists of a jet engine that drives two 3.4 m (11 ft) diameter propellers, which rotate in opposite directions on one shaft at the rear of the engine. Because its blades rotate in opposite directions, some engineers kiddingly refer to this new power plant as a ''Flying Cuisinart.'' The propfan uses 25 to 45 percent less fuel than the standard jet turbofan. To achieve these savings, aircraft engineers required the use of sophisticated com-

FIGURE 14-4 Luxury cruise ships with sails—one example of the paraprimitive solution to our energy crisis. (Courtesy of Windstar Sail Cruises Limited.)

puters to design the ideal propeller shape. New graphite composite materials instead of metal are used for the propellers to give them added strength at high speeds. Prior to these innovations, large propeller-driven airliners could not cruise at the 500 to 600 mph speeds that is now expected by the general public. According to many airline executives, these new energy conserving engines will revolutionize the airline industry, making propeller-driven jetliners once again a common sight at airports. In addition to energy savings, noise pollution will be reduced, since these new propfans are much quieter. Considering that *humans are the noisiest animals on this earth,* any technology that reduces noise while saving energy has got to be a step in the right direction.

Urban Design

It has been shown previously that tremendous energy savings can be made in residential and commercial buildings, in industry, and in transportation in the United States and throughout the world. But what about the city itself—the way that we design and live within cities? This is particularly important since, if the U.S. Population Reference Bureau is correct, more than half of humanity will reside in cities by the year 2000. To help conserve energy within urban areas, various techniques do exist, such as (1) initiating wide-scale tree planting programs, (2) closing nutrient cycles, (3) questioning city size, (4) encouraging alternatives to the auto, (5) planning land use according to energy conservation need, and (6) pioneering multifaceted legislation for energy conservation within the city. We will now briefly look at some of these possibilities.

Tree Planting Programs. The tree is one of Mother Nature's best inventions. Trees can shade underlying buildings, and since they provide regional evaporative cooling as they transpire, they can also help limit the development of urban heat islands, which result from the sun pounding down on large areas of exposed asphalt and dark-roofed surfaces. According to Raloff (1988), planting just three trees next to light-colored homes throughout a community can result in a reduced residential cooling demand on a hot summer day of 18 percent in Phoenix, Arizona, and of 44 percent in Los Angeles, California.

Since trees also absorb carbon dioxide—the principal greenhouse effect gas that traps heat and raises the earth's temperature—wide-scale tree planting programs would not only save much utility-generated energy but also help counteract global

warming (Raloff 1988). The beauty of this energy conservation technique is that tree planting can be encouraged at all levels of society, from the individual homeowner putting in an additional tree or two in the backyard, to local communities and private organizations planting an individual acre at a time, to city governments working with their arborists to rebuild the urban forest.

In Stuttgart, West Germany, for example, the city built *shady, landscaped parks* to cool adjacent neighborhoods (Spirn 1984). In addition to designing new urban parks (or reforesting existing ones), imagine how much cleaner, cooler, and attractive our cities would be if we covered our ugly, flat, gravel and tar roofs with *roof gardens* (landscaped gardens with trees, shrubs, and flowers) or *wet roofs* (ponded water 5–8 cm [2–3 in.] deep installed to help cool the building). Such techniques would also help bring birds and other forms of small wildlife back into the city. Parking lots can also be designed to be more attractive and give off less heat to adjacent buildings, thereby reducing air-conditioning fuel requirements on hot, sunny days. This can be accomplished by strategically placing appropriate trees throughout the parking lot, as well as substituting *turf blocks* (alternating blocks of grass and concrete) for the conventional black asphalt. According to Smith and Sholtis (1981), turf-block parking lots (even without trees) are generally 4°F cooler than nearby asphalt parking lots. Highway departments can also get involved in planting native trees to regenerate the median strips and edges of highways that ring the city. In addition to helping cool the city and thereby conserve energy, improved highway vegetation helps filter pollution, reduces highway noise, and provides an attractive gateway to the city.

Admittedly, tree planting programs are only a stopgap measure while efforts are made to slowdown—and ideally—stop deforestation. Some have argued that tree planting programs will only add to global warming, since when these new trees die or rot, or are cut for firewood, they will release whatever carbon dioxide they have absorbed. But eventually cutting these trees *for lumber*—the notion of harvesting the urban forest on a sustained yield basis—would help solve this carbon-backlash question as well as reduce the strain on our national forests. Tree planting programs should go forward, but only with the knowledge that such programs will not prevent global warming by themselves. They must go hand-in-hand with boosting minimum efficiency standards for automobiles, appliances, and other forms of machinery.

Nutrient Recycling. Energy can also be saved if cities increased their efforts at closing nutrient cycles (Brown and Jacobson 1987). As a city grows, so does its volume of waste products (e.g., sludge in municipal waste treatment plants, wastewater in storage lagoons, yard waste—leaves, branches, lawn clippings—in landfill sites). Rather than treat these waste products as "garbage" (something to be discarded), we can apply the paraprimitive solution to help conserve energy and other natural resources.

For example, we would not have to manufacture as much fossil fuel based fertilizer if we took an old idea, the collection of human waste (known as *night soil*) for use as a fertilizer, and modernized the technique with improved waste management technologies to eliminate any potential health problems. Since sludge is usually not a complete fertilizer, farmers would still have to supplement this "natural" fertilizer on their fields. However, the use of sludge would still substantially reduce the farmer's bill for artificial fertilizer. In addition, sludge has several agricultural benefits, such as adding organic bulk to the soil, which aids aeration and water retention, which, in turn, reduces soil erosion. Although the United States already applies 42 percent of the sludge it generates to farmland, other countries, such as the Netherlands and Sweden, are better at closing the nutrient cycle—recycling 60 percent or more back to farmland (Brown and Jacobson 1987).

Composting is another old idea that is becoming increasingly popular. Yard wastes (leaves and clippings from institutional grounds, such as university campuses, as well as from neighborhood backyards) account for 18 percent of the municipal solid waste stream. Why discard this *precious resource* into a garbage dump when composting it can help reduce the need for additional landfills and save energy. The farmer who uses compost requires less fossil fuel fertilizers, since soils that have been conditioned with compost store and release both natural and synthetic nutrients better. In other words, energy efficiency is gained by closing this nutrient cycle. Many countries in Europe already compost. Sweden composts 25 percent of its solid waste, and West Germany boasts of its Heidelberg operation where approximately 33 percent of its municipal refuse is composted (Fine 1989). In order for composting programs to have optimal success, yard wastes need to be properly sorted by residents for curbside collection, carefully screened by facility operators prior to processing, and processed in properly located and well-maintained facilities so as to not offend homeowners. Furthermore, cities need to promote backyard composting as much as possible to help reduce the amount of solid waste sent to the municipal landfill operation. According to Fine (1989), the city of Seattle has the broad recycling strategy—backyard composting *and* curbside collection—and will likely achieve its plan to achieve 60 percent recycling by 1994.

City Size. According to Brown and Jacobson (1987), ecology and economics are forcing us to question city size. As cities increase in size, they argue, so do the energy requirements needed to transport larger and larger quantities of food, water, and fuel into the city and to transport garbage and sewage out. The larger the city, the more complex and energy intensive is its support system. As an example, they cite the problems that New York and Los Angeles have in acquiring their water. The Greater New York area is so large, using 1.9 billion cubic meters of water per year, that 98 percent of its domestic water must come from surface catchments many miles from the city. Likewise, Los Angeles is so large that it regularly draws part of its water from northern California several hundred miles away, as well as from the Colorado River in Arizona.

Just as the Greeks used to restrict town size so that they could remain largely dependent on the local countryside for food, water, and fuel (Mumford 1961), we, too, need to make our existing and future urban areas more self-sustaining. *New towns* can be developed and planned according to the Greek notion of town sustainability, which will reduce energy requirements for transporting goods to and from the city. Existing metropolitan areas such as New York and Los Angeles can help counter the problem of their large size by developing policies and incentives that encourage a movement toward the *decentralization* of water, power, and food. Individual houses and buildings need to be supplying more (but not necessarily all) of their energy supplies (e.g., by using active and passive solar energy designs), of their water supplies for irrigation (e.g., by using individual water catchment systems that use graywater), of their fertilizers (e.g., by recycling food scraps and composting), and of their food (e.g., by planting fruit trees and vegetable gardens (Figure 14-5). According to Brown and Jacobson (1987), we are slowly moving toward an age of using renewable energy, and this type of energy favors the smaller city and the rural dweller.

Alternatives to the Automobile. New towns and young, rapidly growing cities have an opportunity to achieve enormous savings by designing commercial and residential areas that do not have an over

(a)

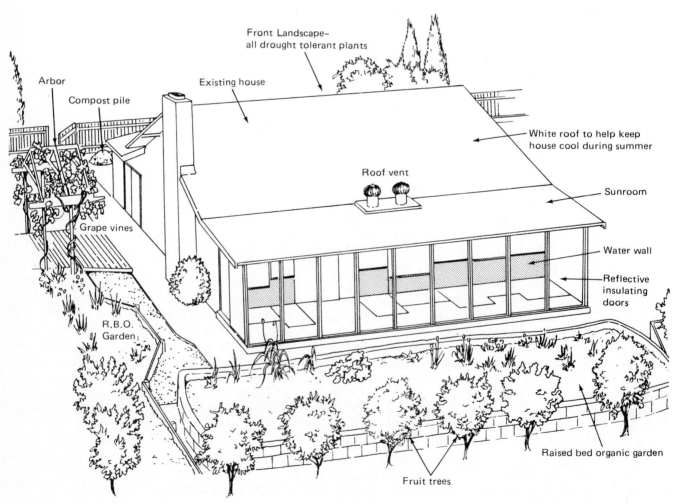

Front Landscape-
all drought tolerant plants

Arbor

Compost pile

Existing house

Grape vines

White roof to help keep
house cool during summer

Roof vent

Sunroom

Water wall

Reflective
insulating
doors

R.B.O.
Garden

Raised bed organic garden

Fruit trees

(b)

reliance on people traveling by car. Transportation in these areas can primarily be by walking and bicycling, both of which use no fuel, create no pollution, and are healthy activities, which allows one to slow down and actually see and enjoy the landscape of which one is apart. Minibuses and other forms of public transportation could be available for longer ventures. Larger and mature cities can also save energy by moving towards greater reliance on the use of van pools, light-rail, and buses. According to Flavin and Durning (1988), buses, light-rail, and railroads require 25 percent less fuel than private automobiles to move each passenger a given distance.

Several traffic-shocked cities in the western United States have already begun to lessen their reliance on the automobile. For example, the cities of Sacramento, San Jose, and San Diego in California, and Portland, Oregon, have selected *light-rail* as the way to go. Once again, its the paraprimitive solution—the blending of an old idea (the old reliable streetcar or trolley) with the new streamline designs and modern technologies. These vehicles are more energy efficient than buses, give off no exhaust fumes, and are more likely to be cost-effective.

Other western cities are jumping on the light-rail revolution, including the automobile-crazed city of Los Angeles, which is planning a 241 km (150 mi) rail network, and San Francisco, which plans to expand its Municipal Railway ("the Muni"), which has been operating electric street cars since 1912. Anyone who has lived in the San Francisco Bay Area for any length of time is familiar with the periodic call by certain public officials for the elimination of the city's trolley cars. They argue that the trolley system is antiquated and ties up automobile traffic. San Franciscans have wisely voted down all such proposals. Perhaps there will be a day when other cities have public transportation systems like San Francisco that are efficient and nostalgic and give a sense of place to their city. Some cities, such as San Jose, have even begun renovating their nineteenth century trollies to put them back on line with its streamlined light-rail system (Figure 14-6). This is a step in the right direction. It is a move not only towards greater energy efficiency, but also a move towards building *city character.*

Energy-Sensitive Land-Use Planning. Additional energy savings can be made within urban areas if land-use planning is done according to energy use. Traditionally, energy planners and land-use planners have worked independently of each other. However, there are signs that these two separate domains may be joining forces to achieve more energy-sensitive land-use plans.

Rejeski (1987) reports on an innovative activity occurring in Hamburg, West Germany. The city's Department of Landscape Planning (part of the Environmental Agency) has initiated a project to integrate energy-relevant parameters into future plans for Hamburg. To facilitate this integration, a comprehensive cartographic process has been developed (see

---

FIGURE 14-5 (a) Frank R. Schiavo and Linda Munn's low-cost energy remodel of a San Jose, California, tract house, on left. Note how it appears no different from the conventional house on the right. Yet, the "conservation house and home" uses far fewer resources. From the front angle, one can see the use of drought-tolerant vegetation to minimize water use, solar collectors to heat water, and a white roof to reflect sunlight, helping to keep the house cool during hot summers. Even the old "recycled" Chevy II automobile runs on propane gas, which is cleaner burning than gasoline. (Photo by author). (b) A south-facing sunroom and a heat-storing water wall are the key components of this same holistic energy-conservation house. The sunroom admits low winter sun for heat gain. Exterior doors, sliding windows, and a roof vent control the flow of warm air from the sunroom into the house and prevent overheating. During cold winter days and nights, a woodburning stove supplements the house with heat. Whereas most San Jose residents pay utility bills of $80 to $150 monthly during the winter, the Schiavo-Munn household pays $12 to $18 monthly. They also recycle almost everything; so much so, in fact, that they require *no* garbage pick-up service—ever! They accomplish this by composting waste scraps for use on their organic raised-bed gardens and, more importantly, by carefully buying only products that come in recyclable containers. *This family is indeed a conservation role model for the rest of the nation, if not the world.*

(a)

(b)

FIGURE 14-6 (a) San Jose's new light-rail transit system. (b) San Jose's nineteenth century streetcars have been renovated to be put back on line with the newer modern version shown above. (Photos by author.)

Figure 14-7) that uses a series of overlay maps to illustrate (1) *existing energy use* to determine energy-use patterns on the land, (2) *building typology and density* to access energy conservation potential, (3) *meso- and microclimatological data* to access information on urban heat islands, air pollution, and human comfort levels, (4) *renewable energy resources* to determine their potential, and (5) *environmental impact analysis* of existing energy sources. In addition to making it easier to assess the spatial distribution of energy-related data and its interrelationship to environmental parameters, this methodology, says Rejeski (1987), has the added benefit of providing a conceptual and methodological framework based on an *interdisciplinary* approach. For an excellent discussion of land-use policy

formation for specific energy types, such as solar energy, see Rao and Sastri (1987).

Multifaceted Legislation for Energy Conservation. Some cities, such as Davis, California, have legislated their way into a new era of energy conservation. Building codes were written that encouraged the use of solar energy systems. Specifically, the new codes regulated the siting (including the solar orientation) and design of new buildings, including the amount of insulation required, the size of windows, the exterior and wall colors, and the overhang shading. With these new designs in place, residents no longer find it necessary to use their air conditioners.

To reduce reliance on the automobile, Davis de-

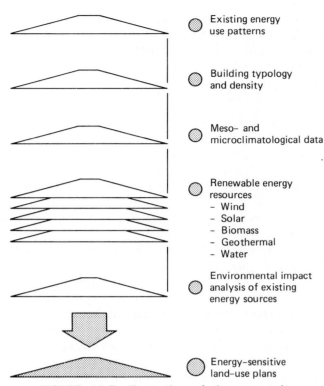

○ Existing energy
   use patterns

○ Building typology
   and density

○ Meso- and
   microclimatological data

○ Renewable energy
   resources
   - Wind
   - Solar
   - Biomass
   - Geothermal
   - Water

○ Environmental impact
   analysis of existing
   energy sources

○ Energy-sensitive
   land-use plans

FIGURE 14-7 Illustration of the composite mapping process. (From David Rejeski, "Energy-Sensitive Land-Use Planning," *Tunnelling & Underground Space Technology*, vol. 2, no. 2 [1987], p. 220.)

cided to develop a system of bikeways. To this day, Davis is considered a "biking town," and in fact, it even has a bike sculpture proudly displayed at the center of town. The city has also developed low-cost public transportation and has encouraged cottage industries to help reduce the need to commute to work.

According to Spirn (1984), the Davis experiment has proved highly successful and, most important, many of the techniques that this town of 33,000 people used can be adapted to larger cities. Larger cities can also be siting and designing new buildings and parks with passive energy conservation in mind, creating bike and car-pool lanes, using building and landscape materials that utilize *nature's gifts*—sun, rain, wind—in an *optimal fashion,* rather than resisting such natural wonders with energy-consuming mechanical devices like air conditioners and furnaces.

PROSPECTS FOR THE FUTURE

One generation passeth away, and another generation cometh; but the earth abideth for ever. (Ecclesiastes 1:4)

But will the earth survive? Continued energy waste and mounting pollutants threaten the economic and environmental health of societies—whether they be large or small, industrial or agrarian. Relying on nonrenewable fossil fuels and uranium has damaged our forests, poisoned our water supplies, contaminated our fisheries, and degraded human health. And, now, our energy systems are even altering the climate, adding 5.4 billion tons of carbon to the atmosphere each year (Flavin 1988).

Positive Signs and Success Stories

Despite such bad news, America (and the world) is definitely in transition—the transition to a new energy system based on conservation and renewable energy. The signs of positive change are all around us.

1. *Tremendous efficiency improvements.* Since 1973, most industrial societies have improved their overall energy efficiency by 20 to 30 percent, and, most important, *without* bringing wrenching societal change. This change did not require shivering through long winter nights, living in darkened rooms, or giving up the family car. As examples, Flavin and Durning (1988) cite the changing office building and automobile. Today, the new American office building uses 50 percent less electricity, despite the fact that room temperatures and illumination remain about the same. Likewise, today's large luxury cars get 20–25 mpg—the same mileage that small cars used to get in the mid-1970s. They also note that since 1973 *the world has conserved far more energy than it has obtained from all new sources combined.* Simply stated, *conservation works!*

2. *Entire communities have been successful at energy conservation.* In 1989, *Time* magazine reported about the good news coming out of Osage, Iowa. Apparently, this town of 3600 people in northern Iowa decided to take energy conservation seriously. Much of the credit goes to Weston Birdsall, the far-sighted general manager of Osage Municipal Utilities, who realized that conserving energy not only saves money but also helps save the environment. He went on a conservation campaign advocating such old-fashioned ideas as plugging leaky windows, insulating walls and ceilings, replacing inefficient furnaces, and wrapping hot-water heaters with insulation. As a result, since 1974, the community has cut its consumption of natural gas by 45 percent and reduced annual growth in electricity demand by 50 percent. The question remains: Why aren't other communities adopting these simple, widely known techniques? Perhaps they just need a person like Weston Birdsall. Perhaps that person is you!

3. *Accelerating shift to low-input agriculture.* America's agricultural systems are undergoing rapid transition. Our energy-intensive conventional systems of growing food are giving way to various alternatives, called by various names, such as *low-input, organic, sustainable, no-spray, transitional,* or *biodynamic.* On August 23, 1988, the *New York Times* reported that even university agricultural researchers and officials at the Department of Agriculture were surprised at the accelerating pace of this transition. On March 21, 1989, the *Wall Street Journal* devoted a quarter page to a feature story entitled ''Big Firms Get High on Organic Farming.'' The author, Sonia Nazario, noted that there is strong evidence that organic farming is becoming *mainstream.* She noted that even before the 1989 scares concerning pesticide-tainted fruit (e.g., apples sprayed with the chemical Alar; potatoes and bananas grown with aldicarb), chemical-using farmers had started converting to alternative methods.

Why are farmers beginning to switch to low-input agriculture? The answer has as much to do with profit as it has to do with environmental consciousness. Farmers have come to realize that people are beginning to *demand* pesticide-free produce, and they are rushing to meet the demand. Nazario reports that large suppliers (e.g., Sunkist Growers, Inc.; Castle & Cooke, Inc.'s Dole Foods Company) as well as smaller farmers are beginning to grow organic produce. Some of these farmers are reacting to a 1989 Louis Harris Poll indicating that 84.2 percent of Americans would buy organic produce if available, and that they would pay more money for it if required. Big supermarket chains and restauranteurs are also listening. According to Organic Farms, the nation's largest organic food distributor, in the six months between October and March 1989, some 20 big supermarket chains started stocking organic produce. Some restauranteurs are also scrambling to meet this demand.

Although America's agricultural system is in transition, and the pace is accelerating, we still have a long way to go. Nazario notes that only about 30,000 of the country's 2.2 million farms practice low-input agriculture. Consequently, less than 1 percent of the nation's produce can be classified as organic. What is really delaying the transition, says the National Academy of Science's agricultural board, are federal farm programs that create strong disincentives for practicing low-input agriculture. There is no question, however, in this author's mind that federal farm policies will change as the public increases its

outcry for food that is safe and of superior quality. For an outstanding article about how one conventional farm family successfully made the transition to low-input farming, while some of their neighbors who remained conventional farmers went bankrupt, see Isenhart (1987).

4. *Greater energy efficiencies are possible.* We have made great strides in achieving energy efficiency since 1973, but there is room for much more improvement. In other words, the good news is that we have not expended all possible ways of achieving greater energy efficiency. The experiences of other countries tells us that we can still live very well in residential communities while lowering per capita energy consumption. For example, Raloff (1988) notes that Japan only spends about 5 percent of its gross national product on energy, as compared with the United States, which spends 11.2 percent. This, of course, gives the Japanese an economic edge on everything they sell in the United States, and they have an advantage as well in foreign markets where they compete with American products.

Rather than remaining a fossil fuel ''junky'' always searching for another ''fix'' (e.g., as seen in President Bush's call in 1989 for oil drilling in the Arctic wildlife refuge on Alaska's north slope), we need to drop this fossil fuel ''habit'' and adopt a common-sense strategy based on energy efficiency and renewable energy resources. According to Timothy Wirth, member of the U.S. Senate Energy and Natural Resources Committee, just a 1.5 mpg increase in the fuel-efficiency standard for new cars, starting in 1993, would save more oil than the Arctic refuge is expected to produce. History has already shown us that, since 1973, improvements in the gas mileage of U.S.–manufactured cars have saved this country 2.4 million barrels of oil every day. This is five times the most optimistic prediction for the production of oil from the Arctic refuge. In fact, according to the World Resources Institute, the world could meet most of its energy needs through the year 2020 simply by making more efficient use of the energy now available. If the world population doubles between 1980 and 2020, only a 10 percent rise in energy production will be needed *if* (and *only if*) existing energy-efficient technologies are adopted.

5. *Renewed interest in energy conservation.* Business, industry, and even the Congress are beginning to take energy conservation seriously. Many businesses have established energy conservation departments, with energy specialists assigned to the task of making their companies more energy efficient, and thus more profitable. Industry, as has already been shown, has taken the path toward substantially improved energy efficiency. Some have done so to make a bigger profit; others have become more energy efficient in order to survive in the market place.

The U.S. Congress, which historically moves at a snail's pace, is increasingly becoming interested in energy conservation. For example, in 1987 it passed the National Appliance Energy Conservation Act. This legislation set efficiency requirements for large household appliances and is expected to save the country billions of dollars in energy bills by the year 2000.

6. *Decreased interest in nuclear power.* Americans, as well as other people around the world, are seriously questioning the repeated promises by authorities that nuclear energy is clean and safe. Over the last 40 years, nuclear power has turned out to be *dirty and outright dangerous*, primarily a consequence of power plants that are based on accident-prone technologies and are confronted with the ever burgeoning problem of what to do with the radioactive waste that is generated. Now almost no one wants a nuclear plant (and especially a waste disposal facility) in their "backyard." Consequently, nuclear power is unpopular with the public—and rightly so. Furthermore, this country (much less the world) cannot economically afford nuclear power plants. According to a recent study by the Rocky Mountain Institute, if the world were to replace all existing fossil fuel plants with nuclear facilities during the next 35 years, it would cost at least $144 billion *annually* (The Worldwatch Institute 1989).

7. *Renewable energy sources are continuing to develop.* Whereas Americans are losing interest in nuclear energy (e.g., no new nuclear plants have been ordered in the last decade), interest in renewable energy sources is soaring around the world, says a recent report of the National Wildlife Federation. New technologies are constantly being developed in the areas of solar, wind, biomass, and geothermal energy. These systems are *readily available*, becoming *more economical by the day*, and are *easily assimilated* into an energy efficient economy. For example, the cost of photovoltaic cells has dropped 90 percent in the last decade (The Worldwatch Institute 1989). Adopting renewables will also put us on a path to climate stabilization.

ACTION FOR ENERGY

Although the United States is clearly moving towards an energy system based on energy conservation and renewables, there is still institutional resistance, inadequate consumer education, and an old way of doing business that must be overcome. For example, the U.S. Department of the Interior still takes actions to benefit the oil industry, such as its 1989 policy making it easier to drill in the environmentally sensitive Arctic National Wildlife Refuge. There are also numerous energy specialists, such as Landsberg (1987), who would like to see a resurgence of coal, uranium, and other nonrenewables in America's energy future. Consequently, there is no time to be apathetic about energy resources. You can help America (and the world) move in the right direction by pursuing some of the following recommendations.

1. *Fight the comeback of nuclear power and other nonrenewables.* In order to survive, nuclear engineers are now claiming that they can "build a better nuke"—one that has fail-safe technology, one that virtually eliminates the danger of a meltdown. But, beware! No nuclear reactor, whether watercooled, gas-cooled, or whatever, is safe and clean as long as it produces radioactive waste. The United States has already created enough nuclear waste so that it will require enough time for three (if not more) *ice ages* to pass before the waste becomes harmless in the environment. Furthermore, we have yet to find a permanent resting place for our existing nuclear waste. We cannot afford to invest in an energy system that will create thousand of tons of additional radioactive materials. Another indication that the fight is not over is President Bush's appointment of James D. Watkins to head the Department of Energy. Watkins is a former chief of naval operations and a nuclear energy expert. Traditionally, so-called experts promote the field of their specialty; they do not dismantle it. Be prepared to rebut (e.g., by sending letters to your representative and letters to the editor) any efforts by our nation's leaders to resurrect the dying dragon of nuclear power.

2. *Help reduce social obstacles to energy conservation.* Although there is plenty of room for additional improvements in energy efficiency, there are a variety of social obstacles that must be overcome. For example, Raloff (1988) notes that although efficient water heaters may only cost slightly more than less efficient models, consumers may avoid the higher priced units because they cannot easily calculate the payback period. Manufacturers (or retailers) need to place stickers on these models that are written in plain language and are understandable. Likewise, more people would pursue drought-resistant landscaping (less water used means less energy used to pump the water) if nurseries stocked and made it easy to identify drought-resistant plants. You can help by bringing things of this sort to the attention of appliance dealers, garden suppliers, and other retailers. Just as U.S. car dealers must now post mileage ratings for new automobiles and appliance dealers must list energy ratings for new appliances, new house and building designers should rate their new buildings for their energy conservation potential. According to Flavin and Durning (1988), this is already a common practice in other countries. Wherever and whenever possible, you can help by insisting that the buyer be fully informed on the energy conservation potential of a product.

3. *Help improve market signals.* To open the market for conservation and renewables, it is essential that the price signals be right. According to Shea (1988), most of the country's existing signals are wrong. For example, the federal government provides tax incentives for coal mining and transportation; it keeps prices for diesel fuel and kerosene artificially low; and it gives tax breaks to petroleum producers. If there are to be tax breaks and other incentives, they should be going to conservation efforts and renewables. Until they do, the development and commercial attractiveness of conservation and renewables will be hampered.

Beginning around 1978, some energy tax credits for businesses and residences were made available and this inspired the markets for solar collectors, photovoltaic cells, windmills, small hydro facilities, and other renewable technologies. By 1985, says Shea (1988), these tax credits were "yanked out wholesale," resulting in a devastating blow to the renewable energy industry. Your voice is needed in calling for tax credits and other incentives for energy conservation and the use of renewables. For additional insight into this aspect of energy resource management, see Flavin (1988).

4. *Support higher energy standards.* Mandatory energy efficiency standards must be reinforced and gradually raised, not relaxed. In 1987, the Reagan administration relaxed automobile efficiency standards. This misguided move virtually told automakers to once again return to the gas-guzzling days of yesteryear. *Just because fuel prices temporarily fall does not mean that we can go back to being wasteful.* Regardless of the price of fuel, Flavin (1988) argues, we need to get the fuel efficiency of the average new car to at least 40 mpg by the year 2000. Similarly, national mandatory energy efficiency standards must also be established for residential and commercial buildings. To date, California has the toughest building efficiency standards, and they have proven to be successful in reducing energy requirements. Why are other states not following suit?

You can help fight for mandatory efficiency standards by joining and financially supporting (through membership fees) such organizations as the Energy Conservation Coalition, an umbrella group that focuses its efforts on increasing national energy efficiency. In 1988, for example, it provided Congress with an alternate energy conservation budget, which called for an 18 percent *increase* over the last year's budget. (By contrast, the Reagan administration had called for a 74 percent *decrease* in funds for energy conservation.)

5. *Support research and development of energy conservation and renewables.* To develop new conservation and renewable energy technologies requires sustained research and development (R & D) so that new theories can be developed, experiments can be made, and demonstration projects can be built. This all requires lots of money. According to Shea (1988), government funding peaked in 1980 at $900 million (in 1986 dollars). Since then, appropriations for this R & D have fallen by 80 percent. Much of this had to do with the Reagan administration's lack of interest in and commitment to renewables.

By contrast, other countries, such as Greece and Portugal, have increased their R & D budgets for renewables. According to per capita expenditures (which factors out population size and funding support for other technologies), Sweden is the real leader in overall government commitment to renewables. In fact, *it even has a national referendum to phase out all 12 of its existing nuclear plants by the year 2010* (Shea 1988). We, too, should be committed to renewables. For additional information on the R & D question, see Gamser (1988) and Setty and Natarajan (1988).

6. *Develop your own personal energy action plan.* Do not sit on the sidelines waiting for the government (whether it be federal, state, county, or city) to save energy for you. There are dozens of books on the market that can inform you how to save energy and money in the realms of transportation, home space heating, hot water heating, appliance use, and lighting. Most of the techniques are simple and affordable—even for university students. For example, there are hundreds of things that you can do in your everyday life, from recycling, to turning off lights, to using mass transit.

7. *Choose a career in energy conservation and renewable resources.* If you are really concerned about this subject, there are a growing number of undergraduate and graduate courses, programs, and degrees on the subject of energy resource management. Furthermore, the job market for energy specialists is already good, and will be expanding rapidly as America (and the world) makes the transition to energy conservation and the renewable energy system. *The world needs leaders that have a fiery sense of mission—not to lead a military or a nationalistic campaign, but to lead a crusade to bring human energy requirements back in line with ecological realities.*

CONCLUSION

As a professionally trained geographer back in the early 1970s, I used to think that one always had to look for sophisticated academic answers to problems regarding the management of energy and other natural resources. I can remember turning my nose up at the "hippie recyclers," the "flaky organic gardeners," and all those who former Interior Secretary James Watt had called the "nuts and berry types." Over the past 20 years of research and teaching, I have come to realize that these so-called ecofreaks were actually pioneering the direction the country (and world) so badly needed to take. My hat is now off to all the individual *conservation pioneers* in our society—the individuals who insist on walking, biking, or riding mass transit rather than using a private automobile; the organic farmers; the patrons of organic produce; the vegetarians; the nonsmokers; the recyclers; the composters; the plastic-boycotters; and especially those individuals such as environmental studies teacher Frank Schiavo (see Figure 14-5) who "buck and override" every governmental policy that tells them to do otherwise. Rather than "poo-poo" their actions as being insignificant, which I admit I used to do, we should *applaud* and *copy* their activities, for they are the new American pioneers—pioneers of a universal *new way of life.*

DISCUSSION TOPICS

1. On March 24, 1989, it was reported that two chemists had discovered the secret to harnessing *fusion* nuclear power. Assuming that their findings are verified, debate whether or not the United States should emphasize the production of fusion nuclear power over energy conservation and renewables energy resources.

2. The United States has several pockets of alternative ways of life that are not exactly mainstream American lifestyles (e.g., the Navaho Indians in Arizona; various Eskimo groups in Alaska; and the Amish in Pennsylvania). Should these people be allowed to hold on to their lands if the country needs the coal, oil, uranium, or other natural resources that may be on their property?

3. How can the energy conservation experiencies of other places, such as Hamburg, West Germany, be applied to America? Give some examples, if possible, from your own experiences of living in other countries. If necessary seek out some ideas from foreign students on your campus.

4. Make an energy conservation plan for yourself by listing every thing that you can possibly do to save energy. Put a "+" by the things that you already do (e.g., turning off lights when leaving a room), an "*" by those things that you would do if conditions were right (e.g., if you had enough money to insulate the windows and doors), and a "−" by those things that you would never consider doing (e.g., living in a house designed like a yurt—a Mongolian-style sheepskin hut). Compare and discuss your list with the lists of others in your class or home. Are there any changes in your opinions after comparing notes and hearing other students' explanations for their choices?

5. Pretend that you are an architect. Design a house so that it could accommodate the use of gray water. Compare your designs with others in class. Submit the best design to your university's School of Architecture or to some local architects. Request a written evaluation of your design.

6. Study the way that indigenous peoples around the world have traditionally captured and conserved energy in their housing designs. In what ways could some of their techniques be adapted to modern architectural designs in America?

7. Is your campus recycling paper? If not, find out why. Start a campaign to recycle paper and save energy.

8. Is your campus located in a drought-prone area? If so, does it have a policy of only planting drought-tolerant trees and shrubs? If not, why not? Again, take action. Do not wait for the campus administration to lead the way.

9. Some conservation organizations have suggested that there be a $1.00 tax per gallon on gasoline, rather than the existing 30 cent tax. Discuss the economic and conservation implications of such a tax if it were enacted. Would you support it? If not, why not?

10. Some key city officials in charge of mass transit use their private cars rather than mass transit to get from one place to another, arguing that they cannot afford to miss an important meeting. Do you consider this a valid reason for them to not ride the mass transit system that they administer?

READINGS

ANON. 1988. ''The Prospects of Renewable Energy Sources,'' *Economic Bulletin for Europe,* vol. 40, no. 1. This special volume of the *Economic Bulletin* covers the 1987 Symposium on the Status and Prospects of New and Renewable Sources of Energy in the ECE Region. It includes the papers presented at the symposium.

ARCO. 1982. ''Photovoltaic-powered Water Pumps Growing in Popularity,'' *Arco Solar News,* vol. 2, no. 4, pp. 4–9. Brief article about using this type of renewable-energy pump to replace the traditional fossil fuel driven irrigation pump.

ARGONNE NATIONAL LABORATORY. 1984. *The Role of Electric Vehicles in the Nation's Energy Future.* Washington, D.C.: U.S. Department of Energy. Excellent summary.

AUBRECHT, GORDON. 1989. *Energy.* Columbus, Ohio: Merrill. Outstanding overview, covering energy topics from A to Z.

BATLY, J., S. N. HAMAD, and J. KELLER. 1975. ''Energy Inputs to Irrigation,'' *Journal of Irrigation and Drainage Division,* ASCE, vol. 101 (IR 4), pp. 293–307. General review.

BEAMAN, DOUG. 1987. ''Aren't Offices Just Big Houses?'' *Sun World,* vol. 11, no. 1, pp. 7–8. Discusses how to achieve greater energy efficiency in office buildings.

BLACKBURN, JOHN O. 1987. *The Renewable Energy Alternative.* Durham, N.C.: Duke University Press. Argues that the United States and the world can prosper without nuclear energy and coal.

BLOOME, P. D., I. W. GREVIS-JAMES, L. K. JONES, and D. G. BATCHELDER. 1981. ''Farm Machinery Ideas that Save Energy.'' In J. Hayes, ed., *Cutting Energy Costs (The 1980 Yearbook of Agriculture),* pp. 115–120. Washington, D.C.: U.S. Department of Agriculture. Good summary.

BROWN, LESTER, et al. 1988. *State of the World.* New York: Norton. Annual Worldwatch Institute progress report on the status of the world.

BROWN, LESTER R., and JODI L. JACOBSON. 1987. ''The Future of Urbanization: Facing the Ecological and Economic Constraints,'' *Worldwatch Paper 77,* May. Contains excellent section on urban energy needs.

CLARK, WILSON. 1975. ''U.S. Agriculture is Growing Trouble as Well as Crops,'' *Smithsonian,* vol. 5, no. 10, January, pp. 59–64. Excellent overview of the problems of our conventional chemical and energy intensive system of agriculture in the United States.

COLLINS, JAMES F. 1987. ''Trends in the U.S. Steel Industry.'' In Ahmad Faruqui and John Broehl, eds., *The Changing Structure of American Industry and Energy Use Patterns,* pp. 271–291. Columbus, Ohio: Battelle Press. Excellent summary.

DOSTROVSKI, I. 1988. *Energy and the Missing Resources.* Cambridge: Cambridge University Press. Argues that long-term technical development will be necessary to ensure future energy sufficiency.

EBINGER, CHARLES. 1987. ''U.S. Energy Security to 2000.'' In Robert Belgrave, Charles K. Ebinger, and Hideaki Okino, eds., *Energy Security to 2000,* pp. 259–303. Boulder, Colo.: Westview Press. Implications for energy decisions within the OECD group of countries and the options available to their governments.

EISENHAUER, D. E., and FISCHBACH, P. E. 1977. ''Comparing Costs of Conventional and Improved Irrigation Systems,'' *Irrigation Age,* vol. 11, no. 8, pp. 36–37. Economic analysis of various irrigation systems for crop production.

ELMORE, R., and D. G. HANWAY. 1984. ''Selecting Varieties and Hybrids,'' *Crop Focus 1984,* pp. 9–11. Lincoln, Nebr.: University of Nebraska. Discusses how selecting the appropriate plant hybrid can eliminate the fossil fuel drying process.

EVANS, DANIEL J. 1987. ''The Future of Federal Energy Conservation Policy,'' *Forum for Applied Research and Public Policy,* Spring, vol. 2, no. 1, pp. 77–81. Good discussion of what the government's role in energy conservation should be.

FINE, SUSAN. 1989. ''Composting Nature's 'Garbage,''' *Worldwatch,* January–February, pp. 5–6. Provides a good argument for composting to help relieve our garbage and energy crisis.

FLAVIN, CHRISTOPHER. 1988. ''Creating a Sustainable Energy Future.'' In Lester Brown et al., *State of the World 1988,* pp. 22–40. New York: Norton. Excellent article on achieving greater energy efficiency.

FLAVIN, CHRISTOPHER. 1987. ''Reassessing Nuclear Power: The Fallout From Chernobyl,'' *Worldwatch Paper 75.* Washington, D.C.: Worldwatch Institute. Raises questions regarding the safety and political feasibility of nuclear power as an energy choice.

FLAVIN, CHRISTOPHER, and ALAN DURNING. 1988. ''Raising Energy Efficiency.'' In Lester Brown et al., *State of the World 1988,* pp. 41–61. New York: Norton. Contains numerous suggestions on how the United States can raise its energy efficiency.

FOLEY, GERALD. 1987. *The Energy Question.* 3d ed. London: Penguin Books. Survey of the world's energy resources and needs from a technical, environmental, and political perspective.

FRANCIS, C. A., and J. W. KING. 1988. ''Cropping Systems Based on Farm-Derived, Renewable Resources,'' *Agricultural Systems,* vol. 27, no. 1, pp. 67–75. Provides several examples of how farmers can use internal resources instead of more expensive external production inputs.

FRYE, W. W., and S. H. PHILLIPS. 1981. ''How to Grow Crops With Less Energy.'' In J. Hayes, ed., *Cutting Energy Costs (The 1980 Yearbook of Agriculture).* Washington, D.C.: U.S. Department of Agriculture. Includes good tables on energy savings with various types of tillage systems.

FULLER, S., and T. MCTIERNAN. 1987. ''Old Crow and the Northern Yukon: Achieving Renewable Resource Utilization,'' *Alternatives,* vol. 14, no. 1, pp. 18–25. Discusses how the Band Council of Old Crow have begun preparation of a renewable resource socioeconomic development plan based on the sustainable use of wildlife, water, and forests.

GAMSER, M. S. 1988. "Power from the People: Technology Users and the Management of Energy Innovation," *Energy Policy,* vol. 16, no. 1, pp. 27–35. Discusses the importance of the participation of users in the development of new energy technologies.

GOLDEMBERG, JOSE, et al. 1988. *Energy for a Sustainable World.* New York: Wiley. Contains an excellent section on agriculture and energy.

GUCERI, S. I. 1983. "Solar Dehydration." In D. Knorr, ed., *Sustainable Food Systems.* Westport, Conn.: AVI. Detailed study.

HEICHEL, G. H. 1978. "Stabilizing Agricultural Needs: Role of Forages, Rotations, and Nitrogen Fixation," *Journal of Soil and Water Conservation,* vol. 33, pp. 279–282. Opportunity for meeting crop nitrogen needs with the use of legumes.

HEID, W. G., JR., and D. F. ALDIS. 1981. "Solar-Supplemented Natural Air Drying of Shelled Corn," *Tech. Bull. No. 1654.* Washington, D.C.: Economic and Statistical Service, U.S. Department of Agriculture. Good technical report.

HEID, W. G., JR., and W. K. TROTTER. 1982. "Progress of Solar Technology and Potential Farm Uses," *Agricultural Economic Report No. 489.* Washington, D.C.: Department of Agriculture. Good summary.

HEIJMAN, W. 1988. "The Need for a Steady State Economy," *International Journal of Social Economics,* vol. 15, no. 3–4, pp. 80–87. Argues that economic theory must take an interest in nature, which consists of renewable and nonrenewable resources.

HIRST, ERIC, et al. 1986. *Energy Efficiency in Buildings: Progress and Promise.* Washington, D.C.: American Council for an Energy-Efficient Economy. Good summary.

HIRST, ERIC, and KENNETH KEATING. 1987. "Dynamics of Energy Savings Due to Conservation Programs," *Energy Systems and Policy,* vol. 10, no. 3, pp. 257–273. Raises questions about whether or not government and utility program-induced energy savings are constant over time.

INSTITUTE FOR ENERGY STUDIES. 1979. *Alternative Energy Futures.* Palo Alto, Calif.: Stanford University. Good discussion of the various ways the paper industry can become more efficient.

INTERNATIONAL ENERGY AGENCY. 1987. *Renewable Sources of Energy.* Paris: OECD/IEA. Comprehensive report of the efforts of the Organization for Economic Cooperation and Development (OECD) to implement an International Energy Program.

ISENHART, CHARLES. 1987. "Two Iowa Farmers Sow the Seeds of Change," *Sierra,* November–December, vol. 72, no. 6, pp. 79–82. Excellent example of a success story in switching from conventional farming to organic farming.

JENKINS, BRYAN M. 1989. "Field-Drying Rice Using Modified Swath Harvesting," *California Agriculture,* March–April, vol. 43, no. 2, pp. 25–27. Discusses how covering rice that is drying with stubble reduces drying costs and energy.

JENSEN, M. E., and E. G. KRUSE. 1981. "Cheaper Ways to Move Irrigation Water." In J. Hayes, ed., *Cutting Energy Costs (The 1980 Yearbook of Agriculture),* pp. 121–132. Washington, D.C.: U.S. Department of Agriculture. Good summary.

KATZEV, RICHARD D., and THEODORE R. JOHNSON. 1987. *Promoting Energy Conservation: An Analysis of Behavior Research.* Boulder, Colo.: Westview Press. Major findings of experimental research on the conditions that promote energy conservation.

KOZLOFF, KEITH. 1987. "Overcoming Barriers to Improved Energy Efficiency: U.S. Experiences and Relevance to Developing Countries." In R. K. Pachauri, ed., *Global Energy Interactions.* Riverdale, Md.: Riverdale. Excellent review of the U.S. experience with energy efficiency.

LANCEY, STANLEY. 1987. "Energy Consumption by the Paper Industry." In Ahmad Faruqui and John Broehl, eds., *The Changing Structure of American Industry and Energy Use Patterns,* pp. 315–327. Columbus, Ohio: Battelle Press. Excellent summary.

LANDSBERG, H. H. 1987. "The Case for Coal in the United States," *Environment,* vol. 29, no. 6, pp. 19–20, 38–43. Argues that coal is the most attractive alternative for U.S. energy policymakers.

MATARE, HERBERT F. 1989. *Energy: Facts and Future.* Boca Raton, Fla.: CRC Press. Highly technical report.

MELOSI, MARTIN. 1987. "Energy and Environment in the United States: The Era of Fossil Fuels," *Environmental Review,* Fall, pp. 167–188. Good historical analysis of changing federal policy toward energy resources.

MILLER, G. TYLER. 1988. *Living in the Environment.* 5th ed. Belmont, Calif.: Wadsworth. Contains excellent chapters on energy for introductory background information.

MORAN, J., M. MORGAN, and J. WIERSMA. 1986. *Introduction to Environmental Science.* 2d ed. New York: Freeman. Excellent introductory text.

MUMFORD, LEWIS. 1961. *The City in History.* Orlando, Fla.: Harcourt Brace Jovanovich. Classic study of the historical evolution of cities worldwide.

NATIONAL WILDLIFE FEDERATION. 1988. "Energy Efficiency Back in Business," *Conservation '88,* June, vol. 6, no. 7, pp. 6–8. Very brief article about the renewed interest in energy efficiency with a special focus on U.S. federal legislation.

NKONOKI, S. R., and E. LUSHIKU. 1988. "Energy Planning in Tansania: Emerging Trends in Planning and Research," *Energy Policy,* vol. 16, no. 3, pp. 280–291. Discusses renewable energy potentials for Tanzania.

OWEN, OLIVER. 1985. *Natural Resource Conservation.* 4th ed. New York: Macmillan. Contains two good chapters on energy for background information.

PACHAURI, R. K., ed. 1987. *Global Energy Interactions.* Riverdale, Md.: Riverdale. Compilation of papers from contributions made at the Fifth International Conference of the International Association of Energy Economists (IAEE) at New Delhi in 1984.

PECK, MERTON J. 1988. "Restructuring the Aluminum Industry," *Resources*, Spring, no. 91., pp. 14–17. Discusses how the world aluminum industry shifted from one region to another after the energy shock of 1973.

POINCELOT, RAYMOND. 1986. *Toward a More Sustainable Agriculture*. Westport, Conn.: AVI. Contains separate chapters on animal husbandry energy conservation, crop energy conservation, greenhouse energy conservation, and post-production energy conservation. Must reading.

PYRDE, PHILIP R. 1983. *Nonconventional Energy Resources*. New York: Wiley Interscience.

RALOFF, JANET. 1988. "Energy Efficiency: Less Means More," *Science News*, May, vol. 133, pp. 296–298. Includes a good discussion of how planting trees can achieve energy efficiency.

RAO, G. L., and M. K. SASTRI. 1987. "Land Use and Solar Energy," *Habitat International*, vol. 11, no. 3, pp. 61–75. Excellent article that considers land-use implications of generating solar energy.

RAO, K. S., et al. 1987. "Khandia—a Solar Village," *Sunworld*, vol. 11, no. 1, pp. 11–13. A village in India is used to illustrate the concept of the Integrated Rural Energy Centre.

REJESKI, D. 1987. "Energy-sensitive Land-use Planning," *Tunnelling & Underground Space Technology*, vol. 2, no. 2, pp. 219–225. Describes the undertaking of Hamburg, West Germany, to address the existing disparity between energy and land-use planning.

ROSE, DAVID. 1986. *Learning About Energy*. New York: Plenum Press. University textbook that presents a broad overview of the energy field. Contains good chapter on energy conservation.

ROSS, MARC. 1987. "Industrial Energy Conservation and the Steel Industry of the United States," *Energy*, vol. 12, no. 10–11, pp. 1135–1152. Excellent review of the manufacturing aspect of energy use in industry.

ROSS, R. 1978. "Colorado Pump Tests Show How to Make Big Dollar Savings," *Irrigation Age*, March, vol. 12, no. 3, pp. 9, 12, 16. Example of how to economize on energy for irrigation pumping, as shown in tests in Colorado.

RUDOLPH, RICHARD, and SCOTT RIDLEY. 1986. *Power Struggle*. New York: Harper & Row. Traces the rich history of the use of electricity.

RUTTEN, B., B. HASPEL, and A. BEEK. 1988. "GISWA: Geographical Information System Wind Resource (Wind Power)," *Journal of Wind Engineering & Industrial Aerodynamics*, vol. 27, no. 1–2, pp. 103–112. Discusses the use of wind resource maps in finding sites for wind systems.

SCHNEIDER, R. 1988. "Renewable Sources of Energy in IEA Countries—A Review of Status and Prospects of NRSE. *Economic Bulletin for Europe*. vol. 40, no. 1, pp. 163–167. Useful summary.

SERI. 1981. *A New Prosperity: Building a Sustainable Energy Future*. Andover, Mass.: Brick House.

SETTY, K., P. SRINIVASA, and R. NATARAJAN. 1988. "Process Analysis of Becoming Committed to Energy Conservation—A Path Analytic Approach," *Energy Convers. Mgmt*, vol. 28, no. 1, pp. 5–9. Interesting article on how to transform society from an extravagant energy user to a frugal user.

SHEA, CYNTHIA POLLOCK. 1988. "Renewable Energy: Today's Contribution, Tomorrow's Promise," *Worldwatch Paper 81*, January. Information-packed report from The Worldwatch Institute.

SHEPPARD, WILLIAM J. 1987. "Trends in the U.S. Chemical Industry." In Ahmad Faruqui and John Broehl, eds., *The Changing Structure of American Industry and Energy Use Patterns*, pp. 293–314. Columbus, Ohio: Battelle Press. Excellent summary.

SMITH, DAVID R., and DAVID A. SHOLTIS. 1981. "Green Parking Lot, Dayton, Ohio: An Experimental Installation of Grass Pavement. 2d Performance Evaluation." Dayton, Ohio: The Heritage Conservation and Recreation Service. Interesting analysis of turf-block paving.

SOBEY, ALBERT J. 1987. "Trends in the U.S. Automobile Industry." In Ahmad Faruqui and John Broehl, eds., *The Changing Structure of American Industry and Energy Use Patterns*, pp. 257–269. Columbus, Ohio: Battelle Press. Interesting summary.

SPIRN, ANNE. 1984. *The Granite Garden*. New York: Basic Books. Must reading for anyone interested in designing cities for energy conservation.

STETSON, L. E., D. G. WATTS, F. C. COREY, and I. D. NELSON. 1975. "Irrigation System Management for Reducing Peak Electrical Demands," *ASEA*, vol. 18, pp. 303–306, 311. Description of a systems management approach to conserving irrigation energy.

THAYER, R. L., and C. M. FREEMAN. 1987. "Altamont: Public Perceptions of a Wind Energy Landscape," *Landscape & Urban Planning*, vol. 14, no. 5, pp. 379–398. Examines public response to the Altamont Pass Wind Energy Development in California.

TIME MAGAZINE STAFF. 1989. "Planet of the Year: Endangered Earth," *Time*, January 2, vol. 133, no. 1. This issue was devoted to the state of the planet in lieu of its usual "Man or Woman of the Year" cover story.

TWIDELL, JOHN, and TONY WEIR. 1986. *Renewable Energy Resources*. New York: E. & F. N. Spon. Renewable energy from a physical science and engineering perspective.

U.S. ENERGY INFORMATION ADMINISTRATION. 1988. *Energy Facts 1987*. Washington, D.C.: U.S. Department of Energy. Useful annual report.

WHITE, J. G. 1978. "Re-use Pits: Cheapest Water on the Farm," *Irrigation Age*, November–December, vol. 12, no. 11, pp. 58, 62. Recycling as a technique to conserve irrigation energy on the farm is discussed.

WILLIAMS, ROBERT H. 1987. "A Low Energy Future for the United States," *Energy*, vol. 12, no. 10–11, pp. 929–944. Argues that we can dramatically reduce energy use without sacrificing economic growth.

WILSON, HOWARD, PAUL B. MACCREADY, and CHESTER R. KYLE. 1989. ''Lessons of Sunraycer,'' *Scientific American*, March, vol. 260, no. 3, pp. 90–96. Discusses the lessons that sunraycer (a solar racing car) have for those considering alternatives to fuel-burning vehicles.

WORLD COMMISSION ON ENVIRONMENT AND DEVELOPMENT. 1987. *Energy 2000: A Global Strategy for Sustainable Development*. Atlantic Highlands, N.J.: Zed Books. Contains excellent strategies for achieving energy sustainability.

WORLD RESOURCES INSTITUTE, and INTERNATIONAL INSTITUTE FOR ENVIRONMENT AND DEVELOPMENT. 1988. *World Resources 1988–89*. New York: Basic Books. Contains a good chapter on energy and the global situation.

WORLDWATCH INSTITUTE. 1989. ''Toward a Climate Sensitive Energy Policy,'' *World Watch*, January–February, vol. 2, no. 1, pp. 11–13. Brief summary of suggestions for reducing the causes of global warming.

GLOSSARY

Abyssal zone. The undulating deep sea plain or ocean floor below 2000 m (6562 ft), marked by an accumulation of pelagic marine deposits, notably ooze. Compare *oceanic zone, euphotic zone,* and *bathyal zone.*

Accelerated erosion. Relatively rapid erosion caused by human intervention. Compare *geologic erosion.*

Acid rain. Rainfall that is more acid than normal because of the absorption of air pollutants; sulfuric acid (H_2SO_4) and nitric acid (NHO_3) are formed when water vapor in the air reacts with such pollutants as nitrogen dioxide (NO_2) and sulfur dioxide (SO_2).

Algal bloom. The rapid growth of algae on the surface of stagnant streams, ponds, or lakes; usually caused by phosphate enrichment.

All-aged forest. A forest stand composed of trees of all ages. Compare *even-aged forest* and *uneven-aged forest.*

Alluvium. Type of *depositional soil;* unconsolidated fragmental material (mostly fine-grained silt and silt-clay, though sand and gravel are also present) laid down by a stream as a cone (*alluvial fan*) in its river bed (*floodplain*) or at a river mouth (*delta*); usually very fertile and therefore of great agricultural value.

Animal unit month (AUM). A measure of the forage or feed required to maintain one animal unit (one cow, one horse, or five sheep) for a period of one month.

Aquaculture. The controlled cultivation and harvesting of aquatic plants, fish, and shellfish in land-based ponds. Compare *mariculture.*

Aquiclude. A rock stratum that is porous and may hold much water (e.g., clay), but cannot transmit water at a sufficient rate for wells or springs. Since an aquiclude is rela-tively impermeable, and, consequently, *retards* the flow of water, some scientists prefer the term *aquitard.* Compare *aquifer.*

Aquifer. A layer of relatively permeable rock (e.g., sandstone, chalk) that not only holds water but can transmit it at a sufficient rate for human consumption. There are two types of aquifers: *confined* (capped on its upper surface by an aquiclude) and *unconfined* (not bounded by an aquiclude). Compare *aquiclude.*

Area surface mining. One of two types of strip mining. It involves cutting deep trenches in level to gently rolling topography. Compare *contour surface mining.*

Artesian well. A well that usually produces a continuous flow of water due to hydrostatic pressure. This phenomenon occurs when a well is dug into an aquifer below the level of the water source.

Azonal soils (immature, young soils). Soils that have indistinct or only slightly developed horizons because of the relatively short time that soil-building forces have been acting on the parent material. An obsolete term based on the 1949 revision of the Great Soils system of soil classification. Compare *zonal soils.*

Bathyal zone. The middle region of the oceanic zone that is below the level of light penetration and that reaches to the bottom of the continental slope, that is, from 200 m (656 ft) to 2000 m (6562 ft), or from the euphotic zone to the abyssal zone. Compare *oceanic zone, euphotic zone,* and *abyssal zone.*

Bedrock. Solid rock underlying the topsoil and subsoil. Compare *regolith.*

384

Benthic. Plants and animals that inhabit the bottom of seas, lakes, or streams.

Biochemical oxygen demand (BOD). A measure of the oxygen *utilized* by aerobic microorganisms in water rich with organic matter. Also known as *biological oxygen demand.* Compare *dissolved oxygen content (DO).*

Biological control. A method of controlling pest organisms by using means other than chemicals, such as natural predators, parasites, sterilization, or sexual reproduction–inhibiting hormones.

Biotic (reproductive) potential. The maximum capacity (rate) at which a population of either plants or animals can reproduce under optimum environmental conditions, including unlimited resources.

Botulism. A highly destructive disease of waterfowl caused by the anaerobic bacteria *Clostridium botulinum* that thrives on rotting vegetation or animal debris. Waterfowl exposed to botulism suffer respiratory paralysis and death.

Capillary fringe. A zone of subsurface water held above the water table by capillary action. Water is held in the soil by surface tension and is not pulled downward by the force of gravity. Since this belt of soil is almost (but not totally) saturated, wells must be dug past the capillary fringe into the zone of saturation.

Capillary water. Type of soil water; water that clings to soil particles after *gravitational water* has been drained from a field. Capillary water clings to solid surfaces by means of capillary film tension. Compare *gravitational water* and *hygroscopic water.*

Carnivore. An organism, whether plant or animal, that eats meat. Compare *herbivore* and *omnivore.*

Carrying capacity. The maximum population size (e.g., number of cattle) that a given habitat (e.g., range of a given acreage) will support indefinitely under normal environmental conditions (e.g., without drought).

Cetacean sanctuaries. Protected regions of the ocean set aside for fishlike aquatic mammals, such as whales, dolphins, and other cetaceans; a marine resource management technique for keeping certain animals from being harassed or killed.

Channelization. The conversion of a natural stream into a theoretically more efficient ditch or waterway for the purpose of flood control. The process involves straightening, widening, and deepening the stream so that water can move faster.

Chlorination. The addition of chlorine to sewage, industrial waste, or drinking water to oxidize or disinfect harmful compounds.

Clear-cutting. A harvesting technique in which all the trees are removed from a given area of forest. Compare *selective cutting* and *shelterwood cutting.*

Coliform bacteria. A certain group of bacteria used as a measure of water quality; their presence indicates dangerous bacterial pollution from inadequate sewage treatment or barnyard wastes.

Colloid. Organic and inorganic matter in a state of extremely fine particle size; it is gelatinous in nature, and when dissolved in liquid, will not diffuse through membranes. Colloids physically impart an adhesive quality to clay particles and chemically attract and hold ions of dissolved substances, especially bases such as calcium.

Companion crop. A crop grown simultaneously with another for the purpose of holding soil in place or improving soil fertility. Compare *cover crop.*

Cone of depression. A local depression of the water table around a water supply well caused by the withdrawal of water at a faster rate than it can move laterally through the aquifer to supply the well. See *drawdown.*

Conservation. To use resources wisely (natural resources) so as to *sustain* the quality of life for humanity and for other organisms. Broadly defined, the term conservation encompasses all the tools, techniques, policies, and philosophies needed to *restore, replace, regenerate,* and *recycle* natural resources. See *natural resources.*

Conservation tillage. A major type of tillage in which ridges are formed and crop residues and clods are left on the soil surface; increases infiltration and reduces runoff and erosion. Compare *contour cultivation* and *emergency tillage.*

Continental shelf. The portion of the sea floor adjacent to a continent or an island, covered by shallow water that is 200 m (656 ft) or less in depth; gently sloping (1 degree or less); generally excellent fishing grounds. Compare *continental slope.*

Continental slope. The 2 to 5 degree slope that decends from the edge of the continental shelf to the deep ocean bed (abyssal zone), ranging in depth from 200 m (656 ft) to 2000 m (6562 ft). Compare *continental shelf.*

Contour cultivation (contour tillage). A type of tillage in which plowing and planting are done at right angles to the slope of the land to prevent erosion and to conserve water. Compare *conservation tillage* and *emergency tillage.*

Contour surface mining. Generally the most destructive of the two types of strip mining, since this technique involves cutting a series of bands in hilly or mountainous terrain. Compare *area surface mining.*

Controlled burn (prescribed burn). The use of fire, under controlled conditions, to improve the quality of forest, range, or wildlife habitat.

Cover. Elements in the environment (e.g., standing trees, fallen logs, shrubs, and boulders) that provide cover (protection) for wildlife, thereby enhancing reproduction and survival.

Cover crop. A quick-maturing crop, generally a legume, that is grown between main crops to protect the soil surface, to decrease erosion and leaching, to shade the ground, and to protect against excessive freezing and heaving. Compare *companion crop.*

Crop rotation. A cropping system in which two or more crops are grown in succession on the same field in order to preserve fertility and minimize soil erosion.

Cultural (bioenvironmental) controls. An umbrella phase

for nonchemical pest control techniques, such as crop rotation, strip cropping, and field planning.

Cultural eutrophication. Acceleration by humans of the natural process of enrichment (aging) of water bodies. Agricultural, urban, and industrial discharge are the primary human-made sources that overnourish aquatic ecosystems. Compare *eutrophication.*

Cyclic population. A wildlife population that has *regular* and *predictable* increases and decreases in population that occur at intervals that are less variable than could be expected by chance. One of three classifications of wildlife populations. Compare *stable population* and *irruptive population.*

Deferred grazing. Discontinuance of livestock grazing on a specific piece of rangeland for a specified period of time. A range management technique used to promote plant reproduction, establish new plants, and restore the vigor of old plants. Compare *deferred-rotation grazing* and *rest-rotation grazing.*

Deferred-rotation grazing. A deferred grazing scheme that is systematic, wherein a range is divided into several pastures that are grazed on a rotational basis (e.g., pasture A and B are grazed, but pasture C is allowed to rest). Compare *deferred grazing* and *rest-rotation grazing.*

Depletion time. The length of time that it takes a society to use up 80 percent of a given mineral supply. The concept uses certain assumptions regarding consumptive practices.

Depositional soils. Soils that have been transported and then deposited mechanically by running water, wind, ice, tides, or ocean currents. Compare *residual soils.*

Desalination (also desalinization). The conversion of seawater or brackish water into potable (sweet) water.

Desertification. Conversion of semiarid rangelands into desert through a combination of prolonged drought and the degradating process caused by overgrazing by livestock.

Detention (depression storage). Precipitation temporarily retained in a surface depression (e.g., small mud puddles), and therefore not available for overland flow. Once depression storage is exceeded, then overland flow and runoff can occur.

Disinfection. A process, usually involving chlorination, done at sewage treatment plants that removes water coloration and kills most organisms that cause infectious disease. The final stage of secondary treatment. See *secondary treatment.*

Dissolved oxygen content (DO). The amount of gaseous oxygen dissolved in water and *available* for aquatic life. Inadequate waste treatment may result in low dissolved oxygen concentrations that are harmful or deadly to aquatic organisms. Compare *biochemical oxygen demand (BOD).*

Drainage basin. A part of the surface of the earth drained by a single river with all its tributary surface streams.

Drawdown. The height of a cone of depression, which is a measurement of the difference between the water table in a well before pumping as compared with the water level in the well during pumping. See *cone of depression.*

Dredging. One of three types of surface mining, the other two being open pit mining and strip mining. Dredging usually denotes the use of chain buckets or suction devices to extract minerals from streambeds or seabeds.

Dryland farming or dry farming. The practice of agricultural production in low rainfall areas without the use of irrigation. Moisture-conserving techniques are used, such as mulches and fallowing.

Dune sand. Type of aeolian landform; low ridge or hill of loose, well-sorted sand, deposited by wind and usually capable of downwind motion. Also called *dune* or *sand dune.*

Ecotone. A transition zone where two adjacent ecosystems merge together, rather than change abruptly. The zone has characteristics of both kinds of neighboring vegetation, yet it still possesses characteristics of its own.

El Niño. An atmospheric-oceanic phenomenon that disrupts normal ocean circulation patterns by bringing a warm-water current to the western coast of South America approximately every seven years; the current occasionally reaches as far north as North America, upsetting normal precipitation rates, the dissolved oxygen content of marine waters, and marine animal life.

Emergency tillage. A type of tillage in which chisels and other implements are used in times of emergency to produce ridges and furrows across the path of the wind. Compare *conservation tillage, contour cultivation.*

Endangered species. Any fish, terrestrial animal, or plant that is in danger of extinction in all or part of its range. Compare *threatened species.*

Energy conservation. A phrase that implies both *reducing energy use* (e.g., composting food scraps in your backyard rather than using an electric garbage disposal) and *increasing energy efficiency* (e.g., buying a refrigerator, stove, washer, dryer that uses less energy to do the same amount of work).

Environmental resistance (ER). Limiting factors in the environment (e.g., lack of food, limited or contaminated water supplies, an overabundance of predators) that suppress the maximum allowable size (biotic potential) of a organism's population. Compare *biotic potential.*

Erosion. The wearing away of the land surface by such geological agents as running water, wind, and ice; includes both *geologic erosion* (natural) and *accelerated erosion* (human influenced).

Estuary. A region in which fresh water from a river or stream mixes with salt water from the sea; an important nursery ground for many marine animals.

Euphotic zone. The uppermost stratum of the oceanic zone into which light can penetrate; thus, it is the region of photosynthesis. Although the depth of this zone is highly variable, it is approximately 200 m (656 ft) on average. Compare *oceanic zone, bathyal zone,* and *abyssal zone.*

Euryphagous. An organism that has a highly varied diet, such as an opossum, a pheasant, or a human animal. Compare *stenophagous.*

Eutrophic. An environment (e.g., a lake) that has a large or excessive supply of plant nutrients (e.g., phosphates and nitrates) and hence has a great abundance of plant and animal species. The nutrients generally come from agricultural fertilizers, and from human and animal wastes. Compare *oligotrophic* and *mesotrophic*.

Eutrophication (natural eutrophication). The natural aging process by which all lakes "die" (i.e., evolve into a marsh and eventually disappear). This natural process is often accelerated by human activities. Compare *cultural eutrophication*.

Evaporation. The physical process by which a liquid changes to a gaseous state. This process is generally a function of air temperature, wind velocity, topography, and vapor pressure.

Evapotranspiration. The combined loss of water from evaporation from soil surfaces and from transpiration from plants per unit of land area during a specific period of time. See *evaporation* and *transpiration*.

Even-aged forest. A forest stand composed of trees of nearly the same age (with a difference in age of not more than 10 to 20 years); often the result of fire or clear-cutting. Compare *all-aged forest* and *uneven-aged forest*.

Field capacity (field moisture capacity). The amount of water retained in a unit of soil after it has been saturated and allowed to drain for several days or even weeks. Except during drought periods, this *capillary water* is sufficient to provide most of the needs of growing plants. Field capacity is usually expressed as a percentage of the oven-dry weight of the soil.

Floccules. Larger soil particles resulting from *flocculation*—the clotting together of colloidal mineral particles, especially fine clay, into small groups or granules. The presence of floccules in agricultural soils is a sign of good soil structure. See *soil structure*.

Flood. An overflow of water from a river or stream channel, which may cause or threaten to cause damage. Floods are usually due to sudden storms, spring snowmelt, or volcanic activity.

Floodplain. Relatively flat alluvial areas bordering one or both sides of a river channel that is subject to overflow flooding.

Floodplain management. One form of water resource management. It involves the use of structural and nonstructural methods of water management to protect or preserve a floodplain. Emphasis is usually on flood prevention. Compare *watershed management* and *groundwater management*.

Forest. A complex community of trees, vegetation, and other living organisms in which the tree canopy is usually closed.

Forest resource management. The management of forests to produce wood and wood-derived products, to safeguard forest grasslands for forage, to protect wildlife habitats, to control floods and erosion, to increase the recreational potential, and to protect the watershed.

Freshwater fisheries management. The manipulation of fish populations and their habitats to maintain or to improve commercial or recreational fisheries. Techniques of freshwater fisheries management include habitat improvement, habitat construction, biotic manipulation, the enforcement of fishing regulations, and habitat protection.

Fungicide. Any synthetic chemical used to kill fungi.

Game laws. Laws that are directed towards sustaining annual crops of *game animals*—animals sought for their fur, flesh, or for trophy value.

Genetic assimilation. The transfer of genetic characteristics from one species of few numbers (e.g., red wolf, *Canis niger*) to the genetic pool of a similar species of greater number (e.g., coyote, *Canis latrans*) by interbreeding. One means by which a wildlife species can become extinct.

Geologic erosion (natural erosion). Erosion caused by natural geological processes acting over long periods; results in the wearing away of mountains and the building up of flood and coastal plains. Compare *accelerated erosion*.

Girdling. A method of killing a tree by encircling the trunk with cuts that sever the bark and cambium, thereby preventing the passage of nutrients from the soil.

Glacial drift. Type of *depositional soil*; general term for rock debris that has been transported by glaciers and deposited directly or indirectly by agents such as meltwater from melting ice sheets.

Grade (mineral). A term designating the concentration of desirable mineral within mineral matter. An ore is generally classified as either *high-grade* (a high concentration of the desirable element) or *low-grade* (a low concentration of the desirable element).

Gravitational water. Type of soil water; water that enters, passes through, and drains out of soil under the influence of gravity. Compare *capillary water* and *hygroscopic water*.

Green manuring. The practice of growing a crop for use as green manure (a *green manure crop*), which is turned into the soil, usually with mechanical disks, to increase fertility.

Groundwater (phreatic water). Subsurface water in the zone of saturation; it originates from the percolation of surface water downward to a layer of impervious material. Compare *surface water*.

Groundwater flow (base flow). The slow, continuous drainage of water in an underground reservoir of saturated material into a stream channel. In other words, that part of the groundwater that is discharged into a stream channel.

Groundwater management. One form of water resource management. It involves groundwater monitoring (regular sampling and analysis of the chemical constitutents in groundwater) as well as the use of incentives and penalties to prevent groundwater overdraft, saltwater intrusion, or groundwater contamination from toxic chemicals. Compare *watershed management* and *floodplain management*.

Gully erosion. A type of water erosion; sudden rainstorms that produce a localized, concentrated runoff over soft material and often create deep gashes in the land surface. Compare *splash erosion*, *sheet erosion*, and *rill erosion*.

Habitat. The natural environment of a particular plant or animal. It includes all the essentials of life for that organism, such as food, water, and cover.

Hardpan. A hard and impermeable soil layer in the lower A or in the B horizon, usually resulting from *illuviation* (the deposition of minerals). There are five types: *ironpan, moorpan, claypan, limepan,* and *duripan.*

Heavy metals. Metallic elements, such as lead, mercury, cadmium, and arsenic, that have a specific gravity of 5.0 or over; generally toxic in low concentrations and apt to accumulate in the food chain.

Herbivore. An animal (e.g., cattle and horses) that feeds on plant materials (e.g., herbs and grasses) only. Compare *omnivore* and *carnivore.*

Home range. The area traversed by an animal or population for its habitat requirements (e.g., food, water, cover) during its life cycle, but not aggressively defended by the animal against others of the same species. Compare *territory.*

Humus. Dark brown to black partly decomposed organic matter in soil; organic tissues are more decomposed in humus than in *raw humus,* but less decomposed than in *peat* or *muck* soils. Humus is the organic constituent of soil.

Hydraulic mining. A type of surface mining wherein the desired mineral is exposed by using water under extreme pressure to wash away the sand and dirt overburden.

Hydrologic cycle. The endless cycle of water transfer that occurs between the sea, air, and land. Its numerous stages or processes include evaporation, transpiration, precipitation, interception, infiltration, percolation, storage, and runoff.

Hydrology. The scientific study of water, including its properties, distribution, and circulation. It includes the study of water in the atmosphere, as well as on surface and underground.

Hydroseeder. A machine used to spray grass seed, water, and fertilizer on steep banks to help control soil erosion.

Hygroscopic water. Type of soil water; the moisture remaining in the soil after *gravitational water* has been drained and *capillary water* has evaporated. Unavailable to plants because it clings tightly to soil particles. Compare *gravitational water, capillary water.*

Infiltration. The downward penetration of water from the ground surface into the soil. See *percolation.*

Infiltration capacity. The maximum rate at which water can percolate into a soil. If precipitation exceeds infiltration capacity, overland flow occurs. See *percolation* and *overland flow.*

Insecticide. Any synthetic chemical used to prevent, repel, or kill insects.

Integrated pest management (IPM). A method of pest management that uses a combination of biological and cultural controls with a minimum use of chemicals.

Interbasin transfers. The practice of using canals, aqueducts, or giant pipes to transfer or divert water from one region to another. Also known as *water diversion projects.*

Interception. The process by which a certain amount of precipitation is *intercepted* or kept from reaching the soil by falling on trees, shrubs, agricultural crops, and other types of vegetation.

Intertidal zone. That portion of the shore (including *estuaries*) that is covered with water at high tide and is exposed at low tide. Compare *neritic zone* and *estuary.*

Intolerant species. Tree species that are unable to grow in the shade of other trees. Compare *tolerant species.*

Introduction. The placement of a species into a habitat where at the time it does not occur.

Irruptive population. A wildlife population that has *irregular* and *unpredictable* peaks and diebacks. Examples of irruptive populations can be found in such species as the jack rabbit and the desert quail. One of three classifications of wildlife populations. Compare *stable population* and *cyclic population.*

Land reclamation (of surface-mined areas). The replacement of *overburden* (the earth, rock, and other materials originally covering the desired ore or mineral deposit) with soil and the revegetation of surface-mined areas.

Leaching. The washing out and removal of *soluable* minerals and other material by infiltrating or percolating water. Much leach material is held in the zone of accumulation (the B horizon). Typical leached soils are podzols and latosols.

Lentic. Water bodies that are standing or slow moving, such as lakes, swamps, or ponds. Compare *lotic.*

Limnetic zone. The surface open-water region of a lake to a depth where sunlight can no longer penetrate.

Littoral zone. The shallow shoreline of a lake, extending between the high-water and low-water tide marks.

Living fences. Any fence made up of living plant material (e.g., bushes, hedges, and trees), as opposed to wire, wooden posts or metal.

Loam. Textural class of soil having *relatively* equal amounts of sand, silt, and clay. Ideal for farming.

Loess. Type of aeolian landform; deposit of yellowish to buff-colored fine-grained dust (similar in appearance to talcum powder) that has been transported by the wind to its present location; frequently fertile.

Lotic. Water bodies that are fast moving, such as rivers or streams. Compare *lentic.*

Macronutrients. Chemical elements required in abundance for organic growth (e.g., nitrogen, calcium, potassium, and phosphorous). Compare *micronutrients.*

Mariculture. The controlled growing and harvesting of fish and shellfish in estuarine and coastal areas. Compare *aquaculture.*

Mass movement (mass wasting). Downward movement of soil, regolith, and/or bedrock on a slope under the influence of gravity (not by the action of fluid agents). Includes slow movement (soil creep) and rapid wasting (*earth-flow, earthslide, slump, rock-slide, rock-fall*).

Mesotrophic. An environment (e.g., a lake) that has a *moderate* supply of plant nutrients (e.g., phosphates and nitrates) and hence is in *transition* from the oligotrophic (nutrient poor) state to eutrophic (nutrient rich) state. Compare *oligotrophic* and *eutrophic.*

Micro-catchment farming. A variation of runoff agriculture, which is a form of water harvesting. With micro-catchment farming, agricultural fields are divided into small basins that are shaped so that water entering the basin will drain to one corner to irrigate where the crop is planted. See *water harvesting* and *runoff agriculture*.

Micronutrients. Chemical elements required by plants in minute or *trace* quantities (e.g., iron, zinc, copper, and iodine). Compare *macronutrients*.

Mineral deposit. Any element or compound found in the lithosphere that remains in solid form.

Minimum tillage farming. A type of tillage that employs fewer operations than normally practiced, especially during the preplant period; creates less soil disturbance than stubble mulch tillage but more than no-till farming. Compare *stubble mulch tillage* and *no-till farming*.

Mixed forest. A forest stand in which less than 75 percent of the trees are of a single species. Compare *pure forest*.

Monoculture. The use of a field for a single crop (such as maize or cotton) to the exclusion of other crops; typical of modern highly energy-dependent agricultural systems in developed countries. Compare *polyculture*.

Multiple-use management. Forest management that encourages several uses in addition to timber production. See *forest resource management*.

Natural erosion. See *geologic erosion*.

Natural eutrophication. See *eutrophication*.

Natural resources. An appraisal by a given cultural group during a given historic period, the term usually encompasses air, soil, water, wildlife, fuel and nonfuel minerals, freshwater and marine fisheries, forests, grasslands, and wilderness and open space.

Neritic zone. A zone of relatively shallow water above the *continental shelf* that includes the *intertidal zone*, extends from the high tide mark to the edge of the continental shelf, and contains extensive neritic deposits derived from the remains of shellfish, sea urchins, and coral. Compare *intertidal zone* and *oceanic zone*.

Nonadaptive behavior. An animal behavior that causes a species to be especially vulnerable to extinction. For example, when a member of a flock of Carolina parakeets was shot, the remaining parakeets would hover over the wounded or dead animal, thereby increasing their chance of also being shot.

Nonpoint source. Pollution arising from a broad, ill-defined source rather than from a discrete point. Nonpoint sources of pollution include runoff from grazing lands, cultivated fields, and manure disposal areas. Leaking sewerage systems and saltwater intrusion are also nonpoint sources of pollution. Compare *point source*.

Nonrenewable energy. Energy resources that are not naturally replenished within the limits of human time. Examples are the fossil fuels (coal, oil, and natural gas) and uranium. Compare *renewable energy*.

Nonrenewable resources. Natural resources that are finite or exhaustible within the limits of human time, for example, old growth forests, fossil fuels, and nonfuel minerals. Compare *renewable resources*.

No-till farming. A type of tillage in which a narrow slot is made in the untilled soil so that seed can be planted where moisture is adequate for germination. Weed control is entirely by herbicides. Compare *minimum tillage farming* and *stubble mulch tillage*.

Oceanic zone. The open sea beyond the continental slope; also known as the *pelagic zone*. Compare *neritic zone*.

Odd area (wildlife). A small, oddly shaped piece of land (e.g., a fence corner, a sink hole, a burrow pit) that acts as a good wildlife habitat.

Old Growth. Ancient timber stands that have never been cut; classified as a nonrenewable resource.

Oligotrophic. An environment (e.g., a lake) that has a minimum supply of plant nutrients (e.g., phosphates and nitrates) and hence has very few plant and animal species, for example, Lake Superior. Compare *mesotrophic* and *eutrophic*.

Omnivore. An organism, such as the human animal, that consumes both animal and vegetable substances. Compare *herbivore* and *carnivore*.

Open pit mining. One of three types of surface mining, the others being strip mining and dredging. The technique extracts minerals by creating a large open pit and is used primarily for extracting sand, gravel, stone, and metalliferous ores.

Open space. Any land on which buildings or other forms of development do not dominate the landscape. Wilderness areas and parks are two major types of open space. See *wilderness* and *park*.

Ore. Earth material containing a mineral in sufficient concentration to be extracted profitably.

Overdraft. The pumping of groundwater at rates perceived to be excessive and that could prove harmful to the aquifer.

Overgrazing. Excessive grazing by livestock to the point that future forage production is reduced. The native grass cover is often replaced by invaders of low nutrient value.

Overland flow. The movement of melted snow or rainwater over the ground surface toward stream channels. One of four types of runoff. Compare *runoff*.

Oxidation. A form of weathering, wherein a substance is combined with oxygen (e.g., rusting). Compare *solution*.

Parent material. Weathered rock material (C horizon) from which soil-forming processes create soil. *Bedrock* (consolidated rock material) rarely but occasionally serves as the parent material.

Park. Usually a tract of public land set aside for recreational purposes. Usually quite developed (containing picnic benches, baseball diamonds, barbeque pits, latrines) in comparision to wilderness areas. Compare *wilderness*.

Pathogen. A virus, microorganism, or other substance capable of producing disease.

Pedology. Scientific study of the origin, characteristics, and utilization of soils.

Pedon. A generic term for the smallest volume that can be called a soil, used mainly by American pedologists. A three-dimensional volume with lateral dimensions large enough to permit the study of soil horizon shapes and relations. Multiple pedons make up a *polypedon*. Compare *polypedon*.

Perched water table.   A smaller water table in a local zone of saturation, located above the main water table and separated from the main water table by an impermeable aquiclude, which is usually composed of clay.

Percolation.   The downward movement of water through the interstices (pores, joints, crevices) of rock or soil. Compare *infiltration*.

Permeability.   A rock or soil horizon that can transmit a fluid, usually the passage of water. Fluids can pass either because the rock is porous (e.g., sand, sandstone, or gravel) or pervious (e.g., chalk or limestone).

Pest.   A plant (e.g., a weed) or animal (e.g., an insect) that can be troublesome, annoying, and detrimental to other vegetation, agricultural crops, livestock, or wildlife.

Pesticide.   Any chemical designed to control pests, such as weeds (herbicides), insects (insecticides), rodents (rodenticides), and other organisms; examples are organophosphates, chlorinated hydrocarbons, and carbamates.

pH scale.   Abbreviation for potential hydrogen; numerical system indicating relative acidity or alkalinity of a soil on a 0 to 14 scale. A neutral soil has a pH of 7.0; an acid soil, less than 7.0; an alkaline soil, more than 7.0.

Point source.   Pollution arising from a discernible, discrete origin, usually stationary, such as the discharge from an industrial site, a sewer pipe, a contaminated well, or a drainage ditch. Compare *nonpoint source*.

Polyculture.   The use of a field for the simultaneous planting of many crops (such as bananas, sugar cane, and taro); typical of highly labor-intensive agricultural systems in Africa, Asia, and Latin America. Compare *monoculture*.

Polypedon.   A *soil body* or landscape unit as perceived by the soil scientist. Each polypedon has a unique set of properties that make it different from the properties of adjacent polypedons. Polypedons are composed of many *pedons*. See *pedon*.

Pond.   Generally a human-constructed water body that is smaller than a reservoir. An example would be a *farm pond*.

Population crash.   A population decline or dieback resulting when a population exceeds the carrying capacity of the land. Compare *population explosion*.

Population density.   The number of organisms per unit of land, such as the number of deer per square mile or the number of mice per acre. An important environmental factor related to wildlife reproduction.

Population dynamics.   The study of the population characteristics of a species (e.g., their number, sex-age compositions, reproduction, mortality rates, and health) and the environmental forces that causes them to change.

Population explosion.   A rapid increase in a population within a given habitat. Compare *population crash*.

Precipitation.   An inclusive term for all forms of moisture coming from the atmosphere, including dew, rain, hail, snow, and sleet. Likewise, the word *rainfall* is a general term. For example, the government's annual rainfall figures include rain and the rainwater equivalent found in snow, hail, and so forth.

Predation.   A powerful selective force, wherein one species (the predator) feeds on another species (the prey), thereby altering the population composition of the prey by removing the injured, diseased, or weak, or by removing one sex or a certain age class of the prey.

Predator.   A free-living organism that exists by killing and eating other organisms.

Primary treatment.   The first stage in wastewater treatment, wherein most floating debris and solids are mechanically removed by screening and sedimentation. Compare *secondary treatment* and *tertiary treatment*.

Profundal zone.   The deep-water zone of a lake, from the lake bottom up to the limnetic zone. This zone characteristically has insufficient sunlight for photosynthesis.

Pure forest.   A forest stand in which at least 75 percent of the trees are of a single species. Compare *mixed forest*.

Rain-drop erosion.   See *splash erosion*.

Rainshadow.   The markedly drier (lee) side of a mountain, as opposed to the wetter (windward) side that first receives the moisture-bearing clouds.

Rainwater harvesting.   A form of water harvesting. An ancient technique to collect rainwater so that it can be concentrated for agricultural or domestic use. Modern systems of rainwater harvesting involve chemically treated soils, asphalt, or using granulated paraffin wax in soil to improve the collection technique. Compare *runoff agriculture*.

Range condition.   A term used by range managers to discribe the quality of the range—the amount of ground cover, the types of plant species, and the forage production.

Rangeland.   Lands that produce primarily herbaceous or shrubby plants suitable for grazing by livestock. The term includes areas within forest lands that support an understory or periodic cover of forage plants. Furthermore, the term includes natural grasslands that are used for purposes other than livestock grazing.

Recycling (mineral).   A mineral conservation technique that goes beyond mere reuse of a product (e.g., returnable bottles). Recycling involves the recovery, reprocessing, and refabrication of the mineral components from society's industrial waste products (e.g., aluminum obtained from aluminum cans).

Regolith.   Unconsolidated mantle of weathered rock and soil material that overlies the bedrock (solid rock). Regolith has superficial deposits of alluvium, loess, and volcanic ash in it. Compare *bedrock*.

Renewable energy.   Energy resources that are *incoming* or *continuous* in that they constantly replenish themselves within the limits of human time. Examples are sun, wind, rivers, tides, waves, and plants. Compare *nonrenewable energy*.

Renewable resources.   Natural resources that are replenishable within the limits of human time if not overexploited or polluted, for example, soil, water, wildlife, freshwater and marine fisheries, and solar energy. Compare *nonrenewable resources*.

Reserves (mineral). A mineral deposit of known location and quality (one desired by society), and one that is economically and technologically feasible to extract. Compare *resource (mineral)*.

Reservoir. An aritificial water body larger than a pond. An example would be Hetch Hetchy reservoir behind O'Shaughnessy Dam in California. See Chapter 5. Compare *pond*.

Residual soils. Soils that have always *resided* (stayed) in the place where they were formed. Compare *depositional* soils.

Resource management. In terms of natural resources, resource management entails a culture's ''inadvertent'' (indirect) and ''intentional'' (direct or conscious) effects upon the environment. Usually, it refers to the introduction of planning programs that seek the improvement, conservation, or protection of natural resources.

Resource (mineral) Useful earth materials (chemical elements or compounds in solid form). Includes mineral reserves and other deposits that may someday become reserves. Compare *reserves (mineral)*.

Rest-rotation grazing. A type of deferred-rotation grazing wherein one grazing unit (e.g., pasture C) is rested from grazing for a full year. Compare *deferred grazing* and *deferred-rotation grazing*.

Rill erosion. A type of water erosion that removes surface soil unevenly and forms numerous small channels. Compare *splash erosion, sheet erosion,* and *gully erosion*.

Rodenticide. Any synthetic chemical designed to kill gophers, rats, mice, and other rodents.

Runoff. The movement of surface waters towards the ocean. There are four types of runoff: channel interception, overland flow, throughflow, and groundwater flow.

Runoff agriculture. A form of water harvesting that is closely related to rainwater harvesting, since it diverts rainfall to specified agricultural fields. In runoff agriculture, stone barriers are placed across intermittent stream channels so that rainwater, when it comes, is diverted to a broad, flat floodplain where crops are planted. Compare *rainwater harvesting*.

Salinization. The process by which soluable salts accumulate in soil particularly prevalent in the arid western states where irrigated land is poorly drained.

Saltation. A type of wind erosion in which wind moves solid particles (sediment along dry stream beds, sand grains in deserts) in short hops. Compare *suspension, surface creep*.

Sanitary landfill. A solid waste disposal site employing engineering methods that minimize air and water pollution, pests, and disease; solid wastes are spread in thin layers, wastes are compacted to the smallest practical volume, and a thin cover of fresh soil is applied each day.

Secondary treatment. The second stage of wastewater treatment, wherein the wasteflow is subjected to (1) bacteria, which consumes the organic wastes and (2) chlorination, which disinfects (kills) disease-carrying bacteria and some viruses. Compare *primary treatment* and *tertiary treatment*.

Sediment. Soil particles derived from rocks and biological materials that have been transported by rivers, wind, ice, and the sea.

Selective cutting. A harvesting technique in which selected trees scattered throughout a forest are periodically harvested, either individually or in small groups; synonymous with thinning. Compare *clear-cutting* and *shelterwood cutting*.

Sheet erosion (sheet wash). A type of water erosion in which runoff water removes a fairly uniform layer of soil from the land surface. Compare *splash erosion, rill erosion,* and *gully erosion*.

Sheet wash. See *sheet erosion*.

Shelterbelts. Extensive rows of trees planted at right angles to the prevailing wind to diminish its eroding effects on agricultural fields and rangeland. Compare *windbreaks*.

Shelterwood cutting. A harvesting technique in which trees are harvested in two or more successive stages. The trees left standing after the first cutting provide a seed source and partial protection for regeneration.

Shooting preserves. A hillside or open area devoted to the shooting of pen-reared game under very controlled conditions. The antithesis of the concept of *balanced biotas*.

Silviculture. The cultivation of forest trees as crops.

Sinkhold. A saucer-shaped or funnel-shaped depression in the earth's surface usually caused by the excessive withdrawal of groundwater. Drainage through underground channels can also dissolve limestone, salt, or gypsum beds, resulting in underground caverns that are susceptible to collapse.

Sludge. The solid or semisolid by-product of wastewater that remains after municipal, commercial, or industrial wastewater treatment. Usually associated with the results of sedimentation at sewage treatment plants.

Soil. Earth material consisting of inorganic matter (unconsolidated minerals), organic matter (decomposed plants and animals), living organisms, air, and water. Responds dramatically to climate (including moisture and temperature effects), parent rock material, macro- and microorganisms (both plants and animals), topography, time, and human use and abuse. A natural medium for the growth of land plants.

Soil horizons. Main divisions or layers of a soil profile, consisting of the A horizon (uppermost layer), B horizon, C horizon, and D horizon (lowermost layer). Each horizon has distinctive characteristics. See *soil profile*.

Soil profile. Succession of zones or soil horizons revealed by a vertical cut of soil, from surface to bedrock. Main soil types have profiles different in color, texture, and degree of gradation. See *soil horizons*.

Soil resource management (soil conservation). The preparation, manipulation, and treatment of soils for the benefit of posterity.

Soil structure. The manner in which soil particles are grouped together into secondary units (lumps or clusters) called *aggregates* or peds. Soils that have good structure for crop production contain *floccules*. See *floccules*.

Soil texture. Designates the classification of soil according to the size of its individual constituent particles. Actual classification is based on percentages of sand, silt, or clay.

Soil water (soil water belt). Subsurface water held in the soil within a few feet of the surface. The water is available to plants through their root systems.

Solum. Upper and most weathered part of the soil profile, consisting of the A and B horizons; the *true soil* as defined by pedologists.

Solution. A form of weathering, wherein a substance is dissolved in a liquid (e.g., the solution of rock salt in water). Rivers carry vast loads in solution. Compare *oxidation*.

Splash erosion (rain-drop erosion). A type of water erosion in which soil particles are displaced by the impact of raindrops, particularly under intense convectional precipitation and bare earth conditions. Compare *sheet erosion, rill erosion,* and *gully erosion*.

Stable population. A population that remains at a rather constant level in terms of numbers, once having reached the carrying capacity of its habitat. One of three classifications of wildlife populations. Compare *cyclic population* and *irruptive population*.

Stenophagous. Any organism (e.g., the Everglade kite; the ivory-billed woodpecker) that has a very specialized or limited diet. Compare *euryphagous*.

Stocking. A program to maintain or increase the number of fish within a freshwater habitat. It entails the actual placement of additional fish within a habitat.

Stream gradient. The general slope, or rate of change in elevation, of a flowing stream.

Stream order. One method of classifying streams as part of a drainage basin network. Tributaries (branches of the stream) are classified according to first order, second order, third order, and so on.

Strip cropping (strip farming). A type of cropping in which crops are grown in alternating strips or bands to protect soil and vegetation from running water or wind.

Stubble mulch tillage. A type of tillage in which organic materials (stubble and other crop residues) are left on the surface as a mulch (protective cover) during the preparation of the seedbed and during at least part of crop growth.

Subsurface (underground) mining. The mining technique that extracts minerals without removing the *overburden* (overlying materials). Basically there are two types of subsurface mining: (1) the room-and-pillar system, and (2) the solution method. Compare *surface mining*.

Superinsulated houses. Such houses have at least twice the average amount of insulation materials in the ceilings; the walls have airtight linings; the heat is generated by sunlight through windows and by body heat and sometimes by active solar collectors. Air-to-air heat exchangers prevent the buildup of air pollutants and excessive moisture inside the house.

Surface creep. A type of wind erosion in which relatively large soil particles (between 0.5 and 1.0 mm in diameter) are rolled or pushed along the surface by the impact of particles in saltation. Compare *suspension, saltation*.

Surface mining. Mining technique used in which the overlying materials (e.g., the topsoil, subsoil, and other overburden) are removed to expose the desired mineral seam for extraction. Compare *subsurface mining*.

Surface water. Water that flows exclusively on the ground surface, it is the opposite of *groundwater*, which is located in underground aquifers. Compare *groundwater*.

Suspension. A type of wind erosion in which winds lift and transport soil particles for long distances. Compare *saltation* and *surface creep*.

Sustained yield. The amount of timber that a forest can produce on a continuing basis under careful management.

Synthetic organic chemicals (SOCs). Artificial (human-created) chemical compounds containing carbon, such as synthetic fertilizers, pesticides, and other petroleum by-products.

Territorial sea. The belt of sea along a coast that a country or state considers to be within its jurisdiction. For most U.S. states, the territorial sea extends 3 nautical miles from shore.

Territory. A more-or-less geographically definable area defended by one member of a species (e.g., a lion) against other members of the same species (e.g., other lions). Compare *home range*.

Tertiary treatment. Advanced cleansing of waste water beyond the primary (mechanical) and the secondary (biological) treatments. Nutrients (e.g., phosphorus and nitrogen) and a high percentage of the suspended solids are removed from the water. Compare *primary treatment* and *secondary treatment*.

Thermal pollution. The warming of a lake, stream, or bay by the industrial discharge of heated water. The heated waste water discharged raises the temperature of the receiving water body, thereby affecting the life processes of its aquatic organisms.

Threatened species. Any species (fish, terrestrial animal, or plant) that is approaching *endangered* status within the foreseeable future. Compare *endangered species*.

Throughflow (interflow). Water that moves laterally through the upper soil horizons (below the ground surface but above the water table) until it intercepts either a stream channel or returns to the ground surface at a point downslope from its origin.

Tilth. The physical condition of the soil in relation to the growth of plants. Good tilth refers to soils that are easy to till and are friable enough for root penetration and seedling emergence.

Tolerant species. Tree species that can grow in the shade of other trees. Compare *intolerant species*.

Trace elements (micronutrients). A chemical element usually within the soil that is needed in only minute or *trace* amounts (less than 1 ppm) for plant growth. Either a deficiency or surplus of the element may have severe adverse effects.

Transpiration. The process by which plants lose water vapor through the minute pores (stomata) of their leaves. The water vapor is released to the atmosphere. Compare *evaporation* and *evapotranspiration*.

Uneven-aged forest. A forest stand in which the trees differ considerably in age. Compare *all-aged forest* and *even-aged forest*.

Upwelling. The movement of cold, nutrient rich bottom water to the surface as a consequence of the effects of winds blowing parallel to or away from the coastal zones; it results in abnormally low surface-water temperatures that are rich in nutrients, thus creating a favorable environment for plant and animal growth.

Urban forestry. The care and maintenance of trees in urban areas.

Volcanic ash. Type of aeolian deposit; pulverized extrusive igneous rock material (particles of lava) ejected from the crater of a volcano during an eruption; capable of being transported by winds for great distances.

Water harvesting. A general term encompassing rainwater harvesting and runoff agriculture (which includes micro-catchment farming). See *rainwater harvesting, runoff agriculture,* and *micro-catchment farming*.

Water pollution. The natural or human-caused degradation of water quality.

Water resource management. The use of structural and nonstructural approaches to obtain added benefits from precipitation, water, or water flow. Encompasses water storage, water diversion, irrigation, and water cleanup. Compare its three subfields: *watershed management, floodplain management,* and *groundwater management*.

Watershed (drainage or catchment basin). The *gathering ground* of a single river system. The crest of a ridge often serves to divide one river system and its watershed from another.

Watershed management. One form of water resource management. The comprehensive management of a particular watershed—its use, regulation, and treatment of water and land resources. Compare *floodplain management* and *groundwater management*.

Water table. The upper surface of the zone of saturation or the top level of the groundwater. Compare *perched water table*.

Weathering. Disintegration and decay of rock material by exposure to the atmosphere; may be *mechanical* or *physical* (frost action or temperature change), *chemical* (solution, carbonation, hydrolysis, oxidation, or hydration), or *biological* (the action of microflora and fauna).

Wilderness. Tracts of land that have been minimally disturbed by humans. Very undeveloped in comparison to parks. Compare *park*.

Wildlife. A term that has both a narrow and broad definition. The narrow definition is that wildlife is all undomesticated (free-ranging) vertebrate animals, except fish. The broad definition is that wildlife is all undomesticated species, including plants, in wild ecosystems.

Wildlife border. A border around an agricultural field that also serves as a wildlife habitat. For example, a double row of grass, autumn olive, and honeysuckle can serve as cover for pheasants and songbirds.

Wilting point. A measure of soil moisture. The point at which plants wilt and fail to recover their turgidity.

Windbreaks. Small groups of trees and shrubs planted to protect houses and farmsteads against severe winds. Compare *shelterbelts*.

Woodlot. A relatively small area of land set aside for the growing of forest trees.

Zonal soils. Soils that have distinct horizons because longtime soil-building forces (climatic forces and living organisms, chiefly vegetation) have been acting on the parent material. An obsolete term based on the 1949 revision of the Great Soils classification system. Compare *azonal soils*.

Zone of aeration. Subsurface zone above the water table that has more air within its pore space than water. Compare *zone of saturation*.

Zone of saturation. Subsurface zone immediately below the water table that is saturated, that is, all the interstices are filled with water. Water within this zone is called *groundwater*. Compare *zone of aeration*.

INDEX